SABR 50 at 50

(SABR)

50 AT 50

THE SOCIETY FOR AMERICAN BASEBALL RESEARCH'S FIFTY MOST ESSENTIAL CONTRIBUTIONS TO THE GAME

Edited by
BILL NOWLIN

Foreword by
JOHN THORN

Associate Editors
MARK ARMOUR,
SCOTT BUSH,
LESLIE HEAPHY,
JACOB POMRENKE,
CECILIA TAN,
JOHN THORN

University of Nebraska Press
Lincoln

Library of Congress
Cataloging-in-Publication Data
Names: Nowlin, Bill, 1945– editor. | Armour,
Mark L., editor. | Bush, Scott, 1982– editor. |
Heaphy, Leslie A., 1964– editor. | Pomrenke,
Jacob, editor. | Tan, Cecilia, 1967– editor. |
Thorn, John, 1947– writer of foreword.
Title: SABR 50 at 50: the Society for American
Baseball Research's fifty most essential
contributions to the game / edited by Bill Nowlin;
associate editors Mark Armour, Scott Bush,
Leslie Heaphy, Jacob Pomrenke, Cecilia Tan;
foreword by John Thorn.
Description: Lincoln: University of Nebraska Press,
[2020] | Includes bibliographical references.
Identifiers: LCCN 2020001902
ISBN 9781496222688 (hardback)
ISBN 9781496223265 (pdf)
Subjects: LCSH: Society for American Baseball
Research—History. | Baseball—History—
Research—United States. | Baseball—
United States—Statistics. | Baseball—
United States—History.
Classification: LCC GV862 .S3255 2020 |
DDC 796.3570973/021—dc23
LC record available at
https://lccn.loc.gov/2020001902

Designed and set in
Minion Pro by L. Auten.

Contents

Foreword

JOHN THORN

Nerds, we members of the Society for American Baseball Research (SABR) call ourselves proudly, flying our freak flag high. The world has countless baseball fans—more than 110 million tickets are sold to major- and minor-league games in this country alone—but SABR membership is steady, year after year counting up to this 50th anniversary, at around six thousand.

Who are we few, we happy few, we band of brothers and sisters? Just ordinary folks in the pursuit of our daily bread, yet different in our approach to what has long been at the core of the American experience: baseball. We are a sort of Nonconformists Club: mild-mannered sorts by day, superheroes by night on our computers or, on our off days, at archives.

To deflect suspicion that he is Superman, Clark Kent adopts a largely passive and introverted personality with odd mannerisms, a higher-pitched voice, and a slight slouch. SABR members wear this disguise, too, sometimes from the inside out. Faster than a speeding bullet, more powerful than a locomotive, able to leap tall buildings in a single bound—that's us. To best be in position to use our amazing powers in a never-ending quest for fresh baseball data and insight, SABR members tend to adopt a bland wardrobe, unfashionable eyeglasses, often a briefcase and, at gatherings, nametags that camouflage our coolness.

What are these amazing powers cited above? Caring deeply about getting it right and about completing the journey, however improbable the prospect of home may have seemed at the outset. We endure the predictable slings and arrows on the whole cheerfully, not only because we know who we are, but also because we live in the age of Steve Jobs, Bill Gates, and other nerds for whom data, when shared, become life's most rewarding currency.

Ernie Harwell once said: "SABR is the Phi Beta Kappa of baseball." This is especially true in the Age of the Nerd, in which knowledge is, at long last, cool. For many years SABR's board members bristled when its members were painted with a broad brush and called sabermetricians. They protested that

Society members were also interested in history, and culture, and ballparks, and the Negro Leagues, and the international game.

Incubated in the pages of the *Baseball Research Journal*, sabermetrics soon flew the coop and soared over the entire baseball landscape. Bill James coined the term to honor the Society not so much for its statistical analysis but for its conviction that significant aspects of the game are invisible to the naked eye, and that received wisdom about the game warranted distrust. All these years later, I think it is a good thing that we no longer protest quite so much about being known as analytics pioneers.

First convened in Cooperstown in August 1971 by L. Robert Davids and fifteen other avid researchers and history buffs, SABR grew slowly but steadily before settling in a bit north of six thousand members in 1987 (I joined in 1981). "Baseball's best-kept secret," Ted Williams once declared. As some of its early members slipped away into the sunset, new nerds would have to be located. Fortunately, that has happened, and the analytics movement has been SABR's fountain of youth. SABR has become a bridge between the game's journalists and its front offices, on the one hand and, on the other, its fans, who consume and argue over SABR research without even knowing the source.

The Society does good works—lobbying for historical markers, providing headstones to baseball luminaries who were buried without them, holding conferences at which speeches and swag are delivered. Through research committees and regional chapters, SABR members share their finds and their expertise, providing a rich experience that links the generations of advanced fans.

SABR is not a secret society with initiation rites—anyone may join and do nothing at all beyond paying annual dues; writers need readers, after all. And boy, do we write! SABR publishes, in print and online, the *Baseball Research Journal* (fifteen hundred articles since 1972), *The National Pastime* (one thousand since 1982), and online stories. Add in SABR's digital library, notably the Baseball Biography Project (more than five thousand profiles since 2002) and the Games Project (two thousand game accounts since 2014). And chalk up another four thousand articles in research committee newsletters, plus six hundred in one-off publications, and the number of articles totals more than fifteen thousand, all written by SABR volunteers.

From these, SABR has, though an arduous process in which I was involved, somehow selected its fifty best to mark its 50th birthday, spanning the half century of its existence while restricting even our most notable authors to a single representative story. The selection committee sought to create a chronological portrait of the Society while balancing the genres represented by its thirty-one research committees: for example, biographical, nineteenth century, deadball, ballparks, records, women in baseball, and, yes, statistical analysis.

In the early days of SABR, many of its most skilled researchers concerned themselves not only with the relative merits of men who played in different eras but with determining who the players *were*. Hundreds of players were absolute ciphers, about whom nothing but a last name was known—a box score entry, that was all. Lee Allen and Bill Haber hunted for headstones; Vern Luse and Bill Carle scoured the squibs in *Sporting Life*. Today the number of major leaguers about whom absolutely nothing is known has been reduced to a relative handful. For this fortunate state of affairs we thank SABR's Biographical Research Committee. This sort of digging seldom yields a full-fledged article but is vital to those who may write another sort of story even a decade later. The recently deceased Richard Malatzky offers a case in point.

I knew Richard by his work, and we spoke excitedly about his progress with new finds when we met at SABR conventions. He was just the sort of guy I like, one who cares deeply, even obsessively, about getting things right. His delights may well have seemed strange to the world at large, but in shunning the noise of that larger world to visit an alternative one in the past, he and I and so many SABR members were brothers under the skin.

Others, especially those in the Biographical Research Committee, knew Richard far better and far longer. Not only did he dispel mysteries of very long standing that had stumped others for decades, he corrected some of the "compromise" errors made in earlier record books whereby, for example, two fairly inconsequential players with the same common last name (Smith, Jones, Miller, etc.) had their records mistakenly grouped under one individual.

Each of the fifty writers whose articles are offered herein will have a capsule biography beginning their piece, but those SABR stars like Malatzky who may have helped in the research will go unidentified; probably that is just the way they would have liked it.

Every SABR writer relies upon the efforts of a colleague or predecessor.

Fred Lieb, whose career in baseball began as a writer for *Baseball Magazine* in 1909, is this book's leadoff hitter, with a profile of Ernie Lanigan, another SABR icon whose career began with *The Sporting News* in 1898 (when Henry Chadwick was still writing baseball). The pair grew up and grew old in baseball, with Lanigan creating the game's first encyclopedia in 1922. Counting the uncounted, in his case RBIs and Caught Stealing before they became official statistics, was Lanigan's specialty . . . a very SABR thing to do. Lieb lived long enough to join SABR and write for the first number of the *Baseball Research Journal*.

The last entry in this volume is by D. B. Firstman, whose first book will be published in the same season as this one. In between are luminaries past and present, all accounted as SABR heroes and all worthy of your attention. I won't list them or their contributions here, as a tease—that's what the table of contents is for—but you will recognize their names or their discoveries.

Finally, you may wonder why I have been asked to write the foreword to this book. In 2011, within days of my appointment by Commissioner Selig as Major League Baseball's official historian, I spoke before the New York City regional chapter of SABR. I said then that, gratifying as this post might be to me, it was also a bouquet toss to SABR, without which I could not have come to understand and serve the game. Several of those in the audience had collaborated with me in *Total Baseball* and other sabermetric efforts, in historical research, and in SABR publications. Truly, I said then and reiterate now, if I occupy a high standing in baseball it is in good measure because I stand on your shoulders. Thank you, SABR.

Acknowledgments

SABR thanks Todd Radom for lending his artistry to our 50th anniversary celebration, and SABR's founders, the "Cooperstown 16," whose vision and hard work made all this possible: L. Bob Davids, Dan Dischley, Paul Frisz, Dan Ginsburg, Raymond Gonzalez, Bill Gustafson, William Haber, Tom Hufford, Cliff Kachline, Bob McConnell, Pat McDonough, Ray Nemec, John Pardon, Thomas Shea, Joseph Simenic, and Keith Sutton.

Editors' Note

The selections for this book were made by a committee of four volunteers: Mark Armour, Leslie Heaphy, Bill Nowlin, and John Thorn. The idea for the book was John's, and to credit him we asked him to write the foreword. In making the included selections, we decided early on to limit ourselves to no more than one piece by any given author. It was a challenging but rewarding process to look over all the work that has appeared in SABR journals and publications and a daunting task to settle on fifty selections.

SABR 50 at 50

Ernie Lanigan—Patron Saint of SABR

FREDERICK G. LIEB

Both author and subject of this piece have been honored posthumously with SABR's Henry Chadwick Award in recognition for their extensive contributions to baseball research. Fred Lieb began writing for *Baseball Magazine* in 1909, wrote for several New York daily papers, contributed articles to *The Sporting News* for many years, and wrote nine valuable baseball history books in the 1940s and 1950s. He became one of the first SABR members (joining four months after its founding) and wrote three pieces for the early *Baseball Research Journal*. Lieb wrote this piece to remember and honor another research giant, Ernie Lanigan, a man he had worked with six decades earlier. This article originally appeared in the *Baseball Research Journal* (1973, issue 2).

Baseball already has had some interesting centennials. In 1939, they celebrated the first 100 years of baseball as an American sport and institution. It was the year the game's shrine in Cooperstown, New York was officially dedicated. In 1969, they celebrated the golden anniversary of baseball's first all-pro team, the unbeaten Cincinnati Reds in 1869, with appropriate functions and ceremonies in Washington DC, Cincinnati, New York, and other cities.

In 1971, the game did honor to the National Association, first professional league to play a regular schedule, with the Athletics of Philadelphia winning the 1871 championship. In 1876, the early National Association was reorganized into the National League, the great and honored major league of today.

In 1973, baseball comes up with another centennial, the 100th birthday of Ernest John (Ernie) Lanigan, early historian of the Hall of Fame, who was king of baseball figures, statistics, records, names, and birthplaces of players, events, and incidents, both ordinary and extraordinary. He was born in Chicago on January 4, 1873, and died in Philadelphia on February 6, 1962.

SABR, the Society for American Baseball Research, may well consider the beloved Ernie Lanigan as its patron saint or guardian angel. No man, living or dead, did as much for baseball research as the diligent, untiring, ever-searching ol' Ernie.

Damon Runyon, a brilliant baseball writer in the New York press box at the Polo Grounds, New York, in the early part of this century, once referred to Ernie as the "Figger Filbert." I am sure Ernie never cared for this cognomen. As author of the book, *The Baseball Cyclopedia*, he referred to himself as the "Fearless Writer." But I feel Damon meant Ernie no harm. Lanigan actually was a nut on baseball statistics, and chased down any odd item on baseball with the zeal of a scientist coming up with a new plant, bug, million-year old human bone, or any early caveman's artifact.

My early New York baseball writing career was closely associated with that of Ernie Lanigan, as I succeeded him as baseball editor of the *New York Press* in 1911. The *Press* gave more attention and space to baseball than any of its competitors. It was Lanigan of the *Press* who was kind enough to teach me how to score, and make out a box score, and some of the tricks of successful metropolitan writing.

However, one must confess that Lanigan was an odd character as a top echelon baseball man. After he spent some two weeks with me in the Giants' and old New York Highlanders' press boxes, helping me with my chores and scores, I never again saw him in a major-league ballpark. I believe he did attend one or two games, and when he worked for the International League as statistician and publicist, he attended a few of their games.

"I really don't care much about baseball, or looking at ball games, major or minor," he once confided to me. "All my interest in baseball is in its statistics. I want to know something about every major-league ballplayer, not only what he is hitting, but his full name with all middle names and initials, where they were born, and where they now live."

He came by his interest in baseball and its statistics, and his writing ability, quite naturally as his mother, Bertha Spink Lanigan, was a sister of the famous Spink brothers, all born on an island off the shore of Quebec, Canada. First to come to the States was William (Willie) Spink, early St. Louis baseball writer and personal telegraph operator to President U. S. Grant. He was followed by Albert H. Spink, who started *The Sporting News* in St. Louis in 1886, and eventually by Charles C. Spink, early South Dakota homesteader, who soon became one of the key men in *The Sporting News* picture. Ernie was a first cousin to J. G. Taylor Spink, for many years the dynamic publisher of *The Sporting News*, and a second cousin of C. C. Johnson Spink, the present publisher and editor.

George T. Lanigan, Ernest's father, was a skillful newspaper reporter-editor and poet; and Ernie's mother, Mrs. Bertha Spink Lanigan, was an early editor of the *Ladies Home Journal.* A younger brother of Ernie, Harold (Hal) was a successful baseball writer and sports editor in both St. Louis and New York.

Ernest never was a robust man, and most of his life he battled with some form of illness, especially pulmonary. Several times he had to go to health sanitariums or live in high altitudes. Despite his health problems, and frequent indulgence in bourbon and rye whiskey, he lived to be 89, and had his fine mental faculties and splendid memory, especially of things concerning baseball, right to the end.

He changed jobs frequently, partly because of health and partly because of his independence and rugged individuality. He left the *New York Press* in 1911 to take a position of assistant to Edward G. Barrow, then the new strong president of the International League. No matter what high positions Barrow later attained, he always demanded almost servile service from his subordinates. Ernie couldn't live, breathe, or function at his best under such a boss. During the latter part of the 1911 season, Ernie wasn't fired from his International League, nor did he officially quit. He just went out to lunch one day, and never returned.

In his frequent moves, Lanigan served stints as baseball editor of the *Cleveland Leader*, press representative and auditor of the Syracuse Stars, and business manager of the St. Louis Cardinals' farm clubs in Dayton, Ohio, and Fort Wayne, Indiana. Eventually, he gravitated back to the International League office when Frank Shaughnessy served as president.

Big names in the world of politics, sports, or the theater meant little to Lanigan; he was strong in his likes, also in his dislikes. On one of Commissioner K. M. Landis's periodic trips to New York, he stopped at the International League offices, then in Gotham. He peered for a moment or two at an elderly man seated behind an outside desk, and asked, "Didn't I meet you in Florida?"

The elderly gentleman in the outer office was Ernie Lanigan. "No, you didn't see me in Florida, or anywhere else," he said through pursed lips. "Because I have carefully avoided meeting you." Judge Landis's face turned livid. In his long career as a Federal judge, and then as the No. 1 man of baseball, no one ever had spoken to him like that. He started to say something, though better of it, and went into the office of the International League president. In the 1920s, when there was a running feud between Landis and

Byron Ban Johnson, first American League president, Ernie's sympathies were entirely with the fighting Ban.

Lanigan worked for his uncles, Al and Charley Spink, of the St. Louis *Sporting News*, when he was only a teenager. His contributions to baseball were many. He was one of the original boosters for a national organization of the major-league baseball writers, and even had his then young friend, Sid Mercer, do missionary work for such an association when Sid took the road, writing about the New York Giants. He saw his dreams become reality when the Baseball Writers Association of America was successfully launched in New York in December 1908.

His big gift to the field of baseball statistics is the important Runs Batted In (RBI) column of today. He and his *New York Press* sports editor, Jim Price, used to enter "Runs Batted In," and "base-runners thrown out by catcher" in the lower part of the *Press* box scores of New York teams. They appeared in no other big city newspapers. Eventually, Lanigan induced John Heydler, then secretary of the National League, to include these figures in his official averages. Later, they were taken up by the Associated Press in their nation-wide coverage of big-league games.

In 1946, Shaughnessy loaned Lanigan to the Hall of Fame at Cooperstown, New York. Although he took a strong distaste to his title as "Curator of the Museum," Lanigan grew roots in the pretty town on Lake Otsego, and stayed there for the remainder of his working days. After a few years, he was able to turn over active direction of the museum, and he concentrated his efforts as historian of the Hall of Fame. He continued in this post until old age caused him to retire. Lee Allen succeeded him as Hall of Fame historian in 1959.

While baseball statistics were Ernie Lanigan's first love, he did have a keen interest in orchestral music. Among his many jobs, he was treasurer and press representative for the Philadelphia Symphony Orchestra in 1902–04. But, even when Ernie was getting his pay and groceries from this great orchestra, he still had time to dabble with baseball "facts and figgers." If the tuba player had a cousin in Oshkosh who played third base for the Cardinals, Ernie would not rest until he had the player's middle name, something on his antecedents, and whether he had been a pitcher before he switched to the hot corner.

As Judge Landis once said of Ernie's cousin, Taylor Spink, "There never could be another like him. After God made him, he threw away the mold." So the same is true of Ernest John Lanigan, and for the same reason.

Relative Batting Averages

DAVID SHOEBOTHAM

One of the fundamentals of sabermetrics is the concept that the value of any statistical event depends on context—a home run hit in 1968 in the Astrodome has more statistical value than a home run hit in 2001 in Coors Field. David Shoebotham, armed with a stack of record books and a handheld calculator, took an early step in taking context into account by considering batting average relative to the league environment for batting averages. SABR's Statistical Analysis Committee began in 1974, and many of the greatest insights in the field of baseball analytics were presented in early SABR publications. This article originally appeared in the *Baseball Research Journal* (1976, issue 5).

Who has the highest single-season batting average in major-league history? The modern fan would probably say that Rogers Hornsby's .424 in 1924 is the highest. Old timers would point out that Hugh Duffy hit .438 in 1894. But the correct answer is Ty Cobb with .385 in 1910.

How can .385 be higher than .438? The answer is when it is compared to the average of the entire league for the year in question. This is the only way performances from different seasons and leagues can be compared. Thus a hitter's *relative* batting average, which is the true measure of his ability to hit safely, is computed as follows:

$$\text{Rel. Avg.} = \frac{\text{Player's Avg.}}{\text{League Avg.}}$$

$$= \left(\frac{\text{Player's Hits}}{\text{Player's ABs}}\right) \Big/ \left(\frac{\text{League Hits}}{\text{League ABs}}\right)$$

As a further refinement (since it is unfair to compare a player to himself), the player's own hits and ABs can be subtracted from the league totals, thus giving an average relative to the remainder of the league.

As an example, compare Bill Terry's National League-leading .401 in 1930 to Carl Yastrzemski's American League-leading .301 in 1968. At first glance the 100-point difference would make it appear that Yastrzemski's average should not be mentioned in the same breath as Terry's. But look at the calculations of relative averages:

$$\text{Terry,} \atop \text{1931 Rel. Avg.} = \left(\frac{254}{633}\right) \Bigg/ \left(\frac{13260 - 254}{43693 - 633}\right) = 1.328$$

$$\text{Yastrzemski} \atop \text{1968 Rel. Avg.} = \left(\frac{162}{539}\right) \Bigg/ \left(\frac{12359 - 162}{53709 - 539}\right) = 1.310$$

The relative averages are almost identical, meaning that had the two performances occurred in the same season, the batting averages would have been within a few points of each other. The big difference, of course, is that in 1930 the National League had a combined average of .303, the highest of any major league in this century (and two points higher than Yastrzemski's 1968 average), whereas in 1968 the American League had a combined average of .230, the lowest for any major league ever. (A relative average of 1.30 indicates that a player's batting average was 30% higher than the remainder of his league.)

Figures 2.1 and 2.2 show league averages since 1900. It can be seen that the 1920s and 30s, following the introduction of the lively ball, were fat times for hitters. Both leagues reached their recent lows in 1968, the "Year of the Pitcher." Note that for the last three seasons the American League's Designated Hitter rule has artificially raised the league's average and thus lowered individual relative averages.

Table 2.1 shows the highest single season relative averages since 1900. The list is clearly dominated by Ty Cobb, who has 10 of the top 19 averages, including the highest of all: 1.594 in 1910. Interestingly, the second highest relative average is Nap Lajoie's 1.592, also in 1910. That epic batting race, enlivened by the offer of a new car to the winner, resulted in a major scandal, the awarding of two automobiles, and incidentally the two highest relative averages of all time. Rogers Hornsby's .424 produced the highest National League mark of 1.51, but this ranks only 14th on the list. (Duffy's .438 reduces to a relative average of about 1.42.) Note that five of this century's .400 averages do not qualify for this list.

With the modern preoccupation with home runs, high relative averages (not to mention high absolute averages) have become rare. The only relative average over 1.45 in recent years is Joe Torre's 1971 mark.

For a look at other recent high marks, Table 2.2 shows the highest relative averages of the last 20 years. It is interesting to note that Rod Carew's 1974

Fig. 2.1. American League Season Averages

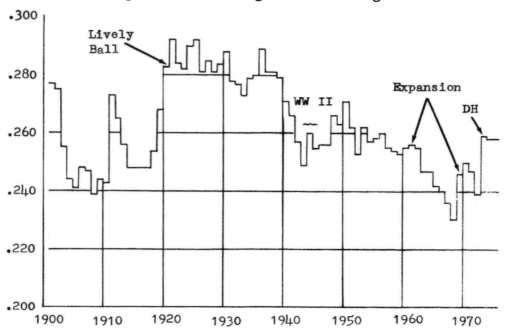

Fig. 2.2. National League Season Averages

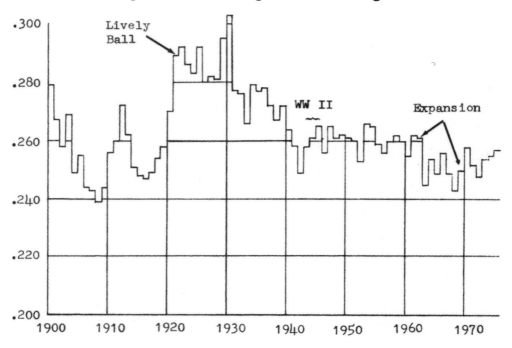

Table 2.1. Single season relative average greater than 1.45

Rank	Player	Year	League	At Bats	Hits	Avg.	League Avg.	Relative Avg.
1	Ty Cobb	1910	Amer.	509	196	.385	.242	1.594
2	Nap Lajoie	1910	Amer.	591	227	.384	.241	1.592
3	Nap Lajoie	1904	Amer.	554	211	.381	.243	1.57
4	Tris Speaker	1916	Amer.	546	211	.386	.247	1.57
5	Ty Cobb	1912	Amer.	553	227	.410	.263	1.56
6	Ty Cobb	1909	Amer.	573	216	.377	.242	1.56
7	Ty Cobb	1917	Amer.	588	225	.383	.246	1.56
8	Ty Cobb	1911	Amer.	591	248	.420	.271	1.55
9	Nap Lajoie	1901	Amer.	543	229	.422	.275	1.53
10	Ty Cobb	1913	Amer.	428	167	.390	.254	1.53
11	Ted Williams	1941	Amer.	456	185	.406	.265	1.53
12	Ted Williams	1957	Amer.	420	163	.388	.254	1.53
13	Ty Cobb	1918	Amer.	421	161	.382	.252	1.52
14	Rogers Hornsby	1924	Nat.	536	227	.424	.281	1.51
15	Joe Jackson	1911	Amer.	571	233	.408	.271	1.51
16	Joe Jackson	1912	Amer.	572	226	.395	.263	1.50
17	Ty Cobb	1916	Amer.	542	201	.371	.247	1.50
18	Ty Cobb	1915	Amer.	563	208	.369	.247	1.50
19	Ty Cobb	1914	Amer.	345	127	.368	.246	1.49
20	Honus Wagner	1908	Nat.	568	201	.354	.237	1.49
21	Cy Seymour	1905	Nat.	581	219	.377	.253	1.49
22	George Sisler	1922	Amer.	586	246	.420	.283	1.49
23	Joe Jackson	1913	Amer.	528	197	.373	.254	1.47
24	Tris Speaker	1912	Amer.	580	222	.383	.263	1.45
25	Stan Musial	1948	Nat.	611	230	.376	.259	1.45
26	George Stone	1906	Amer.	581	208	.358	.247	1.45
27	Joe Torre	1971	Nat.	634	230	.363	.251	1.45
28	George Sisler	1920	Amer.	631	257	.407	.282	1.45
29	Honus Wagner	1907	Nat.	515	180	.350	.242	1.45

and 1975 marks would probably be well over 1.45 except for the Designated Hitter rule in the American League.

Table 2.3 shows the all-time leaders in career relative average. Not surprisingly, Ty Cobb tops the list with an average that is just a few hits short of 1.40. Close behind Cobb is Shoeless Joe Jackson, though the closeness of their averages is deceptive. Jackson's career was abruptly terminated while he was still a star performer, and therefore he did not have the usual declining years at the end of his career that would have lowered his average. During the years that Jackson averaged 1.38, Cobb was averaging a fantastic 1.50.

It can be seen that despite the preponderance of pre-1920 hitters in the single season leaders, the career list contains players from all periods since 1900, including four who are active. Rod Carew, who in 1975 moved past Ted Williams into third place, seems destined to be one of the all-time leaders in relative average. Whether all four active players will finish their careers among the leaders is an open question, but at least they show that hitting for high average is not altogether a lost art.

Table 2.2. Highest single season relative averages during last 20 years (1956–1975)

Rank	Player	Year	League	At Bats	Hits	Avg.	League Avg.	Relative Avg.
1	Ted Williams	1957	Amer.	420	163	.388	.254	1.53
2	Joe Torre	1971	Nat.	634	230	.363	.251	1.45
3	Roberto Clemente	1967	Nat.	585	209	.357	.248	1.44
4	Mickey Mantle	1957	Amer.	474	173	.365	.254	1.44
5	Rico Carty	1970	Nat.	478	175	.366	.257	1.42
6	Norm Cash	1961	Amer.	535	193	.361	.255	1.42
7	Rod Carew	1974	Amer.	599	218	.364	.257*	1.41
8	Harvey Kuenn	1959	Amer.	561	198	.353	.252	1.40
9	Rod Carew	1975	Amer.	535	192	.359	.257*	1.40
10	Pete Rose	1969	Nat.	627	218	.348	.249	1.39
11	Carl Yastrzemski	1967	Amer.	579	189	.326	.235	1.39
12	Ralph Garr	1974	Nat.	606	214	.353	.254	1.39
13	Pete Rose	1968	Nat.	626	210	.335	.242	1.39
14	Roberto Clemente	1969	Nat.	507	175	.345	.250	1.38
15	Bill Madlock	1975	Nat.	514	182	.354	.256	1.38
16	Hank Aaron	1959	Nat.	629	223	.355	.259	1.37

17	Matty Alou	1968	Nat.	558	185	.332	.242	1.37
18	Tony Oliva	1971	Amer.	487	164	.337	.246	1.37
19	Roberto Clemente	1970	Nat.	412	145	.352	.257	1.37
20	Ralph Garr	1971	Nat.	639	219	.343	.251	1.37

*Designated Hitter rule in effect

Table 2.3. Lifetime relative average greater than 1.20 (over 4000 ABS)

Rank	Player	Years	At Bats	Hits	Avg.	League Avg.	Relative Avg.
1	Ty Cobb	1905–1928	11429	4191	.367	.263	1.39
2	Joe Jackson	1908–1920	4981	1774	.356	.258	1.38
3	Rod Carew	1967–1975*	4450	1458	.328	.247	1.33
4	Ted Williams	1939–1960	7706	2654	.344	.261	1.32
5	Nap Lajoie	1896–1916	9589	3251	.339	.258	1.31
6	Rogers Hornsby	1915–1937	8173	2930	.358	.275	1.30
7	Tris Speaker	1907–1928	10208	3515	.344	.266	1.29
8	Stan Musial	1941–1963	10972	3630	.331	.258	1.28
9	Honus Wagner	1897–1917	10427	3430	.329	.258	1.28
10	Eddie Collins	1906–1930	9949	3311	.333	.265	1.26
11	Rob. Clemente	1955–1972	9454	3000	.317	.254	1.25
12	Tony Oliva	1962–1975*	6178	1891	.306	.246	1.24
13	Pete Rose	1963–1975*	8221	2547	.310	.251	1.23
14	Harry Heilmann	1914–1932	7787	2660	.342	.278	1.23
15	Sam Crawford	1899–1917	9579	2964	.309	.252	1.23
16	George Sisler	1915–1930	8267	2812	.340	.278	1.23
17	Babe Ruth	1914–1935	8399	2873	.342	.279	1.23
18	Matty Alou	1960–1974	5789	1777	.307	.252	1.22
19	Joe Medwick	1932–1948	7635	2471	.324	.266	1.21
20	Paul Waner	1926–1944	9459	3152	.333	.275	1.21
21	Lou Gehrig	1923–1939	8001	2721	.340	.281	1.21
22	Bill Terry	1923–1936	6428	2193	.341	.282	1.21
23	Joe DiMaggio	1936–1951	6821	2214	.325	.269	1.21
24	Hank Aaron	1954–1975*	12093	3709	.307	.254	1.21
25	Jackie Robinson	1947–1956	4877	1518	.311	.260	1.20

*Active player

3

The Best Games Pitched in Relief

L. ROBERT DAVIDS

L. Robert Davids, known to the SABR community as Bob, founded SABR in August 1971 when he summoned a group of baseball researchers—most of whom he had not yet met—to a gathering at the National Baseball Hall of Fame Library in Cooperstown, New York. Davids ran the organization for a few years out of his house, served three terms as board president, and edited all SABR publications and newsletters for fourteen years. He wrote many articles throughout his career, including short uncredited lists of accomplishments or interesting numerical feats from the past. This entry is typical of Davids, who was able to use his deep understanding of the game's history to shine a light on some then-unknown performances. Bob received the Henry Chadwick Award in 2010. This article was first published in the *Baseball Research Journal* (1978, issue 7).

There are ways of recognizing the best pitched games of starting hurlers—the record books list the no-hit games and in a special category even the perfect games where no opposition batter got to first base. But what about the relief pitcher? What about the great efforts they have made over the years? There is no record category for best games pitched in relief and consequently these gems are not recorded and soon forgotten.

Well, that is not exactly true. There was one game that was so flawless, the powers that be lifted it from the ranks of relief efforts and called it a perfect game. That really wasn't necessary and wasn't quite accurate anyway.

The game we are talking about, of course, was the first game of the June 23, 1917, twinbill between the Red Sox and Senators where Boston starter Babe Ruth walked the first Washington batter and was dispatched from the field for forcefully disputing the call by umpire Brick Owens. Ernie Shore was brought in to replace Ruth. The Washington runner was thrown out stealing and Shore set down all 26 batters he faced. This should not be considered a "perfect game" like those of Young, Joss, Bunning, et. al., because not quite all the ingredients for "perfect" are there. It should, however, be called the *best relief performance* ever turned in, and that is quite a singular accomplishment.

What were some of the other stellar relief efforts? Considering only regular season games since 1900, we have reviewed several factors including length of performance, fewest runs and hits and men on base, most strikeouts, relieving with men on base, etc. Whether the relief pitcher won the game or not is considered a negligible factor.

One game that evoked some memories of and comparisons with the Ernie Shore performance took place on August 31, 1955, in Cleveland. Bill Wight of the Baltimore Orioles was facing rookie Herb Score of the Indians. In the first inning Wight gave up two walks, five hits, and five runs without getting the first batter out. With two on base, he was replaced by Hector "Skinny" Brown, who could start or relieve as needed. Brown completely cut off the Tribe. He was facing a team that had gotten its first seven batters on base and then suddenly they could not get another hit for the rest of the game. Brown's knuckleball and slider were working marvelously against such batters as Bobby Avila, Ferris Fain, Ralph Kiner, and Al Rosen, and this particular day he also had a live fastball. He fanned 10, and, while he was one of the best control pitchers in modern baseball (only 8 walks in 141 innings in 1963), he did give up five bases on balls in this contest.

Herb Score was also pitching well, and he had the advantage of five runs in the first inning. He fanned 13 and won the game 5–1. The Indians did not have to bat in the ninth, and Brown was credited with eight no-hit innings. He was responsible for all 24 Indian outs. Baltimore management thought he should be credited with a no-hit game, much like Shore, but the American League Office quickly ruled this out.

On July 20, 1914, Hubert "Dutch" Leonard was scheduled to pitch for the Red Sox against the Tigers and George Dauss. He begged off because of a weak ankle and Fred Coumbe took his place. The latter pitched well and the Red Sox had a 2–0 lead going into the ninth. But the Tigers got two runs off Coumbe before anyone was out and Leonard was sent in with Bobby Veach on second. He dispatched the Bengals without a hit that inning, and as the game went into extra innings he kept setting them down. Finally, in the 16th inning Tris Speaker singled in Harry Hooper to give Leonard a 3–2 victory. He had not given up a hit in eight innings, had walked three and fanned nine, pretty good for a pitcher not up to starting.

Some of the best relief efforts were performed by pitchers who won lasting fame as starters. They thereby demonstrated that they could be great under any conditions. In fact, Cy Young had back-to-back performances, one in long relief and the next as a starter, which were faultless.

The rescue effort came on April 30, 1904, in a contest against Washington. George Winter was pitching for the Boston Americans and they were leading 3–0 after two. However, Winter was clipped for three quick hits and a run in the third and Young came in with two men on base and nobody out. He set the Senators down in order and continued his mastery throughout the game. He did not give up a hit or a walk in seven innings and, as his next outing was a perfect game against the Athletics, he was untouchable for 16 straight innings. This was part of his record 25⅓ consecutive hitless innings, which is discussed in another article in *Baseball Research Journal* (1978, issue 7).

Grover Cleveland Alexander won 28 games as a rookie with the Phils in 1911 and one was in a spectacular relief performance against the Reds on May 13. Alex relieved George Chalmers in the top of the ninth with the score tied at 4–4. He pitched eight hitless innings and was returned a victor in the 16th when Pat Moran singled in Fred Luderus. He walked only two and one was caught stealing and the other was wiped out in a double play. Frank Smith, acquired from the Red Sox, went the route for the Reds and lost 5–4.

On the same day there was another notable relief performance, but not a particularly good one. In this game the Giants scored 13 runs off the Cardinals in the first inning. With a 13–0 lead, manager John McGraw wasn't going to waste his ace Christy Mathewson and pulled him after the first inning. In came Rube Marquard who pitched the remaining eight innings in a 19–5 victory. He gave up 12 hits, yet he fanned 14, which was a top mark for a relief hurler up to that point.

Two years later, on July 24, 1913, Walter Johnson fanned 15 (some reports say 16) in 11⅓ innings of relief against the St. Louis Browns. This is not only a record for relief hurlers, but turned out to be the most Johnson ever fanned in any game, and he pitched in two that went 18 innings. Johnson had many great relief performances, but probably none that would rank in the top 10. His best was against the Yankees on July 5, 1912. He relieved Joe Engel in the fourth with one down and two men on. Both scored on an error by shortstop George McBride before Johnson could retire the side. The game was tied 5–5 and went into overtime. The Nats finally won it 6–5 in the 16th. In 12⅔ innings, Johnson gave up only four hits. He walked three, hit a batter, and fanned five.

The longest relief effort in major-league history occurred in a game between the Dodgers and Cubs on June 17, 1915. Chicago hurler Humphries was tapped for one run in the first and he left after Zack Wheat slashed a wicked drive back to the mound which took a fingernail off his pitching hand. With two out and two on, he was replaced by George Washington "Zip" Zabel, who had not had a chance to warm up. Almost immediately George Cutshaw was caught off base at third to retire the side. Zabel gave up an unearned run in the eighth which tied up the game 2–2 and it shortly went into overtime. In the 15th he walked Casey Stengel intentionally and the strategy backfired into another unearned run for the Dodgers; however, Vic Saier of the Cubs tied it up again with a homer in the bottom of the 15th. In the 19th inning the Cubs finally pulled it out when Bob Fisher scored on an error by Cutshaw for a 4–3 win for Zabel over Jeff Pfeffer, who went the distance, but was not especially sharp. In 18⅓ innings, "Zip" had given up only nine hits, two runs, and one intentional walk.

Not all of the really long relief efforts were good jobs. The most notorious example was on July 10, 1932, when the Philadelphia Athletics were caught with a limited pitching staff in Cleveland and Eddie Rommel struggled through 17 innings in relief, giving up 29 hits and 14 runs. Ironically, he was still returned the victor, because Wes Ferrell, his relief opponent through 11⅓ innings, was banged for 12 hits and 8 runs. That was an exceptional game, won by the A's 18–17 in 18 innings.

The longest scoreless relief effort was turned in by Bob Osborn of the Cubs on May 17, 1927. In this game against the Boston Braves, Osborn made his entrance in the eighth with the score tied 3–3. He hurled 14 innings, giving up only six hits and two walks, and won the game in the 22nd when Charlie Grimm singled in Hack Wilson, who had walked. Bob Smith went the entire 22 innings for the Braves and lost a heartbreaker.

Two outstanding relief performances were racked up during the summer of 1959. On July 9, at Milwaukee, Roger Craig of the Los Angeles Dodgers relieved Danny McDevitt in the third with the score tied 3–3. Craig, later a pitching coach and now manager of the San Diego Padres, used only 88 pitches in 11 innings of superb hurling. He gave up a pop-fly double to Joe Adcock and two harmless singles, and did not walk a batter. In fact, it was one of the longest games by a relief hurler without giving up a base on balls.

The Braves even called in their ace southpaw, Warren Spahn, in one of his infrequent relief appearances, to pull this one out. He pitched well, but in the 13th gave up a double to Wally Moon and a single by Rip Repulski and Craig won the contest, 4–3.

On August 6, 1959, it was the battle of the Billies at Baltimore. Billy Pierce of the White Sox was hurling against Billy O'Dell of the Orioles. It was 1–1 in the ninth when Hoyt Wilhelm came in to relieve O'Dell. His knuckleball was working exceptionally well against the Chicago club, which was heading for the pennant that year. Wilhelm hurled 8⅔ innings before he was reached for a hit. In the 18th inning he gave up his second hit, an intentional pass, and catcher Joe Ginsburg was charged with a passed ball, but Hoyt retired the side. It was midnight and the game was called after 18 innings as a 1–1 tie. Wilhelm had given up only two hits in 10 innings, but the hapless Orioles could not score again off Pierce, who went 16 frames, and Turk Lown, who relieved him.

Another 10-inning effort that got more acclaim than the Wilhelm performance was pitched by rookie Bobby Shantz of the Philadelphia A's on May 6, 1949. In a game against the Tigers, Connie Mack called him in with nobody out in the fourth and a man on third. Shantz, in only his second major-league game, retired the side without mishap. He went on to pitch nine hitless innings as the game went into overtime. He weakened in the 13th and gave up two hits and a run, but Wally Moses won the game for the A's with a two-run homer, 5–4. While Shantz did pitch the closest thing to a no-hit game in 1949 (there was no regulation no-hitter that year), his overall performance was marred by seven bases on balls.

While Shantz starred in his second major-league encounter, Pete Richert of the Los Angeles Dodgers actually pitched his best game in his debut on April 12, 1962. Stan Williams of the Dodgers was drubbed for four runs by the Cincinnati Reds in the second inning and the nervous southpaw made his initial appearance with two out and Eddie Kasko on second. Richert fanned Vada Pinson on three pitches to retire the side. In the third inning he struck out Frank Robinson, Gordie Coleman, Wally Post, and Johnny Edwards. Yes, four batters in one inning. Coleman got on when a third strike got past catcher John Roseboro. In the next inning Richert fanned Tommy Harper, giving him six strikeouts for the first six batters he faced in the majors. He was invincible in the 3⅓ innings he hurled, giving no hits and no walks, and fanning seven. He went out for a pinch-hitter in the fifth when the Dodgers scored seven runs and sewed up the victory for him. It was a brief stint compared to the others cited in this article, but he was overpowering, tying three strikeouts records.

One of the marks, six consecutive strikeouts by a relief hurler, fell to young Denny McLain three years later. On June 15, 1965, at Detroit, McLain came to the mound in the first after the Red Sox had roughed up Dave Wickersham for three runs and there was only one out. He fanned the first seven batters he faced and a fantastic 14 in only 6⅔ innings. However, he gave up two runs in the sixth and was lifted for a pinch-hitter in the seventh. The Bengals scored four runs in the eighth and won, 6–5.

There have been many other great relief performances in the past 77 years, but the time has come to make a decision on the top 10. Here is one person's opinion, and the cold statistics to support those selections.

Date of Game	Pitcher and Club	IP	R	H	BB	SO	Outcome
June 23, 1917	Ernie Shore, Red Sox	9	0	0	0	2	Won
August 31, 1955	Hector Brown, Orioles	8	0	0	5	10	No Decision
July 20, 1914	Hubert Leonard, Red Sox	8	0	0	3	9	Won
May 13, 1911	Grover Alexander, Phils	8	0	0	3	8	Won
April 30, 1904	Cy Young, Americans	7	0	0	0	4	No Decision
June 17, 1915	Zip Zabel, Cubs	18.1	2	9	1	6	Won
May 17, 1927	Bob Osborn, Cubs	14	0	6	2	1	Won
July 9, 1959	Roger Craig, Dodgers	11	0	3	0	4	Won
Aug. 6, 1959	Hoyt Wilhelm, Orioles	10	0	2	3	7	Tie
April 12, 1962	Pete Richert, Dodgers	3.1	0	0	0	7	Won

4

The First Negro in Twentieth-Century O.B.

WILLIAM J. WEISS

Bill Weiss had worked for twenty years as a record-keeper and statistician for several minor leagues before the birth of SABR. He joined up a month after SABR's founding and continued working in the game for another thirty years. His largest contribution to his fellow SABR members was as a repository of minor-league records and statistics, particularly in the years before online databases. At the time this article was published, very few people knew the story of the first black player in the twentieth-century minor leagues, but this California-based historian was just the person to tell the tale. Weiss died in 2011, and three years later his family donated his entire collection of books, guides, record books, and research materials to SABR's San Diego chapter and the San Diego Central Library, where it is available to researchers to this day. This article first appeared in the *Baseball Research Journal* (1979, issue 8).

In the last two decades of the 19th century, some 30 Negro players saw service in leagues in Organized Baseball. After 1898, however, the doors of the majors and the members of the National Association of Professional Baseball Leagues were closed to Negroes, although there were no rules anywhere prohibiting them from playing. It is, of course, possible that a light-skinned Negro of mixed racial background may have "passed," to use the expression of the time.

Thus, the first documented instance of a Negro playing in Organized Baseball in the twentieth century was Jackie Robinson, signed by the Brooklyn Dodgers, who made his debut with Montreal of the International League in 1946, right? Wrong!!

Exactly 30 years earlier, in 1916, a Negro named Jimmy Claxton pitched for the Oakland Oaks in the Pacific Coast League, briefly, to be sure, but he was there. Jimmy was a well-known baseball figure in the Pacific Northwest and, in 1969, was elected to the Tacoma-Pierce County Hall of Fame. Claxton was a baseball player for more than 40 years.

James E. Claxton was born in 1892 at Wellington, British Columbia, on Vancouver Island off the west coast of Canada. His family moved to Tacoma, Washington, when he was three months old and he always considered that city to be his hometown. His mother was Irish and English, his father was Negro, French, and Indian.

As chronicled by Tacoma *News-Tribune* sports editor Dan Walton in a 1964 column, "Jimmy began playing baseball as a left-handed catcher with the Roslyn town team as a 13-year-old. He held the job for five years. He started pitching in 1912 with the Chester team, near Spokane, and fanned 18 in his first game." Walton went on to say:

> His travels took him to such teams as the Tacoma Giants; Sellwood of the Portland City League; Good Thunder, Minnesota; Homestead in the Stevens County League; Shasta (California) Limiteds; the Lincoln Giants of the Los Angeles Winter League; the Seattle Queen City Stars; Mukilteo of the Snohomish County League; the Chicago Union Giants; the Tacoma Longshoremen; Eureka, S.D.; the Cuban Stars of the Negro American League; the Nebraska Indians and many way points.

He had a 20–1 record with the Chicago Giants the season they played 43 barnstorming games against the House of David, he won 20 games in 20 starts at Edmonds, managed and pitched Roslyn to three titles in four years in the Central Washington League, and had Luis Tiant Sr. as a fellow left-hander with the Cuban Stars in 1932.

How did he get to the Pacific Coast League in 1916? "I got off to a real good start as a southpaw pitcher with the Oakland Giants in a Colored League in the spring of 1916," Jimmy told Walton.

"A fellow named Hastings, a part-Indian from Oklahoma, I believe, followed every game we played. He introduced me to Herb McFarlin, secretary of the Oakland Coast League club, and told him I was a fellow tribesman. I was signed to an Organized Baseball contract, but the manager was against me and did everything to keep from giving me a fair chance.

"I had been with Oakland about a month when I got a notice that I was released. No reason was given, but I knew. They tried to get out of paying me, but I had my contract and the notice of release. They had to come through with the money."

After 48 years, Claxton's memory was a little off as to the time he spent with the PCL club, but otherwise research indicates he was correct.

The *San Francisco Chronicle* for Sunday, May 28, 1916, reported, "Claxton, the Indian pitcher who works from the port side and hails from an Indian reservation in Minnesota, will make his PCL debut (today)." Being a Sunday, the Oaks were playing a morning-afternoon doubleheader with visiting Los Angeles, then managed by Frank Chance and fielding such players as Harl Maggert, Johnny Bassler, and Harry Wolter.

Claxton started the first game, pitched two-plus innings, allowed four hits and three runs, two of them earned. He walked three, struck out none. Jimmy left the game with the Oaks trailing, 3–0, but got off the hook when his teammates tied the score in the fourth. The Angels won the game, 5–4.

Claxton finished the second game that afternoon, pitching one-third of an inning, giving up no runs or hits and walking one batter. Los Angeles won that contest handily, 10–5.

The press was reasonably kind in the next day's editions. The *Chronicle* stated, "Klaxton (some incorrectly spelled his name with a K), the Indian youngster who made his PCL debut, was obviously nervous and cannot be fairly judged by his showing."

The *San Francisco Call* reported, "Klaxton, the Indian southpaw recently nailed by the Oaks from an Eastern reservation, stepped into the box for the first time yesterday morning. The Redskin had a nice windup and a frightened look on his face, but not quite enough stuff to bother L.A. He lasted two innings. However, he may do better in the future."

Unfortunately, for Claxton there was to be no Pacific Coast League future. His name next appeared in the press on June 3, when his outright release was announced.

The *Call* reported it rather matter-of-fact. "Elliott (Oaks manager Harold 'Rowdy' Elliott) has given the gate to George Klaxton, the Indian southpaw recently secured from an Eastern reservation. Klaxton appears to have a lot of stuff, but he's not quite ripe for this company. He's a free agent and will probably make a stab to secure a job in the Western League."

The *Chronicle*, however, had a little different twist to the story. In his 1964 interview with Walton, Claxton indicated he always suspected that a "supposed friend" had tipped off Oakland officials that he was part Negro.

The *Chronicle's* story, signed by sports editor Harry B. Smith, said, "George Claxton, the Indian pitcher who was signed by Elliott, has been handed his release. According to Rowdy, the heaver had nothing on the ball and he couldn't afford to bother with him. Claxton pitched last year, according

Fig. 4.1. Jimmy Claxton, photographed for a Zeenut candy card in 1916 while making a brief appearance with Oakland in the Pacific Coast League.

to reports, with the Oakland Giants, but Manager Rowdy declared that he appeared at the Oakland headquarters with an affadavit (*sic*) signed before a notary showing him to be from one of the reservations in North Dakota."

The commentary was somewhat different after it became known Claxton was part Negro!

Despite his very brief Pacific Coast League trial, Claxton did have enough ability as a pitcher to say that, had he been born 30–40 years later, he might well have made the majors. For example, in 1919, in what the Oakland *Tribune* called "the greatest semi-pro game ever put on here," Claxton pitched the Shasta Limiteds to the Northern California championship by beating Best Tractors, 2–1, on a five-hitter. His mound opponent that day was Johnny Gillespie, who, three years later, was pitching for Cincinnati. Best's first baseman and cleanup hitter was Babe Danzig, former Red Sox and PCL performer, and their catcher, Andy Vargas, later played several years in the Coast League.

Claxton must have been a pretty fair hitter, too. The box score for that 1919 game shows him batting fourth and, while the game was still a scoreless tie, he drew an intentional walk to load the bases.

Claxton was still pitching once a week at the age of 52, in fast semipro company. According to a nephew, he pitched, and won, a two-hitter when he was 61! He died in Tacoma on March 3, 1970, at the age of 78.

Claxton's "timing!" might not have been the best, in that he was born too soon to be a major league player, but it was uncanny in another context. Believe it or not, Jimmy Claxton is the first Negro player who ever appeared on a baseball trading card.

From 1911 to 1939, a candy company in San Francisco issued the famous "Zeenut" cards, the longest continuous series of baseball cards printed, until they were recently surpassed by Topps. Claxton may have been with the Oaks for just one week, but he happened to be there when the photographer was around taking the pictures for the 1916 set of Zeenut cards, and his card was issued with all the rest that year (see figure 4.1).

5

Average Batting Skill through Major-League History

RICHARD D. CRAMER

Dick Cramer is one of the acknowledged giants in the field of baseball statistical research. Many of Cramer's most famous insights were published in SABR's journals, including his 1977 claim that clutch hitters do not exist—shocking at the time, but today a generally accepted truth. In this brilliant article from a few years later (*Baseball Research Journal* [1980, issue 9]), Cramer broke new ground by trying to quantify the increase in batters' skills over the history of the game, a subject we have been wrestling with ever since. For his extensive body of work Cramer was awarded SABR's Henry Chadwick Award in 2015.

Is the American or the National a tougher league in which to hit .300? How well would Babe Ruth, Ty Cobb, or Cap Anson hit in 1980? What effect did World War II, league expansion, or racial integration have on the caliber of major-league hitting? This article attempts definitive answers to these types of questions.

The answers come from a universally accepted yardstick of batting competitiveness, comparing the performances of the same player in different seasons. For example, we all conclude that the National League is tougher than the International League because the averages of most batters drop upon promotion. Of course, factors other than the level of competition affect batting averages. Consider how low were the batting averages of the following future major leaguers in the 1971 Eastern League:

Player	1971 Eastern League	Lifetime average (through 1979)
Bill Madlock	.234	.320
Mike Schmidt	.211	.255
Bob Boone	.265	.268

Andre Thornton	.267	.252
Bob Coluccio	.208	.220
Pepe Frias	.240	.239

Double A seems a bit tougher than the major leagues from these data because (1) this player sample is biased: most Eastern Leaguers don't reach the majors, and I haven't shown all the 1971 players who did, and (2) large and poorly-lighted parks made the 1971 Eastern League tough for any hitter, as shown by its .234 league average. My study tries to avoid these pitfalls, minimizing bias by using all available data for each season-to-season comparison, and avoiding most "environmental factors" such as ball resilience or rule changes that affect players equally, by subtracting league averages before making a comparison. Of course, direct comparisons cannot be made for seasons more than 20 years apart; few played much in both periods, say, 1950 and 1970. But these seasons can be compared indirectly, by comparing 1950 to 1955 to 1960, etc., and adding the results.

Measures of batting performance are many. In the quest for a single accurate measure of overall batting effectiveness, I have developed the "batter's win average" (BWA) as a "relative to league average" version of the Palmer/Cramer "batter's run average" (BRA). (See *Baseball Research Journal* 1977: 74–79.) Its value rests on the finding that the scoring of major-league teams is predicted from the BWAs of its individual players with an error of ±21 runs (RMS difference) when all data are available (SB, CS, HBP, and GIDP as well as AB, H, TB, and BB) and about ±30 runs otherwise.

A property useful in visualizing the BWA in terms of conventional statistics is its roughly 1:1 equivalence with batting average, provided that differences among players arise only from singles. To make this point more clearly by an example, Fred Lynn's +.120 BWA led the majors in 1979. His value to the Red Sox was the same as that of a hitter who obtained walks, extra bases, and all other statistical oddments at the league average, but who hit enough extra singles to have an average .120 above the league, that is, a BA of .390. The difference between .390 and Lynn's actual .333 is an expression mostly of his robust extra-base slugging.

The first stage in this study was a labor of love, using an HP67 calculator to obtain BWA's for every non-pitcher season batting record having at least 20 BFP (batter facing pitcher) in major-league history. The second stage was merely labor, typing all those BFPs and BWAs into a computer and checking the entries for accuracy by comparing player BFP sums with those in the *Macmillan Baseball Encyclopedia*. The final stage, performing all possible season-to-season comparisons player by player, took 90 minutes on a PDP10 computer. A season/season comparison involves the sum of the difference in BWAs for every player appearing in the two seasons, weighted by his smaller number of BFPs. Other weighting schemes tried seemed to add nothing to the results but complexity.

Any measurement is uncertain, and if this uncertainty is unknown the measure is almost useless. The subsequent treatment of these season/season comparisons is too involved for concise description, but it allowed five completely independent assessments of the level of batting skill in any given American or National League season, relative to their respective 1979 levels. The standard deviation of any set of five measurements from their mean was ±.007, ranging from .002 to .011. This implies that the "true" average batting skill in a season has a two-in-three chance of being within ±.007 of the value computed, and a 19-in-20 chance of being within ±.014, provided that errors in my values arise only from random factors, such as individual player streaks and slumps that don't cancel. However, no study can be guaranteed free of "systematic error." To cite an example of a systematic error that was identified and corrected: If a player's career spans only two seasons, it is likely, irrespective of the level of competition, that his second season was worse than his first. (If he had improved, he was likely to have kept his job for at least a third season!) Another possible source of error which proved unimportant was the supposed tendency for batters to weaken with age (the actual tendency appears to be fewer hits but more walks). It appears that overall systematic error is less than 20 percent of the total differences in average levels. One check is that the 1972 to 1973 American League difference is attributable entirely to the calculable effect of excluding pitchers from batting, plus a general rising trend in American League skill in the 1970s.

Assessment of the relative strength of the major leagues, as might be expected, comes from players changing leagues. Results again were consistent and showed no dependence on the direction of the change. Results from the two eras of extensive interleague player movement, 1901 to 1905 and post-1960, agreed well also.

The results of my study are easiest to visualize from the graphical pre-

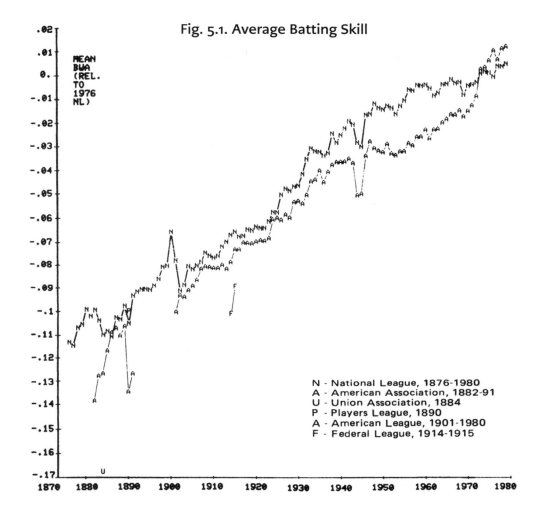

Fig. 5.1. Average Batting Skill

N - National League, 1876-1980
A - American Association, 1882-91
U - Union Association, 1884
P - Players League, 1890
A - American League, 1901-1980
F - Federal League, 1914-1915

sentation in figure 5.1. (Because few readers will be familiar with the BWA units, I have not tabulated the individual numbers, but later convert them to relative BAs and slugging percentages.) Theories on the whys and wherefores of changes in average batting skill I leave to others with greater personal and historical knowledge of the game. But the major trends are clear:

(1) The average level of batting skill has improved steadily and substantially since 1876. The .120-point difference implies that a batter with 1979-average skills would in 1876 have had the value of an otherwise 1876-average batter who hit enough extra singles for a .385 batting average.

(2) The American and National Leagues were closely matched in average batting strength for the first four decades (although not in number of superstars, the AL usually having many more). About 1938 the

25

National League began to pull ahead of the American, reaching its peak superiority in the early '60s. A resurgence during the '70s makes the American League somewhat the tougher today, mainly because of the DH rule.

(3) The recent and also the earliest expansions had only slight and short-lived effects on batting competitiveness. However, the blip around 1900 shows the substantial effect on competition that changing the number of teams from 12 to 8 to 16 can have!

(4) World War II greatly affected competitiveness in 1944 and 1945.

Many baseball fans, myself included, like to imagine how a Ruth or a Wagner would do today. To help in these fantasies, I have compiled a table of batting average and slugging percentage corrections, based again on forcing differences in league batting skill overall into changes in the frequency of singles only. However, league batting averages and slugging percentages have been added back in, to reflect differences in playing conditions as well as in the competition. To convert a player's record in year A to an equivalent performance in season B, one should first add to his year A batting and slugging averages the corrections tabulated for season A and then subtract the corrections shown for season B. The frequency of such other events as walks or stolen bases then can, optionally, be corrected for any difference in league frequencies between seasons A and B.

Table 5.1. Corrections applied to a player's batting average and slugging percentage in a particular season to equate them with 1976 National League play

	American		National	
	BA	SPCT	BA	SPCT
1979	+.003	-.029	-.001	-.017
1978	+.011	-.007	+.005	-.004
1977	+.002	-.031	-.004	-.033
1976	+.016	+.017	(.000)	(.000)
1975	+.009	-.006	.000	-.006
1974	+.007	-.001	+.002	-.004
1973	+.005	-.011	+.002	-.014
1972	+.013	+.015	+.005	-.007
1971	+.001	-.010	.000	-.008

1970	-.004	-.027	-.007	-.035
1969	-.002	-.019	-.003	-.016
1968	+.016	+.013	+.010	+.018
1967	+.008	-.001	+.003	-.005
1966	+.004	-.019	-.002	-.024
1965	+.001	-.021	+.003	-.016
1964	-.006	-.035	-.003	-.017
1963	-.009	-.036	+.003	-.010
1962	-.017	-.050	-.014	-.040
1961	-.022	-.055	-.012	-.049
1960	-.017	-.044	-.004	-.031
1959	-.018	-.043	-.009	-.043
1958	-.019	-.042	-.011	-.048
1957	-.024	-.045	-.011	-.045
1956	-.028	-.056	-.007	-.046
1955	-.029	-.046	-.015	-.057
1954	-.029	-.039	-.023	-.059
1953	-.035	-.050	-.027	-.066
1952	-.026	-.032	-.012	-.027
1951	-.030	-.043	-.018	-.024
1950	-.043	-.068	-.020	-.054
1949	-.034	-.034	-.021	-.042
1948	-.036	-.046	-.018	-.034
1947	-.023	-.025	-.026	-.045
1946	-.030	-.032	-.018	-.011
1945	-.045	-.030	-.040	-.033
1944	-.051	-.038	-.034	-.030
1943	-.026	-.012	-.024	-.007
1942	-.032	-.026	-.013	-.001
1941	-.042	-.059	-.025	-.022
1940	-.047	-.077	-.034	-.040
1939	-.055	-.077	-.046	-.054
1938	-.059	-.087	-.037	-.040
1937	-.062	-.090	-.050	-.054

1936	-.074	-.100	-.057	-.059
1935	-.060	-.076	-.055	-.063
1934	-.063	-.077	-.056	-.065
1933	-.058	-.069	-.042	-.032
1932	-.068	-.089	-.057	-.071
1931	-.072	-.084	-.064	-.068
1930	-.081	-.108	-.095	-.134
1929	-.064	-.081	-.087	-.113
1928	-.081	-.091	-.076	-.086
1927	-.084	-.092	-.076	-.074
1926	-.082	-.087	-.076	-.076
1925	-.092	-.101	-.095	-.111
1924	-.091	-.091	-.086	-.089
1923	-.090	-.090	-.093	-.096
1922	-.106	-.101	-.102	-.108
1921	-.101	-.111	-.099	-.101
1920	-.093	-.091	-.079	-.070
1919	-.079	-.064	-.069	-.042
1918	-.064	-.027	-.064	-.032
1917	-.058	-.024	-.059	-.032
1916	-.061	-.031	-.060	-.035
1915	-.061	-.033	-.059	-.036
1914	-.067	-.036	-.063	-.040

Federal League

1915	-.090	-.069		
1914	-.110	-.096		
1913	-.078	-.052	-.077	-.063
1912	-.085	-.062	-.089	-.080
1911	-.094	-.073	-.082	-.072
1910	-.064	-.029	-.078	-.054
1909	-.065	-.024	-.065	-.029
1908	-.060	-.019	-.059	-.020
1907	-.069	-.026	-.067	-.027
1906	-.075	-.038	-.070	-.030

Year				
1905	-.070	-.037	-.082	-.053
1904	-.075	-.046	-.075	-.042
1903	-.078	-.072	-.103	-.076
1902	-.108	-.096	-.096	-.050
1901	-.117	-.105	-.077	-.065
1900			-.090	-.071
1899			-.108	-.086
1898			-.097	-.067
1897			-.123	-.111
1896			-.124	-.115
1895			-.132	-.129
1894			-.145	-.165
1893			-.103	-.109
1892	American Assn		-.082	-.042
1891	-.127	-.110	-.075	-.075
1890	-.132	-.105	-.086	-.086
1889	-.112	-.098	-.096	-.096
1888	-.092	-.063	-.068	-.068
1887	-.124	-.112	-.123	-.123
1886	-.096	-.070	-.092	-.092
1885	-.107	-.083	-.095	-.070
1884	-.111	-.090	-.102	-.089
1883	-.124	-.097	-.111	-.103
1882	-.127	-.089	-.096	-.082
1881			-.107	-.079
1880			-.089	-.058
1879			-.106	-.074
1878			-.111	-.065
1877			-.131	-.092
1876			-.123	-.073
	Union 1884		Players 1890	
	-.146	-.111	-.108	-.106

One interesting illustration might start with Honus Wagner's great 1908 season (BWA=+. 145). What might Wagner have done in the 1979 American League, given a livelier ball but tougher competition? Table 5.1 yields a batting average correction of—.059-(+.003)=-.062 and a slugging correction of—.020-(-.029)=+.009, which applied to Wagner's 1908 stats gives a 1979 BA of .292 and SLG of .551. (In 600 ABs, he would have, say 30 HRS, 10 triples, 35 doubles). Wagner's stolen base crown and 10th-place tie in walks translate directly to similar positions in the 1979 stats. That's impressive batting production for any shortstop, and a "1979 Honus Wagner" would doubtless be an All-Star Game starter!

These results are fairly typical. Any 20th century superstar would be a star today. Indeed a young Babe Ruth or Ted Williams would out-bat any of today's stars. But of course, any of today's stars—Parker, Schmidt, Rice, Carew—would before 1955 have been a legendary superstar. Perhaps they almost deserve their heroic salaries!

Facts are often hard on legends, and many may prefer to believe veterans belittling the technical competence of today's baseball as compared, say, to pre–World War II. Indeed, "little things" may have been executed better by the average 1939 player. However, so great is the improvement in batting that if all other aspects of play were held constant, a lineup of average 1939 hitters would finish 20 to 30 games behind a lineup of average 1979 hitters, by scoring 200 to 300 fewer runs. This should hardly surprise an objective observer. Today's players are certainly taller and heavier, are drawn from a larger population, especially more countries and races, are more carefully taught at all levels of play. If a host of new track and field Olympic records established every four years are any indication, they can run faster and farther. Why shouldn't they hit a lot better?

6

Runs and Wins

PETE PALMER

Pete Palmer's contributions to SABR and to baseball analysis could fill a book. He has vastly improved or corrected Major League Baseball's historical record, including both the famous (Ty Cobb's hit total) and the obscure. He invented OPS (on-base percentage + slugging percentage) and the concept of using linear weights to measure baseball value. Perhaps most importantly, he was the first researcher to recognize the mathematical relationship between runs and wins, a foundational concept that informs all modern analysis. *The Hidden Game of Baseball*, a book he co-wrote with John Thorn in 1984, remains a fundamental text within the game's literature. Palmer received the Henry Chadwick Award in 2010. This article appeared in the first issue of *The National Pastime*, a new SABR publication launched in 1982 by editor Thorn.

Most statistical analyses of baseball have been concerned with evaluating offensive performance, with pitching and fielding coming in for less attention. An important area that has been little studied is the relationship of runs scored and allowed to wins and losses: how many games a team ought to have won, how many it did win, and which teams' actual won-lost records varied far from their probable won-lost records.

The initial published attempt on this subject was Earnshaw Cook's *Percentage Baseball*, in 1964. Examining major-league results from 1950 through 1960 he found winning percentage equal to .484 times runs scored divided by runs allowed. (Example: in 1965 the American League champion Minnesota Twins scored 774 runs and allowed 600; 774 times .484 divided by 600 yields an expected winning percentage of .630. The Twins in fact finished at 102-60, a winning percentage of .624. Had they lost one of the games they won, their percentage would have been .623.)

Arnold Soolman, in an unpublished paper which received some media attention, looked at results from 1901 through 1970 and came up with winning percentage equal to .102 times runs scored per game minus .103 times runs allowed per game plus .505. (Using the '65 Twins, Soolman's method produces an expected won-lost percentage of .611.) Bill James, in his *Baseball Abstract*, developed winning percentage equal to runs scored raised to the power x, divided by the sum of runs scored and runs allowed each raised to the power x. Originally, x was equal to two but then better results were obtained when a value of 1.83 was used. (James's original method shows the '65 Twins at .625, his improved method at .614.)

My work showed that as a rough rule of thumb, each additional 10 runs scored (or 10 less runs allowed) produced one extra win, essentially the same as the Soolman study. However, breaking the teams into groups showed that high-scoring teams needed more runs to produce a win. This runs-per-win factor I determined to be equal to 10 times the square root of the average number of runs scored per inning by both teams. Thus in normal play, when 4.5 runs per game are scored by each club, the factor comes out equal to 10 on the button. (When 4.5 runs are scored by each club, each team scores .5 runs per inning—totaling one run, the square root of which is one, times 10.) In any given year, the value is usually in the 9 to 11 range. James handled this situation by adjusting his exponent x to be equal to two minus one over the quantity of runs scored plus runs allowed per game minus three. Thus with 4.5 runs per game, x equals two minus one over the quantity nine minus three: two minus one-sixth equals 1.83.

Based on results from 1900 through 1981, my method or Bill's (the refined model taking into account runs per game) work equally well, giving an average error of 2.75 wins per team. Using Soolman's method, or a constant 10 runs per win, results in an error about four percent higher, while Cook's method is about 20 percent worse.

Probability theory defines standard deviation as the square root of the sum of the squares of the deviations divided by the number of samples. Average error is usually two-thirds of the standard deviation. If the distribution is normal, then two-thirds of all the deviations will be less than one standard deviation, one in 20 will be more than two away, and one in 400 will be more than three away. If these conditions are met, then the variation is considered due to chance alone.

From 1900 through 1981 there were 1448 team seasons. Using the square root of runs per inning method, one standard deviation (or sigma) was 26 percentage points. Seventy teams were more than 52 points (two sigmas) away and only two were more than 78 points (three sigmas) off. The expected numbers here were 72 two-sigma team seasons and 4 three-sigma team seasons, so there is no reason to doubt that the distribution is normal and that differences are basically due to chance.

Still, it is interesting to look at the individual teams that had the largest differences in actual and expected won-lost percentage and try to figure out why they did not achieve normal results. By far the most unusual situation occurred in the American League in 1905. Here two teams had virtually identical figures for runs scored and allowed, yet one finished 25 games ahead of the other! It turns out that with one exception, these two teams had the largest differences in each direction in the entire period. Detroit that season scored 512 runs and allowed 602. The Tigers' expected winning percentage was .435, but they actually had a 79-74 mark, worth a percentage of .517. St. Louis, on the other hand, had run data of 511–608 and an expected percentage of .430, yet went 54-99, a .353 percentage.

Looking at game scores, the difference can be traced to the performance in close contests. Detroit was 32-17 in one-run games and 13-10 in those decided by two runs. St. Louis had marks of 17-34 and 10-25 in these categories. Detroit still finished 15 games out in third place, while St. Louis was dead last. Ty Cobb made his debut with the Tigers that year, but did little to help the team, batting .240 in 41 games.

The only team to have a larger difference between expected and actual percentage in either direction than these two teams was in the strike-shortened season last year [1981], when Cincinnati finished a record 88 points higher than expected. Their 23-10 record in one-run games was the major factor. The 1955 Kansas City Athletics, who played 76 points better than expected, had an incredible 30-15 mark in one-run games, while going 33-76 otherwise.

Listed below are all the teams with differences of 70 or more points.

Year	Club	Runs	W/L	Pct.	Expected	Diff.
1981	Cincinnati	464–440	66-42	.611	.523	+.088
1905	Detroit	512–602	79-74	.517	.435	+.082
1955	Kansas City	638–911	63-91	.409	.333	+.076
1954	Brooklyn	778–740	92-62	.597	.523	+.074
1970	Cincinnati	775–681	102-60	.630	.558	+.072

1924	Brooklyn	717–675	92-62	597	.527	+.070
1981	Baltimore	429–437	59-46	.562	.492	+.070
1905	St. Louis (AL)	511–608	54-99	.353	.430	-.077
1946	Philadelphia (AL)	529–680	49-105	.318	.395	-.077
1907	Cincinnati	524–514	66-87	.431	.507	-.076
1935	Boston (NL)	578–852	38-115	.248	.322	-.074
1917	Pittsburgh	464–594	51-103	.331	.404	-.073
1937	Cincinnati	612–707	56-98	.364	.437	-.073
1975	Houston	664–711	64-97	.398	.471	-.073
1919	Washington	533–570	56-84	.400	.472	-.072
1924	St. Louis (NL)	740–750	65-89	.422	.494	-.072
1911	Pittsburgh	744–560	85-69	.552	.623	-.071

The 1924 National League season affords an interesting contrast which is evident in the chart. St. Louis failed of its expected won-lost percentage by 72 points while Brooklyn exceeded its predicted won-lost mark by 70.

The two poor showings by the Pittsburgh club in 1911 and 1917 were part of an eight-year string ending in 1918 in which the Pirates played an average of 37 points below expectations, a difference of about six wins per year. This was the worst record over a long stretch in modern major-league history. Cincinnati was 40 points under in a shorter span, covering 1902 through 1907. No American League team ever played worse than 25 points below expectation over a period of six or more years.

On the plus side, the best mark is held by the current Baltimore Orioles under Earl Weaver. From 1976 through 1981 they have averaged 41 points better than expected. The best National League mark was achieved by the Brooklyn and Los Angeles Dodgers in 1954–63, 27 points higher than expectations over a ten-year period, or about four wins per year.

The three-sigma limit for 10-year performance is 25 points. The number of clubs which exceeded this limit over such a period is not more than would be expected by chance. So it would seem that the teams were just lucky or unlucky, and that there are no other reasons for their departure from expected performance.

Below are the actual results and differences for the four teams covered.

Pittsburgh

1911	85-69	.552	-.071
1912	93-58	.616	-.009
1913	78-71	.523	-.036
1914	69-85	.448	-.025
1915	73-81	.474	-.053
1916	65-89	.422	-.003
1917	51-103	.331	-.073
1918	65-60	.520	-.029

Cincinnati

1902	70-70	.500	-.049
1903	74-65	.532	-.041
1904	88-65	.575	-.025
1905	79-74	.516	-.007
1906	64-87	.424	-.039
1907	66-87	.431	-.076

Baltimore

1976	88-74	.543	+.029
1977	97-64	.602	+.060
1978	90-71	.559	+.042
1979	102-57	.642	+.028
1980	100-62	.617	+.01
1981	59-46	.562	+.070

Brooklyn/ Los Angeles

1954	92-62	.597	+.074
1955	98-55	.641	+.012
1956	93-61	.604	+.025
1957	84-70	.545	-.021
1958	71-83	.461	+.021
1959	88-68	.564	+.041
1960	82-72	.532	-.015
1961	89-65	.578	+.054
1962	102-63	.618	+.032
1963	99-63	.611	+.050

7

Ladies and Gentlemen,
Presenting Marty McHale

LAWRENCE S. RITTER

Larry Ritter drove seventy-five thousand miles across the United States in the mid-1960s, conducting interviews and doing research for what became his 1966 book *The Glory of Their Times*, an oral history of early twentieth-century baseball that is considered one of the best baseball books ever written. He later recounted that he was inspired by the death of Ty Cobb and the realization that Cobb's generation of baseball players was dying off. On his travels, he discovered many nearly forgotten men who were willing to talk to him, and their stories resonate in the book to this day. Ritter's interview with Marty McHale was conducted at the same time but was not transcribed in time for the book's publication. John Thorn, with Ritter's approval, edited it for the first edition of SABR's *The National Pastime*. This is the only such interview that did not make it into either the original or the updated edition of *Glory*. Larry Ritter received the Henry Chadwick Award in 2010.

Damon Runyon once wrote a story about me, saying this fellow McHale, who is not the greatest ballplayer that ever lived, is probably the most versatile man who ever took up the game. This was in the 1920s, after I had left baseball. So Johnny Kieran of the *New York Times* asked Babe Ruth about it, knowing he and I had been on the Red Sox together. Johnny said, "Marty played in the big leagues, he played football in college, he was on the track team, he was on the stage, he wrote for the Wheeler Syndicate and the *Sun*, he was in the Air Service"—and so forth. He went on listing my accomplishments until the Babe interrupted to say, "Well, I don't know about all those things, but he was the best goddamn singer I ever heard!"

You see, I sang in vaudeville for 12 years, a high baritone tenor—an "Irish Thrush," they called it then, and *Variety* called me "The Baseball Caruso." But even before vaudeville, before baseball even, I used to work in a lot of shows around Boston and made trips down to Wakefield, Winchester—minstrel shows, usually—and sometimes these little two-act sketches.

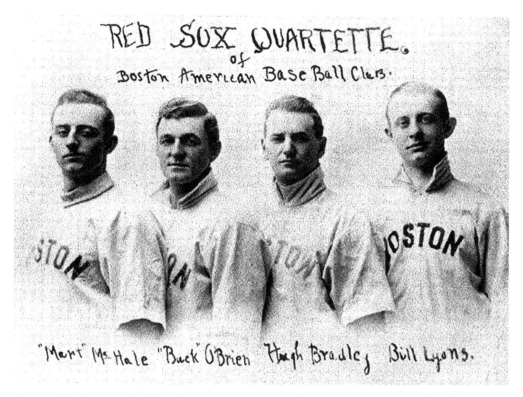

Fig. 7.1. The Boston Red Sox Quartette, second edition (sans Larry Gardner). National Baseball Hall of Fame Library, Cooperstown NY.

So when I joined the Boston club, a bunch of us—Buck O'Brien, Hughie Bradley, Larry Gardner, and myself—formed the Red Sox Quartette. After a while Gardner gave it up and a fellow named Bill Lyons stepped in. This Lyons was no ballplayer, but Boston signed him to a contract anyway, just to make the name of the act look proper. We were together three years, and when we broke up I was just as well satisfied because it was quite an ordeal keeping the boys on schedule. They just couldn't get used to that buzzer that tells you you're on next. They'd be a couple of minutes late and think nothing of it, but you can't do that in vaudeville, you know—you're *on*.

I did a single for about another three years, which was not very good— just good enough so that they paid for it—and then Mike Donlin and I got together. Now, you may not remember Mike, but he was—well, he was the Babe Ruth of his day. "Turkey Mike," they called him, because when he'd make a terrific catch or something he'd do a kind of turkey step and take his cap off and throw it up like a ham, a real ham; but he was a great one, he could live up to that stuff in the field or at the bat. His widow gave me some of his souvenirs: a gold bat and ball that were given to him as the most valuable player in 1905, some cufflinks, and a couple of gold cups, one from the Giants and the other from the Reds. He hit over .350 for both of them.

Mike and I were together for five years, doing a double-entendre act called "Right Off the Bat"—not too much singing, Mike would only go through the motions—and we played the Keith-Orpheum circuit: twice in one year we were booked into the Palace in New York and that was when it was the Palace, not the way it is now! They had nothing but the big headliners. When Mike left for Hollywood, I went back to doing a single. He made a bunch of pictures out there, and that's where he died.

Which did I like better, baseball or vaudeville? Well, I'd call it about 50–50. The vaudeville was more difficult, the traveling. Sure, you had to travel a lot in baseball, but you had somebody taking care of your trunk and your tickets and everything; all you had to do was get your slip, hop onto the train, and go to bed. When you got to the hotel your trunk was there. In vaudeville you had to watch your own stuff. I used to say to Mike, you're the best valet I know, because he was always on time with the tickets and had our baggage checks and everything all taken care of, right on the button all the time.

Of course, Mike and I wouldn't have been such an attraction if it hadn't been for baseball, so maybe I ought to tell you how I came to sign with the Red Sox in 1910. First of all, Boston was almost my home town—I grew up in Stoneham, that's nine miles out and if you took a trolley car and changed two or three times, you could get to the ballpark. Which I'd done only once—I only saw one big-league game before I played in one, and Cy Young pitched it; I wasn't really a Red Sox fan. But here comes the second reason for my signing: they gave me a big bonus. How big? Two thousand dollars, and back then that was money!

You see, that year for Maine University I had thrown three consecutive no-hitters, and the scouts were all over. I had a bid from Detroit, one from Pittsburgh, one from the Giants, and another from the Braves. And there was sort of a veiled offer from Cincinnati, which is an interesting story.

This Cincinnati situation, Clark Griffith was down there managing and when I reported to the Red Sox, which was in June, following the end of the college term, his club was playing the Braves, over at Braves Field across the tracks from the Huntington Avenue park. Now, the Red Sox were on the road when I and some other college boys reported. We had signed, but the Red Sox didn't want us with them right away: they had to make room for us, they could only have so many players. So I remember that Griffith came over to the Red Sox park one morning to watch the boys work out. The clubhouse man told us we were all being watched—like you'd watch horses, you know, working out each morning, and he said if we wanted to stay with the club, better take it easy and not put too much on the ball and so on. See, the club usually asks waivers on the newcomers immediately upon reporting to see if anybody else is interested in them, and if so they can withdraw the waivers after a certain time.

I remember very definitely—I went out there and I was pitching to the hitters and I put everything I had on the ball, because after looking over that bunch of Red Sox pitchers I could see there was not much chance for a young collegian to crack that lineup.

At any rate, Griffith must have put in some claim, you see, because two days later I was on my way to Chicago to join the Red Sox. They had withdrawn the waivers. I joined them in Chicago and we went from there to Cleveland. I remember my pal Tris Speaker hurt his finger in Chicago and he was out for a few days, and Fordham's Chris Mahoney, who was an outfielder, a pitcher, and a good hitter, took his place.

He and I weren't the only college boys on that team, you know: Bill Carrigan, Jake Stahl, Larry Gardner, Duffy Lewis, Harry Hooper . . . even Speaker went to—not the University of Texas, but Texas Polyclinic, Polytechnic or something of that kind out there; only went for two years, but he went. And Ray Collins and Hughie Bradley, too. Buck O'Brien, he came the next year, he said, "I got a degree, I got a B.S. from Brockton." He said B.S. stood for boots and shoes, meaning that he worked in a factory.

Now on this day in Cleveland, we had Chris Mahoney playing right field, Harry Hooper moved over to center, and Duffy Lewis stayed in left, and Patsy Donovan put me in to pitch my first game in the big leagues against Joe Jackson and those Cleveland boys. I wasn't what you'd call sloppily relaxed, but I wasn't particularly nervous, either. You see, I was one of the most egotistical guys that God ever put on this earth: I felt that I could beat anybody. I struck out 10 of those Naps, including Jackson. The first time he was up, I had Joe two strikes, no balls, and I did something that the average big-league pitcher would never do. Instead of trying to fool him with a pitch, I stuck the next one right through there and caught him flat-footed. He never dreamed I'd do that.

So the next time up there the same thing happened. He hit a foul, then took a strike, and then Red Kleinow, an old head who was catching me, came out for a conference. He said, "What do you want to pitch him, a curve ball?" And I said, "No, I'm going to stick another fast one right through there."

He said, "He'll murder it." Well—he did! Joe hit a ball that was like a shot out of a rifle against the right-field wall. Harry Hooper retrieved it in *left* center!

Yes, I had ten strikeouts, but I lost the ball game. It was one of those sun-field things: a fellow named Hohnhurst was playing first base for Cleveland and, with a man on first, he hit a long fly to left-center field. Harry Hooper, who was in center this day, was dead certain on fly balls, but when Speaker was out there, as Harry said afterwards, he used to let Speaker take everything within range. Harry said he and Duffy Lewis didn't exactly get signals crossed, but they were not sure as to who was going to take the ball.

Finally Duffy went for it, and just as he made his pitch for the ball the sun hit him right between the eyes and he didn't get his hands on the thing and the run, of course, scored, and Hohnhurst, the fellow who hit the ball—he got himself to second base. Ted Easterly got a single on top of that, and anyway, the score ended up 4–3. That was it.

I was supposed to be a spitball pitcher, but I had a better overhand curve, what they called a drop curve—you'd get that overspin on it and that ball would break much better than a spitter. I had what they call a medium-good fastball, not overpowering but good enough, and if you took something off your curve and your spitter, your fastball looked a lot better. For my slow one, the changeup as they call it now, I tried a knuckler but never could get any results with it, so I stole Eddie Karger's slow-breaking downer. He and I used to take two fingers off the ball and throw it with the same motion as we used for the fastball.

They still have those fellows today that throw spitters, but it doesn't make much difference—because even when the spitter was legal in my day, in both leagues you couldn't pick six good spitball pitchers. You'd take a fellow like Ed Walsh with the White Sox, the two Coveleskis, Burleigh Grimes, and the lefthanded spitter in the National League, who has since lost both legs, Clarence Mitchell.

Now, Clarence was a good spitball pitcher, but Walsh was the best. He worked harder at it, had a better break, had better control of it, and he pitched in more ballgames than any pitcher in either league over a period of years.

Eddie Cicotte, he was with us in Boston, you know, he was going with a spitter for a while. He used to throw that emery ball, too, and then he developed what we call the "shine" ball. He used to have paraffin on different parts of his trousers, which was not legal, and he would just go over all the stitches with that paraffin, making the other part of the ball rougher. It was just like the emery situation, but in reverse, and an emery ball is one of the most dangerous, not like the spitter, which can be controlled. But Cicotte's main pitch was the knuckleball, and he used that to such an extent that we called him Knuckles.

Joe Wood was with the Red Sox when I joined them, too. Now there was a fellow who could do nearly everything well. He was a great ballplayer, not just a pitcher, he was a good outfielder, he was a good hitter, he was a good baseman, he would run like blazes, he used to work real hard before a ball-game, he was just a good all-around ballplayer and a great pitcher. And he was a fine pool player, too, and billiards. He could play any kind of a card game and well; also he was a good golfer. I think that he could have done nearly everything. If he were playing football he'd be a good quarterback.

Joey was a natural—and talking about egotistical people, there's a guy who had terrific confidence, terrific. Without being too fresh, he was very cocky, you know. He just had "the old confidence."

I wasn't with Boston the year they won the World's Championship and Joey won those 34 games and then three more against the Giants, but I was at the Series and wrote a story about that final game. I saw the Snodgrass muff—he was careless, and that happens. But right after that he made a gorgeous running catch.

Earlier in that game Harry Hooper made the best catch I ever saw. I hear from Harry twice a year or so; he lives in California, and he's got plenty of the world's goods. Harry made this catch—he had his back to the ball—and from the bench it looked like he caught it backhanded, over his shoulder. After I sent my story to him, he wrote to me. "I thought it was a very good catch, too," he said, "but you were wrong in your perspective. When I ran for that ball, I ran with my back toward it and you guys with your craning necks were so excited about it, when I ran into the low fence"—you see the bleachers came up from a low fence in Fenway—"the fence turned me around halfway to the right and I caught the ball in my bare right hand." Imagine!

In 1913 I joined the Yankees—they weren't called the Highlanders any more—and then three years later I went back to the Red Sox. Bill Carrigan, who was the Boston manager then, said, "Now that you're seasoned enough you can come back and pitch for a big-league team." The Yankees in those days were a terrible ballclub. In 1914 I lost 16 games and won only 7, with an earned-run average under three. I got no runs. I would be beaten one to nothing, two to nothing, three to one, scores like that. You were never ahead of anybody. You can't win without runs. Take this fellow who's pitching for the Mets, Roger Craig, what did he lose—22, something like that? What did he win—5? One to nothing, two to nothing, terrible.

When I got to New York, Frank Chance was the manager, a great guy. He had a reputation as a really tough egg, but if you went out there and worked and hustled and showed him that you were interested in what you were doing he would certainly be in your corner, to the extent that he would try and get you more money come contract time.

I have a watch, one of these little "wafer" watches, that Chance gave me in 1914 after I guess about the first month. I had won a couple of games for him, one of them was the opening game against the World Champion A's, and one day, just as a gesture, he said, he gave me this watch.

Frank and I were such good friends that late in 1914, when we were playing a series in Washington, after dinner, one evening he said, let's take a little walk. So we went out to a park across from the hotel and sat down. "I'm going to quit," he said. "I can't stand this being manager, can't stand being the manager of this ballclub."

He said, "We're not going to get anyplace. I've got a good pitching staff"— and he did have a good pitching staff—"but you fellows are just batting your heads against the wall every time you go out there, no runs." The owners wouldn't get him any players, see, and he said, "I just can't take it—I'm going to quit."

He had already talked it over with the front office in New York and one of the reasons he took me out to the park was that he had told them which men he thought they should keep, and I happened to be one of three pitchers along with Slim Caldwell and Ray Fisher, and he said I know that you'll be working in vaudeville next winter and I would advise you to get yourself a two- or three-year contract, if you can, before you leave New York on your tour, which was very good advice—which advice I didn't take. I was too smart—you know how it is, very smart—so Mike Donlin and I went out on the Orpheum circuit that winter after opening at the Palace.

So Mike, before we left New York, he said, you better go over to the Yankee office and get yourself signed in before we leave for Chicago. He said, you never can tell what's going to happen. I, being very, very smart, I said,

"No, I'll be worth more money to them in the spring than I am now after the publicity we will get in vaudeville this winter."

But I was wrong, because during the winter, while we were in Minneapolis at the Orpheum theatre, Devery and Farrell sold the team to Ruppert and Huston. I'm quite sure I could have made a deal with Frank Farrell for a two- or three-year contract before leaving, but as I say I wasn't very smart.

When we got back east Bill Donovan (that's Bill, not Patsy) had been appointed manager of the Yankees, and he was not in favor of anybody having a long-term contract. I didn't even last out the year with him.

It seemed every time I pitched against Washington I had Walter Johnson as an opponent, or Jim Shaw, either one. Griffith, he used to . . . I don't know . . . I had an idea he didn't pitch them against Caldwell. It seemed that every time Slim pitched, the team would get him three or four runs—though he didn't need them, he was a great pitcher.

Was Johnson as great a pitcher as they say? Let me tell you, he was greater than they say. He was with one of the worst ballclubs imaginable, not quite as bad as the old Yankees but almost as bad.

When I got out of the Air Service, after the War—you see, I quit baseball on the 4th of July, I think, in 1917 and went into the Air Service—when I came out I went to work for the *New York Evening Sun*. I wrote articles, and the *Sun* used to run them every Saturday. The Wheeler Syndicate used to sell them to—wherever they could sell them, Boston, Philadelphia, Newark, anywhere they could, you know, and I used to get five, two, four, eight dollars apiece for them, and one of the stories that I wrote was about Walter Johnson.

I wrote one about Joey, too, and about Cicotte, and Mathewson, oh, so many of them. In the story about Johnson, I wondered what would have happened if he had been pitching for the Giants, who could get him five or six runs nearly every time he started, and I'm wondering if he'd ever lose a ballgame. I found out from Joe Vila, who was the sports editor for the *Sun*, that Matty didn't care very much for that.

Matty was a very good friend of Mike's, and so was McGraw, who was my sponsor into the Lambs Club. He was a Jekyll and Hyde character. Off the field he was very affable, but the minute he'd get in uniform, he was one of the toughest guys you'd ever want to know. Mike used to tell me a lot of inside information which of course helped me when I was writing these stories.

Do you know about the movie Speaker and I made? In 1917, just before I went into the Service, we produced a motion picture of the big stars in both major leagues. We had $80,000 worth of bookings for the picture, and then they declared baseball during the War not essential, so all the bookings were cancelled. We sold the rights to the YMCA to use it in the camps all over Europe, in the ships going over and back, and in the camps here.

After the War was over I showed the film to my friend Roxy, God rest him, and he took the thing over and showed it at the Rivoli and the Rialto and down to Fifth Avenue, and then I happened to come into Wall Street to work as a stockbroker—in 1920 I started my own firm, which I still run today—and I forgot all about the film.

It was put in the morgue some place up at the Rialto or the Rivoli, and the YMCA lost their prints somewhere over in France, but I had left in the tins some cuts and out-takes of the shots of—well, Speaker, Hooper, Ruth, Wood, Matty, and Johnson and all, and I still have them. I showed the clips only about two years ago at the Pathé projection room one day and they still look pretty good.

The game's a lot different today from what it was when I played. The biggest change—and the worst one, in my opinion—is the home run. Now, let's first talk of the fellow going up to the plate. Seventy-five percent of the time he goes up there with the thought of hitting the ball out of the ballpark, and it's not too difficult to do, because they have moved the ballpark in on him. Now in right field and center field and left field, you've got stands. They used to have a bleacher, way out, in the old days, but the only home run you'd get would be if you hit it between the fielders. "In grounds," they'd call it, a home run in grounds: if a ball got in between those fielders and if you had any speed, they wouldn't be able to throw you out. Today, if you hit a good long fly it's in one of these short stands.

In the old days they juiced up the ball some, but when they talk about the dead ball—there never was any dead ball that I can remember. I've got a couple of scars on my chin to prove it. I saw Joe Jackson hit a ball over the top of the Polo Grounds in right field—*over the top of it*—off one of our pitchers, and I have never seen or heard of anyone hitting it over since, and that was around 1914–15, in there.

Today's ball is livelier, no doubt of that. They are using an Australian wool now in winding the core of the ball. In the old days they used wool but not one that is as elastic as this wool. The bats are whippier, too. But the principal reason for all these homers is the concentration of the hitter on trying to hit the ball out of the park.

The fielding today? Well, any of these boys in the big leagues today could field in any league at any time. I think the better equipment has more to do with the spectacular play. You take this here third baseman up with the Yankees—Clete Boyer—he's terrific, just terrific. Larry Gardner, who played third on the Boston team with me, he was a great third baseman, and he had that "trolleywire throw" to first, but Larry was not as agile as Boyer. I think Boyer is a little quicker. But, if you want a fellow to compare with Boyer, take Buck Weaver of that Black Sox team. He would field with Boyer any day, and throw with him, and he was a better hitter. He would be my all-time third baseman.

Players of my day, give them the good equipment, and they would be just as good or better. Now, you take a fellow like Wagner—I don't mean the Wagner we had with the Red Sox, but the Pirates' Wagner, Honus Wagner, who came to see us in Pittsburgh at the theatre, and he took up the whole dressing room with that big can of his. There was one of the most awkward-looking humans you ever saw, but he made the plays, without the shovel glove.

And Speaker—could a big glove have made him any better? As an outfielder, Speaker was in a class by himself: He would play so close to the infield that he'd get in on rundown plays! Then the next man perhaps would hit a long fly into center field and he would be on his bicycle with his back to the ball—not backing away, he'd turn and run—and you'd think he had a radar or a magnet or something because just at the proper time he'd turn his head and catch the ball over his shoulder.

Those fellows, Speaker, Lewis, and Hooper, they used to practice throwing, something that you don't see anymore. Those fellows would have a cap down near the catcher and they'd see who would come closest to the cap when they'd throw from the outfield. They all had marvelous arms. Nobody would run on them and I think that most of the people who ever saw them play would say there was no trio that could compare with them.

Mike and I, in our act, we used to do a number called, "When You're a Long, Long Way From Home." In it I used to do a recitation, and the last two lines were, "When you're on third base alone, you're still a long, long way from home." It was serious, about life being like a game of baseball. Times have changed—a boy can't peek through a knothole in a concrete fence—but that's still true.

8

In Pursuit of Bull Durham

BILL HABER

Bill Haber, one of SABR's sixteen founders, is considered one of baseball's all-time greatest researchers. The Biographical Research Committee was an original SABR committee, and Haber was one of its leading lights for many years. Working mainly from his home in Brooklyn, before the internet transformed genealogical work, Haber would often spend years working on leads for a player who played four games a century ago, calling or writing cemeteries, county courthouses, municipal officials, newspapers, and family members. Haber also worked for Topps, Inc. for many years, writing the statistics and text on the back of their baseball cards and organizing their massive photo archive. This article from the 1983 *Baseball Research Journal* provides a glimpse into Haber's dedication and passion for biographical research.

Perhaps the most intriguing mystery in our pursuit of "missing" ballplayers is the case of Louis "Bull" Durham. He pitched briefly in four seasons in the major leagues between 1904 and 1909, and also attracted considerable attention in 1908 when he pitched and won five consecutive doubleheaders for Indianapolis in the American Association. The Macmillan *Baseball Encyclopedia* indicated he was born in Bolivar, New York, in 1881, and was a brother of James Garfield "Jimmy" Durham, a contemporary ballplayer. Both facts proved to be incorrect, the one about their relationship being rather obvious. Both were listed as being born in 1881, one in New York and the other in Kansas.

For 13 years, this writer conducted a serious effort to turn up clues about the life and death of Louis Durham. The newspaper accounts of his baseball exploits indicated that he was married about 1907, but the name of his bride or the site of the marriage was never determined. Newspapers indicated that the player spent the winter of 1906–7 studying law in Geneva, Ohio. However, no such learning institution could be identified in or near that city. A newspaper note indicated that he was a patent medicine specialist, a jack of all trades, but there was no specific information reported which could be used to trace the man.

Although diligent efforts to pursue Mr. Durham were begun in 1969, a definite clue to the man's identity wasn't located until October 1982, when two other SABR members became involved. Ray Nemec of Illinois located a note in a 1906 Pennsylvania newspaper which indicated that Bull Durham's correct name at birth was Charles Staub. Al Kermisch of Virginia, who has researched the early decades of professional baseball, had found a reference to a Louis Staub pitching in Pennsylvania in 1900–02. This Staub reportedly was born in New Oxford, Pennsylvania, in 1879.

With that knowledge in hand, a random phone call was made to several Staub families listed in the current New Oxford telephone directory. One such call referred this writer to a young lady in York, Pennsylvania, who has compiled a genealogy of all the Staub families of southeastern Pennsylvania dating back to the 1700s. A phone call to this lady produced the information that Louis Raphael Staub was born in New Oxford, Pennsylvania, June 27, 1877, the eighth of nine children. Within several weeks after making this discovery, two daughters of this man were found. They were able to provide biographical information needed for the record of their father to be brought up to date.

Louis Staub began playing professional baseball about 1898. In 1902, he found himself with the Cedar Rapids, Iowa, ballclub, a teammate of the above-mentioned Jimmy Durham. The latter, also a pitcher, fared well at Cedar Rapids and earned a trial with the Chicago White Sox. Louis failed at Cedar Rapids and was released by June. By August he was pitching at McSherrystown, Pennsylvania, his hometown. It was just about this time that Louis Staub changed his name to Louis Staub Durham, perhaps because of his liking for the popular Bull Durham tobacco of that period, or because of his friendship with Jimmy Durham, or perhaps a combination of the two. In any event, Louis "Bull" Durham, the silver-haired right-hander, became a better pitcher. He had a pretty good year at Augusta in the South Atlantic League in 1904, although he lost his debut on April 26. This also was the Organized Ball debut of Ty Cobb, the center fielder of Augusta, who broke in with a home run.

The Brooklyn Dodgers brought up Durham in September and on the 22nd of that month, "the white-haired lad from Atlanta" pitched a four-hit, 3–1 win over Pittsburgh. The Atlanta reference was one of the many false leads about Durham, who had a very erratic career. He moved ever so quickly from the minors to the majors to the minors, to semipro ball, to the majors, etc. For one or two years there is no playing record of him at all. He was up with the Washington Senators briefly in 1907 and the New York Giants in 1908–09 after that great 19-6 season with Indianapolis when he won those five doubleheaders. His pro ball career apparently ended in 1913 when he pitched briefly and played the outfield for Long Beach and Pasadena in the Southern California League. At that location, Durham made the transition to a career as a silent screen movie actor in Hollywood.

Backtracking a little, we note that Durham (Staub) had attended George-town University briefly before the turn of the century. His first marriage in 1906 or 1907 ended about 1909 when his wife died of tuberculosis or a similar ailment. He married a Pittsburgh girl about 1914 and had one child, a daughter, by this marriage. In early 1918, his motion picture work came to an end and he moved back to Pittsburgh with his family. By the early 1920s, this marriage ended in divorce and Durham headed back to California. However, he never made it.

For some reason (perhaps to visit Jimmy Durham of Coffeyville, Kansas) Durham stopped off in Kansas on his way west. He met a young lady, married her in 1927, and made his home in Kansas for the rest of his life. Louis Durham adopted his third wife's two children and the couple proceeded to have six more children. He was employed as a geologist in Kansas until his retirement, and died in Bentley, Kansas, June 28, 1960. His obituary in the Halstead *Independent* gave not the slightest indication that he had been a ballplayer, an occupation he had filled for about 15 years.

There still are a number of things we don't know about Louis Durham. We can only speculate about why he changed his name and why he moved to Kansas, and why there was no mention of his long baseball background in his obituary. The family is of the opinion that he used the pseudonym of Bull Durham because of his appreciation for the popular smoking tobacco. However, one can't help but wonder if his friendship with Jimmy Durham had something to do with it. The two had developed a close relationship when they first met as members of the Cedar Rapids pitching staff of 1902. Their friendship continued in 1907 when the two combined to win 34 games at Louisville. As a matter of fact, the 1907 Louisville team photo shows Jimmy seated with Louis standing right behind him. And, it has to be something more than mere coincidence that Louis settled in Kansas, the home state of Jimmy, upon heading west during the 1920s. Also, we know Jimmy was in the oil business in Kansas, and Louis became a geologist. Louis's widow doesn't recall him mentioning Jimmy by name, but then again, we know he was a mysterious sort of fellow, don't we?

9

Out at Home

JERRY MALLOY

Jerry Malloy was a legendary baseball researcher whose untimely death in 2000 so moved his legion of friends and colleagues that they named SABR's annual Negro Leagues Research Conference in his honor. "His articles for SABR were pathbreaking and exceptional and rank among the very best this organization has ever published," Jules Tygiel once said. "Even more so, I doubt that the best among us have ever been as generous with their research and support as was Jerry." Malloy had many baseball interests, but he was especially drawn to the history of baseball's color line: its effects on the game and the African American experience. This groundbreaking 1983 article tells the definitive story of how the segregation of Organized Baseball was established. Jerry received the Henry Chadwick Award in 2015.

> Baseball is the very symbol, the outward and visible expression of the drive and push and rush and struggle of the raging, tearing, booming nineteenth century.
>
> —MARK TWAIN

> Social inequality . . . means that in all the relations that exist between man and man he is to be measured and taken not according to his natural fitness and qualification, but that blind and relentless rule which accords certain pursuits and certain privileges to origin or birth.
>
> —MOSES F. WALKER

It was a dramatic and prophetic performance by Jackie Robinson. The 27-year-old black second baseman opened the 1946 International League season by leading the Montreal Royals to a 14–1 victory over Jersey City. In five trips to the plate, he had four hits (including a home run) and four RBIs; he scored four runs, stole two bases, and rattled a pitcher into balking him home with a taunting *danse macabre* off third. Branch Rickey's protégé had punched a hole through Organized Baseball's color barrier with the flair and talent that would eventually take him into the Hall of Fame. The color line that Jackie Robinson shattered, though unwritten, was very real indeed. Baseball's exclusion of the black man was so unremittingly thorough for such a long time that most of the press and public then, as now, thought that Robinson was making the first appearance of a man of his race in the history of Organized Baseball.

Actually, he represented a return of the Negro ballplayer, not merely to Organized Baseball, but to the International League as well. At least eight elderly citizens would have been aware of this. Frederick Ely, Jud Smith, James Fields, Tom Lynch, Frank Olin, "Chief" Zimmer, Pat Gillman, and George Bausewine may have noted with interest Robinson's initiation, for all of these men had been active players on teams that opened another International League season, that of 1887. And in that year they played with or against eight black players on six different teams.

The 1887 season was not the first in which Negroes played in the International League, nor would it be the last. But until Jackie Robinson stepped up to the plate on April 18, 1946, it was the most significant. For 1887 was a watershed year for both the International League and Organized Baseball, as it marked the origin of the color line. As the season opened, the black player had plenty of reasons to hope that he would be able to ply his trade in an atmosphere of relative tolerance; by the middle of the season, however, he would watch helplessly as the IL drew up a written color ban designed to deprive him of his livelihood; and by the time the league held its offseason meetings, it became obvious that Jim Crow was closing in on a total victory.

Yet before baseball became the victim of its own prejudice, there was a period of uncertainty and fluidity, however brief, during which it seemed by no means inevitable that men would be denied access to Organized Baseball due solely to skin pigmentation. It was not an interlude of total racial harmony, but a degree of toleration obtained that would become unimaginable in just a few short years. This is the story of a handful of black baseball players who, in the span of a single season, playing in a prestigious league, witnessed the abrupt conversion of hope and optimism into defeat and despair. These men, in the most direct and personal manner, would realize that the black American baseball player soon would be ruled "out at home."

I

The International League (IL) is the oldest minor league in Organized Baseball. Founded in 1884 as the "Eastern" League, it would be realigned and renamed frequently during its early period. The IL was not immune to the shifting sands of financial support that plagued both minor and major leagues (not to mention individual franchises) during the nineteenth century. In 1887 the league took the risk of adding Newark and Jersey City to a circuit that was otherwise clustered in upstate New York and southern Ontario. This arrangement proved to be financially unworkable. Transportation costs alone would doom the experiment after one season. The New Jersey franchises were simply too far away from Binghamton, Buffalo, Oswego, Rochester, Syracuse, and Utica in New York, and Hamilton and Toronto in Ontario.

But, of course, no one knew this when the 1887 season opened. Fans in Newark were particularly excited, because their "Little Giants" were a new team and an instant contender. A large measure of their eager anticipation was due to the unprecedented "colored battery" signed by the team. The pitcher was George Stovey and the catcher was Moses Fleetwood Walker.

"Fleet" Walker was born in Mt. Pleasant, Ohio, on the route of the Underground Railroad, on October 7, 1857. The son of a physician, he was raised in nearby Steubenville. At the age of twenty he entered the college preparatory program of Oberlin College, the first school in the United States to adopt an official admissions policy of nondiscrimination by sex, race, or creed. He was enrolled as a freshman in 1878, and attended Oberlin for the next three years. He was a good but not outstanding student in a rigorous liberal arts program. Walker also attended the University of Michigan for two years, although probably more for his athletic than his scholastic attainments. He did not obtain a degree from either institution, but his educational background was extremely sophisticated for a nineteenth century professional baseball player of whatever ethnic origin.

While at Oberlin, Walker attracted the attention of William Voltz, former sportswriter for the Cleveland *Plain Dealer*, who had been enlisted to form a professional baseball team to be based in Toledo. Walker was the second player signed by the team, which entered the Northwestern League in 1883. Toledo captured the league championship in its first year.

The following year Toledo was invited to join the American Association, a major league rival of the more established National League. Walker was one of the few players to be retained as Toledo made the jump to the big league. Thus did Moses Fleetwood Walker become the first black to play major-league baseball, 64 years before Jackie Robinson. Walker played in 42 games that season, batting .263 in 152 at-bats. His brother, Welday Wilberforce Walker, who was two years younger than Fleet, also played outfield in five games, filling in for injured players. Welday was 4-for-18 at the plate.

While at Toledo, Fleet Walker was the batterymate of Hank O'Day, who later became a famous umpire, and Tony Mullane, who could pitch with either hand and became the winningest pitcher, with 285 victories, outside the Hall of Fame. G. L. Mercereau, the team's batboy, many years later recalled the sight of Walker catching barehanded, as was common in those days, with his fingers split open and bleeding. Catchers would welcome swelling in their hands to provide a cushion against the pain.

The color of Walker's skin occasionally provoked another, more lasting, kind of pain. The *Toledo Blade*, on May 5, 1884, reported that Walker was "hissed . . . and insulted . . . because he was colored," causing him to commit five errors in a game in Louisville. Late in the season the team travelled to Richmond, Virginia, where manager Charley Morton received a letter threatening bloodshed, according to Lee Allen, by "75 determined men [who] have sworn to mob Walker if he comes on the ground in a suit." The letter, which Morton released to the press, was signed by four men who were "determined" not to sign their real names. Confrontation was avoided, for Walker had been released by the team due to his injuries before the trip to Richmond.

Such incidents, however, stand out because they were so exceptional. Robert Peterson, in *Only the Ball Was White*, points out that Walker was favorably received in cities such as Baltimore and Washington. As was the case throughout the catcher's career, the press was supportive of him and consistently reported his popularity among fans. Upon his release, the *Blade* described him as "a conscientious player [who] was very popular with Toledo audiences," and *Sporting Life's* Toledo correspondent stated that "by his fine, gentlemanly deportment, he made hosts of friends who will regret to learn that he is no longer a member of the club."

Walker started the 1885 season with Cleveland in the Western League, but the league folded in June. He played the remainder of 1885 and all of 1886 for the Waterbury, Connecticut, team in the Eastern League. While at Waterbury, he was referred to as "the people's choice," and was briefly managed by Charley Hackett, who later moved on to Newark. When Newark was accepted into the International League in 1887, Hackett signed Walker to play for him.

So in 1887 Walker was beginning his fifth season in integrated professional baseball. Tall, lean, and handsome, the 30-year-old catcher was an established veteran noted for his steady, dependable play and admired, literally, as a gentleman and a scholar. Later in the season, when the *Hamilton Spectator* printed a disparaging item about "the coon catcher of the Newarks," *The Sporting News* ran a typical response in defense of Walker: "It is a pretty small paper that will publish a paragraph of that kind about a member of a visiting club, and the man who wrote it is without doubt Walker's inferior in education, refinement, and manliness."

One of the reasons that Charley Hackett was so pleased to have signed Walker was that his catcher would assist in the development of one of his new pitchers, a Negro named George Washington Stovey. A 165-pound southpaw, Stovey had pitched for Jersey City in the Eastern League in 1886. Sol White, in his *History of Colored Base Ball*, stated that Stovey "struck out twenty-two of the Bridgeport [Connecticut] Eastern League team in 1886 and lost his game." *The Sporting News* that year called Stovey "a good one, and if the team would support him they would make a far better showing. His manner of covering first from the box is wonderful."

A dispute arose between the Jersey City and Newark clubs prior to the 1887 season concerning the rights to sign Stovey. One of the directors of the Jersey City team tried to use his leverage as the owner of Newark's Wright Street grounds to force Newark into surrendering Stovey. But, as the *Sporting Life* Newark correspondent wrote, "On sober second thought I presume he came to the conclusion that it was far better that the [Jersey City] club should lose Stovey than that he should lose the rent of the grounds."

A new rule for 1887, which would exist only that one season, provided that walks were to be counted as hits. One of the criticisms of the rule was that, in an era in which one of the pitching statistics kept was the opposition's batting average, a pitcher might be tempted to hit a batter rather than be charged with a "hit" by walking him. George Stovey, with his blazing fastball, his volatile temper, and his inability to keep either under strict control, was the type of pitcher these skeptics had in mind. He brought to the mound a wicked glare that intimidated hitters.

During the preseason contract dispute, Jersey City's manager, Pat Powers, acknowledged Stovey's talents, yet added: "Personally, I do not care for

Stovey. I consider him one of the greatest pitchers in the country, but in many respects I think I have more desirable men. He is head-strong and obstinate, and, consequently, hard to manage. Were I alone concerned I would probably let Newark have him, but the directors of the Jersey City Club are not so peaceably disposed."

Newark planned to mute Stovey's "head-strong obstinance" with the easy-going stability of Fleet Walker. That the strategy did not always work is indicated by an account in the *Newark Daily Journal* of a July game against Hamilton: "That Newark won the game [14–10] is a wonder, for Stovey was very wild at times, [and] Walker had several passed balls. . . . Whether it was that he did not think he was being properly supported, or did not like the umpire's decisions on balls and strikes, the deponent saith not, but Stovey several times displayed his temper in the box and fired the ball at the plate regardless of what was to become of everything that stood before him. Walker got tired of the business after awhile, and showed it plainly by his manner. Stovey should remember that the spectators do not like to see such exhibitions of temper, and it is hoped that he will not offend again."

Either despite or because of his surly disposition, George Stovey had a great season in 1887. His 35 wins is a single season record that still stands in the International League. George Stovey was well on his way to establishing his reputation as the greatest Negro pitcher of the nineteenth century.

The promotional value of having the only all-Negro battery in Organized Baseball was not lost upon the press. Newspapers employed various euphemisms of the day for "Negro" to refer to Newark's "colored," "Cuban," "Spanish," "mulatto," "African," and even "Arabian" battery. *Sporting Life* wrote: "There is not a club in the country who tries so hard to cater to all nationalities as does the Newark Club. There is the great African battery, Stovey and Walker; the Irish battery, Hughes and Derby; and the German battery, Miller and Cantz."

The Newark correspondent for *Sporting Life* asked, "By the way, what do you think of our 'storm battery,' Stovey and Walker? Verily they are dark horses, and ought to be a drawing card. No rainchecks given when they play." Later he wrote that "Our 'Spanish beauties,' Stovey and Walker, will make the biggest kind of drawing card." Drawing card they may have been, but Stovey and Walker were signed by Newark not for promotional gimmickry, but because they were talented athletes who could help their team win.

Nor were other teams reluctant to improve themselves by hiring black players. In Oswego, manager Wesley Curry made a widely publicized, though unsuccessful, attempt to sign second baseman George Williams, captain of the Cuban Giants. Had Curry succeeded, Williams would not have been the first, nor the best, black second baseman in the league. For Buffalo had retained the services of Frank Grant, the greatest black baseball player of the nineteenth century.

Frank Grant was beginning the second of a record three consecutive years on the same integrated baseball team. Born in 1867, he began his career in his hometown of Pittsfield, Massachusetts, then moved on to Plattsburg, New York. In 1886 he entered Organized Baseball, playing for Meriden, Connecticut, in the Eastern League until the team folded in July. Thereupon he and two white teammates signed with the Buffalo Bisons, where he led the team in hitting. By the age of 20, Grant was already known as "the Black Dunlap," a singularly flattering sobriquet referring to Fred "Sure Shot" Dunlap, the first player to sign for $10,000 a season, and acknowledged as the greatest second baseman of his era. Sol White called Frank Grant simply "the greatest ball player of his age," without reference to race.

In 1887, Grant would lead the International League in hitting with a .366 average. Press accounts abound with comments about his fielding skill, especially his extraordinary range. After a series of preseason exhibition games against Pittsburgh's National League team, "Hustling Horace" Phillips, the Pittsburgh manager, complained about Buffalo's use of Grant as a "star." The *Rochester Union* quoted Phillips as saying that "This accounts for the amount of ground [Grant] is allowed to cover . . . and no attention is paid to such a thing as running all over another man's territory." Criticizing an infielder for his excessive range smacks of praising with faint damns. Grant's talent and flamboyance made him popular not only in Buffalo, but also throughout the IL.

In 1890 Grant would play his last season on an integrated team for Harrisburg, Pennsylvania, of the Eastern Interstate League. His arrival was delayed by several weeks due to a court battle with another team over the rights to his services. The *Harrisburg Patriot* described Grant's long-awaited appearance:

> Long before it was time for the game to begin, it was whispered around the crowd that Grant would arrive on the 3:20 train and play third base. Everybody was anxious to see him come and there was a general stretch of necks toward the new bridge, all being eager to get a sight at the most famous colored ball player in the business. At 3:45 o'clock an open car-

riage was seen coming over the bridge with two men in it. Jim Russ' famous trotter was drawing it at a 2:20 speed and as it approached nearer, the face of Grant was recognized as being one of the men. "There he comes," went through the crowd like magnetism and three cheers went up. Grant was soon in the players' dressing room and in five minutes he appeared on the diamond in a Harrisburg uniform. A great shout went up from the immense crowd to receive him, in recognition of which he politely raised his cap.

Fred Dunlap should have been proud had he ever been called "the White Grant." Yet Grant in his later years passed into such obscurity that no one knew where or when he died (last year an obituary in the *New York Age* was located, revealing that Grant had died in New York on June 5, 1937).

Meanwhile, in Binghamton, Bud Fowler, who had spent the winter working in a local barbershop, was preparing for the 1887 season. At age 33, Fowler was the elder statesman of Negro ballplayers. In 1872, only one year after the founding of the first professional baseball league, Bud Fowler was playing professionally for a white team in New Castle, Pennsylvania. [He was said to be playing; no proof has yet emerged.—Eds.] Lee Allen, while historian of baseball's Hall of Fame, discovered that Fowler, whose real name was John Jackson, was born in Cooperstown, New York, in about 1854, the son of itinerant hops-pickers. Thus, Fowler was the greatest baseball player to be born at the future site of the Hall of Fame.

As was the case with many minor league players of his time, Fowler's career took him hopscotching across the country. In 1884 and 1885 he played for teams in Stillwater, Minnesota; Keokuk, Iowa; and Pueblo, Colorado. He played the entire 1886 season in Topeka, Kansas, in the Western League, where he hit .309. A Negro newspaper in Chicago, the *Observer*, proudly described Fowler as "the best second baseman in the Western League."

Binghamton signed Fowler for 1887. *The Sportsman's Referee* wrote that Fowler "has two joints where an ordinary person has one. Fowler is a great ball player." According to *Sporting Life's* Binghamton correspondent: "Fowler is a dandy in every respect. Some say that Fowler is a colored man, but we account for his dark complexion by the fact that . . . in chasing after balls [he] has become tanned from constant and careless exposure to the sun. This theory has the essential features of a chestnut, as it bears resemblance to Buffalo's claim that Grant is of Spanish descent."

Fowler's career in the International League would be brief. The financially troubled Bings would release him in July to cut their payroll. But during this half-season, a friendly rivalry existed between Fowler and Grant. Not so friendly were some of the tactics used by opposing baserunners and pitchers. In 1889, an unidentified International League player told *The Sporting News*:

> While I myself am prejudiced against playing in a team with a colored player, still I could not help pitying some of the poor black fellows that played in the International League. Fowler used to play second base with the lower part of his legs encased in wooden guards. He knew that about every player that came down to second base on a steal had it in for him and would, if possible, throw the spikes into him. He was a good player, but left the base every time there was a close play in order to get away from the spikes.
>
> I have seen him muff balls intentionally, so that he would not have to try to touch runners, fearing that they might injure him. Grant was the same way. Why, the runners chased him off second base. They went down so often trying to break his legs or injure them that he gave up his infield position the latter part of last season [i.e., 1888] and played right field. This is not all.
>
> About half the pitchers try their best to hit these colored players when [they are] at the bat . . . One of the International League pitchers pitched for Grant's head all the time. He never put a ball over the plate but sent them in straight and true right at Grant. Do what he would he could not hit the Buffalo man, and he [Grant] trotted down to first on called balls all the time.

Fowler's ambitions in baseball extended beyond his career as a player. As early as 1885, while in between teams, he considered playing for and managing the Orions, a Negro team in Philadelphia. Early in July 1887, just prior to his being released by Binghamton, the sporting press reported that Fowler planned to organize a team of blacks who would tour the South and Far West during the winter between 1887 and 1888. "The strongest colored team that has ever appeared in the field," according to *Sporting Life*, would consist of Stovey and Walker of Newark; Grant of Buffalo; five members of the Cuban Giants; and Fowler, who would play and manage. This tour, however, never materialized.

But this was not the only capitalistic venture for Fowler in 1887. The entrepreneurial drive that would lead White to describe him as "the celebrated promoter of colored ball clubs, and the sage of base ball" led him to investigate another ill-fated venture: The National Colored Base Ball League.

II

In 1886 an attempt had been made to form the Southern League of Colored Base Ballists, centered in Jacksonville, Florida. Little is known about this circuit, since it was so short lived and received no national and very little local press coverage. Late in 1886, though, Walter S. Brown of Pittsburgh announced his plan of forming the National Colored Base Ball League. It, too, would have a brief existence. But unlike its Southern predecessor, Brown's Colored League received wide publicity.

The November 18, 1886, issue of *Sporting Life* announced that Brown already had lined up five teams. Despite the decision of the Cuban Giants not to join the league, Brown called an organizational meeting at Eureka Hall in Pittsburgh on December 9, 1886. Delegates from Boston, Philadelphia, Washington, Baltimore, Pittsburgh, and Louisville attended. Representatives from Chicago and Cincinnati also were present as prospective investors, Cincinnati being represented by Bud Fowler.

Final details were ironed out at a meeting at the Douglass Institute in Baltimore in March 1887. The seven-team league consisted of the Keystones of Pittsburgh, Browns of Cincinnati, Capitol Citys of Washington, Resolutes of Boston, Falls City of Louisville, Lord Baltimores of Baltimore, Gorhams of New York, and Pythians of Philadelphia. (The Pythians had been the first black nine to play a white team in history, beating the City Items 27–17 on September 18, 1869.) [This finding since superseded. —Eds.]* Reach Sporting Goods agreed to provide gold medals for batting and fielding leaders in exchange for the league's use of the Reach ball. Players' salaries would range from $10 to $75 per month. In recognition of its questionable financial position, the league set up an "experimental" season, with a short schedule and many open dates.

"Experimental" or not, the Colored League received the protection of the National Agreement, which was the structure of Organized Baseball law that divided up markets and gave teams the exclusive right to players' contracts. *Sporting Life* doubted that the league would benefit from this protection "as there is little probability of a wholesale raid upon its ranks even should it live the season out—a highly improbable contingency." Participation in the

National Agreement was more a matter of prestige than of practical benefit. Under the headline "Do They Need Protection?" *Sporting Life* wrote:

> The progress of the Colored League will be watched with considerable interest. There have been prominent colored base ball clubs throughout the country for many years past, but this is their initiative year in launching forth on a league scale by forming a league . . . representing . . . leading cities of the country. The League will attempt to secure the protection of the National Agreement. This can only be done with the consent of all the National Agreement clubs in whose territories the colored clubs are located. This consent should be obtainable, as these clubs can in no sense be considered rivals to the white clubs nor are they likely to hurt the latter in the least financially. Still the League can get along without protection. The value of the latter to the white clubs lies in that it guarantees a club undisturbed possession of its players. There is not likely to be much of a scramble for colored players. Only two [sic] such players are now employed in professional white clubs, and the number is not likely to be ever materially increased owing to the high standard of play required and to the popular prejudice against any considerable mixture of races.

Despite the gloomy—and accurate—forecasts, the Colored League opened its season with much fanfare at Recreation Park in Pittsburgh on May 6, 1887. Following "a grand street parade and a brass band concert," about 1200 spectators watched the visiting Gorhams of New York defeat the Keystones, 11–8.

Although Walter Brown did not officially acknowledge the demise of the Colored League for three more weeks, it was obvious within a matter of days that the circuit was in deep trouble. The Resolutes of Boston traveled to Louisville to play the Falls City club on May 8. While in Louisville, the Boston franchise collapsed, stranding its players. The league quickly dwindled to three teams, then expired. Weeks later, Boston's players were still marooned in Louisville. "At last accounts," reported *The Sporting News*, "most of the Colored Leaguers were working their way home doing little turns in barbershops and waiting on table in hotels." One of the vagabonds was Sol White, then nineteen years old, who had played for the Keystones of Pittsburgh. He made his way to Wheeling, West Virginia, where he completed the season playing for that city's entry in the Ohio State League. (Three other blacks in that league besides White were Welday Walker, catcher N.

Higgins, and another catcher, Richard Johnson.) Twenty years later he wrote: "The [Colored] League, on the whole, was without substantial backing and consequently did not last a week. But the short time of its existence served to bring out the fact that colored ball players of ability were numerous."

Although independent black teams would enjoy varying degrees of success throughout the years, thirty-three seasons would pass before Andrew "Rube" Foster would achieve Walter Brown's ambitious dream of 1887: a stable all-Negro professional baseball league.

III

The International League season was getting under way. In preseason exhibitions against major league teams, Grant's play was frequently described as "brilliant." *Sporting Life* cited the "brilliant work of Grant," his "number of difficult one-handed catches," and his "special fielding displays" in successive games in April. Even in an 18–4 loss to Philadelphia, "Grant, the colored second baseman, was the lion of the afternoon. His exhibition was unusually brilliant."

Stovey got off to a shaky start, as Newark lost to Brooklyn 12–4 in the team's exhibition opener. "Walker was clever—exceedingly clever behind the bat," wrote the *Newark Daily Journal*, "yet threw wildly several times." A few days later, though, Newark's "colored battery" performed magnificently in a 3–2 loss at the Polo Grounds to the New York Giants, the favorite National League team of the Newark fans (hence the nickname "Little Giants.") Stovey was "remarkably effective," and Walker threw out the Giants' John Montgomery Ward at second base, "something that but few catchers have been able to accomplish." The play of Stovey and Walker impressed the New York sportswriters, as well as New York Giants captain Ward and manager Jim Mutrie who, according to White, "made an offer to buy the release of the 'Spanish Battery,' but [Newark] Manager Hackett informed him they were not on sale."

Stovey and Walker were becoming very popular. The *Binghamton Leader* had this to say about the big southpaw:

Well, they put Stovey in the box again yesterday. You recollect Stovey, of course—the brunette fellow with the sinister fin and the demonic delivery. Well, he pitched yesterday, and, as of yore, he teased the Bingos. He has such a knack of tossing up balls that appear as large as an alderman's opinion of himself, but you cannot hit 'em with a cellar door. There's no use in talking, but that Stovey can do funny things with a ball. Once, we noticed, he aimed a ball right at a Bing's commissary department, and when the Bingo spilled himself on the glebe to give that ball the right of way, it just turned a sharp corner and careened over the dish to the tune of "one strike." What's the use of bucking against a fellow that can throw at the flag-staff and make it curve into the water pail?

Walker, too, impressed fans and writers with his defensive skill and baserunning. In a game against Buffalo, "Walker was like a fence behind the home-plate . . . [T]here might have been a river ten feet behind him and not a ball would have gone into it." Waxing poetic, one scribe wrote:

> There is a catcher named Walker
> Who behind the bat is a corker,
> He throws to a base
> With ease and with grace,
> And steals 'round the bags like a stalker.

Who were the other black ballplayers in the IL? Oswego, unsuccessful in signing George Williams away from the Cuban Giants, added Randolph Jackson, a second baseman from Ilion, New York, to their roster after a recommendation from Bud Fowler. (Ilion is near Cooperstown; Fowler's real name was John Jackson—coincidence?) He played his first game on May 28. In a 5–4 loss to Newark he "played a remarkable game and hit for a double and a single, besides making the finest catch ever made on the grounds," wrote *Sporting Life*. Jackson played only three more games before the Oswego franchise folded on May 31, 1887.

Binghamton, which already had Bud Fowler, added a black pitcher named Renfroe (whose first name is unknown). Renfroe had pitched for the Memphis team in the Southern League of Colored Base Ballists in 1886, where "he won every game he pitched but one, averaging twelve strikeouts a game for nine games. In his first game against Chattanooga he struck out the first nine men who came to bat," wrote the Memphis *Appeal*; "he has great speed and a very deceptive down-shoot." Renfroe pitched his first game for Binghamton on May 30, a 14–9 victory over Utica, before several thousand fans.

"How far will this mania for engaging colored players go?" asked *Sporting Life*. "At the present rate of progress the International League may ere many moons change its title to 'Colored League.'" During the last few days in May, seven blacks were playing in the league: Walker and Stovey for Newark, Fowler and Renfroe for Binghamton, Grant for Buffalo, Jackson for Oswego, and one player not yet mentioned: Robert Higgins. For his story, we back up and consider the state of the Syracuse Stars.

IV

The 1887 season opened with Syracuse in a state of disarray. Off the field, ownership was reorganized after a lengthy and costly court battle in which the Stars were held liable for injuries suffered by a fan, John A. Cole, when he fell from a grandstand in 1886. Another fall that disturbed management was that of its team's standing, from first in 1885 to a dismal sixth in 1886. Determined to infuse new talent into the club, Syracuse signed seven players from the defunct Southern League after the 1886 season. Although these players were talented, the move appeared to be backfiring when, even before the season began, reports began circulating that the Southern League men had formed a "clique" to foist their opinions on management. The directors wanted to sign as manager Charley Hackett, who, as we have seen, subsequently signed with Newark. But the clique insisted that they would play for Syracuse only if Jim Gifford, who had hired them, was named manager. The directors felt that Gifford was too lax, yet acquiesced to the players' demand. By the end of April, the *Toronto World* was reporting: "Already we hear talk of 'cliqueism' in the Syracuse Club, and if there be any truth to the bushel of statement that team is certain to be doomed before the season is well under way. Their ability to play a winning game is unquestioned, but if the clique exists the club will lose when losing is the policy of the party element."

Another offseason acquisition for the Stars was a catcher named Dick Male, from Zanesville, Ohio. Soon after he was signed in November 1886, rumors surfaced that "Male" was actually a black named Dick Johnson. Male mounted his own public relations campaign to quell these rumors. The Syracuse correspondent to *Sporting Life* wrote: "Much has been said of late about Male, one of our catchers, being a colored man, whose correct name is said to be Johnson. I have seen a photo of Male, and he is not a colored man by a large majority. If he is he has sent some other fellow's picture."

The Sporting News' Syracuse writer informed his readers that "Male . . . writes that the man calling him a negro is himself a black liar."

Male's performance proved less than satisfactory and he was released by Syracuse shortly after a 20–3 drubbing at the hands of Pittsburgh in a preseason game, in which Male played right field, caught, and allowed three passed balls. Early in May he signed with Zanesville of the Ohio State League, where he once again became a black catcher named Johnson.

As the season began, the alarming specter of selective support by the Southern League players became increasingly apparent. They would do their best for deaf-mute pitcher Ed Dundon, who was a fellow refugee, but would go through the motions when Doug Crothers or Con Murphy pitched for the Stars. Jim Gifford, the Stars' manager, not equal to the task of controlling his team, resigned on May 17. He was replaced by "Ice Water" Joe Simmons, who had managed Walker at Waterbury in 1886.

Simmons began his regime at Syracuse by signing a 19-year-old lefthanded black pitcher named Robert Higgins. Like Renfroe, Higgins was from Memphis, and it was reported that manager Sneed of Memphis "would have signed him long ago . . . but for the prejudice down there against colored men." Besides his talents as a pitcher Higgins was so fast on the basepaths that *Sporting Life* claimed that he had even greater speed than Mike Slattery of Toronto, who himself was fast enough to steal 112 bases in 1887, an International League record to this day.

On May 23, two days after he signed with the Stars, Higgins pitched well in an exhibition game at Lockport, New York, winning 16–5. On May 25 the Stars made their first trip of the season to Toronto, where in the presence of 1,000 fans, Higgins pitched in his first International League game. The *Toronto World* accurately summed up the game with its simple headline: "Disgraceful Baseball." The Star team "distinguished itself by a most disgusting exhibition." In a blatant attempt to make Higgins look bad, the Stars lost 28–8. "Marr, Bittman, and Beard . . . seemed to want the Toronto team to knock Higgins out of the box, and time and again they fielded so badly that the home team were enabled to secure many hits after the side should have been retired. In several instances these players carried out their plans in the most glaring manner. Fumbles and muffs of easy fly balls were frequent occurrences, but Higgins retained control of his temper and smiled at every move of the clique . . . Marr, Bittman, Beard and Jantzen played like schoolboys." Of Toronto's 28 runs, 21 were unearned. Higgins' catcher, Jantzen, had three passed balls, three wild throws, and three strikeouts, incurring his manager's wrath to the degree that he was fined $50 and suspended. (On June 3, Jantzen was reinstated, only to be released on July 7.) *The Sporting News* reported the game prominently under the headlines: "The Syracuse Plotters; The Star Team Broken Up by a Multitude of Cliques; The Southern Boys Refuse to Support the Colored Pitcher." The group of Southern League players was called the "Ku-Klux coterie" by the Syracuse correspondent, who hoped that player Harry Jacoby would dissociate himself from the group. "If it is true that he is a member of the Star Ku-Klux-Klan to kill off Higgins, the negro, he has made a mistake. His friends did not expect it."

According to the *Newark Daily Journal*, "Members of the Syracuse team make no secret of their boycott against Higgins. . . . They succeeded in running Male out of the club and they will do the same with Higgins." Yet when the club returned to Syracuse, Higgins pitched his first game at Star Park on May 31, beating Oswego 11–4. *Sporting Life* assured its readers that "the Syracuse Stars supported [Higgins] in fine style."

But Bob Higgins had not yet forded the troubled waters of integrated baseball. On the afternoon of Saturday, June 4, in a game featuring opposing Negro pitchers, Syracuse and Higgins defeated Binghamton and Renfroe 10–4 before 1,500 fans at Star Park. Syracuse pilot Joe Simmons instructed his players to report the next morning to P. S. Ryder's gallery to have the team portrait taken. Two players did not comply, left fielder Henry Simon and pitcher Doug Crothers. The Syracuse correspondent for *The Sporting News* reported:

The manager surmised at once that there was "a n— in the fence" and that those players had not reported because; the colored pitcher, Higgins, was to be included in the club portrait. He went over to see Crothers and found that he was right. Crothers would not sit in a group for his picture with Higgins.

After an angry exchange, Simmons informed Crothers that he would be suspended for the remainder of the season. The volatile Crothers accused Simmons of leaving debts in every city he had managed, then punched him. The manager and his pitcher were quickly separated.

There may have been an economic motive that fanned the flames of Crothers' temper, which was explosive even under the best of circumstances: he was having a disappointing season when Simmons hired a rival and potential replacement for him. According to *The Sporting News*'s man in Syracuse, Crothers was not above contriving to hinder the performance of another pitcher, Dundon, by getting him liquored-up on the night before he was scheduled to pitch.

Crothers, who was from St. Louis, later explained his refusal to sit in the team portrait: "I don't know as people in the North can appreciate my feelings on the subject. I am a Southerner by birth, and I tell you I would have my heart cut out before I would consent to have my picture in the group. I could tell you a very sad story of injuries done my family, but it is personal history. My father would have kicked me out of the house had I allowed my picture to be taken in that group."

Crothers' suspension lasted only until June 18, when he apologized to his manager and was reinstated. In the meantime he had earned $25 per game pitching for "amateur" clubs. On July 2, he was released by Syracuse. Before the season ended, he played for Hamilton of the International League, and in Eau Claire, Wisconsin, all the while threatening to sue the Syracuse directors for $125.

Harry Simon, a native of Utica, New York, was not punished in any way for his failure to appear for the team portrait; of course, he did not compound his insubordination by punching his manager. The *Toronto World* was cynical, yet plausible, in commenting that Simon "is such a valuable player, his offense [against Higgins] seems to have been overlooked." The sporting press emphasized that Crothers was punished for his failure to pose with Higgins more than his fisticuffs with Simmons.

Thus in a period of 10 days did Bob Higgins become the unwilling focus of attention in the national press, as the International League grappled with the question of race. Neither of these incidents—the attempt to discredit him with intentionally bad play nor the reluctance of white players to be photographed with a black teammate—was unprecedented. The day before the Stars' appointment with the photographer, the *Toronto World* reported that in 1886 the Buffalo players refused to have their team photographed because of the presence of Frank Grant, which made it seem unlikely that the Bisons would have a team portrait taken in 1887 (nonetheless, they did). That Canadian paper, ever vigilant lest the presence of black ballplayers besmirch the game, also reported, ominously, that "The recent trouble among the Buffalo players originated from their dislike to [*sic*] Grant, the colored player. It is said that the latter's effective use of a club alone saved him from a drubbing at the hands of other members of the team."

Binghamton did not make a smooth, serene transition into integrated baseball. Renfroe took a tough 7–6 11-inning loss at the hands of Syracuse on June 2, eight days after Higgins' 28–8 loss to Toronto. "The Bings did not support Renfroe yesterday," said the *Binghamton Daily Leader*, "and many think the shabby work was intentional."

On July 7, Fowler and Renfroe were released. In recognition of his considerable talent, Fowler was released only upon the condition that he would not sign with any other team in the International League. Fowler joined the Cuban Giants briefly, by August was manager of the (Negro) Gorham Club of New York, and he finished the season playing in Montpelier, Vermont.

On August 8, the *Newark Daily Journal* reported, "The players of the Binghamton base ball club were . . . fined $50 each by the directors because six weeks ago they refused to go on the field unless Fowler, the colored second baseman, was removed." In view of the fact that two weeks after these fines were imposed the Binghamton franchise folded, it may be that the club's investors were motivated less by a tender regard for social justice than by a desire to cut their financial losses.

According to the *Oswego Palladium*, even an International League umpire fanned the flames of prejudice: "It is said that [Billy] Hoover, the umpire, stated in Binghamton that he would always decide against a team employing a colored player, on a close point. Why not dispense with Mr. Hoover's services if this is true? It would be a good thing for Oswego if we had a few players like Fowler and Grant."

There were incidents that indicated support for a color-blind policy in baseball. For example:

A citizen of Rochester has published a card in the *Union* and *Advertiser* of that city, in which he rebukes the Rochester *Sunday Herald* for abusing Stovey on account of his color. He says: "The young man simply discharged his duty to his club in whitewashing the Rochesters if he could. Such comments certainly do not help the home team; neither are they creditable to a paper published in a Christian community. So far as I know, Mr. Stovey has been a gentleman in his club, and should be treated with the same respect as other players."

But the accumulation of events both on and off the field drew national attention to the International League's growing controversy over the black players. The forces lining up against the blacks were formidable and determined, and the most vociferous opposition to integrated baseball came from

Toronto, where in a game with Buffalo on July 27, "The crowd confined itself to blowing their horns and shouting, 'Kill the n——.'" The *Toronto World*, under the headline "The Colored Ball Players Distasteful," declared:

> The World's statement of the existence of a clique in the Syracuse team to "boy cott" Higgins, the colored pitcher, is certain to create considerable talk, if it does not amount to more, in baseball circles. A number of colored players are now in the International League, and to put it mildly their presence is distasteful to the other players. . . . So far none of the clubs, with the exception of Syracuse, have openly shown their dislike to play with those men, but the feeling is known to exist and may unexpectedly come to the front. The chief reason given for McGlone's* refusal to sign with Buffalo this season is that he objected to playing with Grant.

[* John McGlone's scruples in this regard apparently were malleable enough to respond to changes in his career fortunes. In September 1888 he signed with Syracuse, thereby acquiring two black teammates—Fleet Walker and Bob Higgins.]

A few weeks later the *World* averred, in a statement reprinted in *Sporting Life*:

> There is a feeling, and a rather strong one too, that an effort be made to exclude colored players from the International League. Their presence on the teams has not been productive of satisfactory results, and good players as some of them have shown themselves, it would seem advisable to take action of some kind, looking either to their non-engagement or compelling the other element to play with them.

Action was about to be taken.

July 14, 1887, would be a day Tommy Daly would never forget. Three thousand fans went to Newark's Wright Street grounds to watch an exhibition game between the Little Giants and the most glamorous team in baseball: Adrian D. (Cap) Anson's Chicago White Stockings. Daly, who was from Newark, was in his first season with the White Stockings, forerunners of today's Cubs. Before the game he was presented with gifts from his admirers in Newark. George Stovey would remember the day, too. And for Moses Fleetwood Walker, there may have been a sense of déjà vu—for Walker had crossed paths with Anson before.

Anson, who was the first white child born among the Pottawattomie Indians in Marshalltown, Iowa, played for Rockford and the Philadelphia Athletics in all five years of the National Association and 22 seasons for Chicago in the National League, hitting over .300 in all but two. He also managed the Sox for 19 years. From 1880 through 1888, Anson's White Stockings finished first five times, and second once. Outspoken, gruff, truculent, and haughty, Anson gained the respect, if not the esteem, of his players, as well as opponents and fans throughout the nation. Cigars and candy were named after him, and little boys would treasure their Anson-model baseball bats as their most prized possessions. He was a brilliant tactician with a flair for the dramatic. In 1888, for example, he commemorated the opening of the Republican national convention in Chicago by suiting up his players in black, swallow-tailed coats.

In addition to becoming the first player to get 3,000 hits, Anson was the first to write his autobiography. *A Ball Player's Career*, published in 1900, does not explicitly delineate Anson's views on race relations. It does, however, devote several pages to his stormy relationship with the White Stockings' mascot, Clarence Duval, who despite Anson's vehement objections was allowed to take part in the round-the-world tour following the 1888 season. Anson referred to Duval as "a little darkey," a "coon," and a "no account n——."

In 1884, when Walker was playing for Toledo, Anson brought his White Stockings into town for an exhibition. Anson threatened to pull his team off the field unless Walker was removed. But Toledo's manager, Charley Morton, refused to comply with Anson's demand, and Walker was allowed to play. Years later *Sporting Life* would write: "The joke of the affair was that up to the time Anson made his 'bluff' the Toledo people had no intention of catching Walker, who was laid up with a sore hand, but when Anson said he wouldn't play with Walker, the Toledo people made up their minds that Walker would catch or there wouldn't be any game."

But by 1887 times had changed, and there was no backing Anson down. The Newark press had publicized that Anson's White Stockings would face Newark's black Stovey. But on the day of the game it was Hughes and Cantz who formed the Little Giants' battery. "Three thousand souls were made glad," glowed the *Daily Journal* after Newark's surprise 9–4 victory, "while nine were made sad." The *Evening News* attributed Stovey's absence to illness, but the *Toronto World* got it right in reporting that "Hackett intended putting Stovey in the box against the Chicagos, but Anson objected to his playing on account of his color."

On the same day that Anson succeeded in removing the "colored battery," the directors of the International League met in Buffalo to transfer the ailing Utica franchise to Wilkes-Barre, Pennsylvania. It must have pleased Anson to read in the next day's *Newark Daily Journal*:

> THE COLOR LINE DRAWN IN BASEBALL. The International League directors held a secret meeting at the Genesee House yesterday, and the question of colored players was freely discussed. Several representatives declared that many of the best players in the league are anxious to leave on account of the colored element, and the board finally directed Secretary White to approve of no more contracts with colored men.

Whether or not there was a direct connection between Anson's opposition to playing against Stovey and Walker and, on the same day, the International League's decision to draw the color line is lost in history. For example, was the league responding to threats by Anson not to play lucrative exhibitions with teams of any league that permitted Negro players? Interestingly, of the six teams which voted to install a color barrier—Binghamton, Hamilton, Jersey City, Rochester, Toronto, and Utica—none had a black player; the four teams voting against it—Buffalo, Oswego, Newark, and Syracuse—each had at least one.

In 1907, Sol White excoriated Anson for possessing "all the venom of a hate which would be worthy of a Tillman or a Vardaman of the present day." (Sen. Benjamin R. ["Pitchfork Ben"] Tillman, of South Carolina, and Gov. James K. Vardaman, of Mississippi, were two of the most prominent white supremacists of their time.)

Just why Adrian C. Anson . . . was so strongly opposed to colored players on white teams cannot be explained. His repugnant feeling, shown at every opportunity, toward colored ball players, was a source of comment throughout every league in the country, and his opposition, with his great popularity and power in baseball circles, hastened the exclusion of the black man from the white leagues.

Subsequent historians have followed Sol White's lead and portrayed Anson as the *meistersinger* of a chorus of racism who, virtually unaided, disqualified an entire race from baseball. Scapegoats are convenient, but Robert Peterson undoubtedly is correct: "Whatever its origin, Anson's animus toward

Negroes was strong and obvious. But that he had the power and popularity to force Negroes out of organized baseball almost single-handedly, as White suggests, is to credit him with more influence than he had, or for that matter, than he needed."

The International League's written color line was not the first one drawn. In 1867 the National Association of Base Ball Players, the loosely organized body which regulated amateur baseball, prohibited its members from accepting blacks. The officers candidly explained their reason: "If colored clubs were admitted there would be in all probability some division of feeling, whereas, by excluding them no injury could result to anybody and the possibility of any rupture being created on political grounds would be avoided."

This 1867 ban shows that even if blacks were not playing baseball then, there were ample indications that they would be soon. But the NABBP would soon disappear, as baseball's rapidly growing popularity fostered professionalism. Also, its measure was preventative rather than corrective: it was not intended to disqualify players who previously had been sanctioned. And, since it applied only to amateurs, it was not intended to deprive anyone of his livelihood.

Press response to the International League's color line generally was sympathetic to the Negroes—especially in cities with teams who had employed black players. The *Newark Call* wrote:

If anywhere in this world the social barriers are broken down it is on the ball field. There many men of low birth and poor breeding are the idols of the rich and cultured; the best man is he who plays best. Even men of churlish dispositions and coarse hues are tolerated on the field. In view of these facts the objection to colored men is ridiculous. If social distinctions are to be made, half the players in the country will be shut out. Better make character and personal habits the test. Weed out the toughs and intemperate men first, and then it may be in order to draw the color line.

The *Rochester Post-Express* printed a shrewd and sympathetic analysis by an unidentified "old ball player, who happens to be an Irishman and a Democrat":

We will have to stop proceedings of that kind. The fellows who want to proscribe the Negro only want a little encouragement in order to establish class distinctions between people of the white race. The blacks have so much prejudice to overcome that I sympathize with them and believe in frowning down every attempt by a public body to increase the burdens the colored people now carry. It is not possible to combat by law the prejudice against colored men, but it is possible to cultivate a healthy public opinion that will effectively prevent any such manifestation of provincialism as that of the ball association. If a negro can play better ball than a white man, I say let him have credit for his ability. Genuine Democrats must stamp on the color line in order to be consistent.

"We think," wrote the *Binghamton Daily Leader*, "the International League made a monkey of itself when it undertook to draw the color line"; and later the editor wondered "if the International League proposes to exclude colored people from attendance at the games." Welday Walker used a similar line of reasoning in March 1888. Having read an incorrect report that the Tri-State League, formerly the Ohio State League, of which Welday Walker was a member, had prohibited the signing of Negroes, he wrote a letter to league president W. H. McDermitt. Denouncing any color line as "a disgrace to the present age," he argued that if Negroes were to be barred as players, then they should also be denied access to the stands.

The sporting press stated its admiration for the talents of the black players who would be excluded. "Grant, Stovey, Walker, and Higgins," wrote *Sporting Life*, "all are good players and behave like gentlemen, and it is a pity that the line should have been drawn against them." That paper's Syracuse correspondent wrote "Dod gast the measly rules that deprives a club of as good a man as Bob Higgins." Said the *Newark Daily Journal*, "It is safe to say that Moses F. Walker is mentally and morally the equal of any director who voted for the resolution."

Color line or no color line, the season wore on. Buffalo and Newark remained in contention until late in the season. Newark fell victim to injuries, including one to Fleet Walker. Grant's play deteriorated, although he finished the year leading the league in hitting. Toronto, which overcame internal strife of its own, came from the back of the pack, winning 22 of its last 26 games; they may have been aided by manager Charley Cushman's innovative device of having his infielders wear gloves on their left hands. On September 17, Toronto swept a doubleheader from Newark at home before 8,000 fans to take first place. One week later they clinched their first

International League title. To commemorate the triumphant season, the Canadian Pacific Railway shipped a 160-foot tall pine, "the second tallest in America," across the continent. Atop this pole would fly the 1887 International League pennant.

Before the season ended there was one further flareup of racial prejudice that received national attention. On Sunday, September 11, Chris Von der Ahe, owner of the St. Louis Browns, canceled an exhibition game that was scheduled for that day in West Farms, New York, against the Cuban Giants. Led by its colorful and eccentric owner, and its multitalented manager-first baseman, Charles Comiskey, the Browns were the Chicago White Stockings of the American Association. At ten o'clock in the morning Von der Ahe notified a crowd of 7,000 disappointed fans that his team was too crippled by injuries to compete. The real reason, though, was a letter Von der Ahe had received the night before, signed by all but two of his players (Comiskey was one of the two):

> Dear Sir: We, the undersigned members of the St. Louis Base Ball Club, do not agree to play against negroes tomorrow. We will cheerfully play against white people at any time, and think by refusing to play, we are only doing what is right, taking everything into consideration and the shape the team is in at present.

The Cuban Giants played, instead, a team from Danbury, New York, as Cuban Giant manager Jim Bright angrily threatened to sue the Browns. Von der Ahe tried to mollify Bright with a promise to reschedule the exhibition, a promise that would be unfulfilled. The Browns' owner singled out his star third baseman, Arlie Latham, for a $100 fine. Von der Ahe did not object to his players' racial prejudice. In fact, he was critical of them not for their clearly stated motive for refusing to play, but for their perceived lack of sincerity in pursuing their objective: "The failure to play the game with the Cuban Giants cost me $1000. If it was a question of principle with any of my players, I would not say a word, but it isn't. Two or three of them had made arrangements to spend Sunday in Philadelphia, and this scheme was devised so that they would not be disappointed."

VI

There was considerable speculation throughout the offseason that the International League would rescind its color line, or at least modify it to allow each club one Negro. At a meeting at the Rossin House in Toronto on November 16, 1887, the league dissolved itself and reorganized under the title International Association (IA). Buffalo and Syracuse, anxious to retain Grant and Higgins, led the fight to eliminate the color line. Syracuse was particularly forceful in its leadership. The Stars' representatives at the Toronto meeting "received a letter of thanks from the colored citizens of [Syracuse] for their efforts in behalf of the colored players," reported *Sporting Life*. A week earlier, under the headline "Rough on the Colored Players," it had declared: "At the meeting of the new International Association, the matter of rescinding the rule forbidding the employment of colored players was forgotten. This is unfortunate, as the Syracuse delegation had Buffalo, London, and Hamilton, making four in favor and two [i.e., Rochester and Toronto] against it."

While the subject of the color line was not included in the minutes of the proceedings, the issue apparently was not quite "forgotten." An informal agreement among the owners provided a cautious retreat. By the end of the month, Grant was signed by Buffalo, and Higgins was retained by Syracuse for 1888. Fleet Walker, who was working in a Newark factory crating sewing machines for the export trade, remained uncommitted on an offer by Worcester, as he waited "until he finds whether colored players are wanted in the International League [*sic*]. He is very much a gentleman and is unwilling to force himself in where he is not wanted." His doubts assuaged, he signed, by the end of November, with Syracuse, where, in 1888 he would once again join a black pitcher. The Syracuse directors had fired manager Joe Simmons, and replaced him with Charley Hackett. Thus, Walker would be playing for his third team with Hackett as manager. He looked forward to the next season, exercising his throwing arm by tossing a claw hammer in the air and catching it. After a meeting in Buffalo in January 1888, *Sporting Life* summarized the IA's ambivalent position on the question of black players: "At the recent International Association meeting there was some informal talk regarding the right of clubs to sign colored players, and the general understanding seemed to be that no city should be allowed more than one colored man. Syracuse has signed two whom she will undoubtedly be allowed to keep. Buffalo has signed Grant, but outside of these men there will probably be no colored men in the league."

Frank Grant would have a typical season in Buffalo in 1888, where he was moved to the outfield to avoid spike wounds. For the third straight year his batting average (.346) was the highest on the team. Bob Higgins, the agent and victim of too much history, would, according to *Sporting Life*, "give up his $200 a month, and return to his barbershop in Memphis, Tennessee," despite compiling a 20-7 record.

Fleet Walker, catching 76 games and stealing 30 bases, became a member of a second championship team, the first since Toledo in 1883. But his season was blighted by a third distasteful encounter with Anson. In an exhibition game at Syracuse on September 27, 1888, Walker was not permitted to play against the White Stockings. Anson's policy of refusing to allow blacks on the same field with him had become so well-known and accepted that the incident was not even reported in the white press. The *Indianapolis World* noted the incident, which by now apparently was of interest only to black readers: "Fowler, Grant, and Stovey played many more seasons, some with integrated teams, some on all-Negro teams in white leagues in organized baseball, some on independent Negro teams. Fowler and Grant stayed one step ahead of the color line as it proceeded westward."

Fleet Walker continued to play for Syracuse in 1889, where he would be the last black in the International League until Jackie Robinson. Walker's career as a professional ballplayer ended in the relative obscurity of Terre Haute, Indiana (1890) and Oconto, Wisconsin (1891).

In the spring of 1891 Walker was accused of murdering a convicted burglar by the name of Patrick Murphy outside a bar in Syracuse. When he was found not guilty "immediately a shout of approval, accompanied by clapping of hands and stamping of feet, rose from the spectators," according to *Sporting Life*. His baseball career over, he returned to Ohio and embarked on various careers. He owned or operated the Cadiz, Ohio, opera house, and several motion picture houses, during which time he claimed several inventions in the motion picture industry. He was also the editor of a newspaper, *The Equator*, with the assistance of his brother Welday.

In 1908 he published a 47-page booklet entitled *Our Home Colony; A Treatise on the Past, Present and Future of the Negro Race in America*. According to the former catcher, "The only practical and permanent solution of the present and future race troubles in the United States is entire separation by emigration of the Negro from America." Following the example of Liberia, "the Negro race can find superior advantages, and better opportunities . . . among people of their own race, for developing the innate powers of mind and body." The achievement of racial equality "is contrary to everything in the nature of man, and [it is] almost criminal to attempt to harmonize these two diverse peoples while living under the same government." The past 40 years, he wrote, have shown "that instead of improving we are experiencing the development of a real caste spirit in the United States."

Fleet Walker died of pneumonia in Cleveland at age 66 on May 11, 1924, and was buried in Union Cemetery in Steubenville, Ohio. His brother Welday died in Steubenville 13 years later at the age of 77.

VII

In *The Strange Career of Jim Crow*, historian C. Vann Woodward identifies the late 1880s as a "twilight zone that lies between living memory and written history," when "for a time old and new rubbed shoulders—and so did black and white—in a manner that differed significantly from Jim Crow of the future or slavery of the past." He continued: "A great deal of variety and inconsistency prevailed in race relations from state to state and within a state. It was a time of experiment, testing, and uncertainty—quite different from the time of repression and rigid uniformity that was to come toward the end of the century. Alternatives were still open and real choices had to be made."

Sol White and his contemporaries lived through such a transition period, and he identified the turning point at 1887. Twenty years later he noted the deterioration of the black ballplayer's situation. Although White could hope that one day the black would be able to "walk hand-in-hand with the opposite race in the greatest of all American games—base ball," he was not optimistic: "As it is, the field for the colored professional is limited to a very narrow scope in the base ball world. When he looks into the future he sees no place for him. . . . Consequently he loses interest. He knows that, so far shall I go, and no farther, and, as it is with the profession, so it is with his ability."

The "strange careers" of Moses Walker, George Stovey, Frank Grant, Bud Fowler, Robert Higgins, Sol White, et al., provide a microcosmic view of the development *of* race relations in the society at large, as outlined by Woodward. The events of 1887 offer further evidence of the old saw that sport does not develop character—it reveals it.

---

* It was the September 4, 1869, game of Olympic vs Pythian. See *Philadelphia Inquirer* September 4 and *New York Times* September 5.

IO

The Federal League and the Courts

GARY D. HAILEY

SABR was formed during an era of increasing friction between owners and players in baseball, and the organization has always shown an interest in exploring the business side of the game. The last marginally successful attempt to take on the big-league monopoly was attempted by the Federal League from 1914 to 1915, and much of its story played out in courtrooms both before and after its folding. Gary Hailey, a lawyer who has practiced in Washington DC for many years, told the story of those legal battles in 1985 in the spring issue of *The National Pastime*, several years before SABR created its Business of Baseball Committee.

THE COURT HOUSE

This is that theater the muse loves best.
All dramas ever dreamed are acted here.
The roles are done in earnest, none in jest.
Hero and dupe and villain all appear.
Here falsehood skulks behind an honest mask,
And witless truth lets fall a saving word,
As the blind goddess tends her patient task
And in the hush the shears of fate are heard.
Here the slow-shod avengers keep their date;
Here innocence uncoils her snow-white bloom;
From here the untrapped swindle walks elate,
And stolid murder goes to meet his doom.
O stage more stark than ever Shakespeare knew
What peacock playhouse will contend with you?

Wendell Phillips Stafford, the composer of "The Court House," was a federal judge in Washington DC, for almost 27 years. One of the thousands of trials Judge Stafford presided over was a 1919 antitrust suit brought against Organized Baseball (O.B.) by the Baltimore club of the defunct Federal

League—a suit that threatened to loosen O.B.'s monopolistic hold on the national pastime.

Antitrust litigation is rarely colorful or dramatic enough to be the stuff of poetry, and it is doubtful that Judge Stafford had *Federal Baseball Club of Baltimore vs. National League* in mind when he wrote his verse. But a reading of the testimony given in the two-week-long trial does bring to mind a number of the poem's phrases. There were few if any heroes to be seen, but "dupe and villain" were well represented in Judge Stafford's courtroom. Certainly "falsehood skulk[ing] behind an honest mask" was present in abundance at the trial, as well as "untrapped swindle."

But more than anything, the evidence presented by the *Federal Baseball* litigants tells the story of a "stolid murder"—the murder of O.B.'s last serious competitor, the short-lived Federal League.

The Federal League War

Late nineteenth century professional baseball was plagued by wars between the established National League and a succession of upstart leagues. The American Association war of 1882, the Union Association war of 1884, the Players League war of 1890, the American League war of 1900—all these bitter conflicts resulted in huge losses for almost everyone involved, not to mention widespread public disenchantment with the professional game.

More than two decades of strife ended in 1903, when the National League and the American League signed a peace treaty. American League President Ban Johnson testified at the *Federal Baseball* trial that the purpose of the peace treaty was to restore "normal conditions" to professional baseball.

Q. Then your purpose was to eliminate competition between the two leagues for players?
A. I don't think we cared for competition at all.

Later that year, the two major leagues and several minor leagues adopted the "National Agreement," which provided for mutual respect for player contracts, reserve lists, and territorial rights. It also established a "National Commission," consisting of the major-league presidents and a third man selected by them, to rule the sport.

Peace—or, to put it another way, the lack of competition between the two leagues—brought prosperity. Attendance and profits reached unprecedented heights, and the World Series added greatly to the public interest in the pennant races. That prosperity attracted the attention of potential rivals. In 1913, several wealthy businessmen organized the Federal League of Professional Baseball Clubs. Prior to the start of the 1914 season, Federal League President James Gilmore asked Ban Johnson if O.B. would allow the Federal League to operate under the National Agreement as a third major league. Johnson told Gilmore that "there was not room for three major leagues."

The Federal League owners declared war. They quickly erected brand-new stadiums in seven of the league's eight cities: Baltimore, Brooklyn, Buffalo, Chicago, Indianapolis, Kansas City, Pittsburgh, and St. Louis. They also declared that the reserve clause in O.B.'s standard player contract was unenforceable, and began to sign up players under reserve by existing major- and minor-league clubs.

The Reserve Clause

Lawyers for the Federal Baseball Club of Baltimore hoped to persuade the jury that the purpose of the "right of reservation," a key feature of the National Agreement, was to enable O.B. "to eliminate the possibility of competition by establishing an absolute monopoly" over the supply of professional baseball players.

Much of the National Agreement and many of the rules and regulations issued by the National Commission dealt with the right of reservation, which National Commission chairman and Cincinnati Reds president August "Garry" Herrmann described as "absolutely necessary" to O.B. For example, Article 8, Section 1 of the National Agreement provided that: "[N]o non-reserve contract shall be entered into by any club operating under the National Agreement until permission to do so has been first obtained." Article 6, Section 1 of that document stated that no club could "negotiate for the purchase or lease of the property"—that is, players—"of another club without first securing the consent of such club." The title of a team to its "property" lapsed only when a team released a player or failed to include the player's name on the reserve list it was required to submit at the end of each season.

The reserve clause itself, which was found in section 10 of the standard player's contract, provided that:

> In consideration of the compensation paid to the [player] by the [team], the [player] agrees and obligates himself to contract with and continue in the service of[the team] for the succeeding season at a salary to be determined by the parties of such contract.

What happened if the player and his team couldn't agree on a salary for the succeeding season? According to Herrmann, the player was free to go elsewhere.

Q. And if he does not want to sign, what happens?
A. That ends it. He becomes a free agent.

Q. Could he go out and play for any other club in Organized Ball?
A. If he got employment, yes. There is no rule against it.

But on cross-examination, Herrmann admitted that the player would have a hard time finding a job with any other team.

Q. Could he get employment with any other club in Organized Baseball?
A. I do not imagine any other club would take him, because I have always felt, and we all feel, that reservation is absolutely necessary to keep the game alive.

Baltimore Federals director and stockholder Ned Hanlon, a veteran baseball man who had managed Baltimore and Brooklyn to five National League pennants before the turn of the century, described what happened if a player didn't agree on contract terms with his team.

Q. At the end of a man's term of employment, under the Organized Ball system, it is provided in these contracts that the club shall have a right to negotiate with him for employment for another year, or another season, upon terms to be agreed upon. Suppose they could not agree on terms, on a salary, for instance, for the next year? What happened?
A. He could not play professional baseball. If they did not agree on terms, he could not go anywhere else, could not play anywhere else under professional baseball.

Q. How long could he be kept in that situation without employment?
A. For year after year.

Q. It would not prevent him from going to blacksmithing or plowing or anything like that, would it?
A. No, sir. If they put him on the reserve list, they could not agree on terms, and they did not see fit to sell him or exchange him to

somebody else, they would reserve his reservation year after year, continuously. That is what it means.

The experience of former major leaguer Jimmy "Runt" Walsh supported Hanlon's claim that the right of reservation could last forever. Walsh was a Phillies utilityman who decided to sign with the Baltimore Federals after Philadelphia sold his contract to Montreal after the 1913 season. After the Federal League folded, Walsh spent the 1916 season with Memphis. When he and that team could not agree on a salary for 1917, Walsh quit baseball and went to work at a Baltimore steel mill. Walsh had not played professionally since then, but he still heard from the Memphis club in following years.

Q. They tendered you a contract at the end of the season of 1916 for the following year for $250 a month, and you would not accept that. Did they tender you another contract at the end of the year 1917?

A. I got a contract frowm them again this spring, yes, sir, this past spring, February, I think.

Q. At the end of each year they have been offering you contracts, have they?

A. Yes sir.

Q. Why do they do that? Do you understand why?

A. I do not understand the reason why, no, sir, with the exception that they still reserve me to their club.

Q. The object is to reserve you, so that you cannot make any other contract without their consent. That is the purpose of their offering you these contracts every year?

A. Yes, sir.

Connie Mack described the situation of holdouts like Walsh very graphically.

Q. Suppose you cannot come to an agreement with him?

A. I will tell you. If a player is at all reasonable we come to terms.

Q. But suppose you don't think he is reasonable; suppose you can't agree?

A. There are cases of that kind.

Q. What happens?

A. We just let him lay there.

The Blacklist

Other rules of O.B. were intended to discourage players under reserve from jumping to "outlaw" organizations that were not parties to the National Agreement, such as the Federal League. Articles 22 and 23 provided that any player who signed a contract or even entered into negotiations with an outlaw team "shall be declared ineligible" for at least three years. Any National Agreement team that signed an ineligible player could be drummed out of O.B. Any player who even appeared in an exhibition game with an ineligible player was himself subject to blacklisting.

As several of the plaintiff's witnesses testified, players were reluctant to sign with the Federal League because they knew that they might be blacklisted for the remainder of their playing days. On November 12, 1913, Herrmann had told the annual meeting of minor-league teams that "there will be no place in Organized Baseball" for players who did not respect their contractual obligations, including the reserve clause. According to Hanlon, his fellow director and part-owner of the Baltimore Federals, L. Edwin Goldman, and Baltimore's player-manager, Otto "Dutch" Knabe, the team had to offer excessively large salaries and long-term, guaranteed contracts to attract players. Moreover, they alleged, most of the players who did take a chance with the new league were veterans who knew they were nearing the end of their playing days.

"Runt" Walsh's testimony supported those witnesses' statements. After the 1913 season, Walsh learned through the newspapers that the Phillies had sold his contract to Montreal of the International League. He had never been to Montreal and was not consulted whether he would care to go to Montreal, so he signed with Baltimore.

Walsh demanded a three-year contract without the usual provision that allowed a team to release a player on ten days' notice. He wanted the security of a guaranteed, long-term contract because he believed there was little if any chance that he would be permitted to return to O.B. A letter he received from Montreal president Sam Lichtenheim after signing with Baltimore proved that Walsh's concern was justified.

> Dear [Mr. Walsh]:
>
> I am very much surprised . . . you signed with the Federals. . . .
>
> [I]f you start to play with them, you are blacklisted from Organized Ball for three years, and if their league blows up I don't know what you will do for three years. . . .

I don't think you want to throw away three years of your future for the sake of a few hundred dollars advance money which you may have received, and which if it is not too much I may be willing to pay back for you. . . .

So don't be foolish and let these people blindfold you, which they have done with several players, and which players would be very glad to come back to Organized Ball but it is too late, because their clubs won't take them back, but in your case I will take you back, if your terms are not too much, before you make this fatal jump, but once you have made the jump and played one game for them, I could not take you back if you were willing to play for me for $100.00 per month, as you must stay out of Organized Ball for three years, the same as any other player who plays one game for the Federal League.

Lichtenheim's letter to Walsh was very helpful to the plaintiff's case. The Montreal team president did not just threaten Walsh with blacklisting. He also encouraged Walsh to break his valid contract with Baltimore and generally libeled the new league.

[I]f the amount that they have advanced you is not too large, perhaps we could arrange to pay it back for you to them, when you report to us, and sign you to a contract, because . . . you know they will not go to the courts.

I am quite sure that Manager Knabe, or any of these other managers, would not do anything for you if you get hurt, or if you took sick, whereas in Organized Ball we have to take care of you, and I think you must know by now that this Federal League started out to be a Major League. I think you have already seen enough to know that they won't even be as good a league as ours, as they have only obtained very few Major League players, and the big bulk of their players come from our league and lower leagues, and I am quite sure that you know the public will not look on them as a Major League.

Don't you see that their whole trick is to get you signed to a contract so as to be taken over by Organized Ball, which will never be the case, but if they were taken over by Organized Ball, you would be in a worse position with them than you would be with us, because they would chop you down quickly, knowing that you could not go anywhere else.

Now just think this over and you will see that it is best to send them back their money, if they advanced you any money . . . and sign another contract with your real employers, who have always taken care of you, and who have made you what you are, and if you sign [a] contract with us we will protect your interests. . . .

[T]here is nothing to stop them throwing you out at any time, and cancelling your contract as soon as they know you cannot get back to Organized Ball for three years and which you know is the case. So I think you are much better off with Organized Ball, and which is the devil you do know, instead of Outlaw Ball, which is the devil you don't know, and it must sound sensible to you, that Organized Ball, for whom you have worked for many years, can and will do more for you, than your new owners, who are only speculators, and who have started out to bluff the public right from the jump, because they have promised Major League Ball, which you know they will not have.

They also promised to have a club in Toronto, which they will not have, and I think you will find before you get through that they have made a great many other promises, which they will not carry out, whereas with Organized Ball we must carry them out, and if you know of any promise I ever made, of any kind, which I did not carry out, I will be glad to hear of it. . . .

P.S. . . . [Y]ou must understand that you have a chance of being captain or manager here later on, whereas with them as soon as your usefulness as a player is finished, or you meet with an accident, which I hope you won't, they would throw you on the street, and you could not work for them. . . . So don't throw the substance away for the shadow, and get caught by these alluring offers which cannot materialise, and you know as well as I do that they cannot pay these salaries and take it at the gates by playing Minor League Ball, and you also know that they will play nothing but Minor League Ball, and will also have to play when we are away, in other words they will have to take our leavings, so I don't see how your future is in any way secure with them. . . . [O]utlaws in business have never been successful, and without organization there cannot be any success, and if we were not organized your position as a player would not be secure, and I think they don't know from week to week what cities they will play in and every week sees them change their cities, so you see they are only making a stab to be taken into Organized Ball, but they have guessed wrongly, and Organized Ball will never recognize them, and I think you know this already, and if you don't know it you may write to President Ban Johnson or [National League President John K.] Tener, and get their reply and find out for yourself that what I tell you is correct.

Johnson Fights Back

Walsh never wrote to American League president Ban Johnson, as Lichtenheim had suggested. But only two weeks after Lichtenheim had written to Walsh, Johnson made his opinions known. In a March 5, 1914, interview with a *New York Evening Sun* writer, Johnson "declared war" on the Federal League.

There can be no peace until the Federal League has been exterminated . . . [W]e will fight these pirates to the finish. There will be no quarter.

Yes, I've heard that peacemakers are at work, but they are wasting their time. The American League will tolerate no such interference. . . .

This Federal League movement is taken too seriously, why, the whole thing is a joke. They are holding a meeting once a week to keep from falling to pieces. Quote me as saying that the Federals have no money in Buffalo, Indianapolis, and Pittsburgh. They have no ball parks in any of their cities, except an amateur field in Kansas City and a ramshackle affair in Pittsburgh. There are some wooden bleachers put up on Hanlon's Park in Baltimore, I believe.

We hear from day to day that the Feds have millions behind them. If that is true they ought to build half million dollar stadium[s] in a few weeks. But getting down to brass tacks, they have neither grounds nor players that amount to anything.

When the list of players is finally announced the baseball public will realize what a bluff these fellows have been putting up. They have many unknown players, taken off the lots[,] and a bunch of Bush Leaguers with a sprinkling of big fellows. But the American League will lose not more than ten men. . . .

We are going to cut and slash right and left from now on. We intend to show up the four flushers and the bluffers in the proper light.

The Johnson interview appeared in print the day before 50-odd major leaguers returned to New York on the *Lusitania* after an around-the-world trip. According to the plaintiff, Johnson's tough talk was intended to frighten those players away from the Federal League as well as to destroy the new circuit's credibility with the public.

The 1914 Season

In spite of Organized Baseball's opposition, the Federal League opened the 1914 season confident of success. Opening day attendance was high, with Baltimore's home opener attracting a standing-room-only crowd of 19,000.

The 1914 pennant race was a close one: Indianapolis, led by outfielder Benny Kauff (who hit .370, stole 75 bases, and scored 120 runs) and pitcher Cy Falkenberg (a 25-game winner with a 2.22 ERA and 9 shutouts), edged Chicago by 1½ games, with Baltimore a close third. Still, total Federal League attendance did not approach that of either the American or National League. The Chicago Federals led the league in attendance, but drew fewer fans than the sixth-place White Sox. The established leagues suffered as well; AL attendance fell from 3.5 million in 1913 to 2.75 million in 1914.

The players were not complaining about the competition between the rival leagues. The Federal League eventually signed 81 major leaguers and 140 minor leaguers to contracts, nearly all of them at much higher salaries. Other players used the threat of jumping to get more money from teams in O.B. Several players—including Ray Caldwell, Walter Johnson, "Reindeer Bill" Killefer, and Ivey Wingo—signed contracts with Federal League teams but were persuaded to jump back to their former clubs. Caldwell made $2,400 in 1913, but the Yankees gave him a four-year contract paying $8000 annually to bring him back into the fold. Killefer's and Wingo's salaries also more than doubled while Johnson's went from $7,000 to $12,500.

Several times, disputes over who had rights to a player ended up in court. Organized Baseball did not take legal action against players who were reserved but not under contract, but it did go to court to restrain players who had signed contracts for the 1914 season from jumping leagues. Early that season, pitchers Dave Davenport and George "Chief" Johnson and out-fielder Armando Marsans of the Cincinnati Reds jumped to Federal League clubs. A Missouri federal judge granted the Reds' request for an injunction against Marsans, but a court in Illinois refused to issue a similar injunction against Johnson because the contract lacked "mutuality." On similar grounds, a New York court denied a White Sox request for a court order to prevent first baseman Hal Chase from jumping to the Buffalo Federals.

The tables were turned in the Killefer case. Killefer's 1913 Phillies salary was $3,200. On January 8, 1914, he signed with the Chicago Federals for $5800; only twelve days later he signed a new Phillies contract for $6,500. A federal appeals court refused to order Killefer to stand by the contract with Chicago on the grounds that the Federal League team, which had induced Killefer to ignore his reserve clause, came into court with "unclean hands." George Wharton Pepper, who represented O.B. in that case as well as in the Baltimore Federal Club litigation, persuaded the court that while the reserve clause was not legally enforceable by Philadelphia, the Chicago Federals had no business luring Killefer away before the Phillies had a fair chance to sign him to a contract for the 1914 season.

On January 5, 1915, the Federal League took the legal offensive by filing an antitrust suit against Organized Baseball. The Chicago federal judge assigned to hear the case was none other than Kenesaw Mountain Landis, who had the reputation of being a committed trustbuster. The trial of that case ended on January 22, and the Federal League hoped for a quick decision from Judge Landis. But the future commissioner seemed to be in no hurry to act. In March, Brooklyn Federals owner R. B. Ward approached Ban Johnson and again asked O.B. to allow its rival to become a party to the National Agreement.

1915: The War Continues

The Federal League opened the 1915 season with high hopes. Over 27,000 fans were on hand for opening day in Newark, where oilman Harry Sinclair had moved the Indianapolis Federals. But attendance fell off rapidly and losses began to mount. By the end of the league's second season, Brooklyn's Ward had lost $800,000; the Kansas City and Buffalo clubs were insolvent. Baltimore lost $35,000 in 1914 and almost $30,000 in 1915.

According to President Gilmore, the league's financial ills became apparent early in the season.

A. [I]t was probably in May that some of us realized that it was going to be a very poor season from a financial standpoint, and I know along about the middle of July we started to hold meetings to discuss the situation, because previous to that time I had been called to Buffalo, and I had been called to Kansas City, in an effort to induce other people to invest money. Their overhead was far in excess of their receipts, and they were all beginning to complain.

Q. When did you say you reached the conclusion that the Federal League was doomed?

A. Along about the middle of June or the first of July. . . . [M]y opinion was that we were fighting a hopeless task. There were two clubs that had practically given up the fight, Kansas City and Buffalo. I had already received an opinion from the other members of the organization that they would not continue with six clubs. . . .

Q. You had no idea from June on that the Federal League would be able to prepare for the next season at all?

A. I did not see any opportunity at all, no sir.

Q. Were you absolutely convinced of that?

A. I felt satisfied in my own mind to the extent that I began to figure out some way that we could at least save the ball players, and save our own reputations.

"It Was One Big Bluff"

Gilmore approached Sinclair and Ward with an audacious plan. First, they rented a suite of Manhattan offices and purchased an option to buy some vacant land at 143rd Street and Lenox Avenue. They then asked Corry Comstock, a New York City engineer and architect who was also the vice-president of the Pittsburgh Federal club, to draw up plans for a grandiose, 55,000-seat stadium. Gilmore then announced to the press that the Federal League planned to "invade" New York in 1916.

The purpose of all this? According to Gilmore, "[i]t was one big bluff," a trick to force O.B. into "coming around and making some kind of offer."

Q. Your real purpose was to get Organized Baseball to buy you out?

A. To reimburse us for some of our expenditures, yes, sir.

Q. To buy you out. Did not they have enough ball parks for the American and National Leagues at that time?

A. I presume they did.

Q. You expected them to buy you out and get rid of you as an annoying competitor; is that the proposition?

A. I think so, yes, sir.

Q. You had statements and interviews in the papers about it [the N.Y. stadium]?

A. Yes, sir.

Q. You said you were going to build it?

A. Yes, sir.

Q. And you had no idea of building it?

A. None at all. We did not know where the money was coming from unless some angel came along.

Q. You mean some devil; you were not associating with angels. Do you mean to tell this jury that you gave out interviews to the papers that you were going to build this stadium, employed an architect and manifested all of the different things that were necessary to accompany a real good faith act and had no idea of building a stadium at all?

A. It was one big bluff.

Q. That is the word you used for it?

A. Bluff, yes, sir.

Q. Might you not also characterize it as false pretense?

A. I do not know what you characterize it.

Q. Were you not engaging in false pretense?

A. We were trying to be protected to the best of our ability.

Comstock described the threatened invasion of New York by the Federal League as a "holdup"; he said there was "not a word of truth" in the announcement of the plans to build a stadium.

Gilmore and his co-conspirators did not tell the other Federal League owners about their scheme. According to Gilmore,

A. [T]he bluff that we had formulated, the plan we had formulated, to put this thing through, was an absolute secret between Mr. R. B. Ward, Mr. Comstock, Mr. Sinclair and myself. . . .

Q. You were putting up a bluff on Baltimore?

A. Baltimore did not know one thing about the plan we were putting up in New York. . . . [W]e decided to keep it a secret from everybody. Mr. Weeghman [of Chicago] knew nothing about it. Mr. Ball of St. Louis knew nothing about it.

Gilmore's machinations certainly fooled the Baltimore club. While he was trying to bluff O.B. into buying out the Federal League, Baltimore officials were naively making preparations for the 1916 season. Colonel Stuart S. Janney, a prominent Baltimore attorney who held stock in the team and served as its lawyer, testified that the club's directors and stockholders had not expected to turn a profit overnight and were prepared to supply whatever additional financing was necessary for the 1916 season.

These preparations were encouraged by a series of letters Gilmore wrote to club officials in the fall of 1915, all of which contained some implication that the Federal League would be alive and well enough to operate in 1916. In an October 13 letter, Gilmore wrote:

[I] hope that your club is signing up some good talent for the coming year. I have wonderful faith in Baltimore as a Major League city, and know if you can get a fighting team there and keep it in the race, you will draw wonderful crowds and easily pay expenses.

On November 1, he wrote:

I also want to suggest that in view of your experience the last year that you make out a statement of the approximate cost to operate your club during the next season. In other words, I would like an idea of how much cheaper you think you can operate in 1916 than you could in 1915. This will be valuable information for our Board Members, and I want you to get it as accurately as possible.

On November 30, Gilmore forwarded to Baltimore club president Carroll W. Rasin a letter from a Williamsport, Pennsylvania fan recommending that the Federal League sign up for the 1916 season a local star who was a "natural-born hitter . . . fast on his feet; a sure catch and a 'find.'" And on December 3, Gilmore wrote again to request the financial information that he had asked for in his November 1 letter.

Peace Talks

Baltimore officials did hear rumors that some Federal League owners were negotiating a settlement. At a November 9 league meeting in Indianapolis, Baltimore President Rasin asked Gilmore, Weeghman, and Sinclair point-blank if there was any truth in newspaper reports to that effect. All three denied that they were in communication with Organized Baseball, but Rasin suspected at the time that their denials "might not be frank." In early December, Rasin saw more "newspaper talk" that O.B. and the Federal League were about to cut a deal. When he called Gilmore, Gilmore again assured him that there was no truth to the rumors.

On December 12, Gilmore ran into three National League officials in the lobby of New York City's Biltmore Hotel. One of them asked Gilmore to "come around and take this matter up" at the National League owners' meeting scheduled for the next day. Gilmore turned down the invitation. "Absolutely nothing doing," he said. "We have gone too far and made too much progress on our New York invasion."

The next day, the same men called Gilmore and asked him to "come over and fix this thing up." Gilmore—hoping to hook his adversaries a little more firmly before reeling them in—feigned disinterest. "I told you the other day I would not have anything to do with it," he said, "and I will not talk about it."

Gilmore then turned to Harry Sinclair and said, in a voice loud enough for his caller to hear, "Harry, these people want [us] to come over and talk to them. Do you want to go?" Also intending the caller to hear him, Sinclair replied, "We might as well go and hear what they have to say." The two of them went to National League president Tener's office to discuss the situation.

Gilmore, Sinclair, and the National League representatives came to a tentative peace agreement. First, the NL agreed to make all blacklisted Federal League players eligible to play in O.B. and to let the Federal League owners sell their players' contracts to the highest bidders. Next, the NL owners offered to buy the Brooklyn Federals' park for $400,000, subject to the American League owners agreeing to kick in half of that sum. They also promised to approve the sale of the Chicago Cubs to Chicago Federals owner Charles E. Weeghman and put up $50,000 of the purchase price. The NL owners then agreed to buy out the Pittsburgh Federals for $50,000. Sinclair was a close friend of St. Louis Federals owner Phil Ball, and he assured the conferees that Ball would be satisfied if he could buy either the Cardinals or the Browns. The Buffalo and Kansas City clubs were no longer members in good standing of the Federal League—their owners had run out of money before the season ended, and the other teams had provided funds to pay their players in order to keep the league's financial problems a secret—so there was little need to worry about them. There was apparently no discussion concerning the Newark franchise, even though owner Sinclair was present.

That left only the Baltimore club. Gilmore testified that he asked for $200,000 for Baltimore's owners, but was laughed at. He later told Sinclair that he thought it was wise "to start high." The meeting then broke up.

On December 16, 1915, Rasin received a telegram from Gilmore: "You and Hanlon be at Biltmore in morning. Important." Rasin, Hanson, and Janney took the midnight train to New York, and went to Gilmore's apartment at the Biltmore Hotel on the morning of December 17. Gilmore explained that he had summoned them to New York to tell them that the 1916 Federal League season was "all off." Gilmore then told the stunned Baltimore officials about the tentative peace agreement of the 13th.

Janney and Rasin asked why Gilmore and the others had agreed to sell out, but Gilmore did not reply. They then asked what arrangements had been made concerning the Baltimore club's interests. None, said Gilmore; however, he was sure that Baltimore would be "taken care of" before the settlement was made final.

Later, Sinclair, Weeghman, and representatives of other Federal League teams joined the meeting. They told the Baltimoreans that the opportunity to make peace had arisen suddenly and unexpectedly, and no one then present in New York felt he had authority to speak for Baltimore; however, like Gilmore, they were all sure that the National Commission would give due consideration to Baltimore's claims.

The Baltimore officials were in no mood to take Gilmore's advice and "accept the situation philosophically." According to Janney, the discussion "grew rather bitter." When Sinclair defended his and his allies' actions, "quite a dispute arose" between him and Janney; "his words and mine," Janney testified, "were not always of the smoothest." Janney argued that the Federal League clubs should get some share of the proceeds of any agreement to dissolve the circuit, but Sinclair said he "would have none of that."

Gilmore and his allies hoped to finalize the December 13 agreement at a meeting with American and National League club owners that evening at the Waldorf-Astoria Hotel. According to Gilmore, Comstock, and Ward, Rasin moved that a committee of three—Gilmore, Sinclair, and Weeghman—be authorized to represent all the Federal League clubs at that meeting. Rasin denied that he made such a motion.

The Waldorf Meeting

The Waldorf meeting was called to order by National Commission president August Herrmann at 9:10 p.m., Friday, December 17, 1915. Among the thirty or so baseball men present at the meeting were American and National League presidents Johnson and Tener; Federal Leaguers Gilmore, Sinclair, Weeghman, and Rasin; American League owners Charles Comiskey (White Sox) and Colonel Jacob Ruppert (Yankees); and National League owners Charles Ebbets (Dodgers), James Gaffney (Braves), and Barney Dreyfuss (Pirates). A stenographer was present, and a transcript was produced.

The conferees quickly ratified those parts of the tentative peace agreement of December 13 that provided that the National League would put up $50,000 toward Weeghman's purchase of the Cubs; that Organized Baseball would pay R. B. Ward's heirs $20,000 a year for 20 years in exchange for the Brooklyn Federals' stadium; that Organized Baseball would pay $50,000 to the owners of the Pittsburgh Federals; and that all Federal League players would be eligible to return to O.B.

Gilmore was asked if his committee was empowered to enter into a binding agreement on behalf of the Federal League.

> GILMORE: I can say for the Federal League that the committee represented here tonight was appointed with full authority to discuss this proposition with you, and conclude any agreement that we might come to, and we are ready to open up the talk and see what can be done.
> HERRMANN: I understand, Mr. Gilmore, you state now that you have authority to act on behalf of the Federal League; that is, your committee?
> GILMORE: We have full authority, Mr. Herrmann.

Rasin did not challenge Gilmore's assertion. At about the time the meeting was beginning, a *Baltimore Sun* reporter went to the Biltmore to tell Janney that it looked as if Baltimore might be able to get a National League team. Janney hurried to the Waldorf, where Rasin also told him that Baltimore had a good chance of landing an established franchise if they asked for one. Herrmann then gave Janney the floor.

We feel just as I suppose everyone feels, that peace is the very best proposition in baseball and for baseball. We are all willing to concede that, and we hope it will come about. There is in the proposal which has been adopted, and which has been signed by certain parties—the situation in Baltimore is not touched upon, and it seems to me important in several aspects. In the first place, Baltimore has a population of seven hundred and fifty or eight hundred thousand people, including the suburbs. . . .

We are willing to purchase and pay for a franchise in the major leagues, if we can get it, and we want that to be the main keynote of our situation this evening. . . .

We are not venturing to suggest to you gentlemen just what franchise we think that would be. You could work that out probably better than ourselves, but that is our starting point, and that is what we would like to see, and which we lay before you.

Baltimore is not mentioned in the proposals that you have heretofore considered, and we think that, that is—we want to be taken up with every consideration, and . . . if you state or suggest that Baltimore would not pay the rest of the teams what the city does from which the franchise might be moved, we would be willing, and we will say that [we] will guarantee to pay as much as the city from which it is moved. In other words, the patronage there, we are willing to stand back of. We know it is there. We know that the people [will] attend the games, and we know we can produce the same revenue for a visiting team that has been produced by the city from which it will be moved. . . .

We represent a large body of representative citizens there, and we will see to it that suitable guarantees are given to back up every word that I have said. That is our position, gentlemen; and . . . we do not ask anything if we could be given the privilege of buying and locating a major league club in Baltimore, at a reasonable price, a franchise in . . . either one or the other of the two major leagues which you represent. We do not ask anybody to sacrifice anything or contribute to us. We are willing to stand in our own position and come forward and back our words with deeds and give you suitable guarantees.

Several of the major league owners present ridiculed the notion that Baltimore could support a major league franchise.

COMISKEY: Well, what would you give for a franchise in Baltimore? Suppose we could blow life into McGraw and Kelley and Jennings and all those players that you had there that you could not support. . . . What would you give for those players if we would guarantee that they would play good ball in Baltimore for ten years, what would you pay for them and how loyally would you support them?

JANNEY: We would support them well.

COMISKEY: What crowd would you draw?

JANNEY: We would draw sufficient to enable us to pay $250,000 for a franchise.

COMISKEY: That is just the proper price for a minor league franchise. . . . Baltimore, a minor-league city, and not a hell of a good one at that.

EBBETS: That's right.

COMISKEY: As sure as you are sitting there now, and your friends will tell you. Charlie, show them what you have got in Baltimore. You are the best evidence in the world. Tell them what you drew in Baltimore. . . .

EBBETS: When [Ned Hanlon] quit Baltimore and came to Brooklyn, he said, "Baltimore is not a major league city." We lost money in Baltimore operating the club with the same players that Mr. Comiskey speaks of.

JANNEY: There are very peculiar circumstances that brought that about.

EBBETS: Nothing peculiar about it; it is a minor league city, positively and absolutely, and will never be anything else.

JANNEY: That is your opinion.

EBBETS: Sure that is my opinion, because I had a piece of experience and lost money down there.

JANNEY: But money has been lost in other towns also in baseball.

EBBETS: Not in major league cities.

JANNEY: Yes, they have been lost in other towns that are major league cities.

EBBETS: It is one of the worst minor league towns in this country.

JANNEY: It will never be a minor league town because the people feel naturally—

EBBETS: You have too many colored population to start with. They are a cheap population when it gets down to paying their money at the gate.

JANNEY: They come across, I think, in good shape. This is perfectly futile, of course. It requires your consent and I am not going to try to convince you when you are so set in your ways.

Janney was right to call further discussion futile. Under both American and National League rules, the transfer of any franchise to Baltimore would require the unanimous consent of the league owners. From the statements of the owners at the meeting, it is clear that any motion to give Baltimore an existing team—Janney and Rasin had thought the Cardinals might be available—would have been met not with unanimous consent, but unanimous refusal.

The two sides agreed that a detailed settlement, including something for Baltimore, should be worked out by the National Commission and a Federal League committee of three. Gilmore proposed that himself, Sinclair, and Weeghman serve as that committee, and neither Janney nor Rasin objected.

There was then some discussion of the Federal League's pending antitrust suit against Organized Baseball, which Judge Landis had still not decided. National League counsel John C. Toole felt that the suit should be withdrawn before any more negotiating was done:

[I]t seems to me that the very first thing that should be done, and that should be done very promptly, to show that the thing is moving along, is that both sides should agree that that action be discontinued, and prompt steps should be taken to discontinue it and get it out of the way. That ought to be done before you have any meeting of the [National] Commission with this committee.

Janney objected that Toole was putting the cart before the horse.

JANNEY: I think that should be part of the agreement ultimately reached, that the suit be discontinued. It would not certainly be any discourtesy to the Court for parties to a litigation to discuss its composition, and when they come to a composition, then to have the dismissal of the action as a part of the composition.

TOOLE: You are not settling that suit, that is the difficulty. If you were settling that litigation, that is another thing, but you are settling a multitude of things in no way involved in that, and reaching agreements on them and this decision has been in abeyance. He may decide it tomorrow, and all this go to nothing, and put you all in a very embarrassing position, although you do not, perhaps, get into contempt of court.

JANNEY: I think the most that could be done, so far as I can see, would be to wire our respective counsel to appear before the Court tomorrow and advise him that there are matters under discussion which may ultimately result in an agreement, and if this agreement is effective, it will involve the discontinuance of the action before him, and suggest it would be proper for him to delay rendering a decision in it until this could be seen, whether the composition was effected, and that would be perfectly compatible with every possible legal or courteous principle. . . . What we do here will be subject to the dismissal. It is not usual to dismiss the case and then compose it. You compose it and then dismiss it. . . . You do not dismiss your suit and then agree how to settle it. That is that whole settlement. You settle this thing, and then, with your settlement, go and dismiss it. I have no objection, of course, to notifying the attorneys and telling them to do everything that is necessary to be courteous and pleasing to the Court.

When the meeting was adjourned, Toole telegraphed Organized Baseball's Chicago attorney:

Negotiations are pending, which if carried out will result in an agreement to withdraw the action brought by the Federal League. Please bring the matter to the attention of Judge Landis, if you think it advisable, and secure his approval of situation. Communicate with attorneys for Federal League, who will be advised by their client.

The Federal League was dead, but Gilmore and his allies weren't shedding any tears over its demise. Fearful that the league was doomed anyway, they decided to cut their losses rather than fight to the finish. Organized Baseball was happy to offer the Federal League a generous peace settlement. After all, there was still a chance that Judge Landis would issue a damaging verdict in the Federal League's antitrust action. The rival league's New York bluff also raised the specter of even more bitter competition for players and fans, with plenty of red ink to go around.

Ban Johnson would have preferred not to call a truce. The Federal League's threat to put a team in New York may have fooled the National League, but the American League knew better: It had considered building a new stadium on the Lenox Avenue property years earlier, but found that it was absolutely impractical to locate a park there. Johnson was characteristically blunt in describing his feelings about the peace pact.

Q. Can you tell us without any lengthy answer why did you pay $50,000 for [the Pittsburgh park]?

A. That was a tentative agreement that the National League entered into, and we abided by their decision in the matter. I could not see any reason why Pittsburgh should be given $50,000. As a matter of fact I did not want to give a five-cent piece to Pittsburgh.

Q. What you wanted to do was to knock them out?

A. Knock them out; that is it.

Q. Not to pay a cent?

A. Not a nickel.

Q. You were not as generous as Mr. Herrmann. Mr. Herrmann said yesterday he wanted to help them out.

A. I did not want to help them out. I am very frank in that regard.

The National Commission and the Federal League committee signed a peace treaty in Cincinnati on December 22. Before the agreement was concluded, Gilmore called Rasin to ask if Baltimore would accept $75,000, but Rasin said no. Another meeting to discuss Baltimore's claims was held in Cincinnati on January 5, 1916, but no settlement was reached. A day or two later, Baltimore filed a complaint with the U.S. Department of Justice, but Assistant Attorney General Todd announced on January 11 that he had no reason to believe that Organized Baseball had violated the antitrust laws.

The War Moves to the Courtroom

On January 27, the Baltimore stockholders voted to authorize the club's directors to spend up to $50,000 on "litigation in such form as they deem advisable" to protect the stockholders' interests. They eventually filed suit in Washington on September 20, 1917.

After a year and a half of legal skirmishing, a jury was sworn in on March 25, 1919. The testimony summarized above was presented, the judge gave his instructions, and the jury retired to deliberate on April 12. Given the judge's instructions to the jury—which, in essence, told the jury that O.B. had in fact violated the federal antitrust laws, and that the Baltimore club was entitled to recover for any damages it suffered as a result—the verdict came as no surprise. The jury found in favor of the plaintiff and assessed damages at $80,000. The antitrust laws provide that guilty defendants pay three times the amount of the actual damages plus attorneys' fees, so the final judgement was for $254,000.

Organized Baseball's lawyers immediately appealed to the U.S. Court of Appeals for the District of Columbia. They attacked the trial court's decision on a number of legal grounds, but focused most of their attention on a single key issue:

> By far the most important question presented by the assignments of error is whether professional baseball is interstate commerce.

In his memoirs, George Wharton Pepper, O.B.'s top lawyer, described his appeal strategy.

> I raised at every opportunity the objection that a spontaneous output of human activity is not in its nature commerce, that therefore Organized Baseball cannot be interstate commerce; and that, it not being commerce among the states, the federal statute could have no application. . . .
>
> [T]he case came on for argument . . . on October 15th [, 1920]. I mention the date because of the coincidence that on the same day there was being played the final game in the [Dodgers vs. Indians] World Series of that year. . . .
>
> Counsel for the Federal League made the grave mistake of minimizing the real point in the case (the question, namely whether interstate commerce was involved) and sought to inflame the passions of the Court by a vehement attack upon the evils of [Organized Baseball], a few of which were real and many, as I thought, imaginary. I argued with much earnestness the proposition that personal effort not related to production is not a subject of commerce; that the attempt to secure all the skilled service needed for professional baseball is not an attempt to monopolize commerce or any part of it; and that Organized Baseball, not being commerce, and therefore not interstate commerce, does not come within the scope of the prohibitions of the Sherman [Antitrust] Act.

If the business of professional baseball was not interstate commerce, it was not subject to the Sherman Antitrust Act or any other federal regulation, even if all of the Baltimore club's allegations of monopoly and conspiracy were found to be true.

On December 6, 1920, the Court of Appeals issued its decision, which was written by its Chief Justice, Constantine J. Smyth. Chief Justice Smyth first stated that interstate commerce "require[s] the transfer of something, whether it be persons, commodities, or intelligence" from one state to another. But, Smyth wrote,

> A game of baseball is not susceptible of being transferred. . . . Not until [the players] come into contact with their opponents on the baseball field and the contest opens does the game come into existence. It is local in its beginning and in its end. Nothing is transferred in the process to those who patronize it. The exertions of skill and agility which they witness may excite in them pleasurable emotions, just as might a view of a beautiful picture or a masterly performance of some drama; but the game effects no exchange of things.

It didn't really matter that baseball players traveled across state lines, or that the players carried their bats, balls, gloves, and uniforms across state lines with them.

> The players, it is true, travel from place to place in interstate commerce, but they are not the game. . . .
>
> The transportation in interstate commerce of the players and the paraphernalia used by them was but an incident to the main purpose of the appellants, namely the production of the game. It was for it they were in business—not for the purpose of transferring players, balls, and uniforms. The production of the game was the dominant thing in their activities. . . .
>
> So, here, baseball is not commerce, though some of its incidents may be.
>
> Suppose a law firm in the city of Washington sends its members to points in different states to try lawsuits; they would travel, and probably carry briefs and records, in interstate commerce. Could it be correctly said that the firm, in the trial of the lawsuits, was engaged in trade and commerce? Or, take the case of a lecture bureau, which employs persons

to deliver lectures before Chautauqua gatherings at points in different states. It would be necessary for the lecturers to travel in interstate commerce, in order that they might fulfill their engagements; but would it not be an unreasonable stretch of the ordinary meaning of the words to say that the bureau was engaged in trade or commerce?

Chief Justice Smyth then cited with approval cases holding that those who produce theatrical exhibitions, practice medicine, or launder clothes are not engaged in commerce.

The Baltimore club tried to persuade the United States Supreme Court to reinstate the original verdict in its favor. But Justice Oliver Wendell Holmes, writing for a unanimous Court, upheld the decision of the Court of Appeals.

[E]xhibitions of base ball . . . are purely state affairs. It is true that, in order to attain for these exhibitions the great popularity that they have achieved, competitions must be arranged between clubs from different cities and States. But the fact that in order to give the exhibitions the League must induce free persons to cross state lines and must arrange and pay for their doing so is not enough to change the character of the business. . . . [T]he transport is a mere incident, not the essential thing. That to which it is incident, the exhibition, although made for money would not be called trade or commerce in the commonly accepted use of those words. As it is put by the defendants, personal effort, not related to production, is not a subject of commerce. That which in its consummation is not commerce does not become commerce among the States because the transportation that we have mentioned takes place. To repeat the illustrations given by the Court below, a firm of lawyers sending out a member to argue a case, or the Chautauqua lecture bureau sending out lecturers, does not engage in such commerce because the lawyer or lecturer goes to another State.

The Supreme Court's decision was issued on May 29, 1922—almost seven years after the Baltimore Federals played their last game.

Given the legal doctrines of its day, the *Federal Baseball* case was correctly decided. The courts of that era applied the federal antitrust laws only to businesses that were primarily engaged in the production, sale, or transportation of tangible goods.

It is popularly believed that Organized Baseball was given immunity from the antitrust laws because baseball was a sport, not a business. That belief has grown out of a passage in the Court of Appeals opinion:

> If a game of baseball, before a concourse of people who pay for the privilege of witnessing it, is trade or commerce, then the college teams who play football where an admission fee is charged, engage in an act of trade or commerce. But the act is not trade or commerce; it is sport. The fact that [Organized Baseball] produce[s] baseball games as a source of profit, large or small, cannot change the character of the games. They are still sport, not trade.

But a close reading of that language and the rest of Chief Justice Smyth's opinion shows that the key to the decision was not the fact that baseball was a sport. The more crucial fact was that baseball—as well as the practice of law or medicine, the production of grand opera, and the other nonsporting activities cited in the opinion—was not commerce.

The Legacy of *Federal Baseball*

Antitrust doctrines have changed radically since *Federal Baseball* was decided in 1922. The cases that the Supreme Court relied upon in holding that baseball wasn't interstate commerce have long ago been overruled. By 1960, the Supreme Court had held that doctors, theatrical producers, boxing promoters, and even the National Football League were subject to the federal antitrust laws.

But baseball has somehow retained its uniquely privileged status. In 1953 and again in 1972, in the celebrated Curt Flood case, the Supreme Court affirmed the holding of *Federal Baseball*. Justice Blackmun, in *Flood vs. Kuhn*, noted that baseball's antitrust immunity was "an anomaly" and "an aberration." But, he noted,

> Remedial legislation has been introduced repeatedly in Congress but none has ever been enacted. The Court, accordingly, has concluded that Congress as yet has had no intention to subject baseball's reserve system to the reach of the antitrust statutes. . . .

> If there is any inconsistency or illogic in all this, it is an inconsistency and illogic of long standing that is to be remedied by the Congress and not by this Court.

Is the *Federal Baseball* ruling of any consequence today? After all, the players' union has managed to decimate the reserve clause through collective bargaining. Free agency, arbitration, limits on trades without consent—no longer is the major league player, in Curt Flood's words, "a piece of property to be bought and sold irrespective of [his] wishes."

But what about the owners? Al Davis and Robert Irsay could move away from Oakland and Baltimore because the antitrust laws prevent the other NFL owners from taking concerted action against such moves. What if Calvin Griffith, rather than selling the Twins, had decided to move them to Tampa—or back to Washington DC—without American League approval? If the other owners simply refused to schedule any games with the Twins and Griffith sued them, would *Federal Baseball* still control?

Or what if the USFL owners decided to start a baseball league, too? (Perhaps they would play in the fall and winter.) If Organized Baseball threatened NBC that it would never again sell broadcast rights to that network if it televised the new league's games, would the "USBL" win the antitrust suit that would undoubtedly follow?

Surely then *Federal Baseball*—a case decided over 60 years ago, long before television, jet airplanes, free agents, and night baseball—would finally be laid to rest. Of course, that was what Curt Flood's lawyers thought would happen in 1972. *Federal Baseball* may be an anomaly and an aberration—but it may also outlive us all.

J. Lee Richmond's
Remarkable 1879 Season

JOHN R. HUSMAN

When John Thorn and Mark Rucker formed the Nineteenth Century Research Committee in 1982, those long-ago ballfields seemed to be filled with strangers playing a strange game. In the years since, SABR has published several hundred research articles, biographies, game accounts, and box scores from that era, and it feels closer than ever before. A nineteenth-century historian and Toledo expert who later chaired the committee himself, John Husman recaptures baseball's brief glory in Worcester, Massachusetts.

J. Lee Richmond played four full seasons and parts of two others in baseball's major leagues. Not a long career. Today, more than 100 years later, a check of his statistical record reveals little that would seem to be worthy of recognition. The record does not, however, tell of the spirit he brought to the game and how he changed it. Nor does this record show that he was the first to accomplish the rarest of all single game pitching feats: a perfect game.

Richmond burst upon the baseball world in 1879, leading Brown University to the college championship early in that season. He then revived the struggling Worcester, Massachusetts entry in the National Baseball Association so successfully that they were admitted to the National League in 1880. Along the way he played for several teams, as both an amateur and a professional. He ended the season as he began it, playing as an amateur at his alma mater during the fall season. His composite record for the 1879 season may be unparalleled in all of baseball history: a lofty claim, but lending credence are his season total of 47 pitching wins and his official number two ranking among the hitters in the National Baseball Association with a batting average of .368.

Richmond had paid his dues, playing at Oberlin College in his home state of Ohio, for the Rhode Islands of Providence, and two full years at Brown before embarking on this remarkable season. His career in baseball had been lackluster to this point, but the experience he had attained would be the basis for the total baseball player that was about to emerge. Added to this experience was a variety of left-handed curve pitches that he had developed and perfected during the 1878–79 winter in Brown's gymnasium. In addition, Richmond was named captain of his university's nine.

The attainment of college baseball's championship would be the crown on a successful season for most, but it was only the beginning for Richmond. Even before the college season was completed, manager Frank Bancroft of the Worcesters attempted, on more than one occasion, to lure Richmond to his professional team. He sent the young pitcher a barrage of telegrams asking for his services.

Professional Debut

Walter F. Angell, Richmond's classmate and lifelong friend, wrote years later of how Richmond came to play his first game for Worcester. The occasion was an exhibition game with the Chicago White Stockings on June 2.

> Richmond received a telegram from F. C. Bancroft, then the manager of the Worcesters, asking him to come to Worcester to pitch the game. The telegram is before me as I dictate this letter. I happened to be with Richmond when he opened it, and he handed it to me with the comment that of course he could not go, but his college catcher Winslow came along and persuaded him to take chances and change his mind, Winslow agreeing to go along with him and play as catcher.

Richmond and Winslow had each been offered $10 plus expenses to play the game. Richmond resisted jeopardizing his standing at Brown and his reputation on the mound. Chicago was one of the country's greatest teams, and was hot, having just beaten Boston three in a row. But in the end the arguments of his friend Winslow prevailed. It seems that Winslow was in need of a new pair of trousers, and thus was launched J. Lee Richmond's professional baseball career!

Anson brought his team to Worcester on June 2 as the leaders of the National League. The Chicagos left Worcester having been shut out 11–0 without having made a single base hit. Richmond had thrown a no-hitter in his first game as a professional! Only three others—Bumpus Jones, Ted Breitenstein, and Bobo Holloman—have done the same in their first start against a major-league nine. This was the first of three exceptional pitching performances he would complete within a nine-day period.

Worcester vs. Chicago

Worcester

	AB	R	H	TB	PO	A	E
Brady, 2b	5	2	4	6	1	2	0
Knight, rf	5	1	1	1	0	0	0
Bennett, 1b	2	2	1	3	12	0	0
Sullivan, cf	4	0	0	0	0	0	0
Bushong, lf	4	1	2	3	0	0	0
Richmond, p	2	1	1	3	0	8	0
Winslow, c	3	1	2	3	6	2	0
Irwin, 3b	3	2	1	1	1	2	0
Nichols, ss	3	1	0	0	1	4	0
Totals	31	11	12	21	21	18	0

Chicago

	AB	R	H	TB	PO	A	E
Dalrymple, lf	2	0	0	0	0	0	0
Gore, cf	3	0	0	0	2	0	1
Anson, 1b	3	0	0	0	6	0	0
Shaffer, rf	3	0	0	0	2	0	0
Peters, ss	2	0	0	0	1	2	2
Quest, 2b	2	0	0	0	0	1	2
Hankinson, p	2	0	0	0	0	6	3
Williamson, 3b	2	0	0	0	4	1	0
Harbidge, c	2	0	0	0	6	0	3
Totals	21	0	0	0	21	10	11

Worcester	3	0	1	3	4	0	0	-11
Chicago	0	0	0	0	0	0	0	-0

Runs earned, Worcester 5; three base hits, Brady, Bennett, Richmond; two base hits, Winslow, Bushong; 1st on errors, Worcesters 1, Chicagos 0; 1st on balls, Worcesters 5, Chicagos 1; left on bases, Worcesters 5, Chicagos 1; struck out, Dalrymple, Gore 3, Shaffer 3, Harbidge, Knight, Sullivan, Nichols 2; balls called on, Richmond 56, Hankinson 111; strikes called off, Richmond 14, Hankinson 12; strikes missed off, Richmond 23, Hankinson 23; fouls struck off, Richmond 11, Hankinson 21; double play, Williamson; time of game, 2 hours 10 minutes; umpire. Wm. McLean of Philadelphia.

Arthur A. Irwin also made his professional debut that day playing third base for Worcester. He went on to play thirteen major league campaigns and to manage eight more. Some 20 years later he recounted the story of that historic game:

I signed a Worcester contract on June 2, 1879, coming to Worcester from my home in Boston, where I had been playing on amateur teams. Although I afterward played shortstop I was sent in to cover third base in that first game. Lee Richmond, the greatest left-handed pitcher this country has ever seen, did the pitching for us, and the game that followed became famous the country over. We had as opponents the Chicago club, and we shut them out by the score of 11–0. Richmond pitched the greatest ball that day I have ever seen in all of my experience. The first Chicago man up reached first on a base on balls, and he was the only one of Anson's men to see first base during the entire nine innings [Author's note: actually seven innings were played]. Before the game was over the Chicago players were betting cigars against dollars that they would hit the ball, not that they would hit safely, but only hit it.

Richmond had marvelous support by his teammates, not an error being committed—a highly unusual occurrence in that era. His domination was so complete that in addition to eight strikeouts in the seven-inning game not a single ball was hit out of the infield. Both teams wished immediately to get Richmond's signature on a contract. Worcester was successful, and some 25 years later Bancroft recalled how he had accomplished the signing.

We had struck one of those ruts that comes to every team every once in so often and had lost 18 straight games. The directors were for firing me and getting a new manager. But the stockholders stepped into the breech and saved my life by giving me 30 days in which to either "make good" or lose my job. The next day we were scheduled to play an exhibition with "Pop" Anson's White Stockings. I had heard of a young fellow with the beautiful name of J. Lee Richmond, with the accent on the Lee, who was doing good work for the Brown University team. I ran down to Providence that night and got the boy to come up to pitch the game against the Chicagos. J. Lee was a slightly built chap, who weighed not much over 135 pounds, and certainly didn't look the part of a pitcher.

I also got Arthur Irwin—the famous Arthur Irwin—then but a boy playing on the lots around Boston, to come down and go in at short for me [Author's note: Irwin actually played third base]. When I told the fans what I had done they gave me the laugh. "What, come out and see those kids play the famous White Stockings?" was their chanted response to my invitation for their money. "Not on your life."

Those who refused to come out missed one of the prettiest games that was ever played on any diamond. J. Lee Richmond shut out Anson and his heavy hitters without a hit. Anson asked me if had signed Richmond, and I—for once in my life—told a lie. But I "coppered" my fabrication in what I think was a clever fashion. The dressing room for the players was under the grandstand, and it wasn't much shucks. So I hired a carriage, and when the game was over got young Richmond by the arm and whispered in his ear:

"Now Mr. Richmond—I used the Mr. because I wished to be diplomatic—there isn't much of a place for you to dress down here, so I've taken the liberty of putting your street clothes in a hack. If you would like I'll drive you down to a hotel, where I have reserved a room and a bath for you. You can dress there."

He fell into the trap and I hustled him off to the tavern. There I had no trouble signing him to a contract which called for $100 a month. He was the goods too.

Irwin recalled that Chicago wanted to sign Richmond as well:

Old man Anson was as much struck with Richmond's playing as President Pratt (of Worcester), and when the young pitcher reached Union Station he found Captain Anson there in uniform. Anson had hustled from the grounds, without stopping to change his uniform, in the hopes of getting Richmond to sign with Chicago before Worcester could have a chance to sign him. Anson's ruse did not work, however, and Richmond remained with Worcester.

Back to College

Richmond's second major win of this fantastic nine-day period was the College Championship contest played at Providence on June 9, 1879. Brown beat Yale 3–2 that day with Richmond hurling as he always did for the Bruins. This was the second meeting of the season between these rivals, Yale having won the first contest 2–0 on Richmond's throwing error. This, then, was a "must win" game for the Brunonians.

Brown lost the toss and was sent to bat first, leaving Yale with the advantage of batting last on Brown's home field. Both teams scored a run in the first inning. Brown scored one more in the sixth and what proved to be the deciding run in the seventh. Richmond himself doubled and scored on two consecutive errors. He then held on for the win. Yale scored again in the eighth on a wild pitch but the tying run was cut down at the plate by second baseman Ladd on a ground ball with only one out.

Richmond "took to the points" to pitch the bottom of the ninth inning leading 3–2 with the College Championship hanging on his ability to retire the side. Yale's leadoff hitter, first sacker Hopkins, singled and moved to second as Richmond threw out Camp. Clark, the Yale center fielder, flied out to White at first. However, Smith was safe on Waterman's throwing error and Hopkins moved to third. Smith then stole second and the game, which had looked to be in hand before Waterman's error, was now very much in doubt. Runners at second and third, two out, bottom of the ninth, one-run game—a classic finish for a championship contest and season. To add further to the drama, Richmond got wild. He ran the count to eight balls and one strike (nine balls then constituting a walk) to Ripley. Reaching back for something extra, he got two more strikes to strike out Ripley and end it—a storybook finish that is recalled at Brown University to this day. Richmond himself is remembered as the first of Brown's athletes to be inducted into her Hall of Fame.

The game remained vivid in Richmond's memory as he wrote about it in *Memories of Brown* years later.

This final game with Yale that gave possession of the championship was the most exciting game I ever saw. When Yale went to bat in the ninth inning, the score stood 3–2 against them. By the time two men were out they had the bases full [Author's note: actually there were runners at second and third]. The game literally turned on one ball pitched, for the next batter waited till he had two strikes and eight balls. The grandstand was as still as death. Numbers of fellows had gone behind the grandstand unable to watch the game. When the last ball was struck at and caught by the catcher—well—I can't tell you my feelings. I remember having Professor Lincoln shake my hand, and wondering if the other fellows found it as uncomfortable to be hoisted up on shoulders as I did.

Fame

Just two days later, Richmond pitched his third gem in this fantastic nine-day stretch. On June 11, 1879, he faced the Nationals of Washington DC at the Driving Park, Worcester. The Nationals were leading the National Baseball Association at the time. It was Richmond's first professional championship contest (one that counted in league standings). He bested the league front-runners 4–1 with a neat two-hitter. Richmond had pitched only two games for Worcester, but he had arrived. His presence would provide the spark that would see Worcester roll through the remainder of the season.

The local press was much impressed. From the *Worcester Gazette*:

> The ball game at the Driving Park, yesterday afternoon, was the neatest game of the day, and the spectators, nearly 1000 in number, cheered themselves hoarse over the numerous fine features of the contest. . . . Richmond's wonderful work against the Chicagos, last week, had raised high hopes, and his pitching yesterday was all that could have been expected, only two safe hits being made off his puzzling delivery.

And now, as pitcher for the Worcester club his every effort would be noted by the national press. The game account as it appeared in the *New York Clipper*:

> Richmond's wonderful pitching enabled the Worcesters to defeat the Nationals at Worcester on June 11 in the presence of over 1200 people. The Nationals could not get the hang of Richmond's left-handed delivery and made but two single basers off him in the entire nine innings. The Worcesters batted very well, Bennett taking a decided lead in that respect. The game was one of the most exciting ever played at Worcester, and the home nine's victory was a most credible one.

Worcester vs. Springfield

JULY 28, 1879, WORCESTER, MASSACHUSETTS

Worcester							
	AB	R	H	TB	PO	A	E
Wood, lf	6	2	4	7	0	0	0
Knight, rf	6	2	1	1	4	0	0
Bennett, cf	5	1	1	2	0	0	0
Whitney, 3b	5	0	2	4	2	0	0

	AB	R	H	TB	PO	A	E
Brady, 2b	5	0	0	0	1	4	1
Sullivan, 1b	5	0	0	0	11	1	0
Irwin, ss	5	2	3	5	1	4	1
Bushong, c	5	3	2	2	8	1	2
Richmond, p	5	4	4	6	0	5	1
Totals	47	14	17	27	27	16	5

Springfield

	AB	R	H	TB	PO	A	E
Cassidy, 1b	4	0	0	0	9	0	2
Pike, cf&p	4	0	0	0	3	4	1
Smith, 3b	4	0	0	0	2	3	0
O'Leary, lf	1	0	0	0	2	1	1
Battin, 2b	3	0	0	0	2	3	2
Mack, ss	3	0	0	0	2	3	1
Goldsmith, p&cf	3	0	0	0	3	1	1
Corcoran, rf	3	0	0	0	0	0	0
Powers, c	2	0	0	0	4	3	5
Totals	27	0	0	0	27	18	13

Worcester	2	4	2	0	0	1	2	0	3	-14
Springfield	0	0	0	0	0	0	0	0	0	-0

Runs earned, Worcesters 4; two base hits, Wood 3, Bennett, Whitney 2, Irwin 2, Richmond 2; sacrifice hits, Wood, Knight, Brady, Richmond; struck out, Knight, Bennett 2, Pike 2, O'Leary; balls called, on Richmond 90, on Goldsmith 28, on Pike 98; strikes called, on Richmond 22, on Goldsmith 6, on Pike 20; bases on balls, O'Leary 2, Powers, Bennett, Whitney; wild pitches, Richmond 1, Pike 1, Goldsmith 1; passed balls, Bushong 2, Powers 5; double play, Irwin, Sullivan and Whitney; left on bases, Worcesters 7, Springfields 3; time of game, 3 hours; umpire, Otis Tilden of Brockton.

So ended Richmond's "fantastic nine days." He had won the College Championship with his Brown University team, pitched a no-hitter against the National League leader, and beaten the National Association leader with a two-hitter. He was on his way to a remarkable season that would be marked by fine composite totals and the instant reversal of form by the Worcester club. He was a control pitcher, giving up few walks and striking out more batters than did most pitchers of his time. His defenses recorded unusually high numbers of ground outs. He also helped his cause with the bat, and he took his turn in the heart of the order. On July 28, he no-hit Springfield while knocking out four hits himself—including two doubles—and scoring four runs.

In championship contests through the rest of the 1879 season, Richmond was 18-10 with a league leading earned run average of 1.06. He batted .368 and had a slugging average of .569, leading his team in both categories.

However, there was still much baseball to play. Worcester was scheduled for a slate of exhibition games that would last until mid-October. Featured were contests with the strongest teams of the National League.

Richmond melded participation in these games with attending classes during Brown's fall term. He played for Worcester in especially prestigious games, the schedule and the game site being the determining factors in whether he would appear. This regimen of pursuing his education and furthering his ballplaying career would continue through 1883, when he would receive his medical degree and play his last full season for the Providence Grays.

The highlights of this postseason exhibition schedule were those contests with Providence, Boston, and Chicago of the National League. Providence would take the pennant by five games over Boston. Chicago, after a fast start, would finish fourth, one-half game behind third-place Buffalo.

Worcester knocked off Boston 4–3 at Worcester, on September 11, to set the stage for a very successful exhibition series. The next league team into Worcester was Chicago, on September 18, for a rematch of Richmond's first professional encounter in June. The White Stockings did not fare much better this trip. Richmond shut them out on four singles.

Mingled among these games with the teams of the "Big League" were almost daily games with other teams, many from the National Baseball Association. Albany, their league's champion, came to Worcester on September 25. The occasion was the first of a five-game series arranged for the championship of their respective cities. Richmond sent them packing 10–3, recording the then unheard of total of 15 strikeouts.

Big Leaguer

Richmond capped off a season of firsts and debuts by playing in his first major-league game on September 27. Manager Harry Wright of Boston secured Richmond to hurl against Providence in his team's final league game.

The regular Boston pitcher was ill and the change pitcher was also unavailable for this wrap-up game with Providence, which had already clinched the flag. Pitching for Providence was John Montgomery Ward, who had recorded a league high 47 wins in leading the Grays to the pennant.

After a shaky first inning by Richmond and his defense, he pitched a solid 12–6 win, allowing but a single base hit over the last eight innings. He recorded a league record five consecutive strikeouts in his debut in the senior circuit. The *New York Clipper* felt that the Bostons were a better team with Richmond on the mound:

> The Bostons, strengthened by Richmond, the famous left-handed pitcher of the Worcesters, defeated the Providence nine on Sept. 27 at Boston, Mass. The contest was a remarkable one, the visitors being badly beaten, although they started off with a lead of 5 to 0. Singles by Wright and Start and Gross' three baser earned two runs for Providence, and they made three more runs on errors in the first inning. Richmond then settled down to his work, and the visitors in the next eight innings made but one base hit on him, and that a lucky one to short right field, and scored but one more run, the result of errors by Burdock and Snyder. Eleven of the visitors struck out, five in succession, and we are safe in saying that the chief credit of the victory belongs to Richmond.

Richmond and Worcester went on to split four more games with Boston and Providence. The final game was something of a homecoming for Richmond as Worcester visited Providence, the home of Brown University. J. Lee prevailed again, 3–2, on October 7 in what was both a home and road game for him. This win made him 7-2 against National League clubs for the season, a prodigious record.

Richmond was a busy man. Keeping up with both his studies and his Worcesters was too much for him on one occasion. He mistakenly took the train from Providence to New Haven rather than Worcester for a game with Providence. Failure to meet his team cost him yet another crack at the Grays.

Richmond then rejoined the Brown U. nine for their fall season. Their first scheduled game was with his own Worcester club. Rain interfered, however, and the game was not played. This must have been a great disappointment to Richmond and to the many fans who came to witness another interesting matchup. Brown played four more games, ending their season on October

22. Richmond ended his season as he began it, playing as an amateur. And what a lot of baseball he had played in between!

Richmond's 1879 exploits paid rich dividends for both him and the Worcester team the next season. Because of Worcester's resurgence under his leadership the team was admitted to the National League for the 1880 season. The league fathers were so much in favor of admitting the Worcesters that qualifying rules concerning the population of candidate cities were "modified" to allow the Brown Stockings entry. As what may have been sports' first "franchise player," J. Lee Richmond was paid a then-record $2,000 salary for his services for the 1880 season. In my view, the admittance of this team from a tiny New England town to the National League was Richmond's greatest baseball achievement.

Perfect Game

The 1880 season was the scene of what others consider as Richmond's greatest accomplishment on the field, his perfect game against Cleveland at Worcester on June 12, 1880. The perfect game is the milestone event of Richmond's baseball career, the game that sets him apart from all other pitchers. He was the first, from the purist's point of view (discounting the efforts of Ernie Shore and Harvey Haddix), to pitch a perfect game in the entire 110-year history of major-league baseball.

The story of the perfect game is an amazing one. Taken in context with other events that surrounded it, the feat becomes even more formidable. On the Thursday before this Saturday contest, Richmond had shut out the Cleveland team 5–0, also at Worcester. He was in the midst of a streak of at least 42 consecutive innings during which he would not allow an earned run. In addition, the perfect game would be his third shutout within nine days. He returned to Brown for graduation festivities and parties, passing up Worcester's Friday exhibition game with the Yale nine.

Graduation events included a class baseball game played at 4:50 on Saturday morning. Richmond had been up all night following the class supper at Music Hall. He took part in the ballgame and went to bed at 6:30 a.m. He rose in time to catch the 11:30 a.m. train to Worcester to pitch the afternoon contest against Cleveland. The train on which he rode was delayed and he was forced to go to the field without his dinner. One would not think that proper preparation for a ballgame would include foregoing sleep and food and playing another game earlier in the day.

This train ride has become almost legendary. As the story goes, Frank Bancroft had hired a special train to stand by and rush Richmond to Worcester upon completion of Brown's graduation ceremonies. The story continues with Richmond proceeding to pitch his perfect game. Great story, but not true. Richmond's graduation day was four days later, on June 16. On that day Bancroft did, in fact, have a special train waiting. Richmond took this train to Worcester and was beaten by Chicago 7–6 in 10 innings.

The Worcester team of 1880 was very young, the players averaging 23 years of age. The team included several rookies, playing the team's initial season in the National League. They were enjoying some success, with a 14-9 record early in the season. This series with Cleveland may have offered an extra incentive for Richmond: Cleveland was essentially his hometown team and this was the first time he had ever faced them.

Richmond and big Jim McCormick locked up in a super duel. Richmond himself got the first hit of the game in the fourth, but was erased on a double play. Worcester would get but two more hits the entire day, both by shortstop Art Irwin. The only run of the day scored in the fifth on a double error by Cleveland second sacker Fred "Sure-Shot" Dunlap.

Like so many games that became classic, the game featured a game-saving play. In this case the "saver" may have been the first of its kind. In the fifth inning Cleveland's Bill Phillips hit a ball through the right side for an apparent base hit. Lon Knight, captain, right fielder, and old man of the team at twenty-six, charged, scooped up the ball, and fired to first. Umpire Foghorn Bradley called the runner out, the no-hitter being preserved. This seems to have been a turning point in the game. Richmond had not struck out a batter. He took complete command, striking out five the rest of the way. His domination was so complete that only three balls were hit out of the infield all day.

An effort was made by Mother Nature to disturb Richmond's concentration and perhaps halt the string of batters being set down in order. A cloudburst halted the game in the eighth inning for seven minutes. Undaunted, Richmond returned to the box and, using a heap of sawdust to dry the ball, completed the game.

Richmond always kept his achievement in perspective. He once remarked in a newspaper interview that catcher Charlie "Bennett and the boys behind me gave me perfect support." On another occasion he said, "I couldn't have pitched it if the fielders had not been so expert in handling the ball." Richmond knew that an errorless game played by barehanded fielders was a rare achievement in itself.

Just five days later John Ward of the Grays turned in a second perfect effort against Buffalo in Providence. Two perfect games within a five-day period defies all odds. Ward had equaled Richmond's standard of perfection, a level of play that was not even thought of as being attainable only a week before. The third perfect game did not occur until May 5, 1904, when the legendary Cy Young threw one for Boston (AL). Young's effort kept the perfect game as an exclusive New England institution. The third perfect game in the National League did not occur for 84 years, when Jim Bunning turned the trick in 1964.

During his remarkable 1879 season, J. Lee Richmond established himself as one of the game's fine all-round players and foremost pitchers. He did this at a time when baseball was undergoing rapid evolutionary change. He was a major contributor to changes in pitching strategies and philosophies. He was not the first breaking-ball pitcher. Nor was he the first left-hander ("heartside heaver") to hurl in the National League. He was, however, the first to combine these two then-unusual attributes. The results were devastating, especially on a hitter's first encounter with his unique delivery and pitch. Richmond employed a change of pace and a sharply breaking curve, which broke down rather than out as did the curves of other pitchers. Slight of stature at 140 pounds, he did not overpower hitters. He studied hitters and kept a book on them. His allies were cunning, deception, and strategy. His remarkable 1879 season set off a search for left-handed pitching talent that continues to this day.

12

Roy Tucker, Not Roy Hobbs

The Baseball Novels of John R. Tunis

PHILIP BERGEN

In the late 1980s, SABR produced an annual series entitled *The SABR Review of Books*, four volumes in total. Besides traditional book reviews, the journals included surveys, articles about authors or book series, and author interviews. In this entry taken from that series, Phil Bergen reviews the work of John R. Tunis, author of several well-loved juvenile baseball novels in the 1940s and 1950s. Bergen has been contributing to SABR publications, projects, and committees for nearly four decades.

A person's first impression of baseball literature usually comes from library books, usually from the juvenile fiction section. Judging from what I see as a librarian, there are no more series of baseball books being published today for 8- to 12-year-olds. But if you are a bit older than the video generation, you may remember the Duane Decker Blue Sox series, each book centering on an individual player from that team. Perhaps you remember the Bronc Burnett series by Wilfrid McCormick or the Chip Hiltons written by basketball coach Clair Bee, rather unrealistic accounts of teenagers playing for high school or American Legion honors.

These boys played other sports (and starred in those, too), abstained from social contact with girls, and hung around with their chums, to use a word which fit in well with that milieu. Fatherly coaches explained "inside baseball" didactically, and usually a glory-seeking teammate or revengeful rival provided the plot's conflict, which invariably came down to a hit in the bottom of the ninth inning (or a strikeout if the hero was on the visiting team). These books were entertaining, easily read, and quickly forgotten.

Certain authors were not so easily digested. Ralph Henry Barbour's sporting novels, while formulaic, described the world of the privileged at the turn of the twentieth century in fascinating terms, mixing accounts of ball games with life at New England prep schools, class distinctions, and a snug sense

117

of a time gone by forever. Barbour's books were fun to read and thought provoking. So were those of John R. Tunis.

John R. Tunis today is regarded as out-of-date for today's youth, and perhaps he is. His novels have been incorrectly written off as typical of all boys' sports fiction, full of derring-do by wildly implausible heroes living in a make-believe world. It does Tunis a disservice to be classified like that, both as an author and as an instructor to the youth of his time.

Examining Tunis is much easier today than with other boy's authors. Tunis wrote nine baseball novels in the period from *The Kid From Tomkinsville* (1940) to *Schoolboy Johnson* (1958) and many of them are still available with a reasonable amount of searching. In addition, students of Tunis are fortunate enough to have his 1964 autobiography, *A Measure of Independence*, which provides an insight to the man and his career.

As with Ralph Henry Barbour, John R. Tunis was born in Cambridge, Massachusetts, in 1889, the son of a Unitarian minister. After his father's death, when Tunis was 6, his mother boarded Harvard students, an occupation which provided income and an impetus for her children to value education:

> Education was her whole being, she believed in it with a passion that not many persons have for anything today. It was a source with her. She held it with both hands, cherished it. That we should receive an education also was her principal aim in life, all her energies were bent toward that goal, to this end she dedicated her tremendous determination. Of course we were going to college! Of course we were going to Harvard! The only question was how.

From his grandfather Roberts, Tunis learned to appreciate American history and the Boston Nationals of Billy Hamilton and Fred Tenney. From his extraordinary mother, Caroline Roberts, he received an enthusiasm for life that never waned, judging from the tone of his autobiography, which is written in a self-mocking tone flavored with an optimistic outlook for life.

Tunis did go to Harvard, graduating with the class of 1911 and passing through his collegiate career with Conrad Aiken, Heywood Broun, and Robert Benchley. But he was an indifferent student and preferred athletics, especially tennis, to study.

Unlike the traditional picture of a Harvard education opening doors for success, Tunis pounded the pavements before finding a job as a manual worker in a Massachusetts cotton mill, making 12½ cents an hour. With the arrival of World War I and a new bride happening simultaneously, Tunis debarked for Europe and began a close association with France. After his separation from the Army he began his writing career from a lack of other prospects and wrote for the *New Yorker* and *New York Post* while stubbornly continuing to freelance articles during the Golden Age of Sport. Tunis quickly specialized in tennis and covered the Davis Cup for many years, wrote a novel about women's tennis which sold quite well and even had it adapted for the movie *Hard, Fast and Beautiful*. During the Depression Tunis kept his head above water with his wits and pen.

In the late 1930s his first juvenile novel, *The Iron Duke*, dealt with a Midwestern boy who comes East and gets lost in the world of Harvard. Not originally planning a juvenile book, Tunis had to be convinced that its appeal would be to young readers, but *The Iron Duke* continues to be a well-read story and it launched a second career for Tunis as a novelist for young people. After a sequel which took Jim Wellington through the 1936 Berlin Olympics, Tunis tried his hand at baseball fiction:

> The next morning I piled in to see Mrs. Hamilton, my editor at Harcourt, Brace. Would she, I asked, be interested in a big league baseball story? Again good fortune intervened. She must have been one of the few junior book editors in New York, and surely the only Phi Beta Kappa from Vassar, who had regular seats behind the plate at the Polo Grounds each week. She nodded to my question, immediately agreed on an advance of $200, with which I hoped to pay my own way south to the baseball training camps in Florida. Without hesitation she gave me that vote of confidence every writer needs at such a moment.

Of Tunis's nine baseball novels, eight center on the fictional Brooklyn Dodgers, including the Roy Tucker trilogy, *The Kid From Tomkinsville*, *World Series*, and *The Kid Comes Back*. The ninth, *Buddy and the Old Pro*, follows baseball from the other end of the spectrum, junior high school baseball in the Midwest. Tunis's Dodger books are fiction, but fiction based to a great degree on fact (the preface to TKFT reads "The author wishes to state that all characters were drawn from real life") and it is part of the charm to a ball fan today to match a character to his real life contemporary.

BERKLEY HIGHLAND BOOKS

C977 45c

JOHN R. TUNIS

A SMALL-TOWN BOY
WITH BIG-LEAGUE COURAGE

THE KID FROM TOMKINSVILLE

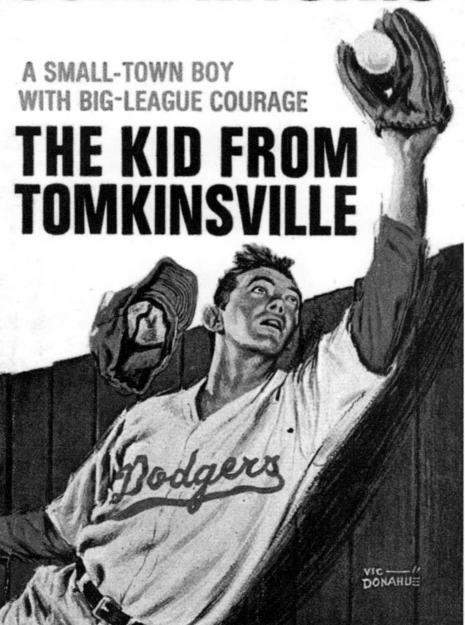

This narrow line between truth and imagination helps contribute to the appeal of the series, especially to young boys whose idea of the major leagues does not include profanity, agreeable women, or long nights on the road. The 40s and 50s were a simpler time, but not as simple as Tunis implies. The idea of creating fiction using real teams and ball parks, and even using an occasional real-life figure (Connie Mack and Al Schacht come to mind) enables the reader to familiarize the setting of many of the events with an understanding gleaned from other accounts of the game. Descriptions of Braves Field, Crosley Field, the Polo Grounds, and even minor-league parks in Nashville and Augusta, give the Tunis books a verisimilitude which other authors lacked.

Although *The Kid From Tomkinsville* was not his first book for youngsters, it was his first baseball novel and the longest, fullest of his attempts to explore the inside world of major-league ball. Roy Tucker, Tunis's penultimate hero, is a Roy Hobbs without flaws and the namesake character. We follow him from his Connecticut hometown to Florida on the day coach, a rookie pitcher in awe of his surroundings.

Tunis wisely starts off the novel with Tucker's departure from the Tomkinsville railroad station, embarrassed by the community's turning out to honor its star athlete while the train's passengers gawk and smirk. (If you imagine Jimmy Stewart in the Tucker role throughout his career, you'll be close.) At the same time Tunis picks up the communal thread of other ballplayers heading to Florida. Some are confident stars roaring down South in their roadsters; others are fading reserve catchers with families, just trying to hang on for another year. Their attraction for the game and its tenuous hold on the players is the string which pulls them south every spring. Tunis started his research with a spring training in Clearwater, so his account of practices, hotel life, and the general bonhomie of the ball club is sharply drawn.

As is typical with most juvenile fiction, Roy Tucker makes the team, pitches a no-hitter in the first night game played in Brooklyn (sound familiar?), and tears up the league the first time around. His mentor, veteran catcher Dave Leonard, steadies him through periods of doubt, catches his no-hitter, and is then released by the Dodgers as being over the hill. Horseplay in the clubhouse leads to a career-threatening elbow injury, and Roy is forced to switch to the outfield in order to stay in the game. He is attacked in his hotel room by a drunken teammate and nearly thrown out the window, an episode that is rather lightly treated by Tunis in a "boys will be boys" manner. It is one of the few episodes of player dissipation shown in his stories. Gabby Gus Spencer, the Durocheresque Dodger manager, is killed off in a fortuitous auto accident (all done very swiftly in a page) and is replaced by Leonard, who challenges the Kid's self-pity with his taunting phrase, "only the game fish swim upstream." Dave Leonard is patterned after veteran Luke Sewell who befriended Tunis in Florida and served as a source of information on the details of a ballplayer's life.

Unlike other Tunis books, TKFT takes place over a two-year period and Roy Tucker, after a year as a pitching phenom, returns to Tomkinsville to reclaim his job as night-time soda jerk and to work on his swing in the barn during the day. His second season is spent chasing down the arrogant Giants—a feat not so easily performed in 1940. Stationed in the outfield for good, Roy battles a late-season slump and saves the pennant with an extra-inning circus catch at the wall of the Polo Grounds. No one body of Tunis's writing is as exciting as the last game of the season when player-manager Murphy is forced to eat his words "Is Brooklyn still in the league?"

TKFT captures the self-doubt and roller coaster emotions of every rookie, and changes Roy Tucker from an exceedingly naive country boy to a seasoned professional ballplayer. Yet never in his long career does Roy lose the earnestness and team spirit that characterizes his rookie season. Capturing the natural skill of Roy Hobbs with the All-American character of Jack Armstrong, Tucker is an ideal hero for a juvenile book, though the adult reader will find him a bit low on human faults.

For Tunis, ever the democrat, writing about Brooklyn and its working-class population of rabid Dodger fans was a wise decision. Throughout his books, most notably *Highpockets*, he expresses the sense of community shared with fan and player and the underdog mentality inherent at Ebbets Field. TKFT, while regarded as a juvenile novel, was of sufficient quality and interest that it was printed as a Victory edition paperback for soldiers during World War II. The plot is fast moving, the baseball scenes are realistic, and Roy Tucker is just the patriotic, aw-shucks hero who would appeal to Americans of all ages during the war. Realistically illustrated with charcoals by Jay Hyde Barnum, TKFT is still an engaging read nearly half a century after its publication.

The immediate sequel to TKFT, *World Series* (1941) is somewhat of a let-down from the excellence of *The Kid*. The Dodgers' Series opponent mysteriously changes from the Yankees (at the end of TKFT) to Cleveland, and the corresponding loss of excitement is evident. The Indians were inserted solely to provide a train ride out and back and to introduce a Bob Feller-like flame thrower who beans the Kid in the first game. The Dodgers fight back to victory from a 1–3 deficit, engage in a brawl after another brushback incident, and capture the Series in seven, but the excitement is less riveting than the drama of the regular season.

Tunis realizes that the months-long tension of the pennant chase is eradicated from the two-week glitz of the Fall Classic. More of the excitement in *World Series* is off the field—a raucous party for the Dodgers when they are on the verge of defeat, a municipal dinner which turns into a Gashouse Gang stunt wherein ballplayers dressed up like painters manage to douse the pompous Dodger owner with whitewash, and the lure of easy money for endorsements and radio shows—but the soul of the novel lacks the intensity of its predecessor. The winning home run is hit by a nondescript teammate, and Roy's only act of note is his slugging an obstreperous sportswriter who has called him washed up. Despite a long series of Dodger successes in subsequent volumes, this is the only one to substantially deal with the World Series, and it does so in a way that suggests that its hoopla is more than the event itself.

The third Dodger novel *Keystone Kids* (1943) is perhaps the most interesting of all the baseball series, for it is more than a sports story. Written during the height of World War II, it is a combination of sports and democracy in action and emphasizes the American way of life through teamwork and a multi-national coalescing. The slumping Dodgers are revived by the arrival of the Russell brothers, up from Nashville to take over at short and second. Both make good, and Spike Russell's leadership abilities are recognized when he is named player-manager of the team. (Did Lou Boudreau have a brother?) For the rest of the series Spike Russell ran the Dodgers firmly, with the sense of an active player.

Complicating the rookie manager's problems is the arrival of rookie catcher Jocko Klein from the minors. He quickly becomes the target of anti-Semitic remarks from opposing bench jockeys and from his teammates who accept his quiet manner for cowardice. Spike Russell's attempts to rally the team behind the catcher are met with indifference and resistance from his younger brother Bob who contends that all Jews are yellow, and that Klein should be abandoned to fight his own battles. Finally, in a showdown with outfielder Karl Case, Klein stands his ground:

"Get outa the way, you k— you; get outa the way and let a man hit who can."[2]

The rookie tottered, stumbled, then found his feet. Old Fat Stuff in the box stood watching; the crowd around the batting cage came alive. Everyone realized something was going to break at last. It did. The boy reacted quickly. He grabbed the nearest bat and, turning, was at the plate in three strides.

"Look, Case." He waved the club at the astonished fielder.

"That stuff's over. I'm the catcher of the Dodgers, get it? If you wanna slug it out, okay."

Case hesitated. He started to lay on with his bat, to go for this fresh busher, when his eyes rested on Klein's hands. They were white and tense around the handle of his club; they looked as if they meant business. The big chap looked down at the stocky figure across the plate, at those hands tightening around the handle. What he saw, he didn't care for. He shrugged his shoulders. "Okay," he murmured casually. "Okay, pal." Then he moved away.

Klein battles his way back to acceptance, until his teammates go into the stands in Philadelphia to fight for him, against a group of redneck fans. In a remarkable passage, Tunis defines teamwork by showing how each member of the team was descended from people who settled America and came together to better their families.

These were some of the things Spike did not know about his team, the team that was lost and found itself. For now they were a team, all of them. Thin and not so thin, tall and short, strong and not so strong, solemn and excitable, Calvinist and Covenanter, Catholic and Lutheran, Puritan and Jew, these were the elements that, fighting, clashing and jarring at first, then slowing mixing, blending, refining, made up a team. Made up America. . . .

Gosh yes. Spike had forgotten about Chiselbeak. Old Chisel, the man no one ever saw, who took your dirty clothes and handed out clean towels and cokes, and packed the trunks and kept the keys to the safe and did the thousands of things no one ever saw. Chisel was part of the team, too; and, though Spike didn't realize it as he followed his team along the concrete runway, part of America also. He was the millions and millions who have never had their names in the line-up, who never play before the crowd, who never hit home runs and get the fans' applause; who work all over the United States, underpaid, unknown, unrewarded. The Chiselbeaks are part of the team, too.

In a very entertaining and thought-provoking way, Tunis explores the reasons why the country is at war and the dangers of one's self-interest overcoming that of the common good. The spectre of anti-Semitism in the major leagues was as far as Tunis would go, although at the same time, his juvenile novels *All-American*, *A City for Lincoln*, and *Yea, Wildcats!*, all set at the high school level, deal with racial segregation and Negro athletes not being able to compete with whites.

Basketball coach Don Henderson, in *Yea, Wildcats!*, stands down an Indiana lynch mob on the courthouse steps, and shames the ringleaders by comparing the town to the integrated high school team which had worked together for a common purpose. Tunis's failure to go further than dealing with Jews in baseball was typical of the period, in which Negroes playing professional baseball were verboten, though they were allowed to compete in high school and college sports. Given Tunis's proven democratic and egalitarian tendencies, it would have been very interesting if *Keystone Kids* could have been extended farther in its stridency; but also, given the time, the book was a refreshing revelation for the general tenor of the time. Aimed at an impressionable audience, it went far in showing how prejudice could hinder all manner of collective effort. *Keystone Kids* won the 1943 Child Study Children's Book Award for breaking ground with its subject matter for that age group.

Rookie of the Year (1944) continues the Dodger season after *Keystone Kids* and follows Spike Russell's team towards a final showdown with the Cardinals. Jocko Klein's troubles are referred to in passing, but the catcher is by now an accepted part of the team and his hustling brand of ball makes him a favorite in Brooklyn. Karl Case has been traded to the Braves, eliminating his aging bat and his prejudice from Flatbush and the problem at hand is with rookie pitcher Bones Hathaway. Hathaway's fondness for John Barleycorn is not as pronounced as with other Tunis characters on the Dodgers (see Raz Nugent in *Young Razzle*) but he and his roommate become pawns in a power struggle between Russell and business manager/traveling secretary Bill Hanson, who resents the young skipper as a Johnny-come-lately. Hanson is a traditional front-office type—glib, brash, and full of baseball tales from days gone by—and is not above sabotaging Dodger morale and success on the field to ingratiate himself with owner Jack McManus. The fact that Hanson is a sideline troublemaker is compared to that of a non-combatant in wartime, a sensitive point in 1944. Spike Russell, as player-manager, can be seen to have shouldered both of the roles of general and foot soldier. Misunderstandings and false accusations abound until Hanson's perfidy is discovered, and Hathaway returns from suspension to walk on the field in the midst of a game to save the team.

It was very difficult to top *Keystone Kids*, and ROTY is among the weakest of the Tunis stories. Certain aspects of wartime America are evident, but the traitorous Hanson is atypical of Tunis's Dodger organization. Hanson is eventually thrown out of baseball by McManus and evidently becomes a publicity man for the Roller Derby or a New Jersey politician.

The Kid Comes Back (1946) returns to the story of Roy Tucker, and carries him from a bomber crash over occupied France to a German prison train to America and Ebbets Field. It is a war story and a baseball story, and expresses through Tucker the uncertainty of the returning veteran.

The conflict in *The Kid Comes Back* lies within Tucker himself and uncertainties about his health (a back problem from the plane crash) and his value to the team at a new position, third base, contrast the differences between personal satisfaction and the value of the team as a whole. While it does not replace Mackinlay Kantor's *Glory For Me* as the best fiction piece about World War II returnees, it does provide a war yarn and a baseball story for young readers and a good deal more for those somewhat older.

Highpockets (1947) is a tall, gangling rookie from North Carolina. Cecil McDade is a great hitter, indifferent fielder, and self-centered individualist more concerned with his average and personal success than the team's. Among the first of his post-war breed, McDade causes resentment among the rest of the Dodgers. Contrasted to McDade is Roy Tucker who is injured (again) in making a wall-crashing catch. Highpockets' self-concern is shaken only when he runs over a Brooklyn boy in his new car after Cecil McDade Day.

The victim, Dean Kennedy, is unusual for his age; he's a Brooklyn boy who is uninterested in baseball, preferring his stamp collection instead. To him Cecil McDade is no hero, just an inconvenient adult who has put him in the hospital. Faced with indifference, Highpockets' struggle to win the boy's friendship and to realize the value of teamwork is the core of the novel.

Tunis's ability to present baseball as a unifying thread throughout New York is evident from the passage reflecting the progress of the big game:

> In the taverns all over town, in Manhattan and the Bronx, and of course in Queens, crowds hung around the television sets, watched Spike Russell have a field day at short, saw Highpockets' tight face when he came to bat, and big Jim Duveen, pitching the game of his life, mow down the Brooklyn sluggers. On the streets, strangers spoke to strangers as they never do in New York, and everybody asked the same thing, "Anybody scored yet?" All afternoon white-coated soda jerkers came out of comer drugstores and posted up goose eggs on the sheet stuck to the front window pane. Folks sat in taxis long after they paid the bill, because for once drivers were content to sit and listen too, and manage the Dodgers for a change. Around the parked cars by the curb, little knots of people bent forward in silence, nodding as the Brooks pulled themselves out of hole after hole, inning after inning. Truck drivers even made peace with their enemies, the traffic cops, hurling the latest score at them as they turned into the main avenues of town.

Highpockets was written during the high-water mark of New York City baseball; this passage expresses the communal sense of the game's ritual before television fragmented the audience. Interposing the ballplayer with the stamp collector, Tunis points out that not everyone is interested in the national pastime, and this makes *Highpockets* a better story. Interestingly, McDade himself is virtually neglected in subsequent Dodger novels; he had served his purpose and was then discarded by Tunis as an uninteresting character.

Young Razzle (1949) is a singular book in the continuity of the Dodger series, but it is not an especially good job by Tunis and is an uninteresting read. It is not a book strictly about the Dodgers. Much of the plot takes place in the minor leagues. The protagonist of the novel is not a Dodger, but a New York Yankee rookie. And the Dodgers blow a 3–1 lead in the World Series and lose in the bottom of the ninth. Not only that, Young Razzle has a slap-dash quality to it that indicates a novel written in haste. An extra-inning pennant-winning game with the Giants is dismissed with a few pages, and the seven-game World Series is condensed into 50 pages. (It rated 300 in *World Series*.)

The problem with YR is that Tunis splits the attention of the book between a father and son; one on the way up, the other hanging on one final year. Joe Nugent is bitterly resentful of his father for abandoning him and his mother over the course of his career. Raz Nugent is a Kirby Higbe type character—very much his own man and unencumbered by discipline or training rules. His colorful antics don't make up for his mediocre pitching, and his inability to control his drinking and his temper push him into the minor leagues, where he faces his son on the field for the first time. Despite his faults Raz appears very proud of Joe and rejoices in his promotion to the Yankees. When Raz is recalled by the Brooks he applies himself, loses weight, and becomes a useful pitcher. Joe, on his side, gradually appreciates his father's courage and skill, and a final reconciliation occurs at the seventh game's conclusion.

With some thoughtful writing, this might have made a passable, if somewhat farfetched tale. (What if Phil Niekro had a son . . . ?) But what develops is a typical boy's story of the period, unremarkable from any other author's, using the interesting characters from the Tomkinsville trilogy and *Keystone Kids* as mere background fillers. If the rest of Tunis's writing were like this, there would be no need to write articles examining his quality.

By 1958 when the last Dodger book was published, both baseball and the Dodgers had undergone changes. Tunis was pressed to catch up with them and it shows in *Schoolboy Johnson*. The most obvious baseball fact about the Dodgers in 1958 was that they were no longer in Brooklyn—instead trying to hit high flies to left 3,000 miles away. Much of the Dodger appeal lay in their location, and Tunis bravely sets his story back in Flatbush, despite facts to the contrary. This in itself was not calculated to win a large readership among boys to whom being up-to-date is more important than tradition. The plot for *Schoolboy Johnson* is centered around a young headstrong pitcher who loses his cool in tight situations. It is unremarkable and no better than those offered by Tunis's competition in the juvenile fiction race. What is remarkable (surrealistic, perhaps) is the Roy Tucker character and his passage through time.

From 1940 to 1958, with time out for war duty, is a long time for a fleet center fielder, even Roy Tucker. In fact, at the beginning of *sj*, Tucker is released, an over-the-hill veteran who winds up playing third base in the Sally League—a counterpoint to the schoolboy who has his career ahead of him. Through a chance set of injuries, Roy is re-signed by the Brooks, and at age 40, returns to dazzle the National League with his speed and ability.

In one sequence he confuses the Braves (Tunis does have them in Milwaukee), getting the winning run across by running wild on the bases (shades of Davey Lopes).

It is evident that all of Tucker's skills and charm are still there, so why was he released? The ultimate team player would have been offered one of those "jobs in the organization" which are always given to loyal sorts who keep their nose clean. Even stranger is the romantic subplot between the schoolboy and Maxine Tucker, Roy's daughter, who has never been mentioned in any previous novel. If Maxine is a store decorator with an established career, she must be in her early twenties, yet neither child nor mother appears in a careful reading of the other Kid novels, and judging from Roy's apple pie and milk character, he has been a bachelor throughout his long career. Just why Tunis felt the need to include this mystery character is puzzling, for no explanation is made about death or divorce. Roy and Maxine live together, but the questions about the Tucker girl and the setting make the novel very disquieting for a fan of the baseball stories and perhaps it was a fitting way for Tunis to end his series. With the Dodgers moved from Brooklyn, and with Roy Tucker's past catching up with him, there was nothing more to write.[1]

The one non-Dodger baseball story, *Buddy and the Old Pro* (1955) takes place on the sandlots of a Midwestern town and is one of Tunis's very best works. Buddy Reitmayer, shortstop and captain of the Benjamin Franklin school team, lives and breathes baseball as does his hero, Mr. McBride, a former major league star cut from the Ty Cobb mold. When McBride moves to Petersburg and gets a coaching job to augment his work as a night watchman, the conflict between playing clean baseball and winning at all costs is presented. What a star major leaguer is doing at a menial job and coaching a school team is not explained satisfactorily, nor is it clear why there is no adult coaching Buddy's team, but here as in no other Tunis story is the conflict between good and evil so well defined.

McBride's team intimidates the Franklin boys with beanballs, bench jockeying and sliding in with spikes high, and the volunteer umpire is no match for the gamesmanship of the ex-big-league terror. Buddy's team, in sneakers and ragtag uniforms, is not able to fight back. When Buddy takes a third strike with the bases loaded to end the game, he throws a temper tantrum that rivals McBride's best, embarrasses his parents, and reflects the doubts he has about the way to play the game. There are nice touches Tunis interjects, such as the closing of the Franklin school at the end of the year (and its consolidation as Curtis P. Gerstenslager Jr. High), and the inability of adults to take the boys' problems seriously. The local sports editor is seen as absent-minded and ineffectual, and only Buddy's father is able to appreciate the injustices of matching boys against a major leaguer, and the wisdom of playing by the rules vs. the winning at-all-cost approach.

As Tunis was in his mid-60s when he wrote *BATOP*, he shows a remarkable appreciation of what it is like to be 12 and playing ball for keeps. Significantly he places the setting away from a Little League, and one can believe that he feels that boys should be allowed to play and have fun on their own—not a novel idea even in 1955 but one which bears repeating. Even at the school level many of the tensions and situations of the game are identical to those of the major leaguers and *BATOP* is not noticeably different from the Dodger books in game description. Buddy Reitmayer's taking a third strike is part of a boy's growing up, and if he is unable to be considered a prospect by the major leagues (as he feels on the way home), he is able to grow up a wiser individual, not as apt to accept the infallibility of his heroes.

In *The Other Side of the Fence* (1953), a non-baseball novel, Tunis takes the unusual step of making his protagonist a comfortable Connecticut teenager who is bound for Yale. Setting out on a cross-country trip with an unreliable friend, Robin Longe decides to set out on his own and hitchhike his way across America. Using his wits and golfing ability to catch rides and provide odd jobs, he meets a variety of people and sees both good and bad sides of America. Tunis's skills describing scenery and regional distinctions are well used, and the historical setting of Connecticut suburban life in the Eisenhower era provides us with an unlikely underdog, the preppie naive traveler. Sport is taken as the great common denominator, as everyone from truck drivers to teenagers to businessmen are bound together from a mutual love of the game. Robin's acceptance in California is sealed by his athletic skill, and his desire to succeed in individual sports is shown to be related to his desire to make it across the country on his own. *TOSOF* is not readily found these days, but it is well worth the search.

After *Schoolboy Johnson* Tunis continued to write juvenile fiction. His book *His Enemy, His Friend* (1967) written when he was 77 and set in the familiar location of France, was a savage indictment of war and its long-term effect on countries and people. It was obviously his personal statement on Viet Nam. Again, the subjugation of individual glory for the sake of the common good is seen as man's ultimate goal.

John R. Tunis died in his beloved Connecticut in 1975. He had written over 30 books and more than 2,000 magazine articles, mostly on sport, and had seen Babe Ruth replaced by Reggie Jackson as the nation's sports hero—both Yankee right fielders who could hit home runs. Throughout his 50-year career he had observed the role that sports played in building the character of adolescents in America and had attempted to better his audience by his stories, which glorified self-sacrifice, team spirit, and the ability to improve oneself through hard work.

The opening words of *A Measure of Independence* puts it best. "I am the product of a parson and a teacher. Any such person is forever trying to reform or to educate, himself if nobody else." Tunis attempted to identify that which is beneficial about sport and character by using the most popular sport of his day—baseball—as the vehicle. That his works are still read and enjoyed today reflects the skill of his writing and the aptness of his lesson. For those persons who grew up with Roy Tucker and the Dodgers it must be rewarding to consider that Roy's number 34 was never retired, and was worn with distinction by Fernando Valenzuela.

NOTES

1. Interestingly enough, Karl Case shows up again in *Schoolboy Johnson* (1958), again playing the outfield for the Dodgers. Instead of being in his dotage, he is described as a hustling veteran with a strong arm. His politics have changed during his exile, as he is shown in an extremely sympathetic light. Unlike his earlier appearances where he is described as figuring his batting average as he runs down to first base, the elder Case is a team player like Roy Tucker. Evidently playing the outfield makes one younger and more liberal. Jocko Klein, in *SJ*, has been released and is managing Birmingham.
2. The ethnic slur originally used by Tunis was removed in the 2020 edition.

13

Zane Grey's Redheaded Outfield

JOSEPH M. OVERFIELD

Another early SABR member, Joseph Overfield joined in 1972 and soon became a prolific contributor. A lifelong devotee of both his native Buffalo and baseball, his passions came together in 1985 with the publication of his well-received book, *The 100 Seasons of Buffalo Baseball*. He wrote often of the stars from Buffalo's nineteenth-century National League club, as well as the city's long minor-league history. In this article from the winter 1985 issue of *The National Pastime*, the great researcher switches gears to reveal the real-life counterparts of the three men at the center of Zane Grey's beloved story.

Zane Grey possesses "no merit whatsoever either in style or in substance," wrote Burton Rascoe, the brilliant but acerbic New York literary critic. And this was the view of another critic, Heywood Broun: "The substance of any two Zane Grey books could be written upon the back of a postage stamp."

The public disagreed. According to the authorized biography of Grey written by Frank Gruber in 1970, the 85 books he wrote sold 100 million copies. Millions more saw the 100 movies based on his books.

Most of Grey's books were about the American West, but those he wrote about deep sea fishing and on his world travels were widely read as well. Often forgotten is the fact he wrote numerous baseball stories that gained wide popularity among young readers. Grey's short story "The Redheaded Outfield" is one of the most famous and widely read baseball stories ever written. Published by the McClure Syndicate in 1915, it was reissued in 1920 along with 10 other baseball stories under the title *The Redheaded Outfield and Other Stories*.

It is not surprising that Grey wrote about baseball. He started to play as a youngster in Zanesville, Ohio, where he was born January 31, 1875. It has been suggested that he was forced to excel in sports to overcome the stigma of the name his mother had given him, Pearl Gray. Eventually he dropped the Pearl and assumed his middle name, Zane, and at the same time changed his surname from Gray to Grey. As a teenager he was recognized as one of Zanesville's better young pitchers. Equally adept as a ballplayer was his younger brother, whose unusual first name, Romer, seems somewhat prophetic for one destined to attain a degree of fame as an outfielder in professional baseball.

When the Gray family moved to Columbus in 1890, the brothers' baseball horizons broadened. Both joined the Capitols, a strong amateur nine, for whom Pearl soon became the star pitcher. A scout for the University of Pennsylvania watched him defeat Denison College of Granville, Ohio, whose star pitcher was Danny Daub, a future major leaguer. Penn offered him a baseball scholarship, and to satisfy his dentist father he decided to enter the dental school. After barely passing his entrance examinations, he began his college career in 1892. His graduation in 1896 was by the slimmest of margins.

Undistinguished as he was in the classroom, he more than made up for it on the diamond. He played college baseball for four years, first as a pitcher and then as an outfielder. In 1896 he helped Penn defeat the New York Giants in an exhibition game, and then in the last game of the season he hit a home run with one man on in the last of the ninth to defeat the University of Virginia. Helped financially by his father and by Romer, who had already started his professional baseball career, Grey set up a dental practice in New York City in 1896. Since the income from his practice was small, or possibly because he much preferred baseball to dentistry, he continued to play baseball in the succeeding summers. The entire story of Grey's professional baseball activity is somewhat shrouded in mystery. Biographer Jean Karr writes that he played in the Eastern, Tri-State, and Michigan State Leagues, but cites no years and no cities. Gruber's book paints another picture. He wrote: "Pearl was sorely tempted to turn professional but he knew it would be the end of his dream of becoming a writer."

According to the Grey obituary in *The Sporting News*, he played for Wheeling in the Iron and Oil League in 1895, Fort Wayne of the Interstate League in 1896, and Toronto of the Eastern League in 1899. SABR members Vern Luse and Robert Hoie have uncovered some pertinent data. Luse found an item in *Sporting Life*, April 15, 1896, reporting that Pearl Zane Gray had signed with Jackson of the Interstate League. Hoie has found he played for Newark of the Atlantic League in 1898, batting .277 in 38 games. The haziness of his baseball career notwithstanding, his exposure to the game was such that it was only natural he should write about it. His first substantial check came from *The Shortstop*, published by A. C. McClurg of Chicago in 1909. Another success was *The Young Pitcher*, in which the author, transformed into "Ken Ward," is the hero and brother Reddie Grey is the shortstop. A few years later he wrote "The Redheaded Outfield," starring Red Gilbat, Reddy Clammer, and Reddie Ray of the Rochester Stars of the Eastern League.

Two of the redheads were trouble personified. "Gilbat was nutty and his average was .371. The man was a jack-o-lantern, a will-o-the-wisp, a weird, long-legged, redhaired phantom." Clammer was a grandstand player "who made circus catches, circus stops and circus steals, always strutting, posing, talking, arguing and quarreling." Reddie Ray, on the other hand, "was a whole game of baseball in himself, batting .400 and leading the league." "Together," wrote Grey, "they made up the most remarkable outfield in minor league baseball."

The story revolves around a single crucial game between the Stars and the Providence Grays, a game in which the Stars' manager Delaney (first name not given) flirts with apoplexy before it is over. First, Gilbat is playing ball with some kids four blocks away and is rounded up only as the game is about to start. In an early inning Clammer is forced to make a one-handed catch (a no-no in those days) because his other hand is filled with the peanuts he is munching on. Then Gilbat, enraged by some remarks about the color of his hair, leaps into the stands to battle the hecklers and is put out of the game. In the sixth Clammer crashes into the wall in making one of his circus catches and is knocked cold. "I'll bet he's dead," moans Delaney. He revives but is through for the day. With no substitutes available for Gilbat or Clammer, the Stars are forced to play the last three innings with just one outfielder, Reddie Ray, "whose lithe form gave the suggestion of stored lightning." It comes down to the last of the ninth, the bases are full, the Stars are down by three and Reddie Ray is at the plate. He smashes one to right center for an inside the park home run and victory for the Stars. "My Gawd!" exclaimed Delaney, "wasn't that a finish! I told you to watch them redheads."

Such was the Redheaded Outfield in fiction. In fact, it was the outfield of the 1897 Buffalo Bisons of the Eastern League, not of the Rochester Stars. In the story Gilbat, Clammer, and Ray make up the redheaded trio; in fact, their names were Larry Gilboy, Billy Clymer, and Romer (R.C. or Reddie) Grey, the author's younger brother. In the story the harassed manager is one Delaney; in fact, the manager was Jack Rowe, a hard-bitten veteran of the baseball wars who had been a member of the famed Big Four (with Dan Brouthers,

Deacon White, and Hardie Richardson) of Buffalo's National League days. Such a dramatic game as described by Grey was never played by the 1897 Bisons. Closest to it was a game played against Scranton on August 5 when the Bisons rallied in the last of the ninth for a comeback win. Clymer and Grey participated in the rally with hits, but the tying and winning runs were driven in by non-redheaded third baseman Ed Greminger.

In the story Grey calls it the greatest outfield ever assembled in the minor leagues; in fact, that would be stretching the truth. But who can say it was not the most unusual? People who know about such things tell us there is one chance in 19 of being a redhead, which makes the emergence of three redheads in one outfield on one minor-league team the longest of long shots.

Perhaps not the greatest, but they were good nonetheless. "Fast and sure, both in the field and at bat," wrote a Buffalo reporter. The headline in the *Express* after the Bisons' opening day win at Springfield was: "Redheads Great Playing!" In the game account we are told that "the redheaded outfield distinguished itself by covering every inch of ground," and that "Gilboy stood the fans on their heads with a spectacular onehanded catch off the bat of Dan Brouthers." In game two of the season, Bill ("Derby Day") Clymer was the star, "catching seven balls that were labeled for hits." On May 8 at Scranton, Gilboy made an acrobatic catch, called "far and away the best catch ever seen at Athletic Park." After a game at Wilkes-Barre, a writer called them great, "as good as any outfield in the game," then added: "Clymer and Gilboy were really sensational. They made some of the most startling plays ever seen in Wilkes-Barre. Both have evidently been with a circus."

When the Bisons opened at home on May 16 against Rochester, they were in first place with an 8-3 record. The highlight of the first game was a miraculous onehanded catch by Clymer, which he topped off by doing a complete flip-flop. On Memorial Day, Clymer provided the one bright spot in what the Express described as an "execrable game" by the Bisons, by snaring a long drive off the bat of McHale of Toronto and then crashing into the fence, just as in the Grey story. According to the *Express*, "It was the most thrilling out seen here this season." Clymer was applauded to the skies when he came immediately to the bat (as so often happens after a spectacular fielding play), and he responded by slashing a hit to left. Not to be outdone by Clymer and Gilboy, Reddie Grey, on June 26 in a game at Rochester, raced to right center to make a one-handed catch of a sinking liner hit by Henry Lynch. His momentum was so great that he turned head over heels after he made the catch.

And so it went all season, with visiting players and managers marveling at the play of the three redheads.

And they were far from slouches at the bat. Gilboy, while not a long-ball hitter (one triple and two home runs for the year), was a gem of consistency. He hit safely in 28 of the first 30 games and then after a couple of blanks proceeded to hit in 14 straight games. For the season he totaled 201 hits (second only to Brouthers' 225), scored 110 runs, hit 44 doubles, stole 26 bases, and batted .350.

Reddie Grey, called by the *Express* writer "the perambulating suggestion of the aurora borealis," played every inning of the Bisons' 134 games, batting .309, with 167 hits, 29 doubles, 13 triples, and 2 home runs. In a game against Scranton in which he was the hitting star, he was, in the quaint practice of that day, presented with a bouquet of flowers as he came to the plate. He responded by doubling to left. Clymer, the most brilliant of the three in the field, was the weakest with the stick. He batted just .279 on 154 hits, but his extra-base totals were strong—32 doubles, 5 triples, and 8 home runs. Five of his homers came in a twelve-day period beginning on August 12 and caused the *Express* writer to inquire: "We wonder what oculist Clymer has seen?" Clymer's fielding average was phenomenal for those days—.969 with just 14 errors. As for the others, Grey fielded .915 and Gilboy .913.

Spurred by the redheads, the Bisons were in the pennant race most of the year, holding first place as late as August 14. A late August slump, however, saw them drop to third by the end of the month. This was where they finished, a disappointing 10 games behind first-place Syracuse and four games behind Toronto. As the team began to fade, so did the early-season euphoria. After a loss to Toronto, the *Express* said, "There are players goldbricking and the fans know who they are." And then the next day, after another loss: "The infield played like a sieve. Could some players be playing for their releases?" First baseman and captain Jim Fields was abused so severely from the stands after making an error that he asked Manager Rowe for his release, which was not granted. In September, after three straight losses to Springfield, the *Express* writer, warming to the task, wrote: "The Eastern League is a beanbag league, just where the Bisons belong. They are playing the type of baseball that made Denmark odiferous in the days of Hamlet."

The 1897 season, which had started on such an optimistic note, came to a merciful end on September 22 with gloom and pessimism pervading the atmosphere. Owner Jim Franklin complained that he was losing money ("This has been no Klondike for me"), the press was vitriolic, the fans were disgruntled, the Eastern League was rocky, and the Western League of Ban Johnson was casting covetous eyes on Buffalo. (Actually, Buffalo did join the Western League in 1899.) But spring has been known to wash away the depressions of falls and winters, and so it was in Buffalo as the 1898 baseball season approached. But what of the fabled redheaded outfield of 1897? Surprisingly, it was destined for a one-year stand. Clymer, who had been with the Bisons since 1894, was the first to go, being shipped to Rochester on March 11. Five days later the *Express* announced: "A Chromatic Deal—Grey for White." In an even exchange of outfielders, Reddie Grey had been sent to Toronto for Jack White. Only Gilboy remained. Not only was he coming back, but he was to get a raise, as well. Word from his home in Newcastle, Pennsylvania, was that "he had spent the winter as one of the leaders of the gay [old connotation] society." When he arrived in Buffalo in early April, the *Courier* noted that "the most prominent thing on Main Street was Gilboy's summer dawn hair, topped with a white hat."

Billy Clymer remained in the game for many years as a player and manager, returning to Buffalo in 1901, 1913, 1914, and from 1926 to 1930. This writer recalls him clearly, as he managed the 1927 Bisons to a pennant—strutting, chest out, argumentative, flamboyant, just as Reddy Clammer had been in the Zane Grey story. Clymer's managerial record is remarkable. He managed 23 complete seasons and parts of six others, all in the minors, compiling 2,122 wins and 1,762 losses for a percentage of .546. He won seven pennants and had an equal number of second-place finishes. Counting only the complete seasons, his record shows just three second-division finishes. He died in Philadelphia, December 26, 1936, at the age of 63. The Macmillan *Encyclopedia* shows he played just three major-league games, those with Philadelphia of the American Association in 1891. Reddie Grey played in the Eastern League with good success until 1903, performing for Toronto, Rochester, Worcester, and Montreal. With Rochester in 1901, he led the league in home runs with 12. In *The History of the International League: Part 3*, author David F. Chrisman picked him as the league's most valuable player for that year. According to the Macmillan *Encyclopedia*, Grey never played in the major leagues. This is disputed by SABR member Al Kermisch, who maintains that Grey played a game for Pittsburgh on May 28, 1903, but was confused with another Grey and therefore has not been listed as a major league player. [This situation was remedied long ago, and Reddy Grey does have his entry in the MLB Player Registers.—Eds.] Once out of baseball, he followed his father and brother into dentistry, but eventually gave it up to become his brother's secretary, adviser, and companion on his world travels. A strong fraternal relationship existed between Romer and Zane throughout their lives. Zane never forgot that it was R. C., along with his father, who helped him financially when he was setting up his dental practice in New York and that it was R. C. who gave him encouragement and monetary assistance when he was struggling to establish himself as a writer. Zane showed his esteem for his younger brother by naming his first son Romer. R.C. died in 1934 at age 59, one year before Zane too passed on.

Little is known about the third member of the redheaded triumvirate, Lawrence Joseph Gilboy. He lasted with the Bisons only until May 27, 1898, when he was released outright because, in the words of owner Franklin, "He was worse than useless when he got on the lines." He signed with Syracuse, played only a few days, was released, played for Utica and Palmyra of the New York State League and for Youngstown of the Interstate. There is no record that he played after 1898. It was a strange and abrupt ending to a career that had started so brilliantly. There was a note in the *Express* that he was entering Niagara University to study medicine. The school cannot find that he ever enrolled. Such is the story of three minor-league outfielders who would have long since been forgotten, were it not for the color of their hair.

14

Honus Wagner's Rookie Year, 1895

A. D. SUEHSDORF

A. D. Suehsdorf joined SABR in 1979, just as he was finishing up a long career as a writer and editor for newspapers, magazines, and book publishers. In "retirement," he became an active SABR writer for the *Baseball Research Journal*, *The National Pastime*, and *The SABR Review of Books*, and eventually served as a copyeditor and as chair of the publications committee. In this 1987 article, Suehsdorf presents a detailed chronicle of the twenty-one-year-old Honus Wagner's peripatetic first year in the minor leagues.

During the summer of 1895, John Peter Wagner—not yet known as "Honus" or "Hans," nor yet as a shortstop—played at least 79 games for teams at Steubenville, Akron, and Mansfield, Ohio; Adrian, Michigan; and Warren, Pennsylvania. He rapped out at least 91 hits in 253 known at-bats for an overall average of .360.

The numbers are approximate, for reasons that will be explained, but they are a factual beginning to the hitherto unsubstantiated, or erroneously reported, record of Wagner's first season in professional baseball.

Gaps in the great man's stats have occurred through a variety of circumstances. His leagues—Inter-State, Michigan State, and Iron & Oil—adhered to the National Agreement. They were acknowledged in the annual Reach and *Spalding Guides* and their organizational details were noted by *Sporting Life*, but by and large their statistics were ignored. Two of Wagner's leagues and three of his teams collapsed while he was with them, leaving only random evidence of their existence. Contemporary newspapers, although the principal sources for this article, were erratic in their coverage and scoring.

Discrepancies in the available box scores raise the possibility that Wagner actually had 93 hits, which would improve his average to .368. There also were 11 games in which he made a total of 15 more hits, but in which, unhappily, at-bats were not scored. (His average at-bats in the games for which box scores are complete was 3.83; for those 11 games that would be, conceivably, 35. Add these to 253, and the 15 hits to 91 or 93, and you reach hypothetical averages of .368 and .375.) Finally, there were 12 games, including four exhibitions, in which Wagner probably played for which no boxes have so far been found.

Honus himself was a fount of misinformation when pressed for biographical detail many years after the event. In an early episode of a nearly interminable life story run by the *Pittsburgh Gazette-Times* in 1924, a boxed tabulation of the Wagner record carries a BA of .365 in 20 games at Steubenville and .369 in 65 games at Warren. Both, Honus claimed, were league-leading averages.

Actually, he played a mere seven games for Steubenville before the franchise was shifted to Akron, where he played five games more. He did hit .367 for Steubenville (or .400 if he deserves an extra hit one box score gave him) and .304 for Akron. Twelve games, however, are obviously too few for him to have been league batting champion.

If he hit .369 at Warren, it was not from 92 hits in 249 ABs in 65 games, as cited by the *Gazette-Times*. Wagner played his first game for Warren on July 11 and his last on September 11, a total of 63 days during which he missed 21 because of an injury to his throwing arm and several others because no ball was played on Sundays. In the playing days available to him, only 34 league games were scheduled (plus 19 exhibitions), hardly enough to support a claim to league batting honors. From the numbers I have at hand, I believe he played all 34 and batted about .324.

For all the uncertainty, a close look at Wagner's rookie season gives us a fascinating look at a youngster developing in the minor leagues of 90 years ago. The enormous skills of his National League years—power hitting, exceptional range afield, base stealing ability—already were apparent. A reporter for the *Mansfield Shield* seems to have printed it first and said it best: "Oh! for nine men like Wagner."

In 1895, John Wagner had just turned 21 and had been playing hometown ball around Mansfield, Pennsylvania—now Carnegie—a coal-and-steel suburb of Pittsburgh, for some six or seven years. He was working in the barber shop of his brother Charley, presumably as an apprentice, but mostly sweeping up, running errands, brushing stray hairs off the customers' suits, and trying to get loose to play ball.

He escaped the barber shop forever when George L. Moreland, owner and manager of the Steubenville club, wired him an offer of $35 a month.

Moreland, who moved in Pittsburgh baseball circles, may have seen Honus as a kid, playing in the Allegheny County League, or he may have asked his third baseman, Al Wagner, Honus's elder brother, if he knew any young prospects. Or maybe both.

At a Pittsburgh spring training camp in the mid-thirties, Moreland, by then a baseball statistician and historian, recalled Al saying: "I've got a brother who is a peach. He's loafing now, and mebbe you could get him to play for you. If so, you won't go wrong on him. He's a great ballplayer."

John tried to squeeze an extra $5 a month and got a wire back: "If you can't accept thirty-five you had better stay home."

Abashed, he jumped aboard a late-night freight hauling coal and was in Steubenville by 5 the following morning.

Steubenville

Games	AB	R	H	PCT	PO	A	E	Other
7	30	7(8)	11	.367	6	6(7)	0	3 HR, 1 3B, 3 2B, 3 SB

Wagner's contract has several points of interest. First, he signed as "William" Wagner and thereafter became known as "Will" throughout the league. William was the name of still another ball-playing Wagner brother, and old Hans occasionally said he signed that way because he thought William was the Wagner Steubenville wanted. Well, perhaps, although that lets the air out of Al's recommendation. On the other hand, Manager Moreland noted that the contract was received February 10, which was a mite early for third-baseman Wagner to be hanging around Steubenville offering advice on young prospects. Honus's comment on the contract obviously was much later; maybe Moreland's was, too.

The club obligates itself to pay expenses on the road, while charging the player for his uniform and shoes, a not-unusual practice in those days. Les Biederman's 1950 biography of Wagner, *The Flying Dutchman*, has 76-year-old Honus recalling with amusement that $32 of his first month's salary went for two uniforms and a pair of shoes.

Steubenville's nine seems not to have had a nickname, but it had handsome "Yale gray suits," with cap, belt and stockings of blue. On the left breast of the shirt was the letter *S*. A "decidedly pretty effect," said the *Steubenville Daily Herald*.

Steubenville was one of seven Ohio teams in the Inter-State League.

Wheeling, West Virginia, the eighth, justified the name. All the clubs were in a 275-by-80-mile area. Steubenville's scheduled road games would have involved about 2,200 miles of travel.

Like many leagues of its time, the Inter-State began bravely, with well-attended games and intense local rivalries, then foundered amid turmoil and confusion, which led the acerbic reporter for the *Shield* to dub it the Interchangeable League.

"Will" Wagner appears in the Steubenville lineup for the first time on April 20, an exhibition victory over Holy Ghost College. He played right field, batted seventh, and went 2-for-5. (E. Vern Luse has backstopped my Steubenville, Akron, and Warren numbers by generously sharing his research into Inter-State and Iron & Oil League statistics.)

The regular Inter-State season opened at home on May 2 with a wild 29–11 win over Canton. Will was in left field, again batted seventh, and went 1-for-6, a homer in the fourth with a man aboard. He also got an outfield assist for nailing at the plate a runner trying to score from second on a single.

On May 4 he stole three bases against Canton, an individual effort not usually credited in game summaries, but available here because the paper published a play-by-play story.

On May 7, with the Kenton Babies in town, Will started in left and went 3-for-5, including a homer and a triple. He also struck out four in two shut-out innings of relief—a short "row of post holes," as scoreboard zeroes were sometimes called in 1895. Always a strong thrower, Wagner had done some impressive relief work in preseason exhibitions, and manager Moreland may have thought to make a hurler of him.

The following day, in a rain-shortened five-inning contest, Wagner pitched all the way. He gave up six runs and seven hits, including three home runs, but won easily as Steubenville teed off on Kenton pitching for 26 runs on 22 hits, two of them Wagner doubles.

Now considered a pitcher exclusively, Wagner sat out the next game and entered the one following in the sixth, with the Mansfield Kids already well ahead. He allowed two runs in two-plus innings.

Meanwhile, Moreland had telegraphed the league president, Howard H. Ziegler, requesting permission to transfer his club to Akron, pleading inadequate support by Steubenville. "Akron has the baseball fever in the most malignant form," said the *Ohio State Journal*, "and has promised Moreland to receive his nine with open arms." Belatedly, Steubenville began to raise money to keep the team in town and urged people in neighboring communities to come by streetcar and support the club.

President Ziegler, always mentioned scornfully by Mansfield's *Shield* as a dilatory and do-nothing leader, acted promptly in this instance. He approved the move over the weekend and by Monday, May 13, the team represented Akron.

				Akron				
Games	AB	R	H	PCT	PO	A	E	Other
5	23	4	7	.304	11	1	1	2 HR, 2 2B, 34 RBI

The first game in its new setting was a rousing 21–5 win over Findlay, whose location at the center of the state's oil and gas producing region earned it the nickname "Oil Field Pirates." Wagner, back in left field, had three RBIs with a homer and two doubles in six at-bats. "The Wagner brothers are little," said the *State Journal* in a sidebar, "but the way they hit the ball is something awful."

In fact, the more experienced Al was judged to be the more promising player. Batting cleanup in 13 games for Steubenville/Akron, he had 26 hits in 56 ABs for an overwhelming average of .464. He also scored 25 runs. Neither man, however, was physically small.

On the 17th, Will pitched a complete game at Canton's Pastime Park, winning 14–7 and contributing three hits and a run. He allowed seven hits, including two doubles and a homer, walked four, hit two, and had a wild pitch. Not an artistic success. Even so, because of five Akron errors only one earned run was charged against him.

Akron's final game was a 5–5 tie in the seventh when one of its players was called out attempting to steal third. A violent protest erupted, and when Moreland refused Canton's request to remove an abusive player, the single umpire gave him five minutes to comply and then forfeited the game to Canton.

(Unaccountably, at-bats were not scored for this game. Since Wagner went hitless, and because of the rumpus probably did not bat in the seventh, I have arbitrarily given him three ABs.)

Following the game, Akron "went to pieces," and its place in the league was awarded to Lima, Ohio, whose team, inevitably, was called the Beans. Canton immediately signed Al Wagner. Will was picked up by Mansfield.

Claude Ritchey, the excellent shortstop, went to the Warren Wonders, where Honus would catch up with him again.

				Mansfield				
Games	AB	R	H	PCT	PO	A	E	Other
17	62	15	24	.387	26	43	15	5 HR, 1 3B, 1 2B, 10 RBI

Honus was in the Mansfield lineup on May 20, batting second and listed as "J. Wagner." Lacking a shortstop of Ritchey's caliber, Mansfield's manager, Frank O'Brien, gave the versatile Wagner his first try at the position.

He played through June 8, a total of 17 games for which box scores of 13 are available. The missing four involve games with the Twin Cities—Uhrichsville and Dennison, manufacturing towns adjoining each other on a bend of the Tuscarawas River—Cy Young country south of Canton. One game, at Mansfield on May 29, was skipped because the *Shield* did not publish on Memorial Day, and got only a paragraph in the issue of the 31st, which also had to report the holiday doubleheader. The other three—June 6, 7, and 8 at the Twin Cities, which meant the park at the fairgrounds, several blocks from beautiful downtown Uhrichsville—are forever lost. The *Shield*, like many small-town papers of the time, did not send a reporter on road trips, and there was no local coverage because the *Uhrichsville Chronicle* did not start publication in 1895 until after the baseball season: The summary under the line score for one of these three credits Wagner with a homer, so there is at least one AB, run, and RBI to add to his totals.

As it happened, Wagner did well when his team was thriving and tailed off when it slumped. While the Kids were winning five of the first six he played for them, his average was a fantastic .467. When they lost 10 of the next 11, he dwindled to .313. All told, he had a countable 24-four hits in a traceable 62 at-bats for a handsome .387 average. (It might even have been .403. In one game—again with the wretched Twins—the box gives him 1-for-5, but the summary credits him with a homer and a double. So, maybe he had 25 hits.)

In a 14–10 loss to Canton (and Brother Al), he had two home runs and three RBIs, then pitched relief in the sixth, evidently shutting down the Dueberites, as Canton was called, with one run in two innings plus. "Wagner Covered Himself with Glory," said the *Shield's* headline bank. And somewhat less kindly, for this could be a harshly critical paper: third baseman Jack

Dunn "Loses His Head and His Stupid Playing Alone was sufficient [sic] to Lose the Game."

There is no indication of the distances to the outfield fences. One of Wagner's homers was described as "a hot shot deep into center" and the other as an inside-the-park drive that the center fielder was slow getting to.

With the glove he did less well: 10 errors in eight games at short, one in two games in center, four in three games at third. This was called "yellow" support in those days. The etymology is unknown, although it probably derives from the many pejorative uses of the word. Here it obviously means sloppy play that lets the side down.

Wagner was nothing if not willing. In one game at short he drifted into the center fielder's territory for a fly and had to be called off. Another postgame note had the second baseman, Billy Otterson, a veteran who had played with the Brooklyn team in the old American Association, chewing him out for backing into the left fielder.

Against Canton on May 24, he nearly put the Kids under all by himself. In the seventh, his "rotten fielding" allowed a batter to reach first. This so occupied the umpire's attention that a Canton player, McGuirk—"McSquirt the robber," the outraged *Shield* called him—"cut third base by at least twenty feet and the umpire allowed the score to count because 'he didn't see it.'"

The Kids went into the ninth leading 7–4 until two Wagnerian errors enabled Canton to tie it up.

> The agony of the rooters was painful, but it couldn't be helped. Smith [Harry, a catcher who would be Honus' teammate at Warren and for six years at Pittsburgh] was safe on Wagner's [second] error and the rooters were ready to faint and were cussing Wagner in language which the pastors of Christian congregations do not use, but Smith was thrown out at second and the church members, who had been swearing like pirates, breathed easier.

Mansfield rallied for nine runs in the 10th and won, 16–9. Wagner's contribution was a walk.

With victory in hand, the *Shield* was more forgiving. "J. Wagner's three errors yesterday," it said, "were sheer awkwardness, but Wagner played a great all-around game and accepted chances outside of his territory which resulted in some of the errors marked against him."

With 26 putouts, 43 assists, and 15 errors, Honus' fielding average was a painful .821.

As May ended, the league's perilous condition became obvious. Canton disbanded and Al Wagner and Harry Smith quickly jumped to Warren. The collapse put Mansfield in a bind. Well entrenched in last place with a record of 8-23, the club now faced an idle week through the loss of six scheduled games with the nonexistent Dueberites. The end came June 14. "Lock the Gates," read the *Shield's* one-column headline. "The Jig is Up with Mansfield for This Season."

Al, looking out for little brother, wired John to join him at Warren. "Will come for sixty-five [dollars per month]," Honus wired back. "Send ticket."

That was too steep for Warren, and Wagner moved on to the Adrian Demons of the Michigan State League—at $50 a month.

Adrian								
Games	AB	R	H	PCT	PO	A	E	Other
16	70	23	27	.386	36 (37)	46 (49)	9 (10)	2 3B, 5 2B, 16 SB

The long jump of an untraveled rube from Ohio to Michigan has a simple explanation. In 1949, Honus told Jim Long, then the Pirates' PR man, that the Mansfield owner, "a man named Taylor," said his brother ran a hardware store and a baseball team in Michigan and would have a spot for a hard-hitting youngster.

This time Wagner's memory was on track. Mr. Taylor would have had to be William H., the father of Rolla L. Taylor of Adrian, who did, indeed, run a hardware store that was known throughout Lenawee County for its reliability. Moreover, Rolla was a prime mover in the consortium of Adrian businessmen who financed the Demons. He served as club secretary, managed the team, and selected as mascot his little son, Grandpa's namesake.

William's connection with baseball can be established only circumstantially today, but he was a member of a pioneer Ohio family, earned a captaincy in the Civil War, and between 1885 and 1895 was a partner in a Mansfield cracker factory which evidently was one of the regional bakeries amalgamated into the National Biscuit Company. He sounds distinguished and wealthy enough to have backed a small-town ball club.

Honus also told Long that, although he was a stripling with 29 games' worth of professional experience, Adrian appointed him manager. Not so. Rolla ran the show.

The Michigan State League was a well-organized, well-run circuit of six clubs, located generally in the lower half of the State. Besides Adrian, which was also known as the Reformers, there were the Lansing Senators, Owosso Colts, Port Huron Marines, Battle Creek Adventists, and Kalamazoo Kazoos, Zooloos, or Celery Eaters, celery being a big local crop.

Adrian, the Maple City, performed at Lawrence Park and Wagner appeared in his first game there on June 20, playing second base and batting cleanup. In the first inning, the semi-weekly *Michigan Messenger* reported, Wagner "made the greatest slide for first probably ever made on the grounds, but in an effort to steal second his great slide failed to save him. He played on second base and did good work."

It wasn't all heroics, however. In his third game, he "took the stick with bases full and had an opportunity to distinguish himself, which he unfortunately did by striking out, and retiring the side." He contributed a double and a triple later on, and Adrian beat Owosso in 10, 12–11.

Against Battle Creek the following day he came to bat with two on in the first and "almost lost the ball over between left and center fielders for a triple." Not bad afield, either, according to the *Daily Times*: "Some of the ground stops he made were handsome plays in every respect."

In a game against Port Huron, the best and worst of the young Wagner's abilities were made evident. In the first he "made a beautiful stop" to retire the side with the bases full. In the third, again with bases full, a Marine drove the ball to right field, and a "wild throw of Wagner"—a relay, no doubt— allowed three Marines to score. Finally, in the eighth with three on, Port Huron "sent a red hot grounder to Wagner, who plays all over his field and half of the adjoining sections, [and who] made the best stop of the day and retired the side."

All told, available stats give him 36 putouts, 46 assists, and 10 errors for .891.

For hitting, I am relying on Ray Nemec's thoroughgoing research into the Michigan State League's 1895 season, which he assembled some years ago. He credits Wagner with 27 hits in 70 ABs for .386. I have confirmed 14 of Wagner's 16 games and am persuaded that the missing two would match Ray's numbers.

An interesting aspect of Honus' experience at Adrian was the presence

Fig. 14.1. The Page Fence Giants, 1895. Bentley Historical Library.

of two excellent black players on the Demons' roster, another piece of history authoritatively researched by Nemec. These were George H. Wilson, a 19-year-old righthander, and Vasco Graham, his catcher. Wilson appeared in 37 games—30 complete—winning 29 and losing 4. He pitched 298 innings, allowed 289 hits and 173 runs. He struck out 280 and walked only 96. He hit .327 in 52 games as pitcher and occasional outfielder. Graham played in 67 and hit .324, with 19 doubles and 18 SB. I encountered one reference to them as Adrian's "watermelon battery," but the town's, and the league's, tolerance seems to have been exceptional and newspaper admiration of their talents genuine.

The two were acquired from the Page Fence Giants, a highly successful team of black barnstormers organized by the legendary John W. "Bud" Fowler and sponsored by Adrian's Page Woven Wire Fence Company. Fowler and many other players from the Page Fence Giants also played for the Demons, though not during Wagner's few weeks. A measure of the Giants' prowess can be gained from an account of an exhibition game between the Demons and the Giants 11 days before Wagner's arrival. Watched by a crowd of 1,400, the Giants walloped the Demons, 20–10. Fowler, in right field, went 5 for 6. Sol White was at second base, got two hits, and took part in three double plays.

In later years, Honus laid his departure from Adrian to homesickness. There may have been more to it than that. During the exhibition with the Giants it was evident that some of the Demons were in a truculent mood. Referring to their haphazard play, the *Messenger* observed: "No club can play a good game unless harmony can prevail among them. When a set of men get to kicking about this and that, and seem dissatisfied, it is time they were called to a halt, and from all appearances the greater part of the team needed a calling down. . . . If Mr. [J. T.] Derrick is manager of the club [he was not, but as pitcher and outfielder may have been field captain], the players under him should be made to obey." Did this have something to do with the Demons' reactions to getting shell-shocked by blacks?

In July, 12 days after Wagner's departure, the *Messenger* reported: "Derrick was released this morning. There seems to have been a strong feeling among members of the club against him in some way, with the result that there was a greater or less lack [*sic*] of harmony in the organization. It is strongly hinted that Wagner left largely on account of that feeling." What feeling? One could wish that the reporter wrote plainer, more felicitous English.

In a retrospective interview with manager Rolla Taylor in 1930, the *Adrian Daily Telegram* offered this paraphrase: "Wagner never 'hitched' so very well with the Adrian team. He didn't like to play with Adrian's colored battery. It was thought this had something to do with his quick departure."

The trail ends there. Efforts to elaborate, or refute, the story through contemporary sources have been futile. I found no one in Adrian today aware of the history, let alone the personal circumstances. Perhaps it is less a comment on Honus than on the perniciousness and relentlessness of baseball's color bar, which would soon be absolute and persist for more than half a century.

								Warren
Games	AB	R	H	PCT	PO	A	E	Other
17	68	15	22	.324	57	49	17	1 HR, 3 2B, 11 SB, 5 DP
9	—	9	15					

Joining Warren was like old home week for Honus. Five of his mates from the disbanded Steubenville club were in the lineup. Aside from Brother Al at third, there were Claude Ritchey at short; Dave "Toots" Barrett, a workhorse lefthander; Jakie Bullach (Bullock in Steubenville boxes), who could play second or the outfield; and outfielder-catcher Jimmy Cooper.

For all the talent, the Wonders were fifth in the Iron & Oil League, two games under .500, when Wagner arrived.

The I&O comprised six small cities in the northwestern corner of Pennsylvania, plus two refugees from the defunct Inter-State: the obscurantist Twin City Twins and Wheeling's Mountaineers (or Stogies), whose factotum, also headed for the big leagues, was Edward G. Barrow. It had the usual dropouts and replacements, but seemed on the way to completing its split-season schedule.

Warren's home field was Recreation Park, which the Pittsburg (no "h" in those days) *Post* called the finest in the league. In his first game there on July 11, Wagner had his one and only trial at first base. He batted fourth, following Al, and produced a double and a stolen base. The following day he was in right field and the day after that at short and batting second. He got four hits, including a home run, scored three, batted in three, and stole two bases. He had six assists afield and the *Warren Evening Democrat* told its readers: "John Wagner covers a great deal of ground at short."

Of his first nine games, eight involved the same opponent representing two towns. Four were with Sharon (Pennsylvania), two of them played as exhibitions after the franchise folded and was transferred to the curious little town of Celoron (New York). Located, with its large neighbor, Jamestown, by Lake Chautauqua, Celoron was at the heart of the era's famous "Chautauquas"—summertime tent meetings where huge crowds gathered for educational lectures, concerts, and revivalist sermons by evangelists. (A year later, a star attraction would be the ex-ballplayer, Bill Sunday.) Two of Warren's four games with the no-nickname Celorons also were exhibitions as the league marked time before starting the split season's second half. The ninth game, still another exhibition, was a loss at Warren, before a crowd of 1,000, to Connie Mack's National League-leading Pittsburg Pirates.

As for Wagner's performance, statistics are available for 17 games, half of those he played, including exhibitions. Several of the I&O League towns reported at-bats irregularly or not at all. This affects nine games in which he got 15 hits. For eight others, particularly those with Celoron, there is no coverage whatever. "The Jamestown people," said the Warren *Evening*

Democrat, "take a great deal more interest in balloon ascensions than they do in baseball." This was an unseemly gripe, considering that the *Democrat* was among those that ignored at-bats.

We know for sure that Honus went 22 for 68 in the 17 games, an average of .324. Fielding stats are complete for all 26 scored games: A not very impressive average of .862.

He played right field and third base, eventually taking over there from Al, who shifted to second. ("J. Wagner put up a good game at third . . . that seems to be a regular Wagner base.")

Then, on Monday, July 29, the *Democrat* reported "while running to catch the train at Titusville, John Wagner fell and received a rather severe cut under his right arm. The muscles were not affected but it took several stitches to close up the wound . . . . It will probably necessitate his being out of the game for a week or so." Actually, three. He rejoined the team for a game with the Franklin Braves and had a week of action before the league started to disintegrate. Three teams disbanded.

A 12-game winning streak in Wagner's absence had moved the Wonders into the league lead, with the strong Wheeling organization some three games behind. When it was clear that the league could not continue, Warren agreed to play a seven-game series at Wheeling to decide the championship.

It was State Fair week at Wheeling, which guaranteed good crowds for the games, even though baseball was playing second fiddle to bike races and Buffalo Bill. One game was scheduled in the morning to avoid a conflict with Bill's street parade of cowboys and Indians. Another was played at four in the afternoon, after the bike races.

Wheeling won four of the first six games, so that Warren's victory in the seventh was technically an exhibition for another payday. Wheeling immediately claimed the championship. The Wonders, although hard pressed to ignore their agreement to a decisive series, could not help noting that their season's record, including the seven at Wheeling, was 26 and 12 for .684, while the Stogies' 27 and 16 was .630. Warren went on to lose two out of three to New Castle, languishing in third place, which thereupon had the temerity to proclaim itself the league champs. For what it's worth, the A. G. Spalding Company, in its wisdom, sent a pennant to Wheeling.

Warren's management wanted to keep the team going. It was only September 12, after all. But there was a small matter of paying the players, who had received nothing since the first of the month. A wrangling negotiation led nowhere and the players voted to go home. Last to leave were manager Bob Russell and the Wagner boys.

Whatever the statistical confusion of his season, John Peter Wagner was on his way. By August he was beginning to be known as "Hannes," though not yet as a shortstop. Of the 67 games for which his position is known, only 10 were spent at short. He played 18 at third, 17 each at second and the outfield, one at first, and five on the mound.

If his fielding left something to be desired, it was not for lack of range or a strong throwing arm. And as a hitter, he already was awesome. He did not escape the notice of "Cousin Ed" Barrow, who would move on to Paterson (New Jersey) in 1896 and arrange to have Hannes with him. Thereafter, it was Louisville, Pittsburgh, and the Hall of Fame.

15

Four Teams Out

The National League Reduction of 1900

BOB BAILEY

A longtime SABR stalwart, Bob Bailey is known as the world's foremost expert on the Louisville club, a major-league team for eighteen years (ten in the American Association and eight more in the National League). In this 1990 article from the *Baseball Research Journal*, he tackles one of the most interesting off-field tales in baseball history, when the National League of 1892–99 contracted from twelve teams down to eight. It is a tale involving intrigue and owner shenanigans and which also, alas, spelled the end of Louisville's major-league story.

Phoenix, Denver, Tampa, Washington, perhaps a dozen cities are all hoping to be tapped by major-league baseball's magic wand and be initiated into the fraternities of American and National League clubs. Expansion has been a topic of discussion for at least 40 years, ever since weak franchises in two-team towns began looking for salvation outside the shadow of their more dominant cousins.

In baseball's more distant past the question was not expansion, but reduction of teams. Back in 1899 the National League went from twelve teams to eight as Baltimore, Cleveland, Louisville, and Washington left the majors. Within two seasons all but Louisville had landed in Ban Johnson's American League. Cleveland is still there. Washington spent many decades in the AL. Baltimore's franchise shifted to New York in 1902 and the Maryland city remained beyond the pale until 1954. Louisville is the only city of the group that was out and stayed out.

This is the story, from the perspective of the almost forgotten Louisville Colonels franchise, of how the National League dropped four teams after the 1899 season.

The seeds for the reduction in 1899 were sown in the Brotherhood war of 1890. With the advent of the Players' League in that year, the fans found three major leagues on the field. The venerable National League and the eight-year-old American Association had been battling for years. But the competition with three leagues caused a massive reorganization in the early 1890s. The Players' League folded after one season and the magnates believed it expedient to merge the Association and National League into one "Big League." The new 1892 National League had twelve teams, with Boston, Philadelphia, Milwaukee, and Columbus of the American Association dropping off the baseball map.

The twelve-team arrangement had trouble from the start. Now eleven teams had a chance to be disappointed at not winning a pennant. Several franchises, including Louisville, were thinly capitalized and could not adequately compete for players. This led to several teams being chronic second-division dwellers, often out of the pennant race by the Fourth of July. Even the strong teams struggled. The expense of traveling to additional cities, fewer home games and a deepening national recession all cut into the teams' revenue.

By 1895 rumors appeared that teams were either folding or moving to lower leagues that year. The League meetings began to discuss reducing the number of franchises.

The embers of reduction glowed softly for several seasons and burst into flame at the close of the 1898 season. Reports began to circulate that Washington, Cleveland, Pittsburgh, New York, and Brooklyn had lost money for the year. The most desperate appeared to be New York, which had major problems drawing fans to the Polo Grounds. Some blamed the Spanish-American War for curtailing attendance as people gave little thought to entertainment while their thoughts were on that conflict.

The Sporting News had time to think about it, and in November 1898, one of the paper's correspondents spoke what many others believed: that the twelve-club league had outlived its usefulness and some adjustments were necessary. He suggested not reduction but expansion. He proposed two eight-team leagues, a return to the pre-1890 status quo.

There can be no doubt that the league was in trouble. Only Boston, Philadelphia, and Chicago consistently made money. Neither the New York nor Brooklyn franchise drew well in the nation's largest city and both were in danger of going under. Baltimore always fielded a competitive, contending team, but the fans did not show up at the ballpark in sufficient numbers to prevent financial losses. St. Louis was tied up in a court case that would cost

Chris Von der Ahe his franchise. Louisville and Washington were perennial losers on the field and at the box office.

On top of this, another phenomenon developed in the 1890s that gave rise to thoughts of reducing the number of teams in the League. It was the development of common ownership of several teams. This practice began in 1892, when A. G. Spalding, owner of a large block of the Chicago franchise, invested in the New York club. He did this more or less as the banker of last resort for the financially troubled Gotham franchise, but nevertheless, he ended up owning stock in both clubs. By 1898 seven of the twelve teams were involved in such arrangements to some degree. Arthur Soden of Boston, John Brush of Cincinnati, and F. A. Abell of Brooklyn had small holdings in the New York club. Abell, H. R. Von der Horst, Ned Hanlon, and Charles Ebbets jointly owned the Brooklyn and Baltimore franchises. The Robison family owned both Cleveland and St. Louis.

These arrangements led to some strange dealing. The Robisons transferred the best players of their two franchises to St. Louis, leaving the woeful Cleveland Spiders of 1899 to achieve the lowest winning percentage in major-league history. Brooklyn and Baltimore engineered the "trade" of nine players with Hughie Jennings, Willie Keeler, and Joe Kelley moving to Brooklyn in 1899 for a mess of pottage and bringing a pennant to the Flatbush faithful. During the 1899 pennant race, anti-syndicalist Arthur Soden got a return on his New York investment when pitcher Jouett Meekin came to Beantown free of charge.

In any event, the dual ownership of several teams by now had led to the idea of consolidating those teams and moving to an eight-team league. The general idea was to merge Baltimore into Brooklyn and Cleveland into St. Louis, and to buy out two teams from among the poor-performing Washington, New York, and Louisville. When the League meeting was held in December 1898, the reduction plan was discussed but so was the idea of two eight-team leagues. The magnates ended up adjourning with instructions for the League office to prepare an 1899 schedule for twelve teams.

As winter turned to spring in 1899 the owners left the twelve-team structure as it was. Not because they wanted to, but rather by the default of uncertainty. However, by July it was clear that something had to be done. By that time Cleveland was playing most of its home games on the road. In August the Louisville ballpark burned down. Makeshift bleachers were erected, but the club's inability to collect an insurance settlement in a timely fashion prevented construction of covered grandstands. With Louisville's summer heat the fans decided to remain home rather than sit in the sun to see a bad ballclub.

In September, *The Sporting News* commented that financial problems might lead to Louisville, Cleveland, Baltimore, and Washington dropping from the League. But Louisville signed ten players to contracts in early October 1899 and Ned Hanlon in Baltimore was having no part of any league reduction if his team was a target.

Finances for the clubs in 1899 had improved over 1898, but still only pennant-winning Brooklyn, Boston, Chicago, Philadelphia and St. Louis were more than marginally profitable. Something would have to be done to return the owners to steady profits.

Three clubs—Louisville, Pittsburgh, and Washington—were for sale. The syndicate clubs of Baltimore-Brooklyn and Cleveland-St. Louis were searching for ways to make both clubs pay.

Publicly, NL President Nick Young was optimistic that the twelve-team league would continue. His basic argument was that the National Agreement that emerged after the Brotherhood war had two years to run. But it was this looming deadline that encouraged the weaker clubs to seek new owners. They believed, probably rightly, that once the National Agreement expired, their franchises would have little value.

Here was the crux of the problem. The powerful clubs of Boston, Chicago, and Philadelphia wanted to reduce the league to eight teams. But they hoped the four clubs, whoever they might be, would be willing to leave quietly. The targeted clubs had no intention of going gently into the night without substantial compensation. All sorts of posturing began. Soden of Boston was adamant that he would not contribute to a *buyout*. Frank De Haas Robison of Cleveland announced that he was ready to field a team for 1900. Louisville was staying but planned to run on the cheap. The owners announced that they were looking for ballplayers who would play for $100 per month or less.

The stage was set for the struggle to reduce the League to eight clubs. The four targets were identified (Louisville, Baltimore, Cleveland, and Washington). These clubs were willing to discuss dropping from the league but wanted to be bought out. The powers of the league were split on the issue of payment. Soden proposed arranging a schedule for the four that would ensure financial disaster. President Young continued to make silly statements that no reduction was contemplated.

The president of the Louisville club at this time was Barney Dreyfuss, a local businessman. The club was in debt to several of the club directors, including Dreyfuss, and had no real prospects of improvement on the field or on the financial ledgers. The club had several solid players—Honus Wagner, Fred Clarke, Rube Waddell among them—but was given to poor starts and strong finishes. Unfortunately the strong finishes never got Louisville out of the second division. Dreyfuss wanted to stay in baseball but saw no future in Louisville. He wanted to sell. But there were no buyers. So Barney looked for greener pastures. He cast his eye about four hundred miles up the Ohio River to Pittsburgh. W. W. Kerr of the Smoky City club wanted to sell. Dreyfuss began negotiations with Kerr. The negotiations were difficult.

Arthur Soden of Boston saw this as a great opportunity to bring about the league reduction. He foresaw Louisville combining with Pittsburgh, Cleveland with St. Louis, and Baltimore with Brooklyn. That would leave just Washington to deal with. But things are never that easy.

Louisville baseball circles were in an uproar. The city still held an NL franchise and intended to play in 1900. Essentially the same line was taken in Baltimore by Ned Hanlon, who was pushing the idea of two eight-club leagues.

To complicate things further, two new figures entered the drama. One was Ban Johnson and his Western League, recently renamed the American League. Johnson was beginning his campaign to create another major league and the NL owners did not wish to cede any territory to him. The other was a group including Francis Richter, the Spink family of St. Louis, and other investors who began to organize a new American Association. So the National League faced another baseball war on one front while trying to trim teams from its loop on another.

On December 6, 1899, directors of the Louisville club confirmed that Dreyfuss had purchased Pittsburgh and had immediately effected a trade between the two clubs. Dreyfuss sent $25,000 and pitcher Jack Chesbro, catcher Paddy Fox, and infielders John O'Brien and Art Madison to Louisville. In return Pittsburgh received Rube Waddell, Deacon Phillippe, Tommy Leach, Honus Wagner, Fred Clarke, Claude Ritchey, Mike Kelly, Tacks Latimer, Chief Zimmer, Walt Woods, Conny Doyle, and Patsy Flaherty. In addition

Dreyfuss announced Clarke as the new Pittsburgh manager and said he was leaving Louisville to establish a permanent residence in Pittsburgh.

The local reaction in Kentucky was strange. Within a few days of the big deal, local papers reported that the "general impression is that Louisville got much the best of the deal."[1] Apparently the Louisville franchise owners did not agree, for the following day they embarked for the league meeting in New York intent on selling the team.

The local press became manic-depressive, assuring people that Louisville would have a big-league team in 1900 in one paragraph and bewailing the loss of the team a few columns later. The *Courier-Journal* on December 12, 1899, displayed these swings by reporting, "Louisville is not going to be wiped off the baseball map." Rather, it went on, the club would either be sold to the NL or join the American League. "At the present time," it reported, "the indications are that the circuit will not be reduced."[2] So, either the team was to be sold to the National League, which was not in the market to add squads, or it was about to join a league which would compete with the baseball establishment.

The truth of the situation was that the NL was going to reduce but had two situations to confront: to keep the buyout price for the targeted four down; and to position itself in such a way as to not harm itself in comparison to the American League or the new American Association.

On the first front, problems for the National League arose immediately. The December league meeting had set up a Circuit Reduction Committee to negotiate the terms of a buyout of Louisville, Washington, Cleveland, and Baltimore. It was rumored that Louisville was looking for $20,000, Baltimore $60,000, Washington $55,000, and Cleveland wanted whatever Louisville got. Nobody expected the league to pony up over $150,000 to become an eight-team circuit.

As the new century opened, the NL was faced with the problems of inflated expectations of the four designated departees and the maneuverings of Ban Johnson and the new American Association. The general strategy of the National League was to lengthen the process so that when the four teams were bought out, the other leagues would have insufficient time to reorganize to occupy those cities. John McGraw, years later in his autobiography, *My Thirty Years In Baseball*, confirmed part of the strategy, writing, "The league heads hesitated to act openly (on circuit reduction) for fear that the new American League, then expanding, would grab the territory."[3] True enough as far as it went. From press reports of the day it appears the established league was even more concerned about the newly proposed American Association. This latter group had promoted Cap Anson as its president and had interested McGraw enough to consider jumping. From the AA's plans to go head-to-head with the NL in most major cities, the League had more to fear from them than from the AL, which still inhabited cities like Minneapolis and Milwaukee and had no real Eastern base.

A group of Louisville businessmen then entered the picture to save major-league baseball for Louisville. They organized quickly and raised about thirty percent of their goal of $20,000 in capital. Their intent was to find a league— any league—that would have Louisville as a member. They negotiated with the NL, which offered to make Louisville a charter member of their own rein-carnation of the American Association. The NL version of the AA was to be a sort of junior varsity to the big clubs. It was really a brilliant tactical move.

While it is doubtful that the NL had any real intention of following through with this venture into a new AA, it gave potential rival financial backers pause to consider that they might be starting a venture that would be in local com-petition with a team backed by the powerful National League. This effectively froze the Louisville contingent, which continued to flirt with the American League and American Association but wanted no part of any baseball war. By mid-February the AA bubble had burst because of a lack of funds and the inability to secure substantial owners in several cities. That left just the American League to deal with.

The game for the NL owners was still the same: reduce the League at the lowest cost without giving any rival league an opening. As one owner put it, "It is not so much a question of buying out Washington and Baltimore as it is of keeping a tight grip on territory slated for abandonment that is keeping the leaders guessing. . . . The League, therefore, is practically forced to decide between two alternatives—either continue the present twelve-club league or pacify the 'little four' by reasonable cash appropriations and then place them in another eight-club league which would work in harmony with the National."[4] This last notion of "harmony" was uppermost in the NL owners' minds. With the purpose of circuit reduction being to return the NL to pros-perity, the shadow of another war cast a pall over their plans.

But now time began to run against the older league. It was March and the teams were making plans for spring training. Negotiations continued with the "little four." Earl Wagner at Washington said his franchise was not for sale. Ned Hanlon of Baltimore was starting to push for a ten-team circuit. Louisville and Cleveland were just looking for as much cash as they could get to cover their debts. Meanwhile, Ban Johnson was preparing another thrust into NL territory. He announced plans to move the St. Paul franchise, held by ex-St. Louis manager Charles Comiskey, to Chicago. The National League owners were aghast and Jim Hart of the Chicago (NL) club announced that a baseball war would erupt if Johnson came into Hart's territory.

As the battle heated up the Circuit Reduction Committee finally had to make its move.

On March 9, 1900, the report of the National League Circuit Reduction Committee was released. The National League would be reduced to eight teams. Washington received $39,000 for its franchise but retained its player contracts. Cleveland received $25,000, $10,000 for the franchise and $15,000 for its stadium, grounds and equipment. Louisville got $10,000 for its franchise. The NL had achieved one of its goals. It had shed four clubs and saved about $50,000 from the original asking price. But the specter of the American League remained.

Ban Johnson immediately began plans to put franchises in Washington, Baltimore and Cleveland. The NL countered with renewed reports of starting an American Association of its own. Johnson correctly divined that "it is a bluff to scare us out."[5]

As far as Louisville was concerned, the bluff worked. A chronically weak franchise with little extra capital to risk had no business in the new league. Although the Louisville committee and Ban Johnson exchanged several sets of telegrams and the local papers reported the securing of an AL franchise as a done deal, the dispute over the Chicago territory scared off the Bluegrass delegation. In all probability, even if they had thrown in with Johnson, they would not have received a franchise. Louisville was well down the AL's list of potential cities and was used by Johnson to keep the NL off balance.

On March 21, 1900, it was announced that there would be no war between the American and National Leagues, with the AL consigned to Chicago's South Side as the terms for entry into that city. But it was too late for Louisville. Insufficient capital, population and support left Louisville on the outside of the major-league candy store looking in. The Kentucky city moved to the minor leagues, where its baseball history continues today.

NOTES

The author has recently published another article on the subject with some newly found material showing Dreyfuss's machinations in purchasing his original block of Pittsburgh stock. (See "Barney Dreyfuss Buys Pittsburgh," *Baseball Research Journal* 48, no. 1 [Spring 2019]: 86–91.)

1. "The New Colonels," *Louisville Courier-Journal*, December 9, 1899, 6.
2. "Their Price is $20,000," *Louisville Courier-Journal*, December 12, 1899, 6.
3. John J. McGraw, *My Thirty Years in Baseball* (New York: Boni & Liveright, 1923), 122–23.
4. "May Injure This City," *Louisville Courier-Journal*, February 26, 1900, 6.
5. "Threat of James Hart," *Louisville Courier-Journal*, March 13, 1900, 8.

16

Jackie Robinson's Signing

The Real Story

JULES TYGIEL AND JOHN THORN

The story of Branch Rickey signing Jackie Robinson has been told in countless books and films over the years, but the details were not firmly and properly detailed until this article by Jules Tygiel and John Thorn first appeared in *Sport* magazine in 1988 and then was revised and republished by SABR in the 1990s. Thorn later wrote, "Jules and I believed that the real story was not only more interesting than the schoolboy version but also made Jackie's pioneering mission even more heroic." Tygiel was a brilliant writer and researcher whose book *Baseball's Great Experiment: Jackie Robinson and His Legacy* is one of the essential classics of baseball literature. Thorn, whose work appears elsewhere in this collection, has contributed as much to baseball scholarship as anyone ever has, and he is Major League Baseball's official historian. Both writers have received SABR's Henry Chadwick Award.

OCTOBER 1945. As the Detroit Tigers and Chicago Cubs faced off in the World Series, photographer Maurice Terrell arrived at an almost deserted minor-league park in San Diego, California, to carry out a top-secret assignment: to surreptitiously photograph three black baseball players.

Terrell shot hundreds of motion-picture frames of Jackie Robinson and the two other players. A few photos appeared in print but the existence of the additional images remained unknown for four decades. In April 1987, as major league baseball prepared a lavish commemoration of the 40th anniversary of Robinson's debut, I unearthed a body of contact sheets and unprocessed film from a previously unopened carton donated in 1954 by *Look* magazine to the National Baseball Hall of Fame in Cooperstown, New York. This discovery triggered an investigation which led to startling revelations regarding Branch Rickey, the president of the Brooklyn Dodgers, and his signing of Jackie Robinson to shatter baseball's longstanding color line; the relationship between these two historic figures; and the stubbornly controversial issue of black managers in baseball.

The popular "frontier" image of Jackie Robinson as a lone gunman facing down a hostile mob has always dominated the story of the integration of baseball. But new information related to the Terrell photos reveals that while Robinson was the linchpin in Branch Rickey's strategy, in October 1945 Rickey intended to announce the signing of not just Jackie Robinson, but of several other Negro League stars. Political pressure, however, forced Rickey's hand, thrusting Robinson alone into the spotlight. And in 1950, after only three years in the major leagues, Robinson pressed Rickey to consider him for a position as field manager or front-office executive, raising an issue with which the baseball establishment grappled long after.

The story of these revelations began with the discovery of the Terrell photographs. The photos show a youthful, muscular Robinson in a battered cap and baggy uniform fielding from his position at shortstop, batting with a black catcher crouched behind him, trapping a third black player in a rundown between third and home, and sprinting along the basepaths more like a former track star than a baseball player. All three players wore uniforms emblazoned with the name "Royals." A woman with her back to the action is the only figure visible amid the vacant stands. The contact sheets are dated October 7, 1945.

The photos were perplexing. The momentous announcement of Jackie Robinson's signing with the Montreal Royals took place on October 23, 1945. Before that date his recruitment had been a tightly guarded secret. Why, then, had a *Look* photographer taken such an interest in Robinson two weeks earlier? Where had the pictures been taken? And why was Robinson already wearing a Royals uniform?

I called Jules Tygiel, the author of *Baseball's Great Experiment: Jackie Robinson and His Legacy*, to see if he could shed some light on the photos. Tygiel knew nothing about them, but he did have in his files a 1945 manuscript by newsman Arthur Mann, who frequently wrote for *Look*. The article, drafted with Rickey's cooperation, had been intended to announce the Robinson signing but had never been published. The pictures, Jules and I concluded, were to have accompanied Mann's article; we decided to find out the story behind the photo session.

The clandestine nature of the photo session did not surprise us. From the moment he had arrived in Brooklyn in 1942, determined to end baseball's

Jim Crow traditions, Rickey had feared that premature disclosure of his intentions might doom his bold design. No blacks had appeared in the major leagues since 1884 when two brothers, Welday and Moses Fleetwood Walker, had played for Toledo in the American Association. [In recent years an earlier African American major leaguer has been identified: William Edward White, a one-game first baseman for Providence of the National League in 1879.] Not since the 1890s had black players appeared on a minor-league team. During the ensuing half-century all-black teams and leagues featuring legendary figures like pitcher Satchel Paige and catcher Josh Gibson had performed on the periphery of Organized Baseball.

Baseball executives, led by Commissioner Kenesaw Mountain Landis, had strictly policed the color line, barring blacks from both major and minor leagues. Rickey therefore moved slowly and secretly to explore the issue and cover up his attempts to scout black players during his first three years in Brooklyn. He informed the Dodger owners of his plans but took few others into his confidence.

In the spring of 1945, as Rickey prepared to accelerate his scouting efforts, advocates of integration, emboldened by the impending end of World War II and the recent death of Commissioner Landis, escalated their campaign to desegregate baseball. On April 6, 1945, black sportswriter Joe Bostic appeared at the Dodgers' Bear Mountain training camp with Negro League stars Terris McDuffie and Dave "Showboat" Thomas and forced Rickey to hold tryouts for the two players. Ten days later black journalist Wendell Smith, white sportswriter Dave Egan, and Boston city councilman Isidore Muchnick engineered an unsuccessful 90-minute audition with the Red Sox for Robinson, then a shortstop with the Kansas City Monarchs; second baseman Marvin Williams of the Philadelphia Stars; and outfielder Sam Jethroe of the Cleveland Buckeyes. In response to these events the major leagues announced the formation of a Committee on Baseball Integration. (Reflecting Organized Baseball's true intentions on the matter, the group never met.)

In the face of this heightened activity, Rickey created an elaborate smokescreen to obscure his scouting of black players. In May 1945 he announced the formation of a new franchise, the Brooklyn Brown Dodgers, and a new Negro League, the United States League. Rickey then dispatched his best talent hunters to observe black ballplayers, ostensibly for the Brown Dodgers, but in reality for the Brooklyn National League club.

A handwritten memorandum in the Rickey Papers at the Library of Congress offers a rare glimpse of Rickey's emphasis on secrecy in his instructions to Dodger scouts. The document, signed "Chas. D. Clark" and accompanied by a Negro National League schedule for April-May 1945, is headlined "Job Analysis," and defines the following "Duties: under supervision of management of club":

1. To establish contact (silent) with all clubs (local or general).
2. To gain knowledge and [*sic*] abilities of all players.
3. To report all possible material (players).
4. Prepare weekly reports of activities.
5. Keep composite report of outstanding players . . . To travel and cover player whenever management so desire.

Clark's "Approch" [*sic*] was to "Visit game and loose [*sic*] self in stands; Keep statistical report (speed, power, agility, ability, fielding, batting, etc.) by score card"; and "Leave immediately after game."

Clark's directions, however, contain one major breach in Rickey's elaborate security precautions. According to his later accounts, Rickey had told most Dodger scouts that they were evaluating talent for a new "Brown Dodger" franchise. But Clark's first "Objective" was "To Cover Negro teams for possible major league talent." Had Rickey confided in Clark, a figure so obscure as to escape prior mention in the voluminous Robinson literature? Dodger superscout and Rickey confidante Clyde Sukeforth had no recollection of Clark when Jules spoke with him, raising the possibility that Clark was not part of the Dodger family, but perhaps someone connected with black baseball. Had Clark himself interpreted his instructions in this manner?

Whatever the answer, Rickey successfully diverted attention from his true motives. Nonetheless, mounting interest in the integration issue threatened Rickey's careful planning. In the summer of 1945 Rickey constructed yet another facade. The Dodger president took into his confidence Dan Dodson, a New York University sociologist who chaired Mayor Fiorello LaGuardia's Committee on Unity, and requested that Dodson form a Committee on Baseball ostensibly to study the possibility of integration. In reality, the committee would provide the illusion of action while Rickey quietly completed his own preparations. "This was one of the toughest decisions I ever had to make while in office," Dodson later confessed. "The major purpose I could see for the committee was that it was a stall for time. . . . Yet had Mr. Rickey not delivered . . . I would have been totally discredited."

Thus by late August, even as Rickey's extensive scouting reports had led him to focus on Jackie Robinson as his standard bearer, few people in or out of the Dodger organization suspected that a breakthrough was imminent. On August 28 Rickey and Robinson held their historic meeting at the Dodgers' Montague Street offices in downtown Brooklyn. Robinson signed an agreement to accept a contract with the Montreal Royals, the top Dodger affiliate, by November 1.

Rickey, still concerned with secrecy, impressed upon Robinson the need to maintain silence. Robinson could tell the momentous news to his family and fiancée, but no one else. For the conspiratorial Rickey, keeping the news sheltered while continuing arrangements required further subterfuge. Rumors about Robinson's visit had already spread through the world of black baseball. To stifle speculation Rickey "leaked" an adulterated version of the incident to black sportswriter Wendell Smith. Smith, who had recommended Robinson to Rickey and advised Rickey on the integration project, doubtless knew the true story behind the meeting. On September 8, however, he reported in the *Pittsburgh Courier* that the "sensational shortstop" and "colorful major-league dynamo" had met behind "closed doors. . . . The nature of the conference has not been revealed," Smith continued. Rickey claimed that he and Robinson had assessed "the organization of Negro baseball," but Smith noted that "it does not seem logical [Rickey] should call in a rookie player to discuss the future organization of Negro baseball." He closed with the tantalizing thought that "it appears that the Brooklyn boss has a plan on his mind that extends further than just the future of Negro baseball as an organization." The subterfuge succeeded. Neither black nor white reporters pursued the issue.

Rickey, always sensitive to criticism by New York sports reporters and understanding the historic significance of his actions, also wanted to be sure that his version of the integration breakthrough and his role in it be accurately portrayed. To guarantee this he persuaded Arthur Mann, his close friend and later a Dodger employee, to write a 3,000-word manuscript to be published simultaneously with the announcement of the signing.

Although it was impossible to confirm in 1987, when I found Maurice Terrell's photos, it seemed to Jules and I highly likely that, inasmuch as they had been commissioned by *Look*, they were destined to accompany Mann's article. (Once we located Terrell himself, he confirmed the linkage.) Clearer prints of the negatives revealed that Terrell had taken the pictures in San Diego's Lane Stadium. This fit in with Robinson's autumn itinerary. After his August meeting with Rickey, Robinson had returned briefly to the Kansas City Monarchs. With the Dodger offer securing his future and the relentless bus trips of the Negro League schedule wearing him down, he left the Monarchs before season's end and returned home to Pasadena, California. In late September he hooked up with Chet Brewer's Kansas City Royals, a postseason barnstorming team which toured the Pacific Coast, competing against other Negro League teams and major- and minor-league all-star squads. Thus the word "Royals" on Robinson's uniform, which had so piqued our interest as a seeming anomaly, ironically turned out to relate not to Robinson's future team in Montreal, but rather to his interim employment in California.

For further information Jules contacted Chet Brewer, who at age 80 still lived in Los Angeles. Brewer, one of the great pitchers of the Jim Crow era, had known Robinson well. He had followed Robinson's spectacular athletic career at UCLA and in 1945 they became teammates on the Monarchs. "Jackie was major-league all the way," recalled Brewer. "He had the fastest reflexes I ever saw in a player."

Robinson particularly relished facing major-league all-star squads. Against Bob Feller, Robinson once slashed two doubles. "Jack was running crazy on the bases," a Royals teammate remembered. In one game he upended Gerry Priddy, Washington Senators infielder. Priddy angrily complained about the hard slide in an exhibition game. "Any time I put on a uniform," retorted Robinson, "I play to win."

Brewer recalled that Robinson and two other Royals journeyed from Los Angeles to San Diego on a day when the team was not scheduled to play. He identified the catcher in the photos as Buster Haywood and the other player as Royals third baseman Herb Souell. Souell was no longer living, but Haywood, who, like Brewer lived in Los Angeles, vaguely recalled the event, which he incorrectly remembered as occurring in Pasadena. Robinson recruited the catcher and Souell, his former Monarch teammate, to "work out" with him. All three wore their Kansas City Royals uniforms. Haywood found neither Robinson's request nor the circumstances unusual. Although he was unaware that they were being photographed, Haywood described the session accurately. "We didn't know what was going on," he stated. "We'd hit and throw and run from third base to home plate."

The San Diego pictures provide a rare glimpse of the pre-Montreal Rob-

Fig. 16.1. One of Maurice Terrell's original photographs from the secret *Look* magazine photoshoot. National Baseball Hall of Fame Library, Cooperstown NY.

inson. The article which they were to accompany and related correspondence in the Library of Congress offer even more rare insights into Rickey's thinking. The unpublished Mann manuscript was entitled "The Negro and Baseball: The National Game Faces a Racial Challenge Long Ignored." As Mann doubtless based his account on conversations with Rickey and since Rickey's handwritten comments appear in the margin, it stands as the earliest "official" account of the Rickey-Robinson story and reveals many of the concerns confronting Rickey in September 1945.

One of the most striking features of the article is the language used to refer to Robinson. Mann, reflecting the racism typical of postwar America, portrays Robinson as the "first Negro chattel in the so-called National pastime." At another point he writes, "Rickey felt the boy's sincerity," appropriate language perhaps for an 18-year-old prospect, but not for a 26-year-old former Army officer.

"The Negro and Baseball" consists largely of the now familiar Rickey-Robinson story. Mann recreated Rickey's haunting 1904 experience as collegiate coach when one of his black baseball players, Charlie Thomas, was denied access to a hotel. Thomas cried and rubbed his hands, chanting, "Black skin! Black skin! If I could only make 'em white." Mann described Rickey's search for the "right" man, the formation of the United States League as a cover for scouting operations, the reasons for selecting Robinson, and the fateful Rickey-Robinson confrontation. Other sections, however, graphically illustrate additional issues Rickey deemed significant. Mann repeatedly cites the costs the Dodgers incurred: $5,000 to scout Cuba, $6,000 to scout Mexico, $5,000 to establish the "Brooklyn Brown Dodgers." The final total reaches $25,000, a modest sum considering the ultimate returns, but one sufficiently large that Rickey must have felt it would counter his skinflint image.

Rickey's desire to show that he was not motivated by political pressures also emerges clearly. Mann had suggested that upon arriving in Brooklyn in 1942, Rickey "was besieged by telephone calls, telegrams and letters of petition in behalf of black ball players," and that this "staggering pile of missives so inspired to convince him that he and the Dodgers had been selected as a kind of guinea pig." In his marginal comments, Rickey vehemently wrote "No!" in a strong dark script. "I began all this as soon as I went to Brooklyn." Explaining why he had never attacked the subject during his two decades as general manager of the St. Louis Cardinals, Rickey referred to the segregation in that city. "St. Louis never permitted Negro patrons in the grandstand," he wrote, describing a policy he apparently had felt powerless to change.

Mann also devoted two of his 12 pages to a spirited attack on the Negro Leagues, repeating Rickey's charges that "they are the poorest excuse for the word league" and documented the prevalence of barnstorming, the uneven scheduling, absence of contracts, and dominance of booking agents. Mann revealingly traces Rickey's distaste for the Negro Leagues to the "outrageous" guarantees demanded by New York booking agent William Leuschner to place black teams in Ebbets Field while the Dodgers were on the road.

Rickey's misplaced obsession with the internal disorganization of the Negro Leagues had substantial factual basis. But Rickey had an ulterior motive. In his September 8 article, Wendell Smith addressed the issue of "player tampering," asking, "Would [Rickey] not first approach the owners of these Negro teams who have these stars under contract?" Rickey, argued Smith in what might have been an unsuccessful preemptive strike, "is obligated to do so and his record as a businessman indicated that he would." As Smith may have known, Rickey maintained that Negro League players did not sign valid contracts and so became free agents at the end of each season. Thus the Mahatma had no intention of compensating Negro League teams for the players he signed. His repeated attacks on black baseball, including those in the Mann article, served to justify this questionable position.

The one respect in which "The Negro and Baseball" departs radically from the common picture of the Robinson legend is in its report of Robinson as one of a group of blacks about to be signed by the Dodgers. Mann's manuscript and subsequent correspondence from Rickey reveal that Rickey did not intend for Robinson to withstand the pressures alone. "Determined not to be charged with merely nibbling at the problem," wrote Mann, "Rickey went all out and brought in two more Negro players," and "consigned them, with Robinson, to the Dodgers' top farm club, the Montreal Royals." Mann named pitcher Don Newcombe and, surprisingly, outfielder Sam Jethroe as Robinson's future teammates. Whether the recruitment of additional blacks had always been Rickey's intention or whether he had reached his decision after meeting with Robinson in August is unclear. But by late September, when he provided information to Mann for his article, Rickey had clearly decided to bring in other Negro League stars.

During the first weekend in October, Dodger coach Chuck Dressen fielded a major-league all-star team in a series of exhibition games against Negro League standouts at Ebbets Field. Rickey took the opportunity to interview at least three black pitching prospects—Newcombe, Roy Partlow, and John Wright. The following week he met with catcher Roy Campanella. Campanella and Newcombe, at least, believed they had been approached to play for the "Brown Dodgers."

At the same time, Rickey decided to postpone publication of Mann's manuscript. In a remarkable letter sent from the World Series in Chicago on October 7, Rickey informed Mann:

> We just can't go now with the article. The thing isn't dead,—not at all. It is more alive than ever and that is the reason we can't go with any publicity at this time. There is more involved in the situation than I had contemplated. Other players are in it and it may be that I can't clear these players until after the December meetings, possibly not until after the first of the year. You must simply sit in the boat. . . .
>
> There is a November 1 deadline on Robinson,—you know that. I am undertaking to extend that date until January 1st so as to give me time

to sign plenty of players and make one break on the complete story. Also, quite obviously it might not be good to sign Robinson with other and possibly better players unsigned.

The revelations and tone of this letter surprised Robinson's widow, Rachel, 40 years after the event. Rickey "was such a deliberate man," she recalled in our conversation, "and this letter is so urgent. He must have been very nervous as he neared his goal. Maybe he was nervous that the owners would turn him down and having five people at the door instead of just one would have been more powerful."

Events in the weeks after October 7 justified Rickey's nervousness and forced him to deviate from the course stated in the Mann letter. Candidates in New York City's upcoming November elections, most notably black Communist City Councilman Ben Davis, made baseball integration a major issue in the campaign. Mayor LaGuardia's Democratic party also sought to exploit the issue. The Committee on Baseball had prepared a report outlining a modest, long-range strategy for bringing blacks into the game and describing the New York teams, because of the favorable political and racial climate in the city, as in a "choice position to undertake this pattern of integration." LaGuardia wanted Rickey's permission to make a pre-election announcement that, as a result of the committee's work, "baseball would shortly begin signing Negro players."

Rickey, a committee member, had long since subverted the panel to his own purposes. By mid-October, however, the committee had become "an election football." Again unwilling to risk the appearance of succumbing to political pressure and thereby surrendering what he viewed as his rightful role in history, Rickey asked LaGuardia to delay his comments. Rickey hurriedly contacted Robinson, who had joined a barnstorming team in New York en route to play winter ball in Venezuela, and dispatched him instead to Montreal. On October 23, 1945, with Rickey's carefully laid plans scuttled, the Montreal Royals announced the signing of Robinson, and Robinson alone.

Mann's article never appeared. *Look*, having lost its exclusive, published two strips of the Terrell pictures in its November 27, 1945, issue accompanying a brief summary of the Robinson story, which was by then old news. The unprocessed film and contact sheets were loaded into a box and nine years later shipped to the National Baseball Hall of Fame, where they remained, along with a picture of Jethroe, unpacked until April 1987.

Newcombe, Campanella, Wright, and Partlow all joined the Dodger organization in the spring of 1946. Jethroe became a victim of the "deliberate speed" of baseball integration. Rickey did not interview Jethroe in 1945. Since few teams followed the Dodger lead, the fleet, powerful outfielder remained in the Negro Leagues until 1948, when Rickey finally bought his contract from the Cleveland Buckeyes for $5,000. Jethroe had two spectacular seasons at Montreal before Rickey, fearing a "surfeit of colored boys on the Brooklyn club," profitably sold him to the Boston Braves for $100,000. Jethroe won the Rookie of the Year Award in 1950, but his delayed entry into Organized Baseball foreshortened what should have been a stellar career. Until I informed him of how he had been part of Rickey's 1945 plan, Jethroe had been unaware of how close he had come to joining Robinson, Newcombe, and Campanella in the pantheon of integration pioneers.

For Robinson, who had always occupied center stage in Rickey's thinking, the early announcement intensified the pressures and enhanced the legend. The success or failure of integration rested disproportionately on his capable shoulders. He became the lightning rod for supporters and opponents alike, attracting the responsibility, the opprobrium and ultimately the acclaim for his historic achievement.

Beyond these revelations about the Robinson signing, the Library of Congress documents add surprisingly little to the familiar story of the integration of baseball. The Rickey Papers copiously detail his post-Dodger career as general manager of the Pittsburgh Pirates, but are strangely silent about the criticial period of 1944 to 1948. Records for these years probably remained with the Dodger organization, which in 1988 claimed to have no knowledge of their whereabouts. National League Office documents for these years have remained closed to the public.

In light of the controversy engendered by former Dodger General Manager Al Campanis's remarks about blacks in management, however, one exchange between Rickey and Robinson becomes particularly relevant. In 1950, after his fourth season with the Dodgers, Robinson appears to have written Rickey about the possibility of employment in baseball when his playing days ended. Robinson's original letter cannot be found in either the Rickey papers or the Robinson family archives. However, Rickey's reply, dated December 31, 1950, survives. Rickey, who had recently left the Dodgers after an unsuccessful struggle to wrest control of the team from Walter O'Malley, responded to Robinson's inquiry with a long and equivocal answer.

"It is not at all because of lack of appreciation that I have not acknowledged your good letter of some time ago," Rickey began. "Neither your writing, nor sending the letter, nor its contents gave me very much surprise." On the subject of managing, Rickey replied optimistically, "I hope that the day will soon come when it will be entirely possible, as it is entirely right, that you can be considered for administrative work in baseball, particularly in the direction of field management." Rickey claimed to have told several writers that "I do not know of any player in the game today who could, in my judgment, manage a major-league team better than yourself," but that the news media had inexplicably ignored these comments.

Yet Rickey tempered his encouragement with remarks that to a reader today seem gratuitous. "As I have often expressed to you," he wrote, "I think you carry a great responsibility for your people . . . and I cannot close this letter without admonishing you to prepare yourself to do a widely useful work, and, at the same time, dignified and effective in the field of public relations. A part of this preparation, and I know you are smiling, for you have already guessed my oft repeated suggestion—to finish your college course meritoriously and get your degree." This advice, according to Rachel Robinson, was a "matter of routine" between the two men ever since their first meeting. Nonetheless, to the 31-year-old Robinson, whose non-athletic academic career had been marked by indifferent success and whose endorsements and business acumen had already established the promise of a secure future, Rickey's response may have seemed to beg the question.

Rickey concluded with the promise, which seems to hinge on the completion of a college degree, that "It would be a great pleasure for me to be your agent in placing you in a big job after your playing days are finished. Believe me always." Shortly after writing this letter Rickey became the general manager of the Pittsburgh Pirates. Had Robinson ended his playing career before Rickey left the Pirates, perhaps the Mahatma would have made good on his pledge. But Rickey resigned from the Pirates at the end of the 1955 season, one year before Robinson's retirement, and never again had the power to hire a manager.

Robinson's 1950 letter to Rickey marked only the beginning of his quest to see a black manager in the major leagues. In 1952 he hoped to gain experience by managing in the Puerto Rican winter league, but, according to the *New York Post*, Commissioner Happy Chandler withheld his approval, forcing Robinson to cancel his plans. On November 30, 1952, the Dodgers star raised the prospect of a black manager in a televised interview on *Youth Wants to Know*, stating that both he and Campanella had been "approached" on the subject. In 1954, after the Dodgers had fired manager Chuck Dressen, speculation arose that either Robinson or Pee Wee Reese might be named to the post. But the team bypassed both men and selected veteran minor-league manager Walter Alston, who went on to hold the job for more than two decades.

Upon his retirement in 1956, Robinson, who had begun to manifest signs of the diabetes that would plague the rest of his life, had lost much of his enthusiasm for the prospect of managing, but nonetheless would probably have accepted another pioneering role. "He had wearied of the travel," Rachel Robinson stated, "and no longer wanted to manage. He just wanted to be asked as a recognition of his accomplishments, his abilities as a strategist, and to show that white men could be led by a black."

Ironically, in the early years of integration Organized Baseball had bypassed a large pool of qualified and experienced black managers: former Negro League players and managers like Chet Brewer, Ray Dandridge, and Quincy Trouppe. In the early 1950s Brewer and several other Negro League veterans managed all-black minor-league teams, but no interracial club at any level offered a managerial position to a black until 1961, when former Negro League and major-league infielder Gene Baker assumed the reins of a low-level Pittsburgh Pirate farm team, one of only three blacks to manage a major-league affiliate before 1975.

This lack of opportunity loomed as a major frustration for those who had broken the color line. "We bring dollars into club treasuries while we play," protested Larry Doby, the first black American Leaguer, in 1964, "but when we stop playing, our dollars stop. When I retired in '59 I wanted to stay in the game, to be a coach or in some other capacity, or to manage in the minors until I'd qualify for a big-league job. Baseball owners are missing the boat by not considering Negroes for such jobs." Monte Irvin, who had integrated the New York Giants in 1949 and clearly possessed managerial capabilities, concurred. "Among retired and active players [there] are Negroes with backgrounds suited to these jobs," wrote Irvin. "Owning a package liquor store, bowling alley or selling insurance is hardly the vocation for an athlete who has accumulated a lifetime knowledge of the game."

Had Robinson, Doby, Irvin, or another black been offered a managerial position in the 1950s or early 1960s, and particularly if the first black manager had experienced success, it is possible that this would have opened the doors for other black candidates. As with Robinson's ascension to the major leagues, this example might ultimately have made the hiring and firing of a black manager more or less routine. Robinson dismissed the notion that a black manager might experience extraordinary difficulties. "Many people believe that white athletes will not play for a Negro manager," he argued in 1964. "A professional athlete will play with or for anyone who helps him make more money. He will respect ability, first, last, and all the time. This is something that baseball's executives must learn—that any experienced player with leadership qualities can pilot a ballclub to victory, no matter what the color of his skin."

On the other hand, the persistent biases of major-league owners and their subsequent history of discriminatory hiring indicated that the solitary example of a Jackie Robinson regime would probably not have been enough to shake the complacency of the baseball establishment. Few baseball executives considered hiring blacks as managers even in the 1960s and 1970s. In 1960 Chicago White Sox owner Bill Veeck, who had hired Doby in 1947 and represented the most enlightened thinking in the game, raised the issue, but even Veeck defined special qualifications needed for a black to manage. "A man will have to have more stability to be a Negro coach or manager and be slower to anger than if he were white," stated Veeck. "The first major-league manager will have to be a fellow who has been playing extremely well for a dozen years or so, so that he becomes a byword for excellence." The following year Veeck sold the White Sox; other owners ignored the issue entirely.

Jackie Robinson himself never flagged in his determination to see a black manager. In 1972, at the World Series at Riverfront Stadium in Cincinnati, baseball commemorated the 25th anniversary of his major-league debut. A graying, almost blind, but still defiant Robinson told a nationwide television audience, "I'd like to live to see a black manager."

"I would have eagerly welcomed the challenge of a managerial job before I left the game," Robinson revealed in his 1972 autobiography, *I Never Had It Made*. "I know I could have been a good manager." But despite his obvious qualifications, no one offered him a job.

On Opening Day 1975, African American star player Frank Robinson took the reins of the Cleveland Indians. But Jackie had not lived to see that; he died nine days after his remarks at the 1972 World Series.

17

Locating Philadelphia's Historic Ballfields

JERROLD CASWAY

Jerrold Casway has written many articles on nineteenth-century baseball and was a featured keynote speaker at the Baseball Hall of Fame. He wrote a 2004 biography of Ed Delahanty (*In the Emerald Age of Baseball*) and wrote *The Culture and Ethnicity of Nineteenth-Century Baseball*, published in 2017. He also contributed several articles to SABR's 2013 book *Inventing Baseball: The 100 Greatest Games of the 19th Century*. In this 1993 article, he presents a detailed look at the many Philadelphia ballparks of the nineteenth century and their locations.

Accompanying an article on the growing popularity of post-Civil War baseball in the last issue of *The National Pastime* was an insert entitled "Where was the Jefferson Street Grounds?" Joel Spivak, who posed this question, asserted that the famous Jefferson Street ballpark of Philadelphia was located not at its actual site at 25th and Jefferson, but at 52nd Street. He credited this placement to transposed numbers. Compounding this conclusion was his claim that the great championship series between the Brooklyn Atlantics and the Philadelphia Athletics could not have been played in the confines of 15th and Columbia. In its stead, he again suggested the 52nd Street "Athletic Grounds." Regrettably, these well-intentioned statements misrepresent the 52nd Street ball grounds, and ignore the existence of two important historic baseball sites.

The Jefferson Street grounds existed in the neighborhood of 25th Street through two ballplaying eras—1864 to 1877 and 1883 to 1890. Another site, the famous Philadelphia Athletics ballpark at 15th and Columbia was prominent from 1865 to 1870. This is where, across from the still-extant Wagner Free Institute, the Athletics played their memorable games with their archrivals, the Atlantics of Brooklyn. As for the "Athletic Grounds" at 52nd and Jefferson, this site was nothing more than an all-purpose sports facility known as the Pennsylvania Railroad/YMCA Athletic Grounds, where amateur baseball and cricket matches were held in the 1890s.

The locations of these ballfields are attested to by daily newspaper accounts, advertisements, pictures, and contemporary local maps. From these sources the following history unfolds.

Philadelphia's major pre-Civil War baseball teams originally played at what might have been the country's first enclosed ball field in Camac's Woods at 12th and Montgomery. Both the Philadelphia Olympics and the Athletics competed on this location. In 1864, the Olympics left these grounds for a new and less congested site at 25th and Jefferson. This location was leased from the city, resodded, and enclosed in 1866 by the new tenants. Until 1871 these grounds were identified solely with the Olympic Club.

Meanwhile, the Philadelphia Athletics, too, had a need to relocate from the suffocating confines of Camac's Woods. In 1865, they moved west across Broad Street to 15th and Columbia Avenue. These grounds were resodded and rolled and enclosed with infield pavilions and a perimeter fence. The Athletics played at 15th and Columbia until 1871, when they were forced out by neighborhood developers. After their eviction, the Athletics took over the Olympics' site at 25th and Jefferson.

By the time the Athletics relocated to 25th Street, they had become the Quaker City's dominant ball club. They won much of their fame in the mid-1860s by playing, and often beating, the powerful New York baseball clubs. They conducted an especially bitter rivalry with the Brooklyn Atlantics, in so-called championship contests.

The Athletics played their end of this home-and-home series at 15th and Columbia. Accessible to a number of horse trolley routes, the 15th Street ball grounds drew large crowds for important games. The game of October 30, 1865, which the visiting Atlantics won 21–15, was attended by 12,000. A year later another Athletics and Atlantics game attracted a huge crowd. Estimated at about 30,000 fans, this multitude forced the postponement of the scheduled game after one inning when the playing field was overrun by spectators. Two weeks later the game was rescheduled. This time only four thousand people were admitted, at $1 a head. But over 12,000 people witnessed the Athletics' 31–12 victory from wagons, trolleys, roof tops, and unobstructed hills. Crowds like this disrupted life for the encroaching neighborhood. By the end of 1870, local property owners sold the ballfield out from under the Athletics baseball club.

With the creation of the new National Association of Professional Baseball Players in 1871, the Athletics moved to 25th and Jefferson and won the championship. The ballfield the Athletics took over was shadowed along the third-base/Master Street side by the old grassed embankment of the Spring Garden Reservoir. But the facility and its playing grounds were in need of great repair. Wasting little time, the Athletics tore down the old grandstands and the encircling fence. They resodded and leveled the playing surface, erected a 10-foot vertical slatted fence and constructed a pair of tiered infield pavilions that abutted near the original home plate at the 25th and Master intersection. Bleacher benches extended along the outfield lines.

The new Jefferson Street grounds had a capacity of 5,000. This figure frequently was doubled for major ball games, when fans lined the outfield fences and stood on boxes and unstable raised wooden planks. Those who could not gain admission purchased 25-cent roof-top seats or climbed a convenient overhanging tree. These trees were eventually taken down, but all calls for a center-field pavilion fell on deaf ears. The club owners were too uncertain about the site's future and their profit margins to start any renovations. Even the advent of the National League in 1876 could not save the old ball field.

The Athletics opened the new league's first season at 25th and Jefferson, but suffering finances led to their expulsion when they could not embark on their final road trip. The old Jefferson Street grounds were left without an affiliated professional team. The Athletics' 1877 nonleague schedule was the last season of games held on this site. At the end of that season it was obvious that more money could be made by turning the grounds over to residential developers.

It took the creation of the American Association, the new "beer ball league," in 1882 to revive the old Philadelphia Athletics and the Jefferson Street ballfield. Unfortunately, the original 25th Street site no longer existed and its remnant, a municipally-owned lot at 27th Street, was scheduled for a high school. As a result, the Athletics played their first Association season on a small renovated post-Civil War site, known as Oakdale Park at 12th and Huntingdon. These grounds, however, were too small to accommodate the city's only professional ball club. With a successful season behind them, the Athletics leased the still-vacant 27th and Jefferson Street location from the city.

On the northwest corner of 27th and Jefferson, the Athletics constructed the "handsomest ball ground in the country." The pitcher's mound of today's softball field approximates the April 1883 batter's box. This corner was backed up by a semi-circular two-tiered grandstand that later doubled as the main entrance. Painted white and adorned in "ornamented . . . fancy cornice work," the pavilion offered patrons armchair seating behind a wire-mesh screen. The structure was topped by 32 private season boxes, each holding five people, and a 22-person press box. A season ticket cost $15. The grandstands sat 2,200 people, but open benches along the outfield foul lines accommodated an additional 3,000 fans. After a successful 1883 championship season, the ballpark's capacity was increased to 15,000. Special features included a private external staircase for box ticket holders and a ladies' toilet room with a female attendant.

Attendance was supported by the Association's standard 25-cent admission fee and the ballfield's accessibility to public transportation. The grounds were five blocks from the 30th and Girard Pennsylvania Railroad Station and a few squares from the busy Ridge Avenue horse-trolley routes. Because of the state's "blue laws," Sunday games were played at the Gloucester Park grounds in New Jersey. A ferry from the South Street wharf took fans to this ball field.

The American Association Athletics played at 27th Street until the 1891 post-Players' League reorganization moved them to Forepaugh Park at Broad and Dauphin. This site belonged to their new owners, the Wagner brothers, who had become involved in baseball when they had invested in the defunct Philadelphia Players' League team. In 1892, the Wagners were forced to abandon the Athletics franchise, and were compensated with a team in Washington DC. This withdrawal left both 27th and Jefferson and Broad and Dauphin without professional occupants. Only the National League's Philadelphia Phillies, playing in a grand wooden stadium on the southwest corner of Broad and Lehigh, remained.

The departure of the Athletics and the demise of the Jefferson Street complex did not dampen the city's enthusiasm for baseball. Each summer, the Quaker City was preoccupied with amateur, semipro, and regional professional leagues. Playing grounds, however, were now located along the new periphery of the expanding city. Prominent among these sporting sites was a facility at 52nd and Jefferson.

Although baseball was not new to this neighborhood, it was not until the summer of 1896 that a sports park was constructed—the Pennsylvania Railroad and YMCA Athletic Grounds. Over 12,000 loads of soil were carted to this site. A large grandstand holding 5,000 spectators was erected, together with a quarter-mile clay and cinder bike track. Tennis, croquet, and cricket were among the other sports played at this facility. But these "Athletic Grounds" were never connected with any of the Philadelphia Athletic[s] baseball clubs. Even Connie Mack's 1901 revived American League Athletics had no association with 52nd Street. They played their first seven seasons on a converted industrial site at 29th and Columbia.

The ball grounds at 25th and Jefferson and 15th and Columbia are long gone, but they helped incubate the sport of baseball, and they deserve recognition as pioneering venues.

18

Smokey and the Bandit

The Greatest Pitching Duel in Blackball History

LARRY LESTER

For three decades, Larry Lester has done as much as anyone to promote the Negro Leagues and their players to a wide audience. Lester co-founded Kansas City's Negro Leagues Baseball Museum and served as Research Director and Treasurer from 1991 through 1995. As the long-time chairman of SABR's Negro Leagues Committee, Lester has organized the annual Jerry Malloy Conference. He has also written or co-written many of the seminal works about the Negro Leagues, including books about the East-West All-Star Game; Rube Foster; black baseball in Detroit, Kansas City, Chicago, and Pittsburgh; and black baseball's first World Series. This selection is Lester's brilliant 1994 look at a classic 1930 pitching duel between Smokey Joe Williams and Chet Brewer. Larry received the Henry Chadwick Award in 2016.

My most desired time-machine dream game happened on August 2, 1930. On a hot, humid summer night in Kansas City, Missouri, two men, one with smoke and the other with fire, engaged in a wild, free-swinging 12-inning contest that would result in a total of 46 strikeouts. Neither man blinked as they mowed down hitter after hitter in one of the first night games ever played in professional baseball. But who were these guys?

Joe Williams

On one mound was Joe Williams, a seasoned 44-year-old fireman with a blazing fastball and diamond savvy. Williams's Homestead Grays, a new entry into the Negro American League, included three future Hall of Famers in Oscar Charleston, Judy Johnson, and rookie Josh Gibson. Owned by Cumberland Posey, the Grays rode into town on a nine-game winning streak over the Kansas City Monarchs that had started back in Pittsburgh. Posey's posse was poised to establish a reputation in this part of the country, and began the three-game series with a victory the night before.

If someone combined a few drops of Roger Clemens's rocket fuel, a couple of ounces of Satchel Paige's control, a tiny pinch of Bob Feller's savvy, a dash of Nolan Ryan's tenacity and a little streak of meanness—they got Joe Williams. At times, Smokey Joe's ball sizzled through the air, and would explode into the catcher's leather mitt with a deep, resounding thump. It was the unmistakable sound of baseball smoke from one of the game's greatest power pitchers.

Everybody called him Smokey, for his fastball filled nostrils with the sizzling aroma of burnt horsehide. At 6-feet-5, the tall Texan was a towering inferno of a pitcher. "Joe didn't wind up. He pitched just like Don Larsen, right from the shoulder," claimed pitcher Sam Streeter. Having no windup to time his delivery, this flame-thrower was a jig-saw puzzle for any batter.

"Let me tell you about Smokey," said Hall of Fame writer and my mentor Sam Lacy in a 1999 interview. "Walter Johnson. He never threw a curve ball. I saw him in Griffith Stadium. He was in his prime then. He threw a sidearm and overhand to spots. But the ball came up there blazing, looking like an aspirin tablet. I thought Smokey was better than Johnson, Bob Lemon, or Mike Garcia."

Perhaps Williams' greatest satisfaction was compiling a career 19-7 record against white major-league teams. Even more remarkable is the fact that two of the losses came at age 45, with two other defeats by slim 1–0 margins. Overall, he shut out major-league clubs 10 times.

Chet Brewer

The other dude on the rubber was from Leavenworth, Kansas. At the age of 4, he lost three toes off his right foot when his home-made scooter ran under a streetcar. Chester Arthur Brewer claimed the injury had no effect on his baseball career. Often the staff workhorse, Chet Brewer had shared in a 1989 interview, "Sometimes, week after week, I would pitch Sunday, Wednesday and Sunday again. But I stayed in shape. The secret to my pitching success was keeping my legs in condition. People would say his arm gave out. No, it was his legs. You have to keep your legs strong and I just ran all the time. In the late innings, my legs were strong and I would still be pumping off that mound."

At just 23 years old, Brewer was pumping and growing into his own as a consummate professional. His Monarchs had pistol-whipped the Negro National League teams the previous season winning 62 out of 79 games.

Brewer had a sneaky change-up, an overhand drop, a lively fastball, an emery ball with an occasional spit ball. His spitter waterlogged batters, while his emery ball made them roller-coaster dizzy. Brewer had a PhD in doctoring the baseball. This medicine man had the gift of deception with an array of placebo pitches. Uncharacteristically, the devious right-hander was known to be notoriously tough on left-handed hitters. Brewer had velocity, command, and poise, making him one of baseball's most successful finesse pitchers.

One teammate thought Brewer's rep for throwing illegal pitches was unwarranted. "Chet wasn't a cheater, but he knew how to throw the spitter," said former Monarch catcher Sammy Haynes. "See, in the Negro Leagues, we would only play with a dozen balls for a whole ballgame—the fans would have to throw them back on the field after a foul ball. If Chet found that little scratch on the ball, he knew what to do with it."

Batter Up!

It was now high-noon drama for this Saturday nightcap, with smoke versus fire. For seven innings the Monarchs might just as well have remained on the bench sipping sarsaparilla. They couldn't buy a hit. In the eighth, however, Smokey Joe threw one down the middle of the plate and Newt Joseph got the Monarchs' first hit, a double. Joseph stole third, as Williams fanned T. J. Young. Seldom-used John Turner, Monarch first baseman, followed with a soft liner over the infield. It looked like a sure Texas League looper, but Grays shortstop Jake Stephens, who once wrote "I am the best short fielder that ever matriculated among the White Roses of York, Pennsylvania," went back and made a spectacular over the shoulder catch, robbing the Monarchs of a run and possible victory. Just like most pitchers trying to be hitters, Brewer ended the inning, going down on three swings.

The showdown continued in the seventh, eighth, and ninth innings along with the first batter in the tenth, as Brewer whiffed 10 straight Grays. Ten up, ten down, pick a tombstone. Overall, Brewer struck out 19 batters. The good doctor held matters even until the 12th frame when the Grays squeezed the trigger for a 1–0 win. Oscar Charleston walked, Judy Johnson popped out, and George Scales grounded out with Charleston moving to second. Next, center fielder Chaney White slapped a leather bullet off the third-base bag, bouncing it into foul territory, and out of the reach of the Monarchs' Newt Joseph. The great Oscar rode home on a cloud of dust.

Once the smoke cleared, Smokey Joe Williams emerged as baseball mythical top gun. At times hotter than a charcoal briquette and with more smoke than a chimney, he owned the inside of the plate and was victorious that day. Williams blazed to glory that night with 27 strikeouts in 12 innings, walking one man. Except for Joseph's double in the eighth, he had not allowed a ball hit out of the infield, as the Grays took their second victory of the series.

On that day, the future Hall of Famer, Smokey Joe was without peer! Oh, I wish I had scored this game. My scorecard would have been littered with K-fetti. Over the years, many scribes have wondered why the letter "K" stands for a strikeout. There are many theories, but no one really knows for sure. Secretly, great speed ballers like Clemens, Feller, Paige, Ryan, Steve Carlton, and Randy Johnson may have known the answer. That is, the letter "S" was already reserved for a man called "S-m-o-k-e-y."

It had to have been a great time to see two outstanding pitchers, one a veteran and the other a newcomer to star status, go head-to-head in the first year of night baseball? Were the night lights a factor in the high strikeout rate? Probably so, but let's not forget that Johnny Vander Meer, the only pitcher in major-league baseball history to throw back-to-back no-hitters— first against the Boston Bees, and, days later, against the Brooklyn Dodgers in the first night game played at Ebbets Field in 1938.

Oh my, what a night it had to be! Star light, star bright. I wish to see that game tonight. I wish I may, I wish I might. As we know, only the "Stars" come out at night.

The Box Score

DATE: AUGUST 2, 1930 / PLACE: MUEHLEBACH FIELD, KANSAS CITY MO / TIME: 8:15 P.M.

	Homestead					
	AB	R	H	PO	A	K
Jake Stephens, ss (a)	5	0	1	1	0	2
Vic Harris, lf	4	0	0	0	0	4
Oscar Charleston, 1b	3	1	0	5	0	1
Judy Johnson, 3b	5	0	0	0	1	3
George Scales, 2b	3	0	0	2	0	1

	AB	R	H	PO	A	K
Chaney White, cf	4	0	2	0	0	1
Bill (Happy) Evans, rf	4	0	1	0	0	3
Josh Gibson, c	3	0	0	27	0	2
Joe Williams, p	3	0	0	1	3	2
Totals	38	1	4	36	4	19

Kansas City

	AB	R	H	PO	A	K
Leroy Taylor, rf	5	0	0	1	0	5
Deke Mothell, 2b	5	0	0	4	1	3
Newt Allen, ss	5	0	0	1	1	4
Goo Goo Livingston, cf	4	0	0	0	0	2
Wilson Redus, lf	3	0	0	0	0	3
Newt Joseph, 3b	4	0	1	1	2	2
T. J. (Tom) Young, c	4	0	0	19	4	4
John Turner, 1b	4	0	0	9	0	1
Chet Brewer, p	4	0	0	0	4	3
Totals	38	0	1	35	12	27

Grays	000	000	000	001	-1	
Monarchs	000	000	000	000	-0	

Stephen bunted for third strike foul

Errors—Pittsburgh 1 (Gibson), Monarch 1 (Mothell)

Left on Base—Pittsburgh 6, Monarchs 3

Stolen Bases—Evans 2, Williams, Taylor, Joseph, Stevens

Two base hits—White, Joseph

Double Plays—Kansas City, Allen to Mothell to Turner

Base on Balls—off Williams 1 (Redus); off Brewer 4 (Harris, Charleston, Scales 2)

Passed Ball—Young

RBI—Chaney White

Time: 2:00

Umpires: Golson and Hawkins

Kansas City American, August 7, 1930

19

The Evolution of the Baseball Diamond

Perfection Came Slowly

TOM SHIEBER

Tom Shieber joined SABR in 1981 while still in high school, and his love of baseball photography, imagery, and film led to his founding of the Pictorial History Committee in 1994. He has also long been interested in the evolution of the playing rules and the ballfield itself, part of which he dissects in this article. In 1998 he moved to Cooperstown to join the staff of the National Baseball Hall of Fame and Museum, and he currently holds the role of senior curator. Here he presents the fascinating story of when and how each of the four bases came to be placed where they are. Shieber received the Henry Chadwick Award in 2018.

Red Smith once wrote: "Ninety feet between bases is the nearest to perfection that man has yet achieved."[1] Technically, this statement is incorrect: there has never been 90 feet between bases. In fact, in the nineteenth century, the distance between bases often varied from season to season as changes in the rules altered the placement of the bases on the infield diamond.[2] This "perfection" of the baseball diamond did not occur spontaneously, but evolved through more than 50 years of tinkering with the rules of baseball.

The modern baseball diamond is a square with sides 90 feet in length, and is used as an aid in the positioning of the bases and base lines. The term "diamond" was used early in the history of the game to differentiate the infield configuration of the "New York" game of baseball from that used in the "Massachusetts" game. In the New York game the batter, or striker, stood at the bottom corner of the infield, thus viewing a diamond-like positioning of the bases. However, the batter in the Massachusetts game would view the infield as a rectangle.

The positioning, orientation, size and make-up of the bases on the infield diamond were not always explicitly stated in the rules of the game. This lack of definition is not unusual, as much of the game itself was not detailed in the early rules. Rather than defining the game of baseball and how it was to be played, these early rules were used to differentiate the particular version of baseball being played from other similar baseball-like games of the era. Nevertheless, it is possible to trace the basic evolution of the baseball diamond.

The Amateur Era

The New York Knickerbocker Base Ball Club, formally organized in 1845, established the first written rules of baseball.[3] Of the original 20 rules, only 14 actually pertained to the game of baseball, and the remaining 6 concerned club matters. Of the 14 game rules, only the first related to the layout of the playing field: "1. The bases shall be from 'home' to second base, 42 paces; from first to third base, 42 paces, equidistant." Simple application of the Pythagorean theorem shows that a square whose diagonal is 42 paces has sides of slightly less than 30 paces. The Knickerbocker rules made no mention of the exact placement or size of the bases in the infield.

In 1856, an article in the December 13 issue of the *New York Clipper* listed the rules of baseball. These rules were essentially identical to the original Knickerbocker rules and were published along with a rudimentary diagram of the baseball infield. Unfortunately, the inaccuracies of the diagram render it useless in determining the exact orientation and positions of the bases of the era. In fact, the diagram shows the distance from home to second base to be noticeably longer than the distance from first to third base, though the rules clearly specify equal distances (see fig. 19.1).[4]

The first convention of baseball players was held in 1857, and a new set of rules, 35 in number, was adopted.[5] Sections 3 and 4 of these rules relate to the layout of the baseball diamond:

> 3. The bases must be four in number, placed at equal distances from each other, and securely fastened upon the four corners of a square, whose sides are respectively thirty yards. They must be so constructed as to be distinctly seen by the umpires and referee, and must cover a space equal to one square foot of surface; the first, second, and third bases shall be canvas bags, painted white, and filled with sand or saw-dust; the home base and pitcher's point to be each marked by a flat circular iron plate, painted or enameled white.

> 4. The base from which the ball is struck shall be designated the home base, and must be directly opposite to the second base; the first base

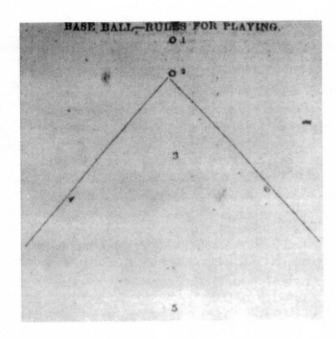

Fig. 19.1. Early baseball diamond diagram. *New York Clipper*, December 13, 1856.

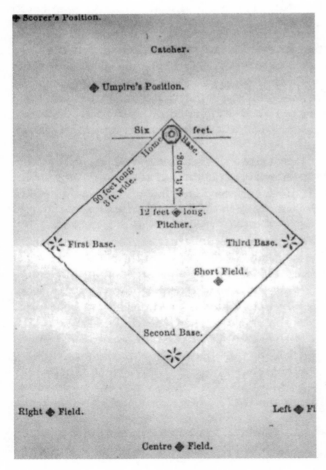

Fig. 19.2. "Diagram of a Base Ball Field." From Henry Chadwick, ed., *Beadle's Dime Base-Ball Player* (New York: Beadle & Co., 1862).

must always be that upon the right hand, and the third base that upon the left hand side of the striker, when occupying his position at the home base.[6]

Rule 3, defining the size of the infield square, was carefully constructed so as to avoid the use of the word "pace." According to Daniel Adams, Knicker-bocker club member and 1857 president of what would later be known as the National Association of Base Ball Players, this rule was rewritten to simply clarify the distances on the ball field, the word "pace" being "rather vague."[7]

Adams's statement implies that the wording of the new rule did not change the size of the infield. Thus, the "pace" was meant to be understood as a measurement approximately equal to three feet. Yet, even today the meaning of the Knickerbocker "pace" is the subject of debate. Some baseball scholars believe the word "pace" should be interpreted as an exact measurement, which, during the 1840s, was defined as 2½ feet.[8] Given a pace of 2½ feet and again employing the Pythagorean theorem, each side of the infield diamond would be roughly 74½ feet in length. Other historians take the point of view that a pace, being a unit of measurement defined solely by the individual doing the pacing, allowed for a scalable diamond dependent on the size of the players. Therefore, since a child's pace is smaller than that of an adult, the diamond as laid out by a child would be proportionally smaller than the adult's diamond.[9]

With the question of the true meaning of the pace yet unanswered, the exact size of the Knickerbocker infield square remains uncertain. The first baseball annual, *Beadle's Dime Base-Ball Player*, was published in 1860. In this guide, the rules regarding the baseball diamond remained unchanged from those adopted at the 1857 convention, but an accompanying diagram was new. The first, second, and third bases are represented by asterisks (certainly not representative of their actual shape), and home base is represented by the curious figure of an octagon inscribed within a slightly larger octagon (see fig. 19.2). Whereas home base was clearly stipulated to be circular, early drawings of baseball games often showed home base as having a smaller circle inscribed upon the plate (see fig. 19.3).

Following the official rules section of the 1860 *Beadle's* guide is an explan-atory section in which editor Henry Chadwick reviewed and elaborated upon some of the rules of the game. With regard to home base, Chadwick stated that it should be "not less than nine inches in diameter."[10] Though

Fig. 19.3. Brooklyn Atlantics vs. Philadelphia Athletics, October 22, 1866. From John Thorn and Mark Rucker, *The National Pastime* 3, no. 1 (Spring 1984): 24.

Fig. 19.4. Rockingham Nine, Portsmouth, New Hampshire, 1865. From John Thorn and Mark Rucker, *The National Pastime* 3, no. 1 (Spring 1984): 8.

there are numerous drawings, there is only one known photograph showing the circular home base (see fig. 19.4).

With regard to the first, second, and third bases, Chadwick stated that: "The proper size of a base is about fourteen inches by seventeen; but as long as it covers one square foot of ground . . . the requirements of the rules will be fulfilled."[11] Note that the official rule required the base to "cover," not necessarily "be," one square foot of surface. Thus, by Chadwick's interpretation of the rule, any base that covers an area greater than or equal to 12 square inches is legal.[12]

Unfortunately, there are no known photographs or drawings clearly showing the bases of the era to be rectangular. The drawings and photographs that do exist show bases that appear to be square, or quite close to square.[13] Nevertheless, the explanatory section in every *Beadle's* guide up to and including that of 1871 states that the proper size of a base was 14 by 17 inches.

The rules as published in the 1861 *Beadle's* guide contained an addition to section 4:

And in all match games, a line connecting the home and first base and the home and third base, shall be marked by the use of chalk, or other suitable material, so as to be distinctly seen by the umpire.[14]

The purpose of this rule was to aid the umpire in determining whether a hit ball was fair or foul.[15]

There were no further rule changes with regard to the layout of the baseball diamond until 1868. However, the 1867 *Beadle's* guide featured a departure from the old diagram of the baseball field to a more accurate representation of the infield. The bases are shown with their correct shapes, and, presumably, in their correct positions on the infield square (see fig. 19.5). Though the rules still did not explicitly state how the bases were to be oriented in the infield, the diagram implied that all four bases were to be centered on their respective corners of the infield square and that the first, second, and third bases were to be positioned such that two corners of each base touched the base lines. In other words, the bases were rotated 45 degrees from their more familiar, modern orientation. This strange orientation of the bases is clearly seen in a number of drawings of ball games of the era (see fig. 19.6).

A major change in the rules regarding the layout of the baseball diamond occurred for the 1868 season, the first such change since the Knickerbocker rules had been written down more than 20 years before: The words "circular

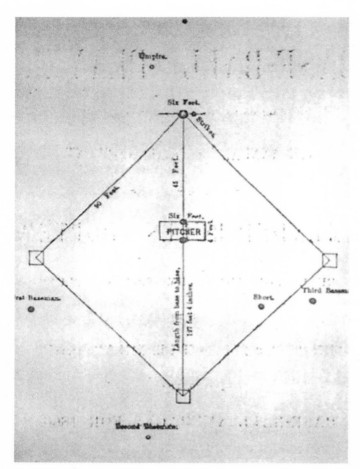

Fig. 19.5. *Beadle's* diagram for 1867. From Henry Chadwick, ed., *Beadle's Dime Base-Ball Player* (New York: Beadle & Co., 1867).

Fig. 19.6. Brooklyn Atlantics vs. Philadelphia Athletics, September 7, 1868. *New York Clipper*, September 12, 1868.

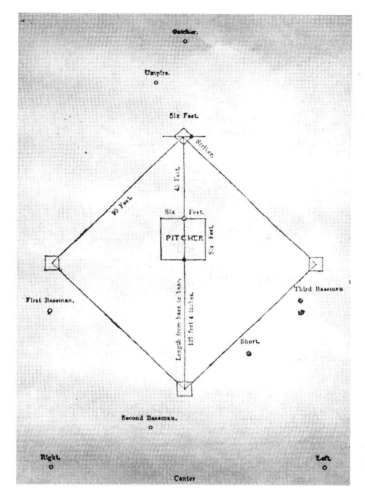

Fig. 19.7. Beadle's diagram for 1969. From "Diagram of the Diamond Field" in Henry Chadwick, ed., *Beadle's Dime Base-Ball Player* (New York: Beadle & Co., 1969).

iron" were stricken from section 3 of the official rules. With this change, the rule regarding the size of the other bases was applied to home base as well: home base to "cover a space equal to one square foot of surface."[16] The official rules as published in the 1868 *Beadle's* guide noted this change in the shape of home base, but the same guide's infield diagram and explanatory section failed to reflect this change.[17] By the following year these mistakes were rectified. Interestingly, while the official rules still failed to stipulate the exact positioning of the bases on the infield square, the 1869 *Beadle's* diagram implied that, unlike the first, second, and third bases, home base was to be oriented with its sides parallel to the base lines (see fig. 19.7).

For most of its life, *DeWitt's Base Ball Guide* was, like *Beadle's*, edited by Henry Chadwick. It, too, contained an explanatory section elaborating upon the rules and play of the game. In the explanatory section of the 1869 *DeWitt's* guide, Chadwick stated that all four bases "should be at least eighteen inches square, although the rules prescribe that they shall cover one square foot of surface."[18] Meanwhile, the explanatory section in the 1869 *Beadle's* guide still stated that the bases should be "about fourteen inches by seventeen." Chadwick's contradictory statements as published in the two guides were repeated for three years. In 1872, the discrepancy was resolved when both guides simply dropped the sections that included the suggested base sizes.

An additional change to the official rules of 1868 occurred with the following amendment to section 4: "The base bag shall be considered the base, and not the post to which it is, or should be, fastened."[19] No doubt, the previous season (or seasons) saw occurrences of bases becoming dislodged from their original position, leaving both runner and fielder dumbfounded as to which one was the true base. The post was a block of wood or stone, sunk into the infield ground and level with the playing surface, to which the bases were attached by stakes (see fig. 19.4).

The Openly Professional Era

With the exception of one minor alteration to the rules, the layout of the infield diamond remained unchanged as the era of openly professional teams dawned. Starting with the season of 1872, home base was no longer to be made of iron, but of "white marble or stone, so fixed in the ground as to be even with the surface."[20]

Whereas diagrams of the baseball infield had long since shown first, second, and third bases centered on their respective corners of the diamond, not until 1874 did the rules officially require this placement. The exact positioning of home, first, and third (but technically not second) base was implied in a new foul line rule (rule 5, section 8) stating:

> The foul ball lines shall be unlimited in length, and shall run from the center of the home base through the center of the first and the third base to the foul ball posts.[21]

A change in the exact positioning of home base occurred for the season of 1874. An addition to rule 1, section 6, required home to be "with one corner of it facing the pitcher's position."[22] This orientation had been implied in diagrams of the baseball infield since 1869. Furthermore, since 1869, Chadwick's explanatory section of the *Beadle's* guide mentioned this orientation of home base.[23] The reason behind the clarification of home base's orientation was simple and well explained by Chadwick in the 1874 *DeWitt's* guide:

> The [home] base [is] to be fixed in the ground with one corner pointing towards the pitcher's position, so as to insure the pitcher's having the full width of the home base to pitch over, instead of the one foot of width he would have were the base to be placed with the square side facing him.[24]

The rules for the season of 1875 further clarified the position of home base. An addition to rule 1, section 6, required that home base be positioned such that the corner that faces the pitcher "touch the foul ball lines where they meet at the home base comer."[25] This amendment moved home base from a position centered on its comer of the infield diamond to a location completely in foul territory. While the infield diagram found in the 1875 *Beadle's* guide failed to reflect this move of home base, the diagram in the De Witt's guide of that year did show the change.

To understand the reason behind this rule change, it is necessary to review what was known as the "fair-foul" hit. The fair-foul hit was a particular technique of hitting that took advantage of the fair and foul ball rules of the day. These rules, from "Rule V-The Batting Department," were as follows:

> 11) If the ball from a fair stroke of the bat first touches the ground, the person of a player, or any other object, either in front of, or on, the foul ball lines, it shall be considered fair.
>
> 12) If the ball from a fair stroke of the bat first touches the ground, the person of a player, or any other object behind the foul ball lines, it shall be declared foul; and the ball so hit shall be called foul by the umpire even before touching the ground, if it be seen falling foul.[26]

In summary, a ball that initially landed in fair territory, regardless of whether it stayed in fair territory or whether it passed first or third base in fair territory, was a fair ball. A fair-foul hit was one in which the batter deftly hit the ball such that it first touched the ground in fair territory and then bounded into foul territory. Often the fielders would have to run a great distance into foul territory to retrieve such a hit ball. To shorten this distance, the first and third basemen would play quite close to the foul lines, which subsequently opened up large gaps in the infield and allowed what would otherwise be easy ground ball outs to safely make it to the outfield as hits.

Henry Chadwick, among others, was eager to lessen the impact of the fair-foul hit. To meet this end, he proposed adding a tenth man (or "right shortstop") to each team so that the large gaps in the infield would be narrowed.[27] Chadwick popularized this idea by writing special sections in both the *Beadle's* and *DeWitt's* guides of 1874 suggesting the use of the 10-man rule. However, though the *Beadle's* guide of 1875 as well as the *DeWitt's* guides from 1875 to 1882 continued to have sections clearly implying that the 10-man rule was the norm for organized baseball, the 10-man game was never adopted into the official rules of the game.[28]

The rule change for 1875 called for home base to move from its former position, centered on its corner of the diamond, back approximately 8½ inches, such that it was located completely in foul territory. This change also moved the batter back a distance into foul territory and thus made it more difficult for him to successfully make a fair-foul hit.[29] This change in the batter's position did not solve the "problem" of fair-foul hitting; in 1877, the fair-foul hit was eliminated from the game altogether by changing the definition of a fair ball essentially to the modern rule.

The Emergence of the National League

For 1876, the inaugural season of the National League, the rules of the game called for an infield diamond that had the following characteristics: The four bases each covered 12 inches square; home base was located in foul territory, its front corner touching the junction of the first- and third-base lines; the first, second, and third bases were centered on their respective corners of the infield square, and oriented such that two corners of each base touched the base lines. The orientation of the first, second, and third bases, as well as the exact position of the second base, were still only implied by the diagrams that supplemented the published rules. Furthermore, while the diagram printed in the new 1876 *Spalding's Official Base Ball Guide* correctly showed this layout of the infield, the diagram in the 1876 *Beadle's* guide still failed to show home base in foul territory.

For the year of 1876 alone, the rules in both *Beadle's* and *DeWitt's* guides, but not those in the *Spalding Guide*, allowed home base to be composed of wood. By the following year, however, none of the guides mentioned a wooden home base.

Two major changes in the infield diamond rules were introduced for the season of 1877. The first change moved home base for the second time in

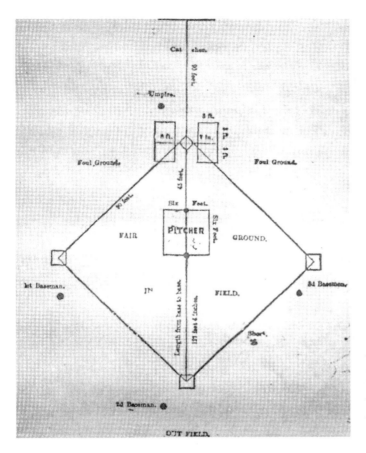

Fig. 19.8. "Diagram of the Diamond Field." Henry Chadwick, ed., *Beadle's Dime Base-Ball Player* (New York: Beadle & Adams, 1877).

three years. This time home base was to be positioned "wholly within the diamond. One corner of said base shall face the pitcher's position, and two sides shall form part of the foul lines."[30] With this change, and after two years of printing erroneous diagrams, the 1877 guide finally contained a diagram that correctly reflected the state of the infield diamond, home base being shown completely in fair territory.

The second infield change for 1877 concerned the size of the bases. "The first, second and third bases must cover a space equal to fifteen inches square."[31] Home base remained a square foot in size.

Whereas the infield diagram in the 1877 *Beadle's* guide still showed the first, second, and third bases rotated 45 degrees from their current orientation (see fig. 19.8), the diagrams in the 1877 *DeWitt's* and *Spalding Guides* no longer showed the bases in this skewed orientation. Instead, they showed the base sides parallel to the base paths, as they are today. Nevertheless, the orientation of these bases was not explicitly stated in the official rules at the time.[32]

The 1880s

Prior to the 1880 season, the official rules of the game were completely rewritten, rearranged, and, in general, improved. Though much of the wording regarding the layout of the infield diamond was altered, the state of the infield itself remained unchanged. However, the positioning of the first, second, and third bases was made explicit by new wording of the rules: "the center of each [base] shall be upon a separate corner of the infield."[33]

No further changes were made to the rules regarding the baseball diamond until 1885. For that season, it was no longer acceptable to have home base made of marble. Home could now be composed only of "white rubber or white stone."[34] The change was made to help prevent players from slipping on the slick marble plate.[35] The rules of the three-year-old American Association departed from those of the National League and called for white rubber home bases only.

The only major differences between the infield diamond of 1885 and that of over a century later are the positions of the first and third bases, and the shape of the home base whereas photographs of the era are numerous, clear pictures of the first and third base bags centered on the base paths are quite difficult to locate. This positioning of the bases is best seen in a photograph that was taken prior to the April 29, 1886, opening day game at the Polo Grounds in New York City (see fig. 19.9).

The year 1887 brought about a single set of rules embraced by both the National League and the American Association. The two leagues compromised with regard to the layout of the infield diamond: the National League adopted the American Association rule requiring home base to be made only of white rubber. Furthermore, the rules for this season altered the positions of the bases:

> The first, second and third bases must be . . . so placed that the center of the second base shall be upon its corner of the infield, and the center of the first and third bases shall be on the lines running to and from second base and seven and one-half inches from the foul lines, providing that each base be entirely within the foul lines.[36]

Why change the positions of first and third base? Prior to 1887, if a batted ball hit first or third base, the umpire was faced with a most difficult decision as to whether the ball was fair or foul. A ball hitting the half of the base that was in fair territory was a fair ball, while a ball hitting the other half of the

Fig. 19.9. Boston Beaneaters vs. New York Giants, April 29, 1886. From John Thorn and Mark Rucker, *The National Pastime* 3, no. 1 (Spring 1984): 50.

base was a foul ball. At times, deciding which half of the base had been hit was practically impossible. Moving first and third base completely into fair territory made the decision academic: if the ball hit the base, it had to be a fair ball.

Note that according to the wording of the rule, the first and third bases were to be positioned such that they straddle the base lines to and from second base. However, the diagram that accompanied the rules in the 1887 *Spalding Guide* shows the bases positioned as they are today, neatly nestled in their respective corners of the 90-foot infield square (see fig. 19.10). Interestingly, it was the diagram, not the wording of the rule, that prevailed. To this day, second base remains "upon its corner of the infield," while the first and third bases lie wholly within the diamond. This rather strange positioning of second base is often overlooked in modern-day representations of the baseball diamond. Even the cover of *The Macmillan Baseball Encyclopedia* shows an infield diamond with second base erroneously placed wholly within the

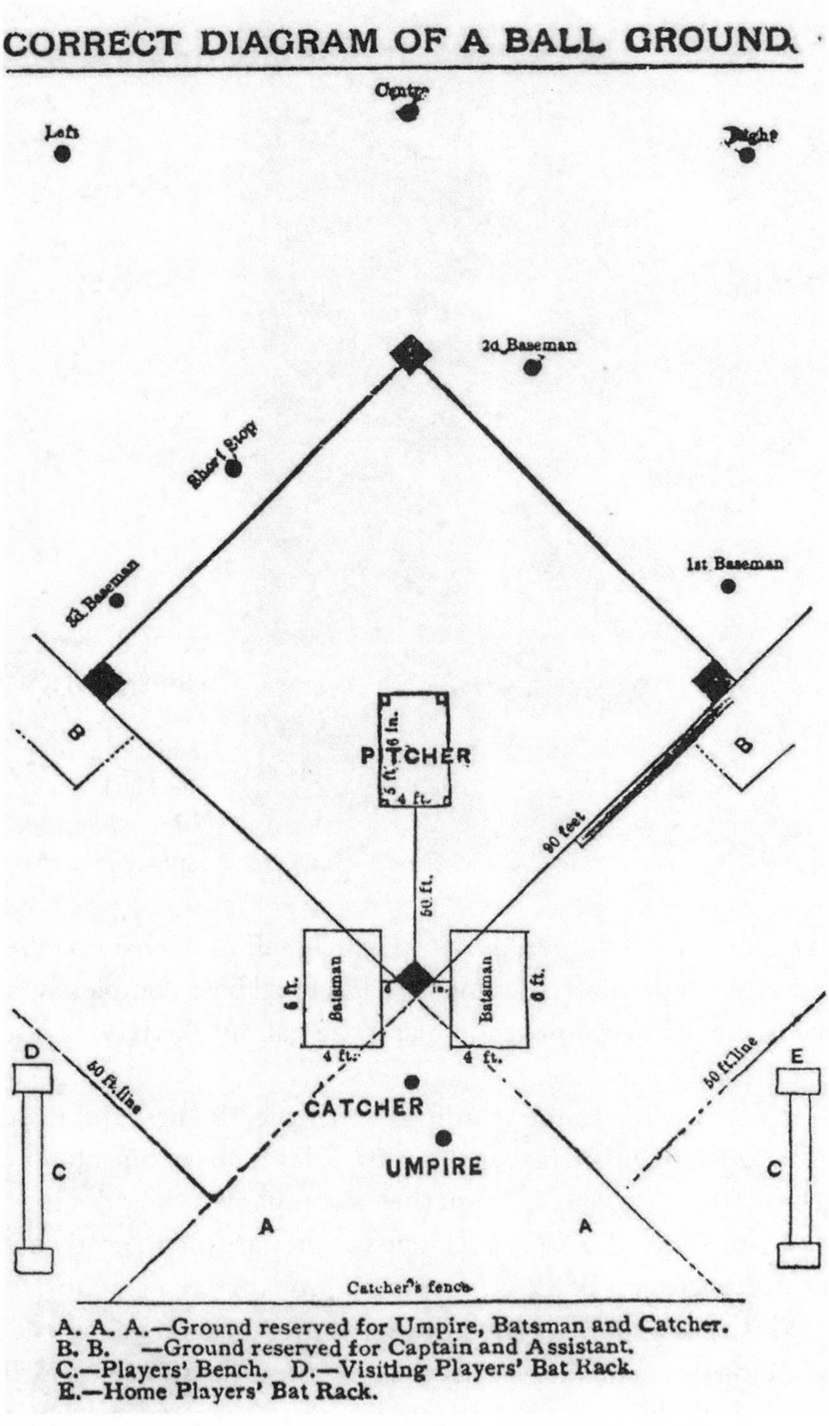
CORRECT DIAGRAM OF A BALL GROUND.
Centre
Right
2d Baseman
Short Stop
3d Baseman
1st Baseman
B
B
PITCHER
5 ft. 6 in.
4 ft.
90 feet
50 ft.
Batsman
Batsman
6 ft.
6 ft.
4 ft.
4 ft.
D
E
50 ft. line
50 ft. line
CATCHER
UMPIRE
C
C
A
A
Catcher's fence
A. A. A.—Ground reserved for Umpire, Batsman and Catcher.
B. B. —Ground reserved for Captain and Assistant.
C.—Players' Bench. D.—Visiting Players' Bat Rack.
E.—Home Players' Bat Rack.

Fig. 19.10. "Correct Diagram of a Ball Ground." From *Spalding's Base Ball Guide for 1887* (Chicago: A. G. Spalding & Bros., 1887), 4.

90-foot infield square. Modern day rules avoid any possible conflict between the written rule and the diagram by essentially stating that the diamond should be laid out so that it looks like the diagram supplied.

The Modern Baseball Diamond

In 1894, a new, more mathematical and geometrical diagram of the baseball diamond accompanied the *Spalding Guide* rules.[37] While the actual layout of the diamond did not change, it was now more precisely defined with labeled points and angles. Henry Chadwick thought the new, complicated description of the infield a bit ridiculous:

> The diagram of the diamond needs a surveyor to lay it out so that it might be made comprehensible to amateurs and novices in the game. What with its "arcs" and its "radiuses" and its algebraic style of description, it is likely to be a greek [sic] puzzle to foreign votaries of the game.[38]

As the turn of the century approached, the infield diamond was basically identical to that of today with but one notable exception: the shape of home base. This final significant change to the diamond rules was implemented for the 1900 season. Two triangular areas were added to the front of the square home base such that the front was no longer a point, but a 17-inch wide, flat side of the now familiar five-sided shape. The *Spalding Guide* of 1900 explained the reason for the change:

> With the plate placed in accordance with the form of the diamond field, that is, with its corner facing the pitcher instead of one of its sides, a width of 17 inches was presented for the pitcher to throw the ball over instead of 12 inches, the width of each side of the base. But this left the pitcher handicapped by having to "cut the comers" as it is called, besides which the umpire, in judging called balls and strikes, found it difficult to judge the "cut the corner" balls. To obviate this difficulty, the Committee [of Rules], while keeping the square plate in its old place—touching the lines of the diamond on two of its sides—gave it a new form in its fronting the pitcher, by making the front square with its width of 17 inches, the same as from corner to corner, from foul line to foul line. The change made is undoubtedly an advantage alike to the pitcher and umpire, as it enables the pitcher to see the width of base he

has to throw the ball over better than before, and the umpire can judge called balls and strikes with less difficulty.[39]

The invention of the five-sided home base was claimed by National League pitcher Crazy Schmit. In a letter he sent to *The Sporting News*, Schmit states that he suggested the five-sided home base to James Hart (chairman of the Baseball Rules Committee) two years earlier. After briefly mentioning his invention, Schmit goes on at length to detail his career in a style uncannily reminiscent of Jack Keefe, the "busher" pitcher made famous in Ring Lardner's story "You Know Me, Al." Recounting the previous season, Schmit writes:

> I pitched some 14 exceptional good games for Cleveland last summer [2-17, 5.86 in 1899]. I am like a gnarled oak and am getting better every year. l may pitch in some smaller league this year. [Charlie] Comiskey says he will give me a chance when things are settled. I had everything arranged to play for [John] McGraw, but if he goes to St. Louis it is all off.[40]

The majority of Schmit's letter is spent listing excuses for many of his 17 losses with the dismal 1899 Spiders. Unfortunately for Schmit, McGraw did go to St. Louis, and Crazy pitched in only four more major-league games, winning none and losing two. Schmit (apparently sensitive of his "Crazy" moniker) ended his letter as follows: "I hope you will not add any nicknames to my name. I remain your humble reader. Frederick Schmit." Whether or not the idea for the five-sided home plate really came from Schmit remains unclear. The fact that he has one of the worst winning percentages (7-36, .163) in baseball history does not.[41]

Former baseball commissioner Ford Frick wrote:

> The establishment of the 90-foot distance between bases must be recognized as the greatest contribution to perfect competition any game has ever known. It is that specification on which our hitting and fielding records are based; that unchanging measurement of success or failure that has set the guidelines for heroes; the great reason why baseball, through the years, has qualified as the most mathematically perfect game ever devised by humankind.[42]

Like Red Smith, Frick describes the baseball diamond as being "perfect." It is the awkward-looking home plate, the strange positioning of the second base, and the first and third bases nestled snugly in their corners of this 90-foot square that we embrace as perfection.

Chronology of Baseball Diamond Rule Changes

1845 First written rules of baseball set down by the Knickerbocker Base Ball Club of New York City. Distance across infield diamond (home to second and first to third) is set at 42 paces.

1857 New set of rules adopted at first convention of baseball players. The sides of the infield square are 30 yards. First, second, and third bases must each cover a square foot in area and are canvas bags filled with sawdust or sand. Home base is circular and made of iron.

1860 In *Beadle's* guide explanatory section, Henry Chadwick suggests that first, second, and third bases be 14 by 17 inches and that home base be at least nine inches in diameter.

1861 Rule requires that chalk lines be drawn between home and first and home and third.

1867 *Beadle's* guide publishes first truly representational diagram of baseball diamond.

1868 Home base changed from a circle to a square. Size of home base same as that of first, second, and third bases. Clarification in the rules states that the base bag, not the post to which the bag should be attached, is to be considered the base. This rule dropped in 1876 according to the *Spalding Guide* 1877 according to *Beadle's* and *DeWitt's* guides.

1869 In *DeWitt's* guide explanatory section, Henry Chadwick suggests first, second, and third bases be eighteen inches square.

1872 *Beadle's* and *DeWitt's* guides no longer contain explanatory sections. Discrepancy between suggested sizes of first, second, and third bases (14 by 17 inches versus 18 inches square) is thus removed. Home base required to be made of white marble or stone.

1874 Foul line rule implies home, first, and third bases are centered on foul lines.

1875 Home base required to have one point facing pitcher and is positioned wholly in foul territory.

1876 *Beadle's* and *DeWitt's* guides allow wooden home base; the *Spalding Guide* does not.

1877 Home base moved wholly into fair territory. First, second, and third bases are to cover 15 inches square. Home base still to cover 12 inches square. Fair-foul hit removed from the game, as definition of fair and foul balls are changed. *Spalding* and *DeWitt's* guide diagrams show bases with sides parallel to base paths. *Beadle's* guide will continue to show first, second, and third bases rotated 45 degrees from their modern orientation through 1881, the final year of its publication. *Beadle's* and *DeWitt's* guides no longer allow wooden home base.

1885 National League home base made of white rubber or stone. American Association home base made only of white rubber.

1887 National League and American Association adopt same set of rules. Home base made only of white rubber. First and third bases moved into fair territory.

1894 New geometric diagram of baseball diamond adopted.

1900 Home base changed to five-sided shape.

ACKNOWLEDGMENTS

Thanks go to Tom Heitz, Liane Hirabayashi, Fred Ivor-Campbell, Larry Webster, and the library staffs of both the National Baseball Library in Cooperstown, New York, and the Paul Ziffren Sports Resource Center at the Amateur Athletic Foundation of Los Angeles.

NOTES

1. Kevin Nelson, *Baseball's Greatest Quotes* (New York: Simon and Schuster, 1982), 183.
2. For example, the distance between first and second base on the modern infield diamond is, at its shortest, 88 feet 1.5 inches.
3. Harold Seymour, *Baseball: The Early Years*, vol. 1 (New York: Oxford University Press, 1960–1990), 15–18.
4. A similar diagram and set of rules were published in *The Spirit of the Times*, May 12, 1855.
5. The initial convention was held January 22, 1857, but the rules were officially accepted at a later meeting, held on February 25, 1857. Not until the convention of the following year, held March 10, 1858, did the organization name itself the "National Association of Base Ball Players."
6. "Rules for Sports and Pastimes," *New York Clipper*, May 2, 1857.
7. John Thorn, "The True Father of Baseball," chap. 1 in *Total Baseball* (New York: HarperCollins, HarperPerennial, 1993), 8.
8. Thorn, "The True Father of Baseball," 6.
9. Frederick Ivor-Campbell argued in favor of this scalable pace in his research presentation "Why Forty-Two Paces'" at the 23rd SABR National Convention, June 26, 1993. Ivor-Campbell also noted that deliberate pacing for an adult male can reasonably yield a three-foot pace and, thus, an infield square with sides 90 feet in length.

10. Henry Chadwick, ed., *Beadle's Dime Base-Ball Player* (New York: Irwin P. Beadle, 1860), 18.

11. Chadwick, *Beadle's Dime Base-Ball Player* (1860), 18.

12. According to an article in the *New York Clipper*, May 20, 1865, bases a cubic foot in size were used in Philadelphia in 1860. However, it is unclear that the game in which these bases were used was what one would refer to as baseball. Certainly the use of such bases was not the norm for the era.

13. One of the earliest patents of a baseball base is U.S. Patent No. 75,076. The device is a base that is attached to a stake by means of a swiveling cap. The diagram accompanying the description of the patent shows the canvas base to be circular, though it is clearly not intended for use as a home base. It is unknown whether the device was ever manufactured.

14. Henry Chadwick, *Beadle's Dime Base-Ball Player* (New York: Beadle, 1861), 12.

15. According to the 1861 *Beadle's* guide, some clubs had adopted this rule during the season of 1860.

16. Henry Chadwick, ed., *Beadle's Dime Base-Ball Player* (New York: Beadle, 1868), 17.

17. Curiously, the *New York Clipper*, December 21, 1867, and December 28, 1867, failed to make note of the change of home from a circle to a square in articles detailing the rule changes for the upcoming 1868 season.

18. Henry Chadwick, ed., *The Base-Ball Guide for 1869* (New York: Robert M. DeWitt, 1869), 30.

19. Henry Chadwick, ed., *Beadle's Dime Base-Ball Player* (New York: Beadle, 1868), 17. In Appendix 4, "Rules and Scoring of Baseball," in *Total Baseball* (New York: HarperCollins Publishers, HarperPerennial, 1993), Dennis Bingham and Tom Heitz state that this rule was dropped in 1876. While the 1876 *Spalding Guide* no longer includes this rule, both the *Beadle's* and *DeWitt's* guides of that year do. All three guides omit the rule for 1877.

20. Henry Chadwick, *The Base-Ball Guide for 1872* (New York: Robert M. DeWitt, 1872), 111.

21. Henry Chadwick, ed., *Beadle's Dime Base-Ball Player* (New York: Beadle & Adams, 1874), 76.

22. Henry Chadwick, *DeWitt's Base-Ball Guide for 1874* (New York: Robert M. DeWitt, 1874), 76.

23. Henry Chadwick, ed., *Beadle's Dime Base-Ball Player* (New York: Beadle, 1869), 14.

24. Chadwick, *Beadle's Dime Base-Ball Player* (1869), 14.

25. Henry Chadwick, *DeWitt's Base-Ball Guide* for 1875 (New York: Robert M. DeWitt, 1875), 74.

26. Chadwick, *DeWitt's Base-Ball Guide* for 1875, 83.

27. John Thorn, telephone conversation with author, June 11, 1993.

28. The idea of a 10-man game was not new. Not uncommonly, box scores of baseball games from the 1860s showed 10 men per team, the extra man noted as playing "RS" or right shortstop.

29. While the batter's box moved back 8½ inches with the move of home base, the same season of 1875 called for a change in the lines of the batter's box that resulted in the batter being moved an extra foot away from fair territory.

30. Henry Chadwick, *DeWitt's Base-Ball Guide for 1877* (New York: Robert M. DeWitt, 1877), 64.

31. Chadwick, *DeWitt's Base-Ball Guide for 1877*, 3.

32. From 1867 to 1881, the final year of its publication, the Beadle's guide diagram of the baseball infield showed the first, second, and third bases to be rotated 45 degrees from their modern orientation.

33. *Spalding's Base Ball Guide for 1880* (Chicago: A. G. Spalding & Bros., 1880), 59.

34. *Spalding's Base Ball Guide for 1885* (Chicago: A. G. Spalding & Bros., 1885), 108.

35. *The Sporting Life*, November 26, 1884, 3.

36. *Spalding's Base Ball Guide for 1887* (Chicago: A. G. Spalding & Bros., 1887), 107.

37. By this time both the *Beadle's* and *DeWitt's* guides were no longer published. *Beadle's* last year of publication was 1881, while *DeWitt's* was 1885.

38. Henry Chadwick, ed., *Spalding's Base Ball Guide for 1894* (New York: American Sports Publishing, 1894), 152.

39. Henry Chadwick, ed., *Spalding's Official Base Ball Guide* (New York: American Sports Publishing, 1900), 201.

40. "The New Home Plate," *The Sporting News*, March 24, 1900.

41. Jack Wadsworth has the worst won-loss percentage for a pitcher with at least five victories: 6-38, .136. However, as of the end of the 1993 season, Anthony Young's record stood at 5-35, 143.

42. Ford Frick, *Games, Asterisks, and People: Memoirs of a Lucky Fan* (New York: Crown Publishers, 1973), 9. Note that, like Red Smith, Frick erroneously states the distance between bases to be 90 feet.

20

The Book

KARL LINDHOLM

Karl Lindholm has been associated with Vermont's Middlebury College as a student, teacher, and Emeritus Dean for more than forty years. His many research interests include the literature of baseball and the Negro Leagues, and he has written many fine articles for SABR and other respected baseball journals. In this 1996 piece for *The National Pastime*, he takes a whimsical look at various definitions of "The Book," encompassing unwritten rules, keeping score, and the literary tradition of the game.

> He begun thinking about baseball a lot, which he never done before, always treating it before like it was football or golf, not a thing to think about but only play. He said to me, "Arthur, tell me, if you was on one club and me on another what kind of book would you keep on me?"
>
> "If I was to keep a book on you," said I, "I would say to myself, 'No need to keep a book on Pearson, for Pearson keeps no book on me.' . . . You must remember. Or if you can't remember you must write it down. The man you are facing is not a golf ball sitting there waiting for you to bash him. He is a human being, and he is thinking, trying to see through your system and trying to hide his own. . . ."
>
> "I will keep a book," he said.
>
> —from *Bang the Drum Slowly*, by Mark Harris

> "I never play by the book because I never met the guy that wrote it."
>
> —DICK WILLIAMS, Oakland A's manager, 1980

Baseball is the most literary of sports in America. Books are important to the game. Every year sees a battery of new books about the diamond game and America's past, often written in the first person by some graybeard wordsmith recalling his youth and the game's timeless heroes. Colleges and universities, even prestigious places like Middlebury College in Vermont, get away with offering courses with grandiose titles such as "A Gentle Trinitarian Mysticism: Baseball, Literature, and American Culture." (The phrase is philosopher Michael Novak's. In *The Joy of Sports*, he asserts that baseball "is suffused with a Gentle Trinitarian mysticism," because of the game's emphasis on the number three and its multiples in its organizational essence.)

The "Book" is a powerful symbol which resides at the center of the game. The immediate suggestion of the Bible and other sacred texts is unavoidable. After all, the Old Testament starts with "in the big inning."

Baseball finds its way into the books of some of our greatest writers. In the 1870s, America's bard, Walt Whitman, observed, "I see great things in baseball. It is our game—the American game." Mark Twain used the game as a pastime for Arthur's (or was it Eddie Feigner's?) knights in *A Connecticut Yankee in King Arthur's Court* (1889). Stephen Crane wore the tools of ignorance for Lafayette College and Syracuse University in 1890 and 1891. Thomas Wolfe was a big fan, and, from high school English, we all know that Hemingway's Santiago, the Cuban fisherman and baseball fan in *The Old Man and the Sea*, was inspired by Joe DiMaggio's bone spurs. Robert Frost was an avid ballplayer in pickup games at the Bread Loaf Writers' Conference in Vermont and even covered the 1956 World Series for the fledgling *Sports Illustrated*. It goes on, even to the present: Bernard Malamud, John Updike, Philip Roth, Marianne Moore, Jack Kerouac, Donald Hall, Robert Coover, Nancy Willard, Garrison Keillor, all players on the varsity, have incorporated their love of baseball into their work.

Playing by the Book

Not all books having to do with baseball encompass the history of the game or explore its imaginative possibilities and cultural relevance. In fact, perhaps the most important book in baseball isn't even written down: It moves through time on the force of its own historical authority.

When was the last time you heard a baseball reference to "the Book"? Maybe it was today . . . when the Voice of the Red Sox intoned that the skipper was "going by the Book" in bringing in the lefty to throw to a like-sided slugger in the late innings of a close game.

The Book has a thousand Commandments. It dictates that you take on 3–0, hit behind the runner, don't throw an 0–2 strike, bunt with runners on first and second with no outs in the late innings of a close game, don't try to stretch a single or steal a base when you're behind. The Book is a guide to life between the lines, a guide to the strategy of baseball, the most complex game among our sporting passions. It is the collected wisdom of the game's practitioners.

Who wrote this book—and where can I get a copy?

Like the Bible, it has many authors. Certainly, John McGraw (hardly a saint), the progenitor of the Baltimore game, was an early and crucial contributor. McGraw's legatee, feisty Earl Weaver, the Earl of Baltimore, wrote new and important chapters in his game strategy. Weaver's approach, based on the big inning, contrasted with McGraw's station-to-station, one-run-at-a-time impulse. "Pitching, defense, and three-run homers" was his credo and formula. "Innovations" such as artificial turf and the designated hitter have occasioned a selective rewriting of aspects of the Book.

You can't buy this Book; it doesn't exist in earthly form. It is thus mystical and mythological, though it has daily practical application in the game itself. Christy Mathewson wrote *Pitching in a Pinch* in 1912; some 70 years later, Tom Seaver wrote *The Art of Pitching*. Cerebral George Will dissected game strategy in *Men at Work* with the baseball's current genius, the (micro-) manager Tony La Russa. Former player Keith Hernandez provides another gem of analysis in *Pure Baseball: The Game for the Advanced Fan*. There are many books, wonderful books, that reflect and contribute to the one essential Book. You can find the Book at any ballpark, any day there's a game, at any level, but you can't find it at B. Dalton.

The Book can be learned, but it can't be *read*. It must be learned if the game is to be played right. Harry Rose taught the Book to Pete; Mutt Mantle taught it to his son, Mickey. High school coaches teach from the Book all the time. It is only when the Book is substantially understood that one can deviate from it and "go against the Book," opening up whole new realms of possibility and appreciation. Knowing the Book of Baseball, understanding the game's chessboard strategy, makes the interstices of the game meaningful and a time for relevant talk: "Think they'll pitch out? I guarantee he's running on this pitch."

Of course, players and managers keep a Book on one another as well, observing and analyzing other players and managers, their skills, weaknesses, and tendencies. We often hear comments like, "the Book on Moose is that he can't lay off the high heater;" or "the Book on Lefty is that he gets rattled with men on base." Tony Gwynn, and many other expert players, keep an extensive book on opposing pitchers, now often assisted by computers and video and other high-tech aids. Managers (supported by advance scouts) keep track of what opponents like to do in certain situations. The Book on Billy Martin was that he practiced the inside game of John McGraw: Roger Angell once said of him, "He loves the suicide squeeze the way a wino loves muscatel." (It turned out, unfortunately, that he also loved muscatel the way a wino loves muscatel.)

No one has ever been more thoughtful and analytical about the game than Ted Williams: his devotion to his craft is legend. He is famous for having said: "All I want out of life is that when I walk down the street folks will say 'there goes the greatest hitter who ever lived.'" He got his wish through the application of great skill, discipline, and knowledge. Nothing infuriated Williams more than being called a "natural hitter." "What about all the practice?" he would demand. He even applied the lessons about aerodynamics from Marine flight school during his war service. Did Williams keep a Book on opposing pitchers and umpires and ballpark idiosyncrasies? Absolutely. In his rookie season, he took the advice of Joe Cronin and wrote down all that he learned in a little black book.

Was there a Book on Williams? According to Detroit manager Del Baker, "The book on Ted when he first came up was that he would chase high balls." This would not be a problem for long. "Boy," Williams said, lamenting the shrinking strike zone to biographer Ed Linn in *Hitter: The Life and Turmoils of Ted Williams* (1993), "a ball above the waist is a helluva ball to hit. The guys who had the best luck with me never gave me anything but quick breaking stuff, down in the dirt." In 1970, he wrote the Book on hitting, *The Science of Hitting*.

Keeping the Book

There is another Book, this one a real, concrete thing, that the game also depends upon utterly—and that's the score book. This is a very different Book from the historical, unwritten Book of fundamental strategy. This Book doesn't just keep score. It is the origin of the miasma of numbers and statistics that envelops the game and absorbs its fans and players. It is the essential starting point, the source, of our evaluation of players' performance: "He's a .300 hitter," we say, or "he's got an ERA under 3.00." These standards of excellence evolve from the daily assembly of scorebook stats.

Go to any game and look on the bench and you will find some solemn individual, a parent, assistant coach, sister, or substitute player, bent over the task of "keeping the book." There is no coach who hasn't asked plaintively before a game, "Who'll keep the Book today?"

In the professional game, writers, sportswriters, fittingly keep the Book. At other levels, it's whoever you can get to do it. The reason it's hard to find keepers of the Book is because it's hard to keep. It is a hieroglyph of black splotches (runs), numbers, letters, combinations of numbers and letters. It is easy to screw up the Book, especially when the ball is winging around the field seemingly unwilled. I love it when the radio announcer says something like, "For those of you keeping score at home, that rundown went 3–6–3–4–2–6." It's damn hard to fit all those numbers in that little box (and, while we're at it, who are these people keeping score at home?).

Keeping the Book (it sounds like a job for a medieval monk—"The Keeper of the Book") is quite a responsibility and a challenge. A mistake affects lives. In a famous scene in the movie *Bull Durham*, Crash Davis talks about how tough it is to hit for a decent average:

> Do you know what the difference between hitting .250 and .300 is? It's twenty-five hits. Twenty-five hits in 500 at-bats is fifty points, okay? There's six months in a season; that's about twenty-five weeks. That means if you get just one extra flare a week, just one, a gork, you get a ground ball, you get a grounder with eyes, you get a dying quail . . . just one more dying quail a week, and you're in Yankee Stadium.

That one hit a week could also be a scorer's decision on a booted ball (or maybe that's what a "gork" is). When I was coaching high school I once read in the morning paper that my team had been no-hit the day before. That was news to me: I could have sworn we got some hits, so I went to the Book, our scorebook, and sure enough, we had three hits. Clearly, their Book-keeping authority (probably the coach) had a different view of some hard ground balls off gloves.

Real Books About Baseball

There are, of course, regular books about baseball, written-down books, published like other books, some of which are quite remarkable in exploring both the hidden and overt dimensions of the game. Among these, is there one that qualifies as the Book, the quintessential baseball story? What is "the Book" about baseball?

Recently, our small, but literate SABR chapter here in Vermont was mailed a membership survey, one of the questions on which asked us to identify our "favorite baseball book?" Lawrence Ritter's *The Glory of Their Times* appeared on the most responses. We could do worse than declare that seminal text of first-person narratives the Book on baseball. Another top vote getter was *The Boys of Summer*, by Roger Kahn, though my choice in the nonfiction category is *Baseball's Great Experiment: Jackie Robinson and his Legacy*, by Jules Tygiel, the best combination of scholarship and narrative appeal in the baseball canon, a great book, a model.

On the fiction side, most readers, I suspect, would anoint Bernard Malamud's *The Natural* as the Book, with W. P. Kinsella's *Shoeless Joe* and Mark Harris's *The Southpaw* running close behind. However, my choices are otherwise. I love Jerome Charyn's *The Seventh Babe* and Nancy Willard's *Things Invisible to See*.

The Seventh Babe tells the tale of Babe Ragland, the seventh "Babe" to play major-league baseball, a lefty shortstop for the Red Sox who plays with a fierce love of the game which ultimately overwhelms the moneyed snakes who try to bring him down. In developing this marvelous character, Charyn imaginatively reworks some of baseball's most dominant myths and cliches, as well as some of its most bizarre footnotes. Full of twists and turns, *The Seventh Babe* explores the imaginative intersection between white baseball and black baseball in the segregated first half of this century.

Nancy Willard's novel is about death and love and war—and baseball. Set in Ann Arbor about the time of WWII, *Things Invisible to See* brings together the young ballplayer, Ben Harkissian, to whom was given "the sinister mysteries of the left hand and the dark meadows of the right hemisphere" (he's also a lefty), and the reticent Clare Bishop, who has the gift of "spirit travel." Ben, along with all of his high-school teammates, is shipped off to war where he encounters Death, and makes a deal with him. The deal involves a ballgame between Death, and his all-star minions, and Ben and his mates, the South Avenue Rovers. Like Charyn in *The Seventh Babe*, Willard makes beautiful use of magical and supernatural devices in this delightful book.

Books and baseball: for those of us who love books, baseball remains the national pastime. So . . . *keep* the book, *read* the book, *learn* the book, *follow* the book—but not slavishly. Sometimes we all need to *defy* the book just to make life interesting.

21

Cricket and Mr. Spalding

TOM MELVILLE

Tom Melville has written books on cricket (*The Tented Field: A History of Cricket in America*) and baseball (*Early Baseball and the Rise of the National League*, which won SABR's Seymour Medal for the best book of baseball history in 2002). In the mid-nineteenth century, many of the country's best athletes played both sports, and Melville was the perfect person to write this story. One of baseball's most important figures, Albert Spalding, was also an avid cricketer and promoter of the game.

As much as any other figure in baseball history, Albert Goodwill Spalding (1850–1915), the Rockford-raised star pitcher, manager, and owner of the Chicago White Stockings (predecessors of today's Chicago Cubs), and the founder of the sporting goods company that bears his name, was most responsible for making professional baseball what it is today.

Though baseball history has long credited William Hulbert, the Chicago coal merchant and founder of the White Stockings, as the architect of the National League, which, in 1876 successfully wrested control of organized baseball away from players to owners, Spalding, his close associate, helped guide the league through its early organizational difficulties, and tirelessly worked to elevate the game into a pastime "worthy of the patronage, support and respect of the best class of people."[1]

For much of his Chicago baseball career, however, Spalding was also associated with another, much less well-known sport, cricket, an association that not only underscored the insecurity of baseball's public image during the late nineteenth century, but also indirectly influenced Spalding's own vision of what baseball should be in American society.

Popular enough with Americans in the 1850s to be heralded, in some sporting circles, as the country's national-sport-to-be, cricket had been quickly displaced by baseball as the country's bat-and-ball sport of choice after the Civil War, the casualty of America's apparently instinctive preference for a rapid transition, "high pressure" game, rather than one, like cricket, that had traditionally emphasized social propriety as much as actual competitive results.[2]

Nonetheless, cricket was still England's national pastime, a sport that enjoyed the prestige of being patronized by "dooks and lawds," a status it held primarily on the strength of its image as the epitome of the amateur ideal, which held that sport should be played and enjoyed as an end in itself, rather than for any extraneous rewards.

The Refined Sport

It was an image that was able to gain for cricket a modest, but sustainable, following among the more status-conscious segments of late nineteenth-century American society, especially those who still looked to England as the model of social propriety. At a time when golf and tennis had not yet arrived on the United States sports scene, cricket was the closest America had to a "gentleman's game," one that respectable Americans were more willing to identify with than baseball, whose reputation during this period was blackened by a succession of gambling scandals, ballpark riots, and owner-player disputes. Even John Montgomery Ward, one of the era's most influential professional players, speaking at a dinner for New York's Cosmopolitan Cricket Club in 1889, believed baseball, in comparison to cricket was becoming too violent a sport.[3]

Not surprisingly, the exclusive suburban cricket club, rather than the local ballpark, became the center of activity for many sports-minded upper-class Americans during the last decades of the nineteenth century, the most notable examples being Philadelphia's Germantown Cricket Club, Boston's Longwood Cricket Club, New Jersey's Seabright Lawn Tennis and Cricket Club, and New York's Staten Island Cricket Club, all of which allowed high society the alternative of a relaxed, highly social weekend of cricket to a frequently unsettling afternoon at the local baseball park.[4]

Cricket in Chicago

In Chicago, cricket began to attract interest as a focal point of high society in 1876, the year the old Chicago Cricket Club, which had enjoyed a moderately active, though not necessarily prestigious, existence before the Civil War,[5] was reorganized on the impetus of a number of the city's Canadian residents, especially the Toronto-born dentist, Dr. E. J. Ogden.[6]

By the early 1880s the club had set itself apart as the wealthiest and most exclusive of the city's half-dozen cricket clubs, with an admission policy that carefully screened applications to exclude "all objectionable persons."[7]

It was an arrangement that paid handsome dividends. By 1885 the club had over 150 members, and within a few years could number among its membership, such prominent Chicago figures as Marshall Field, General Philip Sheridan, Stuyvesant Fish, president of the Illinois Central Railroad, Charles Hutchinson, president of the Chicago Board of Trade, Carter Harrison, the city's five-time mayor, and meatpacking baron Philip Armour, who even granted the club use of his personal property at 63rd and Indiana.[8]

To further enhance its status, the club incorporated in 1889 on the capitalization of $50,000 (a surprisingly large sum, fully half the amount the White Stockings incorporated with three years later) and, the following year, erected an impressive all-purpose clubhouse on seven acres of land at Stoney Island Avenue and 71st Street, which, in addition to its cricket ground, also had a state-of-the-art bicycle track and athletic field.[9]

Spalding seems to have been associated with the Chicago Cricket Club as early as 1880, the year he first appears as a member of the club's standing committee.[10] His involvement with the club, however, was not merely honorary.

He was a playing member of the club team that toured Canada the following year, and was even selected for the All-Midwest team that was to play a team of touring English cricketers at St. Louis that fall, a match that was eventually rained out.[11]

When the club incorporated Spalding was among the select inner circle of investors who held more than $500 of its stock, and a year later donated, in his name, a prize cup to be awarded annually to the winner of the city's newly organized cricket league.[12]

"An Elegant and Cultured Gentleman"

Why Spalding, one of the country's prominent baseball figures, should have been so directly and openly involved with cricket, even to the point of admitting that England's national sport had some features "which I admire more than I do some things about Base Ball," is not hard to explain.[13]

Having assumed the presidency and part ownership of the White Stockings on Hulbert's death in 1882, and already the owner of a thriving sporting goods business, Spalding had by this time completed the transition from the camp of "labor" to "capital."

With this newly acquired status, it was clearly in Spalding's interest to be associated with a sports organization more closely identified with the movers and shakers of Chicago society than baseball, which may have been his bread and butter in the workaday world, but was not something a status-conscious businessman would want to exclusively associate with on his own time, especially for someone like Spalding, who, despite his middle-class roots, seems to have prided himself on being "an elegant and cultured gentleman."[14]

Spalding, however, also seems to have kept tabs on England's national game as part of his grander scheme to make baseball more than just a game for Americans.

His first brush with cricket, in fact, probably came when his old Boston Red Stockings club, in conjunction with the Philadelphia Athletics, toured England in 1874, a scheme that had been hatched by Boston manager Harry Wright to bring baseball to the attention of English society.

Sent to England that winter to work out the details of the tour, Spalding quickly realized that America's fledgling national game stood little chance of being accepted in England unless it could win favorable comparison to cricket. Always the opportunist, Spalding quickly took it upon himself to arrange with English sports authorities a number of cricket matches, so many, in fact, that the American baseballers actually ended up playing as much cricket as they did baseball during the tour.[15]

Spalding seems to have planned to use this same approach for his own, more ambitious, around-the-world baseball tour of 1888–89, even going so far as to persuade his old Red Stockings teammate George Wright, an experienced cricket player, to come along and, using an improvised batting cage, coach his White Stockings at cricket during their long Pacific crossing to Australia. Spalding himself even joined some of these practice sessions, one reporter noting that "standing before a wicket, he is the picture of manly strength and grace." His plan, however, did not seem to go over too well with the baseballers themselves, and after only a single match in Sydney, they played no more cricket during the tour, not even in England.[16]

Spalding was no more successful in his efforts to win the Anglo-Australian world over to baseball in 1889 than he had been in 1874, and following an unsuccessful attempt to personally organize an English baseball league in the 1890s, probably realized that cricket, rather than being a window of opportunity, was, instead, an immovable barrier to his grand dream of making baseball "the universal athletic sport of the world" (which, in his eyes, meant only America, Canada, England, and Australia).[17]

Spalding himself attributed this failure to the different roles cricket and baseball played in their respective cultures. There was little hope, he claimed, that baseball would ever be accepted by upper-class English society because it was "a game for the people," while cricket "is essentially a game for the aristocracy."[18]

For all baseball's popularity as the "people's game," Spalding also seems to have believed that it had to shrug off its image as a hotbed of rowdyism, and incorporate some Old World, upper-class moral constraint into its energetic, New World "pluck and drive," before it could completely and unconditionally become the national game of every American, from the roughest corner sandlot to the most exclusive suburban country club. It's a condition, baseball has long since come to realize, that is not necessary for its national prosperity.

FURTHER READING

Kirsch, George. *The Making of American Team Sports: Baseball and Cricket, 1838–1872.* Urbana: University of Illinois Press, 1989.

Spalding, A. G. *America's National Game.* Lincoln: University of Nebraska Press, 1992.

NOTES

1. Peter Levine, *A. G. Spalding and the Rise of Baseball* (New York: Oxford University Press, 1985), 51.

2. Robert Lewis, "Cricket and the Beginning of Organized Baseball in New York City," *International Journal of the History of Sport* (December 1987): 327.

3. "Gentlemanly Sports," *New York Tribune*, October 31, 1879, 4; "The Base Ball Business," *Western Monthly* (Chicago) 4 (1870): 328–29; *American Cricketer*, September 12, 1889, 81.

4. Will Roffe, "Cricket in New England and the Longwood Club," *Outing*, June 1891, 251–54; Charles Clay, "The Staten Island Cricket and Baseball Club," *Outing*, November 1887, 99–112; John Lester, *A Century of Philadelphia Cricket* (Philadelphia: University of Pennsylvania Press, 1951), 213–18.

5. A. T. Andreas, *History of Chicago* vol. 2 (New York: Arno, 1975), 613–14; *Chicago Tribune*, August 18, 1856, 3; May 26, 1857, 1; May 20, 1876, 5.

6. Andreas, *History of Chicago*, 3: 681–82.

7. *Daily Inter-Ocean*, June 1, 1890, 3.

8. Andreas, *History of Chicago*, 3: 682; *Daily Inter-Ocean*, June 1, 1890, 3; May 8, 1883, 5.

9. *Daily Inter-Ocean*, June 1, 1890, 3; Levine, *A. G. Spalding*, 37.

10. *New York Clipper*, August 27, 1881, 363.

11. *St. Louis Post-Dispatch*, October 11, 1881, 6.

12. *Daily Inter-Ocean*, June 1, 1890, 3; *Chicago Tribune*, June 13, 1891, 6.

13. A. G. Spalding, *America's National Game* (Lincoln: University of Nebraska Press, 1992), 6.

14. Levine, *A. G. Spalding*, 124.

15. *New York Clipper*, August 22, 1874, 163; September 5, 1874, 183.

16. *New York Sun*, December 31, 1888, 3; *Daily Inter-Ocean*, January 21, 1889, 9.

17. Spalding, *Baseball*, 611, 612.

18. Spalding, *Baseball*, 609.

22

Lifting the Iron Curtain of Cuban Baseball

PETER C. BJARKMAN

Peter C. Bjarkman was the leading authority on Cuban baseball history and a 2017 Henry Chadwick Award recipient for his contributions to baseball research. He authored more than forty books on baseball, many of them related to Cuba. His research not only told the stories of Cubans who became famous playing in the United States, but included many of the great players and teams who played only in Cuba or on the Cuban national team. In this 1996 article, Bjarkman brought us up to speed on a long, fascinating story.

For a tradition-minded American baseball fan fed up with ear-piercing Diamond Vision entertainment, cavorting cartoon-style mascots, shopping-mall stadia, luxury-box extravagance, inflated beer and parking prices, plastic-grass fields, and spoiled ballplayers, a trip around the Cuban ballpark circuit in mid-February—during the National Series championships comprising the Cuban postseason—seems a refreshing escape into baseball's pristine past. In Havana and Pinar del Rio and Santiago de Cuba, the diamond action remains pure, the off-field distractions are minimal, and the game continues to thrive at its own beautiful pace and rhythm.

Havana's 55,000-seat Estadio Latinoamericano is a genuine throwback. The park's electronic center-field scoreboard features only lighted displays of lineups and line scores, and is entirely void of video displays or between-inning commercials. The ballplayers' uniforms are equally simple, recalling modern-day industrial league or softball uniforms in the States. The fans are focused on the game alone for nine innings (or less, since Cuban baseball features aluminum bats and an Olympic 10-run rule after seven innings) and they commune joyfully about baseball's timeless rhythms. In a nation of severe material shortages and limited personal freedoms, baseball is a welcome panacea.

Of course, there are stark differences from old-time North American baseball, as well. The outfield wall decorations urge spectators to remain loyal to the Castro revolution. A nationwide paper shortage means no printed score-cards and souvenir stands, and beer vendors are unheard of. Team rosters represent geographical regions, and players are therefore never traded among teams. And a sight entirely foreign to North American ballparks—glowing electric-light foul poles—reminds the visitor that this is not Brooklyn or the Bronx or Philadelphia.

Problems

For Cuban fans, however, the 1997 winter playoffs hardly represented a throwback to past glory days. Cuban baseball has changed drastically in recent seasons and most fans agree that this has been largely for the worse. Many of the nation's top stars have defected to the majors or have, inexplicably, been forced to retire. The defectors—great young pitching prospects like Diamondbacks recruits Larry Rodriguez and Vladimir Nunez, and spectacular Mets shortstop Rey Ordonez—generate little ill-will among the fans and ballplayers left behind. But the forced retirements of perhaps Cuba's best-ever shortstop, German Mesa, and one of its most popular sluggers, outfielder Victor Mesa, have left the fans feeling cheated.

The recent *Series Nacional* season and the following postseason playoffs were often played in half-empty stadiums, especially in Havana. Fans complain that the game is being gutted by the peddling of players to the Japanese Industrial League and to fledgling pro circuits in Italy, Nicaragua, Ecuador, and Colombia. Meanwhile officials of the Cuban League maintain their steadfast insistence that the nation's emphasis remains on amateurism in baseball and on preparing for another Olympic triumph in Australia in the year 2000. One rumored cash deal for Omar Linares and Orestes Kindelan with the Japanese pro circuit was quickly nixed.

Yet veterans like Victor Mesa (reportedly headed to Japan's Industrial League) and 1992 Olympic star hurler Lazaro Valle (bound for Italy) are being retired and sent overseas. Mesa was inexplicably sent packing while only a few homers short of breaking the all-time Cuban career record. German Mesa and exiled hurler Orlando "El Duque" Hernandez—brother of Marlins farmhand Livan Hernandez—were supposedly banned for dealing with a North American agent. (The agent, a Cuban-American with Venezuelan residency, is now serving a 20-year Cuban prison term for his part in the affair.)

Rumors persist that the forced retirements of the two Mesas and others mark an effort to clear space on the national team for young stars like Miguel Caldes, Eduardo Paret, and Jose Estrada, who might otherwise also consider the option of big-league defection.

The crisis has in part been brought on by changes in the economic structure of baseball abroad. Pro ball in the U.S. with its mega-level salaries is now a far greater lure than ever before for low-paid "amateurs" toiling with major-league skills in the talent-rich Cuban League. And Japan is becoming a magnet as well. The unconfirmed story about Linares and Kindelan and top Cuban pitcher Pedro Lazo reportedly involved a $10 million offer from the Japanese.

The Mesa Messes

At the top of the list of retirees and suspensions stand German Mesa and Victor Mesa, unrelated stars of the past half-decade who are two of the finest players in recent Cuban history. The popular and muscular Victor Mesa, who toiled with Villa Clara during the past decade, is a lifetime .313 hitter and extraordinary basestealer, who also stands well up on the career homer list. German Mesa was the starting shortstop on the Cuban national team for six seasons before being dropped from the Olympic squad in favor of hot prospect Eduardo Paret. While Paret flashed his defensive brilliance for two weeks in Atlanta, and Rey Ordonez is already drawing legitimate big-league comparisons with Aparicio and Concepcion in New York, Cuban fans still swear that Mesa is the island's best-ever shortstop.

Most recent defectors have been pitchers. Failures to dominate in the majors as they did in Cuba by Rene Arocha (an arm injury sidetracked his career after 11 wins for the Cardinals in 1993), Livan Hernandez (he labored at AAA Charlotte last season), and Oswaldo Fernandez (7-13 with the Giants in 1996), have raised questions about the true level of Cuban talent. Indeed, the aluminum bats used in the Cuban League spawn throwers, not pitchers. Cuban hurlers are also consistently overused at home as both starters and relievers.

Several new defectors may soon resurrect the Cuban reputation. Ariel Prieto is a top pitching prospect with Oakland despite his slow start in 1996 (6-7, 4.15 ERA). Larry Rodriguez may be even better than Prieto, and was given a $1.25 million signing bonus by Arizona. And Ordonez has caused a storm of excitement in only one season with the Mets. Ordonez is a useful yardstick, since he was far from the best Cuban shortstop at the time of his defection. The future Mets star had been buried behind German Mesa and Paret, who is the best all-around shortstop I have seen since Luis Aparicio. He runs with abandon (swiping 43 bases in this year's short 65-game Cuban season), hits with power, and tracks down aluminum-bat liners with flawless precision. And Abdel Quintana, a hot 17-year-old prospect with the playoff-bound Industriales team, was recently rushed into the starting lineup in Havana and may soon be even better than either Mesa or Paret.

The Old Days

If the talent pool is thinning, this, like much else in Cuba these days, is a sharp departure from the heady years during the '60s, '70s, and early '80s. For three decades, the Cubans maintained the world's greatest showcase of amateur baseball talent. The ballparks in Havana, Holguin, Mantanzas and other cities were home to some of the greatest diamond stars that U.S. fans never saw. Heroes of this era included Wilfredo "El Hombre Hit" Sanchez, Luis Casanova, Fidel Linares (Omar's father), Antonio Munoz, Manuel Alacron, Augustin Marquetti, and Braudilio Vinent. Lefty-swinging Wil Sanchez was one of the greatest hitters in Cuban history, winning no fewer than five batting titles, including the first back-to-back pair in 1969 and 1970. Today, his lifetime mark of .332 trails only those of Linares (.373), the league's first-ever .400 hitter, and Alexander Ramos (.337), the latest Cuban to reach the 1,000-hit plateau.

In the '80s the heavy hitting of Wilfredo Sanchez was replaced by that of Antonio Munoz (370 career homers), Lazaro Junco (the all-time home run leader), and finally Omar Linares. Linares has dominated the hitting of the '90s (with three .400-plus seasons), along with slugger Orestes Kindelan (now only three short of Junco on the homer list with 402), fleet-footed leadoff specialist Luis Ulacia (last year's batting champion), and a group of young stars paced by Jose Estrada and Miguel Caldas.

The pitching of the '70s and '80s was largely dominated by popular flame-throwing right-hander Vinent, considered the greatest Cuban hurler of the Castro era. Most of the lifetime pitching marks are still held by this superb hurler who won (221) and lost (167), more games than any Cuban moundsman, and in 1986 also became the first island hurler to reach the 2,000 career strikeout mark. He also still holds the marks for complete games and games started.

Cuba's rich baseball history stretches back long before Castro and the

1959 revolution. The game was first played there two years before the birth of the National League. Cuban Steve Bellan became the first-ever Latin big leaguer, when he appeared with the National Association Troy Haymakers in 1871. Cubans also appeared in the National League before the First World War (Rafael Almeida and Armando Marsans with Cincinnati in 1911), and Dolf Luque was a legitimate star (27-8 with Cincinnati in 1923) long before major-league integration.

But it was the post–World War II period that saw a full-scale Cuban invasion of the majors—first with a handful of Washington Senators journeymen, then with flashy '50s stars like Minnie Minoso, Camilo Pascual and Pete Ramos, and finally with Zoilo Versalles, Luis Tiant, Tony Oliva, and Tony Perez, who made their marks in the '60s and '70s.

Back home in Havana, the Cubans had been hosting top-flight winter league play between black and white Cubans and North Americans since the mid-'20s. They were also dominating the world amateur scene throughout the '30s and '40s, and the winter professional Caribbean World Series during its first phase from 1949 through 1960. Cuba won the first title in Havana in 1949 and seven of the first dozen competitions.

A top pro league in the '40s and '50s featured legendary teams representing Club Havana, Almendares, Cienfuegos and Marianao, and showcased a mixture of Cuban stars and major leaguers in the sparkling new El Cerro Stadium (today's revamped and renamed Estadio Latinoamericano).

The Cuban Structure

After Castro's takeover, the powers of Organized Baseball pulled the plug on the International League Havana Sugar Kings. (For interested readers the details of Cuban baseball history are laid out in my book *Baseball with a Latin Beat* published in 1994.) Castro's reaction was to mandate a strictly amateur league and a yearly national series between regional teams that consisted of two short seasons and a championship playoff round. It is from this internal season that national teams have long been selected to represent Cuba in Olympic, World Cup, Pan American, and other international competitions. The result in recent decades has been a series of powerhouse Cuban teams that have posted an 80-1 international record between the 1987 Pan American Games in Indianapolis and the 1996 Olympics in Atlanta, captured 15 of 18 world amateur titles since 1969, won both Olympic baseball tournaments, and taken every Pan Am gold medal (and all but one game) since 1963.

The organization of the Cuban League and the Cuban playoff system has undergone several overhauls over the decades. It now consists of a season of 65 games featuring 16 teams in 14 cities (Havana has three teams), which are divided into four divisions (two groups in the West and two in the East). A second Selected Series season with eight teams and 63 games has long been a staple of summer-season play. A February four-team postseason culminates the *Series Nacional* and corresponds to a stateside LCS playoff.

The showcase ballpark is still the 55,000-seat El Cerro. Impressive 25,000-plus capacity parks of AAA quality are also situated in Pinar del Rio, Matanzas, Santiago, Holguin, Cienfuegos, and several smaller cities. What gives Cuban baseball its distinctive appearance within this lavish system of amateur competition is the use of aluminum bats and a total absence of any peripheral commercialism. The one lends a strange feeling of college baseball to games staged in professional venues. The other means that no outfield or scoreboard advertisements or ear-splitting between-innings video ad campaigns contaminate pristine Cuban ballparks.

How Good Are These Guys?

What is the status of the Cuban league and its mysterious cache of potential big-league talent? Are the Cubans really as good as their Olympic and international records suggest? Is a recent claim on the cover of a leading U.S. baseball weekly that Omar Linares is the "best third baseman on the planet" a case of overhype or a bold measure of reality? Stripped of their aluminum bats would the Cuban sluggers who dominated in Atlanta succeed against big-league hurling? Does Cuba really contain a deep untapped talent pool for big-league clubs?

Atlanta provided a clue for American fans privileged to see the Cubans' best players firsthand. Even allowing for aluminum bats, Kindelan and Linares are awesome long ball hitters. Kindelan strokes blasts that remind one of K-brothers Killebrew and Kingman. Paret is as talented at shortstop as any major leaguer of the past several generations, flashier than Ordonez and more potent at the plate (completing this year's National Series with a .290 BA).

There are several others with major-league potential. Miguel Caldes is an impressive outfielder some tout as the next great Cuban star. Luis Ulacia is a leadoff hitter with major-league tools, and rifle-armed Juan Manrique is potentially a solid big-league receiver. Pedro Luis Laso (11-2 with Pinar del

Rio this season) demonstrated in the recent national playoffs that he has a genuine big-league arm, professional savvy, and an overpowering delivery effective even against aluminum rocket launchers.

The rest of the Cuban pitchers are not especially impressive. Jose Contreras (14-1 with Pinar del Rio) throws hard but is undisciplined and features only two pitches. Lazaro Valle is now gone from the scene, and southpaw Omar Ajete (a 1992 Olympic mainstay) is far past his best years. The best up-and-coming young arms—Rodriquez and Nunez—have already defected.

So Cuban talent is a mixed bag. Pitching is thin, but Cuban fielding and hitting is still impressive. Linares stands head and shoulders above the pack. At 28, the slugging third sacker seemed this past winter season to be losing interest. Cuban fans complain that he has put on weight and rarely hustles. But I believe Linares is the best ballplayer this island has ever produced—including Perez, Canseco, Oliva, and perhaps even 1930s-era Negro League wonder Martin Dihigo. He has been described as Brooks Robinson grafted onto Albert Belle. My impression is more along the lines of a mid-career Aaron, Mathews, or Mays. Omar Linares is as good—and as exciting—as anyone I have ever seen, with the possible exceptions of Clemente and Mantle.

The best assessment of Cuban baseball is that the talent is there but the product is waning. The same claim, of course, can be made of the majors. The crisis in Cuban baseball will only be resolved when the sport's top leadership decides to go in one direction or the other-strict amateurism or free-market professionalism. In the meantime Cuba still harbors elements of what appears to an outsider as the last vestiges of the game we all once knew and loved—the game joyfully played more for prideful victory than for bulging bankrolls.

23

The Colorado Silver Bullets

Can Promotion Based on the "Battle of the Sexes" Be Successful?

GAI INGHAM BERLAGE

SABR has published many stories on women in baseball—including articles on players, umpires, and executives. Gai Berlage was a leading authority on the subject and the author of the classic 1994 book *Women in Baseball: The Forgotten History*. In this 1998 article, she captured the history of the women's professional team that played for four years in the 1990s.

Nineteen ninety-seven marked the fourth season of operation for the Colorado Silver Bullets, an all-women's professional baseball team. The team is unique in that it is not part of a women's league. The Bullets barnstorm across the country playing only men's professional, semiprofessional, and amateur teams. They have no home field and, therefore, no hometown fan base. Promotion for the games is based on the "battle of the sexes." Ticket holders are led to believe that they are seeing history in the making—that women are competing against men in baseball for the first time and that spectators are witnessing the establishment of historic milestones.

The idea for the Colorado Silver Bullets emerged not from women ballplayers clamoring for professional opportunities to play, but from the box office success of the movie, *A League of Their Own*, released by Columbia in 1992.

In the wake of the movie's success, Whittle Communications and Coors Brewing Company announced the formation of an all-women's team on December 10, 1993. For $2.6 million, Coors got brand-name sponsorship, and the team became known as the Colorado Silver Bullets, after its brand of light beer. The company hoped to capitalize on the revived interest in women's baseball created by the movie. It hoped that favorable publicity gained from sponsorship would attract more women beer drinkers and increase Coors's market share.

For Bob Hope, president of Whittle Events, the creation of the team was a dream come true. In 1984, he had failed in his bid to win a franchise in the men's Class A Florida State League for the Sun Sox, his proposed all-women's team.[1] His vision for the Silver Bullets was very different from Wrigley's for the AAGBL. Wrigley formed the women's league to keep baseball alive in major league ballparks while the men were off to war. The AAGBL was supposed to be temporary. The Colorado Silver Bullets, on the other hand, were not to be part of a women's league but to play against men's teams. They were to be a permanent barnstorming team.

Hope, the founder of the Silver Bullets, was once described in *Sports Illustrated* as "the most innovative promoter in sports."[2] His experience as public relations and marketing director for the Atlanta Braves and the Atlanta Hawks may have given him experience with creating gimmicks to attract the public to men's baseball games, but it ill-prepared him to deal with marketing women. By having the Silver Bullets play only men's teams, Hope unknowingly doomed them to failure. For the archaic "battle of the sexes" promotion to be successful the women had to be as skilled as the men. They could not be judged on their own merits—the way, say, the 1996 women's Olympic basketball team was—but only in relation to the larger, stronger, and vastly more experienced men they were to play against.

Unlike other sports like basketball, which girls and women play in great and rapidly increasing numbers, few girls or women play baseball. Although Little League Baseball admitted girls in 1974, girls almost always play Little League Softball. Softball is the designated sport for girls at the junior high, high school, and college level. There are no women's baseball teams at the college, high school, or junior high school level.

In fact, only four women have played on college men's teams. In 1985 Susan Perabo played one game for Division III Webster College in Missouri. In 1989 Julie Croteau became the first woman to play National Collegiate Athletic Association baseball when she became a member of the St. Mary's College (Maryland) team. In 1990 Jodi Haller pitched for NAIA St. Vincent's College (Pennsylvania). In 1994 Ila Borders became a pitcher for NAIA Southern California College.

So recruitment immediately became a problem. Where were the Silver

Bullets going to find women who could play baseball? And if they did find these women, how could they realistically expect women with limited baseball experience to compete against men who had played all their lives? On the movie screen, fantasy sells. On the playing field, reality quickly sets in. How could Hope expect these women to be able to compete against AA players when virtually by definition even most men who grew up playing baseball couldn't handle the competition?

In spite of this, Hope announced that the Silver Bullets would play "approximately 50 exhibition games against men's minor-league, semiprofessional, and college teams," and that it would become "an independent member of the AA Short Season Northern League."[3]

The problem of the women's skills became apparent at the inaugural game, which was played—as might be expected—on Mother's Day, May 8, 1994. The Northern League All-Stars crushed the Silver Bullets, 9–0. The women's fielding was not bad, but pitching and hitting were definite problems. Realizing that the women couldn't successfully compete at this level, management quickly adjusted the schedule to drop some minor league games downward and add more against men's amateur teams.

Even with the adjusted schedule the Bullets won only six games during the season, while losing thirty-eight. On the brighter side, 250,000 people paid to see them play—an average of 5,687 per game, including highs of 33,179; 29,896; and 21,654.[4]

Fans and "Firsts"

Even though they were drawing pretty well, the Colorado Silver Bullets had a problem in this area. How could they build a fan base when they were constantly on the road barnstorming? TV could do it, but the few games that were televised on ESPN or Lifetime were often taped and shown days after they were played. It was tough to become a fan.

In an attempt to create media interest, the games were sensationalized. The Silver Bullets's official press kit declared that this was the "first all-women's team recognized for play in the men's minor leagues." Most newspapers omitted the qualifier "recognized for" and merely declared inaccurately that this was the first time a women's team had played against men. Of course, from the 1890s to the 1930s, various Bloomer Girls teams competed against men throughout the United States. As recently as the 1950s, Allington's All-

Americans, former AAGBL players, had barnstormed across the country play-ing local men's teams.[5]

This inaccuracy, though, created the possibility for all kinds of firsts. The implication was that if you went to the games you could see history in the making: the first home run by a woman off a male pitcher or the first woman to shut out a men's team. Bob Hope excelled at this, and would pull off some major coups that involved Silver Bullets players.

In 1994, two Silver Bullets players, pitcher Lee Ketcham and first base-woman Julie Croteau, played in the Class AAA Hawaii Winter Baseball League. Both played for the Maui Stingrays, though neither distinguished herself.[6]

In 1995, Silver Bullets Shannon Mitchum and Ann Williams tried out for the New York Mets. Neither made the team. In 1996 another Silver Bullets player, Pamela Davis, pitched for a major league farm team in an exhibition game. She tossed a scoreless fifth inning and got the win in the Jacksonville Suns's 7–2 win over the Australian Olympic team.[7]

In 1996 the Silver Bullets were invited to Taiwan to play exhibition games against Taiwan major league men's baseball teams. The tour was hyped as "the first time women have competed with men in the same sport in Taiwan." And Bob Hope declared, "It is really gratifying that the Taiwan major league decided to invite our team. American women playing Chinese men in pro-fessional baseball makes a statement that women are accepted as ballplayers." Unfortunately, the Silver Bullets lost the first five games and the sixth was never played.[8]

Failure

For four seasons, 1994–1997, the Colorado Silver Bullets operated as a barn-storming professional baseball team, backed by Coors's annual $2.6 million sponsorship. Gate receipts for games are split between the sponsoring team and the Bullets. Advertising for the games is the responsibility of the spon-soring organization.

The team's record improved year by year, and in 1997, the Silver Bullets had a winning season. But attendance began to decline in mid-1996 and lagged disastrously in 1997 as the novelty of women playing baseball against men waned.

(Those poor 1997 attendance numbers were inflated by a turnout of 27,917 when the Silver Bullets played the Colorado All-Stars at Coors Field. Attendance at that game may have been helped by another Silver Bullets first—the brawl. On June 11, 1997, Kim Braatz-Voisard, at bat, was told by the catcher of the opposing team that the pitcher was going to hit her with the ball. She got hit by the next pitch and claims she saw the pitcher laughing at her. Incensed, she charged the mound. This resulted in a bench-clearing melee. She and the catcher were both ejected from the game. The media loved it and coverage of the "brawl" appeared on nightly television and in newspapers across the country.)

At the end of the 1997 season, Coors announced that it would no longer be a sponsor. According to Bob Hope, Coors Beer's management from the very beginning had ambivalent feelings about sponsoring the Silver Bullets. On the one hand the company hoped to attract women beer drinkers. On the other, it worried about having their Silver Bullet light beer become identified as a "chick beer." They feared alienating their male drinkers.[9]

The season of 1997 marked the end of play for the Colorado Silver Bullets. Without Coors's backing, Hope-Beckham Inc., which purchased the team from Whittle Communications, found it impossible, in the face of low attendance rates, a lack of media interest, and intense competition from other professional women's sports to find new sponsors.

Competition for sponsors is fierce. Currently, there are two professional women's basketball leagues, the American Basketball League (ABL) and the Women's National Basketball Association (WNBA); a professional women's volleyball league; a women's fast pitch softball league, and proposed women's leagues in soccer and ice hockey. All of these sports have greater public recognition than women's baseball. At the summer Olympics in 1996, American women's teams in basketball, softball, and soccer won gold medals. At the Winter Olympics in 1998 women's ice hockey won a gold medal. By relying on an outdated gimmick, "the battle of the sexes," the Colorado Silver Bullets never had a chance to develop an identity of their own.

For women to be judged purely on their own merits as athletes, they need their own leagues. Professional women's golf and tennis circuits have already demonstrated that the public will come out to see women play and that women athletes can be accepted for their athleticism. The future success of the newly formed women's basketball, softball, volleyball, ice hockey and soccer leagues will indicate whether or not women's team sports have finally come of age.

What we have learned from the experience of the Colorado Silver Bullets is that the time of the "battle of the sexes" has passed. Women's teams should not be competing against men's. It is a feminist myth that there are no biological differences between the sexes. Men are, on average, physically bigger and stronger than women. In sports in which size and strength are an advantage, women will come out losers if they play against men. The myth of no physical differences not only deceives women, but sets them up for failure. Women's sports need to be accepted in their own right. The only way to do that is to have women's leagues.

NOTES

1. "Girls of Summer: An All-Female Lineup for the Sun Sox?," *The Sporting News*, October 1, 1984.

2. "Colorado Silver Bullets: 1994 souvenir program," 2.

3. "Colorado Silver Bullets: 1994 souvenir program," 6.

4. Statistics supplied by Colorado Silver Bullets organization.

5. Gai Ingham Berlage, *Women in Baseball: The Forgotten History* (Westport CT: Praeger, 1994), 30–38, 178–91.

6. Robert Collias, "Hawaiian League Reloads with Pair of Silver Bullets," *USA Today Baseball Weekly*, October 12–18, 1994, 8; "Hawaiian Winter League Final Unofficial Statistics," Howe Sportsdata International, Boston Massachusetts, 1994.

7. Anthony L. Gargano, "Diamonds Are a Girl's Best Friend: Women Players Take Their Swings at Becoming Ms. Met," *New York Post*, February 2, 1995, 82–83; "Minor League Baseball: Davis Lives Out Dream with Scoreless Inning, Win," Associated Press via Nando.net, 1996.

8. "Big League Clash of Genders: Bullets Play Six Games in Taiwan," Lifetime On Line, http://www.lifetimetv.com/sports/SilverBullets/taiwan.htm; Summer 1996 Taiwan Game Results: 0–5, November 19, 1996, http://www.inst.eecs.berkeley.edu/~j-yen /SilverBullets/taiwan.html.

9. Author's telephone conversation with Bob Hope, president and owner, Hope-Beckham Inc., which owns the Colorado Silver Bullets, July 29, 1997.

24

Cy Seymour

Only Babe Ruth Was More Versatile

BILL KIRWIN

Bill Kirwin made his most lasting contributions to baseball research with his 1993 founding of NINE: *A Journal of Baseball History and Culture*, and, a year later, with his creation of the NINE Spring Training Conference. Both are still going strong, even after Bill's untimely death in 2007. Bill and his conference cast a wide net, welcoming devotees of history, sociology, economics, statistics, law, and more. Among his many divergent baseball interests was star pitcher-outfielder Cy Seymour, whom he profiled for SABR in 2000.

Imagine if a young major-league pitcher, like Andy Pettitte of the Yankees, decided, for whatever reason, to become an outfielder in the year 2001. And imagine if he hit over .300 for the next five years, culminating in 2005 by winning the league batting crown. And imagine if, upon his retirement in 2010, he had accumulated more than 1,700 hits and generated a lifetime batting average of over .300 to go along with his 60-plus pitching victories. Imagine all the articles that would be written at the close of the first decade of the twenty-first century calling for Pettitte to be inducted into the Hall of Fame.

There was such a player, born a century earlier than Pettitte. He collected 1,723 hits and became a lifetime .303 hitter after he won 61 games as a major-league pitcher. His name was James Bentley "Cy" Seymour, and he is perhaps the game's greatest forgotten name. Seymour won 25 games and led the league in strikeouts in 1898; seven seasons later, in 1905, he won the National League batting crown with a .377 average. Only one player in the history of the game—Babe Ruth—has more pitching victories and more hits than Seymour. The second most versatile player to ever play the game is almost totally unknown!

Of the approximately 14,000 players who have made it to the major leagues since 1893, only a tiny number have enjoyed success both on the pitcher's mound and in the batter's box.[1] A few well-known players, like Sam Rice, Stan Musial, and George Sisler, began their careers as pitchers but became better known as hitters. Others, like Mike Marshall and Bob Lemon, switched from the field to the mound.

Only a handful, however, enjoyed success as both hitters and pitchers. Smoky Joe Wood's blazing fastball enabled him to win 116 games before he blew his arm out. In 1918 he switched to the outfield, and he retired with 553 hits and a respectable .283 batting average. Rube Bressler began his career in 1914 as a pitcher, compiling a 26-32 record with Philadelphia and the Reds. Then he became a full-time outfielder, principally for Cincinnati and Brooklyn. Between 1921 and 1932 he collected 1,090 hits and produced a lifetime .301 batting average. Hal Jeffcoat, on the other hand, played the first six years of his career as an outfielder with the Cubs, and the last six as a pitcher with the Cubs and the Reds. He was 39-37 in 245 games as a pitcher, and accumulated 487 hits for a lifetime batting average of .248.

Since 1893, when the pitching rubber was moved back to 60 feet, six inches, only two major leaguers have pitched in 100 games and collected 1,500 hits.[2] Ruth (1914–1935) stroked 2,873 hits in his career and pitched in 163 games (94-46, 2.28 ERA). Seymour (1896–1913) got 1,723 hits and pitched in 140 games (61-56, 3.76 ERA).

Seymour's pitching career highlights include that 25-victory season with a league-leading 239 strikeouts in 1898, tops during the transition era of 1893–1900. In addition to his hitting crown in 1905, he led both leagues in hits (219) triples (21), RBIs (121), and slugging average (.559). He was second in home runs (8), one behind the leader,[3] and he led the National League in doubles (40). He also led the league and the majors in total bases (325), production (988), adjusted production (175), batter runs (64.7), and runs created (153).

Cy Seymour was a pitcher in the hitting era of the 1890s, and a hitter in a pitching era of the 1900s. Maybe this is why he is forgotten.[4]

"Balloonist" Makes Good

The 24-year-old Seymour began his professional career as a pitcher for Springfield of the Eastern League in 1896. He had been playing semipro ball in Plattsburg, New York, for a reported $1,000 a month.[5] (His good fortune in Plattsburg, if true, undoubtedly delayed his arrival to pro ball.)

His 8-1 record for Springfield earned him a shot with the New York Giants later that year. He won two games and lost four in eleven appearances.

In 1897, he was initially labelled a "balloonist" and an "aerialist" because he was prone to getting wild and excitable.[6] The *New York Times* cited him as "the youngster with a $10,000 arm and a $00.00 head."[7] But the left-hander gradually began to blossom as a major-league pitcher.[8] The *New York Herald* wrote at the end of the season that "Cy is rapidly improving, occasionally he gets a slight nervous chill, but by talking to himself with words of cheer and taking good self advice he lets the wobble pass away."[9]

Seymour's pitching featured a fast ball, a sharp-breaking curve, a screwball, and a wildness (he led the league in walks from 1897 through 1899) that must have induced a certain amount of terror into the 530 league batters that he struck out over the same period. Veteran catcher Wilbert "Uncle Robbie" Robinson said he had never seen anyone pitch like Cy, who would first throw near the batters' eyes and then near their toes, causing them "to not know whether their head or feet were in most danger"[10]

He compiled an 18-14 record with a 3.27 ERA for the third-place Giants (83-48, 9.5 games behind Boston).[11] He led the league in strikeouts per game (4.83) and fewest hits allowed per game (8.23), and he struck out 149 batters, second only to Washington's James "Doc" McJames (156). Batters hit only .242 against him—best in the league. This helped to offset his league-leading 164 walks.

Seymour's 1897 record indicates that he was becoming a peer of teammate and future Hall of Fame member Amos Rusie. Of the 21 pitching categories listing the top five performers in *Total Baseball*, he ranks first in four and second in another. Rusie is first in one category (ERA, 2.54), second in nine, third in one and fourth in one. Future Hall of Famer Kid Nichols of Boston clearly led the league, being first in 10 categories and in the top five in all but three.[12]

In 1898 Seymour improved his record to 25-19, dropping his ERA to 3.18 for the disgruntled seventh place Giants.[13] He led the league in strikeouts with a total of 239, 61 ahead of McJames. He again led the league in strikeouts per game (6.03). He also began to take the field when he wasn't pitching, primarily as an outfielder. As with Ruth 22 years later, the reason had little to do with managerial insight and more with a combination of injuries and the batting ineptitude of the Giants outfielders.[14]

Seymour hit .276 in 297 plate appearances, giving rise to speculation that he might be converted to a full-time outfielder despite the admonition by Wm. F. H. Koelsch in *Sporting Life*: "The suggestion that Seymour be placed in the outfield permanently is more than a rank proposition. As long as Seymour has the speed he has now he is more valuable on the slab than anywhere else."[15] Indeed, the Giants' management was faced with a dilemma. His 45 pitching appearances and his 356⅓ innings were vital. Yet the Giants were an anemic hitting squad that was being carried by the pitching of Rusie (who was also a good hitter) and Seymour.

Seymour's 25 wins in 1898 were nearly one-third of the New York team's total. He threw four shutouts (Nichols had five), two one-hitters, one three-hitter, four four-hitters, and six five-hitters.[16] Compare this with another 25-game winner in 1898. Cy Young threw one shutout, two three-hitters, and one five-hitter.[17] Some felt that he had supplanted Rusie as the ace of the Giants' pitching staff. The New York press said he had the best curve in the league, that "he could win with only five men behind him," and that he had as much speed as Rusie ever had.[18] He led the team in innings pitched, starts (43), and wins.[19] Naturally, he felt he could look forward to a handsome new contract for 1899. But Andrew Freedman stood in his way.

Freedman, a New York City subway financier and Tammany Hall politician, purchased the controlling interest in the Giants in 1895 for $54,000. He quickly antagonized just about everyone in baseball when he attempted to run the team as if it were part of Tammany Hall. He banned sportswriters who were critical of the Giants from the Polo Grounds. When those same reporters purchased a ticket, Freedman had them removed from the park.[20] Freedman regarded his team as a plaything and firmly believed that uppity players must always be put in their place.

In 1897 Rusie held out for the entire season rather than accept a $200 deduction in his 1896 salary for allegedly not giving his best in the concluding games of the season. He agreed to sign for 1898 only after a group of owners got together and paid his legal and "other" costs. Such actions, coupled with a losing team, engendered universal hostility from the world of baseball toward the Giants owner.[21]

Freedman saw no reason to reward either Seymour (25-19, 3.18 ERA) or Rusie (20-11, 3.03 ERA) for their 1898 performances. Rusie choose to retire.[22] Seymour held out for the first month of the season before signing for a $500 raise to $2,000 on May 11.[23] Playing for a dispirited Giants team that was to win only 60 of 150 games, he was able to compile a 14-18 record with an

ERA of 3.56. He finished second in the strikeout race with 142, three behind Noodles Hahn of Cincinnati. He led the league in strikeouts per game (4.76).

How Good a Pitcher?

His pitching career was, for all practical purposes, over. He made only 13 pitching appearances in 1900. Historian and SABR member David Q. Voigt has written that "Seymour was converted to an outfielder because of his penchant for free passes."[24] It is true that Seymour walked 655 batters and fanned 584 in his career, a deplorable ratio by today's standards. But it wasn't so bad in Cy's day. Rusie, for instance, struck out 1,934 batters in his career and walked 1,704. Doc McJames, who nipped Seymour for the strikeout crown in 1897 and finished a distant second to Cy in 1898, walked 563 and struck out 593 in his six years in the majors. Even the premier pitcher of the day, Kid Nichols, walked 854 and struck out 1,062 between 1892 and 1900.[25]

At the same time, Seymour held opposing batters to 67 points below the league average. Seymour's wildness was partially compensated by his superb ability to strike out batters and severely limit their hitting. It is likely that overwork, not wildness, ended his pitching career. He was, for three seasons, a member of that elite fraternity of outstanding pitchers.

Why, then, is his record unappreciated? Context. On the one hand, the lack of a foul strike rule kept league-leading strikeout totals lower than we are used to. On the other, walks weren't as damaging in an era when teams played for a single run as they are in our power-oriented time. A *Sporting Life* report of a 6–2, four-hit victory serves as an example of how Cy's wildness may have been used for positive results when it stated: "Seymour was wild at times, [but] was effective at critical moments."[26] Hall of Famer Elmer Flick maintained that the best pitcher he ever batted against, when he was right, was Seymour, who "was practically unhittable. Cy had a wonderful control of his curve ball."[27]

All players are subject to the limitations of the conventional wisdom of their particular era. An excellent relief pitcher today, for example, would have been nobody in particular 60 years ago.

Leaving the Mound

Cincinnati pitcher Ted Breitenstein warned Seymour not to continue using the indrop ball (screwball) because it would leave his arm "as dead as one of those mummies in the Art Museum."[28] Perhaps he injured his arm in spring training, 1900. At any rate, he found himself playing center field for the "second team" in an intra-squad contest a few days before the regular campaign began.[29] Two days before the opener, the *New York Times* indicated that "Manager Ewing will give particular attention to Seymour"[30] to decide if he would start it, since Rusie had failed to report.[31] However, Cy did not get his first start until the eighth day of the season, when he was shelled. He was lifted in the second inning after he gave up four runs, signaling that something was indeed wrong.

He started again in Chicago in the middle of May, but he couldn't find the plate and was shifted to center field after giving up ten runs in six innings. He collected two singles in the 10–8 loss. He started the next game, in St. Louis, in left field. He again hit safely twice, but also made two errors in a 13–5 defeat.[32] He then disappeared from the lineup except for a couple of mop-up appearances in which he was hit hard.[33] He won his first game of the season in early June, a 10–3 victory over St. Louis. Ironically, it was announced that very day that he was to be farmed out to Worcester, and that Chicago's Dick Cogan had been secured in a trade. Then, mysteriously, the *Times* reports that "Si [a frequent spelling in the press of the time] Seymour put in his appearance again at the Polo Grounds yesterday having been refused by the Worcester management as unfit. It is likely some deal will be fixed up for his retrading [*sic*] with Chicago."[34]

He ended up in Chicago, playing briefly with Charlie Comiskey's then minor-league AL entry. Suggestions were made that perhaps he would devote his time to playing the outfield, although one newspaper report blames "his prancing about in the gardens" (the outfield) as the primary reason for his lost pitching ability.[35] He even had time to pitch for the Schoharie Athletic Club against the Cuban X Giants on August 24.[36]

By the end of the season, Seymour was still on the Giants' reserve list as a pitcher, although Freedman was suspicious of his "habits" and demanded that manager Ewing discover exactly "what he is doing?"[37] "If there is not a change in him, and it is due to his habits, he will be laid off."[38]

This would not be the only time that Seymour's "habits" would be noted. There is little doubt that he was a drinker. We have at least one report of him being removed from a game because he was inebriated. It is known that he suffered from severe headaches.[39] Occasional reports of bizarre behavior find their way into the sporting pages, like the time he was mysteriously sent home from spring training in 1906 because it was simultaneously reported that, (a) he had a bad cold, (b) he needed to rest his tired muscles because the southern climate did not agree with him, and (c) he needed to attend his ill wife. Or the time he was coaching third base for the Orioles and tackled a runner who ran through his stop sign.

To McGraw and the Bat

By 1901 Seymour was no longer a pitcher, but had jumped to John McGraw's American League Baltimore Orioles to play right field. In two days in 1898 Seymour had started for the Giants and pitched three games against McGraw's old National League Orioles. He lost the first game in the Polo Grounds and the first game of a doubleheader the next day in Baltimore, both 2–1. He finally beat the Orioles in the second game, 6–2. McGraw, years later, said that no player, not even Joe McGinnity, deserved the title "Iron Man" more than Cy Seymour.[40] Perhaps it was this determination that convinced McGraw that Cy could be made into a good fielder.

The first seasons of the new century saw Seymour emerge as a star, batting .303 with the Orioles in 1901 and then, following the infamous breakup of the Baltimore team in 1902, going to Cincinnati, where he became the regular center fielder and hit .340 in 62 games. In the following years for the Reds, he hit .342, and .313, before leading the league with .377 in 1905.

He had to beat out the great Honus Wagner for the batting title, and the two met in a season-ending doubleheader. A newspaper account of the time sounds not unlike modern stories about Sosa and McGwire: "10,000 were more interested in the batting achievements of Wagner and Seymour than the games . . . cheer upon cheers greeted the mighty batsmen upon each appearance at the plate and mighty cheering greeted the sound of bat upon ball as mighty Cy drove out hit after hit. The boss slugger got 4 for 7 while Wagner could only get 2 for 7,"[41] allowing Cy to win the crown by .013 points.

He also led the league in hits, doubles, triples, total bases, RBIs, slugging average, and what we would now call Production, Batter Runs, and Runs Created. He was also a close second in home runs, runs produced, and on-base percentage. This was a benchmark season. His average was the best in the National League, 1901–1919. (In the American League only Lajoie and Cobb topped it.)[42] His slugging average of .559 was the best until Heinie Zimmerman's .571 in 1913. His 121 RBIs weren't exceeded again until Sherry Magee drove in 123 in 1910. His 40 doubles were the most hit by a National League outfielder until Pat Duncan collected 44 in 1922.

The first decade of the twentieth century brought the simultaneous development of "scientific baseball"[43] and deadball baseball. The hit-and-run play was the hallmark of the era. A standard practice of the day was for batters to move to the front of the batter's box in an attempt to slap the ball before it began to curve. Seymour eschewed this common practice, staying back in the box[44] and waving his bat around,[45] stating that it allowed him to "get that much more time to be sure which infielder is going to cover second base. A large portion of my base hits were made in this way."[46] He also used a wide variety of bats, depending on the pitcher. Contrary to conventional wisdom, he used a light bat when facing a location pitcher and a heavier one when he was up against a fireballer.[47]

Ned Hanlon, the Brooklyn manager, seemed to sense Cy's unorthodox approach, and said, "I look upon Seymour as the greatest straight ball player of the age, by that I mean he is absolutely all right if you let him play the game in his own way. But if you try to mix up any science on him you are likely to injure his effectiveness."[48]

Cy Seymour comparative offense 1901–1908

	AB	H	BA	2B	3B	HR	RBI
Wagner	4232	1478	.349	288	116	42	756
Seymour	4377	1361	.311	193	82	42	653
Crawford	4493	1391	.310	213	138	44	652
Flick	3811	1171	.307	186	121	26	485

In 1906, the *New York World* listed Cy, along with 10 other notables, such as Christy Mathewson, Ed Walsh, Honus Wagner, Nap Lajoie, and Roger Bresnahan as the best in baseball.[49] Even in 1909, when he became a part-time player, his .311 average left him atop all the reserve players in the league. Take a look at this comparison of offensive figures taken 1901–1908. Seymour is the only non-Hall of Famer listed.[50] From 1901 through 1908 (excluding 1902),[51] Seymour consistently ranked among the league's best offensive players. In 20 categories, he ranked no less than fifth 41 times of a possible 140 (29 percent).[52] Wagner dominated with 111 of the possible 140 (79 percent). Flick was 62 of 140 (44 percent).[53] In contrast, future Hall of Fame third baseman Jimmy Collins was to make the leader category only 19 times (13.5 percent).[54]

Cy Seymour wasn't Babe Ruth, but some comparisons are interesting.

- Each led his league in holding opponents to lowest batting average: Seymour 1897, .242; Ruth 1916, .201.
- Seymour won 25 games in 1898; Ruth won 24 in 1917 and 23 in 1916.
- Each had an 18-game-winning season: Seymour 1897; Ruth 1915.
- Seymour led league in strikeouts (1898); Ruth never did.
- Seymour led league in giving up walks three times; Ruth never did.
- Ruth placed within top five places of league-leading pitcher categories 25 times 1915–1917; Seymour placed 10 times from 1897–1899. (Twelve major-league teams, 1897–1899; twenty-four, 1915; sixteen, 1916–1917.)
- Each won one batting championship: Seymour 1905, .377; Ruth 1924, .378.
- Triple Crown eluded both by the slimmest of margins: Seymour in 1905 was one shy of home run title; Ruth in 1924 was second in RBIS, eight behind Goose Goslin, and in 1926 was .006 behind Heinie Manush for the batting title.
- Seymour stole 222 bases; Ruth 123.
- Ruth led league in RBIS six times; Seymour once.
- Ruth led league in home runs 12 times, but never led league in doubles, triples, or hits; Seymour never led league in HRS but led once each in doubles, triples, and hits.
- Fielding Runs rating: Seymour +81; Ruth +5.

The End of the Line

John McGraw is generally credited with the hiring of baseball's first full-time coach, Arlie Latham. A longtime friend and former Oriole teammate of McGraw, Latham owed his good fortune indirectly at least to Seymour, and, conversely, Arlie was to impact Cy's career.

In the days prior to the hiring of a full-time coach, players took to the coach's box. Seymour was coaching one day when Harry McCormick attempted to stretch a triple into a home run and ran through Cy's hold-up sign. This is when Cy tackled his own teammate. The surprised McCormick scrambled to his feet and was still able to score. When McGraw confronted Seymour about his bizarre behavior, Cy offered a feeble excuse about the sun being in his eyes. From that moment on, according to Christy Mathewson, McGraw realized the need for a full-time coach.[55]

Latham was, in the opinion of Fred Snodgrass, "probably the worst third-base coach who ever lived,"[56] and seemed to ingratiate himself with McGraw with a variety of practical jokes apparently designed in the now time-honored belief that such measures keep a bench loose. During spring training in 1909, Cy took exception to a Latham prank and beat him up, causing McGraw to suspend Seymour from the team for eight weeks.[57]

In his first game back, Seymour received a career-altering injury in the first inning. Chasing a long fly ball, he collided heavily with his right-field teammate, Red Murray, and lay motionless for five minutes. He appeared to have recovered, and he resumed his position in center field. He caught a fly off the bat of the next Boston batter, but when he tried to throw the ball home (there was a runner on third) he collapsed. He had to be carried off the field.[58] The injury to his leg, according to Mathewson, curtailed his effectiveness for the remainder of his career.[59] Exactly two months after the injury he was able to play a few innings in left field in a game in Brooklyn,[60] but speedy Cy (he averaged 20 steals per year) was never the same player after the accident.

Why Forgotten?

Aside from the daily newspaper accounts and the sporting trade papers, little has been written about Seymour.[61] A brief survey of the literature reveals that he was, according to Christy Mathewson, one of the best "batsmen" ever. Alas, he was also a wild pitcher, and there is a dubious claim that he was a poor fielder. This is largely the result of his losing a fly in the sun during the one-game playoff between the Giants and the Cubs in 1908. The misplay allowed three runners to score.

The myth was that Mathewson, just prior to pitching to Joe Tinker, had turned and motioned Seymour to play deeper[62] and that Seymour refused to move. Mathewson always denied this, saying that Cy "knew the Chicago batters as well as I did and how to play them"[63] Mathewson also admitted that day that he "never had less on the ball in my life," and that Cy would have caught the fly 49 times out of 50.[64] In the clubhouse after the game Cy said to Matty: "I misjudged the ball. I'll take the blame for it." And abuse he took; sportswriters looking for an easy story took full advantage of his supposed refusal to take direction from the demigod Mathewson.

Seymour certainly was not a good fielding pitcher, committing 104 of his lifetime 252 errors on the mound. Yet it is hard to believe that John McGraw, his manager both in Baltimore and New York, would have put him in center field if he felt Seymour was a liability. In fact, in 1904 *Sporting Life* claimed that he "is as speedy and graceful as ever in centre field and covers a world of ground out there more than any other centre fielder in the National League."[65] Frank Selee, the Chicago manager called Seymour "a marvel and a pleasure to watch," and was amazed at his range and ability to backpedal.[66] In 1907 he made a spectacular diving barehanded catch that was widely reported to have been the best ever seen in New York City.

A comparison to some of his contemporaries indicates that he was a better than average center fielder. His *Total Baseball* Fielding Runs is +58. Compare that to Cobb's +55, Tommy Leach's +53, and Fred Clarke's +61. Then compare it to Elmer Flick's +24, "Circus"[67] Solly Hofman's +28, Dummy Hoy's +3, and Socks Seybold's +1, not to mention Ginger Beaumont's-26 or Mike Donlin's-31.

Of all the regular center fielders[68] playing in the National League in 1907 and 1908 only one, Roy Thomas, had a better lifetime rating, +71, than Seymour. Making an error at an inopportune time seems to have established Seymour as a poor fielder despite conclusive evidence to the contrary, a condition that Bill Buckner (+121) would undoubtedly understand.

Many have attempted the impossible task of compiling lists of the best players ever. Some are the all-time versions which are usually laden with recent performers; others attempt to categorize them according to specific eras. Almost no one mentions Seymour. David Voigt does include Seymour along with Turkey Mike Donlin and Buck Freeman as players passed over for Hall of Fame consideration in the 1895–1900 era. During that particular era he was primarily a pitcher and for three of those years he ranked among the best in baseball. Yet he had the dubious privilege of pitching in an era when league batters were hitting at a rate of .282 (1897–1899). Then, in turn, he batted in the Deadball Era (1900–1908) when batters for the entire National League averaged but .256. His peak batting career average was .054 above his league's average for the 1901–1908 period, almost identical to that of Crawford (.052) and Flick (.058) His league leading .377 was .122 above the National League average in 1905. This differential would not be topped in the National League until Rogers Hornsby's stupendous mark of .424 in 1924 (.151 above league average).

Personality

It is difficult to assess Seymour's personality from the snippets of data available. Veteran catcher Duke Farrell relates an explosive emotional experience when Cy first started to pitch for the Giants. In Chicago the rookie pitcher was sailing along effectively until the eighth inning when he suddenly became very wild. He gave up nine runs and in the parlance of the day "ascended into the air." His cheeks turned red, he threw his hat off after a bad pitch, then threw his glove away after another. "Finally," Farrell states, "Cy was worked up to such a state that after making a pitch he would run to the plate and grab the ball out of my hands, hustle back and without waiting for my sign shoot it back . . . Nine Chicago runners crossed the plate [before the inning was over] . . . Seymour subsequently had many aerial flights, but nothing like his Chicago performance."[69]

He was not only excitable and high strung, he dressed differently than his teammates and apparently was aloof. All characteristics that would give some fans, sportswriters, and ballplayers the chance to jeer him at the first opportunity.

There is one well-reported incident of him being removed from a game because he was inebriated. A follow-up report suggested, however, that the incident was isolated and that he then played like "a whirlwind."[70] Another said: "J. Bentley Seymour by his good batting is more than making amends to the Reds management for his one jag."[71] In another incident the *Cincinnati Post* complained to the Reds owner, August Herrmann, that Seymour threatened a photographer from the *Post*.[72] Reports by Mrs. McGraw and Hans Lobert[73] indicate that Seymour was a hard-playing, hard-drinking player. One might therefore surmise he was subjected to alcoholic binges and leave it at that.

On the other hand, I think that he saw himself as different. In a world that was determined to be right-handed he was very much left-handed. Conventional wisdom of the day often forced left-handed school children to write with their right hands. Similarly baseball, at the time, could not see left-handed pitchers to be equal to right-handed ones. He was unorthodox; his pitching and his hitting were contrary to the norms of the day.

Seymour seemed sensitive about his name, and came in for a good deal of chiding because he insisted that he was related to the Duke of Somerset.[74] He apparently insisted upon being called J. Bentley or James Bentley rather than the nickname Cy (for Cyclone) that New York sportswriters gave him. He had at least three publicized altercations during his career—an offseason brawl with the ballplaying brothers Jesse and Lee Tannehill,[75] the Latham affair, and a punch-up with Cincinnati pitcher teammate Henry

Thielman during an exhibition game in Indianapolis. Thielman, according to the report, "kidded" Seymour about his name.[76]

On the other hand, he was apparently the person who applied the nickname "Tillie" to Arthur Shafer. Mrs. McGraw reports that in 1909, when her husband introduced the shy, good looking and young Shafer to the Giants in the Polo Grounds clubhouse, "Big Cy Seymour, an Oriole in word and deed, responded first with 'We're all damned glad to meet you Tillie!' Then came the chorus! 'Yes sir Tillie, glad to see you. Yes sir Tillie, glad to see you. Make yourself home, Tillie! Good Luck, Tillie . . . Save Your Money Tillie . . . Get the last bounce Tillie.'"[77] Another report of the same incident has Seymour rushing over to Shafer and planting a kiss on Shafer's cheeks saying "Tillie, how are you?" Shafer hated the nickname, but it stuck with him.[78]

Perhaps this incident, coupled with the Latham episode, paved the way for Seymour's departure to obscurity,[79] and may be one of the reasons that John McGraw never mentions Seymour in his book *My Thirty Years in Baseball*.

Yet while Seymour was playing for Baltimore of the Eastern League in 1911, an opponent, former major leaguer Bobby Vaughn, said that he still had the best batting eye of anyone in baseball. Certainly an exaggeration, but the 39-year-old did hit .296 that year, and one is left to speculate that McGraw and others may have chosen not to employ Cy because of his peculiar personality traits. Vaughn lavishly praised Cy, but then curiously adds: "Many think him a shirker but he is not . . . Seymour is a conscientious ball player whatever else may be said."[80]

He was also plagued by headaches. In the winter of 1904–1905 he sought nasal surgery in an effort to solve his problem.[81] Migraines? Occasionally he would exhibit strange behavior, like the morning that he decided to take on a lion at the Zoo. Mental illness? Some reports later said he was drunk, which was probably so, but he would not have been the first person to use alcohol as a cover-up of other problems.

On the other hand, there are reports that Seymour was "as straight and clean as the Bank of England,"[82] and unlike some other players, he never took advantage of owner Garry Hermann's generosity. Hermann attended Seymour's wedding,[83] added $100 a month to Cy's $2,800 contract when he arrived from Baltimore, and arranged an offseason "job" which according to a newspaper report required him to do little more than walk the streets clad "in swell clothes."

Cy certainly seemed the dandy. Sprinkled throughout the Seymour scrapbooks that reside in the Hall of Fame Library in Cooperstown are accounts and pictures, some of them mocking, about Cy's sartorial splendor. Like many athletes, then and today, he often seemed to take himself too seriously. Be it his dress, or his insistence that he be referred to as J. Bentley[84] rather than Cy, or his reluctance to be photographed, he seemed very much the prima donna.

The 1906 sale of Seymour from the Reds to the Giants for $10,000 was one of the largest in baseball history.[85] After playing but one game for the Giants in which he made a sensational catch—he demanded that he receive a portion of the $10,000 that he insisted Garry Herrmann, the Reds owner, had promised him if the sale was completed. Herrmann denied that a promise had been made. Cy threatened to go on strike. John McGraw was able to convince Seymour to reconsider, and Organized Baseball may have avoided a precedent similar to professional soccer, in which a player transferred from one club to another receives a percentage of the transfer fee.[86]

Seymour was not devoid of humor. Upon his first return to Cincinnati in a Giants uniform after the trade, he wore bright red false whiskers as a disguise that allowed him to receive front page headlines in the *Cincinnati Post*. Descending from the team carriage the bewhiskered Cy announced to the multitude "Cy Seymour I am pained to relate, ladies and gentlemen, is not coming to the park today. He is afraid that the Cincinnati fans will lynch him." When he grounded out his first time at bat he was jeered and cheered by the local fans.[87]

Typical of aging stars of the day, Cy played minor-league ball in 1911 and 1912, for Baltimore and Newark. A newspaper report of his release in Baltimore stated that "although he played good ball his habits were such that it was decided that he would no longer play on the team."[88] Apparently able to correct himself, he was to make it, briefly and unsuccessfully, back to the majors with the Boston Braves in 1913.

The only remaining correspondence[89] written by Seymour are two job enquiries made to Herrmann regarding managerial positions in 1913 or thereabouts. A letter written on November 28, 1913, gives some insight into the character of the man. He saw himself as a loner, but capable of making managerial decisions without being influenced by the press or hangers-on.

His letter also suggests that he may have been regarded as an odd character, because he told Herrmann: "I may seem funny to you the way you know me. I am different on the inside than on the out & I know if I had half a chance

I will make good. I am not much of a talker & [don't] go around talking about myself."[90] On the other hand, his letter suggests that Herrmann be wary of baseball writers' opinions, and is bold enough to say: "I am going to give you a tip now and always remember it. It takes [two] to run a ball club. The manager and yourself."[91] What Herrmann thought of the tip we cannot be certain, except that Cy did not get the job and found himself, at age 41, effectively out of Organized Baseball.

Seymour apparently contracted tuberculosis while working in the ship-yards of New York during the First World War. He died in New York City on September 20, 1919. His death was overshadowed by the talk of the World Series involving Cincinnati and the now-infamous Black Sox. One obituary claimed that he worked on the docks because he was unfit for military ser-vice.[92] Yet he was able to play 13 games for Newark in the International League during the 1918 season, when he was 46 years old. It might be assumed that he was an alcoholic; he was also rumored to have been penniless.[93]

Sporting Life said of Seymour "that he was one of the most brilliant though erratic pitchers the game ever produced."[94] Christy Mathewson said that he "was a mighty batsman . . . one of the best ever."[95] John McGraw thought he deserved the title of "Ironman." Former slick-fielding second baseman turned sportswriter Sam Crane wrote in the *New York Journal* that Seymour "proved himself to be one of the best outfielders in every department" and that Cy "put to rest the notion that pitchers could not hit well."[96] Now he is all but forgotten—the victim of being a pitcher in a hitters' era and a hitter in the Deadball Era. His burial was a simple one: his boyhood chums acted as pallbearers, and although a large throng attended the service, no one from Organized Baseball did.[97] A search of the rural cemetery in his home town of Albany, New York, serves as a final irony. He is buried in the family plot, but no stone marks the accomplishments of the second most versatile player that the game has ever known.[98]

NOTES

1. Thanks to Tom Ruane for this information. He reports that 13,561 have played ball from 1893 until through the 1998 season.
2. David Nemec, *Great Baseball, Feats, Facts & Firsts* (New York: Signet Sports, 1989), 331.
3. See *Total Baseball*, 3rd ed., edited by John Thorn and Pete Palmer (New York: Harp-erCollins, 1993), 1932–33.

4. Prior to 1893 Al Spalding (252 wins and 613 hits), Hoss Radbourne (309 wins and 585 hits) Scott Stratton (97 wins and 379 hits) posted significant pitching and hitting records, yet none of them had two distinctive careers. Only the great John Montgomery Ward (164 wins and 2,105 hits) was able to challenge the accomplishments of Ruth and Seymour. And although Ward played until 1894, he was an infielder for the last ten years of his playing career. Thanks to Larry Gerlach for pointing this out to me.

5. See the *Albany* (NY) *Times-Union*, September 21, 1919. An unusually large salary considering that he only made $2,000 playing for the Giants in 1899! The report indicates that the Northern New York League was supported by millionaire sportsman, Harry Payne Whitney. Prior to playing in the NNYL he played for the Ridgeway team in his hometown of Albany, New York.

6. *Seymour Scrapbook*, 1896. These eight volumes, which are housed at the Hall of Fame Library, Cooperstown, New York, contain comprehensive press clippings of Cy's career apparently compiled by his mother or father, arranged in a fastidious chronological order that is only marred by the fact that the names and dates of publications of the clippings have been eliminated by the compiler. My guess is that his father, Theodore, was the compiler. Correspondence from a Baltimore publisher is addressed to him. Thus, future reference to the scrapbooks shall read as, e.g., HOF SB 1897, except when the exact date or name of the publication is known.

7. *New York Times*, September 5, 1897.

8. The *New York Times* report does not jibe with Amos Rusie's view. Rusie took Seymour under his wing in Cy's rookie season and reported that Seymour was "a willing youngster and a good pupil," See Amos Rusie file, HOF, "Fireball Rusie . . . Tells How He Held Out."

9. *New York Herald*, September 19, 1897.

10. "Cy Seymour's Pitching Arm," HOF SB, July 27, 1898. Sam Crane, among others seemed to think his small hands was an important factor causing his wildness.

11. *Total Baseball* has him at 18-14 while Bill Weiss's stats have him at 20-14. Personal correspondence, Weiss to Kirwin, November 1998.

12. See page 1920 of *Total Baseball*, 3rd Ed.

13. Again, Weiss has him at 25-17.

14. Boston manager Ed Barrow once said: "I would be the laughing stock of the league if I took the best pitcher in the league (Ruth) and put him in the outfield." See Jonathan Fraser Light, *The Cultural Encyclopedia of Baseball* (Jefferson NC: McFarland, 1997), 579.

15. *Sporting Life*, October 15, 1898.

16. A typical 1898 victory saw Cy throw a four-hitter and collect two hits and score one run himself in a 6–2 win over Cleveland on May 30th, striking out seven and issuing as many walks.

17. Nichols had five shutouts, one three-hitter, one four-hitter and six five-hitters.

18. HOF SB 1898.

19. He also again led the league in walks with 213.

20. James D. Hardy Jr., *The New York Giants Baseball Club, The Growth of a Team and A Sport, 1870–1900* (Jefferson NC: McFarland, 1996), 157–61.

21. Seymour himself experienced Freedman's parsimony when as a rookie he was fined $10 for leaving a ticket booth that he was occasionally required to man in order that he might watch his teammates play!

22. He did return to major-league baseball in 1901 to pitch in three games for Cincinnati. In exchange for Rusie, Cincinnati sent the Giants an obscure young pitcher—Christy Mathewson.

23. *New York Times*, May 12, 1899. It is of note that Freedman said a year earlier he would not trade Seymour for $10,000.

24. David Quentin Voigt, *The League That Failed* (Lanham MD: Scarecrow Press, 1998), 123.

25. Cy Young, of course, was a notable exception: although his won-loss record (72-48 vs. 57-51) was not radically different from Seymour's during the 1897–99 seasons, Young walked only 134 batters during the three years in question, seventy-nine fewer than Cy during the 1898 campaign alone! On the other hand, Young, who had won the strikeout crown in 1896, only managed to strike out 300 batters from 1897–99 while Seymour struck out 534 in the same period.

26. *Sporting Life*, June 4, 1898.

27. HOF SB 1902. Flick added, "I have asked many baseball players who batted against him the days past, and they all agreed that he was the star of them all when in condition."

28. HOF SB 1898.

29. *New York Times*, April 8, 1900.

30. *New York Times*, April 17, 1900.

31. *New York Times*, April 19, 1900.

32. *New York Times*, May 16 and 18, 1900.

33. *New York Times*, May 19 and 29, 1900.

34. *New York Times*, June 12, 1900; see also June 8, 1900.

35. HOF SB 1900.

36. HOF SB 1900.

37. Historian Bob Hoie hypothesizes that Seymour probably injured his arm or attempted to take something off his pitches to improve his control and that the Giants merely suspended him because of his arm problems. Personal correspondence, Hoie to Kirwin, December 28, 1998. Also, David Voigt in personal correspondence reflects a changed opinion regarding the pitching demise of Seymour, now believing that it probably had more to do with his arm problems than wildness. Personal correspondence, Voigt to Kirwin, undated, 1998.

38. Andrew Freedman to William Ewing, May 21, 1900; see James Bentley, "Cy" Seymour file, HOF.

39. *Sporting Life*, "The Disappearance of 'Cy,'" March 11, 1905.

40. See HOF Seymour file clipping "Cy Seymour's Iron Man." See also *New York Times*, October 13, 1898. McGraw thought the games were in 1896 or '97 and that the second game of the doubleheader was a shutout. In 1897 Seymour pitched both games of a doubleheader win against Louisville.

41. HOF SB 1905.

42. Lajoie hit .426 in 1901 and .384 in 1910. Cobb equaled Seymour's .377 in 1909 and batted .383 in 1910.

43. The uses of the bunt, hit-and-run, Baltimore chop, and cutoff man were developed by Baltimore manager Ned Hanlon.

44. Bob Rothgeber, "When Hitting Became a Science," *Cincinnati Reds Scrapbook* (Virginia Beach VA: JCP, 1982), 36.

45. *Sporting Life*, January 6, 1906.

46. Rothgeber, "When Hitting Became a Science."

47. Rothgeber, "When Hitting Became a Science."

48. HOF SB 1905.

49. *New York World*, September 22, 1906. The other five were Art Devlin, Giants; George Stone, St. Louis Americans; Johnny Kling, Chicago Nationals; Hal Chase, New York Highlanders; and Rube Waddell, A's.

50. Almost as an afterthought, Seymour was added to the Cincinnati Reds Hall of Fame in 1998. Most of the media attention of that day focused on Tony Perez, who was also inducted.

51. During the 1902 season he ranked high in both RBIS and HRS in the combined league totals. See Top-Five Leading Categories.

52. If one wanted to stretch the case, the claim could be made that Seymour had the fourth highest number of home runs in 1904. The number is correct; however, six players had more home runs that he did. A similar case could be argued for 1906 triples. I choose the more rigid interpretation of including only the top five players wherever possible.

53. Since 1907 was Flick's last year as a regular player, the 1900 season, his second best in category leadership (14) was used for comparison purposes. In 1902 his name does not appear in any of the categories. In the 1901–1907 seasons Flick's category dropped to 34 percent.

54. 1897–1904, excluding the 1902 season when he only played in 108 games.

55. Christy Mathewson, *Pitching in a Pinch* (Lincoln NE: Bison Books, reprint 1988), 120–21.

56. Charles C. Alexander, *John McGraw* (Lincoln NE: Bison Books, reprint 1988), 143.

57. *New York Times*, April 27, 1909.

58. *New York Times*, April 27, 1909

59. Mathewson, *Pitching in a Pinch*, 135–36.

60. *New York Times*, June 26, 1909.

61. Even that his sale of 1906 from the Reds to the Giants for $10,000 (some reports claim it was $12,000) was one of the largest in baseball history up until that time has been ignored.

62. See Rube Marquard, *The Life and Legend of a Baseball Hall of Famer* (Jefferson NC: McFarland, 1998), 5l.

63. Mathewson, *Pitching in a Pinch*, 186.

64. Mathewson, *Pitching in a Pinch*, 186–88.

65. "National League News," *Sporting Life*, June 18, 1904.

66. Seymour HOF SB 1902.

67. Arthur Frederick Hofman was well known for his circus catches and was named after a comic strip character. See James A. Skipper, *Baseball Nicknames* (Jefferson NC: McFarland, 1992), 127.

68. See *Total Baseball*, 3rd Ed., 2327–30. Does not include players who did not play at least 300 games in the outfield.

69. HOF SB 1903, "Seymour's Airship."

70. *Sporting Life*, August 15, 1903. Another report, probably in a Cincinnati newspaper, said that he had called in claiming he was sick when in fact he was drunk, requiring him to miss several games. The record indicates that he played in 135 of the 141 games the Reds played that year.

71. *Sporting Life*, August 29, 1901.

72. Ray Long to August Hermann, Seymour HOF file, January 31, 1906.

73. Lawrence Ritter, *The Glory of Their Times: The Story of the Early Days of Baseball— Told by the Men Who Played It* (New York: Vintage, 1985), 192.

74. "Seymour the Straight," Seymour HOF file, November 17, 1906.

75. Reported, apparently, in the Albany *Times Union* in 1903, citing a Cincinnati dispatch stating that Seymour walked away unmarked from a battle with the two Tannehill brothers. They in turn both required hospital assistance. See HOF SB 1903.

76. *Sporting Life*, October 11, 1902.

77. Mrs. John J. McGraw and Arthur Mann, *The Real McGraw* (New York: David McKay, 1951), 227. Thanks to Darryl Brock for this source.

78. James K. Skipper Jr., *Baseball Nicknames: A Dictionary of Origins and Meanings* (Jefferson NC: McFarland, 1992), 252.

79. Ironically Fred Snodgrass, who was to soon replace Cy as the Giants regular center fielder, was also introduced that day.

80. HOF Seymour file, "Bobby Vaughn Talks of Cy's Batting Eye."

81. "The Disappearance of Cy," *Sporting Life*, March 11, 1905.

82. "Seymour the Straight," Seymour HOF file, November 17, 1906.

83. *Sporting Life*, December 27, 1902.

84. He picked up the name Cy when he first arrived in New York. The name referring to his pitching style derived from the word "cyclone," and was a rather common sobriquet applied to pitchers of the day. He may have wanted to put his pitching

days behind when he resisted being called Cy, yet on the other hand it may have been simply to clarify the fact that he was not a Jew. A letter to the *New York Globe* asks "is Seymour a Hebrew or an Irishman?" and receives the following answer, "He is an American of English descent."

85. Some reports indicated that it was $12,000.

86. Seymour certainly seemed to be not unaware of the upcoming sale, openly saying to the press, "Tell 'em I'm going away." Whether by design or preoccupation, his indifferent play prior was reflected in his .257 batting average.

87. HOF SB 1906, *Cincinnati Post*, August 25, 1906.

88. HOF SB 1908. This scrapbook contains several items after 1908.

89. See "Cy Seymour in Disgrace," SSB 1903.

90. Seymour to Hermann, HOF File, November 28, 1913.

91. Seymour to Hermann, HOF File, November 28, 1913.

92. *New York Times*, September 22, 1919.

93. Rothgeber, "When Hitting Became a Science," 37.

94. *Sporting Life*, June 17, 1905.

95. Christy Mathewson, "'Outguessing' the Batter," *Pearsons Magazine*, May 1911.

96. HOF SB 1902.

97. *Albany Times-Union*, September 23, 1919.

98. Albany Rural Cemetery visit, June 5, 1999. Thanks to John Buszta for his help.

SOURCES

In addition to the sources cited in the notes, the author also consulted:

Demaree, Al. "Tough Customers." *Collier's*, May 14, 1927.

Hertzel, Bob. "Baseball's Hall of Blunders." *Baseball Digest*, January 1973.

Mathewson, Christy. "'Outguessing' the Batter." *Pearson's Magazine* (American Edition), May 1911.

———. *Pitching in A Pinch: Baseball from the Inside*. Lincoln: University of Nebraska Press, 1994.

Rothgeber, Bob. "When Hitting Became a Science: Cy Seymour." In *Cincinnati Reds Scrapbook* (Virginia Beach VA: JCP, 1982).

25

Free Agency in 1923

A Shocker for Baseball

STEVE STEINBERG

Steve Steinberg turned to baseball research only after he sold his family's apparel business in 1998, and he quickly became one of the leading researchers on early twentieth-century baseball. Among several books and dozens of articles, he co-wrote *1921: The Yankees, the Giants, and the Battle for Baseball Supremacy in New York* in 2010 with Lyle Spatz, which was awarded SABR's Seymour Medal. Of all his many thorough and lively research efforts, the one he was drawn to first was the life of Urban Shocker. This article tells of a small episode in the life of that colorful baseball pitcher. His biography *Urban Shocker: Silent Hero of Baseball's Golden Age* was published by the University of Nebraska Press (2017).

Urban Shocker is one of baseball's forgotten stars, even though he was one of the American League's dominant pitchers in the 1920's. He won 156 games in that decade, mostly with the lowly St. Louis Browns, despite the fact that his last decision was in 1927. After going 37-17 for the great 1926–1927 New York Yankees, Shocker died of heart disease in 1928.

Even more forgotten is Shocker's challenge of the reserve system and his fight for free agency, a matter that became the cause celebre of the 1923 winter baseball meetings. Ultimately, Shocker did not win his bid for freedom, but he shook the very foundation of baseball. The incident precipitated a showdown between Commissioner Landis and the owners of baseball that almost ended Landis's reign a mere three years after it began.

The triggering event was straightforward, though unusual in the days when the ballplayer's wife's role was in the home. On the final St. Louis Browns road trip in September 1923, Shocker wanted to take his wife along. Shocker's nephew Roger Shockcor (the original spelling of Urban's last name, before he changed it to simplify matters for reporters) remembered that Urban's wife Irene loved to be "a part of the action." The response of the Browns was swift and clear: They had a well-established rule that wives did not go on road trips. (Some teams, like the Giants, Reds, and White Sox, allowed wives on trips, while others, like the Pirates and Tigers, did not.[1]) When Shocker did not head east, he was fined $1,000 and suspended by the team.

The Sporting News was very much on the side of management, saying the rule was "justified by experience, and for the general good of a team on the road."[2] TSN editorial writer John Sheridan wrote that one of the great values of baseball was "no outsider can help a baseball player in this game of rugged individualism." The logic was a bit unclear, as the *St. Louis Post-Dispatch* wrote, "A tactical blunder appears to have been made, since the presence of a player's wife on a trip certainly should contribute to his good conduct, if he is the least inclined to waywardness."[3]

Shocker felt his personal liberty had been infringed upon, since the team was interfering with his family affairs. On September 27, he asked to be declared a free agent, since the team had voided his contract by suspending him. The *New York Times* wrote on December 4, just before the winter meetings began, "stripped of its legal verbiage, the case simmered down to the question of whether a club had the right to discipline a player as it saw fit."

Commissioner Kenesaw Mountain Landis was the wild card in this dispute once Shocker appealed the case to his office. Hired by the owners in 1920 after the Black Sox scandal (in which the Chicago White Sox "threw" the 1919 World Series), Landis had shown indications that he could not be counted on to rule in the owners' favor in disputes with players. During his long reign, he would surprise the owners with his natural affinity for players in their contract struggles with management. AP reported on December 30 that Landis was reluctant to take a position that might cause the players to feel they were, in effect, "baseball slaves," as was asserted in the Federal League suit against organized Baseball.[4] Years later, Leo Durocher said, "He was always on the side of the ball player. He had no use for the owners at all."[5] Maverick owner Bill Veeck wrote that Landis admonished players, "Don't go to those owners if you get into trouble, come to me. I'm your friend. They're no good." During the December 1923 meetings, Landis explained his support of the underdog: "When he [the player] comes into court against a club owner, he sometimes is not adequately represented."[6]

In November 1923, *The Sporting News* was clearly worried. "One can never tell what stand Landis will take. He is quite capable of assuming arbitrary jurisdiction in the Shocker case." Landis did just that, which TSN declared, would cause "the fur to fly."[7] Shocker then strongly intimated he'd go to court if the case went against him, challenging the Reserve Rule, which would open the door for a legal fight that might shake baseball to its foundation.

In the meantime, the new manager of the Browns, the great first baseman George Sisler, entertained trade offers for his unhappy player. In the first four years of the Lively Ball Era, Shocker was the winningest pitcher in baseball, going 91-51 (.641) on a team that won only 53% of its games. So it was not surprising that many teams inquired about Shocker. The *New York World*, for example, reported that the Yankees offered future Hall of Famer Waite Hoyt. The Yankees had been trying to get Shocker back for years, ever since they traded him in January 1918. The trade, in which Shocker was a last-minute throw-in, was Miller Huggins' first major action as Yankee manager and one of the few mistakes the Yankees made as they built their powerhouse team.

The backdrop to the Winter Meetings was the ongoing battle between Judge Landis and American League President Ban Johnson. On December 10, the *Post-Dispatch* headline shouted "American League Reportedly Ready to Withdraw If Landis Decides Shocker Case Against Browns. Man High in the Councils of Organized Baseball Tells Sports Editor Wray that Owners Will Refuse to Accept Verdict in Favor of St. Louis Pitcher." On December 11, Wray wrote, "Landis is a friend at court for all ball players—and it may cost him his official hand."[8] That very day Landis, ever the tactician, postponed a decision until after the meetings. But he was still on the offensive. On December 12, as the meetings opened Landis made a preemptive move, denouncing Johnson and threatening "any time you [the owners] assert by your votes that I am not wanted, that moment I will tear up that contract."[9] The AL owners quickly fell into line behind Landis, giving him a sweeping victory. It was Yankee owner Colonel Jacob Ruppert who rose in support of Landis and rallied the owners. "Ruppert's Speech Kept Landis in Baseball," declared the headline in the *World*. Johnson's biographer, Eugene Murdock, felt that this showdown was the turning point in Landis's baseball career, when he truly solidified his power base.[10]

On January 18, 1924, just days before Landis's hearing (which had been postponed to late January), Urban Shocker surprisingly withdrew his plea to be declared a free agent and had his case against the club dismissed. Red Sox President Bob Quinn, who was the Browns' business manager earlier in the 1923 season, helped persuade Shocker to accept the settlement. Credit was also given to new Browns manager George Sisler, whose close friendship with Shocker played a role. Before the winter meetings ended, Sisler had telegrammed Browns Business Manager Bill Friel that he wanted to keep Shocker, and the Browns then took Shocker off the trading block. When asked if Shocker would remain a Brown, Ball said, "That is strictly up to George Sisler. There will be absolutely no interference from the business office."[11]

But the key figure behind the scenes was AL President Ban Johnson. On January 23, 1924, the *Globe-Democrat* reported that Johnson, acting as duly appointed proxy by the Browns, signed Shocker to a 1924 contract. On January 31, 1924, *The Sporting News* reported that he had intervened with Quinn, to avert a situation that might have forced the league to walk away from Landis and operate independently. Attorneys for both Shocker and the Browns said report of the settlement was news to them. Even owner Phil Ball, a close friend and ardent supporter of the league president, said he knew nothing, but he had received a wire from Johnson that the case had been settled. Ball's support for Johnson was boundless. In 1926 he would tell the *New York Sun*, "I am with Ban Johnson, first, last, and always."[12]

The *Post-Dispatch* reported that Johnson protected Ball's feelings by letting the fine stand and protected Shocker by substantially raising his salary to reimburse him for the $1,000 fine (January 23, 1924). Exactly what financial incentives were given to Shocker to settle can only be speculated upon. But he said he was completely satisfied and treated better than he anticipated. "If everyone had friends like him [Bob Quinn], there wouldn't be any enemies in this world. Manager Sisler can count on me to pitch my head off once the season starts."[13]

Baseball owners breathed a collective sigh of relief. Back on December 4, Irving Vaughn of the *Chicago Tribune*, saw the explosiveness of this case: "more than a mere dispute between player and club. It involves points that threaten the whole structure of organized baseball, and Landis realizes this." George Daley, sports editor of the *World*, wrote that Landis was saved "from making a decision on a most delicate question." *The Sporting News* summarized the closure this way: "The temperamental and probably ill-advised player had refused to admit the errors of his ways, to take his punishment. Shocker escaped the full consequences of his rank insubordination, but better that than the possible—nay probable—consequences of a decision by Commissioner Landis subversive of club rights and league sovereignty."[14]

Just how Landis would have ruled in this fundamental case can only be surmised, but his "tendency to give the players a chance" almost precipitated fireworks "that would make the Last Days of Pompeii look like a wet match."[15]

It is not surprising that during these winter meetings, all 16 baseball owners made a secret agreement to incorporate into standard player contracts a clause that required the player to abide by all present and future team rules, for the purpose of discipline.[16]

The Baseball Hall of Fame is starting the huge process of cataloguing Commissioner Landis's papers. When "the Shocker file" is found, it will shed more light on this case. A letter found at the Baseball Hall of Fame from AL president Ban Johnson to Phil Ball pointed out that "the real motive and desire of Shocker" was for his wife to see a Philadelphia specialist about her cancer.[17]

NOTES

1. *St. Louis Globe-Democrat*, December 31, 1923.
2. *The Sporting News*, September 27, 1923.
3. *St. Louis Post-Dispatch*, September 20, 1923.
4. G. Edward White, *Creating the National Pastime: Baseball Transforms Itself, 1903–1953* (Princeton NJ: Princeton University Press, 1998), 69–81.
5. Leo Durocher with Ed Linn, *Nice Guys Finish Last* (New York: Simon & Schuster, 1975), 71.
6. *St. Louis Post-Dispatch*, December 11, 1923.
7. Francis C. Richter, "Casual Comment," *The Sporting News*, November 22, 1923.
8. John E. Wray, *St. Louis Post-Dispatch*, December 10 and 11, 1923.
9. *New York World*, December 13, 1923.
10. Eugene C. Murdock, *Ban Johnson: Czar of Baseball* (Westport CT: Greenwood, 1982), 207.
11. *St. Louis Post-Dispatch*, January 19, 1924.
12. *New York Sun*, February 8, 1926.
13. *St. Louis Globe-Democrat*, January 23, 1924.
14. Francis C. Richter, "Casual Comment," *The Sporting News*, January 31 and February 7, 1924.
15. *St. Louis Post-Dispatch*, December 14 and 26, 1923.
16. *St. Louis Post-Dispatch*, December 13, 1923.
17. Steve Steinberg, *Urban Shocker: Silent Hero of Baseball's Golden Age* (Lincoln: University of Nebraska Press, 2017), 134–35.

26

Hack Wilson's 191st RBI

A Persistent Itch Finally Scratched

CLIFFORD S. KACHLINE

Nearly since its founding, members of SABR's Baseball Records Research Committee have been updating and correcting baseball's statistical record. Much of this work has gone unnoticed, adding a run here or a double there to a nearly forgotten player from decades ago. These efforts only garner attention when they change the statistics for a famous player or when a league leadership is at stake. One of the most famous cases is explained in this *Baseball Research Journal* article from 2001, when a group of SABR members worked together to change the all-time record for runs batted in for a single season. Cliff Kachline, the author, was a longtime writer and editor for *The Sporting News*, the official historian of the National Baseball Hall of Fame in Cooperstown, and one of SABR's founders. He served for several years on the SABR Board of Directors (including a term as president) and was the organization's first executive director. Cliff received the Henry Chadwick Award in 2011.

As famed radio news commentator Paul Harvey might expound, "And now for the rest of the story." What story? The one detailing the how and the who of the long-overlooked run batted in that, 69 years after Hack Wilson accomplished the feat, boosted his one-season major-league RBI record to 191.

It's a story that from start to finish spanned almost 22 years and took many twists and turns. It also is a product of the effort of numerous SABR researchers who provided assistance and deserve credit.

It all started in 1977 during my tenure as historian of the Baseball Hall of Fame, when an envelope arrived from *The Sporting News*, where I had earlier been a member of the editorial staff for 24 years. Enclosed were two letters. One was dated November 17, 1977, written by staff member Larry Wigge.

Dear Cliff: We just received this [enclosed] letter from a reader, and since *The Sporting News* box scores from 1930 did not reveal RBI totals, there was no way to answer the man. I thought maybe you have come across this before, and Mac [Paul Macfarlane, another TSN staff member] suggested that you had the official boxes and could check into this.

The enclosed handwritten letter was from a James Braswell, who was living in Chicago at the time.

Gentlemen: I believe if you check Hack Wilson's record from July 24 thru August 5, inclusive, of 1930, you will find Wilson knocked in at least one run in 11 consecutive games, and should be listed in your Baseball Record Book—along with Mel Ott—as the co-holder of this N.L. record [for consecutive games with an RBI].

After making a quick check, my response to Braswell on November 22 (with a copy to Wigge) advised:

Wilson's day-by-day record for 1930, as kept by the National League's official statistician, shows that he was credited with RBIS in only 10 of the 11 games during the period you listed. However, an Associated Press box score of the game for which he is shown with no RBIS on the official sheet does in fact credit him with a run batted in. I am now attempting to obtain a play-by-play of the game in question . . . and will be getting back to you.

Exactly one week later a follow-up letter to Braswell (a carbon again going to Wigge) declared:

We have received copies of accounts appearing in the *Chicago Tribune* and *Chicago Herald-Examiner* of the second game of the July 28, 1930, doubleheader between the Cubs and Cincinnati at Wrigley Field. Both accounts state that Hack Wilson singled home Kiki Cuyler from second base in the third inning. Wilson subsequently moved to third base on an error and scored on Charlie Grimm's single. In summary, the newspaper accounts indicate that Wilson and Grimm should have been credited with one RBI each in this game—rather than Grimm with two and Wilson with none as is shown on the official records. This would then give Wilson a streak of 11 successive games with an RBI. The Official Baseball Records Committee will be meeting next week, and I will arrange to have this matter presented to the group at that time.

The Baseball Records Committee had been founded in Milwaukee during the All-Star Game break in July 1975, prompted by discrepancies between the Elias Bureau's *Book of Baseball Records* and *The Sporting News's Baseball Record Book*, together with the discovery of numerous mistakes in the official records through the years. With the approval of Commissioner Bowie Kuhn and the concurrence of the two league presidents, Joe Reichler of the Commissioner's staff arranged to formally organize such a committee. It originally consisted of 10 members, including two from the Commissioner's staff, the two league public relations directors, three from the Baseball Writers' Association, the head of the Elias Sports Bureau, and one representative each from *The Sporting News* and the Baseball Hall of Fame. Later the committee was expanded to 15 members.

My memorandum on the Wilson RBI matter was presented to the Records Committee at its December 7 session during the 1977 major/minor-league meetings in Hawaii. The report included play-by-play-type accounts by Ed Burns in the *Chicago Tribune* and Wayne Otto in the *Herald-Examiner* of the two innings in which the Cubs scored while edging the Reds, 5–3, in the second half of the July 28, 1930, twin bill. Both clearly stated that Wilson and Grimm each singled in one run in the third inning. (The box score appearing in the *Chicago Herald-Examiner* and the one distributed by Associated Press both show Wilson and Grimm with one run batted in apiece. The *Chicago Tribune* did not include RBIs in its box scores in 1930, while the *Daily News* and *American* seldom listed them.)

In a letter dated December 16, I informed Braswell:

Three factors prompted the Committee to defer any action on the [Wilson] findings:

1. Seymour Siwoff [head of the Elias Bureau] pointed out that his Book of Baseball Records already shows a longer NL RBI streak (12 games by Paul Waner from June 2–16, 1927),
2. Additional data is still needed on other discrepancies in Wilson's 1930 RBI record, and
3. The group simply ran out of time at this particular session [to pursue the matter further].

The letter also noted six other instances where the daily RBI figures that Braswell listed for Wilson differed from the official records. I asked if he was in a position to check Chicago newspapers for play-by-play accounts of these games. About a week later Braswell provided information on the six games and added: "This has spurred me on to doing a complete analysis of Hack's incredible 1930 RBIs. Needless to say, it will take several months of research, but this is a hobby with me so eventually I will complete it."

More Digging . . . and Diggers

Beginning in late December 1977, my involvement in the Baseball Museum's major expansion and total remodeling project increased greatly. As a result, my next contact with Braswell was delayed until the following September. He responded that he had not had a chance to do further research, but hoped to be able to in the future. Unfortunately, this was the last I heard from him. Because of the heightened workload resulting from the Museum expansion/renovation program, I didn't write him again until May 14, 1982, with a follow-up four weeks later. Neither letter brought a response. Braswell, who had joined SABR in 1978, dropped out after 1983, and all contact with him was lost.

I contacted another SABR member living in the Chicago area—Bob Soderman—in January 1981 to ascertain if he might be willing to assist in the research. Ironically, as it turned out, Soderman had been gathering information for several years for a possible biography of Wilson. He advised that his research and writing had carried him through the 1929 season.

Soderman proved to be a key figure in verifying Hack's 191 RBIs. His background made him an ideal choice. As a young man in the late 1940s, he had been a sportswriter with Chicago's City News Bureau. Later he joined the advertising department of the Jim Beam Distilling Company and eventually became vice president of marketing and advertising for the firm. In that role he developed a relationship with *The Sporting News* by placing Jim Beam ads in what then was known as the Baseball Bible. After retiring from Jim Beam, Soderman became active as a boxing historian and has contributed many articles to boxing publications. In 1980 he helped found the International Boxing Research Organization (IBRO). In addition, he continued as an active baseball researcher and was responsible for discovering a unique record: most consecutive at-bats without a home run—Tommy Thevenow, 3,347 in the National League, and Ed Foster with 3,278 in the American League.

Another who became involved in the Wilson project during this period was Paul Macfarlane of *The Sporting News*. We had been colleagues for much of my career with that publication. Among his responsibilities as *TSN* historian/archivist at the time was *Daguerreotypes*, a book containing the lifetime records of the game's greatest players. He was *TSN*'s representative during the last few years of the Official Records Committee and as a consequence of our frequent contacts was aware of the "missing" RBI, and had even changed Wilson's RBI total to 191 in the 1981 edition of *Daguerreotypes*. (A year or two later he changed it back to 190 following Bowie Kuhn's ruling on the 1910 Cobb-Lajoie batting championship dispute.)

By early summer 1982, Soderman's research had uncovered numerous mistakes in RBIs credited to 1930 Cub players. It became obvious that it would be necessary to check every Cub RBI in each game that season if there was to be any possibility of acceptance of a revision of Wilson's total. In a letter dated June 10, 1982, I had asked Soderman whether he'd be willing to do this and reminded him of a day-by-day grid of 1930 Cub RBIs that I had compiled from the official NL records and had sent him. He quickly dug into the assignment full blast. Taking the train or bus from his suburban Mt. Prospect home into the Windy City, he spent days at the Chicago Public Library going through microfilm of four Chicago dailies: *Tribune*, *Times*, *Daily News*, and *Herald-Examiner*.

Early in May 1983, during a conversation with Macfarlane, Soderman said his research up to that point led him to believe Hack had three more RBIs not just one—for a total of 193. However, his "final report" to me and Macfarlane, dated May 30, 1983, scotched that prospect. The 27-page document included a summary of each 1930 Cub game that listed the opponent, home or away, and final score; a daily log of Wilson's home runs and RBIs; a game-by-game grid for all 26 Cub players who had an RBI, and play-by-play descriptions of Cub scoring in 17 games where actual or potential RBI discrepancies were found.

The two "dubious" games in which Soderman originally concluded Hack had been deprived of an RBI were those of June 4 at Boston and the second half of an August 19 doubleheader at Wrigley Field which ended in a 16-inning, 6–6 tie. In the first instance, the *Tribune*'s game account indicated Hack had driven in a run in the fourth inning as well as in the first inning. The play-by-play in the *Chicago Times* refuted this, crediting Riggs Stephenson with both RBIs in the fourth inning.

In the August 19 contest, Soderman's reading of game accounts in two papers originally led him to believe Wilson had driven in Kiki Cuyler in the third inning. As a matter of fact, the Associated Press box score appearing in the *New York Times* and other newspapers did give Hack an RBI. The subsequent discovery of a play-by-play account in the *Chicago Daily News* revealed that, with one out and the Cubs trailing, 4–1, Cuyler scored when Phillies second baseman Fresco Thompson booted Wilson's grounder for an error. Although Cuyler may have taken off for the plate as soon as the ball was hit, Wilson was not credited with an RBI by the official scorer.

Earlier in the season, another Cub player was deprived of an RBI that seemed warranted. It occurred in the second half of a May 30 morning-afternoon bill against St. Louis at Wrigley Field. With the score tied at 8–8, the bases loaded and one out in the bottom of the tenth inning, Riggs Stephenson smashed a grounder to Cardinal shortstop Sparky Adams. He fired to second baseman Frank Frisch, but Frisch's throw to first attempting to double up Stephenson was off-target. Although the winning run scored on the play, the Associated Press and most newspapers listed no RBI for him, and also had no error for Frisch. At the same time, box scores carried a note saying, "One out when winning run scored," thus ignoring the forceout at second base.

However, a check of the NL official records revealed the scorer did include that out and also charged Frisch with an error, thus eliminating the possibility of an RBI for Stephenson. Baseball's official scoring rules in 1930 stated the game summary "shall contain the number of runs batted in by each batsman" but offered no explanation on how to score RBIs in unusual situations. This seeming oversight was corrected at a meeting of the rules committee on December 12, 1930, when the following definition was adopted: "Runs batted in should include runs scored on safe hits (including home runs), sacrifice hits, infield outs, and when the run is forced over by reason of a batsman becoming a baserunner. With less than two out, if an error is made on a play on which a runner from third would ordinarily score, credit the batsman with a Run Batted In."

Did the last sentence starting "with less than two out" represent a new interpretation? The fact that the AP box score credited Wilson with an RBI in the August 19 game would indicate that at least some scorers already may have been following that practice. It's possible the league presidents had previously issued instructions covering the situation, although to date no evidence has been found.

An editorial in the December 25, 1930, issue of *The Sporting News* stated:

When the rules makers were revising the code for the future, they discovered to their surprise that no definition had been made in the rules as to what constitutes a run batted in . . . Of course the major league presidents had their own definition and had instructed the official scorers how to record this play which is presumed to be of such importance to batsmen. . . . When the new rules make their appearance, the run batted in will be defined and in the future this will help the scorers of all games. It is not a play applying directly to the major leagues, it is for all leagues. . . . The run batted in is not a suggestion that is modern. Years ago when Henry Chadwick was fathering baseball, he contended that it should be included in the score and wrote line after line about it. . . . It is with us now, and in the future it is hoped that it will be more valuable than it has been in the past.

The arrival of Soderman's "final report" coincided with my assumption of the newly created position of executive director of SABR. The need to devote full time to this endeavor—together with Commissioner Bowie Kuhn's decision two years earlier in the 1910 Cobb-Lajoie batting controversy ("The passage of 70 years, in our judgment, constitutes a certain statute of limitations as to recognizing any changes in the records with confidence of the accuracy of such changes.")—prompted me to put the Wilson matter aside without even studying and evaluating the results. It would be many years before I pursued it again. Despite Kuhn's edict, Macfarlane proposed doing a story for *The Sporting News* on the Wilson mess. With the Cobb-Lajoie experience in mind, editor Dick Kaegel turned him down. In an inter-office memo dated August 5, 1983, to Macfarlane, with copies to publisher Dick Waters, several TSN staff members and me, Kaegel wrote:

This Hack Wilson RBI research obviously is painstakingly thorough but [there are still] some holes. . . . Our policy on correcting records—particularly records of this significance—must be to first present the evidence to the Official Records Committee. . . . When the Kuhn administration ends, perhaps we'll have better luck with a reorganized Records Committee. One of our first steps should be to impress upon the new commissioner the importance of the records committee and renew our suggestion for implementing a research bureau within the commissioner's office (or possibly under the supervision of Elias [Bureau], SABR or even TSN). . . . Obviously because statistics are such an important part of baseball, it is important to have the correct numbers. Hopefully the new commissioner and his people will be more receptive to this concept. Meanwhile, we will continue to list Wilson's RBIS as 190 for 1930.

Unfazed by the rebuff, Macfarlane proceeded to write an article on the subject for the June, 1986, issue of *The Scoreboard News—About the Chicago Cubs.* I did not learn about this piece until ten years later. The 650-word yarn began: "As long as baseball has been played and will be played, there are people who search for the truth in records. Research is less looking for faults as [*sic*] it is finding an error while looking for something completely non-related."

He then claimed to be the first to find Hack's missing RBI. Completely ignoring Braswell's role, he gave Soderman credit for "painstaking and timeless research [that] proved that I was correct." He also listed the other Cub players whose RBI figures Soderman had found to be incorrect, with their revised totals. (Further study resulted in a subsequent revision.)

A sidebar inserted next to Macfarlane's story by *Scoreboard News* editors pointed out the possibility that Wilson may have been deprived of another RBI, which would have made his total 192. The sidebar cited the 1978 biography of Wilson written by Robert S. Boone and Gerald Grunska. In it, Clyde Sukeforth, a catcher with Cincinnati in 1930, was quoted as saying Hack should have had 57 home runs that season instead of 56. According to Sukeforth, one day when he was sitting in the bullpen in Redland Field, Hack "hit one . . . way up in the seats . . . so hard that it hit the screen and bounced back [onto the field]." Sukeforth said the umpires, apparently not realizing it had cleared the fence, ruled the ball in play and Hack thus was deprived of a home run and RBI. "Of course, we weren't going to say anything," Sukeforth was quoted as saying.

A somewhat similar version appeared in "The Fans Speak Out" section of the August 2001 edition of *Baseball Digest*. According to the writer, then living in Wroclaw, Poland, Wilson allegedly hit a drive into the seats with a runner aboard, but the ball bounced back on the field and Hack wound up with a double instead of a two-run homer. Sukeforth supposedly told Wilson about the incident in 1933, when both were with the Dodgers. Unfortunately, no newspaper reference has been found to confirm Sukeforth's recollection.

As a matter of fact, Sukeforth was the Reds' catcher in eight of the 11 games played against the Cubs at Redland Field that season. In one of the eight, the first half of a July 6 doubleheader, the *Cincinnati Enquirer* stated Wilson smashed homer No. 24 "into the right field seats, which is Hack's favorite spot on this field," and then in the second game drove a ball over right fielder Harry Heilmann's head that "hit close to the top of the screen (but) Hack was held to a single on account of preceding baserunners" [English on second and Cuyler on first], who "feared Heilmann was going to catch the ball." English scored on the hit, but Cuyler was thrown out at the plate and "Hack had to be satisfied with probably the longest single ever made on the [Cincinnati] grounds."

Of the three 1930 Chicago-at-Cincinnati games when Sukeforth conceivably could have been sitting in the bullpen, Wilson had only one hit—a triple on July 9. Accounts in Cincinnati newspapers indicated there was nothing unusual about the hit.

Reawakening

For me, the Wilson dispute remained dormant until SABR's 1996 annual convention in Kansas City. After sitting in on the SABR Records Committee meeting, I mentioned the Wilson matter to committee chairman Lyle Spatz. He immediately expressed deep interest. Another who did was Dave Smith, head of Retrosheet, the group whose goal has been to locate play-by-play accounts of every major league game ever played.

This prompted me to dig out the files and resume evaluating the research that had been done. I looked closely at Soderman's "final report" of 1983, and contacted him directly. His further research clarified matters and led to a few revisions of the figures he had originally provided (and which Macfarlane had listed in *The Scoreboard News* story).

At the 1997 Louisville convention, Spatz asked me to make a presentation on the Wilson matter at the SABR Records Committee meeting. Although a few details still remained to be untangled, the members in attendance seemed convinced that 191 should be accepted. With the assistance of Spatz and another committee member, Joe Dittmar, who on visits to Washington checked accounts in newspapers in the Library of Congress, we tied up the remaining loose ends.

The next significant step in the process was to compile: (1) a box score of the second game of the July 28, 1930, Reds-Cubs doubleheader (in which Wilson's RBI was "missed") from the data shown in the NL official records;

(2) another from the play-by-play account; and (3) compare the two results with the box scores that appeared in the four Chicago newspapers.

There was, incidentally, an obvious mistake in the play-by-play carried in the *Chicago Daily News*. With one out in the Reds' final at-bat, the account stated: "Lucas batted for Ford and singled to left. Callaghan batted for Ford and singled to left." After tapping out the last sentence, the Western Union operator obviously realized his mistake and followed with "Callaghan batted for Durocher and singled to right, Lucas stopping at second."

The process revealed that besides the Grimm-Wilson RBI mixup, the official records for this one game include eight other mistakes. A box score comprised of figures taken from the official National League player and team sheets is shown below.

Based upon the play-by-play in the *Chicago Daily News* and the box scores appearing in various newspapers, the official NL data contain the following mistakes:

1. Wilson had 1 RBI (instead of 0);
2. Grimm had 1 RBI (not 2);
3. Blair had 4 assists (not 3);
4. Chicago had 13 assists (not 12);
5. Gooch had 4 AB (instead of 3);
6. Cincinnati had 34 AB (not 33);
7. Ford had 0 hits (not 1); Callaghan had 1 hit (not 0);
8. Cincinnati had 6 LOB (not 5); 10—Bush faced 36 batters (not 35).

Following are the figures from the official National League records:

July 28, 1930, Box Score

GAME 2: CUBS 5, REDS 3

Cincinnati

	AB	R	H	2B	3B	HR	RBI	PO	A	E	BB	HP	SO	SB
Walker, lf	4	0	1	0	0	0	0	1	0	0	0	0	0	0
Swanson, cf	4	0	2	0	0	0	0	1	0	0	0	0	0	0
Stripp, 1b	4	0	0	0	0	0	0	8	1	0	0	0	0	0
Cuccinello, 3b	3	0	0	0	0	0	0	1	0	0	1	0	1	0
Heilmann, rf	3	1	1	0	0	1	1	0	0	0	1	0	1	0
Ford, 2b	3	0	1	0	0	0	0	0	4	0	0	0	0	0

	AB	R	H	2B	3B	HR	RBI	PO	A	E	BB	HP	SO	SB
Lucas, ph	1	0	1	0	0	0	0	0	0	0	0	0	0	0
Durocher, ss	3	0	0	0	0	0	0	3	7	1	0	0	0	0
Callaghan, ph	1	0	0	0	0	0	0	0	0	0	0	0	0	0
Gooch, c	3	1	1	0	1	0	0	10	1	0	0	0	0	0
May, p	1	0	0	0	0	0	0	0	0	0	0	0	0	0
Johnson, p	1	0	0	0	0	0	0	0	0	0	0	0	0	0
Crawford, ph	1	1	1	0	0	0	1	0	0	0	0	0	0	0
Ash, p	0	0	0	0	0	0	0	0	0	0	0	0	0	0
Sukeforth, ph	1	0	0	0	0	0	0	0	0	0	0	0	0	0
Totals	33	3	8	0	1	1	2	24	13	1	2	0	2	0

Chicago

	AB	R	H	2B	3B	HR	RBI	PO	A	E	BB	HP	SO	SB
Blair, 2b	4	1	2	0	0	0	0	3	3	1	0	0	1	0
English, 3b	3	2	2	1	0	0	0	0	2	0	0	1	0	0
Cuyler, rf	2	1	2	1	0	0	3	0	0	0	1	1	0	1
Wilson, cf	4	1	1	0	0	0	0	4	0	0	0	0	1	0
D. Taylor, Lf	4	0	0	0	0	0	0	2	0	0	0	0	1	0
Grimm, 1b	4	0	1	0	0	0	2	12	0	0	0	0	2	0
J. Taylor, c	4	0	0	0	0	0	0	4	1	0	0	0	2	0
Beck, ss	2	0	0	0	0	0	0	2	3	0	2	0	0	0
Bush, p	3	0	0	0	0	0	0	0	3	0	0	0	2	0
Totals	30	5	8	2	0	0	5	3	12	1	3	2	9	1

LOB—Cincinnati 5, Chicago 6.

DP—Cincinnati 2 (Stripp 2, Ford 1, Durocher 2); Chicago 1 (J. Taylor 1, Beck 1).

Cincinnati

	BFP	IP	H	R	ER	BB	SO	HB
May	15	2	7	5	5	1	4	0
Johnson	17	5	1	0	0	2	4	2
Ash	3	1	0	0	0	0	1	0

Chicago

	BFP	IP	H	R	ER	BB	SO	HB
Bush	35	9	8	3	2	2	2	0

Balancing box score: Cincinnati 3 R, 27 PO, 6 LOB = 36; Cincinatti 34 AB, 2 BB, 0 HB/SH = 36; Chicago 5 R, 24 PO, 6 LOB = 35; Chicago 30 AB, 3 BB, 2 HB/SH = 35.

When I presented this report at the SABR Records Committee meeting during the 1998 convention in the Bay Area, the unanimous feeling was that enough evidence had been developed to justify changing Wilson's total. Soon after my return home from the convention, an enterprising young journalist named Owen S. Good heard about it while chatting with a staff member of the Baseball Hall of Fame Library. Good, who at the time was employed by *The Daily Star* of nearby Oneonta, promptly called and said he'd like to interview me for a story on the subject. At the time, Cleveland's Manny Ramirez was on pace to threaten Wilson's record just as Juan Gonzalez of Texas had been at the All-Star break a year earlier.

Under the headline "Wilson's Lost RBI Has Historians Bothered," Good's 1,200-word article appeared at the top of the first sports page of the July 15, 1998, edition of the Oneonta paper. It quickly caught the attention of the Associated Press, which proceeded to send out a brief item to its clients throughout the country. Because of my long friendship with Seymour Siwoff, head of the Elias Bureau, I immediately called to inform him how the publicity developed. His reaction was that he would need to see play-by-plays of all 1930 Cub games before he could consider supporting a change in Wilson's RBI record.

Siwoff subsequently contacted Retrosheet's Dave Smith. Retrosheet already had complete play-by-plays of 107 of the Cubs' 1930 games and partial accounts of eighteen others. Smith forwarded them to Siwoff, and the Elias Bureau staff began its own study. In December Smith advised that he had sent Siwoff a short note saying "it seems inescapable that Hack's correct total for 1930 is really 191."

Most of the games for which play-by-plays were still lacking involved the second half of Sunday or holiday doubleheaders. In the 1930s it was not unusual for large metropolitan newspapers to publish several editions every day. While the earliest Monday editions usually carried play-by-play accounts of the Sunday games, subsequent editions often replaced them with other sports news, and the files maintained by local historical associations as well as the newspapers themselves usually contain only the later editions.

At this juncture, two other SABR members made significant contributions to finalizing the research effort. They were David Stephan of Culver City, California, and Walt Wilson of Chicago. Stephan, a mathematician who has his own consulting business, asked Wilson to search Chicago newspapers for the remaining play-by-plays. Having heard about the dispute, Walt had already worked up his own compilation of Wilson's 1930 RBIs, and had arranged for his friend Eddie Gold to distribute copies at the 1998 SABR Records Committee meeting. (An article by Walt that includes Hack's game-by-game RBI production of 1930 appeared in last year's *Baseball Research Journal*.)

Walt's efforts, over the next eight or nine months, in digging up most of the missing play-by-plays proved to be a clinching factor. Three other SABR members who assisted in this phase were Mark Stangl of St. Louis, Bill Hugo of Cincinnati, and Denis Repp of Pittsburgh. Stangl was able to dig up data on several Cub games played in St. Louis. Hugo checked out Cub games in Cincinnati and found nothing to corroborate Sukeforth's reference to a phantom homer by Wilson. Repp provided a play-by-play from the *Pittsburgh Post-Gazette* of the Cubs' August 3 game in Pittsburgh.

For the record, the list of mistakes in 1930 NL official RBI statistics of Cub players is presented below. It should be emphasized that it would be unfair to change the season totals for the players involved other than Wilson's record 191—without performing similar research on the entire league, as well as for other seasons. The revised totals of those affected follow, with the original figure in parentheses: Wilson 191 (190), Cuyler 134 (no change), Hartnett 124 (122), Stephenson 69 (68), Grimm 64 (66), English 62 (59), Blair 55 (59), D. Taylor 36 (37), Beck 35 (34), Kelly 53 as a Red and Cub (not 54), Hornsby 17 (18), and Bush 6 (7).

It is worth noting that of the 13 games in which RBI mistakes were found, all except the last two were played in Chicago. Following are the Cub RBI errata by date, with the correct figure shown first and the number credited by the league statistician in parentheses:

June 23—Cuyler 2 (3), Bush 2 (3), Stephenson 4 (3), Blair 4 (2), Hartnett 1 (2), Grimm 1 (2), Beck 1 (0);

July 28 (2nd game)—Wilson 1 (0), Grimm 1 (2);

August 1—English 1 (2), Hartnett 3 (2);

August 2—Blair 0 (1);

August 10 (2nd game)—English 1 (0), Cuyler 4 (3), Blair 1 (3);

August 14—Blair 0 (1);

August 16 (1st game)—Cuyler 2 (3), D. Taylor 1 (0);

August 22—Hartnett 5 (4), Kelly 1 (2);

August 24—D. Taylor 0 (2), Hartnett 2 (1);

August 29—English 2 (1), Blair 0 (1);

August 30—English 2 (0), Blair 0 (2);
September 6—Hornsby 2 (3), Blair 1 (0);
September 12—Cuyler 3 (2).

Official Recognition

The wheels of justice often move slowly. This time, though, the Elias Bureau was simultaneously concerned about a possible mistake in one of the Babe Ruth records that was being threatened. This contributed to quick consideration of the evidence in the Wilson case.

My first inkling that a change in Wilson's 1930 RBI total was going to be officially recognized came on June 17, 1999. Jerome Holtzman, recently named Major League Baseball's official historian following his retirement as a sportswriter for the *Chicago Tribune*, and a longtime friend, called to inform me of the decision. He requested some background information for use in a press release.

The story was given to the media on June 22, the second day of the SABR convention in Scottsdale, Arizona. "I am sensitive to the historical significance that accompanies the correction of such a prestigious record, especially after so many years have passed," Commissioner Bud Selig declared, "but it is important to get it right." The same news release also disclosed that extensive research by the Elias Bureau had discovered six additional walks for Babe Ruth, boosting his record career total to 2,062. The pressure to accept that discovery was driven by the fact that Rickey Henderson was approaching the record, which he exceeded early in the 2001 season.

A week following the official approval of Wilson's 191st RBI, Holtzman posted a story on www.majorleaguebaseball.com explaining why the record was corrected after 69 years and pointing out that "a mystery [still] remains: Where is James Braswell?" He had been living at 1334 W. George Street in Chicago back in the late 1970s and early '80s. Telephone calls made by David Stephan to the current resident of that address and also to several neighbors failed to develop any leads. A check of telephone listings on the internet revealed there are more than 150 men named James Braswell in the U.S. Calls to those shown as living in Illinois and seven nearby states failed to locate the real James Braswell.

At the 2001 SABR convention, Holtzman told Records Committee members that about six months after Wilson's record was officially approved, he received a call out of the blue from Braswell, who mentioned he had been attending Northwestern at the time. Unfortunately, Holtzman had no recollection of the location from which Braswell called, and officials at Northwestern were unable to find any record of him. And so, as Holtzman noted in his 1999 article on the internet, "the only missing piece of the puzzle is the whereabouts of James Braswell, the hero of the story." Even Paul Harvey almost certainly would be intrigued by the story.

Sidebar 1: Runs Batted In Rule

The evolution of the runs-batted-in rule has never been fully documented. Henry Chadwick, the first well-known baseball writer, is said to have originally come up with the concept of such a statistic as far back as 1879, but major league baseball did not officially accept it until some forty years later.

Prior to the 1891 season, baseball's governing board adopted "a new and most important rule" that specified the summary of AL games should include "the number of runs batted in by base hits by each batsman." The proviso apparently proved unpopular. Not only did the National League and American Association averages of 1891 fail to contain any RBI data, but the rule was eliminated the following winter.

In 1907 Ernest J. Lanigan, then a baseball writer with the *New York Press*, suggested to the paper's sports editor, Jim Price, the idea of compiling and publishing RBI data. The proposal was enthusiastically accepted, and Lanigan worked up runs batted in figures for players in both leagues from 1907 through 1919, starting with the Press and later moving on to the *Tribune*, *World*, and finally the *New York Sun*.

Runs batted in became an official statistic starting in 1920, but the scoring rules from then through 1930 simply stated: "The summary shall include . . . the number of runs batted in by each batter," and provided no specifics whatsoever. While the league presidents or the Baseball Writers' Association itself may have issued some scoring instructions during that period covering unusual circumstances, no such interpretations have yet been located.

Baseball's rules committee finally rectified the situation in December 1930, by adopting a description of a run batted in that is essentially the same as that in effect today. The only significant change became effective 1939 when it was specified that no RBI should be credited when a runner scores as the batter grounds into a double play. That later was expanded to include situations where an error was charged on the second part of a potential double play.

Sidebar 2: Why So Many Records Are Wrong

Like Ivory soap, today's major-league averages are 99.44 percent pure, that is virtually 100 percent accurate. By contrast early statistics of both the American and National Leagues, especially for the pre-1950 period, are fraught with mistakes.

The reasons are numerous. First, although many of the sportswriters who served as official scorers were diligent and dedicated, some were incompetent and careless. While the official league statisticians supposedly balanced box scores, they had no way to spot compensating mistakes. It also is obvious that those who entered the figures onto the official sheets sometimes copied them improperly.

Newspapers began barring their baseball writers from serving as official scorers some 30 years ago. The parties who now fill that role are on balance doing a more accurate job.

Another factor was the absence of any crosschecking. Prior to the 1950s few clubs had anyone on their staff who compiled their team's figures. For the past 30 or 40 years all clubs have maintained daily updated stats, and there has been constant contact between the clubs and the league statistician to make certain any differences are immediately resolved. Fans of earlier eras paid far less attention to statistics than they do today. Mistakes in the figures weren't readily observed, so there was less pressure to be thorough and accurate.

While we hope that data for most pre-1950 major-league games were entered correctly, the ten mistakes found in the so-called Hack Wilson 191st RBI contest are dwarfed by those discovered in another game. The questionable listing of a triple play by the New York Yankees during an 11-inning, 11–10 victory at Boston on September 25, 1929—the day Yankee manager Miller Huggins died—prompted me to research that game. Not only did the Yankees not make a triple play as the official American League statistics proclaim (they had two double plays, each coming with one out), but play-by-play accounts indicate the official records for that game contain 22 mistakes involving 10 players. In the early 1900s, the final official league averages were listed as having been prepared by each league's president or secretary. Except for an occasional newspaper, few other sources compiled player stats. There was little opportunity for comparison.

In 1912, the American League hired Irwin M. Howe of Chicago to serve as its statistician. He and the Howe News Bureau produced the official AL figures almost every year through 1972. Sports Information Center then purchased the Howe Bureau and handled the AL averages, 1973–1986.

The National League first went outside its own staff in 1923, when Al Munro Elias of New York was appointed league statistician. The Elias Bureau has filled that role ever since. For years both Howe and Elias also compiled averages of the rival league each season to sell to client newspapers. In 1987, the Elias Sports Bureau became the American League's official statistician, and it has handled both leagues the past fifteen years. Elias receives a play-by-play and official scorer's report of each game via fax shortly after the final out. These are checked before being entered on the computer.

Up until the 1950s and 1960s, most major-league cities had four or more daily newspapers. Some of them prepared their own box scores in order to meet deadlines. The wire services—notably Associated Press and United Press—also produced and distributed box scores. They and the telegraphers for some newspapers tapped out their own play-by-play accounts. This multiplicity of independent sources often resulted in discrepancies, especially in situations where a paper's writer ruled error on a play, unaware the official scorer called it a base hit (or vice versa)—or when the official scorer changed a decision following the game. Differences of this type may well be involved in the question of whether Nap Lajoie had 229 hits or 232 in his banner 1901 season. The American League official team and player stat sheets for 1901 disappeared more than 50 years ago and thus are no longer available as a source against which to check.

Because of the frequency of mistakes in the official records, it has been suggested many times that averages should be recompiled from boxscores. The immensity and expense of such a task have effectively squashed such proposals. Furthermore, as Seymour Siwoff, head of the Elias Sports Bureau, points out: "It would be illogical and impractical to undertake such a project because newspaper boxscores of the same game often differ and even play-by-play accounts sometimes disagree. In most instances there would be no way to reconcile those differences. In cases where the official league statistician's sheets exist, the only logical and practical approach is to limit changes to singular records where mistakes of omission or commission can be readily verified from credible sources."

27

John McGraw Comes to New York

The 1902 Giants

CLIFFORD BLAU

The story of the great skipper John McGraw leaving Baltimore's American League club and coming to the New York Giants in 1902, and the accompanying destruction and rebirth of those two franchises, is the stuff of baseball legend. Its drama is arguably one of the most important stories in the creation of the two-league structure that has brought us to the present day. Cliff Blau, one of SABR's most prolific researchers (and fact-checkers), has been particularly drawn to the details of league and team management operating rules and procedures, writing often about the relationships between leagues, teams, and players over the past 150 years. This story is a perfect one for Cliff to tell.

John McGraw was one of the most successful baseball managers ever, leading the New York Giants to ten pennants in his 30 years with the club. His arrival in mid-1902 marked the turning point in the fortunes of the Giants, a team which had been struggling for years. However, despite an influx of new players whom McGraw brought with him to New York, the Giants barely showed any improvement for the balance of the 1902 season, losing over 60 percent of their decisions in that period. This article will review the Giants' 1902 season and attempt to show why McGraw was unable to make an immediate improvement in the team.

1902 was a season of turmoil not just for the Giants, but for all of Organized Baseball. The National League was at war not only with the American League, but with itself. In its December 1901 meeting, four owners supported a plan proposed by John Brush to convert the National League into a trust which would be owned by all eight owners. This trust would own all eight teams and the contracts of all players. The other four owners supported the candidacy of former league president Albert Goodwill Spalding. Spalding had led the league in its successful battles with the Player's League in 1890 and the American Association in 1891, and these four owners felt he was the perfect choice to defend the league against the upstart American League. The two sides couldn't reach an agreement, and the trust group, including Giants owner Andrew Freedman, left the meeting. The other four owners, claiming a quorum was still present, elected Spalding president. A lawsuit was filed by the trust group and the matter wasn't resolved until the beginning of April 1902. The season schedule was adopted on April 5, just twelve days before opening day.

The American League, under its strong president, Ban Johnson, had moved into several large Eastern cities in 1901 and declared itself a major league on a par with the NL. While its playing talent was probably not on a par with the NL's that year, it did succeed in attracting such top stars as Nap Lajoie and Cy Young. Following the 1901 season, the AL took advantage of the chaotic situation in the NL to step up its player raids. Many of the NL's top players such as Elmer Flick, Jimmy Sheckard, Jesse Burkett, Al Orth, and Ed Delahanty signed with the American League. Meanwhile, the Giants seemed to be making little effort to resign their players or obtain new talent. By the end of 1901, regulars Kip Selbach, Jack Warner, Charley Hickman, and pitcher Luther Taylor, who had led the league's pitchers in games started, had signed with American League teams. Most damaging, future Hall of Fame shortstop George Davis, the Giants' manager in 1901, signed with the Chicago White Stockings. Later, third baseman Sammy Strang jumped ship as well. The decline of the Giants since they were purchased by the petulant, domineering Andrew Freedman in 1894 seemed to be complete. Once one of the league's premier franchises, the team had finished last or next to last the past three seasons. Freedman likely expected the trust scheme to be adopted, and that the Giants would get first pick of the league's stars. Because of the stalemate over that issue, they had to rebuild the club the old-fashioned way. With no National Agreement between the major and minor leagues, there was no draft to provide a cheap source of new talent.

Late in December, the Giants started putting together a team for 1902 by signing minor-league pitchers Roy Evans and John Burke as well as catcher Manley Thurston. They also purchased second baseman/manager George Smith from the Eastern League champion Rochester team. An offer was made to Jesse Burkett, who had just jumped to the AL, but he turned it down. The Giants also tried to woo manager Ned Hanlon away from their crosstown rivals, the Brooklyn Superbas, but that was also unsuccessful. Towards the end of January, Freedman chose Horace Fogel to manage the team.

Fogel's managerial experience consisted of one season at the helm of Indianapolis of the National League. Otherwise, he made his living as a sportswriter and editor, mainly in Philadelphia. Fogel promised to sign some stars, but all he found were college players, American League rejects, and "Roaring" Bill Kennedy, a one-time star pitcher who had been cut loose by the Superbas. As February neared its end, however, the Giants seized an opportunity when Chicago released first baseman Jack Doyle. Fogel quickly signed Doyle and appointed him team captain, giving him responsibility for the team during games. Doyle had been a member of the champion Baltimore Orioles in 1896 and had spent three seasons with the Giants before 1901. He was a good hitter and aggressive baserunner. However, he tended to make enemies wherever he went, as he was demanding and lacking in diplomacy.

The Giants didn't go south for spring training, which was not unusual at the time. Fourteen players reported to the Polo Grounds on March 24 to begin working out under the direction of Jack Doyle. More arrived the next few days. As practice began, the team lined up this way: Captain Doyle at first, Smith at second, Walter Anderson at short, Billy Lauder at third, and Frank Bowerman behind the plate backed up by George Yeager. Veteran George Van Haltren would be the center fielder, with several players competing for the other two outfield spots, including Jim Jackson, Roy Clark, Libe Washburn, Jim Stafford, Jimmy Jones, and Jim Delahanty. The pitching staff was led by the sensation of 1901, Christy Mathewson. Virtually every other pitcher from the prior year was gone. Attempting to replace them were Henry Thielmann (also an outfield prospect), Frank Dupee, Tully Sparks, Burke, Evans, Kennedy, and Bill Magee. Efforts were made to improve the team during spring training; on March 26, it was reported that the manager job was offered to Ed Barrow, then manager of the Toronto team in the Eastern League, and later Red Sox manager and Yankees president. Contracts were supposedly offered to American Leaguers Nap Lajoie, Elmer Flick, Topsy Hartsel, and others, and an unsuccessful attempt was made to purchase shortstop Wid Conroy from the champion Pittsburgh Pirates. Anderson proved inadequate at short, and after Delahanty and Thielmann were tried there, the Giants signed Jack Dunn, who had been released by the Orioles. The weather was cold and rainy throughout spring training. Only 6 exhibition games were played, against college and minor league teams, with the Giants managing to win them all. Five other games were cancelled due to the weather. When that happened, the Giants could work out with weights or exercise machines in the Polo Grounds clubhouse.

Other players failing to make the grade during spring training were Stafford and Dupee, with Clark returning to complete his studies at Brown University. Bowerman and Van Haltren were injured during training camp; thus when the Giants opened the season at home against the Philadelphia Phillies on April 17, the lineup looked like this:

Dunn ss
Delahanty RF
Jones CF
Lauder 3B
Doyle 1B
Jackson LF
Smith 2B
Yeager C
Mathewson P

Jack Dunn began his major-league career in 1897 as a pitcher. He converted to infield in 1901, playing third base and shortstop for the American League Baltimore Orioles. After his release by that team, he was signed by the Giants to fill their gap at short. He ended the season as a utility player, filling in at second and third and playing more games in right field than anyone else. He even started two games as pitcher, and relieved in another. Dunn spent two more seasons with the Giants as a utility infielder. He is best known today as the owner of the minor-league Baltimore Orioles, where he discovered and developed many players, such as Babe Ruth and Lefty Grove.

Jim Delahanty, one of five brothers to play in the major leagues, was a very good hitter who changed teams frequently during his 11-season AL and NL career, most of which was spent as a second baseman. He had spent the bulk of 1901 playing in the Eastern League. After spring training trials at shortstop and center field, he opened the season as the regular right fielder. This was his second major-league trial; his career would begin in earnest in 1904 as the regular third baseman for the Beaneaters.

Jim Jones was a fast runner without much hitting ability. Like Dunn, he had begun his career as a pitcher; Jones had played a few games for the

Giants in 1901. 1902 would be his final major-league season. He was filling in for the veteran George Van Haltren, who was expected to be the Giants' regular center fielder in 1902, as he had been since 1894. Van Haltren was nursing a cold and an injured finger. At 36 years of age, he was one of the oldest players in the league, and was frequently referred to in print as "Rip" Van Haltren. 1902 would be his 16th major-league season.

Billy Lauder was a good field, no hit third baseman. According to Ned Hanlon, Lauder was as good a third baseman as had ever played the game. Unfortunately, he had been out of professional baseball for two years, and was never able to regain his hitting eye.

Jim Jackson was a speedster who spent his rookie season in 1901 with the Baltimore Orioles. He had a .291 on-base average and a .330 slugging average in 1901. Joining the Giants in 1902, where he had to deal with the foul strike rule, his hitting took a predictable fall. In addition, his fielding average fell from a league-leading .971 in 1901 to .897 in 1902.

George "Heinie" Smith was a slick-fielding, weak-hitting second baseman. Smith played for Rochester in the Eastern League in 1901. At 30 years old, this was Smith's first year as a regular in the majors after four previous trials. He would soon be regarded as the best defensive second baseman on the Giants since John M. Ward in 1893–1894, but his big-league career would end the following year with Detroit. Smith and Lauder were the only Giants to play over 109 games in 1902.

George Yeager was a veteran of five big-league seasons as a backup catcher. 1902 would be his last year in the major leagues. He was filling in for the injured Bowerman.

After a band concert which concluded with "The Star-Spangled Banner," and the first ball was thrown out by a former fire commissioner, the Giants got their season off to a rousing start with a seven to nothing victory. Over the next few days, they would lose more than they won before rattling off a seven-game winning streak to close their home stand. As they headed for Chicago, the Giants had a 10-5 record. Their winning streak ended abruptly as Chicago swept the three-game series. However, the first two games were later disallowed by the league as Fogel had discovered before game three that the pitching rubber at West Side Park was two feet too close to home. (Those games were later replayed, with the Giants winning both.) Not including the two protested games, the Giants won four of the first six games on the trip. On May 16 in Cincinnati, as the new Palace of the Fans was dedicated,

George Yeager pinch-hit a two-run single in the ninth to cap a five-run rally and give New York a 14-7 mark. They looked like a pennant contender. However, the good times were over, as the team would lose 43 of its next 51 decisions. A few days after the Giants' come-from-behind victory, Fogel was quoted in a Cincinnati newspaper making disparaging remarks about golden boy Christy Mathewson. He made a quick retraction, but his days at the helm of the Giants were numbered.

Personnel changes were coming fast and furious. Taylor jumped back to the Giants. Bill Magee was released after lasting only two innings in his first start. Delahanty was dropped after seven games. Steve Brodie, a veteran center fielder and former Orioles teammate of Doyle, was signed, released, signed again, released again, and finally signed for a third time the next day after an injury to the Giants' latest outfielder. Indeed, injuries and illnesses would plague the team all season, especially amongst the outfielders. Brodie, despite his multiple comings and goings, was the only person to play more than 67 games in the outfield for New York. The most severe injury occurred on May 22, when Van Haltren broke his leg sliding in Pittsburgh. He missed the remainder of the season, and his major-league career ended the following year. A shortstop, Joe Bean, who had played with Smith at Rochester in 1901, was signed. Unfortunately, Rochester had an option on his services for 1902 and they got a court injunction against the Giants. This matter was resolved in a few days, with the Giants purchasing Bean's contract. Thielman, who was used in the outfield for a trio of games as well as on the mound, was dropped in mid-May as was catcher Thurston, who never got into a game. Outfielders came and went after two or three games. Pitcher Bob Blewett from Georgetown University was given a chance, but he lived up to his name, going 0-2 in five games. Libe Washburn, star pitcher at Brown University, was used in the outfield for a few games but never got a chance on the mound. Roy Clark had rejoined the team, but, like Mathewson and Sparks, didn't play on Sundays. (This was a problem only when the team was playing in three western cities, since Sunday ball was illegal in the four eastern cities and Pittsburgh.)

After losing fourteen of their last 15 games in May, and rumors of dissension spread, changes were made. On June 2, Jack Doyle was stripped of his captaincy, with George Smith taking over that role. The next day, Fogel left the team due to his father's death, and he never returned to the helm, with Smith being promoted to manager on June 11. In an effort to end the dissension on the club, Doyle was released late in June. These changes didn't help the team, as they could only achieve a 5-27 record under Smith.

There had been rumors during the winter about Mathewson having a sore arm. Although he claimed to be fine during spring training and his first pitching appearances were successful, his performance soon fell off. This led to Fogel's threat to bench him. Due to Matty's sore arm and the Giants' infield problems, Smith used him at first base for three games. There was some discussion about converting him to shortstop once his arm healed. While Matty was an excellent fielder on the mound and a good hitter for a pitcher, he proved a flop at first base, making four errors in his three games there, and he returned to pitching.

Meanwhile, on July 1, a new shortstop, Heinie Wagner, joined the team. He had been found playing sandlot ball in New York by Horace Fogel. No one on the team knew anything about him, and some fans thought the Giants had somehow obtained Pittsburgh's star, Hans Wagner. Alas, Heinie, although later a capable major-league player, was not only not Hans, but also wasn't ready for this level of play.

Another newspaper interview in early July gave insight into the Giants' troubles. Jack Hendricks, who had been released after a brief trial in June in right field, spoke candidly to a *Chicago Journal* writer. He claimed that Bowerman and Yeager did all they could to prevent young players from succeeding and that the team had deliberately played poorly behind Blewett to make him look bad. Hendricks, a Northwestern University graduate who would go on to a long career as a manager in the National League and the minors, also had harsh words for Mathewson, calling him a "conceited pinhead" who constantly moaned when things didn't go his way. Matty's teammates rarely spoke to him, and gave him poor support also, according to Hendricks. On the other hand, he had nothing but praise for Doyle, who he said was very helpful to the young players and was a "splendid fellow." He concluded that Freedman should make certain changes in the team, including the manager.[1]

In the meantime, over in the American League, the Orioles' manager John McGraw was having his own problems. McGraw, another veteran of the NL Orioles of the 1890s, had begun his managerial career with that club in 1899. He quickly established a reputation as a genius by leading the team to a strong fourth-place finish even though most of the club's stars had been transferred to its sister team, the Superbas. When the American League moved into the east, McGraw was offered part-ownership of the Baltimore franchise. However, Ban Johnson insisted on supporting his umpires, which put him at frequent loggerheads with McGraw, a notorious ump-baiter. By mid-1902, McGraw was fed up with the frequent suspensions and fines handed him by Johnson. As a player, he had been out of action since being spiked by a baserunner on May 24.

On July 2, McGraw was spotted at the Polo Grounds, and rumors quickly spread that he would take over the helm of the Giants. On the ninth, it became official. The Giants signed McGraw to a three-year contract at $10,000 or $11,000 per year, a munificent sum for the time, when the top player salaries were $6,000–7,000 at best. In his first interview as the Giants' pilot, McGraw stated that he had been given unlimited authority to improve the team. "The only instructions that I have received," he stated, "were to put a winning organization in this city at any cost."[2] Although he admitted that first place was out of reach this year, he did expect the team to finish in the first division and then compete for the flag in 1903.

The details of how McGraw left the Orioles, of which he was part-owner, and how he planned to strengthen the Giants, soon became public. He had arranged for a majority of the Orioles' stock to be sold to Andrew Freedman, who released McGraw and many of the team's stars, including future Hall-of-Famers Joe McGinnity and Roger Bresnahan, as well as first baseman Dan McGann and pitcher Jack Cronin.[3] This quartet joined McGraw and the Giants for his first game as manager on July 19. At the same time, Joe Kelley, who had also played on the Orioles of the 1890s, signed with John T. Brush to be Cincinnati's playing manager; joining him was center fielder Cy Seymour. In the ten days between McGraw being announced as new manager and his first game, he was supposedly trying to sign new players, but was in fact being treated for appendicitis, which would plague him for the rest of the season.

McGraw released seven players upon joining the Giants: Yeager, O'Hagen, Blewett, Wagner, Burke, Sparks, and Evans. Roy Clark received his 10-day notice of release two days before McGraw's signing. In addition to the four Baltimore players, the Giants soon added left fielder George Browne, who had been released by the Phillies, and pitcher Roscoe Miller, who jumped from the Detroit Tigers. Libe Washburn was released on July 25 and Jimmy Jones was suspended and then released after assaulting umpire Bob Emslie on August 6. Bresnahan split time between right field and catcher, while

Browne became the regular left fielder. Both were big improvements over the players the Giants had previously tried. McGraw became the new shortstop.

While the Giants lost their first game under McGraw, the team reportedly showed more "life" than they had in some time. After two days off and an exhibition game versus the Orange (New Jersey) Athletic Club, they took three out of five games against the Superbas. However, despite strong performances from some of the newcomers, the team kept on struggling, and finished the season in last place.

Injuries continued to plague the Giants, and one led to a challenge to McGraw's authority. Frank Bowerman's foot was hurt by a foul ball on August 2. The next day the team played an exhibition game in Bayonne, New Jersey and Bowerman didn't suit up. In fact, due to injuries on the Bayonne club, Roger Bresnahan caught all nine innings for both teams. Since Bowerman hadn't asked permission to sit out, McGraw fined him $50. Bowerman argued that the fine wasn't fair, and he refused to suit up again until it was rescinded. He threatened to jump to the American League but gave in and was back in uniform on August 7. In his first game behind the plate after the incident, however, he committed three errors and five passed balls. While it is not known if his poor fielding was deliberate, it so disgusted Mathewson that in the ninth inning, after the final two passed balls, Christy began lobbing the ball over the plate, and a 3–2 deficit quickly became an 8–2 loss. Despite all this, and later rumors of signing with the St. Louis Browns, Bowerman remained with the team through the 1907 season.

John T. Brush sold most of his stock in the Reds in August, and a few days later was made managing director of the Giants. He worked with McGraw in trying to obtain new players. Late in the season, with McGraw aiding in the negotiations, he bought Freedman's stock and became president of the board of directors. A new era in Giants' baseball was beginning.

Why didn't McGraw turn around the Giants' fortunes in 1902 despite the influx of new talent? The reason seems to be lack of interest. Apparently, he decided soon after arriving in New York that the Giants wouldn't be able to reach the first division and turned his attention to obtaining players for 1903. In this he was successful; he signed several American Leaguers and the team rallied to second place that year. However, this meant that McGraw was away from the team for long stretches. In all, he missed 20 games due to scouting trips and his appendicitis. The team's record in these games was 8-12, little different from their overall mark after McGraw became manager.

As further evidence that McGraw wasn't his usual fighting self, he wasn't ejected from a single game by the umpires with the Giants in 1902. He had promised to contain his temper after coming to New York, and did so. A year later, he was quoted as saying "Baseball is only fun for me when I'm out front and winning. I don't give a hill of beans for the rest of the game."[4]

The Giants continued to be disrupted by injuries as well as rainouts; seven games were postponed between September 9 and October 1. Also, McGraw began the transition from player-manager to bench-manager; 1902 was his last season as a regular player, and he played his last game of the season on September 11. This probably took some getting used to for McGraw.

McGraw made one serious personnel misjudgment, releasing Tully Sparks and signing Roscoe Miller. Miller went just one and eight with a 4.58 ERA. The following season he won two and lost five with a 4.13 ERA. Meanwhile, Sparks was in the midst of a 12-year major-league career which saw him credited with 121 pitching wins and an ERA of 2.79.

The result of the above was that the Giants record under McGraw was just 25-38-2, although 41 of the games were played at home, and they gained only a ½ game on seventh place. By contrast, the Cincinnati Reds after hiring Joe Kelley as manager were 36-26, climbing from seventh to fourth.

OF INJURIES:

4/17 Van Haltren out with cold and infected thumb until 4/19

4/18 Jones hurt sliding / didn't play again until 5/12

4/22 Jackson out with tonsillitis / back 4/25

5/22 Van Haltren broke leg / out remainder of season

5/28 Jones hurt when Long fell on him / back 6/2

6/2 Clark's finger injured-played 6/4 but next day thumb operated on, next played 7/2

6/6 O'Hagen hit by batted ball / back 6/20

6/17 Washburn hit by pitch, broken nose / out until 7/19

8/29 Bresnahan in bed with illness / back 9/8

1902 Giants transactions

Date	Transaction
04/25	Released Magee
04/28	Signed Joe Bean

04/29	Released Jim Delahanty
05/05	Purchased Joe Bean from Rochester
05/08	Luther Taylor rejoined team (had signed over winter but jumped to AL)
05/14	Steve Brodie released
05/20	Released Henry Thielman and Thurston
05/24	Signed Tom Campbell?
05/29	Acquired Hess, Hartley
05/30	Signed Libe Washburn
06/01	Signed McDonald
06/03	Signed O'Hagen
06/04	McDonald retired, Jackson released
06/05	Hartley retired
06/07	Signed Steve Brodie, Nichols, Hendricks
06/14	Signed Blewett
06/17	Released Steve Brodie
06/18	Signed Steve Brodie
06/19	John Hendricks given notice of release
06/20	Jack Doyle released (6/19?)
06/26	Joe Bean given notice of release (6/25?)
07/01	Signed Heinie Wagner
07/08	Roy Clark given notice of release, signed John McGraw
07/15	Released Blewett and Clark
07/17	Released O'Hagen, Burke, Yeager, Sparks, Evans, Wagner; signed Bresnahan, Cronin, McGann, McGinnity.
07/21	Signed George Browne, R. Miller
07/25	Released Libe Washburn
08/01	Signed Joe Wall
08/06	Jim Jones suspended for balance of season
09/01	Borrowed Jack Robinson from Bridgeport

Thanks to Cappy Gagnon, John Pardon, David W. Smith, Darryl Brock, and Bill Deane for sharing their research, and to Paul Wendt, Frank Vaccaro, and Skip McAfee for their help with this article.

NOTES

1. *Chicago Journal* as reprinted in *Sporting Life*, July 12, 1902.
2. *New York Herald*, July 10, 1902.
3. Details of the story vary, with some sources claiming that McGraw had reached agreement with Freedman by mid-June, with team secretary Fred Knowles and possibly John Brush acting as go-betweens. Mrs. McGraw, in her biography of her husband, claimed that the jump to New York was part of a plan between McGraw, Freedman, Brush, and Ban Johnson to put an AL team in New York, but she offers no evidence to support this notion.
4. David H. Nathan, ed., *Baseball Quotations* (New York: Ballantine, 1991).

SOURCES

The main sources used for this article were the *New York Telegram* and the *Sporting Life*. Other newspapers consulted were the *New York Times*, *New York Herald*, *New York Evening World*, *New York Press*, and *The Sporting News*. In addition, the following books and other records were used:

Charles Alexander, *John McGraw*.

Joe Durso, *Days of Mr. McGraw*.

Blanche McGraw with Arthur Mann, *The Real McGraw*.

John Thorn and Pete Palmer, eds., *Total Baseball*, 3rd edition.

Craig Carter, ed., *The Sporting News Complete Baseball Record Book*, 1994 edition.

1902 Official National League Statistics.

Information Concepts Inc. records of 1902 season.

28

Underestimating the Fog

BILL JAMES

Since the 1970s, one of the fundamental tenets of sabermetrics has been the under-standing that clutch hitting is not a repeatable skill—that players who perform well in the clutch one year are no more likely to do so the following year than anyone else. This was most ably demonstrated by Richard Cramer in his 1977 article in SABR's *Baseball Research Journal*. Years later, in this piece from the BRJ in 2004, Bill James argues that our confidence in this area might not be warranted—at least not by the studies Cramer had performed. James was one of the founders of SABR's Statistical Analysis Committee and wrote many articles for the journals in these early years. When he became the most widely read baseball analyst in the 1980s, his promotion of SABR in his annual *Baseball Abstract* fueled a large membership increase. Bill received the Henry Chadwick Award in 2010.

If this was a real scientific journal and I was a real academic, the title of this article would be "The Problem of Distinguishing Between Transient and Persistent Phenomena When Dealing with Variables from a Statistically Unstable Platform." But I was hoping somebody might actually read it.

I have come to realize, over the last three years, that a wide range of conclusions in sabermetrics may be unfounded, due to the reliance on a commonly accepted method which seems, intuitively, that it ought to work, but which in practice may not actually work at all. The problem has to do with distinguishing between transient and persistent phenomena, so let me start there.

If you make up a list of the leading hitters in the National League in 1982 (or any other year) and check their batting averages in 1983 (or the follow-up year, whatever it is) you will quite certainly find that those hitters hit far better than average in the follow-up season. If you look at the stolen base leaders in the National League in 1982, you will find that those players continued to steal bases in 1983. If you look at the hit by pitch leaders in 1982, you will find that those players continued to be hit by pitches in 1983. That is what we mean by a persistent phenomenon—that the people who are good at it one year are good at it the next year as well.

If the opposite is true—if the people who do well in a category one year do *not* tend to do well in the same category the next year—that's what we mean by a transient phenomenon. Here today, gone tomorrow.

All "real" skills in baseball (or anything else) are persistent at least to some extent. Intelligence, bicycle riding, alcoholism, income-earning capacity, height, weight, cleanliness, greed, bad breath, the ownership of dogs or llamas, and the tendency to vote Republican . . . all of these are persistent phenomena. Everything real is persistent to some measurable extent. Therefore, if something *cannot* be measured as persistent, we tend to assume that it is not real.

There are, in sabermetrics, a very wide range of things which have been labeled as "not real" or "not of any significance" because they cannot be measured as having any persistence. The first of these conclusions—and probably the most important—was Dick Cramer's conclusion in SABR's 1977 *Baseball Research Journal* that clutch hitting was not a reliable skill. Using the data from the "Player Win Averages" study by E. G. Mills and H. D. Mills of the 1969 and 1970 seasons, Cramer compared two things—the effectiveness of all hitters in general, and the impact of hitters on their team's won-lost record, as calculated by the Mills brothers. Those hitters who had more impact on their team's won-lost record than would be expected from their overall hitting ability were clutch hitters. Those who had less impact than expected were . . . well, non-clutch hitters, or whatever we call those. There are a number of uncomplimentary terms in use.

"If clutch hitters really exist," wrote Cramer, "one would certainly expect that a batter who was a clutch hitter in 1969 would tend also to be a clutch hitter in 1970. But if no such tendency exists, then 'clutch hitting' must surely be a matter of luck." Cramer found that there was no persistence in the clutch-hitting data—therefore, that clutch performance was a matter of luck. "I have established clearly," wrote Cramer, "that clutch hitting cannot be an important or a general phenomenon."

The argument triggered by this article continues to boil, and has now reached the point at which even *Sports Illustrated* is willing to discuss clutch hitting as an open question, at least for one article. But I am not writing about clutch hitting; I am talking about the method. Cramer's article was very influential. Subsequent to this article, I used a similar method to "demonstrate" that a wide variety of supposed "skills" of baseball players were actually just random manifestations of luck, and many other people have done the same. The list of conclusions which have been bulwarked by this method would be too long to include here, but among them are:

1. There is no such thing as an "ability to win" in a pitcher, as distinguished from an ability to prevent runs. A pitcher who goes 20-8 with a 3.70 ERA is no more likely to win 20 games in the following season than a pitcher who goes 14-14 with a 3.70 ERA on the same team.

2. Winning or losing close games is luck. Teams which win more one-run games than they should one year have little tendency to do so the next year.

3. Catchers have little or no impact on a pitcher's ERA. Whether a pitcher pitches well with a given catcher or does not appears to be mostly luck.

4. A pitcher has little or no control over his hits/innings ratio, other than by striking batters out and allowing home runs. A high hits/innings ratio, if the pitcher has a normal strikeout rate, is probably just bad luck.

5. Base running, like clutch hitting, has no persistent impact on a team's runs scored, other than by base stealing. If a team scores more runs than they ought to score based on their hits, home runs, walks, etc., it is probably just luck.

6. Batters have no *individual* tendency to hit well or hit poorly against left-handed pitching. There is a very strong *group* tendency for all right-handed hitters to hit well against left-handed pitchers, but individual deviations from the group tendency have a persistence of zero, therefore are not meaningful.

7. Batters do not get "hot" and "cold." Hot streaks and cold streaks are just random clusters of events.

8. A quality hitter in the middle of the lineup has little or no impact on the hitters surrounding him. A good hitter will not hit appreciably better with Manny Ramirez in the on-deck circle than he will with Rey Ordonez on deck.

I will revisit these issues later in the article. For now, trying again to keep clear what I am saying and what I am not, I am not saying that these conclusions are false. What I am saying, and will try to demonstrate beginning in just a moment, is that a method used to reach these conclusions is unreliable to the point of being useless—therefore, that some of these conclusions may be wanting in proof. Let me pick up the sixth item listed above, since, as far as I know, I was the only person ever to make this argument, and therefore there is in that case the least chance that someone will take offense when I try to demonstrate the error.

In the *1988 Baseball Abstract* (pages 9–15), I tried to do a thorough analysis of platoon data—data for left-handed hitters against right-handed pitchers, etc. I asked a series of questions about the platoon differential, and tried to work systematically through the data toward the answers.

One of the conclusions of that article was: "The platoon differential is not a weakness peculiar to some players. It is a condition of the game." I based this conclusion on the following research and logic. Suppose that you identify, in last year's platoon data, two groups of players: those who had the *largest* platoon differentials, and those who hit better the wrong way (that is, left-handed hitters who hit better against left-handed pitchers, and right-handed hitters who hit better against right-handed pitchers). Suppose that you then look at how those players hit in the *following* season. You will find that there is no difference or no reliable difference in their following-year platoon differentials. The players who had huge platoon differences in Year 1 will have platoon differences in Year 2 no larger than the players who were reverse-platoon in Year 1.

Individual platoon differences are transient, I concluded, therefore not real. Individual platoon differences are just luck. There is no evidence of individual batters having a special tendency to hit well or hit poorly against left-handed pitchers, except in a very few special cases.

As recently as two years ago I still believed this to be true, although (fortunately) I never succeeded in convincing anybody. The observation was useful, in a sense, because many people pay far more attention to platoon splits for individual hitters than is justified by an understanding of the data—but, in a literal sense, I simply was not correct. Individual batters do have individual platoon tendencies, in many more cases than I at first concluded.

Given a few paragraphs, I could explain how I finally realized that I must be wrong, and how I finally demonstrated that I was wrong, but that's a little bit outside the present article. In any case, this forced me to consider seriously where I had gone astray. My conclusion, which is the basis of this article, was that the "zero persistence equals luck" type of study poses much greater risk of error than I had previously understood.

Suppose that we have two players, whom we will call Allen and Bob. Allen and Bob are both right-handed hitters. Allen hits .290 against right-handed pitchers but .340 against left-handers. Bob hits .290 against right-handed pitchers but .250 against lefties.

From this we attempt to derive a third measurement, which is the player's *platoon differential*. Allen's platoon differential is .050 (.340 minus .290); Bob's is negative .040 (.250 minus .290). The platoon differential is what we could call a *comparison offshoot*—a measurement derived from a comparison of other measures.

The first problem with comparison offshoots is that they have the combined instability of all of their components. Every statistic in baseball is to a certain degree a measurement of a skill, to a certain degree a statement about the circumstances, and to a certain degree simply a product of luck. A pitcher goes 20-8—he goes 20-8 to a certain degree because he is a good pitcher, to a certain degree because he pitches for a good team, and to a certain degree because he is lucky (or unlucky). There is luck in everything, and baseball fans are always engaged in a perpetual struggle to figure out what is real and what is just luck.

In the case of any one statistical record, it is impossible to know to what precise extent it reflects luck, but a player usually bats only 100 to 200 times a year against left-handed pitchers. Batting averages in 100 or 200 at-bats involve huge amounts of luck. If a player hits .340 against lefties, is that 20% luck, or 50% luck, or 80% luck? There is no way of knowing—but batting averages in 100–150 at-bats are immensely unstable. Walter Johnson hit .433 one year in about 100 at-bats; the next year he hit .194. Just luck.

It is hard to distinguish the luck from the real skill, but as baseball fans we get to be pretty good at it. The problem is, that .290 batting average against right-handed pitchers—that also involves a great deal of luck.

When we create a new statistic, platoon *differential*, as a comparison offshoot of these other statistics, the new statistic embodies all of the instability—all of the luck—combined in either of its components. Suppose that you take two statistics, each of which is 30% luck, and you add them together. The resulting new statistic will still be 30% luck (understanding, of course, that the 30% number here is purely illustrative, and has no functional definition).

But when you take two statistics, each of which is 30% luck, and you *subtract* one from the other (or divide one by the other), then the resulting new statistic—the comparison offshoot—may be as much as 60% luck. By contrasting one statistic with another to reach a new conclusion, you are picking up all of the luck involved in either of the original statistics.

But wait a minute—the problem is actually much, much more serious than that. A normal batting average for a regular player is in the range of .270. A normal platoon differential is in the range of 25 to 30 points—.025 to .030.

Thus, *the randomness is operating on a vastly larger scale than the statistic can accommodate.* The new statistic—the platoon differential—is operating on a scale in which the norm is about .0275—but the randomness is occurring on a scale ten times larger than that. The new statistic is on the scale of a Volkswagen; the randomness is on the scale of an 18-wheeler. In effect, we are asking a Volkswagen engine to pull a semi.

But wait a minute, the problem is still worse than that. In the platoon differential example, I reached the conclusion I did by comparing one comparison offshoot with a second comparison offshoot—the platoon differential in one year with the platoon differential the next year. Dick Cramer, in the clutch-hitting study, did the same thing, and catcher-ERA studies, which look for consistency in catcher's impact on ERAs, do the same thing; they compare one comparison offshoot with a second comparison offshoot. It is a comparison of two comparison offshoots.

When you do that, the result embodies not just all of the randomness in *two* original statistics, but all of the randomness in *four* original statistics. Unless you have extremely stable "original elements"—original statistics stabilized by hundreds of thousands of trials—then the result is, for all practical purposes, just random numbers.

We ran astray because we have been assuming that random data is proof of nothingness, when in reality random data proves nothing. In essence, starting with Dick Cramer's article, Cramer argued, "I did an analysis which *should* have identified clutch hitters, if clutch hitting exists. I got random data; therefore, clutch hitters don't exist."

Cramer was using random data as proof of nothingness—and I did the same, many times, and many other people also have done the same. But I'm saying now that's not right; random data proves nothing—and it *cannot* be used as proof of nothingness.

Why? Because whenever you do a study, if your study completely fails, you will get random data. Therefore, when you get random data, *all* you may conclude is that your study has failed. Cramer's study may have failed to identify clutch hitters because clutch hitters don't exist—as he concluded—or it may have failed to identify clutch hitters because the method doesn't work—as I now believe. We don't know. All we can say is that the study has failed.

Dealing now with the nine conclusions listed near the start of the article, which were:

1. Clutch hitters don't exist.
2. Pitchers have no ability to win, which is distinct from an ability to prevent runs.
3. Winning or losing close games is luck.
4. Catchers have little or no impact on a pitcher's ERA.
5. A pitcher has little or no control over his hits/innings ratio, other than by striking batters out and allowing home runs.
6. Base running has no persistent impact on a team's runs scored, other than by base stealing.
7. Batters have no *individual* tendency to hit well or hit poorly against left-handed pitching.
8. Batters don't get hot and cold.
9. One hitter does not "protect" another in a hitting lineup.

On (1), it is my opinion that this should be regarded as an open question. While Dick Cramer is a friend of mine, and I have tremendous respect for his work, I am convinced that, even if clutch-hitting skill did exist and was extremely important, this analysis would still reach the conclusion that it did, simply because it is not possible to detect consistency in clutch hitting by the use of this method.

There have been other studies of the issue (including several by me) which have reached the same conclusion, but these were in essence repeats of the Cramer approach. If that approach doesn't work once, it's not going to work the second time, the third, or the fourth. It just doesn't work. We need to find some more affirmative way to study the subject.

On (2) above (pitchers have no ability to win, which is distinct from an ability to prevent runs), this, I think, has been a very useful observation over the years, and it now has an additional claim to being true, which is: many predictions have been made based on this assumption which later proved to be accurate.

Simple example: in 2002, Dan Wright went 14-12 with a 5.18 ERA for the Chicago White Sox. It's a data mismatch; a 5.18 ERA should not produce a 14-12 record. Anyone in sabermetrics would immediately recognize this as a strong indication that Wright would not be able to continue to win in 2003—and in fact he couldn't, finishing the season 1-7. We have made hundreds of observations/predictions of that nature based on this understanding, and most of these have proven correct. I'm not even going to bring up Storm Davis. Therefore, we probably would not wish to abandon the insight simply because the original proof thereof was faulty.

However, I would have trouble now with my original argument that the pitcher has no ability to win, other than what is reflected in his runs allowed. There may in fact be some ability to win, in the way the old-time baseball guys imagined that there was. There may be some pitchers who have some ability to win games 3–2 and 9–8. Sabermetrics has traditionally discounted the existence of this ability at *any* level. I would now argue that it may exist at some fairly low level.

On (3) above (winning and losing close games is luck) . . . it would be my opinion that it is probably not all luck.

On (4) above (catchers have little or no impact on a pitcher's ERA), I don't think that there is a scintilla of evidence that that is true. It is my opinion that it is impossible to evaluate a catcher's defensive contribution by a comparison based on catcher's ERAs.

Many of the pitcher/catcher combinations which have been studied to reach this conclusion worked together for 40 or 50 innings. ERAs in less than 100 innings pitched have immense instability due to randomness. Further, since the catcher's defensive skill is only one of many, many factors in the prevention of runs, the randomness occurs on a scale which must be 20 times larger than the scale on which the catcher's ERA contribution must be measured—even if you assume that the catcher's defensive contribution is very large.

Obviously, if a catcher makes a defensive contribution, this must result in a lower ERA for his pitchers. It *seems*, intuitively, that this difference would *have* to be visible in the stats at least at some level, that there would at least have to be *some* measurable consistency in the data. That intuitive sense is what misled me, on this issue, for 25 years. But, in fact, it doesn't. There is so much instability in the data that the catcher's defensive contribution simply cannot be isolated in this form.

On (5) above (the Voros McCracken observation), this seems to me different from the others, for this reason. Voros's observation relies on something which is near to a historical constant. When a ball is in play—not a home run, not a strikeout, not a walk—that ball will be turned into an out about 70% of the time. That is the nature of the game. Okay, it's 72% for some teams; it's 67% for other teams; it's 69.5% in some years, it's 68.8% in others. But it doesn't vary crazily from team to team or park to park, and it's really about the same now as it was in 1930 or 1960.

This creates something close to a "stable platform" against which to measure the individual variable, and this makes an important difference. What Voros was saying, in essence, was: "When you see a pitcher who gets outs on 75% of his balls in play, he's just been lucky, because *no pitcher can actually do that*. It's not the nature of the game." This may have been overstated by some people sometimes, but I have little doubt that this observation is more true than false.

On (6) above (base running has no persistent impact on a team's runs scored, other than by base stealing), that's probably not true, and that's probably mostly my error, again. Base running can be measured in simple, objective terms—bases gained, base running errors, etc. A much better way to think about the problem is to measure those things and study what impact they have on runs scored, rather than starting with the proposition that they are probably not meaningful.

On (7) (batters have no *individual* tendency to hit well or hit poorly against left-handed pitching), that, as I said, was just wrong. My mistake.

On (8), this almost becomes a brain teaser. Most baseball fans believe that players get "hot" and "cold." Many analysts believe (and a popular web site is devoted to proving) that this is nonsense, that hot streaks and cold streaks are just random clusters.

Everyone agrees that a hot streak is a transient phenomenon. Therefore, why doesn't everyone agree that it is a non-real phenomenon—a random sequence?

Because people believe that there is *some* persistence to the transient phenomenon—in other words, that the persistence is not zero.

My opinion is that, at this point, no one has made a compelling argument either in favor of or against the hot-hand phenomenon. The methods that are used to prove that a hot hitter is not really hot, in my opinion, would reach this conclusion whether hot hitters in fact existed or whether they did not.

Stated another way, the hot-hand opponents are arguing—or seem to me to be arguing—that the absence of proof is proof. The absence of clear proof that hot hands exist is proof that they don't. I am arguing that it is not. The argument against hot streaks is based on the *assumption* that this analysis would detect hot streaks if they existed, rather than on the proven fact. Whether hot streaks exist or do not I do not know—but I think the assumption is false.

On (9) (batting ahead of a good hitter does not ordinarily cause anyone to hit better), I still believe this to be true. While this analysis relies on part on comparison offshoots, it does so in a more tangential way. I believe that a more careful study, steering clear of comparison offshoots, is still likely to demonstrate that hitters perform (essentially) independent of one another, except in a few isolated cases.

In a sense, it is like this: a sentry is looking through a fog, trying to see if there is an invading army out there, somewhere through the fog. He looks for a long time, and he can't see any invaders, so he goes and gets a really, really bright light to shine into the fog. Still doesn't see anything.

The sentry returns and reports that there is just no army out there—but the problem is, he has underestimated the density of the fog. It *seems*, intuitively, that if you shine a bright enough light into the fog, if there was an army out there you'd have to be able to see it—but in fact you can't. That's where we are: we're trying to see if there's an army out there, and we have confident reports that the coast is clear—but we may have underestimated the density of the fog. The randomness of the data is the fog. What I am saying in this article is that the fog *may* be many times more dense than we have been allowing for. Let's look again; let's give the fog a little more credit. Let's not be too sure that we haven't been missing something important.

29

Which Great Teams Were Just Lucky?

PHIL BIRNBAUM

Students, critics, and fans of baseball analysis have always struggled mightily with the concept of "luck" in baseball. The "best" team doesn't always win—not today, not over seven games, not even over 162 games. There are many forms of luck—the sequencing of game events, the health of your players, the confluence of good player seasons—that can make a fair team into a good team, or a good team into a great one. Phil Birnbaum has been a leading baseball analyst for many years, the long-time editor of SABR's "By the Numbers" newsletter, the chairman of the Statistical Analysis Committee, and the statistical editor of *Total Baseball*'s final edition in 2004. In this typically insightful piece, Phil examines all the ways a team can be lucky and tells us which teams in particular were blessed with good fortune.

A team's season record is massively influenced by luck. Suppose you take a coin and flip it 162 times to simulate a season. Each time it lands heads, that's a win, and when it lands tails, that's a loss. You'd expect, on average, to get 81 wins and 81 losses. But for any individual season, the record may vary significantly from 81-81. Just by random chance alone, your team might go 85-77, or 80-82, or even 69-93.

Suppose you were able to clone a copy of the New York Yankees, and play the cloned team against the real one. (That's hard to do with real players, but easy in a simulation game like APBA.) Again, on average, each team should win 81 games against each other, but, again, the records could vary significantly from 81-81, and the difference would be due to luck.

As it turns out, the range and frequency of possible records of a .500 team can be described by a normal (bell-shaped) curve, with an average of 81 wins and a standard deviation (SD) of about six wins. The SD can be thought of as a "typical" difference due to luck—so with an SD of six games, a typical record of a coin tossed 162 times is 87-75, or 75-87. Two-thirds of the outcomes should be within that range, so if you were to run 300 coin-seasons, or 300 cloned-Yankee seasons, you should get 200 of them winding up between 75 and 87 wins.

More interesting are the one-third of the seasons that fall outside that range. If all 16 teams in the National League were exactly average, you'd nonetheless expect five of them to wind up with more than 87 wins or with fewer than 75 wins. Furthermore, of those five teams, you'd expect one of them (actually, about 0.8 of a team) to finish more than two SDs away from the mean—that is, with more than 93 wins, or more than 93 losses.

This is a lot easier to picture if you see a real set of standings, so Table 29.1 shows a typical result of a coin-tossing season for a hypothetical National League where every team is .500.

Table 29.1. Games gained/lost because of luck

Mets	94	68	—	+13
Nationals	82	80	12	+1
Phillies	78	84	16	-3
Braves	77	85	17	-4
Marlins	70	92	24	-11
Brewers	84	78	—	+3
Cardinals	83	79	1	+2
Pirates	82	80	2	+1
Reds	80	82	4	-1
Cubs	79	83	5	-2
Astros	78	84	6	-3
Padres	93	69	—	+12
Dodgers	89	73	4	+8
Giants	84	78	9	+3
Rockies	75	87	18	-6
Diamondbacks	67	95	26	-14

In this simulated, randomized season, the Mets in the East and Diamondbacks in the West were both really .500 teams—but, by chance alone, the Mets finished ahead of Arizona by 27 games!

As it turns out, this season is a little more extreme than usual. On average, the difference between the best team and the worst team will be about 24 games, not 27. Also, there should be only one team above 93 wins (we had two), with the next best at 89.

Real Seasons

So far this is just an intellectual exercise because, of course, not every team is a .500 team. But even teams that aren't .500 have a standard deviation of around six games, so a similar calculation applies to them.

For instance, suppose you have a .550 team, expected to win 89 games. That's eight games above average. To get a rough idea of the distribution of wins it will actually get, you can just add those eight games to each row of table 29.1. So, if our .550 team plays 16 seasons, in an extremely lucky season it'll finish 102-60, and in its unluckiest season it will go only 75-87—still a swing of 27 games (although, as we said, 24 is more typical). It's even possible that those two seasons will be consecutive, in which case the team will have fallen from 102 wins down to 75 in one season—and only because of luck!

If, in an average season, one team will drop 12 or more games out of contention for no real reason, and some other team will gain 12 games, it's pretty obvious that luck has a huge impact on team performance.

Which brings us to this question: is there a way, after the fact, to see how lucky a team was? The 1993 Philadelphia Phillies went 97-65. But how good were they, really? Were they like the top team in the chart that got 13 games lucky, so that they really should have been only 84-78? Were they like the bottom team in the chart that got 14 games unlucky, so that they were really a 111-51 team, one of the most talented ever? Were they even more extreme? Were they somewhere in the middle?

This article presents a way we can find out.

Luck's Footprints

A team starts out with a roster with a certain amount of talent, capable of playing a certain caliber of baseball. It ends up with a won-lost record. How much luck was involved in converting the talent to the record?

There are five main ways in which a team can get lucky or unlucky. Well, actually, there is an infinite number of ways, but those ways will leave evidence in one of five statistical categories.

1. Its Hitters Have Career Years, Playing Better than Their Talent Can Support

Alfredo Griffin had a long career with the Blue Jays, A's, and Dodgers, mostly in the 1980s. A career .249 hitter with little power and no walks, his RC/G (Runs Created per Game, a measure of how many runs a team would score with a lineup of nine Alfredo Griffins) was never above the league average.

Griffin's best season was 1986. That year he hit .285, tied his career high with four home runs, and came close to setting a career high in walks (with 35). He created 4.16 runs per game, his best season figure ever.

In this case, we assume that Alfredo was lucky. Just as a player's APBA card might hit .285 instead of .249 just because of some fortunate dice rolls, we assume that Griffin's actual performance also benefited from similar luck.

What would cause that kind of luck? There are many possibilities. The most obvious one is that even the best players have only so much control of their muscles and reflexes. In *The Physics of Baseball* Robert Adair points out that swinging one-hundredth of a second too early will cause a hit ball to go foul—and one-hundredth of a second too late will have it go foul the other way! To oversimplify, if Griffin is only good enough to hit the ball randomly within that .02 seconds, and it's a hit only if it's in the middle 25% of that interval, he'll be a .250 hitter. If one year, just by luck, he gets 30% of those hits instead of 25%, his stats take a jump.

There are other reasons that players may have career years. They might, just by luck, face weaker pitchers than average. They may play in more home games than average. They may play a couple of extra games in Colorado. Instead of 10 balls hit close to the left-field line landing five fair and five foul, maybe eight landed fair and only two foul. When guessing fastball on a 3–2 count, they may be right 60% of the time one year but only 40% of the time the next.

I used a formula, based on his performance in the two seasons before and two seasons after, to estimate Griffin's luck in 1986. The formula is unproven, and may be flawed for certain types of players—but you can also do it by eye.

Here's Alfredo's record for 1984–1988:

Year	Outs (AB-H)	Batting runs	RC/game
1984	318	-28	2.46
1985	448	-20	3.43
1986	425	-5	4.16
1987	364	-16	3.52
1988	253	-22	2.15

Leaving out 1986, Griffin seemed to average about -22 batting runs per season. In 1986, he was -5: a difference of 17 runs. The RC/G column gives similar results: Griffin seemed to average around three, except in 1986, when he was better by about one run per game. 425 batting outs is about 17 games' worth (there are about 25.5 hitless at-bats per game), and 17 games at one run per game again gives us 17 runs.

The formula hits almost exactly, giving us 16.7 runs of "luck." That's coincidence, here, that the formula gives the same answer as the "eye" method—they'll usually be close, but not necessarily identical.

Griffin is a bit of an obvious case, where the exceptional year sticks out. Most seasons aren't like that, simply because most players usually do about what is expected of them. The formula will give a lot of players small luck numbers, like 6 runs, or -3, or such. Still, they add up. If a team's 14 hitters each turn three outs into singles, just by chance, that's about 28 runs—since it takes about 10 runs to equal one win, that's 2.8 wins.

And, of course, the opposite of a career year is an off-year. Just as we measure that Alfredo was lucky in 1985, he was clearly unlucky in 1984, where his 2.46 figure was low even for him.

2. Its Pitchers Have Career Years, Playing Better than Their Talent Can Support

What's true of a hitter's batting line is also true of the batting line of what the pitcher gives up. Just as a hitter might hit .280 instead of .250 just by luck, so might a pitcher give up a .280 average against him instead of .250, again just by luck.

Using Runs Created, we can compute how many runs per game the pitcher "should have" given up, based on the batting line of the hitters who faced him (this stat is called "Component ERA"). And, just as for batters, a career year (or off-year) for a pitcher will stick right out.

Here's Bob Knepper, from 1980 to 1984:

Year	IP	ERA	Component ERA
1980	215.1	4.10	4.13
1981	156.2	2.18	2.26
1982	180	4.45	4.14
1983	203	3.19	3.62
1984	233.2	3.20	3.28

Leaving out 1981, Knepper seemed to average a CERA of about three-and-a-half. But in '82, he was at 4.14. That's about .7 runs per game, multiplied by exactly 20 games (180 innings), for about 14 runs lost due to random chance.

The formula sees it about the same way, assigning Knepper 17 runs of bad luck.

A pitcher's record necessarily includes that of his fielders—and so, whenever we talk about a pitcher's career year, that career year really belongs to the pitcher and his defense, in some combination.

3. It Was More Successful at Turning Baserunners into Runs

The statistic "Runs Created," invented by Bill James, estimates the number of runs a team will score based on its batting line. Runs Created is pretty accurate, generally within 25 runs a season of a team's actual scoring. But it's not exactly accurate, because it can't be.

Run scoring depends not just on the batting line, but also on the timing of the events within it. If a team has seven hits in a game, it'll probably score a run or two. But if the hits are scattered, it might get shut out. And if the hits all come in the same inning, it might score four or five runs.

The more a team's hits and walks are bunched together, the more runs it will score. That's the same thing as saying that the better the team hits with men on base, the more runs it will score. Which, again, is like saying the better the team hits in the clutch, the more runs it will score.

But several analyses, most recently a study by Tom Ruane of 40 years' worth of play-by-play data, have shown that clutch hitting is generally random—that is, there is no innate "talent" for clutch hitting aside from ordinary hitting talent. So, for instance, a team that hits .260 is just as likely to hit .280 in the clutch as it is to hit .240 in the clutch.

And if that's the case, then any discrepancy between Runs Created and actual runs is due to luck, not talent.

And so when the 2001 Anaheim Angels scored 691 runs, but the formula predicted they should score 746, we chalk the difference, 55 runs, up to just plain bad luck.

4. Its Opposition Was Less Successful in Turning Baserunners Into Runs

If clutch hitting is random, it's random for a team's opposition, too. So when the 1975 Big Red Machine held its opponents to 70 fewer runs than their Runs Created estimate says they should have scored, we attribute those

70 runs to random chance. The Reds' pitchers were lucky, to the tune of seven wins.

5. It Won More Games than Expected from
Its Runs Scored and Runs Allowed

The 1962 New York Mets achieved the worst record in modern baseball history, at 40-120. That season they scored only 617 runs and allowed 948—both figures the worst in the league.

There's another Bill James formula, the Pythagorean Projection, which estimates what a team's winning percentage should have been based on their runs scored and runs allowed. By that formula, the Mets should have been 7.6 games better in the standings than they actually were—that is, they should have been 47-113.

Any difference between expected wins and actual wins has to do with the timing of runs—teams that score lots of runs in blowout games will win fewer games than expected, while teams that "save" their runs for closer games will win more than their projection. But studies have shown that run timing, like clutch hitting, is random. Teams don't have a "talent" for saving their runs for close games, and therefore any difference from Pythagorean Projection is just luck.

So we judge that seven of the Mets' 1962 losses were the result of bad luck, and that based on this finding, they weren't quite as bad as we thought. Of course, 47-113 is still pretty dismal.

Putting It All Together

Earlier, we mentioned the 1993 Phillies. How lucky were they? Let's take the five steps, one at a time:

1 / 2. Career Years or Off-Years

Everything came together in 1993, as individual Phillies hitters had career years, to the tune of a huge 131 runs.

Lenny Dykstra had a monster year, hitting 19 home runs (his previous high was 10) with a career-high .305 average. He was 37 runs better than expected. Rookie Kevin Stocker was lucky by 19 runs—he hit .324, but would never break .300 again. John Kruk and Pete Incaviglia were a combined 33 runs better than expected. Of the hitters, only Mickey Morandini, at -9, had an off-year of more than three runs.

The pitchers, for their part, were lucky by 39 runs, led by Tommy Greene, who had the best year of his career, 37 runs better than expected. Other than that, the staff performed pretty much as expected. A full list:

Player	Luck (runs)
Dykstra, Lenny	37
Stocker, Kevin	19
Kruk, John	17
Incaviglia, Pete	16
Daulton, Darren	11
Chamberlain, Wes	11
Eisenreich, Jim	10
Pratt, Todd	7
Batiste, Kim	6
Hollins, Dave	5
Amaro, Ruben	5
Jordan, Ricky	1
Millette, Joe	0
Bell, Juan	-2
Thompson, Milt	-3
Duncan, Mariano	-3
Manto, Jeff	-3
Morandini, Mickey	-9
Greene, Tommy	37
Mulholland, Terry	24
West, David	9
Jackson, Danny	9
Andersen, Larry	5
Pall, Donn	4
Williams, Mitch	3
Williams, Mike	2
Mauser, Tim	2
Brink, Brad	2
Mason, Roger	1
Thigpen, Bobby	-1

DeLeon, Jose	-2
Davis, Mark	-3
Green, Tyler	-7
Ayrault, Bob	-9
Foster, Kevin	-9
Schilling, Curt	-10
Rivera, Ben	-16

3. Runs Created by Batters

The Phillies scored 24 more runs than expected from their batting line.

4. Runs Created by Opposition

The Phillies' opponents scored almost exactly the expected number of runs, exceeding their estimate by only one run.

5. Pythagorean Projection

Scoring 877 runs and allowing 740, the Phillies were Pythagorically unlucky. They should have won 3.1 more games than they did—at 10 runs per win, that's about 31 runs worth. Adding it all up gives:

Career years/off years by hitters: +131 runs
Career years/off years by pitchers: +39 runs
Runs Created by batters: +24 runs
Runs Created by opposition: -1 run
Pythagorean projection: -31 runs
Total: +162 runs (16 wins)
Actual record: 97-65
Projected record: 81-81

We conclude that the 1993 Phillies were a dead-even .500 team that just happened to get lucky enough that it won 97 games and the pennant.

This shouldn't be that surprising. The Phils finished last in the division in 1992, and second last in 1994, with mostly the same personnel. You can argue, if you like, that the players caught a temporary surge of talent in 1993, which they promptly lost after the season. But the conclusion that they had a lucky year makes a lot more sense.

The Best and Worst "Career Years"

Which players had the worst "off-years" between 1960 and 2001? Here's the chart:

1986	TOR	AL	P	Stieb, Dave	-60
1999	SEA	AL	P	Fassero, Jeff	-56
1997	CHA	AL	B	Belle, Albert	-53
1997	OAK	AL	B	Brosius, Scott	-50
1973	PIT	NL	P	Blass, Steve	-50
1980	CHN	NL	P	Lamp, Dennis	-48
1962	CHN	NL	B	Santo, Ron	-47
1997	CHN	NL	B	Sosa, Sammy	-45
1961	CHA	AL	P	Baumann, Frank	-45
1971	HOU	NL	B	Wynn, Jimmy	-45

It's an interesting chart, but also shows a limitation of the formula—it can't distinguish between players who were lucky, and players who had a real reason for their performance problem.

Take Steve Blass, for example. His well-documented collapse in 1973 was not because he was just unlucky, but that he suddenly was unable to find the strike zone. While succumbing to "Steve Blass disease" is, I guess, a form of bad luck, it's not really the kind of luck we're investigating, which assumes that the player has his normal level of talent, but things just don't go his way. If you're doing an analysis of the 1973 Pirates, you might want to subtract out those 50 runs, based on the known understanding that they weren't really bad luck.

Dave Stieb in 1986—the worst "unlucky" season of the past 40 years—is another interesting case. Stieb was arguably the best pitcher in the AL in 1984 and 1985; he was legitimately bad in 1986, but went back to excellent in 1987 and 1988. What happened in 1986? Bill James suggested that Stieb had lost a little bit of his stuff, and was slow to accept his new limitations and pitch within them. I looked over a couple of game reports in the *Toronto Star* from that year, and the tone seemed to be puzzlement at Stieb's bad year—there was no suggestion that Stieb was injured or such.

The next page lists the luckiest years. It shows that Steve Carlton's awesome 1972 season, when he went 28-10 for a dismal .378 team, comes in as the luckiest of all time. Norm Cash is second, for his well-documented cork-aided out-of-nowhere 1961 (note that the system is unable to distinguish luck from cheating). And it's interesting that Sammy Sosa appears on both lists.

1972	PHI	NL	P	Carlton, Steve	63
1961	DET	AL	B	Cash, Norm	60
1980	OAK	AL	P	Norris, Mike	60
1963	CHN	NL	P	Ellsworth, Dick	58
1993	TOR	AL	B	Olerud, John	58
1986	TEX	AL	P	Correa, Ed	54
1970	LAN	NL	B	Grabarkewitz, Billy	54
1991	BAL	AL	B	Ripken Jr., Cal	52
1999	OAK	AL	B	Jaha, John	51
2001	CHN	NL	B	Sosa, Sammy	50

You would expect that the luckiest season of all-time would be one like Cash's, where an average player suddenly has one great year. But, instead, Carlton's 1972 is a case where a great player has one of the greatest seasons ever. Of course, it's a bit easier for a pitcher to come up with a big year than a hitter, because there's a double effect—when his productivity goes up, his impact on the team is compounded because he gets more innings (even if only because he's not removed in the third inning of a bad outing). On the other hand, a full-time hitter gets about the same amount of playing time whether he's awesome or merely excellent.

Again, you can visit these cases to see if you can come up with explanations other than luck—Mike Norris, for instance, is widely considered to have been mortally overworked by Billy Martin in 1980, destroying his arm and, in that light, perhaps 60 runs is a bit of an overestimate.

Lucky and Unlucky Teams

The lists of players are interesting but probably not new knowledge—even without this method, we were probably aware that Norm Cash had a lucky season in 1961. On the other hand, which were the lucky and unlucky teams? I didn't know before I did this study. Not only didn't I know, but I didn't even have a trace of an idea.

Table 29.2 shows the 15 unluckiest teams between 1960 and 2001. The unluckiest team over the last 40 years was the 1962 New York Mets—the team with the worst record ever. This is not a coincidence—the worse the team, the more likely it had bad luck, for obvious reasons.

Table 29.2. The 15 unluckiest teams, 1960–2001

Team	Season	Career Year Hitters (Runs)	Career Year Pitchers (Runs)	Pythagoras Luck (runs)	Batting RC Luck	Opposition RC Luck	Total Luck (runs)	Actual W/L	Luck-Adjusted W/L
NYN	1962	24	-71	-76	-21	-62	-206	40 120	61 99
OAK	1979	-132	-142	42	23	7	-203	54 108	74 88
CLE	1987	-46	-83	2	-29	-40	-196	61 101	81 81
TOR	1995	-72	-50	-24	-43	-6	-196	56 88	76 68
SEA	1998	-35	-55	-49	-63	10	-192	76 85	95 66
PHI	1961	-53	-38	-69	9	-37	-188	47 107	66 88
CHN	1962	-75	-67	-7	-23	-12	-185	59 103	77 85
COL	1999	-61	-178	12	-22	68	-181	72 90	90 72
KC1	1964	-11	-162	-6	-23	24	-178	57 105	75 87
DET	1996	-67	-146	-13	38	9	-178	53 109	71 91
PIT	1985	-10	-54	-61	-17	-29	-171	57 104	74 87
DET	1960	-115	25	-47	-16	-8	-161	71 83	87 67
CLE	1985	-62	-57	-76	50	-15	-161	60 102	76 86
CHA	1970	-31	-89	-43	9	-7	-161	56 106	72 90
ATL	1977	-55	-151	19	20	8	-160	61 101	77 85

Most of the Mets' problems came from timing—poor hitting in the clutch, opponents' good hitting in the clutch, and poor hitting in close games. That poor timing cost them about 15 wins. Bad years from their pitchers cost them another seven wins, which was partially compensated for by two wins worth of good years by their hitters.

On the other hand, the 1979 Oakland A's had good timing—seven games of good luck worth. But their players had such bad off-years that it cost them 27 games in the win column. Of their 33 players, only five had career years of any size. The other 28 players underperformed, led by the 2-17 Matt Keough (43 runs of bad luck), off whom the opposition batted .315.

The 1995 Blue Jays were actually the unluckiest team by winning percentage—they were -196 runs in a shortened 144-game season. They wound up tied for the worst record in the league when in reality their talent was well above average.

But the 1998 Mariners could probably be considered the most disappointing of these 15 teams. Their talent shows as good enough to win 95 games, surely enough for the post-season—but they had 19 games worth of bad luck, and finished 76-85. It's not on the chart, but the Mariners were unlucky again the next season, by 13 games this time—they should have been a 92-win wild-card contender in 1999, but again finished down the pack at 79-83.

The luckiest team (table 29.3), by a runaway margin, was the 2001 Seattle Mariners, who won 116 games. And they did most of it through career years.

Of the lucky runs, 127 came from the hitters (in this study, second only to the 1993 Phillies), and the pitchers contributed 116 of their own (fifth best). Thirteen separate players contributed at least one lucky win each—Bret Boone (40 runs), Freddy Garcia (38), and Mark McLemore (23) topped the list. Only one player was more than 10 runs unlucky (John Halama, at -11). Despite all the luck, the Mariners were still an excellent team—with average luck they would have still finished 89-73.

The 1998 Yankees are considered one of the best teams ever, and it's perhaps surprising that they emerge as the second luckiest team. Like the 2001 Mariners, the '98 Yankees got most of their luck from their players' performances—about eight games each from their hitting and pitching. In talent, they were 92-70, which is still a very strong team. Indeed, of the 15 luckiest teams, the 1998 Yankees show as the best.

The Miracle Mets of 1969 were 17 games lucky—but this time most of

Table 29.3. The 15 luckiest teams, 1960–2001

TEAM	Season	Career Year Hitters (Runs)	Career Year Pitchers (Runs)	Pythagoras Luck (runs)	Batting RC Luck	Opposition RC Luck	Total Luck (runs)	Actual W/L		Luck-Adjusted W/L	
SEA	2001	127	116	49	-21	3	273	116	46	89	73
NYA	1998	88	84	32	9	8	220	114	48	92	70
PIT	1960	77	67	18	-1	29	191	95	59	76	78
OAK	1992	81	18	67	0	20	186	96	66	77	85
SLN	1985	94	56	-11	16	29	183	101	61	83	79
LAN	1962	115	13	41	60	-49	180	102	63	84	81
NYA	1961	51	57	43	17	9	178	109	53	91	71
SFN	1993	64	67	30	6	11	178	103	59	85	77
SLN	2000	68	78	27	-23	24	174	95	67	78	84
NYA	1963	45	52	26	29	21	173	104	57	87	74
NYN	1969	-2	60	65	33	16	172	100	62	83	79
NYN	1986	74	47	31	12	5	169	108	54	91	71
CLE	1995	31	83	54	-27	26	167	100	44	83	61
SLN	1987	30	-2	27	60	52	166	95	67	78	84
CIN	1995	99	66	1	-9	9	166	85	59	68	76

their luck was timing luck—10 wins in Runs Created, and about two wins in Pythagoras. Still, they were a respectable 83-79 team in talent.

The worst of these lucky teams was the 1960 Pirates. Bill Mazeroski's famous Game Seven home run brought the World Series championship to a team that, by this analysis, was worse than average, at 76-78. The 97-57 Yankees, whom they beat, had been eight games lucky themselves, but were still the most talented team in the majors that year, at 89-65.

The Best Teams Ever

Which teams were legitimately the best, even after luck is stripped out of their record? Perhaps not surprisingly, the list is dominated by the "dynasty" teams:

Team	Season	Actual		Talent	
		W	L	W	L
BAL	1969	109	53	102	60
ATL	1998	106	56	102	60
ATL	1997	101	61	100	62
BAL	1970	108	54	99	63
LAN	1974	102	60	98	64
CIN	1975	108	54	98	64
NYA	1977	100	62	98	64
ATL	1993	104	58	98	64
SEA	1997	90	72	98	64
ATL	1995	90	54	87	57
BAL	1971	101	57	95	63
CIN	1977	88	74	97	65
NYA	1997	96	66	97	65
OAK	2001	102	60	97	65
BOS	1978	99	64	98	65

The 1969, '70, and '71 Orioles all appear in the top 15, as do four Braves teams from the '90s. The ill–fated victims–of–Bucky Dent 1978 Red Sox come in at number 15. (The list may not appear to be in the correct order because of rounding—but it is.)

The 1975 Reds made the list, but the 1976 Reds don't (they came in at number 42). Interestingly, the unheralded 1977 Reds, whose nine games of bad luck dropped them to 88-74, appear at number 12. The 1978 Reds, with a projected talent of 96-65, were 21st. This suggests that the Big Red Machine stayed Big and Red longer than we think, but bad luck made it look like the talent had dissipated.

I've never heard the 1974 Dodgers described as among the best of all time, but they're fifth on the list. It was Steve Garvey's first full season, and the Dodgers had a solid infield and legitimately strong pitching staff.

Arguably the biggest surprise on this list isn't the presence or absence of any particular team, but that only three teams over the last 40 years were talented enough to win 100 games. This is legitimate—if there were lots of 100–game teams, we'd see a substantial number getting moderately lucky and winning 106 games or more. Also, it's consistent with a different study I did back in 1988, which found that, theoretically, a team that wins 109 games is, on average, only a 98-game talent. But there is no assurance that this is correct—it's possible that my algorithm for "career years" overestimates the amount of luck and underestimates the amount of talent. Here are the worst teams ever:

Team	Season	Actual	Talent
		W-L	W-L
NYN	1965	50–112	54–108
TOR	1977	54–107	54–107
TEX	1972	54–100	54–100
SDN	1969	52–110	57–105
SEA	1977	64–98	57–105
SDN	1971	61–100	58–103
NYN	1964	53–109	58–104
SDN	1973	60–102	59–103
NYN	1963	51–111	59–103
WS2	1961	61–100	59–102
HOU	1963	66–96	60–102
HOU	1964	66–96	60–102
SDN	1972	58–95	57–96
HOU	1962	64–96	60–100
FLO	1993	64–98	61–101

With expansion, it's a lot easier to create a team that loses 100 games than a team that wins 100 games. The 100-game loser list is 23 teams long.

Interesting here is the repeated presence of the expansion San Diego Padres, with four teams in the top 15 abysmal list. It's actually worse than that—the 1970 team finished 19th, and the 1974 Padres were 29th. For six consecutive years San Diego fielded a team in the bottom 30. That they have not been recognized as that futile a team probably stems from the fact that, unlike the expansion Mets, they never had enough bad luck to give them a string of historically horrific records. From 1970 to 1973, their luck was positive each year.

Missing from this list are the 1962 Mets—as we saw, they really should have been 61-99, for 19th worst ever.

The bottom 14 teams are all from the '60s and '70s, suggesting—or confirming—that competitive balance has improved in recent decades.

How Often Does the Best Team Win?

In 1989, a Bill James study found that because of luck, a six- or seven-team division will theoretically be won by the best team only about 55% of the time.

I checked the actual "luck" numbers for all 96 division races from 1969 to 1993 (excluding 1981), and found that 59% (57 of 96) were won by the most talented team—very close to Bill's figure.

Of the 39 pennant races that went to the "wrong" team, the most lopsided was the 1987 National League East. The Cardinals finished first by three games—but were a 78-game talent, fully 16 games worse than the second-place Mets.

Also of note: the 1989 Mets should have finished 15 games ahead of the Cubs instead of six back. The 1992 White Sox should have won the division, beating the A's by 14 games, instead of finishing third. And the hard-luck Expos were the most talented team in the NL East in 1979, 1980, 1981, 1982, and 1984. They made the postseason only in 1981. In 1982, they were good enough to have finished first by 11 games.

In his 1989 article Bill James speculated that a sub-.500 team could conceivably win the World Series, though it was unlikely. He wrote, "Did we see it in '88?" For the record, the 1988 Dodgers come out as an 82-80 team—close but not quite. The '82 Cardinals came the closest in the four-division era—they won the Series with 81.2-game talent.

But the 1960 Pirates fit the bill. Without luck, they were 76-78. Nineteen games of good fortune pushed them to 95-59, the World Series, and set the stage for Bill Mazeroski's heroics. Table 29.4 shows every World Series team from 1960 to 2001.

Table 29.4. World Series Teams 1960–2001

Year	Team	Talent	Luck (games)	Actual
1960	Pirates	76-78	+19.1	95-59
1961	Yankees	91-71	+17.8	109-53
1962	Yankees	92-70	+3.6	96-66
1963	Dodgers	90-72	+8.9	99-63
1964	Cardinals	82-80	+10.6	93-69
1965	Dodgers	89-73	+8.1	97-65
1966	Orioles	89-72	+8.5	97-63
1967	Cardinals	87-74	+14.4	101-60
1968	Tigers	92-70	+10.7	103-59
1969	Mets	83-79	+17.2	100-62
1970	Orioles	99-63	+8.7	108-54
1971	Pirates	96-66	+1.5	97-65
1972	A's	90-65	+2.7	93-62
1973	A's	94-68	+0.2	94-68
1974	A's	94-68	-4.0	90-72
1975	Reds	98-64	+9.9	108-54
1976	Reds	95-67	+7.3	102-60
1977	Yankees	98-64	+2.2	100-62
1978	Yankees	97-66	+2.9	100-63
1979	Pirates	86-76	+11.8	98-64
1980	Phillies	86-76	+5.2	91-71
1981	Dodgers	66-44	-2.9	63-47
1982	Cardinals	81-81	+10.8	92-70
1983	Orioles	85-77	+13.4	98-64
1984	Tigers	95-67	+8.7	104-58
1985	Royals	84-78	+7.4	91-71
1986	Mets	91-71	+16.9	108-54

1987	Twins	81-81	+3.5	85-77
1988	Dodgers	82-79	+12.3	94-97
1989	A's	94-68	+5.3	99-63
1990	Reds	86-76	+5.4	91-71
1991	Twins	88-74	+6.8	95-67
1992	Blue Jays	95-67	+1.4	96-66
1993	Blue Jays	88-74	+7.0	95-67
1995	Braves	87-57	+3.3	90-54
1996	Yankees	94-68	-1.8	92-70
1997	Marlins	93-69	-0.5	92-70
1998	Yankees	92-70	+22.0	114-48
1999	Yankees	96-66	+1.9	98-64
2000	Yankees	95-66	-8.4	87-74
2001	D-Backs	91-71	+0.7	92-70

Table 29.4 makes it evident that, to win the World Series, it's not enough to be a good team—you have to be lucky, too. Of the 41 champions, 35 of them had a lucky regular season. Of the six unlucky teams, only the 1974 A's and the 2000 Yankees were unlucky by more than three games.

Before 1969, all the winning teams were lucky, some substantially. Between 1969 and 1993, in the four-division era, luck was a little less important. Since 1995 the champions were, on the whole, only marginally lucky (with the exception of 1998).

This makes sense—back in the one-division league, one lucky team could blow away nine others. Now that team eliminates only three or four others, and even then, those other teams have a shot at the wild card. And the lucky team now has to win three series against superior opponents, instead of just one, which increases the chance that a legitimately good team, instead of just a lucky one, will now come out on top.

From 1995 to 2001 every champion was at least a 90-game talent (adjusting 1995 for the short schedule). Before the wild card, champions with talent in the 80s were very common.

Table 29.5. Luckiest and unluckiest seasons for every Major League team, 1960–2001

		Luckiest season		
Team	Year	Talent	Luck (games)	Actual
Angels	1986	76-86	+15.8	92-70
D-Backs	1999	84-78	+16.4	100-62
Braves	1991	81-81	+12.8	94-68
Orioles	1964	82-81	+15.0	97-65
Red Sox	1995	76-68	+9.8	86-58
White Sox	1983	83-79	+15.8	99-63
Cubs	1984	80-81	+16.1	96-65
Reds	1995	68-76	+16.6	85-59
Indians	1995	83-61	+16.7	100-44
Rockies	2000	79-83	+3.0	82-80
Tigers	1961	86-76	+14.7	101-61
Marlins	1995	59-85	+8.5	67-76
Houston	1986	80-82	+16.1	96-66
Royals	1971	73-88	+12.3	85-76
Dodgers	1962	84-81	+18.0	102-63
Twins	1965	92-70	+10.5	102-60
Brewers	1982	83-79	+11.8	95-67
Expos	1994	61-53	+12.7	74-40
Yankees	1998	92-70	+22.0	114-48
Mets	1969	83-79	+17.2	100-62
A's	1992	77-85	+18.6	96-66
Phillies	1993	81-81	+16.2	97-65
Pirates	1960	79-78	+19.1	95-59
Padres	1996	78-84	+13.3	91-71
Mariners	2001	89-73	+27.3	116-46
Giants	1993	85-77	+17.8	103-59
Cardinals	1985	83-79	+18.3	101-61
Devil Rays	2000	70-91	-1.3	69-92
Rangers	1986	76-86	+11.1	87-75
Blue Jays	1993	88-74	+7.0	95-67

		Unluckiest season		
Angels	1996	85-76	-15.4	70-91
D-Backs	2000	90-73	-4.5	85-77
Braves	1977	77-85	-16.0	61-101
Orioles	1967	90-71	-14.1	76-85
Red Sox	1965	78-84	-15.5	62-100
White Sox	1970	72-90	-16.1	56-106
Cubs	1962	77-85	-18.5	59-103
Reds	2001	77-85	-10.7	66-96
Indians	1987	81-81	-19.6	61-101
Rockies	1999	90-72	-18.1	72-90
Tigers	1996	71-91	-17.8	53-109
Marlins	1998	63-99	-8.5	54-108
Houston	1975	78-83	-13.9	64-97
Royals	1997	79-82	-11.7	67-94
Dodgers	1992	74-88	-11.5	63-99
Twins	1964	95-67	-16.0	79-83
Brewers	1977	78-84	-11.2	67-95
Expos	1969	66-96	-13.9	52-110
Yankees	1982	89-73	-10.3	79-83
Mets	1962	61-99	-20.6	40-120
A's	1979	74-88	-20.3	54-108
Phillies	1961	66-88	-18.8	47-107
Pirates	1985	74-87	-17.1	57-104
Padres	1990	84-78	-9.4	75-87
Mariners	1998	95-66	-19.2	76-85
Giants	1972	81-74	-11.5	69-86
Cardinals	1990	83-79	-13.1	70-92
Devil Rays	1998	66-96	-2.8	63-99
Rangers	1985	75-86	-13.2	62-99
Blue Jays	1995	76-68	-19.6	56-88

Table 29.5 lists the luckiest and unluckiest seasons for every major-league team from 1960 to 2001. The Blue Jays and the Red Sox have had good success over the years, but never had a huge season where they won 108

games or something and ran away with the division. That seems to be because they never had the kind of awesome luck you need to have that kind of record. The Jays were never more than 7 games lucky, and Boston never more than 9.8.

For the flip side, look at the San Diego Padres—they were never unlucky by more than 9.4 games. As we noted earlier, that perhaps spared them the reputation as one of the worst expansion teams ever—with a bit of bad fortune, their record could have rivaled the Mets for futility.

And the negative sign in Tampa Bay's "best luck" column is not a misprint—in the first four years of their existence, they were unlucky all four years.

Finally, take a look at the Twins. Their luckiest season immediately followed their unluckiest. As a result, they went from below .500 in 1964 to 102 wins in 1965—even though they actually became a worse team!

Summary

What can we conclude from all this? First, luck is clearly a crucial contributor to a team's record. With a standard deviation of six or seven games, a team's position in a pennant race is hugely affected by chance—seven wins is easily the difference between a wild-card contender and an also-ran.

Second, you have to be lucky to win a championship. As we saw, 85% of world champions had lucky regular seasons.

Third, teams with superb records are likely to have been lucky. Very few teams are truly talented enough to expect to win 100 games. The odds are very low that the 2005 White Sox (99-63) and Cardinals (100-62) are really as good as their record. Despite all this, it should be said that while luck is important, talent is still more important. The SD due to luck was 7.2, but the SD due to talent was 8.5. It's perhaps a comfort to realize that talent is still more important than luck—if only barely.

Appendix

The Algorithm

This is the algorithm to calculate a player's career-year or off-year luck for a given season. The procedure is arbitrary. I used it because it seems to work reasonably well, but it no doubt can be improved, probably substantially. But, hopefully, any reasonable alternative algorithm should give similar results in most cases.

Of course, any algorithm should sum to roughly zero, since over an entire population of players the luck should even out.

A batter's luck is calculated in "runs created per 27 outs" (RC/27). To calculate a batter's luck for year X:

1. Take the player's average RC27 over six years: two years ago counted once, last year counted twice, next year counted twice, and two years from now counted once. Weight the average by "outs made" (hitless AB + CS + GIDP) so that seasons in which a batter had more playing time will have a higher weight. Adjust each RC27 for league and park.

2. Add a certain number of "outs made" at the league average RC27:

   — if the player had more than 2,100 outs made in the six seasons, add 100 league-average outs made;
   — if the player had fewer than 1,200 outs made in the six seasons, add 900 league-average outs made; and
   — if the player had between 1,200 and 2,100 outs made, subtract that from 2,100 and add that number of league-average outs made.

The purpose of this step is to regress the player to the mean. Just as a player who goes 2-for-4 in a game probably isn't a .500 hitter, a player who hits .300 in 1,200 outs made is probably less than a .300 hitter. This adjusts for that fact.

3. If the player had less than 1,600 outs made over the six seasons (not including those added in step 2), subtract 0.0006 for each out made under 1,600. In addition, if the player had less than 800 outs made over the six seasons, subtract another .0006 for each out made under 800. The purpose of this step is to recognize that players with fewer plate appearances are probably less effective players.

4. Add .09 if the player had more than 1,600 outs made (not including those added in step 2).

5. This gives you the player's projected performance, expressed in RC27. To figure the luck, subtract it from the actual RC27, multiply by outs made, and divide by 27. So if a player projects to 4.5, his actual was 5.5, and he did all that in 270 outs that year, then (1) he was lucky by 1.0 runs per game; (2) he was responsible for 10 games (270 outs divided by 27); so (3) he was "lucky" by 10 runs.

PITCHERS

A pitcher's luck is calculated in "component ERA" (CERA), which is the number of runs per game the opposition should score based on its batting line against him. To calculate a pitcher's luck:

1. Take the player's average CERA over six years: two years ago, last year counted twice, next year counted twice, and two years from now counted once. Weight the average by "outs made" (IP divided by three) so that seasons in which a pitcher had more playing time will have a higher weight. Adjust each CERA for league and park.

2. Add a certain number of "outs made" at the league average CERA:

   — if the player had more than 900 outs made in the six seasons, add 900 league-average outs made;
   — if the player had fewer than 400 outs made in the six seasons, add 400 league-average outs made; and—if the player had between 400 and 900 outs made, add that number of league-average outs made.

3. Temporarily add this year's outs made to the total of the six seasons (not including those added in step 2). If that total is less than 1,200, add 0.0006 for each out made under 1,200.

4. Add .35.

5. If the player started more than 70% of his appearances, add .1.

6. If the player had more than 300 outs made this year, but less than 300 outs made total in the six seasons from step 1, ignore the results of the previous five steps, and use the league/park average CERA instead. (That is, assume he's an average pitcher.)

7. This gives you the player's projected performance, expressed in CERA. To figure the luck, subtract the actual CERA, multiply by outs made, and divide by 27. So if a player projects to 3.50, his actual was 4.50, and he did all that in 270 outs that year, then (1) he was unlucky by 1.0 runs per game; (2) he was responsible for 10 games (270 outs divided by 27); so (3) he was "unlucky" by 10 runs.

30

Why Is the Shortstop "6"?

KEITH OLBERMANN

People have been keeping score at baseball games almost as long as the game has been played in an organized way. In this 2005 article, Keith Olbermann explores not just the single issue of why a shortstop is designated as "6," rather than "5," but how such a numerical system took hold at all. Like many of the rules of the game ("three strikes and you're out!"), there were plenty of missteps before we ultimately settled on scorecard perfection. Olbermann became involved with SABR while in high school in the 1970s, officially joined up in 1984, and has contributed articles and insight throughout his eventful career in the media. The formation of SABR's Baseball Cards Research Committee in 2016 gave Keith (an avid and expert collector his entire life) another opportunity to contribute, culminating with a wonderful talk at the 2017 SABR annual convention in New York.

As a baseball artifact, it's pretty special as it is.

It's a scorecard from August 5, 1891—a day when Buck Ewing drove in four runs off Cy Young and the New York Giants managed to hold off the Cleveland Spiders, 8–7, at the Polo Grounds. The book still shows the partial vertical fold its original owner might have created while stuffing it into a pocket as he raced to catch the steam-powered elevated train that would take him back downtown. And the scorecard pages themselves tell of a Cleveland rally thwarted only in the last of the ninth, when Spiders player-manager Patsy Tebeau, rounding third base, passed his teammate Spud Johnson going in the opposite direction—running his team into a game-ending double play.

The program is actually an embryonic yearbook. There are 14 photos and biographies of Giants players, and a wonderful series of anonymous notes under the heading "Base Hits" ("Anson next week. If we win three straights [*sic*] from him, we will be in first place"). But amid all the joyous nostalgia of a time impossibly distant—stuffed between the evidence that the owner saw Cy Young pitch in his first full major league season—hidden among the ads that beckon us to visit the Atalanta Casino or try Frink's Eczema

Ointment or buy what was doubtlessly an enormous leftover supply of Tim Keefe's Official Players League Base Balls—we can throw everything out, except the top of page 10.

There, in six simple paragraphs, the scorecard's buyer is advised how to use it. "Hints On Scoring" tells us, simply, "On the margin of the score blanks will be seen certain numerals opposite the players' name. . . . The pitcher is numbered 1 in all cases, catcher 2, first base 3, second base 4, short stop 5, third base 6."

This is no mistake caused by somebody's over-indulgence at the Atalanta Casino.

The unknown editor offers a few sample plays, including: "If a ball is hit to third base, and the runner is thrown out to first base, without looking at the score card, it is known that the numbers to be recorded are 6–3, the former getting the assist and the latter the put-out. If from short stop, it is 5–3."

If we need any further confirmation that more has changed since 1891 than just the availability of Frink's Eczema Ointment, the scorecard pages themselves provide it. In the preprinted lineups, third basemen Tebeau of Cleveland and Charlie Bassett of New York each have the number "6" printed just below their names. And the two shortstops, Ed McKean of the Spiders and Lew Whistler of the Giants, each have a "5."

We may view the system of numbers assigned to the fielding positions as eternal and immutable. But this 1891 Giants scorecard suggests otherwise, and is the tip of an iceberg we still don't fully see or understand—a story that anecdotally suggests a great collision of style and influence in the press box, no less intriguing than the war between that followed the creation of the American League.

The shortstop used to be "5," and the third baseman used to be "6."

We do not know precisely how and when it changed—there is a pretty good theory—but we do know that by 1909, the issue had been decided. In the World Series program for that year, Jacob Morse, the editor of the prominent *Base Ball Magazine*, gets seven paragraphs—the longest article in the book—to offer not "Hints On Scoring" but the much more definitive "How To Keep Score." And he leaves no doubt about it. "Number the players," Morse almost yells at us. "Catcher 2, pitcher 1; basemen 3, 4, 5; shortstop 6." The New York Giants themselves had reintroduced scorekeeping suggestions by 1915, and conformed to the method demanded by Morse, as if it had always been that way.

We can actually narrow the time frame of the change to a window beginning not in 1891, but closer to 1896. In the same pile of amazingly simple artifacts as that Giants scorecard is the actual softcover scorebook used by Charles H. Zuber, the Reds' beat reporter for the *Cincinnati Times-Star* five years later. Zuber employed a "Spalding's New Official Pocket Score Book" as he and the Reds trudged around the National League in the months before the election of President McKinley. Inside its front cover, one of the Great Spalding's many minions has provided intricately detailed scoring instructions. "The general run of spectators who do not care to record the game as fully as here provided," he writes with just a touch of condescension, "can easily simplify it by adopting only the symbols they need."

That this generous license was already being taken for granted is underscored by the fact that the Spalding editor suggests "S" for a strikeout, but writer Zuber ignores him completely and employs the comfortingly familiar "K." But the book's instructions are not entirely passé. They include the suggestion that the scorer use one horizontal line for a single, two for a double, etc.—which is exactly the way I was taught to do it, in the cavernous emptiness of Yankee Stadium in 1967.

The Spalding instructions go on for 11 paragraphs, and the official *rules* for scoring fill another 20. But remarkably, there are is no guidance about how to numerically abbreviate the shortstop, third baseman, or anybody else who happened to be on the field. There isn't even the suggestion that a scorer must number the players, or abbreviate the players, according to their *defensive* positions: "Number each player either according to his fielding position or his batting order, as suits, and remember that these numbers stand for the players right through in the abbreviations."

In other words—use any system you damn well please. Number the shortstop "5" if you want, or "6." Or, if he's batting leadoff, use "1." Or if he's exactly six feet tall, try "72."

If by now you have wondered if the father of scorekeeping and statistics, Henry Chadwick, was not sitting there with smoke pouring from his ears over all this imprecision and laissez-faire, don't worry—he was. As early as his 1867 opus *The Game Of Base Ball* he was an advocate of one system and one system only—numbering the players based on where they hit in the order.

I realize that some of the most ardent of you, who have little shrines to Chadwick (in your minds, at least) as the ancient inspiration for SABR itself, must be reeling at the thought. Even if you think using "6" for the third baseman instead of the shortstop is a bit silly, it's a lot better than Chadwick's idea, surely the worst imaginable system of keeping score, based on the *batting lineup* ("groundout to short, 1 to 7 if you're scoring at home—no, check that, I forgot, the relief pitcher Schmoll took Robles' spot in the batting order in the double switch, so score it 9 to 7").

Before we knock down the Chadwick statue outside SABR headquarters, this caveat is offered in his defense. In 1867, random substitutions were not permitted at all, and not until 1889 did they become even partially legal. Within a game, the batting order changed about as frequently as the designated hitter today assumes a defensive position. Chadwick's insistence on defensive numbering based on offensive positioning still doesn't make sense on a game-to-game basis, but at least he wasn't completely nuts.

But, as Peter Morris points out, Chadwick wanted to keep his system even as the substitution rule was changing. That same series of "Hints On Scoring" from the 1891 Giants scorecard first appeared, word for word, in a column in the *New York Mail and Express* in early 1889.

Weeks later, Chadwick is railing against it in the columns of *Sporting Life*. This new defensive-based scoring system is, he writes, "in no respect an improvement on the plan which has been in vogue since the National League was organized. If you name the players by their positions, and these happen to be changed in a game, then you are all in a fog on how to change them."

Chadwick was wrong about the ramifications but right about the coming fog.

Certainly, as the Giants scorecard and Charles Zuber's Spalding scorebook suggest, confusion would reign through the 1890s and into the new century. The New York scorecards soon reverted to "3B" and "ss" and dropped all hinting on what the bearer was supposed to do. Zuber's scoring system starts with the first baseman at "1," has the shortstop as "4," and the pitcher and catcher as "5" and "6." Only the Hall of Fame manager Harry Wright seems to have nailed it. In the voluminous scorebooks he kept through to his death in 1893, he has penciled in, in perfect, tiny lettering, the third baseman as "5" and the shortstop as "6."

So how was this chaos resolved?

This proves to have been the unexpected topic of conversation in the late 1950s between a budding New York sportswriter and one of the veterans of the business. Bill Shannon, now one of the three regular official scorers at Yankee and Shea Stadiums, was talking scorekeeping with Hugh Bradley.

[Bill Shannon died in 2010, after this article was initially published.—Eds.] Bradley had been covering baseball in New York since the first World War, had been sports editor of the *New York Post* in the '30s, and was at the time of his conversation with Shannon a columnist with the *New York Journal-American*.

Shannon recalls that, out of nowhere, Bradley began talking about a great ancient conflict between rival camps of scorers, one of which favored the shortstop as "5" and the other as "6." The inevitable clash occurred, Bradley told him, at the first game of the first modern World's Series.

The World's Series, of course, had gone out with a whimper and not a bang in 1890. Though the Brooklyn Bridegrooms and Louisville Cyclones had been tied at three wins apiece, disinterest in that war-ravaged season was so profound that attendance at the last three games had been 1,000, 600, and 300, respectively. They didn't even bother to play the decisive game.

Thus when the series was restored 13 years later, every attempt was made to keep haphazardness and informality out of the proceedings. Not just *one* official scorer was required, but two—and the two foremost baseball media stars of the time: Francis C. Richter of Philadelphia, the publisher and editor of *Sporting Life*, and Joseph Flanner of St. Louis, editor of *The Sporting News*.

Hugh Bradley could not have witnessed it, but he could have heard it second- or third-hand. As the rivals from the two publications filled out their scorecards, somewhere in the teeming confusion of the Huntington Avenue Grounds in Boston, somebody—probably the more volatile Flanner—peeked.

And he didn't like what he saw.

Richter was numbering Pittsburgh shortstop Honus Wagner as "5" and third baseman Tommy Leach as "6."

Questioned by Flanner, Richter supposedly responded that that was the way they kept score where *he* came from, and why would anybody do it any differently?

The basis of their argument was supposed to have been regional. The shortstop, Bradley told Shannon, was still a comparatively new innovation in the game, and it really defined two different positions. In Flanner's Midwest, he was positioned much like the softball short-fielders, not truly an infielder and thus not meriting an interruption of the natural numbering of the basemen. In Richter's East, the shortstop had developed into what he is today—the second baseman's twin. So what if he didn't anchor a bag?

It was second baseman "4," shortstop "5," third baseman "6" and don't they have any good eye doctors out there in St. Louis, friend Flanner?

Bradley's recounting of the conflict had voices being raised and dark oaths being sworn before the more malleable Richter gave way, little knowing that he was ceding the issue forever on behalf of generations to come who saw the same logical flaw he had seen.

Bill Shannon's authority on such matters is near absolute. He can not only recount virtually every game he's ever seen, but can also run down the personnel histories of the sports departments at the dearly departed of New York's newspapers. He believes in the long-gone Bradley's saga of near-fisticuffs between Richter and Flanner—while "Nuf Ced" McGreevy and his Royal Rooters worked themselves into a frenzy before the first pitch of the 1903 Series—because of its likely provenance.

One of Bradley's writers when he was sports editor of the *Post* in the '30s was Fred Lieb, himself almost antediluvian enough to have witnessed the Flanner-Richter showdown. Shannon suspects Bradley got the story from Lieb, and that Lieb had gotten it from his fellow Philadelphian Francis Richter.

For now, that's all we've got—a pretty good-sounding anecdote. There is nothing yet found in the files of *The Sporting News*, *New York Times*, *Washington Post*, or even in any of the contemporary Spalding or Reach annual guides. No Flanner-Richter screaming match, no ruling on whether the shortstop or the third baseman was "5," no verified explanation as to how we got from the *hints* in the 1891 Giants scorecard to the *instructions* of the 1909 World Series program, no smoking gun proving when it became this way, as if there had never been any *other* way.

Needless to say, further research is encouraged and its results solicited.

In the meantime, dare I even mention that the 1891 Giants book also identifies the right fielder as "7" and the left fielder as "9"?

31

Do Batters Learn During a Game?

DAVID W. SMITH

In 1989 David Smith founded Retrosheet, a group of volunteers dedicated to digitizing (among other things) play-by-play accounts of major-league games. As of 2019, they had done so for 174,000 games, profoundly affecting our understanding of baseball records, statistical analysis, and even the memories of our long-ago childhood outings to the ballpark. One of the more active users of Retrosheet data is Smith himself—he annually presents at SABR's convention new research he has discovered within the massive trove of Retrosheet data. His talk on whether batters improve their performance throughout a game, originally presented in 1996 and then revamped with additional data for this 2005 article, is typical of David's great work: well-presented and well-received. David was honored with the Henry Chadwick Award in 2012.

It is common to hear batters and pitchers comment on the value of being able to "make adjustments" during a game. For example, pitchers speak of "setting a batter up" by a certain sequence of pitches, which may take several at-bats to accomplish. Similarly, batters often remark that they "look for" a certain type of pitch or in a certain location after considering what the pitcher has thrown before. Although it makes sense that a player might very well alter his mental approach as a result of earlier success or failure, I decided to go beyond the anecdotal interviews and ask if there were any tangible evidence indicating that this learning actually takes place.

My approach was to examine matchups between starting batters and starting pitchers, giving the greatest opportunity to discover changes during the course of a game. Given the realities of modern relief pitcher usage, it is very uncommon for a batter to face the same relief pitcher more than once in a game, and therefore the relievers were excluded. The batting performance of pitchers was also removed. I analyzed every play of every game from 1960 through 2005, which is 92,271 games and more than seven millon plate appearances. The play-by-play information comes from Retrosheet.org.

There are a variety of performance measures used today within the baseball analysis community. I report here the three standard aggregate measures: batting average, on-base average and slugging average. These three quantities reflect different aspects of batter performance and I therefore suspected that they might not all show the same patterns of change during a game. Table 31.1 presents the results for the first 4 matchups within a game for all games from 1960 through 2005. There were a few cases of a batter facing a starting pitcher five times in one game, but these are too rare to be useful in this analysis.

Table 31.1. Batting by number of appearances within a game, both leagues, 1960–2005

	PA	BA	OBA	SLG
1st	1,530,593	.259	.328	.393
2nd	1,456,880	.269	.331	.416
3rd	1,151,387	.274	.336	.427
4th	394,251	.275	.335	.418

In addition to noting how uncommon it is for a starting batter to face a starting pitcher four times in a game, we see clear patterns of improvement, or batter learning, in all three values as the game progresses. However, the three averages do not increase at the same rate. On-base average rises slowly, only 2.1% from the first to fourth time at bat, while batting average and slugging average go up much more rapidly, 6.1% and 6.4%, respectively.

In the 1950s Branch Rickey and Allan Roth developed a measurement called "isolated power" to examine extra-base hits separately from singles. Isolated power is simply the difference between slugging average and batting average. For all at-bats over the 46 years studied (not just for the starters) the isolated power is .135 (batting average of .259 and slugging average of .394; see table 31.3). For the data in figure 31.1, the isolated power values for the four times at bat are .134, .147, .153, and .143. My interpretation is:

a. the first time up batters are more concerned with making contact than hitting with power and;

b. the second and subsequent times up they are adjusting with the result that they are able to swing more confidently and with greater power;

c. the isolated power of the non-starter appearances is lower than that of the starters.

This pattern was remarkably constant over the period studied (data not shown), even though the total level of baseball offense varied considerably over the years. There was also no discernible difference between the two leagues, either before or after the advent of the DH in the American League in 1973. However, there was a definite in the pattern for home and road teams, as shown in table 31.2 and figures 31.1 and 31.2.

Table 31.2. Home and road batting, by number of appearances, 1984–1985

Home teams				
	PA	BA	OBA	SLG
1st	209,837	.266	.337	.405
2nd	222,576	.272	.336	.424
3rd	173,057	.277	.341	.433
4th	53,727	.278	.340	.425

Road teams				
	PA	BA	OBA	SLG
1st	201,033	.266	.337	.405
2nd	201,458	.272	.336	.424
3rd	160,769	.277	.341	.433
4th	50,943	.278	.340	.425

Fig. 31.1. Batting by Number of Appearances

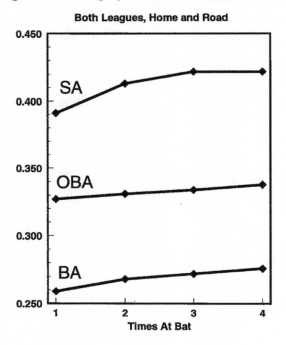

Both Leagues, Home and Road

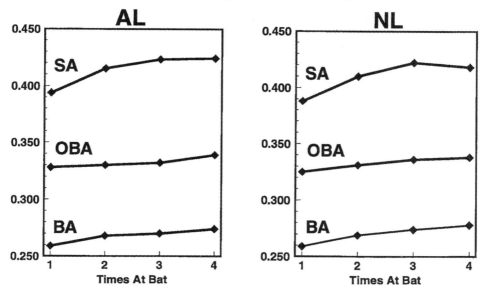

Fig. 31.2. League Batting by Number of Appearances

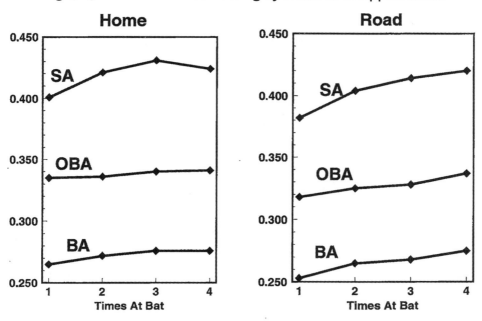

Fig. 31.3. Home and Road Batting by Number of Appearances

There are rather large differences between the two, both in absolute value of the numbers and in the pattern of changes. The home team has an overall nine to 17 point superiority in these three measures, as shown in the bottom portion of table 31.2. However, the greatest differences are in the pattern of the changes (figure 31.1 and 31.2), which come from the data in the first two portions of table 31.2. In all three parameters, the rates of increase are steeper for players on the visiting team than they are for those who are playing at home. Interestingly enough, slugging average for all players drops from the third to fourth times at bat. By the fourth time at bat, the performance differences for the home and road players are much more similar than they were earlier in the game.

This pattern is initially surprising, since it is not obvious why the road team batters should display so much more learning than the home team batters. However, we must remember that there are two sides to each matchup and consider the pitchers as well, since both are presumably capable of making adjustments. One of the great differences usually identified between different parks is the mound and many visiting pitchers comment that it takes time to get used to a new mound on the road. Therefore, it is reasonable to consider that there are two kinds of learning going on. The first is the mental part of the pitcher-batter confrontation, which we have seen to favor the batter, and the second is the physical adjustment by the pitcher to the mound. Presumably the home team pitchers are more familiar with the mound than the road team pitchers are and they should have less of this adjustment to do. Let us consider the home vs road differences again, remembering that the difference between home and road batters narrow as the game proceeds. By this argument, the learning displayed by the road team batters would therefore result mostly from the mental aspects, since the home team pitchers are not affected as much by the mound. On the other hand, the road team pitchers are starting the game at a relative disadvantage as they deal with the idiosyncrasies of that particular mound. Therefore, the performance by home team batters starts off at a higher level, but does not increase as rapidly, because there is less room for improvement before they reach the maximum. However, it must be true that the road team pitchers have been successful in their adjustments, or else one would expect that the performance by home team batters would continue beyond what is actually observed.

There is one additional factor which might affect the batters, and that is the nature of the hitting background. Although the center-field background does vary between parks, there is much less variation here than there is in the mound. One way to examine the effect of the hitting background would be to compare the performance of road team batters in the first game of each series to the later games in the series. If the background were a significant factor, then one would expect the first game performance to be different. I did not subdivide the results in this way, so this possibility remains unexplored.

There are many aspects of batter performance which have changed since 1960, including strike zone rule changes, the rise and decline of artificial surface fields, the designated hitter (DH) rule and profoundly new patterns of relief pitcher usage. It occurred to me that the percentage of plate appearances which were between starters might show variation as well. Figure 31.3 addresses the DH effect. From 1960 to 1972, the two leagues were very similar in the percentage of plate appearances that involved starting batters and starting pitcher, with variation from about 61% to 67%. In 1973 with the advent of the DH, the curves for the two leagues diverge sharply, as the American League percentage jumps to nearly 72% while the National League values show little change. Both leagues have seen a continual decline since then, as the difference between the two has narrowed from a maximum of about 8 percentage points to the current difference of about 4 points. The relationship now is essentially what it was in the pre-expansion era. However, even with these striking changes over time, the results in terms of batter learning did not change in a corresponding way (data not shown).

One more interesting feature of this analysis is the different performance levels of the starters and non-starters. Table 31.3 shows that the starting batters are noticeably more effective than the overall average, as would be expected. However, it must be noted that the overall values include pitchers as batters as well as the effect of specialist relief pitchers.

Table 31.3. Batting performance of starters vs all batters, 1960-2005

	BA	OBA	SLG
Starter vs Starter	.267	.331	.411
All batters vs All pitchers	.259	.326	.394

I would like to emphasize that I presented no information for individual teams or players. It is always true in a study such as this that the results get less clear as the sample size gets smaller, with random statistical nose playing a larger part. I therefore studied aggregates, with home vs. road as the only subdivision. When the results are divided more finely, to single teams or single batters, there will inevitably be many exceptions that cloud the issue, largely because of their statistical unreliability. I have chosen to avoid this confusion.

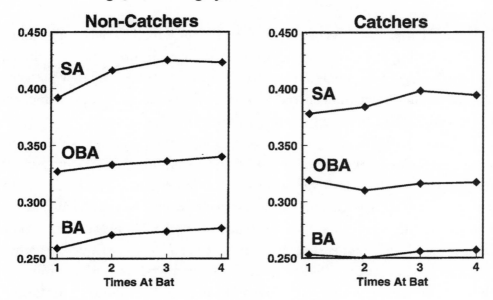

Fig. 31.4. Batting by Catchers and Non-Catchers

I did subdivide the data in one interesting way: to consider catchers separately from players at other positions. Since catchers clearly endure greater physical demands during a game, it is reasonable to ask if this leads to a difference in results. Fig. 31.4 shows that there is a definite effect. The overall totals are lower, and catchers show only a slight increase when compared to other batters. Since catchers can certainly make adjustments similar to other players, it appears that their learning as batters is largely overcome by the rigors of playing behind the plate.

In conclusion I note that I began this study with the question that is the title of the presentation: Do Batters Learn During a Game? It is clear that the general answer is: yes, they do. However, it is also clear that the situation is a little more complicated than that and that a better understanding can be obtained by considering other factors. The biggest one I could identify was the effect of playing at home vs. on the road.

So the next time you hear a batter say that he improved his performance by making adjustments during a game, there is a good chance you should believe it. On the other hand, if you hear a pitcher say it, then you might be a little suspicious.

32

New Light on an Old Scandal

GENE CARNEY

Gene Carney had been researching baseball for many years, active in his upstate New York SABR chapter and writing his own newsletter, but truly made his mark on the wider SABR community when he turned his attention to the Black Sox scandal full-time. Besides his newsletter, his efforts led to the 2006 book, *Burying the Black Sox: How Baseball's Cover-Up of the 1919 World Series Fix Almost Succeeded*, and the 2008 formation of SABR's Black Sox Scandal Research Committee. Carney's untimely death in 2009 shocked friends and colleagues, but the path he forged has remained active in the past decade, leading to a SABR book (*Scandal on the South Side: The 1919 Chicago White Sox*) and a 2019 symposium in Chicago to mark the 100th anniversary of the scandal.

My interest in the Black Sox Scandal began at summer's end in 2002, and by the following June, I was sufficiently addicted to the subject that I simply had to visit Milwaukee. Why Milwaukee? Because I had learned that in 1924 that city was the site of a trial that pitted Shoeless Joe Jackson against his old employer, the Chicago White Sox, who were incorporated in Wisconsin. For B-Sox addicts, it was the Trial of the Century.

Jackson had signed a three-year contract in 1920, and when he was suspended in September that year, he had two years left—that is, unless his contract contained the standard "ten days clause" (if it did, the Sox could release him on short notice without cause). Jackson contended that the clause had been negotiated out of his contract; his team said otherwise. Acquitted with seven other players of conspiracy charges in 1921, Jackson sued for back pay, forcing the Sox to prove that he had done *something*, on the field or off, to deserve termination.

It seemed only Donald Gropman, a sympathetic biographer of Jackson, and Jerome Holtzman, a most unsympathetic historian, used the material from the 1924 trial in their writings. While Gropman thought this information exonerated Jackson, Holtzman believed it condemned him. I had to see for myself.

Jackson was not, however, my main interest. I was focused on the cover-up of the Fix, and how it finally came undone, almost a year later. My Milwaukee research in June 2003 into "the trial nobody noticed" became the first chapter of *Burying the Black Sox: How Baseball's Cover-Up of the 1919 World Series Fix Almost Succeeded*, released in March 2006 by Potomac.

But the B-Sox story is a cold case, not a closed case. Since June 2003 I have learned a lot more, and am still learning. I have often wondered what I missed in Milwaukee on that first visit. How many more pieces to this giant puzzle remained in that treasure trove? So when SABR offered me the chance to return and do more digging (via a Yoseloff grant), I could not resist. Here is what I found, the second time around.

Surveying the Terrain

On my first visit I had set the goal of trying to read through the nearly 1,700 pages of trial transcripts. Skimming here and there, I did that, and I also mapped the three volumes that contain the proceedings.

This time I wanted to go through all of the other material, mostly depositions but also the exhibits: reports from Comiskey's detectives, some newspaper clippings, and handwriting samples used by the experts who testified. This trial hinged on the circumstances under which Jackson had signed his 1920 contract—did the illiterate plaintiff sign in his house, with his wife handy to read it and check for the 10-days clause that Jackson believed was not in the contract? Or did he sign in his car, with only team secretary Harry Grabiner present? Incidentally, among the treasures in Milwaukee is a kind of "Rosetta Stone." Attached to the pretrial depositions of Sox owner Charles Comiskey and Grabiner are "photostatic copies" of Jackson's 1919 and 1920 contracts. In 1919 (and previous years), Kate Jackson signed for her husband; in 1920, Joe signed himself. This document enables us to distinguish between the signatures when Jackson's autograph appears.

Lawyer Ray Cannon had filed three different lawsuits, on behalf of Oscar "Happy" Felsch, Joe Jackson, and Charles "Swede" Risberg. Their cases were numbered 64442, 64771, and 64772 respectively, indicating that his first client was Felsch. Cannon then contacted Jackson and Risberg, who both agreed to file similar suits. Jackson's went to trial first, in January 1924. The material that was collected in preparation for all three suits was used. A former ballplayer, Cannon was hoping that these cases would attract more players to another cause, a players' union that would enable them to battle the reserve clause, which bound players to their teams.

The Risberg and Felsch Cases

All three cases were prepared along the same lines. Each player asked for $1,500 they felt was owed them from 1917; they said that Comiskey had promised each player would receive $5,000 for winning the pennant, no matter what the Series gate receipts turned out to be. When the players' shares turned out to be around $3,500, they all expected another $1,500. In the Jackson trial, the jury said they believed that the promise was made, but they awarded no money, because there was nothing in writing—no contract. This prompted Commy's lawyers to get Schalk, Collins, and Faber on record, stating that their manager in 1917, Pants Rowland, had made no such promise to the team.

The players also asked for the balance due from the contracts they claimed were breached when they were suspended in 1920 and later released. (Monies due from the Sox's second-place finish in 1920 was mentioned, but that was a bone to pick with the league or Commissioner Landis, so it was not featured in these suits.)

Initially, the players also asked for $100,000 in damages to their reputations and careers. In Felsch's suit, filed first, another $100,000 was asked for, because Happy had been blacklisted and unable to play ball in any professional league. These items were eventually removed from each suit when the plaintiffs were unable to substantiate the charges with facts.

Risberg's case is the easiest to summarize. He asked for $750 still due from his 1920 salary; for a $1,500 bonus that he said he was promised in 1920 for "good and efficient baseball"; for the $1,500 from 1917; and (initially) $100,000 because his reputation and career had been "annihilated." Risberg settled out of court in February 1925 for $288.88 plus interest ($75.23) and court costs ($37.20), or a total of $401.31.

Felsch had asked for $1,120 from 1920 (he claimed a paycheck had been missed), the 1917 bonus, and initially those large damages, which were later dropped. In his initial suit, we get a hint of where Ray Cannon was heading. Comiskey's lawyers succeeded in having the following removed, because it was "a sham, frivolous, irrelevant and scandalous": The Sox had been guilty of a cover-up in order to prevent the American public from discovering and learning the true facts about the deception, trickery and fraud that had been practised [*sic*] by the defendant [the Sox] . . . in fooling and deceiving the public as to the baseball games and in deliberately causing games to be lost and won by certain clubs or teams as the defendant . . . desired.

Cannon had intended to complicate things for Comiskey and his lawyers by bringing up three different "scandals" from 1917 involving the White Sox and the Detroit team. Detroit lost back-to-back doubleheaders to the Sox around Labor Day; they also beat the Sox's rival, Boston, later in the pennant race; then, after the pennant was clinched, the Sox lost three games to Detroit. The Sox had taken up a collection and paid off the Detroit pitchers that month. Was it a bribe, for tossing games to the Sox? Or a reward, for knocking off Boston? Did the Sox then pay back the favor by helping Detroit get closer to third-place money? These were old questions—Ban Johnson, American League czar, knew all about them, and Landis had looked into them soon after taking office in 1921. But they were ammunition for Cannon. The loose ends would not be tied up in these cases, however, and became front-page news in 1927, after Swede Risberg went public with the charges when the Cobb-Speaker allegations were in the news.

Felsch's case was settled in February 1925, too, for the two 1920 paychecks ($583.33 each, plus 6% interest, or $1,470.15), and court costs of $105.20.

Among the fascinating items in the Felsch material is a note from Ray Cannon to Comiskey's lawyers when he was preparing the complaint. This laundry list of questions that he wanted to ask appeared in the papers— Cannon was knowledgeable about using the press. It appears that Cannon had picked up from some player(s) a story that he asked the Sox about:

14. What steps were taken and what threatened through Louis Comiskey [Commy's son and team officer], with the aid of a battery of detectives in the spring of 1920, to scare and intimidate the players . . . to admit connection with the framing of the 1919 World Series, and against what players were the threats made, and by what persons were they made, and what statements were made by Louis Comiskey and others, to the effect that all members of the Chicago White Sox baseball team who were connected to the 1919 World Series scandal, *were to be handcuffed together on the opening day of the 1920 pennant race in Chicago, and*

displayed before the large audience in the grandstand and bleachers, and then led away to jail? (emphasis added)

This could be sheer and unfounded bluff on the part of Cannon, but it's nevertheless a striking image. He was sending the Sox a message that he knew what they knew on Opening Day, that they had signed seven of eight players who had been publicly accused (in the press, not by baseball) of suspicious play the previous October, and of at least plotting with known gamblers.

How the Plot Thickened . . . Then Fizzled

The gambling-fixing side of the B-Sox story is by far the murkiest, where little is certain—something I tried to convey in my book by a "Who's on First?" sketch which would be comic relief if only the subject were not so sad. The 1920 grand jury seemed ready to indict gamblers from several syndicates and a roster of cities that stretched from Pittsburgh to New Orleans. But most of those fellows vanished along with Hal Chase (after California refused to extradite him). So the main impression we have today of what happened is from *Eight Men Out*, aversion heavily colored by interviews with Abe Attell and by newspaper accounts of the 1921 trial, focused on just one syndicate.

In the Milwaukee depositions of Bill Burns and Billy Maharg, we get—in the words of those two go-betweens—an account of events in unprecedented detail. This may or may not be the way things unfolded, but it's a fascinating tale.

The testimonies of Burns and Maharg agree substantially with those they gave at the 1921 trial, but there are some differences, and a comparison of the two versions is another project.

When he was deposed on Octobers, 1922, Bill Burns was a confectioner, running a chocolate shop in Texas. But in 1919 he sold oil leases, and his sales route took him to Cincinnati, Chicago, New York, Montreal, and Philadelphia. Here is Burns's story, along with that of Maharg (whose role in this seems to be that of Burns's bodyguard):

> With three weeks to go in the season, before the Sox had clinched the pennant, Eddie Cicotte told Burns in the Ansonia Hotel in New York that "something good was coming up," and if it went through—if the Sox got into the Series—Burns would be informed. A few days later at

the same spot, Burns saw Cicotte again, this time with Chick Gandil. Billy Maharg, visiting Burns from Philadelphia, was also present.

Burns had known Maharg for years; they often hunted and fished together near Burns's Texas home. Burns had wired Maharg an invitation to come to New York for a social visit. Maharg stayed at the Ansonia several days, seeing most of the Sox. But what he overheard at the Ansonia that day would change his life.

Burns was told that six were willing to deal: Cicotte, Gandil ("the chief spokesman"), Risberg, McMullin, Williams, and Felsch. When Burns testified at the 1921 trial that the players initiated the Fix, some who had been sympathetic (thinking that vulnerable, gullible, underpaid athletes had been victimized) were shocked. The asking price was $100,000. Maharg recalled just five names (not McMullin), but also recalled that the players "would throw the first two, or all five in a row—whichever way the financiers wanted it."

Burns left New York City for a 10-day stop in Montreal, and Maharg returned to Philadelphia. There, a gambler friend called "Chrissy" or "Rossy" said "only one man" had the funding for such a project. Rossy gave Maharg a letter of introduction to Arnold Rothstein, then called The Big Bankroll on the phone and told him Maharg was coming over to Considine's, a 42nd Street saloon. But Rothstein was a no-show, and Maharg left.

Burns sent Maharg a telegram from Canada. He'd be back in New York in a few days and would call. Burns met with Maharg in Philadelphia, and this time they made an appointment to see Rothstein, traveling together to the Aqueduct race track on Long Island. But "A.R." was busy "making book," so they agreed to meet at the Astor at 9:00 p.m. Rothstein listened to the scheme, then "said he would not handle it."

Four or five days later, Burns ran into Hal Chase. What seemed a poor risk to Rothstein looked like "a sure shot" to Chase. Burns had received a letter from a Sox player, from St. Louis, saying that now *eight* Sox were in the deal, and that is what Burns told Chase.

Within three or four days Burns and Chase met again, at the Ansonia. Enter Abe Attell and a fellow who went by "Bennett"—as it turned out, this was David Zelcer. Attell claimed to be representing Rothstein, and said A.R. was backing The Big Fix.

Burns remained in New York until two days before the Series, then bought a train ticket to Cincinnati. Before he left, he telegrammed Maharg again, telling him to meet him on the 4:30 train, that the fix was in, and Rothstein was backing it.

With "financiers" lined up, Burns still had to make the connection between the fixers and the players. The day before the Series started, in Cincinnati, Burns met with Attell and Zelcer at the Gibson Hotel, then walked them over to the Sinton, where the White Sox were staying. Seven players were waiting in 708 [Gandil and Risberg's room]; Joe Jackson was not present. Burns announced that Arnold Rothstein was behind the plan.

Burns then introduced the players all around to Attell, "the Little Champ," and "Bennett." Burns recalled that the door to 708 was partly open, and Weaver checked constantly so that manager Kid Gleason would not join the meeting. The negotiation went on until 1:00 or 2:00 a.m. M. Gandil insisted on $20,000 before Game One . . . then the players insisted that their $100,000 be held by someone. Finally, the deal was made: $20,000 paid after each loss. The money would be divided nine ways, eight players—and Bill Burns. Burns had the impression that Lefty Williams was "kind of representing Jackson," and that anything Williams okay'd would be okay with the star outfielder.

Maharg was not in Cincinnati yet. He arrived the morning of Game One. Burns said he saw the players that morning again, in the Sinton lobby. He saw Attell again, too, in the Havlin Hotel.

Neither Burns nor Maharg attended Game One. After the game, which the Reds won 9–1, Maharg caught up with Burns, and they went to a hotel (it's not clear which, the Havlin or the Gibson or the Sinton) looking for Attell and the payoff. When they caught up with him, Attell said the money was "out on bets."

Burns delivered the bad news to the players at the Sinton. He met with Risberg, McMullin, Cicotte, Gandil, and Williams, telling them that Attell was collecting money and they'd have to wait till the morning. Gandil was angry and said Attell was "not living up to his agreement." Burns saw Williams and Gandil again after dinner, and there was a meeting with Attell and Zelcer on a side street. Abe was upbeat, and the conversation was all about tossing Game Two.

On the next morning Burns and Maharg saw Attell again, at the Havlin, but instead of showing him the money, Attell showed him a telegram, saying that Rothstein had wired him cash. Maharg recalled the message: "Have wired you 20 grands. Waived identification. A.R." Burns was skeptical and took the telegram, with Attell in tow, to the nearest telegraph office. There was no sign of it in the log. Attell said the office "must've lost or misplaced the record." Then Attell said that he would go and get the money due, and Maharg could come with him. Maharg could then give the cash to Burns, who would signal the players that all was going smoothly.

But, as Maharg put it, it "never came off that way." "I told him that I thought he [Attell] was a liar, myself," Maharg said. Burns took the telegram—it was all he had—to the Sinton, and went to Room 708. It was about 10:00 a.m. The two pitchers were present, along with the three pals, Gandil, Risberg, and McMullin. Gandil was now sure Attell was double-crossing them. Chick and Swede did all the talking. Burns held out hope that the $20,000 would still appear before game time. Attell would get it to Burns, and Burns would signal the players "in the lines"—that is, from the front row of the stands.

Burns received no cash, gave no signal. He did not go to the park.

After Game Two, Attell and his men were jubilant and flush with winnings. Burns and Maharg "had a date" to meet Attell at the Havlin. They waited, and Attell no-showed. But they caught up with him at the Sinton; he was in his room [660] with the Levi Brothers, Ben and Lou, and Zelcer (whom Maharg described as "Rothstein's First Lieutenant"). Burns told Attell that the players were "sore" and asked for the $40,000 they were due. Attell reached under a mattress and extracted a roll of money—$10,000—and lobbed it to Burns. Attell and Zelcer then complained that "everybody in the East and West" knew about the fix, and it was really hard to make anything in the betting.

Burns took the 10 grand to the players by himself, while Maharg waited with Attell. It was about 9:00 p.m. Risberg, McMullin, and Cicotte were there, and Burns also thought Weaver was present. Then Gandil and Felsch came in and the counting commenced. It was done on a bed, with all of the players standing around, watching: 10 G—not 40. Burns reported, "One of the boys put it under his pillow"—if they were in 710, that would have been Cicotte's pillow, but Burns didn't say. Gandil and Risberg again were noisy about the double-crossing going on. Burns said maybe Attell was swindling them. "I was not." Burns said the meeting then amounted to a lot of swearing.

Burns was upset and returned to Attell, telling him that he was "jamming the whole thing up." Maharg recalled that while Burns was gone (about 30 minutes), someone said Rothstein had bet "about 300 G" ($300,000) on the Series. Attell was sorry about the shortfall, but it couldn't be helped. "Another ring is in on it." The players would have to wait until the Series was over to get the rest. "They asked Burns to ask the players if they would try to win the next game, so they could get better odds for their money. Burns said he would ask them."

Burns left again, then came back. The players had said no, they would not win for "a Busher" (Dickie Kerr, a rookie in 1919; it "was generally known," according to Maharg, that Kerr was getting the start in Game Three). "The same way tomorrow." Maharg: "Burns said the players were not satisfied, and they hollered like hell." Burns set a date to meet with them again the next day, in Chicago. The trains left Cincinnati about midnight.

The morning of Game Three, Maharg and Burns saw Attell at the Sherman Hotel. Attell asked Burns to phone Gandil. Chick told him it was "going the same way." Burns relayed the message to Attell.

But Game Three did not "go the same way"—Kerr pitched brilliantly, and the Sox won, 3–0. Gandil knocked in two runs.

Burns and Maharg went to Zelcer's room at the Astor (next to the Sherman Hotel) after the game. Attell was there, too. Zelcer wanted Burns to go to the players and talk to them about Game Four, but Burns protested that they would not trust him. Zelcer understood, and said he'd put up $20,000 of his own money, give it to Burns to hold as a bet if the Sox lost, Burns would turn the money over to the players. Burns could bet the money on the Reds. Burns agreed to take the offer to the players, and hailed a cab.

Burns found Gandil at his apartment. Chick said they won Game Three because they had been double-crossed. The fix was off, the players were through. Burns ran into Risberg and McMullin on the street later, and Swede confirmed that the players had met by themselves before Game Three and decided to win it. But Swede added that he "was going through with it." [There is some evidence that Swede Risberg was the most sensitive about the dangerous position the players put themselves in; crossing Arnold Rothstein could indeed be hazardous to one's health. If Burns's recollection is accurate, Swede may have been sending A.R. the message that he, at least, was keeping his part of the bargain.] McMullin said nothing; he was riding the bench in this Series.

Burns returned to the Sherman Hotel and told Attell and Zelcer—no deal. Maharg's glum comment: "The next day, Cincinnati won anyway."

Attell was disappointed. It was just hard luck that the money was out on bets; it would be there after the Series was lost. Too bad the players couldn't wait.

This is where Maharg's story ends. He left Chicago for Cincinnati, but had no further doings with the plot. He said he never saw Attell again; and he next saw Zelcer at the 1921 trial. When he read about the 1920 grand jury looking into the Fix, he went to "Jimmie Isaminger," a personal friend and reporter on a Philadelphia newspaper. Why? I "wanted his opinion of it more than anything else, of what they would do with me when this thing came up."

Ain't Over Till It's Over

But for Bill Burns there was one more meeting. It was arranged by Abe Attell, and there Burns was introduced to a group of gamblers from St Louis, including a "short, red-complected man"—Carl Zork. They wanted to offer more money to the players, put the fix back in.

Burns went to the players one more time and made the offer. They rejected it. Burns gave Attell the information. To the best of Bill Burns's knowledge, no more money was exchanged between the gamblers and the players. He did not speak with the players again.

In the Wake of the Fix

Bill Burns lived in Texas. He did not travel to Chicago to give this deposition because he was anxious to tell his story. No, he was asked to make the trip by Ban Johnson, at the suggestion of Alfred Austrian, Comiskey's lawyer— for Buck Weaver's suit against the Sox. As in 1921, when Burns came north for the trial, the American League paid his expenses.

Burns was questioned about why he had not come forth sooner with the tale. He said that right after the Series, he went to New York, then right back to Texas. He spoke with "several private men down there" about the fix but no reporters. When his name popped up in one of Hugh Fullerton's articles about the rumors (in December 1919), he did nothing.

During the 1920 season, Burns said that he did speak with several ballplayers and a manager about the fix. But he refused to name anyone else. After Landis's edict banning anyone connected in any way to fixing games, implicating more men could ruin their careers.

Burns did not mention that he had received a telegram from Judge McDonald, inviting him to come and talk to the grand jury in September 1920. McDonald said that he invited Maharg, Attell, and Rothstein, too, but couldn't force anyone from another state to testify. (Rothstein did come, voluntarily.)

Asked why he did not go for the $10,000 reward that Comiskey had offered, Burns replied, "Well, I didn't want that kind of money . . . I didn't want to bring the ballplayers out." Asked if his motive now was "solely revenge," Burns repeated that he did not want to harm any players. Why then, did he tell all (in the trial) in 1921? "They had it planned to lay everything on me." Maharg, when he tracked Burns down in Texas, had told him that unless he came north to defend himself, he'd be "the fall guy" in the trial. "So you didn't do it for revenge?" Burns: "Well, I did to a certain extent, yes sir."

Burns seemed upset that Cicotte, Jackson, and Williams "started the whole thing"—the unraveling of the cover-up by going to the 1920 grand jury. He recalled that when he came to Chicago and told his story to Hartley Replogle (the assistant state's attorney), Replogle told him that his account of things "dovetailed" with the versions the players gave the grand jury.

Judge McDonald's Recollection

The Cook County grand jury had been called together in September 1920 by Judge Charles A. McDonald. Ban Johnson said that he had given McDonald the green light to hand the grand jury the duty to investigate the ties between gambling and baseball. When the focus fell on the 1919 World Series, McDonald had a problem. He was a baseball fan, and his team, the White Sox, were in another dandy pennant race. He discussed this with Alfred Austrian, and they agreed that no Sox would be subpoenaed until the race had been decided. So the appearance of Cicotte and Jackson on September 28 must have been upsetting.

McDonald had known Comiskey "very well and very favorably" for about 25 years. In the 1924 trial he appeared for the defense (Comiskey). He was quizzed about his meeting with Joe Jackson on September 28, 1920.

Earlier, McDonald had spoken with Eddie Cicotte, then accompanied him for moral support to the grand jury chamber. Cicotte had mentioned Jackson as one of the players involved in the plot. So when Jackson phoned McDonald, from Austrian's office, to say that he wanted to clear his name, McDonald told him it was too late, that Cicotte had given him up, along with six others.

McDonald had no notes from the meeting that followed. Austrian brought Jackson to the courthouse, introduced him to McDonald, and left. The judge said that he did not go with Jackson to the grand jury after their talk.

And that is significant, because McDonald and Jackson sparred in the press after some reporters characterized his grand jury statement as a confession—to throwing games. Jackson disputed that he said that, and the statement we have from the grand jury seems to bear that out. McDonald, recalling only what Jackson had told him earlier (that he might have played harder) and what Cicotte had told him, concluded that Jackson had helped throw the Series. McDonald never heard Jackson tell the grand jury that he played every game to win.

What Did Eddie Say?

The statements made by the three players were among the documents that vanished the winter after the grand jury. But they were reconstructed from stenographer's notes for the 1921 trial. Ray Cannon, deposing Charles Comiskey in March 1923, had pressed Commy's lawyers for a copy of Jackson's grand jury statement. George Hudnall, the Sox's lead lawyer in the 1924 trial, objected when Cannon asked Comiskey if the team had a copy. He instructed Commy not to answer, because "the grand jury proceeding is supposed to be secret. If he got it, he has no business to it."

When Cicotte and Williams were first deposed in 1923, neither were cooperative. But apparently sometime later that year the grand jury statements were deemed admissible evidence, and in January 1924, just weeks before the Jackson case went to trial, Cicotte and Williams were deposed again (separately). This time their grand jury statements were read into the record.

Joe Jackson's testimony from 1920 did not appear until the trial in Milwaukee was under way. George Hudnall produced it from his briefcase. Jackson had given a different version of events in 1924 (for example, he said he received the $5,000 from Williams after the Series, instead of after Game Four), so his 1920 grand jury statement meant that he was guilty of perjury, either in 1920 or 1924; that fact ruined his case and caused the judge to set aside the jury's verdict, which had gone for Jackson on every count by 11–1.

It is not clear that the Milwaukee trial depositions contain every word from the 1920 statements, but they contain a substantial amount of fascinating material, in Q and A format, embedded in the "live" questioning. This is especially important for Cicotte, because we have little from his 1920 statement today (unlike Jackson and Williams), and it is not clear that what we have is reliable, or whether it was embellished by the press.

And the Cicotte grand jury testimony for the 1924 trial has more information than that which was read into the 1921 trial, because many names of players and gamblers were omitted in 1921 at the direction of the judge.

Before Cicotte was deposed, his lawyer advised him not to say anything that might incriminate himself. Cicotte wound up saying very little. When his grand jury testimony was read, he did not disagree with anything he had said in 1920. "What I told the grand jury was the truth." Some highlights of what he said:

- Cicotte indeed named all of the players later banished to the grand jury. He said the idea of the fix had originated in a conversation with Gandil and McMullin, and maybe one other teammate. Gandil: "We ain't getting a devil of a lot of money, and it looks like we could make a big thing." Asked how much it would take for Cicotte to join in, he replied, $10,000.
- He recalled a pre-Series meeting in his room at the Warner Hotel that followed soon after, with Gandil, Felsch, Weaver, and perhaps McMullin and Williams. "I was the first one that spoke about the money end of it. I says, there is so much double-crossing stuff, if I went in the Series ['to throw ball games'] I wanted the money put in my hand." Gandil assured him that he'd get his money in advance. Cicotte left his room to visit with teammates Red Faber and Shano Collins, while the other players left, one by one, to avoid the appearance of having been in a meeting. When he later returned to his room, about 11:30 p.m., there was $10,000 under his pillow. He pocketed the cash and took it to Cincinnati.
- After the Series, he said he took the money home to Detroit and hid it. Four thousand dollars paid off the mortgage on his farm; the rest went to put in new floors in the barn and house and to buy livestock and feed. Cicotte didn't know where the money had come from: "I never asked them" [his teammates]. Some gamblers, he supposed.
- Cicotte admitted that he put on base the first batter he faced in Game One, Morrie Rath. He tried to walk him, but instead hit him. He made no mention that this was a signal that the fix was in. "You wanted Rath to get on base?" "Yes. But after he passed, after he was on there, I don't know, I guess I believe I tried too hard. I didn't care, they could have had my heart and soul out there. That is the way I felt. I felt—I didn't want to be that way after I had taken the money."

- Cicotte spoke at some length about a play in the fourth inning that started his undoing. "That's the play they incriminate me on, but I was absolutely honest on that play." With a runner on first, Cicotte stopped Kopf's smash up the middle and threw to Risberg for the force-out at second. Swede stumbled or threw slowly to first, and the runner beat it out, keeping the inning alive. "Everybody saw me make that play," Cicotte insisted. All of the hits that inning "was clean base hits." Cicotte did not think Swede intended to miss the runner on that play.

- After the 9–1 loss, "I went up in the room. I was too ill, I had the headache after the game. I stayed in my room and was sick all night long. I couldn't hit in St Louis." [The lawyers were puzzled by this phrase, and Cicotte did not offer to explain it.] His roommate, Felsch, offered him some aspirin tablets. "Happy, this will never be done again."

- According to Cicotte, the players did not discuss the fix after Game One, "because we didn't trust nobody."

- Cicotte said he saw nothing fishy in Game Two, except that Williams was wild. Asked if he thought the walks were intentional, he said, "Sure, that is the way I thought."

- Back in Chicago for Game Three, Cicotte did not tell his brother about the fix or the money. His wife was in Detroit, and he didn't tell her, either. "She don't know I paid off the mortgage," he told the grand jury. In Game Three, "Kerr pitched great."

- The next game Cicotte pitched, Game Four, "I tried to make good but I made two errors. I was very anxious to get the ball and I didn't make any runs. [The Sox lost, 2–0.] If we could make four or five runs—I would have won that game." Asked if he had tried to make a bad throw in that game, Cicotte said, "No sir, I didn't, I tried to get my man." "I tried to win [Game Four]."

Cicotte said in effect that he had played the Series to win. "I was going to take a chance. I wanted to win. I could have given [the money] back with interest, if they only let me win the game that day." Tris Speaker consoled Cicotte after the Game Four loss (Spoke was covering the Series for a Cleveland paper).

Asked by someone in the grand jury how he could win with seven players on his own team against him, Cicotte said, "They never talked to me at all. If they talked to me, I was deaf ears. I was a man of another country."

Cicotte said that he never saw any other players receive any money. Asked by Replogle if he would come back to the grand jury if they wanted to hear more from him, he replied, "Yes, sir." He was not asked back.

The newspapers had their story. Cicotte confirmed that the fix had been in: the Sox sold out the Series for $100,000. Never mind that Cicotte and Jackson both said they played the Series to win. Their admission that some players had plotted with gamblers was immediately translated into eight Sox playing crooked for the entire eight-game series. Down in history.

Historian Harold Seymour thinks that the spin given to the players' stories may have been for their protection—that is, for the consumption of the gamblers. See, they tried to lose. Victor Luhrs in his 1966 *The Great Baseball Mystery* argued that Cicotte played to win. But *Eight Men Out* had appeared in 1963, and the film version would color perceptions even more.

The material from the 1924 Milwaukee trial suggests that the fix was in—but not for very long. And that even players assumed to be committed to the fix—like Cicotte—may have played to win.

33

Roberto Clemente's Entry into Organized Baseball

STEW THORNLEY

The story of Roberto Clemente's signing by the Brooklyn Dodgers, his season with their Montreal farm team, and his subsequent loss to the Pittsburgh Pirates, has been told many times over—including by some of the key participants. Like any great researcher, Stew Thornley decided he'd rather figure it all out for himself, and what he found differed quite drastically from the well-known tale. Thornley has been a SABR stalwart for many years, focusing on a wide variety of subjects, including the Polo Grounds, baseball graves, baseball in Minnesota, and official scoring. For the past several years he has been the official scorer for Minnesota Twins games.

"A lie can travel halfway round the world while the truth is putting on its shoes." Although this quote is often attributed to Mark Twain, at least one Twain researcher claims a different source.[1] Beyond the content of the quote, its disputed derivation highlights the need to resist the urge to assume something to be true just because it is repeated often enough or is viewed as "common knowledge."

So it is with Roberto Clemente's sole season in the minor leagues, with the Montreal Royals of the International League in 1954. This saga provides a striking example of a story retold so many times that it takes on a life of its own, eventually becoming so accepted as factual that even a careful researcher may fall into the trap of assuming the claims to be true and not feeling the need to verify them.

Although Clemente spent his entire major-league career with the Pittsburgh Pirates, he was originally part of the Brooklyn Dodgers organization. He signed with the Dodgers in February 1954 for a reported salary of $5,000 as well as a bonus of $10,000.[2] Rules of the time required a team signing a player for a bonus, including salary, of more than $4,000 to keep him on the major-league roster for two years or risk losing him in an offseason draft. Thus, the Dodgers' choice to have Clemente spend 1954 in the minors meant that they might lose him to another team at the end of the season.[3]

What has been written about Clemente in Montreal contains an assertion that the Dodgers and Royals tried to hide him—that is, play him very little so that other teams wouldn't notice him. The claim was expressed by Clemente at least as early as 1962 in an article by Howard Cohn in *Sport* magazine. "Clemente, on the other hand, felt—and still does—that the Royals kept him out of the regular lineup so big-league teams would think him a weak prospect and ignore him in the post-season draft for which he'd be available as a bonus player if he weren't elevated to the Brooklyn roster," wrote Cohn.[4]

Since then, this claim has been trumpeted in much that has been written about Clemente's entry into organized baseball, including several biographies; one of them, by Arnold Hano, was written during Clemente's career, in 1968, and revised following Clemente's death in 1972; two biographies, by Kal Wagenheim and Phil Musick, were written shortly after Clemente's death while another, by Bruce Markusen, came out a quarter-century later. In early 2006, noted biographer David Maraniss, whose works include books on Vince Lombardi and Bill Clinton, had a biography of Clemente published.[5]

The biographers and others who maintain that Clemente was hidden—and beyond that, that the organization may have tried to frustrate Clemente to the point that he would jump the team, making him ineligible to be drafted by another team[6]—offer numerous supporting examples. The examples, with few exceptions, turn out to be false.

Decision on Clemente's Destination

The first question, however, concerns not what happened in Montreal but why the Dodgers did not keep Clemente in Brooklyn in 1954. Many bonus players of this period were kept at the major-league level, even though it meant pining on the bench for two years rather than developing in the minors.

As vice president of the Dodgers, Emil "Buzzie" Bavasi had the power to determine Clemente's fate. In 1955, Bavasi told Pittsburgh writer Les Biederman that the team's only purpose in signing Clemente had been to keep him away from the New York Giants, even though they knew they would eventually lose him to another team.[7]

Other explanations offered center around an often cited but never documented informal quota system said to be in effect in the years following the breaking of the color barrier in organized baseball.[8] The Dodgers already had five blacks who would play at least semi-regularly on their parent roster in 1954, presumably leaving no room for another player of color. (The claim of an informal quota is another possible myth that has become widely accepted over time. A check of a specific claim made in Wagenheim's biography—that the Dodgers would never start all five blacks at the same time—is false, and there are other reasons to question the general claim of a quota system, but it is beyond the realm of this article to fully explore the issue.)[9]

Although Bavasi had claimed at the time that they signed Clemente only to keep him from the Giants, in 2005 he offered a different reason. "I know your sources are not idiots," he wrote in e-mail correspondence with the author, "but not one of those things you mentioned are [sic] accurate. Let's start from the beginning." Bavasi then wrote that while there was not a quota in effect, race was the factor in their decision to have Clemente play in Montreal rather than Brooklyn:

> [Dodgers owner] Walter O'Malley had two partners who were concerned about the number of minorities we would be bringing to the Dodgers. . . . The concern had nothing to do with quotas, but the thought was too many minorities might be a problem with the white players. Not so, I said. Winning was the important thing. I agreed with the board that we should get a player's opinion and I would be guided by the player's opinion. The board called in Jackie Robinson. Hell, now I felt great. Jackie was told the problem, and, after thinking about it awhile, he asked me who would be sent out if Clemente took one of the spots. I said George Shuba. Jackie agreed that Shuba would be the one to go. Then he said Shuba was not among the best players on the club, but he was the most popular. With that he shocked me by saying, and I quote: "If I were the GM [general manager], I would not bring Clemente to the club and send Shuba or any other white player down. If I did this, I would be setting our program back five years."[10]

Clemente in Montreal

So Clemente was headed for Montreal to play for manager Max Macon. According to statements attributed to Clemente in a 1966 *Sports Illustrated* article by Myron Cope, and later picked up by the biographers, the treatment he faced went beyond an attempt to hide him: "The idea was to make me look bad. If I struck out, I stayed in there; if I played well, I was benched."[11] Musick, in *Who Was Roberto?*, added, "A free swinger, Clemente suffered through stretches when he was not making contact with the ball. Fighting those slumps, he was showcased to disadvantage and stayed in the lineup days at a time."[12]

Box scores from *The Sporting News* reveal that Clemente was in the starting lineup against left-handed starting pitchers and did not start him against right-handers through the first 13 games of the season. At that point, Clemente had four hits in 18 at-bats for a .222 batting average, and he played sparingly over the next 2½ months.

Clemente may have, in part, been a victim of a crowded outfield situation in Montreal, which included Jack Cassini, Dick Whitman, and Don Thompson as well as Sandy Amoros, who was sent down from Brooklyn in mid-May and recalled by the Dodgers in mid-July, and Gino Cimoli, who was transferred to Montreal from the Dodgers' other Triple-A farm team, the St. Paul Saints, in early May. (Clemente's opportunities to play may not have been any greater had he been assigned to St. Paul rather than Montreal. With Bud Hutson, John Golich, Bert Hamric, Ed Moore, and Walt Moryn, the Saints, like the Royals, were also heavy on outfielders.)

When Clemente did play, he struggled with his hitting. In early July, his batting average was barely above .200. Part of that may be attributed to his infrequent playing time; it's hard for a batter to get in a groove and hit well when he doesn't play regularly. On the other hand, it's hard for a player to get regular playing time if he's not hitting well.

Macon said the reason he didn't use him much at that time was that he "swung wildly," especially at pitches that were outside of the strike zone. "If you had been in Montreal that year, you wouldn't have believed how ridiculous some pitchers made him look," Macon said of Clemente.[13]

Macon was known around the league for platooning his hitters,[14] and that is what happened with Clemente over the latter part of the season. In the first game of a doubleheader against Havana on July 25, Clemente entered the game in the ninth inning, came to the plate in the bottom of the 10th, and hit a game-ending home run.

He started the second game of the doubleheader, against left-hander Clarence "Hooks" Iotts; for the rest of the regular season and through the playoffs, the right-handed-hitting Clemente started every game in which the opposing starter was left-handed and did not start any games against right-handed starters. After July 25, Clemente's usage was determined by the status of the opposing starting pitcher.

Other claims made to support the notion of Clemente being hidden:

- Clemente hit a long home run in the first week of the season and was benched in the next game. (Clemente did not homer until July 25, and he started the next game. His only other home run came on September 5, and, like his earlier homer, was a game-ending shot. Clemente did not start the next game as a right-hander, Bob Trice, was the starting pitcher for Ottawa.)
- Clemente was benched after a game in which he had three triples. (Clemente did not have three triples in any game in 1954.)
- Clemente was often used only in the second game of a doubleheader, after the scouts had left. (No such pattern of usage is indicated.)

The errors noted above were made by Wagenheim, Musick, and Markusen in their biographies. Maraniss, who went through Montreal newspapers for the 1954 season, avoided many of the inaccurate supporting examples made by the others. However, Maraniss parroted the claim that Clemente was being set up to fail, writing, "It seemed that whenever he got a chance to play and played well, Macon benched him."[15] Maraniss also wrote, "After the first four games, Clemente was leading the team in batting, going four for eight. Then he disappeared again."[16] However, Clemente's disappearance after getting three hits in the team's fifth (not fourth) game was not that abrupt; he started two of the next three games and was hitless before going back to the bench.

Overall, Maraniss stuck to the standard story of Clemente being hidden and did not perform any real analysis of the claim. He also did not pick up on the pattern of usage that eventually developed, in which Clemente started regularly against left-handed pitching. As a result, Maraniss cites instances of Clemente not playing over the final seven weeks as evidence of attempts to hide him, rather than the fact that a right-handed pitcher was starting for the opposing team.[17]

One claim made by biographers that is true regards Clemente being pulled for a pinch-hitter in the top of the first inning of a game. It occurred June 7 at Havana. The Royals had two runs in and the bases loaded with two out when Havana changed pitchers—right-hander Raul Sanchez coming in for left-hander Hooks Iotts. Left-handed Dick Whitman then hit for Clemente. Although the story is presented as more evidence of how poorly Clemente was treated by Max Macon, it appears clear from the circumstances that it had more to do with Macon's affinity for platooning and a desire to try and break the game open.

An essentially opposite situation occurred two months later as Toronto manager Luke Sewell, trying to counteract Macon's platooning, employed a decoy starter. In the first game of an August 3 doubleheader, Sewell started right-hander Arnie Landeck against the Royals and then relieved him with left-hander Vic Lombardi in the second inning. As a result, Dick Whitman started for Montreal and was pinch-hit for by Clemente before Whitman could bat even once. Conveniently, this counterpoint to the June 7 story is never mentioned.

Also, the details of Clemente getting pulled in the first inning get botched by the biographers. Markusen says the incident happened against Richmond in the second week of the season.[18] Musick also says it occurred in a game against Richmond.[19] However, a few pages later, Musick contradicts himself and says the game was in Rochester (wrong in both cases), that it was the last game of the season (not true), and it was against Rochester's Jackie Collum (strike three).[20]

The name of Jackie Collum comes up again in an unrelated story by Wagenheim, who wrote that Clemente had two doubles and a triple off Collum and then was pulled for a pinch-hitter his next time up.[21] Nothing like this happened—regardless of the pitcher.

And one has to wonder about references to Collum by two different biographers. Collum did not even pitch for Rochester, or in the International League at all in 1954.

SABR member and Montreal Royals historian Neil Raymond cross-checked the summary compiled by the author from *The Sporting News* box scores with game accounts and box scores from Montreal newspapers. (See Clemente's game-by-game compilation at the end of the article.) "What becomes apparent going through the Montreal papers daily (*La Presse*, the *Gazette*, the *Star*) is that this team was not perceived as a player-development exercise," maintained Raymond. "They were expected to win. Translation: Sandy Amoros's at-bats were deemed a lot more valuable than learning what Clemente could do, building his confidence, or training him by exposing him to opportunities to fail by being overmatched.

"I feel safe in saying that Clemente made very little impression on those who wrote about him during the 1954 campaign. These were iconoclastic writers. Their copy was eagerly sought-after breakfast or dinner fodder. If Clemente was being 'hidden' to the detriment of the team's ability to perform, they would have peeped up. Not once in my newspaper research is there an allusion to this possibility, or a subtle wink at the canniness of the 'brain trust.' As difficult as it may be to accept to those who, like me, marveled at Clemente's multifarious skills and dynamism throughout the 1960s (the bad-ball hitting, the cannon-like arm, the heady base running, etc.), it's abundantly clear that he was almost an invisible man in Montreal in 1954."[22]

A More Plausible Argument?

It's possible that the strongest argument for a theory of hiding could revolve around the timing of the Pittsburgh Pirates' discovery of Clemente and when Clemente began starting regularly against left-handed pitching.

The accounts surrounding the discovery are consistent in some ways, albeit consistently inaccurate on some details: Clyde Sukeforth, then a Pirates coach, was dispatched on a scouting mission by Branch Rickey, then the Pirates executive vice president/general manager, to check out Montreal pitcher Joe Black. All accounts say this occurred during a Royals series against Richmond in July. Almost every story says this series was in Richmond, with some of the accounts specifically mentioning Richmond's Parker Field, although the only series between the two teams that month was in Montreal.

Sukeforth said Black did not pitch that series (not true, he did) and that Clemente's only appearance was as a pinch-hitter (also not true; his only appearance in the series was as a pinch-runner). Even though Clemente barely appeared in the series, Sukeforth said he noticed, and was impressed by, Clemente while watching him bat and throw in pregame practice. On the basis of Sukeforth's report, Rickey sent scout Howie Haak for a follow-up visit.

The accounts vary to a much greater degree as to when the Pirates informed the Dodgers and/or Royals that they had discovered Clemente and planned on drafting him. Some reports contend that Sukeforth immediately told Macon of the Pirates' interest in Clemente.[23]

The key is when the Dodgers organization found out that the Pirates were planning to draft Clemente. *If* Clemente was first discovered in the Richmond series in July (meaning that the essence of the story of Sukeforth's scouting trip is correct even if the specific details are not), and if Sukeforth imme-diately informed Macon, it raises an interesting possibility. The Richmond series was immediately before the Havana series in which Clemente began starting regularly against left-handers.

If the Royals began playing Clemente more after being informed of the Pirates' interest, then perhaps it could be argued that the Royals had been hiding Clemente up to that point; however, informed that their gambit had failed, they then decided to play Clemente more.

Even if all these *ifs* line up, the argument is still a stretch and nothing more than conjecture; however, it is still the most plausible one.

Interestingly, however, this is not the argument advanced by the biog-raphers or anyone else claiming that Clemente was being hidden. In fact, most go in the other direction, saying that the Royals used Clemente even less after being informed of Pittsburgh's interest. Wagenheim and Markusen even make the outrageous and totally incorrect claim that Clemente did not play in any of the Royals' final 25 games.[24] Although Musick does not make the claim of Clemente not playing in the last 25 games, he writes that Macon restricted Clemente's playing time even more[25] after Sukeforth's scouting trip and alleged revelation to Macon.[26]

Treatment of Max Macon

Markusen at least provided some balance with quotes from Macon in which the manager denied being under orders to hide Clemente.[27] Musick also provided some of Macon's denials as well as Macon's contention that pitch-ers were making Clemente look ridiculous. However, Musick offered these explanations on Macon's part in a patronizing manner as he wrote, "Macon pleads innocence for his former employer twenty years after the fact, but his pleas bring bemused grins to the faces of his contemporaries. And he is part of a baseball establishment that is super-protective of its leaders. There are no skeletons in baseball's closet: They are quickly ground to dust and scattered to the four winds, lest men of stature be embarrassed." Musick also refers to Macon's "southern drawl" becoming "increasingly less reassuring to the player's Puerto Rican ears."[28]

Drafted by Pittsburgh

By the end of the 1954 season, it had become clear to Bavasi and the rest of the Brooklyn brass that other teams were interested in Clemente. However,

Bavasi said he still wasn't ready to give up. The Pirates, by having the worst record in the majors in 1954, had the first pick in the November draft.

If Bavasi could get the Pirates to draft a different player off the Montreal Royals roster, Clemente would remain with the Dodgers organization. (Each team could lose only one player, so if a different Montreal player was taken, then no other team could draft Clemente or any other Royals player.)

Bavasi said he went to Branch Rickey, who had run the Brooklyn Dodgers before going to Pittsburgh. Bavasi had declined Rickey's offer at that time to follow him to the Pirates, but, according to Bavasi, Rickey then told him, "Should I [Bavasi] need help at anytime, all I had to do was pick up the phone."

Bavasi said he used this offer of help in 1954 to get Rickey to agree to draft a different player, pitcher John Rutherford, off the Royals roster. However, Bavasi was dismayed to learn two days later that the deal was off and that the Pirates were going to draft Clemente. "It seemed that Walter O'Malley and Mr. Rickey got in another argument, and it seems Walter called Mr. Rickey every name in the book," Bavasi explained. "Thus, we lost Roberto."[29]

Summary

Some stories and claims may be difficult to fully verify or refute, and it's possible that the contention that Clemente was being hidden and/or mistreated in Montreal is one of them. While this analysis may not provide a definitive answer one way or another, it is telling that the examples used to support the hiding claim are so consistently incorrect.

In a rather supercilious manner, Phil Musick wrote, "Whether or not the Dodgers consciously tried to hide Clemente from the prying eyes of scouts from other major league clubs is questionable—barely. The evidence insists that the Dodgers ordered him into virtual seclusion in Montreal; Macon insists otherwise. The evidence does not support his claim."[30]

In reality, the claims not supported by the evidence are those made by Musick and the other biographers.

[The author prepared a substantial game-by-game appendix of Clemente's season in Montreal, which has been omitted here for space considerations. It is available on sabr.org.—Eds.]

NOTES

1. Barbara Schmidt's web site on Mark Twain (www.twainquotes.com/Lies.html) says this quote has never been verified as originating with Twain and that a related quote

may have originated with British preacher Charles Haddon Spurgeon, who attributed it to a proverb that he once used in a sermon.

2. *The Sporting News*, March 3, 1954, 26.

3. The bonus rule in effect at that time is chronicled in *Baseball's Biggest Blunder: The Bonus Rule of 1953–1957*, by Brent Kelley (Lanham MD: Scarecrow Press, 1997). The rule is also discussed in a *Baseball America* article ("Despite Baseball's Best Efforts, Bonuses Just Keep Growing" by Allan Simpson, June 20–July 3, 2005, 10–12). This article says, "Players with less than 90 days of pro experience were designated as bonus players if they signed multi-year contracts or were promised more than $4,000 from a major league team. Bonus players kept their tag for two years. They had to be placed on major league rosters immediately and could not be optioned to the minors unless they cleared waivers."

4. Howard Cohn, "Roberto Clemente's Problem," *Sport*, May 1962, 56.

5. Arnold Hano, *Roberto Clemente: Batting King* (New York: G. P. Putnam's Sons, 1973); Kal Wagenheim, *Clemente!* (New York: Praeger, 1973); Phil Musick, *Who Was Roberto? A Biography of Roberto Clemente* (Garden City NY: Doubleday, 1974); Bruce Markusen, *Roberto Clemente: The Great One* (Champaign IL: Sports Publishing, 1998); David Maraniss, *Clemente: The Passion and Grace of Baseball's Last Hero* (New York: Simon & Schuster, 2006).

6. Musick, 80, 87; Markusen, 26.

7. Les Biederman, "Dodgers Signed Clemente Just to Balk Giants," *The Sporting News*, May 25, 1955, 11.

8. Wagenheim, 35; Markusen, 33–34.

9. The claim that the Dodgers would not start five blacks in the same game was made by Wagenheim on page 35 of *Clemente!* Box scores of Brooklyn Dodgers games in 1954 from *The Sporting News* indicate four instances in which Jim Gilliam, Jackie Robinson, Don Newcombe, Sandy Amoros, and Roy Campanella were all in the starting lineup: July 17, August 24, September 6 (second game), and September 15. (The Dodgers had one other black player, pitcher Joe Black, briefly on their roster in 1954, but Black did not start any of the five games in which he pitched.)

10. Email correspondence with Buzzie Bavasi, June 3, 2005.

11. A quote from Clemente that contains these claims is in Myron Cope, "Aches and Pains and Three Batting Titles," *Sports Illustrated*, March 7, 1966, 34. One or both of the sentences in the Clemente quote listed in this article are from Wagenheim, 40; Musick, 81; and Markusen, 26.

12. Musick, 81.

13. Musick, 89.

14. *The Sporting News*, August 18, 1954, 34.

15. Maraniss, 46.

16. Maraniss, 43.

17. On page 51, Maraniss tells of a visit by Dodgers front-office personnel but that "it was back to the bench" upon their departure. He also does the same thing on pages 51–53 with stories of the trips by Pittsburgh Pirates scouts to see Clemente, claiming that Macon refused to play Clemente when scout Howie Haak visited. In reality, from the time that Clemente began platooning regularly, there were never more than two consecutive games in which he did not play, and, of course, these were games in which the opposing starting pitcher was right-handed.

18. Markusen, 19.

19. Musick, 81.

20. Musick, 87.

21. Wagenheim, 42.

22. E-mail correspondence with Neil Raymond, July 2005.

23. The discovery of Clemente is described in Cope's 1966 *Sports Illustrated* article, 34; also by Hano, 29–30; Wagenheim, 41–42; Musick, 84–87; and Markusen, 22–24; Maraniss, 51–53, and it is also covered in Andrew O'Toole, *Branch Rickey in Pittsburgh: Baseball's Trailblazing General Manager for the Pirates, 1950–1955* (Jefferson NC: McFarland, 2000), 140–43.

24. Wagenheim, 42; Markusen, 26–27.

25. Musick, 84, 86.

26. The "More Plausible Argument" theory actually disappears with the confirmation that Sukeforth's scouting visit, in which he allegedly discovered Clemente, was in Richmond in early June, not July, as noted in accounts from the *Montreal Star* provided by researcher David Speed. Sukeforth scouted Joe Black on June 2, even though Sukeforth was quoted as saying that he never saw Black pitch. There is no indication of whether or not Sukeforth informed Max Macon of his interest in Clemente at that time; even if he did, however, that didn't keep Macon from starting Clemente in two of the final three games in Richmond. These were Clemente's first starts since his early-season flurry of activity. After another start a few games later, Clemente dropped back to limited appearances over the next seven weeks. Nothing in his game-by-game record seems to indicate that the Royals used Clemente differently following the visit by Sukeforth.

27. Markusen, 26–27.

28. Musick, 86, 88–89.

29. E-mail correspondence with Buzzie Bavasi, June 3, 2005.

30. Musick, 80.

34

The Effects of Integration, 1947–86

MARK ARMOUR

In this article, Mark Armour vividly describes the pace of integration in baseball (by African Americans and Afro-Latinos) in the years following Jackie Robinson's debut with the Dodgers. Since its publication in 2007, there has been an increased interest in the decline of African Americans in the game, so Armour later expanded his study to bring it up to the present day. He joined SABR in 1983, created the Biography Project in 2002, created SABR's Baseball Card Research Committee in 2016, and has written or co-written six books on baseball. Mark received the Henry Chadwick Award in 2014. He is currently serving as the president of SABR's board of directors.

In early 2007 major-league baseball marked the 60th anniversary of Jackie Robinson's first season with the Dodgers, bringing an end to a 60-year ban on black players in the major leagues. The story of Robinson and the brave men who followed his lead and helped change the game has been told often and well over the succeeding years. The story tends to focus on the moral and ethical implications of the game's integration, the righting of baseball's great wrong, as well as on the troubles endured by the heroic men who led the way.

The study presented here begins with 1947, but it concerns itself not with social justice or heroism, but with the effect of integration on the playing field. Jackie Robinson improved baseball ethically and morally, which is plenty, but he also made it better because he was a great player, and his playing time came at the expense of someone who was a lesser player. Robinson opened the doors for a vast new source of baseball talent, and that talent could not help but dramatically improve the game.

I began following baseball a generation after Robinson, in the late 1960s. The baseball I grew up with was well integrated, as far as I knew. In fact, many of the best players seemed to be black men, people who would not have been able to play 25 years earlier. Commentators of the time, and the occasional outspoken player, would whisper that it remained difficult for a black man to make a team if he was not a star—for example, few teams carried black utility infielders. After mulling this over for 40 years, I finally decided to try to determine if this was true.

The first, and ultimately most difficult, step in this study was to determine which players were "black" and which were not. The so-called "color line" was never acknowledged, let alone defined. For other purposes, one might be interested in differentiating between African-American players and dark-skinned Latinos, and in today's culture we would consider certain players "bi-racial." For my purpose, such distinctions are unnecessary. I only needed to determine which players would not have been able to play during the days when black players were prohibited from playing. For almost all players the determination is straight-forward. Lou Brock is black, Al Kaline is not black, etc. For the players I could not recall or never knew, I had to scout down pictures or baseball cards, or solicit the help of other SABR members. To summarize, when I refer to "black" players in this study, I am using the term generically to include any player who would have been prohibited from playing major-league baseball before 1947.

I do not claim that this is an exact science, but the types of questions I am trying to answer here would not be affected by the misidentification of a few players. Ultimately, I made a determination for every player who played in this 40-year period, a total of 5,490. According to my findings, there were 933 black players in this period, beginning with Jackie Robinson in 1947, and ending with Ruben Rodriguez, who caught two games for the Pirates in September of 1986. Putting all of these players in a database, I can answer any number of questions. I present a few of these here.

How Quick Was the Pace of Integration?

The graph in figure 34.1 shows the percentage of major-league players in a given season who were black. The number increased slowly at first, but accelerated in the mid-1950s and was still growing at the end of this 40-year period. Black players first accounted for 10% of rosters in 1958, reached 20% in 1965, and 28% in 1986. Recent studies suggest the number is over 30% today (to reiterate, I am including dark-skinned Latinos as well as African-American players).

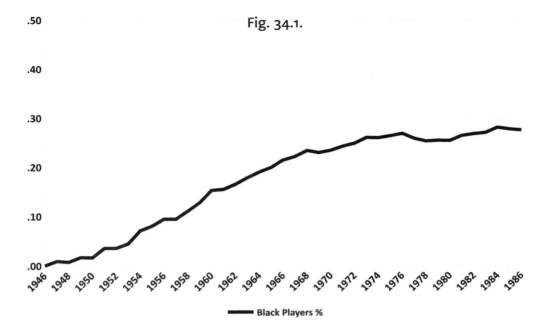

Fig. 34.1.

Black Players %

This is part of what I wanted to know, but this graph gives all players—Willie Mays and Julio Gotay—equal weight. I next needed to separate the quality from the quantity.

How Integrated Were the All-Star Teams?

In figure 34.2, the solid line again shows the percentage of blacks on major-league rosters, while the new line shows the percentage of blacks on the two mid-season All-Star teams. This graph clearly shows that there were more black players on All-Star teams than one would expect if All-Stars were randomly distributed. In 1965, for example, while 20% of all players were black, they accounted for 38% of the All-Stars. Based on the overall percentage of black players in the majors, one might have expected roughly 11 of the 53 players on the All-Star teams to be black; in fact, there were 20. As the graph highlights, this discrepancy was quite common during the era under study.

All-Star teams are not a precise representation of the best players, of course. Besides the human biases that go into the selections, the All-Star rosters require a player from each team and a balancing of positions. What we really want to know is: who were the real star players in baseball, and who were providing the most value?

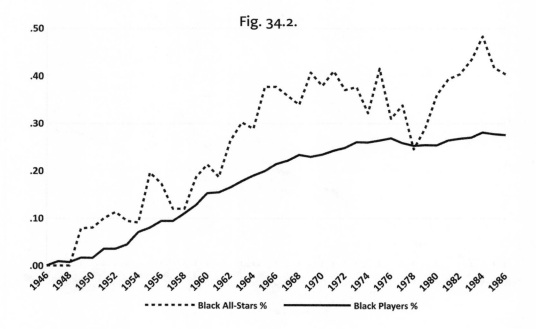

Fig. 34.2.

Black All-Stars %   Black Players %

How Many of the "Real" Star Players Were Black?

Win Shares, a system invented by Bill James that allocates team wins to individual players, lends itself well to studying large pools of players. One can always argue about some of the individual components of the highly complex formula, but when aggregating 5,500 players over 40 seasons one would expect any imbalances to average themselves out. As a point of reference, James suggests that a player who earns 20 Win Shares had a star-quality season. Again, one can find examples of 19 Win Share seasons which are better than 22 Win Share seasons, but over tens of thousands of player-seasons, these anomalies are of little importance. It turns out that the number of 20 Win Share seasons in a league is similar to the size of All-Star rosters—20 or 25 per league or so in the 1950s, and about 35 today with the larger league sizes.

When contrasted with figure 34.2, figure 34.3 shows that the "real" star players were even more likely to be black than the All-Star teams. Returning to 1965, black players made up 20% of team rosters, and fully 44% of the "star" players in baseball. This is not an anomalous season—these results are repeated to some extent for most every season for 20 years.

From another perspective this discrepancy is even starker. In 1965, 6.4% of white major leaguers (36 out of 562) were star players, while 20% of black players (28 of 140) were stars, a percentage three times as large.

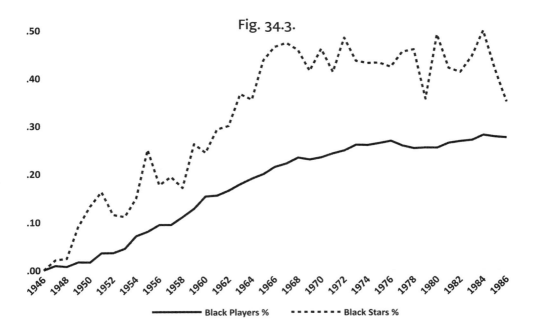

Fig. 34.3.

Black Players % ········ Black Stars %

What Was the Total Contribution of Black Players?

A more thorough way to examine the contributions of black players is to figure how much value the entire group was providing. To examine this question, I summed the Win Shares accumulated by every black player, and calculated the percentage of total Win Shares these men accounted for.

Figure 34.4 confirms the evidence of the previous two graphs: the black players were consistently doing more than their share of the work. The solid line again is the percentage of black players in the major leagues, while the dotted line represents the value they were producing. In 1965 when black players made up 20% of major-league players, they accounted for 28% of the value, a huge difference when considering the size of the pool.

As an aside, it is ironic that many people consider baseball post-1960 as diluted by expansion, even as this great talent source was finally being mined. If 28% of the talent in the league was not allowed to play a generation before, how likely is it that the game was of lesser quality? Baseball in the 1960s had 25% more teams (20 versus 16), but the addition of black players easily accounts for that increase, even as blacks likely remained underrepresented.

As I pushed this study further out, I expected the two lines in figure 34.4 to converge. In fact, although they got closer, there remained a significant gap in 1986, strongly suggesting that lesser skilled black players still had a

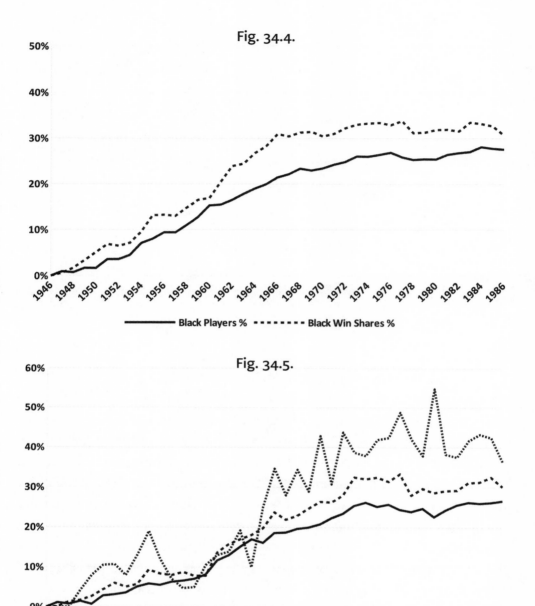

Fig. 34.4.

Black Players %　Black Win Shares %

Fig. 34.5.

Black Players %　Black Win Shares %　Black Stars %

tougher time getting work. It would be interesting to see how this trend has evolved over the past 20 years.

How Large Was the Difference Between the Two Leagues?

Let's first take a closer look at the American League.

Figure 34.5 shows the percentage of American League players who were

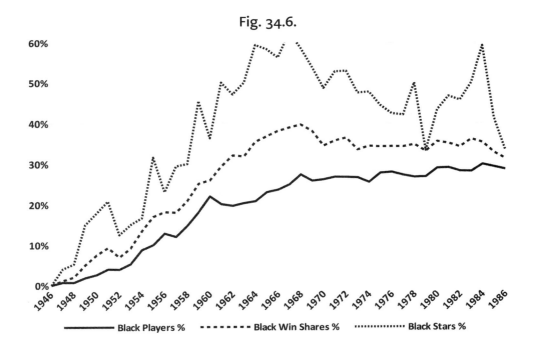

Fig. 34.6.

——— Black Players %   - - - - - - Black Win Shares %   ·············· Black Stars %

black (solid line), the percentage of star players who were black (dashed line), and the overall value of the black players. The American League integrated slowly, and other than for a few years in the mid-1950s, the black players in the league were performing about as one would expect from their share of the rosters through the mid-1960s. During the late 1960s, however, as the American League became more fully integrated, black stars began to make up larger percentage of the talent base than suggested by their numbers alone.

In the National League, the story is much more dramatic, as shown in figure 34.6.

By the early 1960s, half of the stars in the league were black, and the number was over 60% by 1967. The dramatic effect of the star players illustrated in figure 34.3 is nearly completely fueled by the NL; the AL did not begin to field many black stars until the late 1960s.

Finally, one can just plot the difference in the value of the black player in the two leagues.

In figure 34.7 we do not plot lines for the two leagues, but just look at the difference in the value of each league's black players, subtracting the AL share from the NL share. The NL had a small advantage in the early years of integration, but their edge grew rapidly in the late 1950s and remained strong

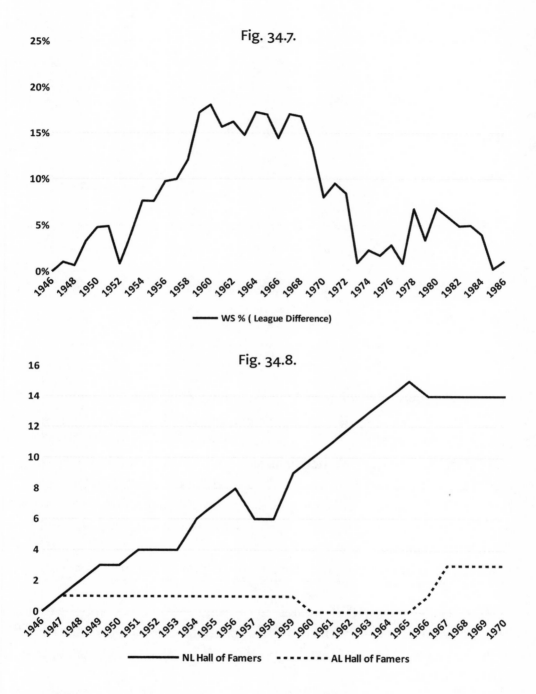

Fig. 34.7.

WS % (League Difference)

Fig. 34.8.

NL Hall of Famers   AL Hall of Famers

into the early 1970s. This graph highlights the National League's superior ability to not only find black players but to find the best black players. In the National League they accounted for roughly 30% of the league's player value by 1961, more than 15 percentage points ahead of that achieved in the less integrated junior circuit—a gap that persisted for the next decade. To put this more concretely, the difference in the two leagues was about 40 Win Shares per team, which is a peak-level Willie Mays season.

Why did the leagues take different paths in this area? Perhaps it is as simple as teams imitating the best clubs in their league. In the National League, the Dodgers provided a model of excellence for the other teams to follow, and first the Giants and Braves, and later the Cardinals brought in black players and became consistently competitive. In the American League, the Yankees won every year with very little help from black players.

How About the Top-Flight Stars, the Future Hall of Famers?

I will conclude with a look at the career superstars, the future Hall of Famers. Rather than using percentages, I focused on the number of these players who were performing in each league. For the purposes of this chart, I have not included Satchel Paige or Willard Brown, deserving Hall of Famers inducted for their great careers outside of the major leagues.

In 1947, each league had a single Hall of Famer—Jackie Robinson, and Larry Doby. Doby remained the sole American Leaguer until his retirement in 1959—at which point there were no black Hall of Famers in the AL for six years.

Meanwhile, the NL added a new Hall of Famer nearly every season, until 1965 when their gap on the Americans was 15–0. In 1966, Frank Robinson was traded to the Orioles, reducing the gap to 14–1, and, perhaps not surprisingly, he was immediately the best player in the AL, winning the Triple Crown.

It should be noted that the players represented on this chart were all top-flight stars. The Veterans Committee, the so-called "back door" into the Hall of Fame, has inducted only two black players—Larry Doby and Orlando Cepeda—along with several white players from this period. Furthermore, if one removed the contributions of the 15 National League Hall of Famers from 1965, the remaining black players in the NL still accumulated more Win Shares than their AL counterparts. The NL dominance extends past the superstars.

What Can One Conclude About the Talent Levels in the Two Leagues?

Win Shares is inadequate to definitively answer a question like this. If you add up the Win Shares of the players in the two leagues they will be exactly equal, because Win Shares begins with the assumption that the two leagues are the same—Win Shares is a parsing out of credit for all of the wins a team achieves. Since each league has the same number of wins, they will also have the same number of Win Shares. To the point, in order for the leagues to be of comparable strength in the 1960s, the white American Leaguers would have to have been significantly better than the white National Leaguers.

Could This Be True?

Returning to 1965 again, who were the best players, of any color, in the American League? According to Win Shares, the best players were Tony Oliva, Zoilo Versalles (who won the league's MVP award), and Don Buford, three fine black players. Going down the list, the best AL white players that year were Rocky Colavito, Brooks Robinson, Curt Blefary, and Jim Hall. How much better could they really have been than Sandy Koufax, Don Drysdale, Pete Rose, Jim Bunning, and Ron Santo, each of whom had excellent seasons that year in the NL?

Admittedly, this is not proof. But I suggest we should all take with a grain of salt comparisons of, for example, Willie Mays and Mickey Mantle, which do not include a huge adjustment for the quality of the two leagues. According to Win Shares, Mickey Mantle deserved his third MVP Award in 1962, beating out Norm Siebern and Floyd Robinson. Meanwhile, Willie Mays competed with a large crop of superstars to win just two MVPs. He might have won every year had he changed leagues.

How Much Did the Black Players Improve the Game?

One argument often used in making the case to induct players from the Negro Leagues into the Hall of Fame is that there were just as many great black players playing before 1947 as there were afterwards. This argument, while not without holes, is a compelling one. There were players like Willie Mays and Frank Robinson playing in the 1930s, the theory goes, and they should be honored just as their successors were.

A parallel argument is to consider the game of the 1960s without its great black players. The baseball of the 1930s, I propose, was comparable to the baseball of the 1960s if all of the black players were somehow removed from the game. Had segregation continued for another generation, players like Harmon Killebrew, Ron Santo, and Norm Cash would have been the superstars and we would not have known that there were better players who were not able to play. Mays and Aaron and Clemente, those wonderful players who remade the game, would have remained in the shadows, and we would be wondering today whether they really could have competed in the great major leagues.

What would baseball have been like in 1965 without Willie Mays and the 27 other black stars? It would have been immeasurably worse. It would have been, I suggest, comparable to the baseball played in 1946.

RELATED LINK

For an update to this study, see "Baseball Demographics, 1947–2016" by Mark Armour and Dan Levitt: http://sabr.org/bioproj/topic/baseball-demographics-1947-2012.

SOURCES

The main data I relied on for this study was gathered by hand, poring over baseball cards and hundreds of pictures found on the internet. Many SABR members helped me in determining the "race" of the 5,490 players, but I want to especially mention three: Rick Swaine and Steve Treder have each been working on research that overlaps what I present here, and were generous with their findings; and Bill Hickman found pictures of many of the most obscure players that had eluded me from this period. Once I had the black players identified, Dan Levitt provided me year-by-year Win Shares totals for each of my players, and (as usual) helped me think through many of the ideas contained in this paper. Bill James's *Win Shares* (Stats Publishing, 2002) was also necessary, of course.

35

Pots & Pans and Bats & Balls

JOHN THORN

In this piece, John Thorn presents his thoughts on the writing of baseball history and a plea to embrace the inherent subjectivity of the craft. No one knows this subject better than John, who has written or co-written several essential books on baseball, including *The Hidden Game of Baseball* (presenting the fundamentals of sabermetrics), eight editions of the encyclopedia *Total Baseball*, and *Baseball in the Garden of Eden: The Secret History of the Early Game*. John co-founded SABR's Nineteenth Century Research Committee, served as SABR's publications director for several years, and has helped countless SABR projects and members for forty years. John received the Henry Chadwick Award in 2013. He has been the official historian of Major League Baseball since 2011.

This essay is modified only slightly from the keynote speech delivered at the twelfth annual Seymour Medal Conference, sponsored by the Society for American Baseball Research (SABR) in Cleveland, April 27–29, 2007. It was published in print that year in the Society's annual *Baseball Research Journal*. The presentation theme of the conference was "How Did We Come to Understand the History of the Game?" The author took brief note of that theme and then shifted his gaze from the rearview mirror to the road ahead.

Before entering upon my remarks, I would like to thank the Society for American Baseball Research for hosting this conference, the Cleveland Indians for sponsoring it, this year's five Seymour Medal nominees for making it necessary (Yogi, can ya hear me?), and Dorothy Seymour Mills and her late husband, Dr. Harold Seymour, for inspiring it; their example encouraged so many of us to hunt for gold in baseball's attic. Even those who may only have found brass came away with a better understanding of our game and, just maybe, the nation whose pastime it is.

Geoffrey C. Ward, with whom I worked happily on Ken Burns's 1994 documentary *Baseball*, said recently that "Working on the film and book taught me [that] . . . while most Americans care too little about their history, the baseball community is different. The real meaning of all those apparently impenetrable stats is that the past matters. Without them no player would know where he stood, no fan could measure his or her heroes against those who have gone before. That fact alone should endear the game to any historian." That it had not, until Dr. Seymour's 1956 dissertation at Cornell, is a fact that may seem puzzling to attendees of this conference.[1] Because the academy still looks askance at baseball history, regarding it as a merely descriptive exercise, despite a proliferation of theses and credit courses related to the game, we have an opportunity at this conference to ask the worthwhile question that forms our presentation theme, "How did we come to understand baseball history?"

This formulation is parallel but not identical with other questions that will concern us this afternoon: "What is baseball history good for?" "How has baseball history been practiced?" And "How might it be better going forward?"

As to the first—"What is baseball history good for?"—some in the audience might reply with umbrage that history, like art, is for its own sake and must serve neither master nor cause; that while it offers tools for discovery, it is itself imperiled when held up to a standard of utility. This is a position with which I will agree . . . and disagree . . . if I may be permitted to make a perhaps old-fashioned distinction between History and The Past, the former being rooted in what happened, the latter in what some annalist thought might be useful to the game or even to the nation. So much of what today passes muster as history was created as propaganda or simple cheerleading, from the fibs of Henry Chadwick and Albert Spalding,[2] to the pinning of Jim Creighton's death on cricket rather than baseball, to the heart-rending tale of the Babe and little Johnny Sylvester. This is the sort of history that Henry Ford described in 1916 as bunk. What he actually said was even more incendiary: "History is more or less bunk. It's tradition. We don't want tradition. We want to live in the present, and the only history that is worth a tinker's damn is the history that we make today."[3] George Santayana, take that!

Another description of The Past might be "what binds and sustains," or mythology. History is what we at this gathering practice, but what we meet, out in the world, sometimes with astonishing rapidity, is this notion of The Past, in the form of that word heavy with nothing but trouble: heritage. At its best, acknowledging a common heritage allows us to form communities and maintain vital traditions, Henry Ford notwithstanding. At its worst, it abuses real history for chauvinistic gain. In a personal example, within hours of the May 2004 press conference in which I revealed that baseball was played by that name in Pittsfield, Massachusetts, in 1791, well-meaning but benighted locals were celebrating their city's usurpation of Cooperstown as the game's Garden of Eden.[4] As David Lowenthal notes in *Possessed by the Past*, history "differs from heritage not, as people generally supposed, in telling the truth, but in trying to do so despite being aware that truth is a chameleon and its chroniclers fallible beings. The most crucial distinction is that truth in heritage commits us to some present creed [or need]; truth in history is a flawed effort to understand the past on its own terms."[5]

In the hands of nearly all its practitioners today, baseball history is a moated activity, in which "what happened" is all that matters. Only occasionally will the drawbridge drop down to connect with not only "what it might be good for" but also with what it might mean in some larger analytical or social context. Finding Walter Johnson's missing strikeout from 1913; revoking Roger Maris's bogus RBI in 1961; getting Ty Cobb's hit totals and batting average right once and for all . . . these are not means to an end but ends in themselves. I attest to having spent many years in such pursuits: getting things right simply because with effort one could, and because "cleaning up" seemed morally superior to "going along," accepting what was wrong. Besides, it was fun to debunk the notion, held for generations, that the pitching distance had retreated 10½ feet in 1893 when it had only moved back five. Or to deny that the width of home plate had been expanded from 12 inches to 17 inches when it became a pentagonal shape, or to affirm that neither Abner Doubleday nor Alexander Cartwright had much if anything to do with inventing baseball. It was pleasant to accumulate and sort baseball facts, like some dotty lepidopterist, and it was sometimes useful to others if we published our research, no matter how trivial and disconnected it might be from larger themes in American life, from analysis, from interpretation.

Historian Kenneth Stampp, author of *The Peculiar Institution: Slavery in the Ante-Bellum South* (1956), once said of a colleague in an interview: "Carl [Bridenbaugh] was very sensitive about his brand of social history. It was rather old-fashioned social history. Somebody once called it pots-and-pans social history. He probably felt that emerging American intellectual history was in some way a negative commentary on his kind of history."[6] By "pots and pans," Stampp explained, he meant "the kind of social history where you talk about things like baseball and recreation—it was not analytical social history. . . . It was descriptive . . . and I suppose some people thought that Bridenbaugh's history was rather old-fashioned, some mod social historians. Every generation has [its new approach]."[7]

Myth and mythmaking are far more useful to the public understanding than mere findings of fact. And from the perspective of the historian of ideas and attitudes, what a man believes to be true, or purports to be true (including willful lies) may reveal more about himself and his era than the truth itself. So in trying get the facts straight about what really happened in baseball (Cartwright, Doubleday, or who?) or to slow the rush to judgment (Pittsfield), baseball's historians may feel that they are bailing against the tide with a teacup. Who cares about their pursuit of truth? *Give us a simple story*, the people cry.

However the history of baseball begins, the history of baseball history begins for most of us with Henry Chadwick. He recalled his first experience of playing baseball[8] as taking some hard hits in the ribs in 1848—if true, his remark reveals that the Knickerbocker rules did not sweep aside all that had gone before—and he dated to 1856 his realization that this game might become to America what cricket was to England. Today most of us think of Father Chadwick cavorting at the Elysian Fields with the Knickerbockers, pausing only to invent the scoring system and the box score or to cluck about the pernicious influence of gamblers and rotters. But as Will Rankin would point out in the first years of the next century, Chadwick had for decades, while elevating the game to the status of national metaphor, elevated himself as well, campaigning on a platform of *Le jeu c'est moi*.[9]

He was not baseball's first reporter—that distinction goes to the little-known William H. Bray, like Chadwick an Englishman who covered baseball and cricket for the *Clipper* from early 1854 to May 1858 (Chadwick succeeded him on both beats and never threw him a nod afterward). Isolated game accounts had been penned in 1853 by William Cauldwell of the *Mercury* and Frank Queen of the *Clipper*, who with William Trotter Porter of *Spirit of the Times* may be said to have been baseball's pioneer promoter. Credit for the shorthand scoring system belongs not to Chadwick but to Michael J. Kelly of the *Herald*. The box score—beyond the recording of outs and runs—may be Kelly's invention as well, but cricket had supplied the model.

Chadwick had the good fortune to team up with Irwin P. Beadle and his Dime publication series, penning the *Base-Ball Guide* for 1860 on up to 1881. He also had the good fortune to outlive his contemporary sporting scribes.

Today we call him a historian—along with Charles Peverelly, Jacob Morse, Al Spink, Francis Richter, and Tim Murnane—but in his own day he and they were journalists, sometimes given to gauzy reminiscences or club-supplied copy when deadlines neared and space yawned. These writers possess the advantage of having been witnesses to events that interest us today but that ought not to accord their writing blanket credence. As Dixon Wecter wrote some 50 years ago:

> A readable historian of his own times will be accepted as the foremost witness par excellence, generation after generation. But by way of compensation, the historian who arrives on the scene long afterwards enjoys advantages too. Though a million details, important and unimportant, will be lost for lack of recording or proper preservation, the disclosure of diaries and secret archives, the fitting together of broken pieces from the mosaic, the settling of controversial dust and cooling of old feuds, and the broad perspective down the avenues of time, all make it possible for him to know an era in its grand design better than most men who lived through it.[10]

Baseball's tradition of mixing—and confusing—contemporary journalism with *ex post facto* history continued into the mid-twentieth century, with working-press types from Fred Lieb and Frank Menke to Tom Meany and Lee Allen working both sides of the street. In recent years we have labeled some outstanding baseball journalists and statisticians as historians—I won't mention names so as not to give offense—but then again the term "baseball historian" is an odd one, a diminutive on the order of Billy Joel's "real-estate novelist." Even those who have made great contributions to the appreciation of baseball's history—I think of Larry Ritter and Donald Honig—are not themselves historians of the game in its entirety as Jules Tygiel or Charles Alexander or David Voigt or Ben Rader are. And then there are the "boutique baseball historians"—Milwaukee Brewers historian, Ty Cobb historian, and so on—who are what used to be called experts, or worse.

At the dawn of the last century, baseball's origins were already too old to be remembered, so stories were devised to rationalize what was otherwise baffling. Baseball history then was in the hands of folklorists, not historians. Members of the Mills Commission, lacking the mundane primary documents that typically aid historians of everyday life in the reconstruction of events and the tenor of the times, looked to octogenarian reminiscences of events witnessed long ago if at all; the most celebrated of these implanted memories was, of course, that of Abner Graves. Thus was the history of baseball supplied with a starting point, a crucial requirement for being viewed seriously. (A similar sense of necessity led to the creation of baseball's statistical record and the rapid and vertiginous climb to its current ascendancy.)

A century later we find ourselves still in the realm of eyewitnesses, as history is a term now accorded to events very recently transpired, and today's scribes may accord more importance to documents. Baseball's historians have largely—and thankfully—been unmoved by post-structuralist, post-Marxist, and post-Freudian siren songs, content to stay in the kitchen with the pots and pans of descriptive history, oblivious to the catcalls of political and intellectual historians. The respectable cousin of pots 'n' pans, the "bottom up" (i.e., not "top down") approach to history, based its claim to legitimacy, and in some measure hipness, on quantification and purported social relevance. Baseball-player studies certainly could be described as coming up from the bottom, but the continued emphasis was on story— what happened; and biography—by whom. There is some evidence of late, however, that baseball history may finally run aground in this generation's perfect storm of race, class, and gender, so perilous to frail, tentative, hopeful insight. Styles blow through the corridors of history no less than on Seventh Avenue; if we can wait it out, this too shall pass.

Where the American Studies movement has long provided a big tent to those who sought to describe American life as it was lived by those outside the political, military, and intellectual elites, it has also come under fire from the academy for its perceived lack of social relevance and scholarly rigor, if not outright triviality (I exclude statistically based studies, which get a pass on the rigor test but not when it comes to relevance). As Daniel Boorstin and Russel Nye, household gods of mine, demonstrated 40 and 50 years ago,[11] a fella could learn a thing or two about America through its media, its advertising, and its patterns of consumption. The perspectives of Larry Ritter and Dr. Seymour were similarly revelations to many of us in this room. And in other approaches to the game, in the 1970s Roger Angell, Bob Creamer, Roger Kahn, and Jim Bouton proved that baseball is the Trojan Horse by which we come to understand ourselves. Knock on the door and say, "I've got history for you," and that door does not budge. Offer baseball and the door swings open wide; once inside, a little history and useful knowledge may be imparted.

Baseball history is not so different from other forms, in the end. Solid research and command of the evidence underlie all of it. Dixon Wecter, not yet a household god but new in my experience and highly congenial in his approach, wrote:

> Industry minus art, accumulation lacking charm, data without digestion—such shortcomings explain this popular allergy against American history as written. . . . The re-creation of a dominant personality, or daily life of an era, or the power generated by its ideas, calls for exact knowledge fired by historical imagination. . . . If the author's saturation in his subject is so real that he develops affections and dislikes, his writing is sure to be more warm and vigorous than if he strikes the attitude of a biologist dissecting a frog.[12]

My friend and protoball pioneer Larry McCray, with his taxonomic bent, likes to say that he is a tree person and I am a forest person, and sometimes we just cannot see the other, cannot grasp one another's perspective. Wecter clearly believes that a first-rate historian must be a forest person—it is the leap of imagination that makes him a big leaguer—but he has to have a lot of little tree in him too. (Echoing another catcher there, Roy Campanella.)

It seems to me that what is lacking in baseball history is its last five letters. Even more than in general American historical writing, because it is the toy shop of history departments (the baseball beat at a newspaper used to be called the toy department), baseball must be pushed by event, driven by character, and have a freight-train narrative drive. As with a novel, there must be a truth of fact and a truth of feeling, illuminated by sensibility. In short, we may not, in the name of accuracy, neglect the speculative and aesthetic possibilities in baseball history. Issue-driven baseball history is simply baseball history unread.

Rather than depersonalize the writing of history, we should fess up to its intrinsically subjective element—the historian—and make way for passion, for intimations of sentiment if not sentimentality . . . itself a lesser crime, it seems me now, than before the current age of irony. Tell us what it felt like to be alive then, in that distant age. Insert yourself and your tale of the hunt into the story.

There may be no "I" in "team"—nor in "research," nor in "SABR"—but there is one in "history" . . . and there ought to be one in the writing of it.

NOTES

1. Harold Seymour, Ph.D., *The Rise of Major League Baseball to 1891* (Ithaca NY: Cornell University, 1956).

2. For more on this, see "Four Fathers of Baseball," a speech the author delivered at the Smithsonian Institution on July 14, 2005, at http://thornpricks.blogspot.com /2005/07/four-fathers-of-baseball.html.

3. Interview in *Chicago Tribune*, May 25, 1916.

4. For more on this subject, see the author's "1791 and All That: Baseball and the Berkshires" in *Base Ball: A Journal of the Early Game* 1, no. 1 (Spring 2007): 119–26.

5. David Lowenthal, *Possessed by the Past: The Heritage Crusade and the Spoils of History* (New York: Free Press, 1996), 119.

6. "Historian of Slavery, the Civil War, and Reconstruction, University of California, Berkeley, 1946–1983: Kenneth M. Stampp," with an Introduction by John G. Sproat. Interviews conducted by Ann Lage in 1996, p. 162, http://content.cdlib.org/xtf/view ?docId=kt258001zq&doc.view=frames&chunk.id=d0e7572&toc.id=d0e7119&brand =oac.

7. "Historian of Slavery," 173.

8. From Henry Chadwick, *The Game of Base Ball* (New York: Munro, 1868), 9–10: "About twenty odd years ago [i.e., 1848] I used to frequently visit Hoboken with base ball parties, and, on these occasions, formed one of the contesting sides; and I remember getting some hard hits in the ribs, occasionally, from an accurately thrown ball. Some years afterwards the rule of throwing the ball at the player was superseded by that requiring it to be thrown to the base player, and this was the first step towards our now National game."

9. Rankled by Rankin's challenges to his recollection and veracity in several *Sporting News* articles in 1904–5, Chadwick wrote to his friend "Joe" (Vila?) in April 1907: "Reference will show you that I knew of base ball in the sixties when—according to 'mine enemy'—I knew nothing about any game but cricket. Although in November 1848 I played as short stop in a field adjoining the old Knickerbocker grounds at Hoboken." Per photocopy in the Giamatti Center "Origins" file.

10. Dixon Wecter, "History and How to Write It," *American Heritage* 8, no. 5 (August 1957): 87.

11. Among many notable works, I take pains to cite Boorstin's *The Image: A Guide to Pseudo-Events in America* (originally published by Athenaeum Press in 1962 as *The Image or What Happened to the American Dream*) and Nye's *The Unembarrassed Muse: The Popular Arts in America* (New York: Dial Press, 1970).

12. Wecter, 25–26.

36

History vs. Harry Frazee

Re-Revising the History

DANIEL R. LEVITT, MARK L. ARMOUR, AND MATTHEW LEVITT

In the early 2000s, there were attempts to revise the longstanding claim that a need for money caused Red Sox owner Harry Frazee to sell off all his stars to the Yankees in the early 1920s. Using access to recently discovered Frazee papers at the University of Texas at Austin, this article serves as a corrective—a restoration of that claim. Principal author Dan Levitt has been one of SABR's best researchers and writers for many years and has written or co-written several books on the game. He and Armour collaborated on *Paths to Glory* and *In Pursuit of Pennants* (both extensive looks at team building) while Dan also wrote a biography of Ed Barrow and a history of the Federal League. Dan won the Henry Chadwick Award in 2017. The following version is as the article appeared in 2019 on the SABR Bio-Project website.

When the Boston Red Sox won the World Series in 1918, it was their fifth triumph in the 15 years of the modern classic. The club had the best player in baseball, outfielder-pitcher Babe Ruth, another top hitter in Harry Hooper, star catcher Wally Schang, and four other pitching stars—Carl Mays, Dutch Leonard, Joe Bush, and Sam Jones—each younger than 27. With the ending of the Great War, Ernie Shore, Duffy Lewis, and other stars were returning from military service. Local fans were optimistic—not only because the ballclub was loaded with talent but because Bostonians had become accustomed to great teams since the early days of professional baseball.

Within a few years all of the above players were gone, mostly traded or sold to the New York Yankees, and the Red Sox had become a laughable franchise, finishing dead last in nine of 11 years from 1922 through 1932. The Yankees, Boston's previously irrelevant neighbor to the south, took advantage of the Red Sox largesse to build a dynasty, winning their first-ever pennant in 1921 and going on to win a total of 29 in a 44-year period.

The man who owned the Red Sox and presided over this change of fortunes was Harry Frazee. A New York–based theater owner, producer, and director, Frazee bought the two-time defending champions after the 1916 season and then oversaw another championship in the war-ravaged 1918 season. After divesting his club of all its best players, the team he sold to Bob Quinn in 1923 was a wreck, and he took his place as one of the more vilified people in Boston's 85-year championship drought. As recounted in Fred Lieb's 1947 history, *The Boston Red Sox*, Frazee dismantled his team because he needed capital to help finance his plays—when he didn't have any players left to sell, he bailed out and sold the entire team.[1] This depiction of Frazee and the team's dismantling was prevalent throughout most of the twentieth century.

In 2000, Glenn Stout and Richard Johnson published their book *Red Sox Century*, which famously revised the Frazee story.[2] According to their version and several subsequent articles written by Stout, Frazee was not a villain but a victim.[3] He was in no way short of money—in fact, he was a wealthy man throughout his years in baseball, and he died rich. Why was Frazee a victim? According to Stout and Johnson, Frazee was being actively forced out of his position by American League president Ban Johnson, and many of Johnson's allies would not trade with Frazee. One team that would was the Yankees, and, all things considered, Frazee made good deals that turned out poorly because of some unforeseen bad luck.

Why did Johnson want Frazee out in Boston? Mainly, according to Stout, because Johnson hated Jews and he believed Frazee was Jewish. Frazee wasn't, but he made his money in an industry where Jews played a prominent role, and the false claim that Frazee was Jewish was suggested in at least one published story. Fred Lieb, according to Stout, was also anti-Semitic and his bigotry led to the revival of the anti-Frazee angle in 1947.

This article will show that the Stout/Johnson thesis is almost completely false. Fred Lieb was not a historian in the way we think of baseball historians today. He was a baseball reporter and storyteller who lived through many of these events, and his books are filled with (mostly small) errors due to his reliance on memory, either his or someone else's. But Lieb got the Frazee story right, and recent attempts to rewrite history are misguided and a disservice to the historical record. The Harry Frazee Papers, recently available at the University of Texas,[4] and New York Yankees business and financial records on file at the National Baseball Hall of Fame and Museum make clear both Frazee's financial distress and the large dollar amounts involved in his player transactions with the Yankees. Harry Frazee sold Babe Ruth and several other players (before and after the Ruth sale) to the Yankees for upward of $450,000 because he needed the money.

Brief Success in Boston

Harry Frazee and his theater pal Hugh Ward purchased the Red Sox along with Fenway Park in November 1916 from Joseph Lannin for a total capital obligation of $1 million. The duo paid $662,000 for the club itself: $400,000 in cash to Lannin (of which Lannin used $100,000 to repay outstanding loans to parties from whom he had purchased the club) and a three-year note for $262,000, due November 1919. The team had also issued $150,000 of preferred stock held by Charles Taylor, the owner prior to Lannin; Frazee's new ownership group was now responsible for both the dividend and the eventual principal repayment of this nonvoting equity interest. Frazee's personal ownership interest in the franchise was 70 percent.[5]

Additionally, Frazee assumed a mortgage of $188,000 as part of the Fenway Park acquisition. (This was technically an indenture of trust, which is identical to a mortgage in terms of the loan security.) Frazee technically owned the stadium through an entity called Fenway Realty Trust, and the team leased the facility from this company—a fairly typical arrangement between two sister companies. The stock of the Fenway Realty Trust (i.e., Frazee's ownership interest in Fenway Park) was pledged as security for the $262,000 note.[6] Taylor and a couple of associates held the mortgage on Fenway Park; on the sale from Lannin to Frazee, Lannin also apparently joined the mortgagees.[7]

The precise nature of Frazee's capital sources are, of course, impossible to reconstruct at this late date, but it is fairly clear that he also borrowed his share of the $400,000 in cash necessary to purchase the team. In an unsigned loan-consolidation document dated May 1921, Frazee considered refinancing $343,250 of debts (exclusive of a new mortgage loan on Fenway Park, to be discussed later), of which $250,000 was owed to the Federal Trust Company and secured by 700 shares in the Red Sox franchise (the remainder was owed to various individuals and banks on behalf of his theater interests)—undoubtedly the major source of Frazee's portion of the funds used to purchase the club. As further evidence of his large borrowings, Frazee and the Red Sox had large interest obligations: In 1920, the only year for which we have a complete team financial statement, the club paid $34,061 in interest (again, exclusive of the interest on the mortgage, which was a separate line item on the team financial statement—apparently the interest on the $250,000 was run through the club's books), and, according to his tax return, he personally paid another $12,475 in interest that year. Looked at another way, if we assume an average interest rate of 6 percent,[8] Frazee and the Red Sox needed to support payments of more than $50,000 based on roughly $850,000 of principal ($250,000 loan secured by the team + $262,000 note to Lannin + $150,000 preferred stock + $188,000 mortgage, and this does not include any potential borrowing by Ward).

The purchase by Frazee from Lannin was the first sale of an American League franchise not vetted and approved by American League president Ban Johnson. For many years Johnson had ruled the American League with dictatorial authority, earned through successes at the birth of the league and long-term bonds forged with the league's early owners. Newcomer Frazee felt little allegiance to Johnson and showed none of the deference Johnson had come to expect, and the two strong personalities disliked each other from the start. At the time, bookies and organized gamblers operated relatively openly in many ballparks, and it was reputedly most blatant in Boston.[9] Johnson seized on this gambling problem in Fenway Park in 1917 as a pretext to condemn Frazee.

Johnson and Frazee appeared to reach some sort of detente during the 1917–18 offseason. Frazee hired Johnson's friend Ed Barrow as Boston's manager, and Johnson likely facilitated the sale of three Philadelphia Athletics stars to Frazee, who was still optimistic about his baseball business, for $60,000. But any reconciliation quickly unraveled in the struggles of the confused, war-shortened 1918 season. Frazee was outspoken in his criticism of Johnson's handling of the war complications and controversies. When the season ended, Johnson began campaigning to oust Frazee from ownership of the Red Sox, while Frazee lobbied to curb Johnson's authority, going so far as to approach former U.S. president William Howard Taft about becoming a "one-man National Baseball Commission" that would oversee all of baseball.[10] The Carl Mays incident in 1919 finally cemented the divide of the American League into two warring factions. Mays, one of the league's top pitchers, jumped the Red Sox in July, and, as the other league owners began offering packages of players and money for Mays, Frazee looked to cash in. Johnson argued that an insubordinate player should not be able to force a trade and demanded the Red Sox instead suspend Mays. Frazee and the Yankee owners, Jacob Ruppert and Tillinghast L'Hommedieu Huston, ignored Johnson's edict: The Yankees bought Mays for $40,000 and two players. Johnson ordered Mays suspended and decreed he could not play for New York. The Yankees owners defied Johnson and obtained a court injunction permitting Mays to play for them. With this act of defiance, the Yankees owners became, at least as much as Frazee, the focus of Johnson's enmity. Chicago White Sox owner Charles Comiskey, also feuding with Johnson, joined Frazee and the Yankees owners in a triumvirate committed to the dismissal, or at least neutering, of Johnson.

Financial Struggles Begin

At the time Frazee purchased the Red Sox, they were one of the most valuable franchises in baseball. When Frazee offered to sell a piece of the team to Ed Barrow after the 1917 season and make him a club executive, Barrow attempted to raise the funds by borrowing from his wealthier baseball friends. In his solicitation letter Barrow called the franchise one of baseball's most profitable, behind only the New York Giants and Chicago White Sox.[11]

Unfortunately for Frazee, profits from the club declined sharply after 1916 as attendance collapsed. The total gate decreased from 496,397 in 1916 to 387,856 in 1917 and then, in the war-shortened 1918 season, to 249,513. In 1919, Red Sox home attendance rebounded to 417,291, but the increase was smaller than what most other American League teams enjoyed. During these years the team's revenue could not have been sufficient to service Frazee's required interest payments. In 1920, for example, one of the most profitable years in baseball up to that time and the earliest one for which we could discover team financial statements, the Boston franchise turned a profit of only $5,970 after paying interest and the 6 percent dividend on the preferred stock.[12]

Although moderately successful with his theater ventures, Frazee was not earning anything close to enough capital to cover the costs of his baseball team, much less to accumulate substantial wealth. Frazee had two principal sources of theater-related income: the Cort Theatre in Chicago and the production of his own plays. Frazee was president of the Cort Theatre Company and a 54 percent owner. As president he earned a salary of $12,000 per year, and as an owner he was entitled to his share of the profits.[13] Unfortunately the profits were not particularly strong. The fiscal year ending July 31, 1916, saw a profit of $68,192, by far the theater's best year. These substantial earnings may have helped convince Frazee that he could afford to buy the Red Sox that November. But the Great War and its aftermath significantly cut into the operation's earnings. For the fiscal years ending July 31, 1918, and July 31, 1919, the theater turned profits of only $4,544 and $5,225, respectively.[14]

The specific economics of Frazee's plays are almost impossible to reconstruct at this point, nearly a century later, but it is clear from his tax returns and snippets of financial information related to his plays that he was not generating significant wealth prior to his hit *No, No, Nanette* in the mid-1920s (at least relative to the ownership of a baseball team and his other obligations). In an article on the economics of producing theatrical plays, Tino Balio and Robert G. McLaughlin highlight the difficulty of making money in this business: "One of the ironic and yet accepted truths of Broadway economics: productions, both large and small, can have substantially long runs and still show a loss when they close." The authors examined a number of plays over the period 1938 to 1960 to underscore how difficult it was to turn a profit.[15]

Although his career fell outside this time frame, Frazee clearly suffered from similar economics. On his 1920 income-tax return, for example, he shows a net loss of $42,534 for his theatrical companies. He claimed losses of $33,000 for *My Lady Friends* (B and C companies), $13,305 for *Ladies' Day*, $5,989 for *Toy Girl*, and $2,335 for *Song Bird*. He turned a profit on only one company, $12,096 on *My Lady Friends* (A company). Table 36.1 spotlights the profits (or lack thereof) for touring *A Good Bad Woman* through the Midwest in 1919.[16] This gloomy picture mirrored a downward trend in road productions during this period. In New York the theater rebounded for two seasons after the war but then hit another downturn when the country fell into a brief recession.[17]

Table 36.1. Profit from Midwest summer tour, *A Good Bad Woman*, 1919

Week Ending	Location	Profit ($)
10 May	Erie, PA	(36.0)
17 May	South Bend, IN	1,105.0
24 May	Peoria, IL	1,747.0
31 May	Madison, WI	416.0
7 Jun	Wausau, WI	14.0

14 Jun	Duluth, MN	133.0
21 Jun	Minneapolis, MN	(2,171.0)
28 Jun	Several small towns: Minnesota, Wisconsin	(2,426.0)
5 Jul	Several small towns: Minnesota, South Dakota, North Dakota	(1,579.0)
12 Jul	Several small towns: Montana, Wyoming	(447.0)
19 Jul	Salt Lake City, UT	(963.0)
	Ending Cash on Hand	**58,631**

Furthermore, Frazee often needed to sell off a significant ownership percentage to finance his productions, leaving him only a small percentage of the profits. According to the Internet Broadway Database, Frazee's longest-running show in the late 1910s was *Nothing But the Truth*, which ran from September 1916 through July 1917. (Notably, after this run Frazee had no play in production—presumably because of the war—until October 1918, a long time to be without theater revenue when his baseball team was struggling at the gate.) Frazee, however, needed to sell off a majority interest in *Nothing But the Truth*, and it is unlikely he received a substantial premium.

In a letter dated June 13, 1917, Lawrence Weber, a sometime backer of Frazee, chastised him for his distribution of the profits from *Nothing But the Truth*: "You certainly seem to be laboring under a misapprehension as to your ownership of a considerably bigger interest than you think you have."[18] Weber complained that, when they had repurchased Sam Friedman's 10 percent interest for $3,500 (using Weber's money), the "agreement was that this money was to be repaid to me out of the net balance of interest or 8% before any profits were declared," later adding that "it is just five years since you made your first touch from me and it is about time that matters are cleaned up." Hardly the tone or dollar amounts to be used with someone flush with cash.

Specifically, Weber pointed out that Frazee owned only 38 percent of the play and that, when he further sold out to Gilbert M. Anderson, Frazee was reduced to only a 3 percent interest. The letter noted that through June 9, 1917, the show made $42,778, a decent return but not the kind of profit needed to generate the resources necessary to meet Frazee's looming obligations.

While the analysis of the incomplete baseball and theater documents available in the Frazee Papers may allow a little room for interpretation, his tax returns clearly testify to his unexceptional income. We have summarized Frazee's individual income-tax returns in table 36.2. His financial affairs were not particularly well organized, and he may have been exaggerating the deductible expenses associated with his plays. But even acknowledging that Frazee's tax returns may have understated his actual cash available does not change the basic fact that he was earning well short of the amounts necessary to continue to service his considerable debts for the team and park. The loose papers and revenue and expense schedules attached to his returns further corroborate his modest income (by baseball-franchise standards). As a confirmation of the validity of the tax returns, several years after Frazee died a final appraisal of his estate was released. He left $1,152,390 in gross assets and $714,935 in debts and other deductions, resulting in a net estate of $437,455 ($94,952 going to his widow, $189,125 to his son, and $153,378 being owed to his first wife).[19] These amounts seem reasonable when compared with the last few years of available tax returns, which reflect the large profits he made from *No, No, Nanette*.

Our examination of Frazee's tax returns revealed that in the late 1910s his earnings were falling well short of his commitments. After showing a negative taxable income of $26,699 in 1915, he earned $24,928 in 1916, his best year up to that point. This solid income and an expectation of more good years was almost certainly a key factor in his acquisition of the Red Sox that November. The next few years, however, were not kind to Frazee financially. In 1917 his income dropped to $15,626; in 1918 it actually dipped into the red, with a negative net income of $13,364; in 1919 his income rebounded all the way to $721. Again, Frazee may have been overstating his expenses; he certainly lived beyond the means indicated by his taxable income. But his income would have had to have been a full order of magnitude larger to have met his looming financial obligations. Note, too, that when Frazee had his biggest hit several years later with *No, No, Nanette*, his tax returns did in fact reflect a much higher income.

Frazee's continued personal borrowing from the Red Sox, often in relatively small amounts, further testifies to his relatively straitened economic circumstances. He often had the club pay some of his non-baseball-related expenses. Additionally, in 1919 he overdrew his salary by $5,850; in 1920 he overdrew his salary by $21,659 and pocketed another $5,000 on a note. At the end of 1920, according to the team's financial statements, Frazee owed the club $38,293.

Table 36.2. Harry Frazee's income tax returns, 1913–1926

Income	1913	1914	1915	1916	1917	1918	1919
Salary: Boston Red Sox					9,000.00	15,000.00	10,000.00
Salary: Cort Theatre Company					12,000.00	12,000.00	12,000.00
Salary: Other (incl expenses allowed against salary)						(9,450.00)	
Salary: Subtotal	5,150.00	12,200.00	7,800.00	3,700.00	21,000.00	17,550.00	22,000.00
Profit from plays and theater company	19,715.00		23,114.00	65,265.00	17,775.00		600.00
Income from rent	315.00				1,341.00	572.50	231.00
Other income		540.00	540.00				
Installment income from sale of Red Sox							
Income subtotal	25,180.00	12,740.00	31,454.00	68,965.00	40,116.00	18,122.50	22,831.00
Deductions							
Interest	3,250.00	6,600.00	8,200.00	12,600.00	7,312.50	20,811.00	14,860.00
Taxes on real property	82.00	127.00	125.00				
Net costs attributable to plays	48,969.00	11,500.00	50,053.00	19,137.50	17,178.00	8,750.00	
Other deductions (bad debts, etc.)			2,775.00	12,300.00		1,925.00	7,250.00
Deductions subtotal	52,301.00	18,227.00	61,153.00	44,037.50	24,490.50	31,486.00	22,110.00
Taxable income before exemptions	(27,121.00)	(5,487.00)	(29,699.00)	24,927.50	15,625.50	(13,363.50)	721.00
Other income (tax paid elsewhere)		65,426.76					

Income	1920	1921	1922	1923	1924	1925	1926
Salary: Boston Red Sox	15,000.00	15,000.00	25,000.00	11,666.67			
Salary: Cort Theatre Company	12,000.00	35,877.77	12,000.00	12,000.00	12,000.00	12,000.00	12,000.00
Salary: Other (incl expenses allowed against salary)	(7,800.00)	1,900.00			9,000.00		
Salary: Subtotal	19,200.00	52,777.77	37,000.00	23,666.67	21,000.00	12,000.00	12,000.00
Profit from plays and theater company	2,500.00	3,805.89	20,669.54	3,667.43	21,389.75	302,363.43	29,767.14
Income from rent					3,827.81		
Other income			2,302.50				
Installment income from sale of Red Sox				15,937.50	15,937.50	15,937.50	15,937.50
Income subtotal	21,700.00	56,583.66	59,972.04	43,271.60	62,155.06	330,300.93	57,704.64
Deductions							
Interest	12,475.00	18,965.00	9,502.00	10,668.12	13,953.28	13,141.23	11,321.14
Taxes on real property	125.00		1,126.00	1,352.28	3,358.00	1,985.13	1,831.85
Net costs attributable to plays	42,533.54	37,256.45	62,581.98	20,435.29			
Other deductions (bad debts, etc.)	1,150.00			13,140.00	13,890.00	76,512.50	14,133.37
Deductions subtotal	56,283.54	56,221.45	73,209.98	45,595.69	31,201.28	91,638.86	27,286.36
Taxable income before exemptions	34,583.54	362.11	(13,237.94)	(2,324.09)	30,953.78	238,662.07	30,418.28

Soon Frazee not only found himself squeezed by the interest on all his debt; in November 1919 the $262,000 principal on Lannin's note came due as well. Magnifying the problem, Ban Johnson would gladly use Frazee's financial distress to try to lever him out of baseball. Furthermore, Frazee was looking to purchase the Harris Theatre on West 42nd Street in New York, which would cost $410,000 later in 1920. Although Frazee and his partner John Heyer eventually arranged for a mortgage of $310,000 on the theater, the partners still needed to contribute $100,000 in equity. Frazee clearly needed fresh funds—and quickly—to support his two businesses.[20]

The Sale of Truth

With his financial squeeze mounting, on January 5, 1920, Frazee announced the notorious sale of Babe Ruth to the New York Yankees. For Ruth, Frazee received the record sum of $100,000: $25,000 up front and three promissory notes of $25,000 each at a 6 percent interest rate, due in November 1920, 1921, and 1922. In addition, Ruppert gave Frazee a three-month commitment that he would lend him $300,000 to be secured by a first mortgage on Fenway Park.[21] With Ruth dispatched, the Red Sox would not finish in the first division again until 1934.

All parties to the transaction consistently maintained that Frazee needed money. Ed Barrow, the Red Sox manager at the time, later recalled that Frazee set up a meeting in the cafe of the Hotel Knickerbocker in New York to tell Barrow about the deal. "Lannin is after me to make good on my notes," Frazee told Barrow.

> And my shows aren't going so good. Ruppert and Huston will give me $100,000 for Ruth and they've also agreed to loan me $350,000 [*sic*]. I can't afford to turn that down. But don't worry. I'll get you some ballplayers, too.

Barrow further added that Frazee "showed me how much he owed, how much he had lost at Fenway Park, and how urgent it was that he get the $500,000 which would be made available by the sale of Ruth."[22]

Yankees owners Ruppert and Huston each stated that Frazee sold Ruth because he needed the funds. Both, particularly Huston, were close friends of Frazee and were well acquainted with his financial situation. They recognized that Frazee was being squeezed and needed to pay off Lannin's note. Ruppert also later remarked on how small Frazee's initial cash investment was relative to the price of the franchise: "Joe Lannin, from whom Frazee had bought the Boston club on a shoestring, was hollering for his money."[23] In a separate account, Huston told the same story: "Frazee found it necessary to do some financing in his baseball ownership," he recalled. "There was a mortgage of about $300,000 on the Boston club and grounds and the holders of this paper called it insisted on having the money."[24] This certainly referred to the $262,000 note due Lannin, the security for which was actually Frazee's equity interest in Fenway Park.

Fred Lieb, a longtime baseball writer and author of several baseball books in the 1940s and 1950s, is another primary source for these details. "Harry Frazee," he wrote,

> once told the author the rape wasn't premeditated. He didn't plan it that way; it just happened. He needed money, and the Yankee colonels, Ruppert and Huston, hungry for a winner, had plenty of it.

(Lieb credited sportswriter Burt Whitman with coining the phrase "the rape of the Red Sox" to describe the sale of Ruth and other players, mostly to the Yankees.) Lieb continued: "'The Ruth deal was the only way I could retain the Red Sox,' Frazee once told the author in a moment of confidence."[25]

Financial Struggles Worsen

Unfortunately, the sale of Ruth did not immediately clear up Frazee's financial obligations. For one thing, Frazee's finances were relatively disorganized, and his attorneys were having difficulty cleaning up the existing mortgage so that the new one from Ruppert could be secured. In the meantime, Frazee immediately began trying to borrow against his three $25,000 notes from the Ruth sale. On December 30, 1919, Colonel Huston wrote to his partner Jacob Ruppert: "I told Mr. Frazee that I would try to get him a short-time loan at my bank, with one of the notes we gave the Boston Club as collateral." In February 1920, Huston again sent a message to Ruppert on financing the notes:

> Mr. Harry Frazee is asking us to aid in getting three $25,000 notes discounted. He says events with Mr. Lannin have made it impossible to follow his original intention of having the notes discounted in Boston.

Frazee wanted cash immediately by either selling or borrowing against the three $25,000 notes.[26] In a friendly but supplicating letter to Frazee on January 11, 1920, Joseph Lannin, expressing dismay at the delay in Frazee's repayment of his $262,000 note after Lannin had extended the date, stipulated, "as agreed by you, that payment would be made before December 4." Lannin added that he needed the money for several of his own obligations:

> I have purchased some property and have been granted two extensions, but the owners refuse to give me a further extension of time, so I must get this money or meet with considerable financial loss, as I would forfeit a substantial payment that I have already made. I have also agreed to take an interest in the Mercedes Automobile Agency, depending on receiving this money from you.[27]

In February 1920, as Frazee's attorneys struggled through the outstanding mortgage issues with Taylor's group, Lannin sued to have his security (Frazee's ownership interest in Fenway Park) auctioned off, with the proceeds going to payoff his note. To delay and mitigate repayment of his debt to Lannin, Frazee claimed that, when he had acquired the club, he had unexpectedly taken on an additional obligation of $60,000 to $70,000 that was rightfully owed by Lannin as part of a legal settlement baseball owners made with the Federal League.[28]

On March 8, Frazee's and Lannin's attorneys signed a stipulation resolving the dispute wholly in favor of Lannin. The settlement called for Frazee to pay $25,000 by March 8, another $25,000 by March 22, and the $215,000 balance by May 3, and Lannin would earn interest on all funds not paid by April 5. (Why this settlement included an extra $3,000 to Lannin is not clear, but several items were in play, and the extra payment could have been for interest, legal fees, or some other associated cost.) To access Ruppert's loan, however, the cash-strapped Frazee still had to clear up the existing mortgage on Fenway Park (including refinancing Taylor's preferred stock). Otherwise, the ballpark could not be used as collateral for the $300,000 loan from Ruppert. In April 1920, as his attorneys finalized arrangements for the release of the existing mortgage, Frazee sent a letter to Ruppert asking for the loan, to which Ruppert agreed:

> You remember that I phoned you about ten days before the expiration of your agreement to make a loan of $300,000 on Fenway Park and asked you to extend the time, which you advised me you would tell Mr. Grant to do. However, I have received no word from Mr. Grant. I telephoned Col. Huston today, as I could not reach you on the phone,

asking the Colonel to see you and advise that I have cleaned up all matters upon the Preferred Stock which your Attorney wanted before making the loan and I am now ready to accept it on May 15.

You can understand how important this is to me as my plans have all been based on my ability to secure this loan. Therefore, will you please send me signed agreement, copy of which Mr. Grant has, stating that you will advance the $300,000 . . . and if possible make the date May 20th. . . . *I need this agreement signed by you here very badly to complete the balance of my negotiations.* (emphasis added)[29]

The mortgage would have netted Frazee about $175,000 in new funds ($300,000 less the balance on the existing mortgage of roughly $125,000).[30] And so, in total, the Ruth transaction freed up about $275,000 for Frazee to meet his financial obligations. Eventually Frazee purchased his theater, renaming it the Frazee Theatre, and settled with Lannin, sending him the final payment of $216,003 (including some additional interest) on May 3.[31]

As evidence for the claim that Frazee had no financial worries, Stout has suggested a couple of other reasons for the Ruth sale. As it is now obvious that Frazee desperately needed money to pay off Lannin and purchase his theater, these alternative explanations are basically irrelevant. They also do not hold up to careful scrutiny. Stout makes much of the fact that at the time Boston writers and fans did not universally pan the sale of baseball's biggest star to what would become their biggest rival. Of course one of the main reasons for the wait-and-see attitude was Frazee's announcement in the wake of the sale: "With this money the Boston club can now go into the market and buy other players and have a stronger and better team in all respects than we would have had if Ruth had remained with us."[32] Many writers believed Frazee's story, though eventually they would learn differently.

Moreover, by the end of the 1919 season, Ruth's status as the game's best player and biggest celebrity at the tender age of 24 belied Frazee's later claim that Ruth was actually a detriment to the club. In 1919 he set the single-season home-run record with 29, when no one else hit more than 10. He also hit .322, led the league in RBIS, and went 9-5 in 133⅓ innings pitched for good measure. He may have been hard to manage, but the Red Sox had already won three world championships with Ruth, and on the Yankees he would help win another seven pennants and four World Series, while the New York club typically led the league in attendance. Ruth was a player who created a winner both on the field and at the box office. Frazee, a clever theatrical promoter, naturally recognized Ruth's value—so much so that he leveraged him into $100,000 and a $300,000 loan. Ruth's purchase price was by far the highest in baseball history at the time, higher than the prices paid for Tris Speaker and Eddie Collins just a few years earlier, surely a sign of just how valuable he was perceived to be.

The remortgage of Fenway Park only prolonged Frazee's need for a steady influx of cash, and over the next few years he became addicted to financial injections from the Yankees owners. As confirmed in the Yankees' financial records and shown in table 36.3, subsequent to the Ruth sale Frazee sold the rest of his top players to the Yankees for more than $300,000. When the Yankees won their first World Series in 1923, four of the eight starting position players and four-fifths of their starting rotation had come from the Red Sox. The Red Sox finished last in the American League, and their skeletal remains would be the doormat of the league for many years.

Table 36.3. Yankee player purchases from Red Sox, 1918–1923

Date	Cash ($)	With Players	For Players
December 18, 1918	25,000	Frank Gilhooley Slim Love Ray Caldwell Roxy Walters	Duffy Lewis Ernie Shore Dutch Leonard[1]
July 29, 1919	40,000	Alan Russell Bob McGraw	Carl Mays
December 26, 1919	100,000		Babe Ruth[2]
December 15, 1920	50,000	Muddy Ruel Hank Thormahlen Del Pratt Sammy Vick	Waite Hoyt Wally Schang Mike McNally Harry Harper
December 20, 1921	150,000	Roger Peckinpaugh Rip Collins Jack Quinn Bill Piercy	Everett Scott Joe Bush Sam Jones
July 23, 1922	55,000	Elmer Miller Chick Fewster Johnny Mitchell Lefty O'Doul	Joe Dugan Elmer Smith

January 3, 1923	—[3]	Al Devormer	George Pipgras
			Harvey Hendrick
January 30, 1923	50,000	George Murray	Herb Pennock
		Camp Skinner	
		Norm McMillan	

1. Leonard did not report, and the Yankees refunded $10,000.

2. Owner Jacob Ruppert also made Boston owner Harry Frazee a $300,000 loan secured by a mortgage on Fenway Park.

3. The Yankees' financial records for 1923 do not show a specific cash outlay for the purchase of Pennock and Pipgras. On September 5, 1922, however, the Yankees gave Boston two notes, totaling $50,000, with no apparent rationale. The Yankees paid the first of these on January 5, 1923, and the second on May 5, 1923. As the two teams had no known transaction between the Dugan and Pipgras deals, the most probable scenario is that these two notes were issued for future-player consideration.

Somewhat quixotically, Stout and Johnson claim that Frazee made sound baseball deals with the Yankees and that he could not have foreseen what the trades would do for either club. This argument does not hold up either. Ed Barrow, manager of the Red Sox from 1918 through 1920, left the Red Sox and became general manager of the Yankees. Barrow knew the Red Sox players as well as anyone, and he spent the next few years grabbing all of the good players, like future Hall of Fame pitchers Waite Hoyt and Herb Pennock, catcher Wally Schang, shortstop Everett Scott, third baseman Joe Dugan, and pitchers Joe Bush and Sam Jones, among others. In fact, Barrow liked his former players enough that he got the Yankee owners to give Frazee $305,000, convincing evidence that both teams agreed that the talent was imbalanced. To argue that Frazee made good deals is to suggest both that Barrow and the Yankees somehow lucked into their dynasty and that the money was not the central piece of the deal for Frazee.

In July 1923, Frazee sold the team for $1.15 million—$850,000 for the team plus the assumption of Ruppert's $300,000 mortgage—to a group led by baseball man Bob Quinn and money partner Palmer Winslow.[33] Under the terms in the draft contract available in the Harry Frazee Papers, Quinn's group paid $350,000 down ($150,000 went to payoff Frazee's refinanced note to Taylor for his preferred stock) and then $500,000 over the next eight years.

During the 1920s, Frazee continued to produce plays, and in 1924 he launched his biggest hit, *No, No, Nanette*. It opened in Detroit and achieved hit status several weeks later when it reopened at the Harris Theater in Chicago after some fine-tuning by Frazee. A year later Frazee opened the musical on Broadway to popular acclaim, in line with the top productions of the era. It ran for 321 shows,

> considerably fewer than the 477 for *Wildflower*, the Youmans hit that preceded it, or 352 for *Hit the Deck*, which followed it. But the short run could be easily excused: Audiences in New York were already so familiar with the show from its Chicago and road success that they did not have to see it on Broadway to enjoy it.[34]

As his tax records indicate, Frazee netted more than $300,000 on *No, No, Nanette* in 1925, by far his most profitable year ever.

After *No, No, Nanette*, Frazee opened only one more Broadway production, *Yes, Yes, Yvette*, which flopped and was cancelled after forty performances.[35] He died on June 4, 1929, from Bright's disease, a kidney ailment. Frazee, a Mason, had no religious service; Masonic rites were performed by Judge Peter Schmuck as chaplain. New York mayor Jimmy Walker delivered the eulogy.[36]

Frazee and the Press

By the time of Frazee's death, the reasons for his dismantling of the Red Sox (to raise cash) had become accepted wisdom. In his syndicated column just before Frazee died, Westbrook Pegler of the *Chicago Tribune* compared the destruction of the Red Sox to the case of the Giants' Phil Douglas offering to throw a game in exchange for money. "The drunken pitcher would have done the same things to the Giants that Mr. Harry Frazee did to the Red Sox, *only to a much smaller degree*," Pegler wrote.[37] Upon Frazee's death in June 1929, the Associated Press story claimed that, after the World Series triumph of 1918, Frazee "began meeting his obligations by converting star Boston players into cash."[38]

Sportswriters began to vilify Frazee's destruction of the Red Sox by the middle of the 1920s as the magnitude of the Yankees dynasty and the depth of the Red Sox ineptitude became clear. Of particular interest to this story are the views of Shirley Povich, a prominent Jewish sportswriter (see sidebar "The Jew," reprinted below) for the *Washington Post* for seven decades. On Bill Carrigan's return to manage the Red Sox in 1926, Povich wrote that Carrigan would never have worked for Frazee, who "dispos[ed] of his good ball players to the highest bidder."[39] A year later, in a story about his hometown

Senators, Povich wrote that "cash does not have the same magnetic property . . . it boasted a few years ago, when Harry Frazee was selling Boston Red Sox in wholesale consignments to the Yankees."[40] In a story about Tom Yawkey's purchase of the team in 1933, Povich sounded the same theme: "Frazee proceeded immediately to wreck the team."[41]

More telling still is an Associated Press story that ran when Ruth was acquired by the Boston Braves in 1935. "And Boston fans," wrote the AP, "who still shudder when the name of the late Harry Frazee is mentioned, will never forget how he ruined a championship club to make the Yankees a winner."[42]

When Lieb's history of the Red Sox was published in early 1947, it received a generally favorable review from Harold Kaese, one of the more respected Boston writers at the time. In recounting the section on Frazee, he wrote that a "mass transferral of manpower led to the long period of Yankee supremacy, while wrecking the Red Sox until Tom Yawkey bought them in 1933." Kaese says of the book that "little that has not been hitherto revealed is brought to light."[43] Including, of course, Lieb's even-handed and decidedly accurate account of Harry Frazee's gutting of the Red Sox for cash.

Having written all of this, we can easily see how an indictment of Frazee could go too far. What Frazee did to the Red Sox—sell off the assets of a championship club without reinvesting in other players—has been done many times in baseball history, including twice by the much-revered Connie Mack. Frazee was a man struggling to pay his bills, and he was able to sell all of his good players and then sell the club at a profit. There is a certain charm in his brazenness. Has there been a tendency on the part of some Red Sox fans to blame Harry Frazee for the team's entire 85-year-championship drought, fans who believed that Frazee's dealing of Ruth placed a curse on the club? We doubt the prevalence of this point of view among serious observers but, to the extent that Frazee was blamed for the state of the franchise beyond the mid-1930s, that is obviously unfair. The club was economically competitive once Tom Yawkey bought the team, and other scapegoats will have to be found for the years between 1933 and 2003. But for Frazee's tenure at the helm, the historical record is clear. The Boston Red Sox won the World Series in 1918, and over the next five years Harry Frazee sold Babe Ruth and other players to the Yankees for $470,000. The shell of a baseball team he sold in 1923 was the doormat of the league until Tom Yawkey reinvigorated the franchise a decade later.

"The Jew"

On what evidence have Glenn Stout and others come to reject the conventional wisdom and revise the historical record, effectively exonerating Frazee from the wrecking of his team? Stout attributes Frazee's problems with Ban Johnson and his later negative portrayal in the press to anti-Semitism. According to Stout, Ban Johnson and Fred Lieb were anti-Semitic. Therefore Johnson's actions and Lieb's writing should be disregarded as the work of bigots. Relative to Stout's charge, two items are clear. First, regardless of the motivation of Frazee's detractors, the historical record is unmistakable: Frazee sold Ruth and others because he needed money for his theatrical ventures and baseball debts, not as a way to improve his ballclub. Second, his charge of anti-Semitism is baseless.

Although Frazee was a Mason and his activities of a religious nature were generally focused on Freemasonry, he came from a well-established line of Presbyterians, which the family traced back to colonial times.[44] Stout postulates that both the general public and close associates believed Frazee was Jewish because of a couple of relatively flimsy details: Frazee, born in Peoria, Illinois, was a New York theatrical producer, an occupation with a disproportionate number of Jews; and an article in the September 10, 1921 *Dearborn Independent*, a virulently anti-Semitic weekly published by Henry Ford, referred to him as a Jew in an article headlined "How Jews Degraded Baseball."

The reference in the *Independent* is the solitary piece of evidence we are aware of suggesting Frazee was Jewish, and it needs to be viewed with a healthy dose of skepticism. Regarding its accuracy, on occasion Ford referred to people as Jews if he disliked them and they exhibited what he considered Jewish characteristics, even if they were not actually Jewish.[45] It is certainly possible that readers—even sympathetic ones—would not have taken all of Ford's accusations literally. (Ford did not write the articles; he conveyed his themes and thoughts to writer William Cameron, who then articulated them in print.)

Furthermore, by late 1921 the impact of the *Independent* within mainstream society was waning. As historian Neil Baldwin points out, the *Independent*'s circulation in late 1920 was about 300,000, but by early 1921 it had fallen to less than half that. Ford initially urged his car dealers to purchase the weekly and pressed them to sell subscriptions to their customers. Many bought them on their own or for their friends and families simply to placate

Ford. As these burned off and were not renewed, circulation fell.[46] To put the circulation in context, in 1920 there were at least 10 magazines with a circulation of more than one million.[47] A review of Ayer's annual directory of circulation indicates that in 1920 roughly 85 magazines had a circulation of at least 300,000.[48] Obviously a magazine with such a divisive theme and well-known publisher could attract attention disproportionate to its circulation, but it was clearly a small voice among many competing interests.

Perhaps even more significantly, in response to the *Independent's* maliciousness, a statement titled "The Perils of Racial Prejudice" and undersigned by more than one hundred well-known Americans, including two presidents and president-elect Warren Harding, was published in many newspapers around the country on January 16, 1921. Baldwin, quoting an historian of anti-Semitism, argues that, several weeks after this piece appeared, "it was clear that Henry Ford stood alone in the United States."[49] And so, by the time the article implying that Frazee was a Jew appeared in September, the *Independent* had been marginalized, even if it remained a terrifying channel for anti-Semitism. The point here is not to minimize the danger from even peripheral voices of hate but to highlight how many people in the mainstream may not have seen the reference to Frazee as a Jew or may not have believed it if they did.

The Frazee Papers include many items one might expect, such as personal tax records, receipts on his theater productions, and business correspondence. They also include a wide range of other material—tax-record notes scribbled on scraps of paper or the backs of envelopes, press clippings about his son being jailed for speeding, unredeemed baseball tickets, a letter from a young man requesting employment. In all of this material, other than a copy of the offending *Dearborn Independent*, we could find no references to, or implications of, Frazee's supposed Judaism.

In fact, we came across only two "religious" references in all of his collected papers. These are two undated Christmas cards that the Frazees had sent out. One says "Yo Ho and a Merry Christmas. Mr. and Mrs. Harry Herbert Frazee." The other, underneath a picture of a dog pulling a leash held by a couple of children, reads: "The Frazee jrs. Ann, Harry, Harry III, Robert & 'the Duke' himself, are pulling for a Merry Xmas and a Happy New Year to all."

In sum, we find it highly unlikely that the Peoria-born Frazee, who sent out Christmas cards and was descended from a long line of Presbyterians, would be mistaken as Jewish. Moreover, the two individuals Stout most specifically charged with anti-Semitism in their treatment of Frazee—Johnson and Lieb—both knew Frazee well and would have known whether he was Jewish. And even if they did believe he was, can we really determine that their deeds and words were dictated by anti-Semitism? What evidence is there that the two men hated Jews at all?

The single item of circumstantial evidence for Johnson's anti-Semitism is that, in contrast to the National League, the American League, after its inaugural 1901 season (when the majority Baltimore stockholder was Sidney Frank, who was Jewish) had no Jewish owner until after Johnson left the presidency in 1927. This is a flimsy piece of evidence on which to tar a man. Moreover, that a Jewish owner still did not come into the American League until after 1946 partially exonerates Johnson from being singled out as uniquely anti-Semitic.[50] A strain of anti-Semitism in the form of negative Jewish stereotypes and quotas limiting Jews in colleges and occupations was common in the early twentieth century. This may have been in play among baseball executives, but it seems unreasonable to single out Johnson.

Stout and Johnson also theorize that Frazee sold Ruth to bolster his alliance with the Yankees owners against Johnson. This argument makes no sense. Most obviously, there is no cause and effect between the sale and the bolstering of the alliance unless one claims that Ruth was sold at a large discount in exchange for a nebulous agreement from the Yankees owners to support Frazee against Johnson. One cannot suggest that Ruth was a detriment to the Red Sox (as Stout does) and simultaneously claim he was worth more than $100,000. More importantly, the Yankees owners were even more at the forefront of the imbroglio with Johnson than was Frazee; they would have needed Frazee's support against Johnson more than vice versa. Any transaction between the Yankees owners and Frazee was a consequence of their social relationship and alliance against Johnson, not a cause. Johnson's feuds with the Yankees owners and with Comiskey were just as bitter as the one with Frazee; there is no reason to attribute anti-Semitism to this quarrel.

Stout wrote that anti-Semitism against Frazee gained traction from the *Dearborn Independent* article, that Frazee received balanced press before the article and generally bad press after it.[51] But the *Independent* article ran in September 1921; Johnson's feud with Frazee was most bitter in the years 1917 to 1920. By the end of the 1921 season both Frazee, with his lousy team, and Johnson, now second fiddle to newly appointed commissioner Kenesaw

Mountain Landis, were largely irrelevant. Furthermore, if the baseball press was more critical of Frazee after the fall of 1921, it is certainly understandable. The Red Sox finished in last place in eight of the nine years following the publication of the *Dearborn Independent* article, while the Yankees won pennants with stars purchased in Frazee's fire sale. One would expect his press coverage to change as the reality of the pillaging of his team began to take hold. In 1920 there were members of the press who bought his line about reinvesting the money he received from the Ruth sale. Once it became clear that he would not, and would also pocket $300,000 more from the Yankees, his defenders understandably had dwindled.

Stout saves worse opprobrium for baseball writer Fred Lieb. According to Stout, the anti-Frazee sentiment died down for 20 years after Frazee's departure from the baseball scene, only to be reintroduced by Lieb in his 1947 history of the Red Sox. (As noted in the main body of this article, this is false.) "Yet underneath his button-down exterior," Stout writes, "Lieb was rife with prejudice."[52] Unfortunately, Stout's evidence for Lieb's anti-Semitism is embarrassingly thin, amounting to Lieb holding "the easy anti-Semitism so rampant within American society during the era between the wars."[53] Lieb was a giant in his profession for more than 60 years, and any prejudices he may have held (and we know of none) did not extend to his writing.

In an article in *The Sporting News*, Lieb directly addresses the issue of Jews in baseball. This lengthy piece, published years before Lieb's supposed anti-Semitic book on the Red Sox, focused on Hank Greenberg as the greatest Jewish baseball player, but Lieb also included the top Jewish players at each position; what Lieb described as "a first class all-Jewish team could now be picked from major leaguers past and present."[54] Lieb began the article by trying to answer the question "Why isn't there a real outstanding Jewish ballplayer?" He answers that "it was my theory that the race had been held back in developing along baseball lines by lack of opportunity." Lieb continues: "It was my contention the Jew did not possess the background of sport that was the heritage of the Irish. . . . Therefore he became an individualist in sport, a skillful boxer and ring strategist, but he did not have the background to stand out in a sport which is so essentially a team game as baseball."

This could be read unsympathetically, but Lieb follows up in the next paragraph with the argument that "this theory may once have had something to it, but in the past few years, it has been knocked into a cocked hat by the big bat of Hefty Hank Greenberg of Detroit and the Bronx." The rest of the article raves about Hank Greenberg and his excellent chance to be the American League's Most Valuable Player, points out how the New York teams let Greenberg slip away, and discusses the positive performances of other Jewish major leaguers. Throughout the article, Lieb's tone is supportive and appreciative.

Stout also imputes anti-Semitism to Lieb because of Lieb's belief in the occult. While Lieb was an occultist, we have been unable to find an association that would make him anti-Semitic. In *Sight Unseen*, one of his two books on the occult, Lieb claimed that Mark Anthony—in Lieb's story Antony spelled his name with an *h*—communicated with him and his wife through their Ouija board. Lieb described Anthony's thoughts on current events (the book was published in 1939): "He is anti-Mussolini . . . he is more friendly to Hitler. Once he said Hitler's treatment of the Jews was partly justified. Inasmuch as I am of German descent, psychologists might attribute this favorable attitude toward Hitler to personal leanings in my subconscious mind, but neither my wife nor I are admirers of the Fuhrer; being religious and political liberals and friends of humanity we strongly condemn his intolerance, his gag on free speech and his medieval anti-Semitic crusade."[55]

Lieb later tells the story of Jewish umpire Albert "Dolly" Stark favorably and sympathetically. Lieb admired Stark's single-minded determination to reach the major leagues, a virtue that eventually paid off when he became one of baseball's top umpires in the 1930s. Lieb is sensitive to Stark's disillusionment on finally reaching his goal and uses him as a sympathetic figure of what happens when one directs his single-mindeness toward earthly goals.[56]

Lieb also wrote a popular history of the Pittsburgh Pirates. He writes admiringly about Jewish owner Barney Dreyfuss: "When the former Paducah bookkeeper closed his earthly books, his contribution to baseball was large. He was one of the game's greatest and most far-seeing club owners."[57] Yet we are to believe that Lieb decided to destroy Frazee's reputation (it was already ruined) because he was Jewish (he wasn't)? This simply does not agree with the record of Lieb's long and distinguished writing career, in which he repeatedly wrote favorably of other Jewish baseball people.

To further make his flimsy case, Stout attempts to tie Lieb to Henry Ford through Lieb's acquaintances. Stout writes that "Lieb was almost certainly aware of the *Independent*. He was well read and the first editor of the *Independent* was journalist E. G. Pipp, uncle of Yankee first baseman Wally Pipp, who Lieb regularly covered on the Yankee beat. Detroit sportswriter H. G.

Salsinger, a close friend of Lieb, occasionally contributed innocuous baseball features to the *Independent*."[58]

As if that is not enough of a stretch, E.G. Pipp was not anti-Semitic, and he strongly objected to the anti-Semitic content of the paper. In April 1920, he resigned in disgust as editor of the *Independent*, before the publication of the first anti-Semitic article on May 22, 1920. E. G. Pipp went on to found a newspaper to counter Ford's anti-Semitism.[59] Additionally, that a baseball-writing colleague "occasionally contributed innocuous baseball features to the *Independent*" is absurd evidence that Lieb shared Ford's anti-Semitism. Stout himself writes that Salsinger's articles were "occasional" and "innocuous." Undoubtedly, given the easy anti-Semitism of the era, Lieb had friends who held negative stereotypes of Jews. To jump from this to claim that Lieb's accurate portrayal of Frazee was driven by anti-Semitism is fantastic.

Ironically, Stout's complete lack of documentary evidence (supporting the charge of anti-Semitism directed against Frazee) is precisely the criticism Stout levels at Fred Lieb. Contrary to Stout's assertion that Frazee died with his reputation intact and that it remained so until Lieb smeared him in 1947, Lieb's sympathetic treatment did nothing to change the generally held opinion of Frazee. The story of Harry Frazee recounted by Fred Lieb in his book, an account no different from the commonly accepted view, is well told and fundamentally true.

NOTES

1. Fred Lieb, *The Boston Red Sox* (New York: Putnam, 1947).
2. Glenn Stout and Richard A. Johnson, *Red Sox Century* (Boston: Houghton Mifflin, 2000).
3. The most extensive treatment of his Frazee thesis is Glenn Stout, "A 'Curse' Born of Hate," espn.com, October 3, 2004, http://sports.espn.go.com/mlb/playoffs2004/news/story?page=Curse041005.
4. Frazee Papers, Harry Ransom Humanities Research Center, University of Texas at Austin; hereinafter, Frazee Papers.
5. *Boston Globe*, February 11, 1920. Two documents from the early 1920s refer to Frazee's 70 percent interest: a draft refinancing agreement from May 1921 that was apparently never consummated, and a Frazee financial statement for year ended October 31, 1922. It is certainly possible that Frazee's interest had changed slightly since he first acquired an interest in the team several years earlier, but this would not affect the basic outline of his finances.
6. *Boston Globe*, February 11, 1920.

7. The Frazee Papers contain a letter dated January 12, 1920, from attorney T. J. Barry to Frazee, conveying an alternative mortgage loan proposal from a potential lender other than Yankee owner Jacob Ruppert. In the proposal reference is made to the fact that the "present de facto Trustees are Messrs. Taylor, Lannin and Lannin. The records at the registry of deeds do not show that . . . the election of Messrs. Lannin and Lannin were accomplished in accordance with the requirements of the declaration of trust."

8. The dividend rate on the preferred stock and the interest rate on the loan proposal in note 7 above were both 6 percent, as was the rate on the notes taken back by Frazee in the Ruth sale.

9. Daniel E. Ginsberg, *The Fix Is In: A History of Baseball Gambling and Game Fixing Scandals* (Jefferson NC: McFarland, 1995), 84–85.

10. For more details on this offer see the *New York Times*, November 24, 1918. Frazee and Giants President Harry Hempstead made a joint announcement from the Lambs Club in New York.

11. Letter from New York Yankees documents auctioned by Sotheby's, June 24, 2006.

12. Frazee Papers.

13. Frazee Papers.

14. Frazee Papers.

15. Tina Balio and Robert G. McLaughlin, "The Economic Dilemma of the Broadway Theatre: A Cost Study," *Educational Theatre Journal* 21, no. 1 (March 1969): 82.

16. Frazee Papers.

17. Jack Poggi, *Theatre in America: The Impact of Economic Forces, 1870–1967* (Ithaca NY: Cornell University Press, 1968), 29–33, 51–52.

18. The letter does not specifically state the name of the play, but the relatively large dollar amounts and the fact that *Nothing But the Truth* was the only Frazee show running anywhere near 1917 make it almost certain that Weber was referring to *Nothing But the Truth*.

19. *New York Times*, August 23, 1933.

20. Freyer Realty Company tax returns for 1920, 1921, 1922, 1923, and 1924, Frazee Papers.

21. Stout mistakenly believes that this mortgage was not part of the Ruth sale; see, for example, Glenn Stout in *When Boston Still Had the Babe: The 1918 Champion Red Sox* (Burlington MA: Rounder Books, 2008; republished by SABR in 2018), 166. This view is certainly incorrect; the mortgage loan of $300,000 was an integral component of the Ruth transaction. In addition to the document quoted below, Ruppert wrote: "We paid $100,000 for Ruth. And I personally made a loan of $370,000 [*sic*] to Frazee, taking a mortgage on Fenway Park as security" (*New York World-Telegram*, February 19, 1938). Moreover, Lannin expected a mortgage loan to be part of Frazee's capital raising. In a letter (January 11, 1920) to Frazee, pleading for his money, he wrote: "I was mightily pleased to learn from you yesterday that you had arranged your finances so that permanent loans may be placed on the Park and

that it is now only a matter of retiring the bonds [the existing mortgage that took Frazee another couple of months to clear up]." Even more convincingly, on January 19, 1920, Ruppert's attorneys sent Frazee a letter stating that they had received the invoices and asking for payment to the real-estate appraisers who "supplied us with the valuations of Fenway Park, which were necessary to be submitted to Col. Ruppert before he could make a decision as to whether to agree to make a loan against mortgage."

22. Edward Grant Barrow, with James M. Kahn, *My Fifty Years in Baseball* (New York: Coward-McCann, 1951), 108.

23. Colonel Jacob Ruppert, as told to Dan Daniel, "Behind the Scenes of the Yankees," *New York World-Telegram*, February 19, 1938.

24. Bozeman Bulger, "The Baseball Business from the Inside," *Collier's*, March 25, 1922.

25. Lieb, *The Boston Red Sox*, 178, 182–83.

26. Robert Creamer, *Babe: The Legend Comes to Life* (New York: Simon and Schuster, 1992), 208.

27. Frazee Papers.

28. *Boston Globe*, February 11, 1920.

29. Creamer, 209.

30. *Boston Globe*, February 11, 1920.

31. Boston Red Sox, 1920 financial statements, Frazee Papers.

32. *Boston Globe*, January 6, 1920.

33. James Quirk and Rodney W. Fort, *Pay Dirt: The Business of Professional Team Sports* (Princeton NJ: Princeton University Press, 1992), 401; draft purchase and sale agreement, Frazee Papers.

34. Don Dunn, *The Making of No, No, Nanette* (New York: Citadel, 1972), 38.

35. Internet Broadway Database, www.ibdb.com.

36. *New York Times*, June 5, 1929.

37. Westbrook Pegler, *Chicago Tribune*, May 8, 1929, 29.

38. Associated Press, *Hartford Courant*, June 5, 1929, l.

39. Shirley Povich, *Washington Post*, December 14, 1926, 17.

40. Shirley Povich, *Washington Post*, December 2, 1927, 15.

41. Shirley Povich, *Washington Post*, February 27, 1933, 29.

42. Associated Press, *Hartford Courant*, February 27, 1935, 11.

43. Harold Kaese, "Fenway Park Special," *New York Times*, April 27, 1947.

44. Frances Frazee Hamilton, *Ancestral Lines of the Doniphan, Frazee and Hamilton Families* (W. M. Mitchell Printing, 1928).

45. Neil Baldwin, *Henry Ford and the Jews: The Mass Production of Hate* (New York: Public Affairs, 2001), 106, 243–44.

46. Baldwin, *Henry Ford*, 146.

47. Carl F. Kaestle et al., *Literacy in the United States: Readers and Reading Since 1880* (New Haven CT: Yale University Press, 1991), 263.

48. *N.W Ayer and Son's American Newspaper Annual and Directory, 1920.*

49. Baldwin, 150–51.

50. Michael T. Lynch Jr., *Harry Frazee, Ban Johnson, and the Feud that Nearly Destroyed the American League* (Jefferson NC: McFarland, 2008), 162.

51. Glenn Stout, "A 'Curse' Born of Hate."

52. Stout, "A 'Curse' Born of Hate."

53. Stout, "A 'Curse' Born of Hate."

54. *The Sporting News*, September 12, 1935.

55. Frederick G. Lieb, *Sight Unseen: A Journalist Visits the Occult* (New York: Harper and Brothers, 1939), 112.

56. Lieb, *Sight Unseen*, 227–29.

57. Frederick G. Lieb, *The Pittsburgh Pirates* (originally published 1948; Carbondale: Southern Illinois University Press, 2003), 47.

58. Stout, "A 'Curse' Born of Hate."

59. Stock Maven, at http://www.stockmaven.com/logsdon99_F.htm; http://freemasonry .bcy.ca/anti-masonry/dearborn.html; Baldwin, *Henry Ford and the Jews*, 98–100.

37

The Quest for Dick McBride

PETER MORRIS

Here Peter Morris describes the long and winding trail to pin down vital information about the life and death of an 1860s baseball star. This effort is typical of Morris, whose tireless biographical research has tracked down many nineteenth-century players over the years. His research has led to dozens of scholarly articles and several books, including *Baseball Fever* (a detailed look at Michigan baseball from its beginnings up to the 1870s), the two-volume *Game of Inches* (examining the origins of every aspect of baseball, from the game itself to the first use of an exploding scoreboard), and *But Didn't We Have Fun?* (which recreated the spirit of bygone days in the words of old-time players and fans). Morris has received countless awards from SABR for his writing and his presentations, and received the Henry Chadwick Award for his body of work in 2010.

The main purpose of the Biographical Committee of SABR is to fill in the remaining gaps in major leaguers' vital information. But another important mission is to ensure the accuracy of the information currently listed. The need to do this was dramatically illustrated recently in the instance of nineteenth-century star Dick McBride.

McBride was one of the greatest players of the 1860s, with his pitching skill being crucial to the emergence of the Athletics of Philadelphia as the first team outside the New York City area to contend for the national championship. Yet when Richard Malatzky, one of the top contributors to SABR's biographical research efforts, began to determine whether McBride was a Civil War veteran, he found something amazing.

While all of the standard reference sources list McBride as dying in Philadelphia on October 10, 1916, there was in fact no evidence for that listing.

The state of Pennsylvania is notoriously difficult for this sort of research, and the absence of documentation doesn't mean that something didn't happen. Yet the lack of even a death notice for such a major figure was still extraordinary, and Malatzky's research prompted a reexamination of the evidence. Emails flew back and forth between such accomplished researchers as Civil War historian Bruce Allardice, David Lambert of the New England Historic Genealogical Society, Biographical Committee chairman Bill Carle, and Gabriel Schechter of the Hall of Fame.

It soon became clear that McBride was indeed a Civil War veteran, who served in the same company with his older brother Francis. Additional research established that his correct name was John Dickson McBride, not James Dickson McBride as had been listed. He came from a prominent Philadelphia family and worked at a clerk at the post office until 1915, at which point he disappeared from the city directories.

Pinning down his date of death remained problematic. A 1922 newspaper article was discovered that seemed to imply that McBride was still alive. Allardice found a Civil War disability pension that appeared to be dated from 1918, but unfortunately the handwriting was too poor to be certain that it wasn't from 1908. So was McBride actually alive after his listed death date?

Going back to square one, Richard Malatzky traced the family and discovered that both of McBride's parents were buried in Philadelphia's Monument Cemetery. This information was passed on to Bob Bailey, a Bio Committee contributor who has an interest in ball players and cemeteries. Bob knew that Monument Cemetery no longer existed and that all of its bodies had been reinterred in Lawnview Cemetery. Having done some previous work at this cemetery, he contacted the cemetery office and was informed that a John D. McBride was buried in the family plot in Monument Cemetery on July 19, 1916, and that their records included a note that he was a baseball player.

They subsequently forwarded a copy of the original interment record, which included a newspaper clipping about McBride's baseball career. The source of the clipping was not identified, but a hand-dated note gave the date as July 29, 1916. The article included these words: "In one of our talks last week on the numerous men in Philadelphia who have passed their three score and ten and whose lives are still full of vitality and usefulness, mention was made of John Dickson McBride, the once famous pitcher and captain of the Athletic Club in the early days of base ball. But I was in error in assuming that he was still living. I am informed that 'Dick' passed away on the 20th of January last and that he was buried in Monument Cemetery."

So it appears that McBride actually died on January 20, 1916, but some questions remain. For one thing, why was there apparently a six-month gap between his death and burial? Bob Bailey notes that most cemeteries of the period had receiving vaults in which caskets were temporarily kept, and suggests that McBride's body may have been kept there until either he was identified or until a burial site was chosen. Since he was the last family member buried in the plot, this seems plausible. A delay in identifying his body would also explain the lack of immediate mention of his death in the Philadelphia papers. (Neither the *Inquirer* nor the *Public Ledger*, the two newspapers I've been able to check, had any mention of his death in January.)

It thus seems that this once legendary pitcher died in obscurity and even his body may not have been identified for some time afterward. But the matter is far from closed, and research continues. The lesson of Dick McBride is therefore one that experienced researchers know all too well—that even when all the information appears to have been discovered, it is always worth checking and rechecking.

38

Zooming In on a Great Old Photo

MARK FIMOFF

Ever since the 1994 formation of the Pictorial History Committee, photography and imagery has been a significant aspect of SABR research and publications. In this article, Mark Fimoff turns photographic detective, exploring a fascinating subgenre of study that shows SABR at its very best. Fimoff has been the co-chairman of the Pictorial History Committee since 2012, and has shepherded the newsletter, including its photo supplement highlighting mystery photos like this one, for many years. He was the photo editor of SABR's 2013 book *Inventing Baseball: The 100 Greatest Games of the Nineteenth Century.*

Wide-angle views of early baseball games provide an unending source of fascination and speculation: What ballpark? Which teams? What year? Can we identify any of the players? Of these, for obvious reasons, the last question is usually the most difficult one to answer.

Rarely, absent a highly credible contemporary source, is such a photo published with anything approaching definitive player IDs. When such claims are made, one wonders: How can you really know who the players are?

The wonderful photo below appeared in *Brooklyn Dodgers* by Mark Rucker (2002).[1]

The original caption included these points:

- Washington Park [Brooklyn], probably ca. 1912
- Cubs were in town . . .
- If . . . 1912, Tinker, Evers, and Chance . . . would be on the field
- The pitcher, **who looks like Three-Finger Brown** . . .

Since we can neither see his face nor count his fingers, it is certainly difficult to decide whether or not the pitcher looks like Three-Finger Brown. Three years later, the same photo was used by the same author in *Chicago Aces: The First 75 Years* (2005).[2] This time there is no hesitation in the caption:

- Cubs . . . playing in
- Washington Park in Brooklyn,
- 1912
- **Mordecai Brown *is* pitching** . . .
- Johnny Evers is at second base, Joe Tinker at shortstop . . .
- Frank Chance had already left for New York

Brown is clearly the reason for including this photo in a book about "Chicago aces." But, how can anyone be so certain about this ID? Can we confirm or refute it? Let's start with a magnifying glass.

To the right we see the pitcher greatly magnified. There's his glove on his right hand, so he must be throwing with his left hand. But, as we know, Miner Brown pitched with his three-fingered *right* hand.

Furthermore, if this is a 1912 Cubs-at-Brooklyn game, a bit of newspaper-article and box score research shows that, in 1912, Brown did not pitch at all in Brooklyn—not to one batter, not one pitch. Conclusion: **Mordecai Brown is *not* pitching**.

This great photo deserves a more careful analysis. Is it possible to determine who that pitcher is? Since the given caption seems untrustworthy, let's start by confirming the teams, location, and year.

"Cubs"

The Cubs wore dark jerseys and pants on the road for three seasons, 1911, 1912, and 1913. From the National Baseball Hall of Fame Uniform Database[3]:

Note the image of the pitcher above right. It is clear that his uniform, socks, and logo match either the 1911 or 1912 Cubs road uniforms. No other Deadball Era MLB team wore a similar uniform. Conclusion: **It's the Cubs, *1911 or 1912*.**

Also, we note that Frank Chance did not leave for New York until after the 1912 season. So, on that point, perhaps the caption was right the first time the photo was used in 2002—Chance *could* be in the scene.

"Washington Park in Brooklyn, 1912"

The Hall of Fame Uniform Database shows the following outfits for the Brooklyn club's final three years at Washington Park. Comparison to the magnification (note the socks), below right, indicates that the home team could be Brooklyn and therefore the site could be Washington Park, but this is not conclusive. Also, the cap/socks combination seems to favor 1911, but cap colors in the Uniform Database are not always perfectly accurate.

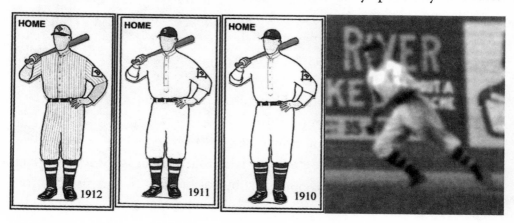

Below is shown a bird's-eye view of Brooklyn's Washington Park.[4] Just across First Street, beyond the right-field wall, is the large rectangular Guinea Flats building. Just across Whitwell Place from the Flats, at the corner of First Street and Whitwell, is a smaller three-story building, about the same height as that of the Flats building.

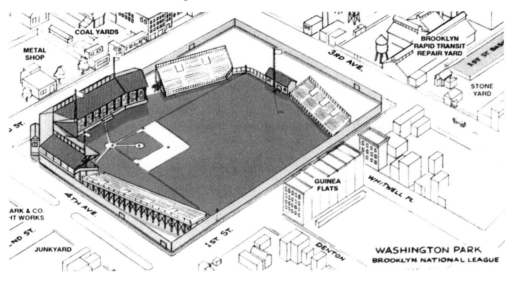

A confirmed 1915 Washington Park Federal League opening-day photo, below, shows the smaller building, left, and the Guinea Flats building, right, beyond the right field wall.[5] These same buildings are seen below in the photo in question.

Conclusion: **This is Washington Park.**

It will be much easier to determine who the pitcher is if there is certainty as to the year. One thing that works in our favor is that the billboards are readable. Though one or two advertisers might keep the same design and location over a period of a few years, in most cases outfield-wall billboards changed every year. Since there were no NL games at Washington Park after 1912, and given that the Cubs uniforms are from 1911 or 1912, what is needed are confirmed photos of the right-field wall from 1911 and 1912.

An "Ajax Tire" sign in right field is seen in our Washington Park photo, below left. It is magnified and shown below. Note the circular tire, partially overlaid with the letters X and T between the words *Ajax* and *Tire*.

This next photo is from the *Brooklyn Daily Eagle*, April 16, 1912.[6] The same circular tire, over-laid with part of the T, is evident.

Another photo, this one from the *Brooklyn Daily Eagle*, October 5, 1911, shows a different sign at that same right-field wall location.[7]

It's clear that the photo in question has the 1912 right-field billboard, which differs from the 1911 sign. Further comforting confirmation can be had from the following: According to box scores and accompanying newspaper articles, Cub lefties did pitch in Brooklyn in 1912 but not in 1911. Conclusion: **Photo taken in 1912**.

So—Who Was Really on the Field?

A lot of effort has been expended to confirm the author's original claimed location, teams, and year. This provides a firm foundation for proceeding with an attempt at identifying the pitcher. The next step is to check the Chicago-at-Brooklyn box scores for 1912.[8] These reveal that three left-handed Cubs pitchers made appearances in Brooklyn in 1912.

- Lefty Leifield—27 innings, with these lineups: *Note that either Ward Miller or Tommy Leach played center field.*
- Len "Lefty" Madden—1 inning, with lineup: *Note that Cy Williams played center field.*
- George Pierce—7 innings, with lineup: *Note that Cy Williams played center field.*

Newspaper articles indicate that, when any of the Cub lefties pitched, Frank Chance was there managing, but the above lineups show that without substitution Vic Saier played first base. Also without substitution Evers was at second, Tinker at shortstop, and Jimmy Archer was behind the plate. Conclusion: **Chance was there, but Saier played first and Archer was the catcher**.

The above lineups also reveal the following:

- When Madden or Pierce pitched, **left-hander** Cy Williams was always in center field
- When Leifield was on the mound, **righties** Ward Miller and Tommy Leach were in center.

Now, note that, when a magnified fielder has his glove hand in front of a light background, the glove is easily discerned as a dark blob. This is clear, for example, in the magnification of second baseman Evers, shown left, compared to the distant center fielder, shown right:

With that in mind, let's take a closer look at the center fielder. After zooming in, it is clear that he has no glove on his right hand. Therefore he is either Ward Miller or Tommy Leach. Checking the above lineups leads to the key finding: Conclusion: **Lefty Leifield is pitching**.

The lineups also indicate that when Leifield pitched, Frank Schulte played right field. So we can also conclude that **Frank Schulte is in right field**.

Putting it all together:

- Cubs . . . playing in
- Washington Park in Brooklyn
- 1912
- *Lefty Leifield* is pitching
- Johnny Evers is at second base, Joe Tinker at shortstop . . .
- Vic Saier at first base, Jimmy Archer catching
- Frank Schulte in right field

Well, maybe . . .

It's indisputable that the pitcher in the photo is not Mordecai Brown. Can we be so sure of the other conclusions, which of course are based on a presumption—the accuracy of the box scores with respect to lineups and substitutions? The records, as given in both the *New York Times* and the *Chicago Tribune*, do match. However, quoting researcher Cliff Blau on the question of confidence in Deadball Era box scores, "No, we can't be confident. . . . As for missing a player substitution, very possible."

So has a misplaced trust in circa-1912 scorekeeping provided an erroneous assumption leading to superficially clever but naïve conclusions? I don't think so. While these box scores alone do not provide absolute proof, they are entirely consistent with the accompanying articles describing the games.

Also, the pitcher's proportions do indicate a tall man, and Leifield was 6'1". Leifield pitched three complete games at Brooklyn in 1912. The Cubs' other tall lefty, 6'2" Len Madden, pitched only one inning, and George Pierce is listed at just 5'10". Therefore I stand by the identifications made here.

Note on Another Washington Park Photo

The National Baseball Hall of Fame has another similar image, just below. Comparison of the warm-up plate in that photo to the warm-up plate visible in the uncropped version of the photo that has been the subject of this article reveals an identical dirt pattern. That and other details indicate that both photos were taken on the same day. This additional photo yields another view of Leifield's delivery.

NOTES

Thanks to researcher John Zinn for going through two seasons' worth of *Brooklyn Daily Eagle* microfilm to find just the right views of the Washington Park right-field fence, and to Tom Shieber at the Hall of Fame for pointing out the other Washington Park photo taken on the same day.

1. Mark Rucker, *The Brooklyn Dodgers, Images of Sports* (Charleston SC: Arcadia, 2002).
2. John Freyer and Mark Rucker, *Chicago Aces: The First 75 Years* (Charleston SC: Arcadia, 2005).
3. National Baseball Hall of Fame, "Dressed to the Nines—Uniform Database," http://exhibits.baseballhalloffame.org/dressed_to_the_nines/database.htm. Note corrections added to Cub uniforms for this article—1911 collar added, 1912 buttons made dark.
4. Marc Okkonen, *Baseball Memories, 1900–1909* (Sterling, 1992).
5. George Grantham Bain Collection, Library of Congress, Prints and Photographs Division.
6. *Brooklyn Daily Eagle*, April 16, 1912.
7. *Brooklyn Daily Eagle*, October 5, 1911.
8. *Chicago Tribune*, June 8, 1912; August 1, 1912; August 4, 1912; September 20, 1912; September 21, 1912.

39

The Georgia Peach

Stumped by the Storyteller

WILLIAM R. COBB

In the long and complicated life of the great Ty Cobb, no event is more mysterious and notorious than the night that his mother killed his father (perhaps accidentally, perhaps not). The auction of the supposed shotgun with which this nefarious deed was performed is the starting point for an extensive investigation into the story and how Cobb's life was co-opted by his ghost writer and biographer. The author of this piece, William Cobb, who is a distant relative but not a direct descendant, has been researching Cobb's life for many years and has served on the Board of Advisors for the Ty Cobb Museum since 2004.

In his December 29, 2005, internet blog, John Thorn, the noted baseball author and SABR member, mentioned that the shotgun that killed Ty Cobb's father in 1905 had been part of the famous Barry Halper collection of baseball memorabilia—an incredible, if not unbelievable, assertion.[1] How could such an artifact of tragedy have survived for 100 years to become part of the most famous collection of baseball memorabilia ever assembled? And more importantly, why?

As a lifelong fan of Ty Cobb (but not a descendant or close relative) and a member of the Board of Advisors to the Ty Cobb Museum in Royston, Georgia, I was fascinated by these questions when I discovered Thorn's blog in mid-2006. A discussion among the museum board members resulted in an email to John Thorn, seeking further information about his assertion and about the relic itself. This exchange digressed quickly into a disagreement as to whether a pistol or a shotgun had actually been used in the incident that took William Herschel Cobb's life, and Thorn declined to discuss his statement further.[2]

A few months later, the Ty Cobb Museum received a phone call from a representative of the New York Yankees organization, inquiring about the shotgun that was used to kill Ty Cobb's father.[3] The caller, who identified herself only as a member of the Yankees' marketing department, wanted to know if the museum had any information that could be used to confirm that a shotgun, which the caller said was now held in the collection of an undisclosed Yankees player, was actually the weapon that had been used in the shooting of W. H. Cobb.

These two events inspired me to begin a thorough investigation to review all of the information that could be located about the August 8, 1905, shooting of Ty Cobb's father at the hand of Ty's mother. I wanted, once and for all, to either confirm or disprove the shotgun element of this tragic event in Ty Cobb's life story. And, if disproved, I wanted to identify and understand the source of this particularly distasteful part of the myth. An unintended result of this investigation has been to provide new insights into other myths about Georgia's most famous baseball player—where they began and how they grew. This investigation also demonstrates that new information to be found in the realm of high-end baseball memorabilia, often well known among collectors and authenticators but not widely publicized, can be highly relevant to the efforts of baseball researchers and historians.

The Shotgun

The first step in my investigation was to review the Sotheby's catalog for the 1999 sale of the Barry Halper Collection, which had netted something over $20,000.000.[4] This unindexed, three-volume set, which provides descriptions, some photos, and the realized prices of the auctioned items, is practically a baseball history in itself and would be an interesting read for any SABR member. My first perusal, however, yielded no information on the Cobb shotgun.

Recalling that I had once read that Major League Baseball had purchased about 20 percent of the Halper collection before the auction and donated it to the Cooperstown Hall of Fame Museum, I asked friend and research director Tim Wiles if the Cobb shotgun was among the Halper items that had been received by the Hall of Fame. His reply a few days later was that no such item was in their collection and that he and his colleagues could not imagine that the Hall of Fame Museum would ever accept such a sordid relic were it to be offered.[5]

A subsequent e-mail exchange with Robert Lifson, the memorabilia expert who managed the auction of the Halper collection for Sotheby's, revealed that the John Thorn blog had indeed been correct.[6] The Cobb shotgun had been listed in the Sotheby's auction catalog. This discovery prompted my second review of the Halper catalogs, in which I found this description on page 439 of volume 1, with no accompanying photo:

1227 Ty Cobb's Shotgun . . .

"Tyrus R. Cobb" is engraved near the trigger of this early twentieth-century double-barrel shotgun. Cobb's biographer Al Stump told Barry Halper that this was the gun that Mrs. Cobb used to shoot Mr. Cobb, when Ty was still young. The younger Cobb kept the gun throughout his life and used it on many of his hunting expeditions.[7]

Lifson also replied that the shotgun originally was to be included in the auction and thus had been included in the catalog, but that ultimately it had been rejected because the only provenance was Al Stump's statement. There was also a question as to whether Sotheby's was licensed to auction such a firearm.[8] The shotgun, as lot 1227, did not appear in the published prices realized list, confirming Robert Lifson's recollection that it had been pulled from the auction.

According to the Sotheby's catalog, the source of the shotgun in the Halper collection was sportswriter Al Stump, who had collaborated with Ty Cobb on his 1961 autobiography and during that process spent time with Cobb in the last year of his life. I was to later learn that Al Stump was very well known to experts and collectors of high-priced baseball memorabilia. But some obvious questions remained.

Why would Ty Cobb, who according to all accounts had been deeply and permanently affected by the untimely death of his beloved father at the hand of his mother, have kept the shotgun supposedly used in the tragedy for the rest of his life? Why would he have used this weapon in many of his later hunting expeditions? Indeed, why would he have had his own name inscribed on the weapon?

The Record

The August 8, 1905, death of William Herschel Cobb, a former Georgia state senator, Franklin County school board commissioner, and owner and editor of *The Royston Record*, was widely covered in newspapers throughout the state. All discovered contemporary news articles that provided details of the shooting death of W. H. Cobb and the subsequent trial of his wife, Amanda Cobb, referred to the weapon used in the shooting as a revolver or pistol. The August 11, 1905, *Atlanta Constitution* includes this description of Amanda Cobb's testimony before the coroner's jury: "When she heard a noise at the window during the night, she took a revolver from the reading table where she had left it and fired two shots at a figure crouching outside." Mrs. Cobb's full testimony before the coroner's jury was included in the same article (see figure 39.1).[9] A diligent online search by researchers at the State of Georgia Archives discovered numerous other newspaper articles available digitally and some legal documents from the Franklin County court records.[10] The weekly *Macon Telegraph* carried this description of Amanda Cobb's testimony on September 28, 1905: "According to a statement made by her soon after the shooting she was roused in the night by someone at her window. She rose quickly, and with a revolver fired at a crouching form. Then she screamed."[11]

Mrs. Cobb's Statement.

Mrs. Cobbs' statement to the jury was as follows:

"Mr. Cobb left home Tuesday morning, telling me that he would not be back until Thursday. Mr. Cobb bought me a pistol in Atlanta since we moved here. This I generally kept under my head, but last night I was reading and had it on my table and left it there.

"I retired about 10:30 o'clock, and woke up some time during the night. I heard a kind of rustling noise at the lower window of my room. I got up and got my pistol. As I approached the window I saw a form some distance from the window. As it went behind the chimney I went to the upper window.

"I went from window to window, two or three times, maybe more. The form seemed to get nearer to the upper window, and I pulled down the shade so that I could see just below it. The form seemed to crouch down. I stood at the upper side of the window and pulled the shade to one side and shot twice.

"After shooting I thought everything. I began to scream and went to send Clifford Ginn after a doctor. I called Mr. Welborn. I couldn't call very loud.

"After shooting I threw the pistol down. I don't know how long it was between shots."

Fig. 39.1. A copy of an excerpt from an article in the *Atlanta Journal*, August 11, 1905, quoting Amanda Cobb's statement to the jury of the coroner's inquest. Amanda testified that she fired two shots from a pistol that her husband had bought for her. No newspaper or court records have been found that dispute her testimony. She also testified that Clifford Ginn was first to assist her and made no mention of Joe Cunningham having been the first to arrive on the scene.

Several articles in *The State* (Columbia, South Carolina), the *Savannah Tribune*, and the *Augusta Chronicle* covered the 1905 coroner's jury and the March 1906 trial but failed to mention the weapon used.[12]

The Superior Court records found online at the State of Georgia Archives include the 1905 criminal docket, the 1905 application for bail, and the 1906 jury verdict, none of which make any reference to the weapon used in the shooting. In a 2004 SABR Deadball Committee e-mail group dialogue, some of these newspaper articles casting doubt on the shotgun theory were presented and discussed. From the ensuing e-mails, the consensus conclusion seemed to be that these documents were insufficient to dispel the well-known and long-accepted "fact" that a shotgun had been used in the shooting death of W. H. Cobb. The principal argument was that press coverage would have been friendly, even lenient, toward Mrs. Cobb, due to the prominence of W. H. Cobb and the entire family.[13]

This conclusion is contradicted by a close reading of the articles, which reveals that the coverage was in fact harsh, even discussing rumors of infidelity and the revelation that W. H. Cobb had a revolver and rock in his coat pocket at the time of his death, which served to heighten the speculation about this sensational case.

The court itself was hardly lenient on Amanda Cobb. Not until September 29, 1905, did the court grant her request for bail, requiring a $10,000 bond "with good security," an extremely large sum in 1905.[14] When the trial finally began on March 30, 1906, the court denied a motion for continuance requested by Amanda Cobb on the grounds of the absence of a principal defense witness. Still further, in 1907, after being acquitted, Amanda Cobb had to file suit against the administrator of her late husband's estate, forcing a division and sale of lands in order for her to receive the "twelve-months support" for her family as provided by Georgia law.

A notable result from this exhaustive search of the record is the absence of any mention whatsoever of a shotgun in the press coverage or in the surviving Superior Court records. To conclude as a result of this study that a handgun was used in the shooting death of W. H. Cobb, against the widely held belief that a shotgun was used, would hardly be unreasonable. However, as described above, it is doubtful that such a conclusion would be widely accepted, even among the SABR community.

To finally conclude that the shotgun story is false, a more compelling piece of evidence is required. Thanks to the research of Wesley Fricks, also a board

Goergia
Franklin County: To any Sheriff, Deputy-Sheriff, Constable, Coroner or Marshal of said State , Greeting:-

It appering to me , upon the oaths of witnesses sworn and examined upon an inquest held by me, on the 8th day of August 1905, over the body of W. H. Cobb, deceased , andthat the said W. H. Cobb came to his death by a pistol bullet wound XXXXX from a pistol in the hands of Amanda Cobb, and there is sufficient grounds to suspect the said Amanda Cobb of being guilty of the crime of voluntary manslaughter in shooting and killing the said W. H. Cobb.

These are, therefore , to cammand you to arrest the body of the said Amanda Cobb, and carry her before some judicial officer of this State to be dealt with as the law, directs.

Given under my hand and official signature. This 9th day of August 1905.

[illegible]
Coroner of Franklin County.

Fig. 39.2. A copy of the coroner's report and arrest warrant for Amanda Cobb, issued August 9, 1905, by the Franklin County coroner. The coroner concluded, based on his examination of the body of the deceased W. H. Cobb and on the sworn oaths of witnesses, that the death was a result of a bullet wound from a pistol fired by Amanda Cobb.

member at the Ty Cobb Museum, such a document has been discovered.[15] The official Franklin County coroner's report, dated August 9, 1905, which served as the arrest warrant for Amanda Cobb, states clearly and unequivocally that a pistol was used by Amanda Cobb and that the death of W. H. Cobb resulted from a pistol bullet. Ecce signum! (See figure 39.2.)

The Shotgun Story

Having proven the shotgun story false, my investigation turned to an interesting and obvious question: what is the origin of this sensational and widely believed story that Ty Cobb's mother killed his father with a shotgun? I completed a thorough review of the biographical literature on Ty Cobb in a search for the answer.

Sverre Braathen's 1928 biography, *Ty Cobb: The Idol of Baseball Fandom*,[16] did not mention the death of Ty Cobb's father at all. Ty Cobb's 1925 autobiography, *My Twenty Years in Baseball*,[17] also fails to mention his father's death, as does H. G. Salsinger's 1951 *Sporting News* biography.[18]

Gene Schoor's 1952 biography, *The Story of Ty Cobb: Baseball's Greatest Player*, stated only that W. H. Cobb was shot and killed "under circumstances which were clouded, in an atmosphere of enigma and cloaked in mystery."[19] John D. McCallum's 1956 biography, *The Tiger Wore Spikes*, was essentially a juvenile biography and provided no specific details about the shooting incident. It did, however, state that W. H. Cobb was killed by a "bullet," which indicates that a handgun, not a shotgun, was the weapon used, since a shotgun shoots "shot" or "pellets," not "bullets." This wording is consistent with the coroner's report in the use of the term "bullet," but McCallum makes no mention of having seen that report.[20]

Cobb's 1961 autobiography, *My Life in Baseball: The True Record*, written in collaboration with Al Stump, states only that his father had been killed in a gun accident. No details were provided.[21]

Shortly after Ty Cobb's death in July 1961 and the release of Cobb's autobiography, Al Stump wrote an article for *True Magazine* titled "Ty Cobb's Wild 10-Month Fight to Live."[22] This article is the first recounting of the shotgun story in the literature that was reviewed in this investigation. It will be examined in detail in the following sections.

In 1975, John D. McCallum expanded his earlier 1956 book and published the first detailed Cobb biography, titled simply *Ty Cobb*. McCallum devotes a full chapter to describing the details of the shooting incident, even including supposed dialogue between Amanda Cobb and Clifford Ginn, a boy who lived nearby who had come to the Cobb house upon hearing the shots and then had gone upstairs to the bedroom where Amanda Cobb stood in shock. Amanda Cobb's testimony in 1906 was that she had summoned Clifford Ginn to come over. This chapter also included three lengthy quotations from articles in *The Royston Record* that ran in the days following the incident. In this 1975 biography, McCallum leaves no doubt that he believed the weapon that killed W. H. Cobb was a pistol. Within this chapter, McCallum states that Amanda "took a pistol out of a drawer"; that Amanda "clutched the pistol between her hands"; that Amanda "stood there clutching a smoking pistol"; and that she had "instinctively reached for her pistol, which she always kept on her nightstand alongside her bed when she was alone nights." McCallum also states that "one gossip said it was a shotgun, while another said it was a revolver." McCallum was thus familiar with the shotgun story, and he apparently dismissed it completely.[23]

Robert Rubin's 1978 juvenile biography *Ty Cobb, the Greatest* mentions only that Ty Cobb's father "had been shot to death by his mother, who mistook him for a prowler."[24]

In 1984, Charles Alexander wrote a detailed biography of Ty Cobb, also titled simply *Ty Cobb*. In it he relates the shotgun story in much the same way that it appeared in Al Stump's 1961 *True Magazine* article. Alexander describes the incident as the "bizarre and ghastly" death of Cobb's father from two shots from a shotgun, with an intervening time interval between the shots. He also states that Joe Cunningham was the first person to come to the Cobb residence and identify the slain intruder as W. H. Cobb and then quotes Joe Cunningham's daughter as stating that her father had said that the sight of W. H. Cobb's body was "the worst thing I ever saw": he viewed a "gaping hole in the abdomen" and Cobb's "brains literally blown out."[25]

Since its publication, Alexander's biography has become the nearest thing to the definitive biography of Ty Cobb. It was written by a professional historian and university professor and is presented as scholarly, comprehensively researched, and uncontroversial. It is thoroughly indexed and references a wide variety of sources. It is generally recognized as complete and, more important, unbiased. It is not without errors, however, such as the statement that W. H. Cobb had married Amanda Cobb when she was only 12 years old, an assertion that probably adds to the sensationalism of the shotgun story. Her actual age was 15, a not uncommon age for marriage at the time, as is clearly shown by examination of the available census and marriage records.[26]

For the next 20 years, all of Cobb's biographers, including Richard Bak (in both his 1994[27] and 2005[28] biographies), Norman Macht (1992),[29] S. A. Kramer (1995),[30] Patrick Creevy (fictionalized biography, 2002),[31] and Dan Holmes (2004),[32] relate the shotgun version of the shooting story. Their shotgun stories vary only in the level of detail presented.

Included also is Al Stump's 1994 biography *Cobb: The Life and Times of the Meanest Man Who Ever Played Baseball*, which amplified and expanded on the 1961 Ty Cobb autobiography on which Stump collaborated. This biography also included a slightly rewritten and expanded version of Stump's 1961 *True Magazine* article. Stump prefaces this book by stating that he had lacked editorial control over the 1961 Cobb autobiography, asserting that what Cobb had allowed into the book was self-serving and implying that this new book would correct the omissions of the earlier work. Stump retells the shotgun story along the same lines as his 1961 article, describing how Amanda "grabbed up a twin-barreled shotgun from a corner rack in the room and in fright fired one load" and then, panic stricken, had "screamed and triggered a second blast. . . . She could barely identify the body of her husband. From the neck up not much was left."[33]

Tom Stanton's 2007 book *Ty and the Babe*, which focuses principally on the post-career relationship of the two megastars, mentions the shooting only in passing, without providing any details.[34]

Don Rhodes, a long-time reporter for the *Augusta Chronicle*, wrote *Ty Cobb: Safe at Home* in 2008. Rhodes quotes extensively from the 1905 and 1906 articles that were printed in the *Chronicle*, taking advantage of the full archives of the *Chronicle* that were available to him.[35] He quotes liberally from the "innuendo-filled articles" published by the *Chronicle*, including one that relates Amanda Cobb's testimony about using her pistol in the incident. He does not mention the shotgun story.

Based on this review of the available biographical literature on Ty Cobb, no account of the shotgun story is found prior to Al Stump's 1961 *True Magazine* article. With the exception of John McCallum's 1975 book and Don Rhodes's 2008 book, every biography and every article written since 1961 that made mention of the weapon used in the shooting of W. H. Cobb has accepted and retold in one form or another this now-disproved shotgun story.

The First Appearance of the Shotgun Story

Ty Cobb's autobiography was released shortly after his death in July 1961. In December, Al Stump turned to *True, The Man's Magazine* to publish his article "Ty Cobb's Wild 10-Month Fight to Live." *True Magazine* was a leader at the time in the men's adventure genre, which featured lurid covers and provocative titles that oversold allegedly true stories that were usually fictional or mostly so. Besides the "true stories" of war, demented rulers, love-starved Amazons, and so on, magazines in this genre often included pin-up photos, love-life articles, and exposés of vice in cities throughout the world. These often near-pornographic magazines were nevertheless sold openly at newsstands and drug stores—thus the provocative titles and covers to "hook" the macho-male population.

The cover of the December 1961 issue showed a full-color photo of four ornate and deadly swords as a lead-in to an article titled "They Live by the Sword." The cover byline for that issue trumpeted Al Stump's article with: "Exclusive! The Strange, Wild, Tragic End of Ty Cobb." Among the other articles in this issue were: "Psychic: The Story of Peter Hurkos," who was world famous for using ESP to solve baffling crimes; "Daring Dive for Derelict Gold," about the salvaging of sunken treasure in a deadly minefield of World War II ordinance; and "The Monster Makers," describing various natural-born and intentionally-mutilated human freaks of the Middle Ages, with grotesquely drawn illustrations. "Men's adventure" is definitely not the genre from which scholars and historians usually seek truthful, insightful, and unembellished information about anyone or anything. Nevertheless, this is where the Cobb shotgun story began.

In the 1961 *True Magazine* article, Stump has Ty Cobb confess, as they visit the Royston, Georgia, tomb of his father and mother, that "my father had his head blown off with a shotgun when I was 18 years old—by a member of my own family. I didn't get over that. I've never gotten over that." Later in the article, Stump quotes "family sources and old Georgia friends of the baseball idol" as being his source for the story. He describes the shooting event simply by saying that Amanda Cobb "kept a shotgun handy by her bed and used it." In this version of the story, he has the shooting occur inside the Cobb house, by placing Amanda in the bedroom "all alone when she saw a menacing figure climb through her window and approach her bed. In the dark she assumed it to be a robber."

Among the many sports-related articles written by Stump, this was by far the most successful of his career and the most widely read. It received several awards and was later reprinted in two editions of *True Magazine Baseball Yearbook* (1962 and 1969),[36] in the resurrected *Baseball Magazine* in 1965,[37] and in the *Third Fireside Book of Baseball*.[38]

The Source of the Shotgun Story

In 1994, an ill and aging Al Stump wrote *Cobb: The Life and Times of the Meanest Man Who Ever Played Baseball*. This book went much farther than the earlier Cobb autobiography, adding details that Stump said had been withheld by Cobb in the 1961 autobiography. It also included an expanded version of Stump's 1961 *True Magazine* article, which had achieved prominent recognition in sports literature over the years. This book was subsequently made into a movie titled *Cobb*, directed by Ron Shelton. The movie was a commercial flop that received mixed reviews, grossed less than $850,000, and was pulled from domestic theaters just weeks after its opening.[39]

Unlike his *True Magazine* article, in the 1994 book Stump identified his source for the details of the shooting of W. H. Cobb as Joe Cunningham, the childhood friend and next-door neighbor of Ty Cobb in Royston. Stump provides several quotations attributed to Cunningham detailing not only the circumstances of the shooting but also Ty's physical and mental reaction to the tragedy.

It is impossible that Al Stump ever had any interaction with Joe Cunningham. Stump never had occasion to be in Royston, with or without Ty Cobb, prior to the 1960 collaboration on Cobb's autobiography. Joe Cunningham died in 1956.[40] The quotations were therefore fabricated to enhance the believability of his story. Possibly, Stump's information came from interactions with Cunningham's daughter, Susie, who was still alive in 1960 and who had been interviewed and quoted by biographer Charles Alexander for his 1984 book. Or Stump could have fabricated this dialogue based solely on Alexander's 1984 biography.

The question naturally arises about Joe Cunningham, who, either directly as falsely asserted by Stump or indirectly as asserted by Charles Alexander, was the source of the shotgun story: If he was the first to arrive at the scene of the shooting, why was he not mentioned prominently in the widespread newspaper coverage of the incident and in the subsequent trials? If he was the first to arrive on the scene of the shooting, why was there no challenge to Amanda Cobb's court testimony that Clifford Ginn, her brother-in-law, was first to arrive? This type of controversy, if it occurred, would have been widely reported in the press, which sensationalized practically every other aspect of the incident. Yet there is no mention of Cunningham in any of the articles or other records that I was able to locate, and thus there is no evidence that Cunningham had even the smallest part in the shooting tragedy or its aftermath.

There are no clear answers to these questions for several reasons, first among them being that neither Stump nor Alexander had any direct interaction with Joe Cunningham. In Stump's case, the story was either fabricated, obtained at second hand from Cunningham's daughter, or copied and expanded from Alexander's 1984 biography. In Alexander's case, as he points out, it came second-hand as a family story from Cunningham's daughter, and is highly suspect for this reason alone.

A recent interview with noted Atlanta sportswriter and editor Furman Bisher clouds the veracity of the Cunningham story even further.[41] Bisher knew Ty Cobb well, having written a widely-read 1953 article which addressed the death of W. H. Cobb and an in-depth *Saturday Evening Post* article about Cobb's return to Georgia in 1958. Bisher stated in this recent interview that he also knew Joe Cunningham well and had spoken to him on several occasions. Furman Bisher stated that Joe Cunningham had told him directly in the early 1950s that Amanda Cobb was not the one who shot W. H. Cobb but that the shots had been fired by her paramour when they were caught together by Professor Cobb after he returned home unexpectedly. However, Susie Cunningham Bond, Joe Cunningham's daughter and Alexander's source, told writer Leigh Montville in 1982 that "her father did not think another man shot Ty's father, that Amanda Chitwood Cobb did, indeed, pull the trigger, and that Amanda knew who her target was."[42] These conflicting stories from Cunningham and his family about what Cunningham did and did not believe cast serious doubt on the truth of anything sourced to Joe Cunningham or his family. More likely, Joe Cunningham, who lived his entire life in the small town of Royston and became the town undertaker, found an outlet in his old age for foggy or perhaps fantasized recollections about the town's most famous citizen and recounted differing versions of the story to family and to visiting sportswriters and historians.

Who Was Al Stump?

Alvin J. Stump was born in 1916 in Colorado Springs, Colorado. He was raised in the Pacific Northwest, attended the University of Washington, and shortly after graduation landed his first reporter's job at the *Portland Oregonian*. Following a stint as a correspondent in the wartime Navy, he settled in Southern California and worked as a freelance writer.[43]

Prior to beginning his collaboration with Ty Cobb in 1960, Stump had written many sports-related articles on the lives and careers of other notables, including Mel Ott, Bob Lemon, Gil McDougald, Ralph Kiner, Eddie Mathews, Duke Snider, Jackie Jensen, and Jack Harshman.[44] These articles appeared in *Sport Magazine*, *American Legion Magazine*, *The Saturday Evening Post*, *Argosy*, and *Saga* (as well as in *True Magazine*), and many were anthologized in a 1952 book, *Champions Against Odds*.[45] No doubt Cobb, an avid reader, was familiar with these articles and was impressed enough to hire Stump to work on his autobiography.

Ty Cobb's 1961 autobiography was the first book that Al Stump actually wrote. He went on to complete five more books, including a collaboration with Sam Snead in 1962 on another autobiography, *The Education of a Golfer*. After the 1961 Cobb autobiography, Stump also continued writing sports-related articles for men's magazines, covering such notables as Albie Pearson,

Brooks Robinson, Hank Aaron, Frank Howard, Vada Pinson, Curt Flood, Babe Pinelli, and Tommy Lasorda.[46]

Stump always focused on the adventurous and provocative side of the subjects he wrote about, seeing himself as an investigative reporter who sought out the "truth" where others failed. Many of his subsequent titles bore out this approach, such as his 1969 book *The Champion Breed: The True, Behind-the-Scene Struggles of Sport's Greatest Heroes*.[47] He never again achieved the success his 1961 Ty Cobb efforts gave him—until his 1994 Cobb biography and its subsequent movie adaptation. But he did score a significant scoop in 1972 that brought him notoriety outside the sports world as a key player in the Marilyn Monroe murder conspiracy and cover-up investigation. Stump arranged and attended the first of many meetings between his friend Bob Slatzer, who claimed to have been Marilyn's husband for three days in 1952, and Milo Speriglio, a prominent Hollywood private detective. Slatzer claimed to have the inside scoop on Marilyn's murder and the cover-up that followed and had come to Stump with the story after his life had been threatened by powerful people. Al Stump thus became the first link and the principal channel for information through which many interesting questions were ultimately answered, such as whether the father of Marilyn's 12th aborted child was Jack Kennedy or his brother, Bobby; whether Bobby Kennedy and Peter Lawford had been with Marilyn at the time she was murdered; and what explosive political and personal secrets Marilyn had intended to reveal at the press conference that was scheduled for the morning after her death. After a 14-year investigation, Milo Speriglio published his book *The Marilyn Conspiracy*, without listing Stump as an author. But Speriglio gave prominent credit to Stump for bringing him the story and convincing him to take on the case.[48]

Stump's second wife, Jolene Mosher, also a writer, said in describing Stump's writing method that he "liked to sit back, have a few drinks, and egg someone on. . . . He'd encourage them to act up, to be really bad. He'd get good stories like that." She also disclosed about Stump: "His only hobby was drinking."[49] No doubt this tactic, and possibly this hobby, was at play as Stump interacted with Cobb in their 1960 collaboration, producing fodder for the sensational and fictionalized parts of the *True Magazine* story.

Al Stump's literary hero was Ernest Hemingway, a role model for many young postwar writers who imitated his writing style, even if they were unable to live his adventurous lifestyle.[50] Hemingway died in 1961 at his own hand from a shotgun blast to the head—only two weeks before Ty Cobb died. This tragic but sensational event was widely reported around the world, and the resulting months-long flurry of articles was surely followed closely by an admiring Al Stump. Afterward, Hemingway's wife told Idaho authorities that the shotgun had discharged accidentally while Hemingway was cleaning it.[51] His estate later sought to prevent the publication of details of the gruesome death scene,[52] and a family friend took the shotgun that Hemingway had used, disassembled it into a dozen different pieces, and buried the pieces in widely different locations to prevent memorabilia collectors from later profiting from the gruesome relic.[53] There is no evidence on which to conclude that the widely publicized shotgun death of Hemingway, Stump's idol, influenced him as he crafted the fictionalized shotgun account of the death of W. H. Cobb. But the similarities to the W. H. Cobb shotgun story created by Stump are striking, particularly the gruesome descriptions of the death scenes. These similarities, and the coincidence of the shotgun death of Hemingway at precisely the same time as Stump's 1961 writing efforts, make for interesting speculation about a possible influence.

Despite the substantial volume of work that Stump produced in his otherwise mediocre 50-year career, he received no national publicity or recognition, and certainly no acclaim, for anything unrelated to Ty Cobb. His only real career success—and his only lasting legacy—was based exclusively on Ty Cobb. Having saved all his notes and papers from the 1960 collaboration to produce his magnum opus in the 1994 Cobb biography and movie, Stump never escaped from the shadow of Ty Cobb hovering over him as the defining subject in his life's work—but, perhaps he never really tried.[54] In the intervening years, he either saved or created a large amount of additional material relating to Ty Cobb to sustain a newly found and profitable fascination with baseball memorabilia.

Al Stump's Collection of Ty Cobb Memorabilia

At the time of Ty Cobb's death, Stump came into possession of a very large number of Cobb's personal effects. Stump claimed that Ty Cobb had given him many personal possessions that had been in his Atherton home when he died and ultimately offered a note from Ty Cobb as evidence of the gift (see figure 39.3). Almost two decades later, Stump began a concerted effort to sell a substantial part of his "collection," and thus began an interesting but little-known story that illuminates another method that Al Stump chose—

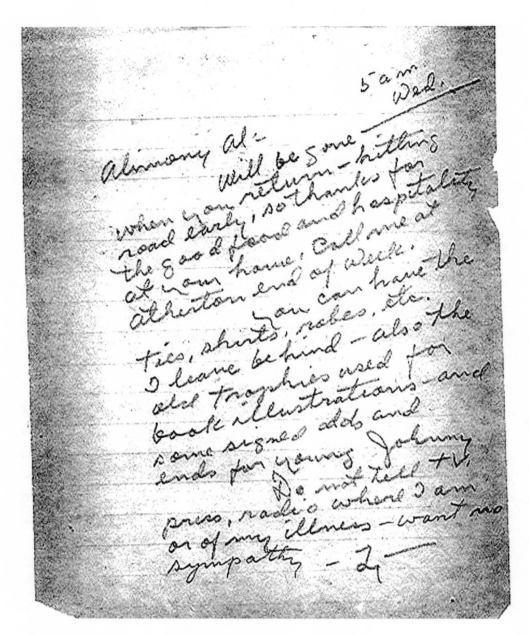

Fig. 39.3. The note to Al Stump from Ty Cobb that gives Stump some of Cobb's personal items, date uncertain. This note was offered in Stump's letter (December 16, 1980) to auctioneer Howard Smith as evidence that Ty told him "to help myself to a bunch of his things stored at Atherton." The original of this note was auctioned by Butterfields in 2001, and copies often accompany the sale of purported Ty Cobb items as evidence that they are authentic. Close examination of the content of the note shows that it refers to items left by Ty Cobb at the Stump residence after Ty departed from a working session there. Stump offered no other evidence that any memorabilia was gifted to him by Ty Cobb.

beyond gory shotgun stories and sports fantasy writing—to ride Ty Cobb's coattails to personal fame and fortune.

On November 29, 1980, Stump wrote to Howard G. Smith, a memorabilia auctioneer in San Antonio, Texas, offering "museum-quality" Ty Cobb pieces itemized as follows:

> Cobb's leather-bound hip-pocket whisky flask, his silver-plated shaving mug and brush, straight-edge razor from the thirties, silver pocket knife, German-made, Damascus barreled shotgun used by Cobb in bird-hunting, a snakeskin-wrapped cane he used in 1960 (real oddity), razor strop, tobacco humidor, wrist watch, pen-and-pencil set and set of decoy ducks. All of these items are prominently engraved or otherwise inscribed with Cobb's name or initials. I also have numerous photos, autographed, of Cobb, with Babe Ruth, in action poses, at the wheel of his racing cars, posed formally at home, even his baby picture, etc.

He told Smith that these items were only a portion of his personal collection of Ty Cobb memorabilia, which was "the largest privately owned collection in the U.S." He stated that had offers for the items from three New York–area collectors but that he wanted to further explore the market for possible auction before deciding how best to dispose of this part of his collection (see figure 39.4).[55]

In a follow-up letter on December 16, 1980, Stump sent Smith a list and photos of the 13 items he was offering, along with his asking price for the more expensive items. Most pertinent to this investigation is the engraved double-barreled shotgun, offered at $2,500 and shown in the set of photos that Stump provided to Smith (see figures 39.5 and 39.6). This is the shotgun that ultimately became part of the Barry Halper collection and was initially listed in (but withdrawn from) the 1999 Sotheby's auction. Its description is precisely the same as that printed by Sotheby's, even including "Tyrus R. Cobb" being engraved near the trigger.[56]

Weeks later, on January 15, 1981, Stump again wrote Smith to provide a more detailed list, now including 18 items, some with descriptions enhanced in ways that belie their credibility. In the first list, Stump itemized a "Benrus watch with leather band (watch doesn't work)." In the second list, this item had suddenly become even more valuable, as Stump implied that this was the watch that Cobb was wearing when he died: "Wristwatch—a Benrus of 1940–1950 period with his full name burned into the brown leather strap.

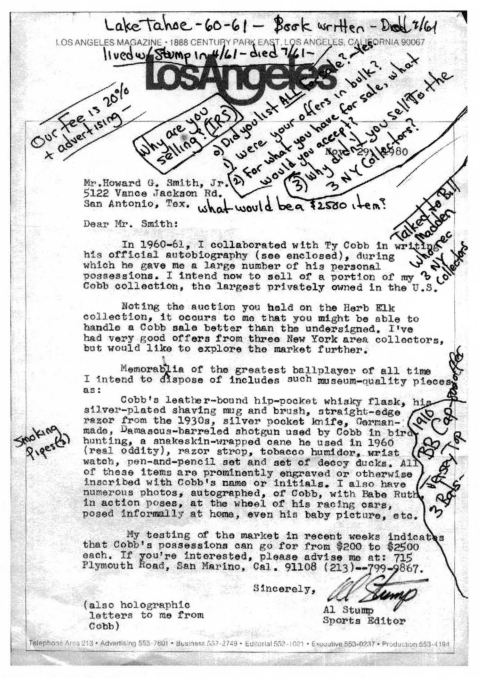

Fig. 39.4. A letter from Al Stump to auctioneer Howard G. Smith offering the sale of a portion of his collection of Ty Cobb memorabilia, which he describes as the largest privately owned collection of Cobb memorabilia in the country. The handwritten notes on the letter (other than Al Stump's signature) are questions and comments written by Smith as he reviewed the letter and subsequently discussed the sale in phone conversations with Stump.

Figs. 39.5 & 39.6. Photos of the Damascus-barreled double-barreled shotgun sent by Al Stump to Howard G. Smith. Stump noted in his letter that the shotgun has "Tyrus R. Cobb" engraved in the steel above the trigger. Stump would later fraudulently claim that this was the shotgun used by Amanda Cobb to shoot Ty's father, William H. Cobb, in 1905. This is the shotgun that found its way into the Barry Halper collection and ultimately into the 1999 Sotheby's auction catalog, only to be pulled because of its questionable authenticity.

Face of watch is worn. Watch is stopped at 1:20 P.M. Cobb died between 1:15 P.M. and 1:30 P.M., according to doctors. Fair shape."[57]

The shotgun was described as: "Twin-barrel shotgun used by Cobb in bird hunting in the 1920s–30s: Damascus barrel makes it an antique. About 7 pounds with fancy scrollwork on the butt and 'Tyrus R. Cobb' engraved in the steel above the triggers. 'I killed a few hundred ducks with it,' he told me. Gun is Rusty." No mention was made of this gun having been the one used by Amanda Cobb in the shooting of W. H. Cobb—that only became part of the story when the shotgun was sold into the Halper collection and ultimately described in the 1999 Sotheby's catalog for the Halper auction.

Apparently, no agreement was reached between Stump and Smith as a result of this exchange of letters, because the items they discussed all found their way into other auctions and collections, many ultimately landing in Barry Halper's. Even today, when an item from Stump's collection appears at auction, there most often is also a photocopy of the note, handwritten by Cobb, which tells Stump: "You can have all the ties, shirts, robes, etc. I leave behind—also the old trophies used for book illustrations—and some signed odds and ends for young Johnny." This note is the supposed permission that Stump had for having taken the very extensive number of personal items from Cobb's Atherton residence. Stump's December 16, 1980, letter offered a copy of this letter to Howard Smith, describing it as: "A copy of a letter Ty to me—in which he tells me to help myself to a bunch of his things stored at Atherton." But the letter actually gives Stump only a few items that Cobb left at Stump's Santa Barbara residence when he departed after a working session there on the 1961 autobiography. It is clear that the limited scope of what Ty Cobb actually gave to Al Stump was far exceeded by the essential cleanout from Cobb's Atherton home of every conceivable item that could in any way be associated with Cobb—even his false teeth. The following is a partial listing of the Ty Cobb memorabilia items from the Al Stump collection offered or sold at various times between 1980 and 2001. Comparison of this list to the six specific items gifted to Stump by Ty Cobb in the note of figure 39.3 raises the question of the legitimacy of Stump's possession of these Ty Cobb collectibles.

TY COBB ITEMS OFFERED OR SOLD BY AL STUMP AFTER 1980:
Leather-bound hip-pocket whiskey flask
Silver-plate shaving mug and brush
Straight-edge razor for the 1930s
Silver pocket knife
German-made, Damascus-barreled antique shotgun
Snake-skin-wrapped cane
Engraved wooden cane
Razor strop
Tobacco humidor
Wrist watch
Pen-and-pencil set
Set of decoy ducks
Numerous photos, all autographed, 16x20 & 8x10
    – Ty with Babe Ruth
    – Ty standing at the plate
    – Ty at the wheel of his racing car
    – Ty posed informally at home
    – Ty's baby picture

1910 Detroit Tigers uniform shirt game-worn by Ty Cobb
1910 Detroit Tigers cap game-worn by Ty Cobb
Ty Cobb signed baseball
Circular poker-chip holder and 200 chips
Deck of cards
Monogrammed dressing gown
Yellow bone-handled knife
Three smoking pipes
Smoking pipe holder
Corncob pipe given to Ty by Gen. Douglas McArthur
Rusty cowbell from Cobb's ranch
3 baseball bats
Ty Cobb signed game-used bat—forged
Fishing hat
Ty Cobb's dentures
Cobb & Co. brass belt buckle—falsely attributed to Ty Cobb
Christmas card signed by Ty Cobb dated 1960
12 smoking pipes
Brass ashtray
Brass and leather ashtray
Cigarette case with matching ashtray
Wooden tea canister, "Ty Cobb" written in pencil on bottom
Tape measure in leather case
Servant's bell
Stampette set with three stamps
2 cork lifters
Small ceramic tiger
Wooden key ring holder with mallard design
Large carving knife set in wooden case
Hunting knife in leather case
Pocket knife
Pen knife
Comb in pewter case
Wooden tackle box with lure
6 Ty Cobb signed baseballs—forged signatures
50 to 100 signed letters on Ty Cobb letterhead—forged
Dozens of Ty Cobb signed baseball magazine pages—forged

What the Memorabilia Experts Know

Item 13 of the December 16, 1980, list sent to Howard Smith by Al Stump is described as: "Letters to me from Cobb, typed for him on his personal letterhead stationary and signed 'Ty,' in which he discusses what he wanted to go into his autobiography and other matters: 6 x 7 inches." These letters, estimated by experts in the autograph business to be as many as 50 to 100 in number, created much excitement in the collecting community when they surfaced, principally because of their extensive baseball content—a fact that adds considerable value to any famous player's correspondence. On cursory inspection, they appear authentic, since they are typed on apparently genuine Ty Cobb letterhead and signed in the green ink that Ty Cobb was well known for using. Ultimately these letters were sold into the market and then were discredited as forgeries by numerous authenticators.

They were first offered to Mike Gutierrez, a prominent authenticator, who authenticated them as genuine and then sold them directly and at auction to trusting buyers. Although the signatures on these letters displayed a more shaky hand than authentic Cobb signatures, Gutierrez explained that to be a result of Cobb's advancing age and declining health and strength—something modern authenticators have disproved through a thorough analysis of steady Cobb signatures dated as late as May 1961, only two months before his death. The fantastic baseball content contained in these forged letters has been quoted by unsuspecting historians, and the incorrect and falsified information has become part of accepted history.[58] One example of these Ty Cobb letters forged by Al Stump is in figure 39.7.

The forged Stump letters are very well known among memorabilia authenticators and collectors. Jim Stinson, a veteran authenticator and collector, wrote at length about the Stump forgeries in *Sports Collectors Digest*,[59] and Ronald B. Keurajian, the premier expert on Ty Cobb autographs, has covered them in detail in the definitive article on authenticating Cobb autographs.[60] Harvey Swanebeck, another long-time autograph collector who purchased one of the Stump-forged Cobb letters in the 1980s, had the unique experience of later finding for sale at a national convention a Ty Cobb letter with the exact same textual content as his own. Evidently Al Stump had created multiple "original" copies of some of the Cobb letters he forged, assuming that the duped purchasers would never meet and compare the content of their forged documents.[61] Even autograph expert Mike Gutierrez, who orig-

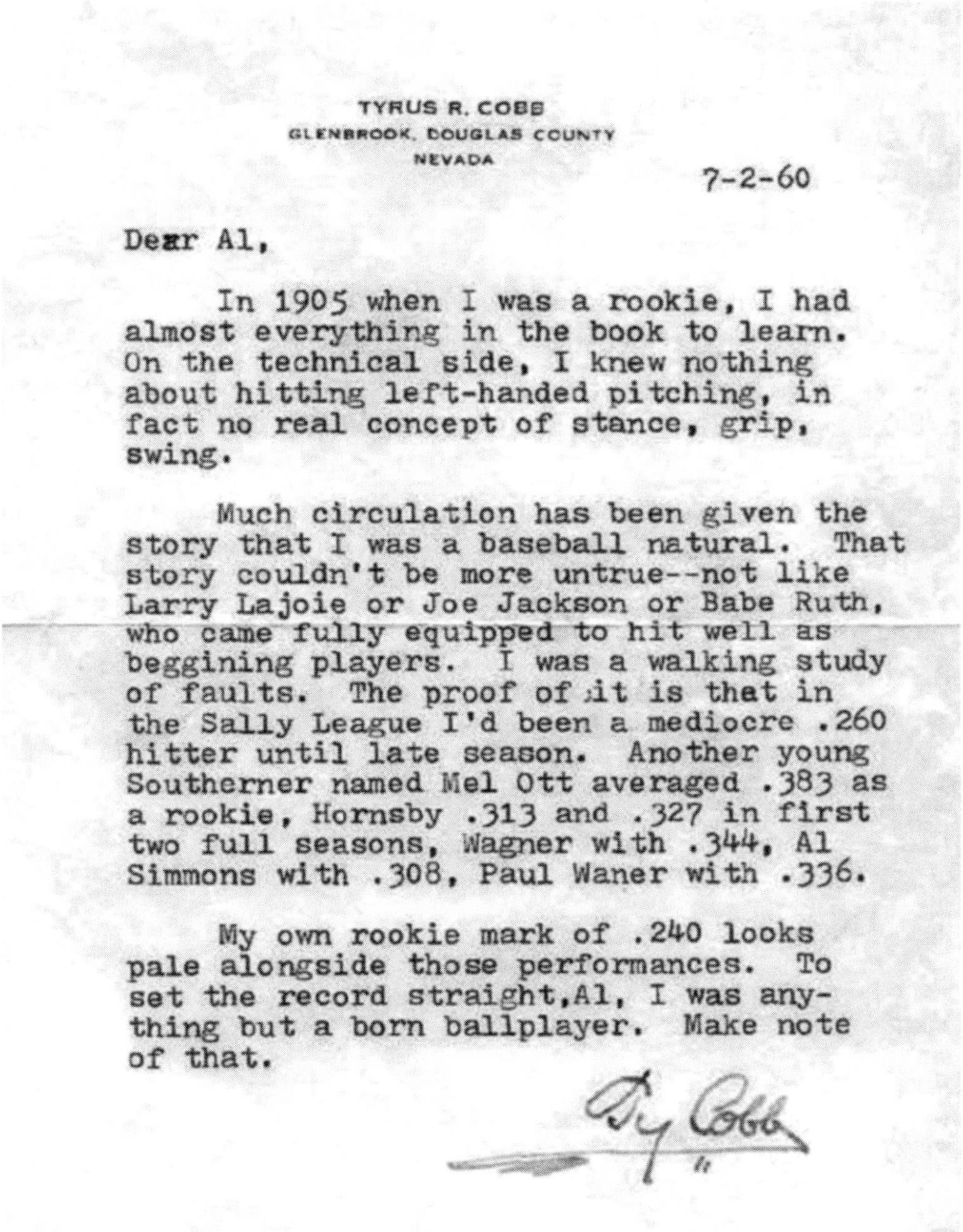

TYRUS R. COBB
GLENBROOK, DOUGLAS COUNTY
NEVADA

7-2-60

Dear Al,

In 1905 when I was a rookie, I had almost everything in the book to learn. On the technical side, I knew nothing about hitting left-handed pitching, in fact no real concept of stance, grip, swing.

Much circulation has been given the story that I was a baseball natural. That story couldn't be more untrue--not like Larry Lajoie or Joe Jackson or Babe Ruth, who came fully equipped to hit well as beggining players. I was a walking study of faults. The proof of it is that in the Sally League I'd been a mediocre .260 hitter until late season. Another young Southerner named Mel Ott averaged .383 as a rookie, Hornsby .313 and .327 in first two full seasons, Wagner with .344, Al Simmons with .308, Paul Waner with .336.

My own rookie mark of .240 looks pale alongside those performances. To set the record straight,Al, I was anything but a born ballplayer. Make note of that.

Ty Cobb

Fig. 39.7. One of the estimated fifty to one hundred letters from Ty Cobb to Al Stump that were forged by Stump on apparently genuine letterhead taken from Cobb's Atherton residence after Cobb's death. These forgeries contained much baseball-related content, which made them more valuable to collectors. Some of the quesionable "facts" in these forged letters became part of baseball history when they were accepted by historians as truthful.

inally authenticated the Stump-forged Ty Cobb letters, later agreed that the Stump letters were indeed forgeries.[62]

Stump's forgeries went far beyond written material that he created using genuine Ty Cobb letterhead that he had taken from Cobb's Atherton residence. They also included many, many photos and pages from baseball-related publications on which were written tidbits of baseball history, wisdom, or advice (often personalized to Stump) along with a forged Ty Cobb signature in his trademark green ink.[63] Figures 39.8 and 39.9 are several examples of these fake artifacts, which were again offered at auction in 2009 and then withdrawn because experts pointed them out as forgeries. As another example of the extent of Al Stump's deception, in the mid-1980s Stump offered a lot of six Ty Cobb–signed baseballs to Ron Keurajian in a phone conversation. Keurajian declined the offer because he lacked the funds to complete the deal. A month later, Keurajian met the Michigan collector who purchased this lot, and after inspecting the six Cobb signatures, he concluded that all six were forgeries.[64]

Fig. 39.8. A copy of one of many photographs of Ty Cobb onto which Al Stump forged comments that he attributed to Ty Cobb along with Ty Cobb's signature. This photo was offered at auction in May 2009 but was withdrawn when experts notified the auction service that it was a forgery.

Fig. 39.9. Four examples of the dozens of baseball-related pages from publications onto which Al Stump forged Ty Cobb's autograph and comments attributed to Ty Cobb. These four were offered at auction in May 2009 but withdrawn when experts notified the auction service that they were forgeries.

Al Stump's efforts to create and sell off Ty Cobb artifacts was so blatant that the entire high-end memorabilia collectors' industry even today dismisses out of hand the authenticity of anything that has the name of Al Stump in its provenance. Ron Keurajian, now one of the country's leading Cobb autograph experts, recently confided, "I, personally, would not trust anything that originated from Stump."[65] Robert Lifson, the memorabilia expert who managed the 1999 sale of the Barry Halper collection, examined dozens of Ty Cobb artifacts and Cobb-signed documents sourced to Al Stump, many of them identical to those described by Stump in his 1981 correspondence with Howard Smith. Lifson said in a recent interview that all Stump items in the Halper collection became suspect after it was proven conclusively that a Ty Cobb game-used bat that Stump supplied to Halper was not authentic, based on the dating of the bat by detailed analysis. Of the large number of Ty Cobb documents from Stump that came to Sotheby's, practically all were judged by Lifson to be fraudulent. Lifson went on to say, after reading the content of these letters and examining the forged signatures, that "Stump must have thought that he was creating history, or something." His faking of so many Ty Cobb documents "must have been a pathological issue with Stump, something deep-seated within him. It was just crazy how Stump went to such elaborate lengths to create the forged Cobb documents."[66]

Josh Evans, a widely respected memorabilia expert and principal in the very successful Leland's Auctions, has a much more serious indictment of Al Stump. Evans, a young collector and authenticator in the mid-1980s when Al Stump was actively trying to sell Cobb memorabilia, worked with Mike Guttierez on selling the Cobb items that Stump supplied. Many of the items were sold to Barry Halper, one of Evans' best customers. After seeing multiple batches of purported Cobb items arrive from Stump via Guttierez, and becoming ever more suspicious with each batch, Evans notified Guttierez that, in his judgment, the items were all fakes—not just the now-infamous Stump letters on Cobb stationary, but many other personal items that had supposedly been owned by Ty Cobb. In a recent interview, Evans stated: "The Cobb stuff that was coming to me through Gutierrez all looked like it had been made yesterday. It seemed that Stump was buying this old stuff from flea markets, and then adding engravings and other personalizations to give the appearance of authenticity." Young Evans was so distressed by the fake Stump material that Gutierrez continued to sell that he first told

Barry Halper of his suspicions and then contacted the FBI in an attempt to get an official investigation of Al Stump started.

Finally, he tracked down Al Stump and phoned him at home to tell him: "I know what you are doing, forging all this memorabilia. I've contacted the FBI. You had better stop!" Evans also related in a recent interview: "To this day, I've never seen any piece of Cobb memorabilia from Al Stump that could be definitely said to be authentic. And I have seen a lot of things over the years." In closing the interview, Evans added: "It was not just Ty Cobb signatures that Al Stump forged. He did a Jim Thorpe signature that I identified as fake. Stump developed a 'style' in his illegal forgeries that I came to recognize, always accompanying them with fantastic content that he knew would increase the value to collectors."[67]

Al Stump's Forged Ty Cobb Diaries

The most recent and perhaps most embarrassing episode in the Stump forged memorabilia saga first came to light, as did the fake Cobb shotgun, via the Barry Halper collection. Among the 180 Halper items purchased in 1998 by MLB and donated to the Hall of Fame Museum was a 1946 diary of Ty Cobb's (see figure 39.10). This diary was an important addition to the Cooperstown collection, which was accompanied by other truly significant relics such as *Shoeless Joe Jackson's* 1919 White Sox jersey and the contract that sent *Babe Ruth* from the Red Sox to the Yankees.

The Cobb diary was a prized acquisition, covering the entire month of January 1946 and containing daily handwritten entries in Cobb's famous green ink. The museum made a realistic looking copy of the diary to assure that the valuable original would not be damaged while displayed from 1999 through 2001 in the "Halper Memories of a Lifetime" exhibit in the Barry Halper Gallery. Visitors to this exhibit could view the original Cobb diary, wall-mounted in a clear protective case, and then peruse this realistic-looking copy, turning page by page with their own fingers, reading and relishing each daily entry of very personal notes and comments that Cobb had made to himself. The entries were tantalizing to museum visitors and to writers and historians as well, providing new insights into this complicated icon of the game. The diary, never before seen by the public, included musings Cobb made to himself like "drinking too much" and "I stayed sober" and many other secret tidbits that Cobb wrote as comments or criticisms about other

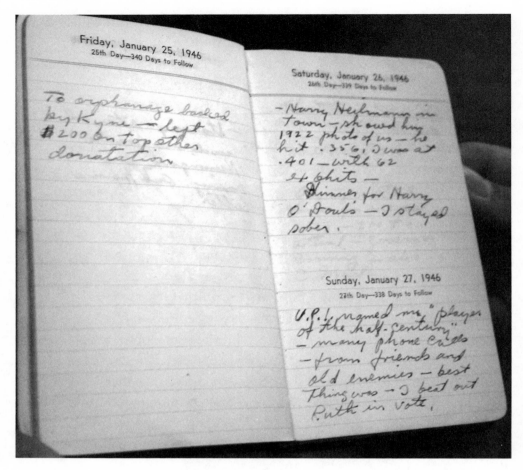

Fig. 39.10. Ty Cobb's 1946 diary, purchased by Major League Baseball from Barry Halper and donated to the Baseball Hall of Fame Museum in 1998. This diary was exhibited from 1999 through 2001 in the Barry Halper Gallery at the Hall of Fame. An FBI investigation in 2009 determined that the diary was a forgery. A recent comparison of the writings in this diary to the writings of Al Stump on the baseball-publication pages shown in fig. 39.9 led autograph expert Roland B. Keurajian to conclude that Al Stump was the forger who created this diary.

players. These entries had obviously been written with no inkling that they would ever be seen by the any but Cobb's own eyes. Or, so it appeared.

In December 2008, Ron Keurajian, the Ty Cobb autograph expert, examined the HOF Cobb diary and compared its entries to known genuine examples of Ty Cobb's handwriting. He concluded that the diary entries were definitely not written by Ty Cobb. Keurajian notified the HOF Museum of his opinion, and officials there ultimately told him that the diary would be submitted to the FBI for further investigation.[68]

Concerns about the diary's authenticity were closely guarded while the FBI investigation was underway in early 2009. The actual date that the FBI delivered their final report to the HOF was not released, nor was the FBI report itself. However, by July 5, 2009, Ernie Harwell, the veteran Detroit sportscaster, was onto the story and went public with it in a *Detroit Free Press* article titled: "Questions Remain about the Fake Cobb Diary."[69] Harwell quoted Ron Keurajian's opinion: "The quality of the forgery is rudimentary, at best. It is far from being well-executed, as the hand evidences unsteady lines and the handwriting seems almost child-like. The entries appear contrived. For example, there is one about Joe DiMaggio which states 'he can't putt for big money' and another entry states 'also drinking too much.' Anybody who has ever read Cobb's writings knows that he would not write in such a fashion. Cobb was well-versed in the art of the written word and would never write crude comments such as these." Harwell closed his article with the remaining questions he alluded to in the title: "Who was the forger? How did he con Halper into buying the diary? Did Halper have it authenticated? If so, by whom? Do any other copies of the fraudulent diary exist?"

Evidently, Ernie Harwell was not aware of a 1995 *Sports Illustrated* article by Franz Lidz titled "The Sultan of Swap," which provided an in-depth look at Barry Halper and his extensive memorabilia collection.[70] Along with details about many of Halper's relics, this article describes in text and photographs many of the items of "Cobbabilia" that Halper had collected. Lidz had access to the entire Halper collection, and had grouped many Cobb items to be photographed for his article, including a game-worn Detroit jersey, Cobb's dentures and the infamous Cobb shotgun. Lidz wrote: "Halper has the Georgia Peach's straightedge razor, shaving cup, shaving strop, bathrobe, *diaries*, dentures, fishing hat, corncob pipe, pocket flask and even the shotgun Cobb's mother used to blow away his father. *Halper wheedled all this out of Al Stump*" (emphasis added).

The first and second questions posed by Ernie Harwell seem to have been answered by Lidz in 1995. Al Stump was the forger of the HOF diary, just as he was for the large number of letters on Ty Cobb letterhead and the many autographed and annotated baseball publication pages and photographs so well known among collectors and authenticators. And, it was Halper who "wheedled," i.e. persuaded and cajoled, Stump out of the forgery. To confirm beyond any doubt that Al Stump was the forger of the 1946 HOF diary, autograph expert Ron Keurajian recently made a detailed comparison of its entries to the Stump annotations on the baseball publication pages shown in figure 39.9 and concluded that they were "all the same hand."[71]

As to the last question Harwell poses: Yes, there are other forged Cobb diaries, as is clearly implied in Lidz's use of the plural "diaries" in his 1995 article. The Elliott Museum in Stuart Florida has in their collection a Ty Cobb diary covering a full month of 1942. When asked to compare their diary with the HOF diary, Janel Hendrix, the curator there, replied that the HOF diary "looks to be the same as ours. Although ours is a 1942 diary, it is the same type of diary and the writing samples appear to be very similar." Hendrix added that she had been contacted by the HOF about the disproved authenticity of the diary in the HOF collection and, on that basis, had removed 1942 diary from the Elliott Museum display.[72]

With this episode now in the public light, it is evident that the Ty Cobb fantasies and forgeries created by Al Stump have infected the very heart of baseball myth and history—the hallowed Hall of Fame at Cooperstown. The legitimacy of the Stump-forged items had seemed reasonable enough when they first began to appear in the 1980s, based on Stump's well-known collaboration with Cobb on the 1961 autobiography. Stump had a believable reason to possess writings by Ty Cobb and other pieces of Cobb memorabilia. The apparent legitimacy of many of these items was further enhanced by the inclusion of the Stump fakeries in the famous and highly publicized Barry Halper collection and by their prominent display in the prestigious Hall of Fame Museum. Nevertheless, we now know that Al Stump forged the Ty Cobb diaries, letters, and other autographed items that made up his memorabilia "collection."

What Other Writers Know

Furman Bisher, sports editor and writer for the *Atlanta Constitution* for 59 years, knew Ty Cobb well. He wrote several articles on Cobb and spent three full days with him in 1958 when he was writing the *Post* article about Ty moving back to Georgia and building his final retirement home. Furman knew Al Stump from his writings and as a result has a very low opinion of him. In my recent interview with Furman, he stated strongly that "the *True Magazine* article was a disgrace" and that "Al Stump took advantage of a dying man." When asked about the provocative stories that Stump wrote about Cobb, he went further: "I would not believe a thing he said." Furman Bisher felt so strongly about the injustice done to Ty Cobb by Al Stump that he took more than an hour away from the time he had devoted to writing the last column of his 59-year career with the *Constitution* to be interviewed on Cobb and Stump.

Historian Charles Alexander, in his more recent writings, took direct aim at Stump's credibility, asserting that Stump had not actually spent the amount of time with Cobb that he had claimed, describing the Stump interaction with Cobb instead as a "14-month intermittent collaboration."[73] Alexander also charged that much of Stump's writings on Cobb had borrowed heavily, and without attribution, from the 1975 John McCallum biography. Alexander later said that the 1961 *True Magazine* article "read like a gothic horror story." Alexander also wrote recently that he had been the first author to "pin down the particular circumstances of William Herschel Cobb's death from gunshots fired by his wife, Amanda Chitwood Cobb, and her trial and acquittal the following spring."[74] Charles Alexander did indeed "pin down" details on the shooting of W. H. Cobb, but unfortunately his source of information was both second hand and faulty. He was incorrect in the retelling of the now disproved shotgun story and, as a result, was incorrect in writing his own somewhat gory description of the crime scene.

Other Stump Stories in the Ty Cobb Myth

This investigation dispels perhaps the most distasteful element of the Ty Cobb myth with definitive proof. A pistol, not a shotgun, was used in the shooting of W. H. Cobb, and therefore there was no crime scene in which W. H. Cobb's head was practically blown off at the neck, nor did his abdomen pour forth its contents onto the porch roof of the Cobb home in Royston. Two pistol shots were all that were fired, and even at close range, these could not produce the grotesque scene that myth would have us believe.

Another of the more outrageous stories written by Stump was the "Cobb killed a man" story, which also first appeared in Stump's 1961 *True Magazine* article and then was enhanced in his 1994 Cobb biography. In Detroit, on August 12, 1912, Ty Cobb and his wife were attacked by three robbers, whom Cobb managed to fight off, sustaining only a knife wound to his back. Ty then traveled by train to Syracuse and played in a game the following day. This attack was reported widely in the press in the days following the incident. Al Stump, who misdates the attack to June 3, 1912, has Ty confessing to having killed one of his three attackers. After Ty's pistol wouldn't fire, he supposedly told Stump that he had killed one attacker by using the gunsight of his pistol to "rip and slash and tear him . . . until he had no face left." To the 1994 Cobb biography Stump adds this substantiation of the story: "A few days later a press report told of an unidentified body found off Trumbull in an alley." That a death occurred in this incident was conclusively disproved in the 1996 *National Pastime* article "Ty Cobb Did Not Commit Murder."[75] SABR member Doug Roberts, a criminal lawyer, former prosecutor, and forensics specialist, performed an exhaustive study of the Detroit autopsy records for the time period around the 1912 attack and found not a single piece of evidence that a death such as Stump described had actually occurred. Further, Roberts found no Detroit newspaper article describing such a death or the discovery of an unidentified body, as Stump had asserted. Doug Roberts concluded that no murder occurred at the hands of Ty Cobb.

Practically all of Stump's sensationalized story of the last ten months of Ty Cobb's life is outrageously false. Stump would have us believe that these months were the alcohol-and-drug-crazed nightmare of a raging lunatic with whom Stump lived in a state of constant fear. Actually, Stump spent only a few days on and off with Ty Cobb, collectively no more than a few weeks during the 11 months between June 1960 and May 1961—three months before Cobb's death.[76] Cobb's constant companion for the last two months of his life told a much different story in a 1982 *Sports Illustrated* interview.[77] Dr. Rex Teeslink of Augusta, Georgia, then a medical student on summer break, was hired in May 1961 by Cobb as his full-time nurse. Teeslink describes a much different Ty Cobb from the demon Stump created. Concerned that he was becoming addicted to the strong painkillers he was taking for terminal cancer and end-stage diabetes, Ty Cobb proposed and withstood a 36-hour test during which he took no medication at all for pain—hardly the behavior of the addict of Stump's fantasy. When Teeslink drove Ty to the Cobb family mausoleum in Royston, he was somber—but Ty was whimsical and upbeat. Cobb suggested that they should have a signal so Cobb would recognize Rex when he visited the tomb after his death, so they "could sit down and talk the way we do now."[78] Throughout this experience, Teeslink saw none of the rage and unbalance that Stump described. He came to know and genuinely respect Ty Cobb. "He was a master of psychology," Teeslink said. "Grantland Rice wrote about it. No one ever had done the things he did, thought the way he did. He was amazing. You always had the feeling he knew what you were going to say before you said it. He'd always be looking around the room, sizing up people. If he was playing cards, he'd know what all six people were holding. He always was thinking, but he never wanted people to know what was going on in his mind. He always wanted the edge." Reflecting on Al Stump's *True Magazine* portrayal of Cobb, Teeslink added: "I'm talking now because I want to set the record straight. . . . The things that have been written, the way he has been portrayed. . . . None of them are true."[79]

Other medical professionals who cared for Cobb in his last days also failed to observe the antics that Stump fictitiously portrayed in *True Magazine*. Jean Bergdale Eilers was a young nurse when she cared for Ty Cobb for a night in May 1961, filling in for his regular private-duty nurse, who was ill. Describing her experience with Cobb, which occurred barely two months before his death, she recently wrote: "Mr. Cobb was up most of the night. He sat in a chair and dictated letters to me. He required a lot of pain medicine and I remember giving him frequent back rubs. . . . He was pleasant and never caused me any problems. I took a baseball with me that night, and he gladly signed it for my 13-year-old brother. . . . When Mr. Cobb was re-admitted in June for his final days . . . I left another ball with him and after about three days I was told he had signed it. That was only about 3 weeks before he died."[80]

So what other outrageous Stump stories about Cobb are either completely false or overblown and exaggerated? That Cobb's close friendship with Ted Williams ended completely after an argument over which players should be on the all-time All-Star team—refuted by Williams himself, who said Stump invented the story and bluntly generalized about Stump: "He's full of it."[81] That Cobb refused to sign autographs for fans and was unfriendly to kids—refuted by Jean Eilers affidavit described above and further disproved by the hundreds of genuine Cobb-signed baseballs, postcards, photos, and other items, many personalized to children, which survive and now sell for thousands of dollars each in the memorabilia market. That he carried a loaded Luger with him to his last hospital stay in the same brown bag that contained a stack of negotiable securities—refuted by Jimmy Lanier, Cobb's personal batboy in 1925 and 1926, who with his son, Jim, visited Cobb in his last days at Emory Hospital, listened as Cobb showed and described the Coca-Cola stock and other securities in the brown bag, and saw no evidence of a gun, either in the bag or elsewhere in the room.[82] That Ty Cobb's funeral was shunned by all but a few baseball players and dignitaries—refuted by *The Sporting News*, which reported shortly after Ty's death that the family had notified Cobb's friends and baseball dignitaries that the funeral service, held only 48 hours after Cobb passed, was going to be private and asked them not to attend.[83] A more appropriate question would surely be: What Stump stories about Ty Cobb are not either outright fantasy or gross exaggerations based loosely on questionable fact?

Ron Shelton, who directed the movie *Cobb* based on Al Stump's writings, called Stump a "supreme storyteller" in the eulogy he delivered at the memorial service after Stump's death.[84] It is a longstanding Southern tradition to call someone a "storyteller" as a polite way of calling him a liar. Although Shelton surely missed this regional nuance, it nevertheless seems an appropriate moniker for Al Stump. There is no doubt that Al Stump is a proven liar, proven forger, likely thief, and certainly a provocateur who created fabricated and sensationalized stories of the *True Magazine* ilk. Can there be any doubt that scholars and historians should adopt the same approach to Al Stump—written material that the memorabilia experts have adopted toward Stump's forged memorabilia: dismissing out of hand as untrue any Ty Cobb story that is sourced to Al Stump?

Conclusion

Ty Cobb created more than the normal amount of controversy during his lifetime, and he lived to suffer the negative effects of his actions on his reputation. Until his death in 1961, Ty was genuinely concerned with his baseball legacy, often expressing concern about being remembered for spikings, fighting, and aggressive play. Even more controversy, beyond that related to Cobb's playing style, has arisen since his death, practically all of it deriving from the sensationalized and fictional writings of Al Stump. These are the writings that are responsible for many, if not most, of the more outrageous—and mostly untrue—elements of the Cobb myth.

I urge each SABR member, and indeed any baseball fan or historian who seeks to know and support the unexaggerated truth, to reexamine his own beliefs about Ty Cobb in light of the results of this investigation. For the others whose inquiring minds insist on believing untruths and exaggerations or who thrive on the excitement and provocation of the *True Magazine* style of history, there will likely never be a proof or revelation that will dispel their beliefs. Sadly, many widely read contemporary sports bloggers, writers, and commentators fall into this latter category, much to the continuing detriment of Ty Cobb's memory.

NOTES

1. John Thorn, blog post dated December 29, 2005, http://thornpricks.blogspot.com.

2. Personal communication from Wesley Fricks, historian for the Ty Cobb Museum, email dated July 16, 2006.

3. Personal communication, Candy Ross, curator of the Ty Cobb Museum, October 2006.

4. *The Barry Halper Collection of Baseball Memorabilia*, Sale 7354, 3 vols. (New York: Sotheby's, 1999).

5. Personal communication, Tim Wiles, director of research, National Baseball Hall of Fame, email dated August 9, 2006.

6. Personal communication, Robert Lifson, email dated November 26, 2006.

7. *The Barry Halper Collection of Baseball Memorabilia*, Sale 7354, vol. 1: *The Early Years*, 429.

8. Lifson email.

9. "Cobb Was Told to Keep Watch Over His Home," *Atlanta Constitution*, August 11, 1905, 1.

10. Personal communication, Joanne Smaley, Georgia Archives researcher, email dated June 30, 2009.

11. *Macon* (Georgia) *Weekly Telegraph*, September 25, 1905, 1.

12. Smaley email.

13. Messages posted to the SABR Deadball Committee Yahoo Group site, June 22–23, 2004. http://groups.yahoo.com/group/deadball.

14. Franklin County, Georgia, Superior Court minutes, Book 5: 1901–1905, p. 478, GAR. RG-159-1-58.

15. Personal communication, Wesley Fricks, historian for the Ty Cobb Museum, email dated July 17, 2009.

16. Sverre Braathen, *Ty Cobb: The Idol of Baseball Fandom* (New York: Avondale Press, 1928).

17. Ty Cobb, *My Twenty Years in Baseball* (Mineola NY: Dover, 2009).

18. H. G. Salsinger, "Which Was Greatest: Ty Cobb or Babe Ruth?," *The Sporting News Baseball Register* (1951).

19. Gene Schoor, *The Story of Ty Cobb* (New York: Julian Messner, 1966).

20. John McCallum, *The Tiger Wore Spikes: An Informal Biography of Ty Cobb* (New York: A. S. Barnes, 1956).

21. Ty Cobb, *My Life in Baseball: The True Record* (New York: Doubleday, 1961).

22. Al Stump, "Ty Cobb's Wild 10-Month Fight to Live," *True—The Man's Magazine*, December 1961: 38.

23. John McCallum, *Ty Cobb* (New York: Henry Holt, 1975).

24. Robert Rubin, *Ty Cobb: The Greatest* (New York: G. P. Putnam, 1978).

25. Charles Alexander, *Ty Cobb* (New York: Oxford University Press, 1984).

26. Don Rhodes, *Ty Cobb: Safe at Home* (Guilford CT: Lyons Press, 2008), 24.

27. Richard Bak, *Ty Cobb: His Tumultuous Life and Times* (Dallas: Taylor, 1994).

28. Richard Bak, *Peach: Ty Cobb in His Time and Ours* (Ann Arbor MI: Ann Arbor Media, 2005).

29. Norman Macht, *Ty Cobb* (New York: Chelsea House, 1993).

30. Sydelle Kramer, *Ty Cobb: Bad Boy of Baseball* (New York: Random House, 1995).

31. Patrick Creevy, *Tyrus* (New York: Forge, 2002). A fictionalized biography of Ty Cobb.

32. Dan Holmes, *Ty Cobb* (Westport CT: Greenwood Press, 2004).

33. Al Stump, *Cobb: The Life and Times of the Meanest Man Who Ever Played Baseball* (Chapel Hill NC: Algonquin Books, 1994).

34. Tom Stanton, *Ty and the Babe* (New York: Thomas Dunne Books, 2007).

35. Rhodes, *Ty Cobb: Safe at Home*.

36. Stump, "Ty Cobb's Wild, 10-Month Fight to Live."

37. Al Stump, "The Last Days of Ty Cobb," *Baseball Magazine* 95, no. 1 (January 1965): 14–18.

38. Charles Einstein, ed., *The Third Fireside Book of Baseball* (New York: Simon & Schuster, 1968).

39. Bak, *Peach*, 210.

40. Personal communication, Candy Ross, curator of the Ty Cobb Museum, email dated October 21, 2009.

41. Personal communication, Furman Bisher, sports editor for the *Atlanta Constitution*, interview on October 9, 2009.

42. Leigh Montville, "The Last Remains of a Legend," *Sports Illustrated* 77, no. 17 (October 1992): 60.

43. Bak, *Peach*, 194.

44. The Baseball Index, Society for American Baseball Research, www.baseballindex.org.

45. Al Stump, *Champions Against Odds* (Philadelphia: Macrea Smith, 1952).

46. The Baseball Index.

47. Al Stump, *The Champion Breed: The True, Behind-the-Scene Struggles of Sport's Greatest Heroes* (New York: Bantam Books, 1969).

48. Milo Speriglio, *The Marilyn Conspiracy* (New York: Pocket Books, 1986), 26–31.

49. Bak, *Peach*, 195.

50. Bak, *Peach*, 195.

51. *New York Times*, July 3, 1961, 1.

52. Ron Martinetti, *Hemingway: A Look Back*, www.americanlegends.com/authors/index.html.

53. Private communication, email from Ron Stinson, August 5, 2008.

54. Private communication, interview with Lewis Martin, Al Stump's 1994 researcher in Michigan, November 12, 2009.

55. Personal communication, Al Stump to Howard G. Smith, letter dated November 29, 1980. This letter and several follow-up letters, along with memorabilia item lists and photographs, are in the personal collection of the author.

56. Personal communication, Al Stump to Howard G. Smith, letter dated December 16, 1980. Original in the author's personal collection.

57. Personal communication, Al Stump to Howard G. Smith, letter dated January 15, 1981. Original in the author's private collection.

58. Jim Stinson, "Ty: Pariah or Peach," *Sports Collectors Digest*, May 5, 2006, 36–42.

59. Stinson, "Ty: Pariah or Peach."

60. Ronald B. Keurajian, "Ty Cobb Autographs," www.autograph-club.org/autograph-article/ty-cobb-autographs.html.

61. Personal communication, Harvey Swanebeck, SABR member and collector, interview on November 4, 2009.

62. Personal communication, Swanebeck.

63. Personal communication, Karl Stone, email dated June 5, 2009.

64. Personal communication, Ron Kerurajian, interview on November 20, 2009.

65. Personal communication, Ron Kerurajian, email dated October 18, 2009.

66. Personal communication, Robert Lifson, interview on October 9, 2009.

67. Personal communication, Josh Evans, interview on November 11, 2009.

68. Ernie Harwell, "Questions Remain about the Fake Cobb Diary," *Detroit Free Press*, July 5, 2009, www.freep.com.

69. Harwell, "Questions Remain."

70. Franz Lidz, "The Sultan of Swap," *Sports Illustrated*, May 22, 1995, 66–77.

71. Personal communication, Ron Keurajian, email dated May 20, 2010.

72. Personal communication, Janel Hendrix, curator of The Elliot Museum, email dated April 10, 2010.

73. Charles C. Alexander, "Introduction," in *My Life in Baseball: The True Record* (Lincoln: University of Nebraska Press, 1993), xi.

74. Charles Alexander, *Ty Cobb* (Dallas: Southern Methodist University Press, 2006), 263.

75. Doug Roberts, "Ty Cobb Did Not Commit Murder," *The National Pastime* 16 (1996): 25–28.

76. Bak, *Peach*, 198.

77. Montville, "The Last Remains of a Legend," *Sports Illustrated*, 1982.

78. Montville, "Last Remains."

79. Montville, "Last Remains."

80. Jean Bergdale Eilers, affidavit signed in 2008, held in the private collection of Ronald B. Keurajian.

81. Bak, *Peach*, 198.

82. Personal communication, Jim Lanier Jr., interview on October 29, 2009.

83. Bak, *Peach*, 203.

84. Geoff Boucher, "This Raconteur Was Simply the Best of the Best," *Los Angeles Times*, January 26, 1996, http://articles.latimes.com/1996–01–26/news/ls-28983_1_al-stump.

40

Babe Ruth, Eiji Sawamura, and War

ROBERT K. FITTS

Rob Fitts presents the story of Eiji Sawamura, a Japanese pitcher most famous for facing—as a seventeen-year-old—a team of American barnstormers that included Babe Ruth. In 2012 at SABR 42, Fitts's presentation about the 1934 tour won the annual Doug Pappas Award for best research presentation. Rob has firmly established himself as the preeminent English-speaking historian of Japanese baseball. He has written several books on the topic, including biographies of Wally Yonamine and Masanori Murakami, as well as the 2012 book *Banzai Babe Ruth: Baseball, Espionage, and Assassination during the 1934 Tour of Japan*, which won SABR's Seymour Medal in 2012. Rob is also a leading authority and collector of Japanese baseball cards in the U.S.

November 20, 1934: Shizuoka, Japan

With a flick of his wrist, the boy received the ball from the catcher. He felt confident as if his opponents were the fellow high schoolers he had shut out just a few months before. The one o'clock sun came directly over Kusanagi Stadium's right field bleachers, blinding the batters. He knew this. It had enabled him to retire the leadoff batter, Eric McNair, on a pop fly and to strike out Charlie Gehringer. The batters saw his silhouette windup, then a white ball exploded in on them just a few feet away. It was nearly unhittable. Fanning Gehringer thrilled the boy as he saw no flaws in his swing. When facing the Mechanical Man, the pitcher imagined them as samurai dueling to the death with glittering swords. It was a spiritual battle, who could outlast the other—who could will the other to submit. Gehringer, alone among the Americans, showed the spirit of a samurai.

The third batter strode to the plate. He was old—more than twice the boy's 17 years—and with a sizable paunch, he outweighed the boy by some 100 pounds. His broad face usually bore a smile, accentuating his puffy cheeks and broad nose. His twinkling eyes and boyish, infectious good humor forced smiles even from opponents. Instinctively, the boy looked at his face . . . this time, a mistake.

There was no friendly smile. The Sultan of Swat glared back like an *oni*—those large red demons that guard temple gates. The boy's heart fluttered, his composure lost. Babe Ruth dug in.

Eiji Sawamura breathed deeply, steadying himself. This was, after all, why he had left high school early and forfeited a chance to attend prestigious Keio University—an opportunity to face Babe Ruth.

Just three months ago, Sawamura had been pitching for Kyoto Commerce High School when Tadao Ichioka, the head of the *Yomiuri Shimbun*'s sports department, approached his grandfather. Ichioka explained that the newspaper was sponsoring a team of major-league stars, including Babe Ruth, to play in Japan that fall. There were no professional teams in Japan, so Yomiuri was bringing together Japan's best to challenge the Americans. Ichioka wanted the 17-year-old pitcher on the staff. The newspaper would pay 120 yen ($36) per month, more money than most skilled artisans made. The Sawamura family needed the extra income to support Eiji's siblings, but the invitation carried a price. The Ministry of Education had just passed an edict forbidding both high school and college students from playing on the same field as professionals. If Sawamura joined the All-Nippon team, he would be expelled from high school and would forfeit his chance to attend Keio University the following semester.

But to pitch against major leaguers! To pitch against Babe Ruth! The boy accepted.[1]

Sawamura wound up, turning his body toward third base before slinging the ball toward the plate. The blinded Ruth lunged forward, his hips and great chest twisting until they nearly faced the wrong direction. The fastball pounded in catcher Jiro Kuji's mitt. Strike one.

The All-Americans were even better than Ichioka had promised—one of the greatest squads ever assembled. The infield of Lou Gehrig, Gehringer, Jimmie Foxx, and defensive wizard Rabbit Warstler at short would be tough to top. The outfield contained Bing Miller in center, flanked by sluggers Earl Averill and Ruth. Only at catcher was the team weak. Star Rick Ferrell cancelled at the last minute, his spot filled by Philadelphia A's rookie Frankie Hayes and an amusing fellow named Moe Berg, who did his best to address Sawamura in Japanese. Lefty Gomez led a staff that also included the intense

Earl Whitehill and Cleveland hurler Clint Brown. Connie Mack, the grand old man of American baseball, led the team with lovable Lefty O'Doul as his coach.

Baseball exchanges between Japan and the United States had become common by this time. Between 1905 and 1934, more than 35 collegiate, semipro, and professional teams crossed the Pacific. The Chicago White Sox and New York Giants had come to promote the game in 1913; teams that included major leaguers barnstormed in Japan in 1920 and '22; and a Negro league team known as the Philadelphia Royal Giants played top collegiate teams in 1927 and '32. In 1931, the Yomiuri newspaper decided to bring over a team of true stars. A squad that included Gehrig and O'Doul, as well as Lefty Grove, Al Simmons, Mickey Cochrane, and Frankie Frisch, had played 17 games against Japan's best, winning each contest. Although these exchanges created close friendships among Japanese and American players, relations between the nations' governments were becoming increasingly tense.

After emerging from isolation in 1853, Japan modernized with dizzying speed and began its own policy of colonialism in the 1890s. The bellicose nation defeated China in 1894–95 and Russia in 1904–05 and annexed Korea in 1910. Throughout the 1920s, Japan increased its interests in Manchuria before seizing control of the province in 1931 and creating the puppet state of Manchukuo. Faced with international condemnation, Japan withdrew from the League of Nations in February 1933 and threatened the following year to withdraw from the Washington and London Naval Treaties which limited the size of their navy. As the United States and Japan vied for control over China and naval supremacy in the Pacific, it was apparent that the countries were drifting towards war.

Politicians on both sides of the Pacific hoped that the goodwill generated by Babe Ruth and the two nations' shared love of baseball could help heal these growing political differences. Many observers, therefore, rejoiced when nearly 500,000 Japanese lined the streets of Ginza to welcome the American ballplayers on November 2, 1934. As the ballplayers traveled by motorcade from Tokyo Station to the Imperial Hotel, rows of fans—often 10 to 20 deep—surged to catch a glimpse of Ruth and his teammates. The pressing crowd reduced the broad streets to narrow paths just wide enough for the limousines to pass. Confetti and streamers fluttered down from well-wishers leaning out of windows and over the wrought-iron balconies of the avenues' multi-storied office buildings. Cries of "*Banzai! Banzai*, Babe Ruth!" echoed through the neighborhood as thousands waved Japanese and American flags and cheered wildly. Reveling in the attention, the Bambino plucked flags from the crowd and stood in the back of the car waving a Japanese flag in his left hand and an American in his right.

Finally, the crowd couldn't contain itself and rushed into the street to be closer to the Babe. Downtown traffic stood still for hours as Ruth shook hands with the multitude. The following day, the *New York Times* proclaimed: "The Babe's big bulk today blotted out such unimportant things as international squabbles over oil and navies." Umpire John Quinn added "on the day the tourists arrived there was war talk, but that disappeared after they had been in the empire twenty-four hours."[2]

The All-Americans won each of the first nine games. At first the fans divided their loyalty. Many reveled in seeing former Japanese collegiate stars play on the same team and believed, or maybe just hoped, that they could match the major leaguers. Others came to see the American stars, especially Ruth. *Yakyukai*, Japan's top baseball magazine, reported "the fans went crazy each time Ruth did anything—smiled, sneezed, or dropped a ball." Once the crowds realized their hometown heroes were unlikely to win, most switched allegiance to the visitors—clamoring for home runs. The fans' enthusiasm impressed and flattered the Americans, helping them overcome cultural differences to develop a deep appreciation for their host country.[3]

The All-Americans had pounded Sawamura in his first start 10 days earlier on November 10. The 17-year-old remembered how nervous he was before taking the field. It didn't help when Ruth homered in the first inning, delighting the sold-out Meiji Jingu stadium crowd of 60,000. Sawamura had lasted eight innings, giving up 10 runs on 11 hits, including home runs to Ruth, Averill, and weak-hitting Warstler. But the *Japan Times* noted that he "pitched courageously to the murderers row" as he struck out both Ruth and Gehrig.[4]

Fanning Ruth and Gehrig helped the boy grasp that even the greatest had weaknesses. Ruth, for example, had difficulty with knee-high inside curves. As Sawamura told a writer for *Yakyukai*, "I was scared but I realized that the big leaguers were not gods." He was noticeably calmer and more effective three days later in Toyama when he relieved Shigeru Mizuhara in the fourth after the starter had surrendered 11 runs. The schoolboy ace held the Americans scoreless until Jimmie Foxx belted a three-run homer in the eighth.[5]

Fig. 40.1. Eiji Sawamura. Courtesy of Konbusha Press.

Recalling how he had struck out Ruth before, Sawamura wound up and fired another fastball.

In 1934, Ruth was no longer the American League's best player. He was 39 years old and had grown rotund. He knew his career was finished, or at least in its twilight. In August, he announced that he would not return as a full-time player in 1935. The reception in Japan, however, had revitalized the Babe. He reveled in the chants of "Banzai Babe Ruth" and the constant attention. His ego bolstered, his bat responded. After 10 games, the Sultan of Swat had belted ten home runs with a .476 average.

Sawamura's fastball burst through the glare. The Bambino flailed his 36-inch, 44-ounce Louisville Slugger at the ball, but it was too late. The ball smacked into Kuji's glove. Strike two.

The sellout crowd at Kusanagi Stadium roared. The park was small, by both American and Japanese standards. Only 8,000 spectators could fit into the grandstands ringing the field. The fans, primarily men, wore light wool overcoats with fedoras or wool driving caps in the pleasant 48-degree afternoon. (Once home, they would remove their western garb, bathe, and don the traditional kimono.) Here and there, however, a man dressed in the traditional manner could be seen in the stands. The fans cheered and shouted on every play, making them louder than an average American crowd. But to the Americans, a familiar sound was missing from the din: no vendors were advertising their wares. No "Hot dogs! Get your hot dogs here!" No "Popcorn!" or "Cracker Jack!" or even the heavenly sound of "Beer! Ice cold beer here!" Eating in the stands was not a Japanese tradition. In fact, eating while walking or sometimes even standing was considered rude. Those who wanted to eat would purchase a small *bento* (boxed lunch) from an outside vendor or a stand just inside the stadium's entrance, then quietly eat fish or octopus with rice, or maybe fried noodles with chopsticks.

Both the fans and players noticed differences between American and Japanese baseball. The much smaller Japanese were solid fielders and quick runners but weak hitters. Most still hit off their front foot and hadn't mastered the hip rotation technique that had enabled Ruth to change the way Americans played the game. They played the field with precision acquired from hours of repetition but without flair—seemingly without joy. John Quinn described them as playing with the seriousness of a professor.[6]

The Japanese also approached the game differently. They believed that it took more than just natural ability and good technique to win a ball game; it also took a dedicated spirit. Borrowing from a heavily romanticized version of samurai behavior, Japanese players in the 1880s created a distinctive approach to the game. One that emphasized unquestioning loyalty to the manager and team as well as long hours of grueling practice to improve both players' skills and mental endurance. This "samurai baseball" offered hope to the All-Nippon team. Infielder Tokio Tominaga explained, "Many fans think that the small Japanese can never compete with the larger Americans, but I disagree. The Japanese are equal to the Americans in strength of spirit."[7]

With Ruth in the hole, Sawamura knew just what to do. Like any good warrior, he attacked his adversary's weakness. As he readied himself, the boy twisted his lips in a peculiar fashion. He then raised his arms, kicked his leg high, and fired.

Ruth brought his bat back, raising his rear elbow to shoulder height before taking a short stride with his front foot and snapping his hips forward. The bat followed along a level plane through the strike zone. Just before contact, the ball "fell off the table." Fooled by the curve, Ruth's momentum carried him forward, his body twisting around like a corkscrew.

As Ruth walked back to the dugout, a surge of confidence and hope swelled through Sawamura and the crowd. Maybe today would be the day. The Japanese had improved with each game. Both their fielding and pitching were shaper even if their hitting was still weak. Maybe today their fighting spirit would be strong enough to defeat the Americans.

By the next morning, as readers unfurled their newspapers and scanned the headlines, Sawamura had become a national hero. He held the All-Americans hitless into the fourth and scoreless into the seventh, when Gehrig belted a solo home run to win the game 1–0. Although the Japanese had not won, they showed that they were capable of conquering their opponents. Many Japanese felt that with enough fighting spirit their countrymen could surpass the major leaguers, just as they believed their military would surpass the Western powers. As years passed, the duel between Sawamura and Ruth took on greater meaning as the nations battled in the Pacific.

The All-Americans stayed in Japan for a month, winning all 18 of their games. Many declared the tour a diplomatic coup and marveled over Ruth's success as an ambassador. "Ruth Makes Japan Go American" proclaimed *The Sporting News*.[8] Connie Mack summed up the consensus that the trip did "more for the better understanding between Japanese and Americans than all the diplomatic exchanges ever accomplished." Soon after the All-Americans returned, Mack told reporters, "When we landed in Japan the American residents seemed pretty blue. The parley on the naval treaty was on, with America blocking Japan's demand for parity. There was strong anti-American feeling throughout Japan over this country's stand. Things didn't look good at all and then Babe Ruth smacked a home run, and all the ill feeling and underground war sentiment vanished just like that!"[9]

A month later at the 12th Annual New York Baseball Writers' Association meeting, Mack told the assembly, "that there would be no war between the United States and Japan, pointing out that war talk died out after his All-Star team reached Nippon."[10] Many Americans wanted to believe Mack. With the isolationist movement dominating foreign policy and national sentiment, Americans eagerly seized on signs of peace, turning a blind eye to Japan's increasingly aggressive military.

Of course, the war that could never be eventually came. Babe Ruth was in his 15th-floor Manhattan apartment on December 7, 1941, when he heard the news. For the Babe, Pearl Harbor was a personal betrayal. Cursing the double-crossing SOBs, he heaved open the living room window. His wife Claire had decorated the room with souvenirs from the Asian tour—porcelain vases, plates, exquisite dolls. The Babe stormed to the mantle, grabbed a vase and heaved it out the window. It crashed on the street below. Other souvenirs followed as Ruth kept up a tirade about the Japanese. Claire rushed around the room, gathering up the most valuable items before they joined the pile on Riverside Drive.[11]

The Sultan of Swat knew how to take revenge. Using the same charisma that made him an idol in Japan, he threw himself into the war effort, raising money to defeat the Japanese and their allies. Ruth worked closely with the Red Cross, making celebrity appearances, playing in old-timers games, visiting hospitals, and even going door-to-door seeking donations. He became a spokesman for war bonds, doing radio commercials, print advertisements, and public appearances to boost sales, and even bought $100,000 worth himself.

Perhaps the Babe's most publicized event came on August 23, 1942, when 69,136 fans packed Yankee Stadium to watch Ruth play ball for the first time in seven years. The 47-year-old Babe faced 54-year-old Walter Johnson in a demonstration before an old-timers game. Johnson threw 15–20 pitches and the Bambino hit the fifth one into the right-field stands. In the hyperbolic style of the time, sports columnist James Dawson wrote, "Babe Ruth hit one of his greatest home runs yesterday in the interest of freedom and the democratic way of living."[12] The event raised $80,000 for the Army-Navy relief fund. Ruth's biographer Marshall Smelser concluded that "Ruth . . . had become a patriotic symbol, ranking not far below the flag and the bald eagle."[13]

The attack on Pearl Harbor did not surprise or upset Eiji Sawamura. On December 7, 1941, Sawamura sat in a staging area on the Micronesian island of Palau awaiting orders. Soon, he would board a crowded transport as part of a massive assault group. He did not know where he would land, but he hoped that he would get to fight the Americans, whom at this point he considered to be little more than animals.[14]

After the tour, Sawamura and most of the All-Nippon players signed pro contracts with the newly-created Yomiuri Giants. The Giants toured the U.S. before participating in the inaugural season of the Nippon Professional

Baseball League in the Fall of '36. Sawamura was the circuit's top pitcher, leading the league in wins that year, then capturing the MVP award in '37. On July 7, 1937, after Eiji finished a one-run complete game, Japanese troops provoked a skirmish at the Marco Polo Bridge, setting off the Second Sino-Japanese War. The conflict would last eight years, cause over 22 million casualties, and spiral into World War II.

Eiji received a draft notice in January 1938 and was assigned to the 33rd Infantry Regiment of the 16th Division. Most of the regiment was currently in Nanking, becoming notorious as "the most savage killing machine among the Japanese military units."[15] Sawamura's 33rd Regiment was at the center of the atrocities against both civilians and prisoners of war during "The Rape of Nanking" and would become one of the perpetrators of the notorious Bataan Death March.

Like most Japanese, Sawamura supported his country's military expansion and did not question the decision to go to war. Since 1890, when the Meiji government announced the Imperial Rescript on Education, all Japanese school children had been trained to obey the Emperor and state. American Ambassador to Japan Joseph Grew told readers in his 1942 book *Report from Tokyo*, "In Japan the training of youth for war is not simply military training. It is a shaping . . . of the mind of youth from the earliest years. Every Japanese school child on national holidays . . . takes part in a ritual intended to impress on him his duties to the state and to the Emperor. Several times each year every child in taken with the rest of his schoolmates to a place where the spirits of dead soldiers are enshrined. . . . Of his obligation to serve the state, especially through military service, he hears every day. . . . The whole concept of Japanese education has been built upon the military formula of obeying commands."[16]

As a result of this education, most Japanese believed that the Western powers were not only thwarting Japan's right to control Asia through the so-called Greater East Asian Co-Prosperity Sphere but were also unfairly strangling the nation through oil and material embargoes. When Japanese radio announced the attack on Pearl Harbor, "the attitudes of the ordinary people," according to literary critic Takao Okuan "was a sense of euphoria that we'd done it at last; we'd landed a punch on those arrogant great powers Britain and America, on those white fellows. . . . All the feelings of inferiority of a colored people from a backward country, towards white people from the developed world, disappeared in that one blow . . . Never in our history had we Japanese felt such pride in ourselves as a race as we did then."[17]

Whereas most of the All-Americans finished the 1934 goodwill tour with warm feelings toward Japan, Sawamura had grown to hate Americans. His loathing began during the Yomiuri Giants's first visit to the United States in 1935. Just before returning to America in 1936, a piece by Sawamura entitled "My Worry" appeared in the January issue of *Shinnseinen*. He wrote: "As a professional baseball player, I would love to pitch against the Major Leaguers, not just in an exhibition game like I pitched against Babe Ruth, but in a serious game. However, what I am concerned about is that I hate America, and I cannot possibly like American people, so I cannot live in America. Firstly, I would have a language problem. Secondly, American food does not include much rice so it does not satisfy me, so I cannot pitch as powerfully as I do in Japan. Last time I went to America, I could not pitch as well as I do in Japan. I cannot stand to be where formal customs exist, such as a man is not allowed to tie a shoelace when a woman is around. American women are arrogant."[18]

Eiji completed his basic training and joined his regiment in Shanghai. Soon after his arrival, the 33rd joined an offensive against Chiang Kai-shek's nationalist army. Relying on his baseball skills, Sawamura became renowned for his grenade throwing and was often given the task of cleaning out strong Chinese positions with a difficult toss. But in September 1938 he took a bullet in his left hand. He spent an undisclosed amount of time in a military hospital before being discharged in October 1939.[19]

Sawamura took the mound again for the Yomiuri Giants during the 1940 season, but throwing heavy grenades had damaged his arm, limiting him to a sidearm motion. He no longer had the velocity of his pre-service years but he remained crafty, tossing a no-hitter against the Nagoya team on July 6. It was the third no-hitter of his career, but it lacked the luster of his first two as the war in China had depleted the pro baseball rosters. Five no-hitters were thrown in 1940, more than any other season in Japanese pro baseball. Eiji finished the 1940 season with a seemingly strong 2.59 ERA, but in truth, his mark fell well above the league ERA of 2.12.

As the military furthered their control of Japan in the late 1930s, the movement to cleanse Japan of Western influence and trappings strengthened. Pulitzer-prize winning historian John Dower has shown that Japanese of the 1930s and 40s did not necessarily see themselves as physically or intellectually superior, but they did view themselves as more spiritually virtuous than others.[20] Propaganda of the time focused on the development of a pure Japanese spirit, *Yamato Damashii*. This entailed a return to traditional Japanese life ways, emphasis on self-denial and self-control, and reverence for the Emperor. Western influences were viewed as corrupting, as they emphasized individuality and undermined Japanese culture and spirit. Army General Sadao Araki, for example, proclaimed, "frivolous thinking is due to foreign thought."[21] Imported amusements fell out of fashion. By the mid-1930s, military marches had replaced jazz as the most popular music. During the war, jazz would be outlawed and even musical instruments used in jazz, such as electric guitars and banjos, were banned. In the late 30s, the Ministry of Education decreed that scholastic sports should be stripped of "liberal influences" and replaced with traditional Japanese values and physical activities designed to enhance national defense. In 1940, Nippon Professional Baseball's board of directors followed suit. They declared that all games would be played following "the Japanese spirit" and banned English terms. Henceforth, the game would only be known as *yakyu* (field ball) and not *besuboru*. "Strike" would now be "*yoshi*" (good), and "ball" became "*dame*" (bad). Other English terms were also replaced with Japanese equivalents. Team nicknames, such as Giants and Tigers, were abandoned. Yomiuri became known as *Kyojin Gun* (Giants Troop) and the Hanshin Tigers became *Moko Gun* (the Fiery Tiger Troop). Two years later (1942), uniforms were changed to khaki, the color of national defense, and baseball caps were replaced with military caps.[22]

Not surprisingly, Babe Ruth was no longer revered. The jovial, overweight, self-indulgent demi-god of baseball became a symbol of American decadence. In 1944, Japanese troops were screaming, "To hell with Babe Ruth!" as they charged to their deaths across the jungles of the South Pacific. The Babe's response to the insult was classic Ruth, "I hope every Jap that mentions my name gets shot—and to hell with all Japs anyway!" He then took to the streets to raise money for the Red Cross telling reporters that he was spurred on by the Japanese war cry.[23]

Although still hampered by his damaged arm, a continuing bout with malaria, and difficulty sleeping, Sawamura threw 153 innings for Yomiuri during the 1941 season. He was no longer a top pitcher. His 2.05 ERA was the highest of the team's five regular pitchers and was .19 runs above the league average. Just before the end of the season, Eiji married his long-time girlfriend Ryoko, but marital bliss was short-lived. Only three days later, Sawamura received a second draft notice. He was to report immediately to the 33rd Regimental headquarters. Units across Japan were being mobilized on the double.[24]

The 33rd left Nagoya on November 20, 1941, (the seventh anniversary of his near-win against the All-Americans) and headed by transport to the island of Palau in Micronesia, where they joined a 130,000-strong invasion force. In early December, the 33rd split. The second and third Battalions left with the majority of the assembled troops, while Sawamura and his first Battalion remained on Palau. On the night of December 16, Sawamura and his comrades boarded a transport and set sail for the Philippines.

As the main body of the invasion force attacked the island of Luzon and pushed toward Manila, Sawamura's force invaded the city of Davao on the island of Mindanao. They occupied the city without a fight as the outnumbered American/Filipino garrison withdrew. Davao was the only area in the Philippines with a significant Japanese population; nearly 20,000 had immigrated to work on the nearby hemp plantations. With Davao secured, the Japanese pushed into the surrounding jungles in pursuit of the American and Filipino troops. The Allies retreated before the superior Japanese force, only to mount swift counter-attacks when they spotted a weakness. Sawamura found such behavior dishonorable and cowardly. "When we were strong and solid, the western devils got quiet as a cat. But, when they saw that we were not prepared, they would attack like a cruel evil." To Sawamura's shock, the outnumbered Americans soon surrendered. "They surrendered immediately even if they had enough bullets and guns," he later wrote with disgust. "While Japanese put their hands up in the sky in a banzai cheer at victory, Americans put their hands up in a halfway manner shamelessly as soon as they realized that they could not win and there was no way out."[25]

As Sawamura's First Battalion fought in Mindanao, the rest of his regiment and division had just defeated the main American force at the Battle of Bataan. The Japanese took 75,000 American and Filipino prisoners and force-marched them 60 miles through tropical jungles without water or food. Stragglers were killed. Escorting Japanese, including members of Sawamura's regiment, beat, shot, and beheaded prisoners for sport as they traveled by the winding column. Over a quarter of the prisoners died before they reached an internment camp at Capas. Known as the Bataan Death

March, the incident became one of the most famous atrocities committed by the Japanese army.

Sawamura stayed in the Philippines for just over a year, returning to Japan with his regiment in January 1943. He rejoined the Yomiuri Giants for the 1943 season, but three years in the Imperial Army had taken its toll. His famous control was gone. Eiji pitched just 11 innings, giving up 17 hits and walking 12. He finished out the season as a pinch-hitter.

No longer a soldier, Sawamura capitalized on his baseball fame to support the war effort. In November 1943, he published a nine-page article about his combat experiences in the baseball magazine *Yakyukai*.[26] Articles supporting the war effort were common in Japanese magazines. Unlike the Nazis or Soviets, who had centralized bureaus responsible for propaganda, in both Japan and the United States private enterprises willingly created propaganda to boost morale on the home front.[27] The piece includes themes common in most Japanese propaganda. Sawamura depicts both the suffering and daily toil of military life to remind readers that self-sacrifice was the moral obligation of all Japanese to support the war effort. Civilians were expected to bear their difficulties without complaint as the military faced the true hardships. He praises the uniqueness of the Japanese spirit, emphasizing the virtues of self-sacrifice, respect, and duty. Following a universal theme of wartime propaganda, Sawamura depicts the enemy as cruel, demonic savages. One particularly unbelievable story has the American garrison of Davao gathering the entire Japanese population of 20,000 in basements rigged with mines. The Americans, according to Sawamura, were planning on blowing up the prisoners before the Imperial Army entered the city but the speed of the Japanese advance startled the Americans and caused them to retreat before setting off the explosives. Another story, which Sawamura admits he did not witness, has American soldiers executing prisoners by pouring boiling water over their heads. With Sawamura's popularity and *Yakyukai*'s wide circulation, thousands, if not millions, read the article. Just as Babe Ruth was using his popularity to support the America war effort, Japan's great diamond hero did what he could to support his nation. Sawamura, however, would ultimately give more than the Bambino.

Before the start of the '44 season, the Giants decided not to renew Sawamura's contract. Devastated, Eiji announced his retirement. In October, another letter arrived from the Imperial Army. The 33rd was being reactivated and sent into combat. By the fall of 1944, the tide of the war had turned against the Japanese. The Battle of Midway in June 1942 had crippled the Japanese Navy allowing the Allies to begin their offensive. In the spring and summer of '44, Americans captured Saipan, Guam, and Palau and readied to retake the Philippines. On October 20, 1944, 200,000 American forces, commanded by General Douglas MacArthur, landed on Leyte to begin the campaign. The Imperial Army's 16th Division, Sawamura's old combat group, defended the area. Heavily outnumbered, the Japanese rushed reinforcements to the area.

The 33rd left Japan on November 27 and steamed toward the Philippines, but Sawamura never reached his destination. On December 2, an American submarine intercepted his transport off the coast of Taiwan and sank it. The hero of the 1934 goodwill tour was dead, killed by the creators of the game he loved.

After his death, Eiji Sawamura became an icon of Japanese baseball. In 1947, the magazine *Nekkyo* created the Sawamura Award to honor the best pitcher in Nippon Professional baseball. Twelve years later, he became one of nine initial members of the Japan Baseball Hall of Fame. Later, statues of the pitcher would be raised outside Shizuoka Kusanagi Stadium and his old high school in Kyoto. Sawamura's image would also be placed on a Japanese postal stamp. Many consider him to be the country's greatest pitcher. But in truth, he was only a standout pitcher for two years. Why then, was he elevated to the pantheon of immortals?

In his short life, Sawamura personified the trials of his country. In 1934, as Japan strove to be recognized as an equal to the United States and Britain, he nearly overcame the more powerful American ballclub. Many viewed his performance as an analogy of Japan's struggles against the west—with the proper fighting spirit Japan could overcome their rivals. In late 1930s and early 1940s, Japan and Sawamura went to war. Eiji wholeheartedly supported the war effort, both as a soldier and spokesman. The press updated fans on his life at the front and upheld him as a patriot who sacrificed his career and endured hardships to serve his Emperor and country.

After the war, Sawamura's life took on a different meaning. Many Japanese felt betrayed by their leaders for initiating a futile war that destroyed their country and lives. To help reconcile the two nations, American occupational forces propagated the myth that a cadre of military extremists had pushed Japan into an unwanted conflict. This enabled the Japanese populace to view themselves as victims of wanton militarism and a repressive government.[28]

Sawamura came to symbolize an entire generation whose dreams and lives were shattered by evils of war.

Eiji Sawamura had become more than a ballplayer. Like Babe Ruth, he had become a national symbol.

NOTES

1. Sotaro Suzuki, *Sawamura Eiji: The Eternal Great Pitcher* (in Japanese) (Tokyo: Kobunsha, 1982), 65–75.
2. *New York Times*, November 3, 1934; Spalding, *Spalding Official Base Ball Guide 1935*, 264.
3. *Yakyukai* 25, no. 3 (1935): 184.
4. *Japan Times*, November 11, 1934, 1.
5. *Yakyukai* 25, no. 1 (1935): 160–61.
6. John Quinn, "Radio Address on NBC November 9, 1934," John Quinn Scrapbook, private collection.
7. *Yakyukai* 25, no. 1 (1935): 138.
8. *The Sporting News*, November 15, 1934, 3.
9. *Daily News* (New York) January 7, 1935, 34.
10. *The Sporting News*, February 7, 1935, 1.
11. Interview with Julia Ruth Stevens, November 7, 2007.
12. Dawson quoted in Robert Elias, *The Empire Strikes Out* (New York: New Press, 2010), 137.
13. Marshall Smelser, *The Life that Ruth Built* (Lincoln: University of Nebraska Press, 1975), 525–27; Gary Bedingfield, "Babe Ruth in World War II," *Baseball in Wartime*, www.baseballinwartime.com, accessed March 17, 2010.
14. Eiji Sawamura, "Memoirs of Fighting Baseball Player" (in Japanese), *Yakyukai* 33, no. 11 (1943): 92–100.
15. Masahiro Yamamoto, *Nanking* (New York: Praeger, 2000), 92.
16. Joseph Grew, *Report from Tokyo* (New York: Simon & Schuster, 1942), 51.
17. Quoted in Ian Buruma, *Inventing Japan, 1853–1964* (New York: Modern Library, 2003), 111.
18. Eiji Sawamura, "My Worry" (in Japanese), *Shinnseinen*, January 11, 1936, 258–59.
19. Sotaro Suzuki, *Sawamura Eiji: The Eternal Great Pitcher* (in Japanese) (Tokyo: Kobunsha, 1982).
20. John Dower, *War Without Mercy* (New York: Pantheon, 1986), 203–33.
21. Harry Emerson Wilde, *Japan in Crisis* (New York: Macmillan, 1934), 52.
22. *The Sporting News*, November 7, 1940, 10; Joseph Reaves, *Taking in a Game: A History of Baseball in Asia* (Lincoln: Bison Books, 2004), 78–79; Ian Buruma, *Inventing Japan, 1853–1964* (New York: Modern Library, 2003), 93; Ikuo Abe, Yasuharu Kiyohara, and Ken Nakajima, "Sport and Physical Education Under Fascism in Japan,"

Yo: Journal of Alternative Perspectives (June 2000); Masaru Ikei, *White Ball Over the Pacific* (in Japanese) (Tokyo: Chuokoron, 1976); Ben-Ami Shillony, Politics and Culture in Wartime Japan (Oxford: Clarendon, 1981), 144.

23. *New York Times*, March 3, 1944, 2; *New York Times*, March 5, 1944, 37.

24. Sotaro Suzuki, *Sawamura Eiji: The Eternal Great Pitcher* (in Japanese) (Tokyo: Kobunsha, 1982).

25. Eiji Sawamura, "Memoirs of Fighting Baseball Player" (in Japanese), *Yakyukai* 33, no. 11 (1943): 92–100.

26. Sawamura, "Memoirs."

27. For discussion of Japanese wartime propaganda see Barak Kushner, *The Thought War* (Honolulu: University of Hawaii Press, 2007) and John Dower, *War Without Mercy* (New York: Pantheon, 1986).

28. James J. Orr, *The Victim as Hero* (Honolulu: University of Hawaii Press, 2001).

SOURCES

This narrative on the November 20, 1934, game is based on *Japan Times*, November 21, 1934, 5; *Osaka Mainichi*, November 21, 1934; Sotaro Suzuki, *Sawamura Eiji: The Eternal Great Pitcher* (in Japanese) (Tokyo: Kobunsha, 1982), 75–77; *Yakyukai* 25, no. 1 (1935): 160–61; *Yomiuri Shimbun*, November 20, 1934, 5.

41

Lou Gehrig's RBI Record

1923–39

HERM KRABBENHOFT

SABR members have been correcting baseball's record books from the very beginnings of the Society. For many decades beginning in the nineteenth century, records were kept and maintained in large hand-written ledgers and were only as accurate as the humans who transcribed and tabulated the game accounts. Herm Krabbenhoft has spent much of the past several years trying to improve the accuracy of various baseball statistics, especially runs scored and runs batted in, by poring over daily game accounts and box scores from multiple independent newspapers. His quest had led him to correct season totals for some of baseball's greatest players including Babe Ruth, Hank Greenberg, and Lou Gehrig, detailed here.

In his Hall-of-Fame career, Lou Gehrig established himself as a premier RBI player. According to the 2012 edition of *The Elias Book of Baseball Records*, Gehrig led the American League in runs batted in five times: 1927, 1928, 1930, 1931, and 1934. Furthermore, according to Elias, Gehrig holds the American League records for most RBIs for both a single season and lifetime.[1] However, as it turns out, many of the RBI statistics in Gehrig's official baseball records are erroneous. In a previous *Baseball Research Journal* article (Fall 2011), I presented my research on Lou Gehrig's RBI records from 1923 through 1930. I reported that I discovered—and corrected—more than 30 RBI errors in his official baseball records, including his AL-leading seasons of 1927, 1928, and 1930.[2]

In this article, I present the results of my research for the second half of Gehrig's major-league career, covering the seasons 1931 through 1939. Again, my research has demonstrated that Gehrig's official RBI records are afflicted with several errors.[3]

Research Procedure

In order to ascertain an accurate RBI record for Lou Gehrig, I applied the most rigorous approach: obtaining the complete details for every run scored by the Yankees in all games Gehrig played. "Complete details" means the following three facts were determined for each run-scoring situation:

(1) The identity of the player who scored the run.
(2) The run-scoring event. For example, a two-RBI single, a one-RBI groundout, a one-RBI grounder (batter safe on a fielding error), a no-RBI grounder (batter safe on a fielding error), a one-RBI bases-loaded walk, a no-RBI balk, etc.
(3) The identity of the player who completed his plate appearance during the run-scoring event. (Note: When a run scores on an event such as a steal of home, passed ball, or wild pitch, no batter completes his plate appearance during the run-scoring event.)

I was aided in my research by the complete (although unproofed) Retrosheet Play-By-Play (PBP) accounts—graciously provided to me by Dave Smith—for most of the 2,164 games that Gehrig played in his major-league career. For the 1923–1930 period, I had access to complete (unproofed) Retrosheet PBP accounts for 727 of Gehrig's 921 games. For the other 194 games I obtained the requisite run-scoring and RBI information from the game accounts in several relevant newspapers. For the 1931–1939 period, I had access to complete (unproofed) Retrosheet PBP accounts for 577 of Gehrig's 1,243 games. For the other 666 games I obtained the complete details from the game accounts in the relevant newspapers (see table 41.1).

Altogether, there were 51 games for which I was unable to acquire complete details. However, for each of these 51 games, the box score RBI information is identical to the RBI statistics in the official baseball records, suggesting that it is highly likely that the official information is accurate.

By comparing the run-scoring and RBI information presented in the unproofed Retrosheet PBP accounts and the various newspaper articles (including box scores), I identified discrepancies with the RBI statistics given in the official DBD records. Next, I resolved the discrepancies by carefully examining the game descriptions presented in multiple newspaper accounts. Then, I provided my conclusions and the supporting documentation to Retrosheet's Tom Ruane and Dave Smith for their review of the evidence and their assessments of my conclusions. I also provided the identical information to Pete Palmer, whose database is utilized by some baseball websites and the most-recently published hardcopy baseball encyclopedias. For those who would like to examine the evidence themselves, the supporting documentation for the corrections to Gehrig's official record is provided in the Supplementary Material, available on the SABR website.

Results

1923–1930

Two adjustments to the RBI record presented in my previous article need to be made.

First, for the 1926 season, I actually discovered and corrected 10, not nine, RBI errors in Gehrig's official baseball record. I inadvertently neglected to include the RBI-error game on July 20, 1926. For this game, baseball's official Day-By-Day (DBD) records (compiled by the Howe News Bureau, the official statistician for the American League during Gehrig's career) show Gehrig with one RBI and Babe Ruth with two. In actuality, Gehrig had zero and Ruth three. This results in Gehrig's season total for 1926 actually being 109 RBIS (not 110 RBIS as previously claimed).

Second, for the 1928 season, Retrosheet deemed that the official DBD record is correct for the second game of the double header on July 26, 1928. Gehrig did have only one RBI (not two) in this game. Thus, Gehrig's season total for 1928 is actually 147 RBIS (not 148 as previously claimed). Now on to the second half of Gehrig's career, 1931–1939.

1931

As described in a presentation given at the annual national SABR Convention in 2011, Trent McCotter discovered and corrected five games with RBI errors involving Lou Gehrig.[4] Subsequently, I carried out an independent review of the runs scored and RBIS by the players on the 1931 Yankees. In addition to corroborating McCotter's findings for Gehrig, I also discovered and corrected yet another RBI error for Gehrig—in the game on May 3, 1931 (see table 41.1). The net result of correcting these six RBI errors is plus-one RBI for Gehrig. Thus, Gehrig's season total for 1931 is actually 185 RBIS, not 184 as shown in the official records. (See also table 42.2.)

1932–1939

My research revealed that Gehrig was involved in eight games with RBI errors in during the 1932–1939 seasons. As indicated in table 41.1, there was at least one RBI-error game for Gehrig in each of his full seasons except for the 1932 campaign. Table 41.2 presents the consequences of correcting the RBI errors I discovered.

Table 41.1. RBI errors and corrections in Lou Gehrig's official baseball record, 1931–39

Year	Month	Day	Game	Opp	Gehrig RBI (off)	Gehrig RBI (act)	Other Players	RBI (off)	RBI (act)	Ret	Supporting Documentation
1931	Apr	21		PHI	2	3	Babe Ruth	1	0	R	NYT-NYHT-NYWT-PINQ
1931	Apr	22		BOS*	2	1	Tony Lazzeri	2	3	R	NYT-NYHT-NYWT-BG-BH-BP
1931	May	03		BOS	0	1	–	–	–	R	NYT-NYHT-NYWT-NYA-NYDN-BG-BH-BP
1931	Jul	01		DET*	2	1	Ben Chapman	0	1	R	NYT-NYHT-NYWT-DFP-DN
1931	Jul	02		DET*	2	1	See Note	–	–	R	NYT-NYHT-NYWT-DFP-DN
1931	Jul	08	1	BOS	0	2	Sammy Byrd	2	0	R	NYT-NYHT-NYWT-BG-BH-BP
1933	Sep	29		WAS	1	2	–	–	–		NYT-NYHT-WP
1934	May	18		DET*	1	2	Harry Smythe	1	0	(R)	NYT-NYHT-NYP-DFP-DN-DT
1935	Jun	08	2	BOS*	0	1	Ben Chapman	1	0	(R)	NYT-NYHT-BG-BH-BP
1936	Apr	15		WAS*	0	1	George Selkirk	1	0		NYT-NYHT-NYP-WP
1936	Sep	04		BOS*	1	0	Jake Powell	0	1	R	NYT-NYHT-BG-BH-BP
1937	Jun	07		DET*	2	1	Bill Dickey	0	1		NYT-NYHT-DFP-DN-DT
1938	May	13		PHI	3	2	–	–	–		NYT-NYHT-NYP-NYDN-PINQ
1938	May	28		PHI*	1	2	J. DiMaggio	1	0	R	NYT-NYHT-PINQ

Key: "Opp" identifies the team that opposed the Yankees; an asterisk indicates that the opposing team was the home team. "Ret" indicates when Retrosheet PBP information was used to identify an RBI error: an "R" indicates that the PBP information covers the entire game; and "(R)" indicates that the PBP information covers only a portion of the game. Newspaper sources: The relevant text accounts and box scores were found in these newspapers: *New York Times* (NYT), *New York Herald Tribune* (NYHT), *New York World Telegram* (NYWT), *New York American* (NYA), *New York Daily News* (NYDN), *New York Post* (NYP), *Boston Globe* (BG), *Boston Herald* (BH), *Boston Post* (BP), *Detroit Free Press* (DFP), *Detroit News* (DN), *Detroit Times* (DT), *Philadelphia Inquirer* (PINQ), *Washington Post* (WP).

Note: Other players in addition to Gehrig with RBI errors in the official DBD record for July 2, 1931, are Bill Dickey (who actually had two RBIs, not three), Lyn Lary (who actually had three RBIs, not two), and Jimmie Reese (who actually had two RBIs, not one).

Discussion

As previously mentioned, the evidence in support of the correcting the RBI errors I discovered in Lou Gehrig's official baseball records is compiled on the SABR website under Supplemental Material. This documentation was provided to Retrosheet (specifically Tom Ruane and Dave Smith) and to Pete Palmer. Both agreed with the conclusions I reached with regard to correcting the RBI errors in Gehrig's official records.[5] Retrosheet has already implemented the corrections in the box score file and Gehrig's daily file; Palmer indicated that he would be making the changes after the conclusion of the 2012 season.

With regard to the Elias Sports Bureau, they have not yet taken a position on corrections of the RBI errors in Gehrig's official baseball record for the 1931–1939 seasons. In the 2012 edition of *The Elias Book of Baseball Records*, Gehrig is shown with league-leading RBI totals of 184 in 1931, and 165 in 1934. As shown above in table 41.2, according to my research, Gehrig actually had 185 RBIs in 1931 and 166 RBIs in 1934. Whether or not Elias updates future editions of the book remains to be seen, however, subsequent to the publication of my previous research on Gehrig's RBI record, 1923–1930, Elias did incorporate the corrections for Gehrig's league-leading RBI totals for the 1927, 1928, and 1930 seasons in the 2012 edition.

Gehrig's lifetime total is also affected by my findings. According to my research, Lou Gehrig accumulated a total of 1,995 RBIs in his career, five more than the 1,990 given in the official baseball records (see table 41.2). The official website of Major League Baseball (MLB.com) has Gehrig credited with 1,995 RBIs, but not because of the needed corrections. MLB.com's 1,995 lifetime total is merely fortuitous because the site has erroneous RBI stats for each of Gehrig's individual seasons (except for 1924, 1929, 1936, 1938, and 1939). It remains to be seen when/if the correct RBI statistics will be included on MLB.com. The 2012 edition of *The Elias Book of Baseball Records* states that Gehrig holds the American League record for most career RBIs with 1,994. Previous editions showed Gehrig with other lifetime totals:[6]

Edition	Total
1973	1,991
1974–1995	1,990
1996–2006	1,995
2007–2011	1,996

To facilitate consideration of corrections to Gehrig's RBI totals on MLB. com and in *The Elias Book of Baseball Records*, the final draft of this manuscript (including the Supplementary Material) was provided to John Thorn, the official historian for Major League Baseball, and Seymour Siwoff, President of the Elias Sports Bureau, the official statistician for Major League Baseball.

Table 41.2. Lou Gehrig's RBI record, 1923–39

Year	Games Played by Gehrig	Official RBIS for Gehrig	Games with RBI-Errors for Gehrig	Net Change in RBIS for Gehrig	Correct RBIS for Gehrig
1923	13	9	1	-1	8
1924	10	5	0	0	5
1925	126	68	4	0	68
1926	155	107	10	+2	109
1927*	155	175	4	-2	173
1928*	154	142	7	+5	147
1929	154	126	5	-1	125
1930*	154	174	3	-1	173
1931*	155	184	6	+1	185
1932	156	151	0	0	151
1933	152	139	1	+1	140
1934*	154	165	1	+1	166
1935	149	119	1	+1	120
1936	155	152	2	0	152
1937	157	159	1	-1	158
1938	157	114	2	0	114
1939	8	1	0	0	1
Total	2,164	1,990	48	+5	1,995

* Gehrig led the AL in RBIS.

Editorial Update, August 2019

Since the publication of this article a great deal of additional research has been carried out. Complete *proofed* PBP accounts have now been posted by Retrosheet for 1,969 of Gehrig's 2,164 ML games. Furthermore, utilizing game accounts provided in numerous independent newspapers the complete PBP details have been ascertained for each Yankee run in 185 of the 195 Gehrig games for which Retrosheet does not yet have complete PBP accounts. Thus, there are now only 10 games for which there are not yet complete details for each Yankee run, compared to 51 such games when the article was published in 2012. This additional research has led to changes impacting Gehrig's RBI record in two games: (1) May 10, 1926 (vs. Detroit)—Gehrig is now credited with four RBIS (instead of three); this change results in Gehrig's 1926 full-season RBI total being 110 (instead of 109). (2) July 26, 1928 (second game) (vs. Detroit)—Gehrig is now credited with two RBIS (instead of one); this change results in Gehrig's 1928 full-season RBI total being 148 (instead of 147). Together, these two individual-season changes result in Gehrig's career RBI total being 1,997 (instead of 1,995).

ACKNOWLEDGMENTS

It is with tremendous gratitude that I thank the following people for their outstanding cooperation in helping me carry out the research for this article: Freddy Berowski, Cliff Blau, Steve Boren, Keith Carlson, Bob McConnell, Trent McCotter, Pete Palmer, Tom Ruane, Dave Smith, Gary Stone, and Dixie Tourangeau. And, special thanks to the "Retrosheeters"—all the people who volunteer their superb efforts to produce the database for Retrosheet—enablers of baseball research (see http://sabr.org/node/25736).

NOTES

1. Seymour Siwoff, *The Elias Book of Baseball Records* (New York: Elias Sports Bureau, 2012) 380, 26.
2. Herm Krabbenhoft, "Lou Gehrig's RBI Record," *Baseball Research Journal* 41 (Fall 2011), 12.
3. Herm Krabbenhoft, "Most Runs Batted In . . . Individual Player . . . Lifetime . . . American League," presentation at SABR 42 (June 2012, Minneapolis, Minnesota).
4. Herm Krabbenhoft and Trent McCotter, "Most Runs Batted In . . . Individual Player . . . Single Season . . . American League," presentation at SABR 41 (July 2011, Long Beach, California).
5. Tom Ruane, personal communications via email correspondence, June 16 and 18, 2012; Pete Palmer, personal communication, via email correspondence, June 24, 2012.
6. *The Little Red Book of Baseball* (the direct precursor to *The Elias Book of Baseball Records*) also lists Gehrig with 1,991 lifetime RBIS in each edition from 1940 through 1966.

42

Clutch Hitting in the Major Leagues

A Psychological Perspective

LEONARD S. NEWMAN

SABR members have tackled the issue of "clutch hitting" many times over the years. Leonard Newman's article here examines the psychology of the phenomenon and wonders if the pool of major leaguers might be so specialized that they are actually all clutch hitters compared with the rest of us. Newman is an associate professor of psychology at Syracuse University. He is the former editor of the journal *Basic and Applied Social Psychology* and coauthor of the textbook *Social Psychology: A Storytelling Approach*.

In the 2011 postseason, David Freese made a name for himself with his spectacular and timely hitting and won both the National League Championship Series and World Series MVP awards. It cannot be denied: Freese hit well in the clutch that October. But would it have been reasonable to expect the same from him in the future? Is he in fact a "clutch hitter"? Do clutch hitters even exist?

Sabermetricians have been arguing about the reality of clutch hitting for quite some time now (see, for example, the special section of the 2008 issue of *Baseball Research Journal*). At this point, an impressive group of sophisticated researchers has carefully analyzed large data sets using a variety of statistical methods to test the hypothesis that some players consistently outperform others in high-pressure situations. For example, Phil Birnbaum analyzed batting data from the years 1974 through 1990 to test for the consistency of players' clutch hitting from one season to the next.[1] A clutch hit was defined as one occurring in the "seventh inning or later, tied or down by three runs or less, unless the bases are loaded, in which case down by four runs." For all players with at least 50 at-bats in clutch situations, batting averages in clutch situations (corrected for batting averages in non-clutch situations) were calculated, and consistency across consecutive seasons was assessed with a simple linear regression analysis.

Needless to say, however one defines and measures clutch hitting, for any given season, some players will have higher scores than others. Those players can without argument be said to have hit better in the clutch during that baseball season. But if clutch hitting is not just subject to random variation, and if some individual players are truly more "clutch" than others, then those players should consistently perform well in the clutch relative to other players—just as extroverted people are consistently more extroverted than introverts, and honest people are consistently more honest than dishonest people. But Birnbaum found no evidence for that sort of consistency.

Although there is some disagreement about the correct interpretation of these and related findings, the following would arguably be a consensus statement: Clutch hitting either does not exist or is a marginal, difficult-to-detect phenomenon that accounts for only a tiny amount of the variance in batting performance.[2] Birnbaum's samples, for example, were large enough so that even correlations as low as approximately .17 would have reached conventional levels of statistical significance. Relationships of that magnitude are not very impressive, and are typically not "perceptible on the basis of casual observation."[3]

Note that even if compelling evidence were presented for the existence of clutch hitting, that would not necessarily mean that what observers perceive to be clutch hitting is real, and not an illusion. The effects of being "clutch" on performance could be so tiny that they would not necessarily even correlate with people's subjective assessments of individual players' clutch hitting abilities. People's intuitions about both the presence and meaning of patterns in athletic performance are often flawed. For example, ample research has demonstrated that the "hot hand" in basketball—the increased likelihood of players making a successful shot if their previous shot was successful—is more illusory than real.[4]

However, two aspects of the debate over the existence of clutch hitting, while they might seem to go without saying, arguably have important ramifications for the question "does clutch hitting exist?"—

- The question "does clutch hitting exist?" can essentially be rephrased as "do some hitters have psychological characteristics that enhance their performance in high pressure situations?"

- Published research on the topic has actually addressed the question "does clutch hitting exist at the *major-league level*?" That might in fact be the question of most interest to researchers, but SABR (the Society for American Baseball Research) is not SAMLBR (the Society for American Major League Baseball Research)

In tandem, those two observations highlight the fact that existing research has, for all intents and purposes, been based on the assumption that major-league ballplayers vary significantly in the psychological characteristics associated with clutch hitting. What might those characteristics be? And is it reasonable to expect major leaguers to represent different levels of those characteristics? If not, what are the implications for the search to find convincing and replicable evidence for clutch hitting?

The Psychological Characteristics of Clutch Performers

What traits (that is, stable dispositions) might be especially pronounced in players who perform exceptionally well in the clutch? The following is not meant to be an exhaustive list of all possible personal characteristics, but the three I focus on here represent three general ways in which clutch hitters might stand out from others specifically, in terms of their affective, cognitive, and/or motivational qualities.

Trait anxiety. Anxiety, of course, is a state that certain experiences trigger in people. Everyone has encountered situations that that are threatening, challenging, and unpredictable enough to at least temporarily trigger somatic effects like increased heart rate and perspiration, trembling, or even, in extreme cases, nausea. Situations in which a person's social reputation and self-esteem are at stake are especially potent sources of anxiety—situations like those involving publicly observable athletic performances taking place when the outcome of a contest is at stake.

Some people, though, are less prone to experiencing anxiety than others; such people are said to be low in trait anxiety.[5] These individuals have been found to be less susceptible than others to stress-induced deterioration of performance. Relative to athletes high in trait anxiety, those low in trait anxiety should thus consistently perform better in clutch situations. Although direct evidence involving baseball players is lacking, this hypothesis has been supported in the context of other sports, such as basketball.[6]

Self-consciousness. In high-pressure athletic situations, your attention should of course be focused on the task at hand (e.g., hitting the pitched ball). You could, though, attend to other things, such as whether or not other people are observing you, and what they might be thinking about you. In addition, you could carefully monitor your own internal states to determine how confident you are feeling or how you are reacting physiologically to the situation. You might also pay careful attention to the positions of your limbs (for example, focusing on your batting stance and how you are gripping the bat).

People high in self-consciousness are those who are most prone to let their attention drift to those other things and to become acutely self-aware in high-pressure situations. Unfortunately, becoming preoccupied with one's physical, psychological, and/or social self can undermine one's performance. Indeed, dispositional self-consciousness has been found be negatively correlated with performance under pressure.[7] Relative to baseball players high in self-consciousness, those low in self-consciousness should consistently perform better in clutch situations.

Achievement motivation. Coming through in the clutch and playing a central role in your team's victory is a major accomplishment, and ballplayers who hit walk-off home runs are more respected and celebrated than those who hit home runs in the ninth inning of a 13–1 blowout. When Yankees owner George Steinbrenner tagged Dave Winfield "Mister May" the nature of the criticism—by comparing him to "Mister October" Reggie Jackson—was clear to everyone. Similarly, most baseball fans remember Francisco Cabrera's two-out pinch hit in the bottom of the ninth inning in Game Seven of the 1992 National League Championship Series; the two runs he knocked in won the game, the series, and the pennant. Fewer fans, it can be assumed, remember that that was his only hit of the series, and it is unlikely that many could identify the Braves' leading hitter for the series: Mark Lemke, with a .333 batting average. He knocked in two runs also—but one was in the Braves' 5–1 victory in Game One and the other in their 13–5 victory in Game Two.

But people differ in terms of how strongly they desire to overcome challenges, outperform others, and stand out from their peers. In other words, there are individual differences in achievement motivation.[8] According to an influential definition of this personal characteristic, it is associated with "intense, prolonged and repeated efforts to accomplish something difficult," having "the determination to win," enjoying competition, and being "stimulated to excel by the presence of others."[9] Relative to baseball players low in achievement motivation, those high in achievement motivation should consistently perform better in clutch situations.

Major-League Baseball Players: An Extreme Population

If clutch hitting is related to the personality traits described above (and related ones), and if major league ballplayers vary in terms of their consistent ability to hit in the clutch, then it follows that major league ballplayers must also vary in terms of those traits. Is that a reasonable expectation? Data from a battery of personality tests administered to major leaguers would answer that question. Such data, alas, do not exist. But an educated guess is still possible.

Consider, for example, what one can learn from SABR's Biography Project (BioProject) website (http://bioproj.sabr.org/). There is, of course, no shortage of sources of information about Hall of Fame-caliber ballplayers or other perennial All-Stars. But the BioProject is notable for its exhaustively researched stories about players who might be memorable to passionate baseball fans, but who are far from household names. Consider, if you will, the following quartet: Ken Frailing, Duffy Dyer, Dalton Jones, and Jerry Adair (selected for, among other things, being prominent in the baseball card collections of my youth). Collectively, they represent 41 years of major-league service—and also, a grand total of zero All-Star Game appearances. None ever led the league in a significant batting or pitching category (although Adair grounded into the most double plays in the American League in 1965). With the exception of Adair, none ever received a single MVP award vote.

Of course, all had one other distinguishing characteristic: they were extraordinarily talented athletes. Frailing, for example, had an eye-popping 13-0 record with an ERA of 0.17 during his senior year in high school. That same school later selected him as their "Athlete of the Century." Dyer, when he was in high school in Arizona, was recognized "as one of the state's top ballplayers," and he led his team to a state championship in 1963. Dalton Jones also led his high school team to the state championship game (in Louisiana)—but scouts had already started "flocking around" him when he was 14 years old. As for Adair, "no athlete from Oklahoma had a more storied pre-professional career than Adair, not even Mickey Mantle." A sportswriter in Oklahoma describes him as "the best athlete to come out of the Tulsa area in his lifetime."[10]

In short, even unremarkable major-league baseball players are elite performers. To reach the major leagues, players undergo an extremely rigorous selection process. In fact, given the number of people who would find a career in professional sports to be appealing, the reference group used to evaluate their aptitude for the game is essentially most of the male population of the United States (and increasingly, a number of other countries as well).

It could conceivably be the case that once a player reaches the majors, the level of pressure and the stakes involved rise to levels that players have not previously experienced, and so the threshold at which different psychological limitations and vulnerabilities might matter are reached for the first time. Nonetheless, anyone with characteristics that inhibit top-flight performance—either physical *or* psychological ones—will be weeded out well before the call-up to the majors. Although no direct evidence is available, high levels of trait anxiety and low levels of achievement motivation are unlikely to be found among men on major-league rosters. The same is true of high levels of self-consciousness; indeed, the rare exceptions to that rule are notable enough to have become legendary, as in the "Steve Blass Disease," or the "Steve Sax Syndrome." Professional ballplayers who suddenly become incapable of completing routine plays report that their problems are associated with excruciating self-awareness. As Dale Murphy put it, "Your mind interferes, and you start thinking, Where am I throwing? What am I doing? instead of just throwing. Your mind starts working against you."[11]

Statistical Implications

To ask "Do some hitters have psychological characteristics that enhance their performance in high pressure situations?" is to ask the question "Is the relationship between game situation (high stakes, low stakes) and batting performance (hitting safely, knocking in runs) *moderated* by psychological variables?" Moderator variables are variables that affect the relationship between two other variables (in this case, game situation and performance); in other words, moderation is in evidence when the relationship between two variables depends on a third variable. But if that third variable hardly varies, it is not much of a variable, and it cannot be a moderator.

That point can probably be understood intuitively, but it can also be formalized in statistical terms. Moderation is typically assessed with a multiple regression analysis. Essentially, one tries to predict or estimate a dependent variable, Y (e.g., performance), on the basis of an independent variable or variables, **x** (e.g., game situation), a moderating variable, **m** (e.g., trait anxiety, self-consciousness, achievement motivation), and most crucially, the interaction of **x** and **m** (**xm**). One or more of the predictor variables might account for statistically significant variance in the dependent variable.

However, a variable that itself has little or no variance cannot account for variance in another one. Thus, if **m** does not vary across observations, it (and the interaction term, **xm**) drops out of the equation, and there can be no moderation effect. All that would be left in the statistical model would be a general estimate of how well batters in general perform in clutch versus non-clutch situations.

Looking for Clutch Hitting in the Right Places:
A Challenge and Prediction

An implication of this analysis is that clutch hitting is unlikely to be detected in data from the major leagues; major league batters simply do not vary enough in terms of the personal qualities that would lead some to perform better and some to perform worse in the clutch. Unmotivated, highly self-conscious men with trouble controlling anxiety are unlikely to be found on the rosters of teams in the American and National Leagues.

There is, however, no reason clutch hitting should not exist in populations of baseball players for whom the relevant moderating variables *are* associated with a significant amount of variance. In other words, clutch hitting should be detectable at lower levels of competition, among players who have not undergone the rigorous selection process experienced by major leaguers. Among such players one could reasonably expect to find people with relatively high levels of anxiety and self-consciousness and low levels of achievement motivation.

Assembling an appropriate data set, however, could be quite a challenge. To assess consistency in clutch hitting at a particular level of competition in a manner consistent with past investigations of the phenomenon, one must find a reasonably large group of batters who (1) stay at that level for more than one year, and (2) accrue enough plate appearances during each of those years to provide a reliable and valid performance measure. Minor-league rosters, however, are quite unstable from year to year. In addition, those players who stay mired at a particular level might differ in systematic ways from those who do not, and thus might not be a representative sample of ballplayers. Another possible source of data might be high school baseball, but high school teams do not play enough games in a given year to satisfy the second criterion.

More promising would be college baseball. Players in college have multiyear careers, and their teams play dozens of games—enough so that players end seasons with hundreds of at-bats. In addition, although most people would not have a realistic chance of making the cut for a college team, it is still the case that the physical skills and psychological attributes required at this level are not what they have to be at the major-league level.

As a result, with a fair amount of confidence, I end this essay with the following prediction: if anyone can construct a data set involving a large number of college players who had substantial amounts of playing time across multiple seasons, and conducts a "Cramer test" of the kind conducted by Birnbaum, evidence for stable levels of clutch hitting will be detected.[12] A failure to find such evidence would not, of course, provide definitive evidence that the phenomenon of clutch hitting is nonexistent. It could instead suggest that the standard criteria for distinguishing between high-pressure batting situations and less pressured ones do not correspond closely enough to how batters directly experience those situations. In other words, faced with null data (that is, a failure to detect the existence of consistent clutch hitting), one might choose to re-examine standard definitions of clutch hitting. But the odds of finding straightforward, unambiguous evidence for clutch hitting would seem to be much more favorable for almost any other sample of batters other than major leaguers.

NOTES

1. Phil Birnbaum, "Clutch Hitting and the Cramer Test," *Baseball Research Journal* 37 (2008): 71–75.

2. Bill James (2008), "Mapping the Fog," *Baseball Research Journal* 37, 76–81; P. Birnbaum, "Response to 'Mapping the Fog,'" *Baseball Research Journal* 37, 82–84.

3. Jacob Cohen, *Statistical Power Analysis for the Behavioral Sciences* (New York: Academic Press, 1977), 79.

4. Thomas Gilovich, Robert Vallone, and Amos Tversky, "The Hot Hand in Basketball: On the Misperception of Random Sequences," *Cognitive Psychology* 3 (1985): 295–314; Alan Reifman, *Hot Hand: The Statistics Behind Sports Greatest Streaks* (Washington DC: Potomac, 2012).

5. Michael W. Eysenck, *Anxiety and Cognition: A Unified Theory* (East Sussex, UK: Psychology Press, 1997).

6. Sian L. Beilock & Rob Gray, "Why Do Athletes Choke Under Pressure?" in Gershon Tenenbaum & Robert C. Eklund, eds., *Handbook of Sport Psychology*, 3rd ed. (Hoboken NJ: John Wiley & Sons, 2007): 425–44; Guiying Hu, Baihua Xu, and Qi Xu, "An Experimental Study on the 'Choking' Psychological Mechanism of Adolescent Basketball Players," *Psychological Science 31* (China, 2008): 528–31; J. Wang, D. Marchant, T. Morris, & P. Gibbs, "Self-Consciousness and Trait Anxiety as Predictors of Choking in Sport," *Journal of Science and Medicine in Sport 7* (2004): 174–85.

7. Sian L. Beilock & Rob Gray, "Why Do Athletes Choke Under Pressure?," in Gershon Tenenbaum and Robert C. Eklund, 425–44; Georgia Panayiotou, "Chronic Self-Consciousness and Its Effects on Cognitive Performance, Physiology, and Self-Reported Anxiety," *Representative Research In Social Psychology* 28 (2005): 21–34; J. Wang, D. Marchant, T. Morris, and P. Gibbs, 174–85.

8. Joan L. Duda, "Motivation in Sport: The Relevance of Competence and Achievement Goals," in Andrew J. Elliot and Carol S. Dweck, eds., *Handbook of Competence and Motivation* (New York: Guilford Publications, 2005), 318–35; Andrew J. Elliot & Holly A. McGregor, "A 2×2 Achievement Goal Framework," *Journal of Personality and Social Psychology* 80 (2001): 501–19.

9. Henry A. Murray, *Explorations in Personality* (New York: Oxford University Press, 1938), 164.

10. All quotations and information about the players discussed in this paragraph were retrieved from the SABR Baseball Biography Project at http://sabr.org/bioproject.

11. Richard Demak, "Mysterious Malady," *Sports Illustrated*, April 8, 1991.

12. Richard D. Cramer, "Do Clutch Hitters Exist?," *Baseball Research Journal* 6 (1977): 74–79.

43

Do Hitters Boost Their Performance during Their Contract Years?

Evidence from the 2006–11 Collective Bargaining Agreement's Years Says "Yes"

HEATHER M. O'NEILL

Ever since the advent of free agency in the 1970s, fans and analysts alike have wondered whether a player can or does improve his play in anticipation of striking it rich in the off-season. This issue has been studied many times before, but never as thoroughly as in this article that first appeared in the Fall 2014 *Baseball Research Journal*. Its author, Heather O'Neill, is a professor of economics at Ursinus College who teaches a variety of applied microeconomics courses, including the Economics of Sports.

Each season, baseball fans and journalists alike identify which players are in the final years of their contracts because a lot rides on how the players produce in their "contract year." Will a player boost his effort and performance in an effort to improve his value and bargaining power? Or will he crumble under the pressure? Or are players' performances uncorrelated with where they stand in their contract cycles? Legendary manager Sparky Anderson believed players rose to the occasion in their contract years declaring, "Just give me 25 guys on the last year of their contract; I'll win a pennant every year."[1] Although anecdotal evidence abounds, this paper uses a robust data set and appropriate player-specific econometric modeling highlighted in O'Neill to show that Anderson was right—players' performances improve during their contract years.[2] To find the answer requires following players throughout their careers to tease out changes predicated on contract status, rather than comparing players to one another given their contract status.

For example, in the last year of a three-year contract with the Mariners in 2006, Raul Ibañez sported an .869 OPS (on-base plus slugging percentage), up from .792 OPS the previous year.[3] He subsequently signed an $11 million, two-year contract with the Mariners. In his next contract year, 2008, his OPS of .837 slightly exceeded his 2007 OPS of .831. Ibañez then signed a $31.5 million, three-year contract with the Phillies. At the end of that deal, in 2011, Ibañez's .707 OPS dipped lower than his previous year's OPS of .793 and the Yankees signed him to a one-year deal at $1.1 million. Two of Ibañez's three contract years show boosts in performance, while the third demonstrates a significant drop. He was also 39 years old in 2011, suggesting age must be accounted for while searching for the answer.

The parties in contract negotiations—players, agents, and team owners—understand that incentives affect performance and that performance impacts pay and contract length. Players seek job security, income, and championships, while profit-seeking owners want players to perform well to win games and championships and secure fan enthusiasm. In contract negotiations, how a player has performed over his career serves as an imperfect predictor of his future performance. If players believe that team owners weigh a player's most recent season more heavily than preceding years, it sets the stage for the contract year phenomenon. The attraction of a lucrative future contract provides ample incentive for a player to put in additional time and effort to boost performance in his contract year. After signing a new guaranteed contract, both pay and contract length are set regardless of actual performance, which removes the previous incentive.[4] For longer-term contracts, this may lead to shirking. Eventually, a new contract year arrives and the incentive to boost performance reappears.

Difficulty arises in separating the individual performance of a baseball player from his team's capabilities. This proves especially true for pitchers since decisions made about their pitch selection, pitch location, and strategy may depend on their team's fielding proficiency and the strength of the bullpen. For a hitter, the type of pitch he sees may depend in part on the hitters adjacent to him in the lineup and the situation. This paper analyzes individual data on hitters (position players), rather than pitchers, while cognizant of the potential measurement errors. Adjusted OPS (OPS100) serves as the measure of the hitter's performance. Although random variations in OPS100 from one year to the next can occur, it is unlikely for a large group of players that above average performances would randomly occur during contract years. I contend that effort and performance change from one year to the next depending upon where the player sits in his contract cycle.

Major League Baseball's use of salary arbitration, contract extensions, and free agency provides avenues for enhanced contract conditions for players. This paper focuses on free agents with six or more years of MLB service for the following four reasons:

(1) free agency is associated with the greatest financial gains for players as teams bid for players' services;

(2) at least six years of service enable more observations per player to capture more robust results;

(3) free agents with fewer than six years are those who have been demoted to the minors or released; and

(4) there will be a sufficient number of players who may retire at the end of their contract year, an intention that is expected to impact contract year performance.

Previous Research Findings

Previous research on MLB contract year performance shows mixed results. As detailed in O'Neill, the choice of performance measure and statistical technique employed often create contradictory results.[5] Researchers generally analyze hitters, believing hitting statistics are less contaminated by team play than pitching statistics. The use of slugging percentage (SLG), at-bats (ABS), days on the disabled list (DL), wins above replacement player, OPS, and runs created per 27 outs (R27), show the range of offensive performance measures investigated. Given differences in players' abilities, changes in a player's output should be relative to his ability, indicating why several studies use the deviation between current and three-year moving average of a player's offensive statistics to capture changes in a player's output. A deviation-based model by Maxcy et al. finds no significant change in SLG for players in their contract year.[6] Maxcy et al. does find that players seeking new contracts spend fewer days on the DL and have more ABS, contending they do so to make themselves more attractive to team owners. Birnbaum does not find a boost in R27 during contract years, whereas Perry does using WARP.[7]

Using ordinary least squares (OLS) regression enables one to predict changes in output during the contract year while controlling for observable player traits, such as age, years of MLB experience, team success, etc. However, compiling data on many players (cross sectional data) over several years played (time series data) creates a "panel" dataset. OLS estimation leads to biased results with panel data. Previous studies show robust statistical evidence of the contract year boost when using appropriate panel data estimation techniques, whereas those applying OLS models do not, as discussed in O'Neill.[8] Analyzing data on hitters between 2001 and 2004, Dinerstein uses seemingly unrelated regression (SUR) and finds statistically significant increases in a hitter's SLG during his contract year.[9] Interestingly, from the team owners' perspectives, Dinerstein finds that consistency of a player's performance mattered more than the most recent performance. If teams are seeking consistency, they will pay for it, and players will begin to aim for steady hitting performances. If Dinerstein is correct, we should see a reduction toward zero in the magnitude of the contract year boost. Hummel and O'Neill employ fixed effects estimation with data on free agents playing 2004–8 and find 4.2–5.5 percent boosts in OPS during contract years.[10] They note that players intending to retire no longer have financial incentive to boost effort, although they may desire to go out on top. Their results suggest the former effect dominates, shown by an 11.2–13.2 percent decrease in OPS for retiring players in the last year of their contracts, after controlling the diminishment of performance due to age and age-related injury.

Ability, Effort, and Performance

Team owners and general managers observe differences in players' performances through easily available statistics. The difference between innate ability and effort, however, which together account for the differences in players' performances, proves difficult to discern. In a given year, a player's ability generally remains relatively constant, but his effort can change and lead to differences in performance levels. While unlikely that effort changes much during a game, offseason effort and effort between games in-season can vary. Players can exert effort to enhance their productivity by engaging in more intense workouts, restricted leisure activities, and eating healthier diets.

Players alter their effort when their interest dictates. If players believe team owners place greater weights on more recent performances, this motivates players to increase their effort and (ideally) performance during their contract year. But if players perceive that owners value consistent performance, then boosting performance in the contract year remains unlikely. When a player intends to retire at the end of the contract cycle, the incentive to perform and acquire another contract disappears, which is expected to reduce effort and performance during all years of the final contract, including the last year.

Multiple Regression Model to Estimate
Adjusted On Base Plus Slugging Percentage

The dependent variable for this study is OPS100, preferred over OPS because it accounts for league play and the player's home baseball park. This offensive measure accounts for power and reaching base frequently, two events contributing to scoring runs. OPS100 does not depend upon playing time and captures offensive prowess better than RBIs, batting average, HRs, etc.[11] Albert and Bennett find OPS a better predictor of scoring runs than its two components separately.[12] Barry Bonds holds the single-season record for unadjusted OPS at 1.4217 in 2004 when his SLG was .812 and his OBA was .609.[13] During that season he typically walked or hit a home run during a plate appearance.

The suggested regression model for OPS100 for player $\underline{i}$ in season $\underline{t}$ is

$$\overset{(+)}{}\overset{(+)}{}\qquad\overset{(+)}{}\qquad\overset{(-)}{}$$
$$OPS100_{i,t} = \beta_0 + \beta_1{}^* GAMES_{i,t} + \beta_2{}^* PLAYOFF_{i,t} + \beta_3{}^* PROBRET_{i,t} + \beta_4{}^* CONTRACTYR_{i,t}$$
$$+ a_i + u_{i,t,}$$

where: GAMES represents the number of games played; PLAYOFF is a binary variable equal to 1 when the player's team makes the playoffs and 0 otherwise; PROBRET is the estimated probability of retirement; and CONTRACTYR is a dummy variable denoting whether season t is a contract year (=1) or not (=0). The sign above each β coefficient denotes the expected impact on OPS100 given an increase in the independent variable, holding all else constant. The stochastic error comprises two terms impacting a player's performance: a_i is the unobserved player effect representing all time-invariant factors that cannot be measured or observed, such as innate ability, work ethic, drive, etc.; and $\mu_{i,t}$ represents random errors, due to accidents, weather, etc.[14]

The GAMES and PLAYOFF variables serve as control variables to mitigate potential bias. Playing more games helps a player gain confidence at the plate, likely raising his OPS100. Similarly, players with higher OPS100 statistics likely play in more games. The expected positive association between OPS100 and GAMES implies $\beta_1 > 0$. Several reasons suggest $\beta_2 > 0$. If a player's team is in the playoff hunt, he is expected to boost his performance to help his team make the playoffs and potentially win a championship. Teams in a playoff race may trade for high performing hitters at the trade deadline, suggesting another reason for the positive association. A financial incentive to perform better also exists, since team members earn playoff revenues. Lastly, higher OPS100 figures may lead to teams making the playoffs.[15]

At the end of a player's contract, he may or may not sign a new contract. He may willingly choose to retire, retire reluctantly due to advanced age or injuries, or be forced to retire because no team is willing to hire him despite his desire to keep playing. Unfortunately, it is not feasible to know which case prevails for all players. The variable NOPLAY=1 denotes a player is not on an MLB team the year after a contract year and NOPLAY=0 indicates he is on a roster. If NOPLAY switches from 0 to 1 because a player willingly chooses to retire, the expected impact is a decrease in OPS100 due to the lack of incentive to sign another contract. If NOPLAY switches for one of the other reasons for retirement, it may be due to a low OPS100, in which case the impact of NOPLAY on OPS100 is biased. To mitigate the bias and introduce the potential reasons behind retirement-advanced age, injuries, and poor performance, a new variable that predicts the likelihood of retirement is created, PROBRET, following work by Krautmann and Solow.[16] The estimated probability of retirement, discussed and shown later, is used to predict the retirement intention for each player for each year. Using PROBRET instead of NOPLAY as an independent variable reduces bias. Players who choose to retire do not seek another contract, therefore are expected to have a lower OPS100. Additionally, a player with a low OPS100 is more likely to have a higher probability of retirement as he goes unsigned or reluctantly hangs up his cleats. These suggest $\beta_3 < 0$.

MLB hitters are expected to engage in opportunistic behavior and increase their performance during the contract year, thus $\beta_4 > 0$. This presumes team owners value the most recent performance as a solid indicator of future performance, making way for the contract year boost. CONTRACTYR is the only independent variable in (1) that satisfies causal inference, rather than simply correlation, since a player's contract status is known a priori.

Data

Data are collected on all free agent hitters playing during the most recently completed 2006–2011 Collective Bargaining Agreement (CBA) who had six or more years of MLB experience, a minimum of two years of observation, and played in at least seven games in a year. Choosing players under the same CBA helps reduce potential impacts due to changes in CBAs, since all players and team owners are subject to the same contract and free agency guidelines, and revenue-sharing rules.[17] Signing new local and national TV contracts also affect revenue-sharing streams and hence salaries, but these are not captured in the data set.

Hitters with one-year and longer-term contracts are used. Players with longer term contracts generally represent those with higher ability; eliminating those with one-year contracts would potentially bias the results.[18] Ultimately, 256 MLB free agent hitters meet the data selection criteria. The panel dataset is unbalanced, meaning the number of observations per player need not be the same.

ESPN.com's Major League Baseball Free Agent Tracker lists the positions played, age, current team and new team unless re-signed, for all free agents in each year. Players who do not receive another contract are listed as retired or free agent again. Baseball-Reference.com provides OPS100 statistics, the number of games played each season, and the year in which a player debuted in the major leagues. Josh Hermsmeyer unselfishly provided me with the number of days on the disabled list (DL) for all players in 2006–2009 from his MLB Injury Report. Backseat Fan (2010) and FanGraphs (2011) provide the days on the disabled list for players in 2010 and 2011, respectively. For players who change teams via an in-season trade, the playoff status of the final team is used.

Table 43.1 presents the format of the unbalanced data set for two players. The first player is outfielder (POSITION=9) Bobby Abreu, given an identification code of 2, who was 32 years old in 2006. Abreu appears on MLB rosters in all six years of the 2006–2011 CBA and with the Dodgers in 2012, thus NOPLAY = 0 for all of his years. In his 2008 contract year and prior year, he played with the Yankees, having been traded from the Phillies in 2006. The Yankees made the playoffs in 2006 and 2007 but not in 2008, shown by PLAYOFF=1 and 0, respectively. In 2007, Abreu shows an OPS100 of 113 playing in 158 games, compared to his OPS100 of 120 in 156 games in his 2008 contract year. Abreu debuted in the majors in 1996, implying 11 years of experience (EXP) by 2006. With no days on the DL over the six years, DL=0.

Table 43.1. Unbalanced dataset example

Name	CODE	YR	YEAR	TEAM	AGE	CONT-YEAR	OPS100	GAMES	POS.	NOPLAY	EXP	PLAY-OFF	DL
Bobby Abreu	2	1	2006	Phil/Yank	32	0	126	156	9	0	11	1	0
Bobby Abreu	2	2	2007	Yank	33	0	113	158	9	0	12	1	0
Bobby Abreu	2	3	2008	Yank	34	1	120	156	9	0	13	0	0
Bobby Abreu	2	4	2009	Angel	35	0	118	152	9	0	14	1	0
Bobby Abreu	2	5	2010	Angel	36	0	118	154	9	0	15	0	0
Bobby Abreu	2	6	2011	Angel	37	0	105	142	9	0	16	0	0
Moises Alou	4	1	2006	Giant	39	1	132	98	9	0	17	0	50
Moises Alou	4	2	2007	Mets	40	0	137	87	9	0	18	0	76
Moises Alou	4	3	2008	Mets	41	1	107	15	9	1	19	0	163

The second player, outfielder Moises Alou, shows two contract years, in 2006 with the San Francisco Giants and in 2008 with the New York Mets. He had 15 years of MLB experience by 2006 at age 39. Alou did not play on a MLB team in 2009, thus NOPLAY = 1 for 2008. His teams did not make the playoffs in any of the three years. Injuries led to increasing numbers of days on the DL and fewer games played between 2006 and 2007, and by 2008 two major injuries limit Alou's playing time to only 15 games with 163 days on the DL. Three observations for Alou and six for Abreu indicate an unbalanced dataset.

Sorting the descriptive statistics by contract year status, interesting results appear in table 43.2. The differences in means for all variables, except playoffs and days on the DL, are statistically significantly different at p<.001. There are 546 player-year observations for contract years and 470 for non-contract years. The average OPS100 for the contract year is 85.9 compared to 97.2 for the non-contract year, which appears contrary to the contract year boost hypothesis. This contrary result arises chiefly from the ex-post retirements (NOPLAY=1) of 23.1 percent in the contract year observations swamping the 3.2 percent in the non-contract year that may be due to poorer hitters receiving only one-year contracts. Ten fewer average games played in the contract year observations also suggests that less capable hitters have shorter contracts. Comparing the two means proves misleading and too simplistic. Predicting OPS100 via appropriate regression analysis can account for the influence of retirement and other factors to offer a more robust test of the contract year phenomenon.

Table 43.2. Descriptive statistics for
contract year versus non-contract year

	Contract Year					Non-Contract Year				
	N	MEAN	ST. DEV.	MIN.	MAX.	N	MEAN	ST. DEV.	MIN.	MAX.
OPS 100	546	85.9	30.41	-21	182	470	97.2	29.87	-39	192
NOPLAY	546	0.231	0.42	0	1	470	0.032	0.18	0	1
AGE	546	33.59	3.28	26	48	470	32.25	3.02	24	47
DL	546	19.39	33.74	0	163	470	17.53	31.99	0	193
EXP	546	11.6	3.29	7	26	470	10.6	3	6	25
PLAYOFF	546	0.333	0.47	0	1	470	0.309	0.46	0	1
GAMES	546	95.23	40.57	7	162	470	115.49	36.88	10	162

Ordinary Least Squares versus Fixed Effects Estimation

Given panel data, estimation of the model via ordinary least squares (OLS) may be inappropriate due to omitted variable bias that occurs when immeasurable player characteristics in the error term a_i are correlated with some independent variables. For example, a player's ability, captured in a_i, is expected to be positively correlated with the number of games he plays, GAMES, since higher ability players are likely to play in more games. Suppose higher ability players do have higher OPS100s and that playing in more games does increase OPS100. Ignoring the influence of ability, as in the case of OLS, means that GAMES receives more credit than warranted as the cause of the high OPS100. Consequently, the estimated coefficient of β_1 will be positively biased. Similarly, if a player has an exceptional (albeit non-measurable) work ethic, he will likely contribute more to his team success and increase his team's chances of making the playoffs. This implies an expected positive correlation between a_i and PLAYOFF. If high OPS100s are attributable to both strong work ethics and playing on a playoff team, then the estimated coefficient of β_2 will also be positively biased in OLS.[19] Eliminating bias requires a different technique, namely fixed effects (FE) estimation.

Studying a player's motivation to perform across the contract cycle suggests concentrating on the within-player behavior. Estimating how each player alters his effort and performance over his contract cycle must be measured against his metrics, not against those of others. FE estimation calculates the mean of each variable over time for each player and subtracts it from the actual observation for each year to demean the data. For example, Bobby Abreu's average OPS100 over his six years of playing is 116.5, which is subtracted from his actual OPS100 for each of his six years to yield six deviations or demeaned observations for his OPS100. After doing so for all players, the demeaned dependent variable of OPS100 is regressed on the demeaned independent variables via OLS producing the fixed effects within-player coefficients. Time-invariant unobserved traits in a_i, such as ability, have demeaned values of zero, eliminating them from affecting outcomes. Dropping out the unobserved traits via demeaning eliminates correlations and associated biases between unobserved traits and independent variables.[20]

While FE estimation addresses bias and focuses on changes in players' behaviors, it comes with a cost. Finding statistical significance for estimated coefficients may be compromised. The variation in OPS100 across 256 players is expected to be much greater than the variation in OPS100 for individual players over their free agency careers. For example, the dataset shows a range in OPS100 from -39 to 192 with a standard deviation of 30.67, while Bobby Abreu's only vary between 105 and 126 with a 7.09 standard deviation. Other players generally have smaller OPS100 deviations too. Since FE estimation concentrates on the within-player variation and dismisses the between-player differences in OPS100, it reduces the sample variation in OPS100 and lessens the likelihood of statistical significance for the estimated β coefficients. Demeaning the data also reduces the degrees of freedom by 255, further diminishing chances of statistical significance. Therefore, finding a statistically significant FE result for β_4, in spite of these perils, occurs because evidence from the dataset is compelling.

Estimating the Probability of Retiring

Players generally retire at the end of a contract. However, the predicted probability of retiring can change over time until actual retirement occurs and it should be considered by the team owner during negotiations. A player's likelihood of retiring depends on how many years he has played, how many days have been spent on the DL, and his offensive performance per Krautmann and Solow.[21] Equation (2) denotes the regression equation for the probability of retirement for player i in season t as

$$PROBRET_{i,t} = \alpha_0 + \alpha_1 {}^* EXP_{i,t} + \alpha_2 {}^* EXP2_{i,t} + \alpha_3 {}^* DL_{i,t} + \alpha_4 {}^* OPS100_{i,t} + a_i + v_t + u_{i,t,}$$

Players with more years of experience are expected to have increasingly greater likelihoods of retiring since they have signed several contracts and amassed income. Additionally, the aging process that accompanies years of experience takes its toll on bodies often coinciding with familial demands to be home more often. With EXP2 representing years of experience squared, $\alpha_1 > 0$ and $\alpha_2 > 0$ are expected. More days on the DL are expected to increase PROBRET, i.e., $\alpha_3 > 0$, since injuries inhibit playing ability and reduce interest by team owners. If a decline in OPS100 portends reduced future performance, it increases retirement likelihood, $\alpha_4 < 0$. The stochastic error comprises both the unobserved time-invariant player traits a_i and unmeasured time-variant traits v_t such as family issues.

Using NOPLAY as the dependent variable, estimating (2) via FE leads to the linear probability model (3) below. Since NOPLAY is determined after the season, all of the independent variables yield causal inference. The p-values for one-tailed hypotheses tests for the estimated slope coefficients are in parentheses below the estimates.

$$PROBRET = -3.38 + .157*EXP + .006*EXP^2 + .0004*DL - .004*OPS100$$
$$(.0475) \quad (.0001) \quad (.135) \quad (.001)$$
$$\text{Correctly Predicted} = 94\%[23]$$

Days on the disabled list do not statistically predict likelihood of retiring, but remaining variables do. Each additional year of MLB experience increases the likelihood of retiring exponentially and a one point increase in OPS100 reduces it the probability of retirement by .4 percent. Since the -3.38 intercept pertains to the last player's last year, the predicted output for all players for all years occur as changes from -3.38. For brevity, they are not provided. For example, Bobby Abreu could have retired after his 2008 contract year, but his predicted probability was .001 (near zero) and he did not retire.[22] His likelihood rose to 1.5 percent in 2009 due to his two-point decrease in OPS100 and extra year of experience. By 2010, despite no change in his OPS100 from 2009, the additional year playing leads to a probability of 12.7 percent. In 2011, his sixteenth year in the majors and drop in OPS100 to 104 increases his likelihood to 33 percent. For Moises Alou the model predicted a 60 percent chance of retirement following his 2008 season, when he did in fact retire. The predicted values of PROBRET for all 1,106 observations are calculated and ultimately used to estimate (1).

Results from Estimating OPS 100

Regression model (1) derives from two improvements in the model estimated in O'Neill.[23] First, traditional theory suggests that as players age, their offensive performance increases at a decreasing rate as they become more comfortable in hitting, until it peaks, and eventually declines as age depreciates hitting skills. O'Neill includes the quadratic form of age, AGE and AGE squared, as independent variables impacting OPS100. Additionally, O'Neill's PROBRET estimation employs performance, injury, and the quadratic form of years of experience in place of age. O'Neill finds the odd result that OPS100 increases at an increasing rate after age 33. Having age enter PROBRET through its correlation with years of experience, and then using PROBRET along with age in predicting OPS100, may have led to that usual result. Second, O'Neill segregated catchers and shortstops as defensive players, believing that they sport lower OPS100 statistics in exchange for better defensive play. However, since FE estimation demeans the data and players who are shortstops or catchers generally do not change positions, it does not seem appropriate to segregate them.

The 1,016 player-year observations yielding equation (4) presents the FE multiple regression equation for predicted OPS100 (OPS100^) with one-tailed p-values in parenthesis.[24] The Buse-R^2 indicates that 78 percent of the variation in adjusted OPS is explained by the model with these independent variables.[25] Games played and being on a playoff team indicate the expected positive sign, but they are not statistically significant at 5 percent.

$$OPS100^\wedge = 114.52 + .03*GAMES + .60*PLAYOFF - 100.34*PROBRET +$$
$$(.091) \quad (.321) \quad (.0001)$$

$$+ 6.11* CONTRACTYR \qquad R^2 = .78$$
$$(.0001)$$

The highly significant PROBRET coefficient says that a one percentage point increase in the likelihood of retiring reduces expected adjusted OPS by 1.0034 points or 1.1 percent decline relative to the mean OPS100 of 91.12. A 10-percentage point increase in the likelihood of retiring, about one half standard deviation in PROBRET, reduces predicted adjusted OPS by 10.034 points.

The estimated model provides evidence of the contract year phenomenon, but the phenomenon depends upon the likelihood of retirement. If a player is in a contract year, holding all else constant, the expected increase in his adjusted OPS is 6.11 points or 6.7 percent increase relative to the mean. But for two otherwise identical players, one in his contract year and the other not, the expected OPS100 for the former is 6.11 points higher. Using the Grossman heuristic that every .100 increase in OPS raises salary by $2,000,000 and converting OPS to OPS100 enables monetizing the 6.11 bump.[26] The contract year boost is expected to increase annual salary by $470,000, about 15.2 percent of the average salary of $3.1 million in 2011.

The impact from the likelihood of retiring offsets the contract year boost. Each additional percentage point increase in a contract year player's retirement probability reduces the 6.11 boost by 1.0034. A complete offset of no expected change in OPS100 during the contract year occurs with a jump in retirement likelihood of about 6.1 (6.11/1.0034) points. With years of experience driving retirement likelihood exponentially, a decline in expected OPS100 reasonably appears at the end of contracts for players with many years of experience. For instance, a 10-point increase in the probability of retirement leads to a 3.9 (6.11–10.034) decline in expected OPS100 during a contract year.

Conclusions

By using FE estimation to account for changes in each player's behavior and reducing bias due to unobserved player traits pervasive with OLS estimation, the data show strong support for the contract year boost. From FE estimation, two important contract year findings follow. First, the adjusted OPS of a free agent hitter in his contract year is expected to be 6.7 percent greater than in non-contract year periods—higher than previously noted studies. Second, "retiring" players show a decline in their contract year performance and any models which ignore retirement will be mis-specified. OLS estimation of the same dataset (not shown) yields a negative impact on OPS100 during the contract year, albeit not statistically significant. This biased result coincides with the contrary findings in table 43.2 that show lower average OPS100 for contract year observations than non-contract year observations.

The model may prove helpful during contract negotiations as one can compare a hitter's actual performance relative to expectations. Take Albert Pujols as an example. In 2008 and 2009, his OPS100 statistics of 192 and 189 greatly exceeded his predicted statistics of 175 and 176, respectively. In 2010, his OPS100 dropped to 173 to his expected value. In 2011—his contract year— the model predicts an OPS100 of 155, yet he hit only 148. Despite two years of declining OPS100 values that failed to meet the model's expectations, the Angels still signed Pujols to a 10-year, $240 million contract. His OPS100 has continued to decline, dropping to 138 in 2012 and 117 in 2013. This type of post-contract performance leads me to the next related research project: whether players shirk after getting a new long-term contract.

NOTES

1. John Lowe & John Erardi, "Baseball Hall of Fame Manager Sparky Anderson Dies at 76," *USA Today*, http://usatoday30.usatoday.com/sports/baseball/2010-11-04-sparky -anderson-obit_N.htm (accessed July 20, 2014).
2. Heather O'Neill, "Do Major League Baseball Hitters Engage in Opportunistic Behavior?," *International Advances in Economic Research* 19(3) (2013): 215–32.
3. Baseball-Reference.com. "Major League Baseball Statistics and History," Sports Reference LLC, http://www.baseball-reference.com/players, accessed September 28, 2012.

4. Players with year options or incentive clauses written into contracts maintain motivation to boost performance.

5. Heather O'Neill, "Do Major League Baseball Hitters Engage in Opportunistic Behavior?"

6. Joel Maxcy, Rodney Fort, and Anthony Krautmann, "The effectiveness of incentive mechanisms in Major League Baseball," *Journal of Sports Economics*, 3(3) (2002): 246–55.

7. Phil Birnbaum, "Do Players Outperform in Their Free-agent Year?," http://philbirnbaum.com, accessed April 27, 2009; Dayn Perry, "Do Players Perform Better in Contract Years?," *Baseball Between the Numbers* (New York: Basic, 2006), 199–206.

8. See Heather O'Neill, "Do Major League Baseball Hitters Engage in Opportunistic Behavior?" for differences in outcomes due to OLS versus FE estimation.

9. Michael Dinerstein, "Free Agency and Contract Options: How Major League Baseball Teams Value Players," PhD. diss, Stanford University, May 11, 2007.

10. Matthew Hummel and Heather O'Neill, "Do Major League Baseball Hitters Come Up Big in Their Contract Year?," *Virginia Economics Journal* 16, (2011): 13–25.

11. Jonah Keri, "What's the Matter with RBI? and Other Traditional Statistics," *Baseball Between the Numbers* (New York: Basic Books, 2006), 1–13.

12. Jim Albert and Jay Bennett, *Curve Ball: Baseball, Statistics, and the Role of Chance in the Game* (New York: Copernicus, 2001).

13. Baseball-Reference.com, "Major League Baseball Statistics and History" Sports Reference LLC, http://www.baseball-reference.com/players, accessed September 28, 2012.

14. One could include v_t in the error term to denote time-variant, unobserved or measured traits such as changes in family structure. The effects were tested econometrically, found to be insignificant, and excluded in (1). Lawrence Kahn, "Free Agency, Long-Term Contracts and Compensation in Major League Baseball: Estimates from Panel Data," *Review of Economics and Statistics* 75(1) (1993): 157–64.

15. Playoff teams generally have better players and their surrounding presence can enhance a hitter's performance, which introduces the aforementioned measurement error associated with seeking an individual's performance.

16. Anthony Krautmann & John Solow, "The Dynamics of Performance over the Duration of Major League Baseball Long-term Contracts," *Journal of Sports Economics* 10(1) (2009): 6–22.

17. Although the CBA was signed at the end of the 2006 season, I include player observations from 2006. As noted at the time, the negotiations taking place during the 2006 season proceeded without much acrimony, in fact yielding ratification prior to expiration of the previous CBA. I am assuming the players were aware and in agreement of what the new agreement would bring, thus working with shared

expectations and incentives. See "MLB players, owners announce five year playing deal," http://sports.espn.go.com/mlb/news/story?id=2637615, October 25, 2006.

18. Kahn, "Free Agency."

19. See Heather O'Neill, "Do Major League Baseball Hitters Engage in Opportunistic Behavior?" for in-depth analysis of bias mitigated by FE estimation.

20. Unfortunately, the impact of time-invariant observable traits, such as race, height, etc. cannot be estimated since they too would drop out of the demeaned variables.

21. Anthony Krautmann and John Solow, "The Dynamics of Performance over the Duration of Major League Baseball Long-term Contracts," *Journal of Sports Economics* 10(1) (2009): 6–22.

22. To preclude predicted linear probabilities below zero, all negative predictions are assigned a probability of .001, essentially zero.

23. Heather O'Neill, "Do Major League Baseball Hitters Engage in Opportunistic Behavior?"

24. The Hausman test with p<.0001 rejected random effects in favor of fixed effects. Random effects assumes no correlation between traits in a_i and any independent variables.

25. When ex-post retirement, NOPLAY, is used instead of the predicted probability of retirement, the Buse-R2 falls to .68, suggesting less predictive power.

26. Mitchell Grossman, Timothy Kimsey, Joshua Moreen & Matthew Owings, "Steroids in Major League Baseball" (2007), http://faculty.haas.berkeley.edu/rjmorgan/mba211/steroids%20and%20major%20league%20baseball.pdf, accessed October 23, 2012.

44

The Double Victory Campaign and the Campaign to Integrate Baseball

DUKE GOLDMAN

Few subjects have been studied more by SABR members than the attempts toward integration in baseball—or resistance against it—in the many years before Jackie Robinson signed with the Dodgers. Duke Goldman is a longtime SABR member and brilliant researcher who has specialized in baseball integration and the Negro Leagues. His extraordinary essay, "1933–1962: The Business Meetings of Negro League Baseball," received the McFarland-SABR Research Award in 2018. In this article, which appeared in the SABR book *Baseball's Business: The Winter Meetings, 1958–2016*, he tells the story of how the Black press paired the causes of fighting fascism overseas and fighting racism at home.

The war against the forces of fascism in Nazi Germany and Japan mirrored another war fought in the trenches of American life—that between the entrenched forces of racism and its ugly operating system of segregation, and a Black populace straining to achieve equal treatment in a land ostensibly promising "liberty and justice for all."

Coincidentally, the tenure of Adolf Hitler as the head of the National Socialist government in Germany–1933–1945—mirrored the time frame of an informal campaign to integrate major-league baseball. In 1933 several sportswriters began to publicly question why major-league baseball should not have Black performers. Several of these writers wrote in the mainstream press—Heywood Broun of the *New York World-Telegram* and Jimmy Powers of the *Daily News* both came out against baseball's color line early that year, with other notable sportswriters such as Dan Parker of the *New York Daily Mirror* and Shirley Povich of the *Washington Post* weighing in later on during this period. The *Daily Worker*, the most prominent Communist newspaper, also produced hundreds of columns, starting in 1933, castigating major-league baseball for excluding Black players. But not surprisingly, the prime participants in the battle to integrate baseball were the members of the Black press, especially Sam Lacy and Wendell Smith. During his lengthy career (extending into the twenty-first century), Lacy wrote for several important Black newspapers and was sports editor of the *Baltimore Afro-American*. Smith plied his trade during this time frame for the *Pittsburgh Courier*.[1] The *Courier* was the leading Black newspaper of the time, reaching a high of 350,000 in circulation in 1945—in part because of the bold stands it took on the issues of the day.[2]

The *Courier*, with Smith as its sports editor, stepped up its campaign to integrate baseball in 1942, while at the same time championing a cause expressed in a letter it published on January 31, 1942, written by 26-year-old cafeteria worker James G. Thompson. He asked: "Is the kind of America I know worth defending?" His answer to this question stressed that dedication to victory abroad must be paired with a fight for victory against similar forces at home: "The first V for victory over our enemies without, the second V for victory over our enemies within. For surely those who perpetrate those ugly prejudices here are seeking to destroy our democratic form of government just as surely as the Axis forces."[3] This crusade came to be known as the Double Victory campaign.

Thompson's letter squarely addressed the "American Dilemma" examined by Swedish sociologist Gunnar Myrdal in his landmark study of America's race problem, to be published in 1944. Myrdal's study explicated what he deemed a failure of the United States to exemplify its "creed"—that of a country dedicated to equality and liberty for all—by the relegation of the Black population to second-class status.[4] Thompson's letter presaged Myrdal's work by asking how America could fight a war abroad against prejudice and blind hatred while failing to address its racial issues at home.

One of those racial issues was the continuing segregation of the national pastime. As the Double V campaign swept Black (and to a limited degree, even elements of White) America, especially in 1942 but to a lesser degree until v-j day in 1945, wartime Negro League baseball and some of its prominent figures championed the cause. One such champion, Cumberland "Cum" Posey, owner of the legendary Negro League powerhouse Homestead Grays, suggested in his weekly *Courier* column, called "Posey's Points," that every team in organized Negro baseball wear a Double V symbol on its uniform, stating his belief that the cause of "victory abroad and at home is more vital than any athletic victory any of us may attain."[5] Posey was prominent among those who worried about the future of the Negro Leagues if the White major leagues were integrated, so his eloquent dedication to the cause of Double Victory is noteworthy, as "victory at home" clearly would include ending employment discrimination such as the color line in baseball.

Another Negro League owner, Effa Manley, engaged in many activities supporting the war effort, including an active promotion of the Double V campaign.[6] Similarly, Satchel Paige biographer Donald Spivey indicated that Paige was a supporter of the Double V.[7] Paige was not shy in expressing his opinions, as he proved in the run-up to the 1942 East-West All-Star game, Negro League baseball's preeminent showcase.

During the heat of the summer and the heyday of the Double V campaign, Paige felt compelled to speak over the public-address system to a throng of over 48,000 attendees before he came on in relief in the seventh inning. The reason: to deny reports that he questioned whether integration of major-league baseball was possible at that time. Paige claimed he was misquoted: He merely said that he doubted that a major-league team would pay him a salary commensurate with the $37,000 he earned in 1941 and that it would be better for a team of Black players to integrate baseball rather than an individual who would face Jim Crow alone.[8]

Fans watched Satchel as he "gummed up the program with a three-minute pointless statement"[9] in trying to defuse the controversy he created, and subsequently lost the All-Star game for the West, his first such loss after three earlier All-Star game wins. Meanwhile, the large crowd also saw symbols of the Double V displayed and distributed. The front page of the August 22 edition of the *Courier* carried a photograph of a woman wearing a Double V logo on her back selling "vv" buttons at the game. Inside the edition, a picture of a woman flashing "vv" with her fingers was captioned "At Chicago East-West All-Star Game."[10]

By the time of the East-West All-Star game, the Double V campaign as covered by the *Courier* was slowing down, although it was by no means at an end. Starting with its February 7, 1942, edition through the end of 1942, the *Courier* printed 970 Double V items, peaking with 50 such items in its April 11 issue. The campaign spread throughout Black America—"there were Double V dances and parades, Double V flag-raising ceremonies, Double V baseball games between professional Black teams, Double V beauty contests, Double V poems, and a double V song, 'Yankee Doodle Tan.'"[11] In the June 13, 1942, issue the *Courier* reported on a Double V game in St. Louis. The thousands who attended watched as the New York Black Yankees defeated the Birmingham Black Barons, 8–4. They also saw a drum and bugle corps form a Double V on the mound, and a $50 Double V certificate being presented to the winner of a Miss Mid-West contest.[12]

The Double V campaign was also supported by other Black newspapers. In another instance where Black baseball was involved, the *Atlanta Daily World* reported on what it called a "true double-V victory" by the Birmingham Black Barons winning an opening day Negro American League doubleheader over the Memphis Red Sox in late May 1943. The article mentioned as well that a high-school band formed a "V" before the game—the first victory of the day.[13] All the prominent Black newspapers of the day—the *Chicago Defender*, the *Baltimore Afro-American*, the *Cleveland Call and Post*, the *New York Amsterdam News*, the *World*, and many others—reported on the progress of the Double V campaign even if it was not with the sustained attention of the *Courier*.

During 1942 especially but also throughout the war, sportswriters Smith and Ches Washington of the *Courier*, Fay Young of the *Defender*, Mabray "Doc" Kountze of the *Call and Post*, Dan Burley of the *Amsterdam News*, and Lacy and Art Carter of the *Afro-American* were promoting the breaking of the color line, often invoking the theme, if not the explicit terminology, of the Double V. Washington told the story of a victorious boxer who invoked the themes of Double V. He also trumpeted the triumphs of Black track stars and boxers over the "enemy abroad" while wishing that baseball stars like Josh Gibson be given a chance at home.[14] Smith used military terminology as he suggested that Negro fans organize and fight the battle for baseball integration with a "concentrated, nationwide action" much like that of the Double V campaign.[15] And on the same day, April 11, 1942, that the *Courier* provided its peak coverage of the Double V campaign, Kountze echoed the words of the American Negro Press's Claude Barnett that "if a colored man is good enough to fight for his own country, he certainly ought to be good enough to work here" as Kountze made the case that "something ought to be done. This very year. I mean, yeah, 1942" to integrate major-league baseball.[16]

While the Double V campaign's momentum slowed down throughout the war, it did not disappear entirely from the pages of the *Courier* until victory was declared over Japan in September 1945. Until then, the *Courier* continued the practice started at the commencement of the Double V campaign of putting a "v v" at the end of each article to separate it from the article appearing beneath it. Meanwhile, the calls for baseball integration continued to build to a crescendo in the *Courier* and the other Black newspapers from 1942 through the end of the war. In the summer of 1942, the Black press reported that Bill Benswanger, owner of the Pirates, would be trying out Negro League stars Leon Day, Willie Wells, Josh Gibson, and Sam Bankhead. It never came to pass. At the end of 1943, the Negro Newspaper Publishers Association met with the American and National Leagues. Baseball Commissioner Kenesaw M. Landis, an ardent segregationist, went on record as not being against the move to place Negro players in the major leagues. Everyone knew otherwise. Yet *Courier* president Ira Lewis spoke at this meeting, and invoked the concept of national unity in suggesting that baseball integration would bring joy to 15 million Black Americans and millions of White Americans as well.[17] Even though the *Courier* was no longer actively promoting the Double V by then, it was certainly continuing the "campaign for the integration of Negro players into the major leagues,"[18] as described by Wendell Smith in late 1943. As history would later prove, a partial victory against racism at home—the signing of Jackie Robinson by the Brooklyn Dodgers—would virtually coincide with the victory against fascism abroad in the fall of 1945.

Jackie Robinson had his own indirect connection to Double V. According to essayist and cultural critic Gerald Early, Jackie likely would not have become an officer in the Army without the publicity created by the Double V, along with a behind-the-scenes campaign started in 1937 by *Pittsburgh Courier* owner Robert Vann to start the process of getting Black officers in the military.[19] Joe Louis also applied pressure on the military to commission Black officers; Jackie said that without Louis "the color line in baseball would not have been broken for another ten years."[20] Louis was another supporter of the Double V campaign,[21] and his wife, Marva, was the Double V girl of the week in the *Courier* of April 11, 1942.[22]

In the end, there is a consensus among historians who have researched the Double V, the Black press, and African American history. The successful campaign to integrate baseball naturally fit within the larger themes of Double Victory. As Henry Louis Gates put it, one of the two most important legacies of the Double Victory campaign is that "through the columns of its sportswriter, Wendell Smith . . . it doggedly fought against segregation in professional sports, contributing without a doubt to the Brooklyn Dodgers' decision to sign Jackie Robinson."[23] The other legacy was the ultimate desegregation of the U.S. Army by Harry Truman in 1948. A double victory—integrating baseball and one year later, the military—had now been accomplished. But the larger struggle for racial justice had just begun.

NOTES

1. On sportswriters supporting baseball integration, see Brian Carroll, *When to Stop the Cheering? The Black Press, the Black Community, and the Integration of Professional Baseball* (New York: Routledge, 2007), 69–87; Chris Lamb, *Conspiracy of Silence: Sportswriters and the Long Campaign to Desegregate Baseball* (Lincoln: University of Nebraska Press, 2012), 3–21; Arnold Rampersad, *Jackie Robinson: A Biography* (New York: Alfred A. Knopf, 1997), 120–21.

2. Patrick S. Washburn, *The African-American Newspaper: Voice of Freedom* (Evanston IL: Northwestern University Press, 2006), 180.

3. *Pittsburgh Courier*, January 31, 1942.

4. Gunnar Myrdal, *An American Dilemma, Volume 1: The Negro Problem and Modern Democracy* (1944; rpt. New Brunswick NJ: Transaction, 1996), 8.

5. *Pittsburgh Courier*, April 18, 1942.

6. According to Sarah L. Trembanis, *The Set-Up Men: Race, Culture and Resistance in Black Baseball* (Jefferson NC: McFarland, 2014), 118.

7. Donald Spivey, *If Only You Were White: The Life of Leroy "Satchel" Paige* (Columbia: University of Missouri Press, 2012), 186.

8. Associated Press, August 6, 1942, reprinted in *Chicago Defender*, August 15, 1942; *New York Amsterdam News*, August 15, 1942; *Baltimore Afro-American*, August 22, 1942; *Pittsburgh Courier*, August 22, 1942.

9. Art Carter, "From the Bench," *Baltimore Afro-American*, August 22, 1942.

10. *Pittsburgh Courier*, August 22, 1942, 1, 13.

11. Patrick S. Washburn, "The Pittsburgh Courier's Double V Campaign in 1942," *American Journalism* 74, no. 2 (1986): 73, 74.

12. *Pittsburgh Courier*, June 13, 1942.

13. *Atlanta Daily World*, June 1, 1943.

14. Ches Washington, "Sez Ches," *Pittsburgh Courier*, March 21, 1942.

15. *Pittsburgh Courier*, July 25, 1942.

16. *Cleveland Call and Post*, April 11, 1942.

17. *Pittsburgh Courier*, December 11, 1943.

18. *Pittsburgh Courier*, December 25, 1943.

19. Author conversation with Gerald Early, October 11, 2012.

20. Rampersad, *Jackie Robinson*, 92.

21. Spivey, *If Only You Were White*, 186.

22. *Pittsburgh Courier*, April 11, 1942.

23. Henry Louis Gates, *What Was Black America's Double War?*, theroot.com/articles/history/2013/05/double_v_campaign_during_work.

45

The Black Sox Scandal

WILLIAM F. LAMB

The creation of the Black Sox Scandal Research Committee in 2008 ignited a new interest in the subject within SABR. Its renewed attention culminated in the 2015 publication of the book *Scandal on the South Side: The 1919 Chicago White Sox*, in which this article appeared. Bill Lamb, a retired state and county prosecutor, has been publishing articles on nineteenth-century and Deadball Era baseball for many years, and has always been especially drawn to the Black Sox in his study. His book, *Black Sox in the Courtroom: The Grand Jury, Criminal Trial and Civil Litigation*, broke new ground in its detailed examination of the long legal trail of the scandal.

Over the decades, major-league baseball has produced a host of memorable teams, but only one infamous one—the 1919 Chicago White Sox. Almost a century after the fact, the exact details of the affair known in sports lore as the Black Sox Scandal remain murky and subject to debate. But one central and indisputable truth endures: Talented members of that White Sox club conspired with professional gamblers to rig the outcome of the 1919 World Series.

Another certainty attends the punishment imposed in the matter. The permanent banishment from the game of those players implicated in the conspiracy, while perhaps an excessive sanction in certain cases, achieved an overarching objective. Game-fixing virtually disappeared from the major-league landscape after that penalty was imposed on the Black Sox.

Something else is equally indisputable. The finality of the expulsion edict rendered by Commissioner Kenesaw Mountain Landis has not quelled the controversy surrounding the corruption of the 1919 Series. Nor has public fascination abated. To the contrary, interest in the scandal has only grown over the years, in time even spawning a publishing subgenre known as Black Sox literature. No essay-length narrative can hope to capture the entirety of events explored in the present Black Sox canon, or to address all the beliefs of individual Black Sox aficionados. The following, therefore, is no more than one man's rendition of the scandal.

The plot to transform the 1919 World Series into a gambling insiders' windfall did not occur in a vacuum. The long-standing, often toxic relationship between baseball and gambling dates from the sport's infancy, with game-fixing having been exposed as early as 1865. Postseason championship play was not immune to such corruption. The first modern World Series of 1903 was jeopardized by gambler attempts to bribe Boston Americans catcher Lou Criger into throwing games. Never-substantiated rumors about the integrity of play dogged a number of ensuing fall classics.

The architects of the Black Sox Scandal have never been conclusively identified. Many subscribe to the notion that the plot was originally concocted by White Sox first baseman Chick Gandil and Boston bookmaker Joseph "Sport" Sullivan. Surviving grand jury testimony portrays Gandil and White Sox pitching staff ace Eddie Cicotte as the primary instigators of the fix. In any event, the fix plot soon embraced many other actors, both in uniform and out. Indeed, dissection of the scandal has long been complicated by its scope, for there was not a lone plot to rig the Series, but actually two or more, each with its own peculiar cast of characters.

Since it was first deployed as a trial stratagem by Black Sox defense lawyers in June 1921, motivation for the Series fix has been ascribed to the miserliness of Chicago club owner Charles A. Comiskey. The assertion is specious. Comiskey paid his charges the going rate and then some. In fact, salary data recently made available establish that the 1919 Chicago White Sox had the second highest player payroll in the major leagues, with stalwarts like second baseman Eddie Collins, catcher Ray Schalk, third baseman Buck Weaver, and pitcher Cicotte being at or near the top of the pay scale for their positions.

But the White Sox clubhouse was an unhealthy place, with the team long riven by faction. One clique was headed by team captain Eddie Collins, Ivy League-educated and self-assured to the point of arrogance. Aligned with Cocky Collins were Schalk, spitballer Red Faber, and outfielders Shano Collins and Nemo Leibold. The other, a more hardscrabble group united in envy, if not outright hatred, of the socially superior Collins, was headed by tough guy Gandil and the more amiable Cicotte. Also in their corner were Weaver, shortstop/fix enforcer Swede Risberg, outfielder Happy Felsch, and utilityman Fred McMullin.

According to the grand jury testimony of Eddie Cicotte, his faction first began to discuss the feasibility of throwing the upcoming World Series during a train trip late in the regular season. Even before the White Sox clinched the 1919 pennant, Cicotte started to feel out Bill Burns, a former American League pitcher turned gambler, about financing a Series fix. Again according to Cicotte, the Sox were envious of the $10,000 payoffs rumored to have been paid certain members of the Chicago Cubs for dumping the 1918 Series against the Boston Red Sox. The lure of a similar score was enhanced by the low prospect of discovery or punishment.

Although they surfaced periodically, reports of player malfeasance were not taken seriously, routinely dismissed by the game's establishment and denigrated in the sporting press. And the imposition of sanctions arising from gambling-related activity seemed to have been all but abandoned. Even charges of player corruption lodged by as revered a figure as Christy Mathewson and corroborated by affidavit were deemed insufficient grounds for disciplinary action, as attested by the National League's recent exoneration of long-suspected game-fixer Hal Chase. By the fall of 1919, therefore, the fix of the World Series could reasonably be viewed from a player standpoint as a low risk/high reward proposition.

In mid-September the Gandil-Cicotte crew committed to the Series fix during a meeting at the Ansonia Hotel in New York. Likelihood of the scheme's success was bolstered by the recruitment of the White Sox's No. 2 starter, Lefty Williams, and the club's batting star, outfielder Joe Jackson. In follow-up conversation with Burns, the parties agreed that the World Series would be lost to the National League champion Cincinnati Reds in exchange for a $100,000 payoff.

Financing a payoff of that magnitude was beyond Burns's means, and efforts to secure backing from gambling elements in Philadelphia came up empty. Thereafter, Burns and sidekick Billy Maharg approached a potential fix underwriter of vast resource, New York City underworld financier Arnold Rothstein, known as the "Big Bankroll." In all probability, word of the Series plot had reached Rothstein well before Burns and Maharg made their play. According to all concerned (Burns, Maharg, and Rothstein), Rothstein flatly turned down the proposal that he finance the Series fix. And from there, the plot to corrupt the 1919 World Series thickened.

The prospect of fix financing was revived by Hal Chase who, by means unknown, had also gotten wind of the scheme. Chase put Burns in touch with one of sportsdom's shadiest characters, former world featherweight boxing champ Abe Attell. A part-time Rothstein bodyguard and a full-time hustler, the Little Champ was constantly on the lookout for a score. Accompanied by an associate named "Bennett" (later identified as Des Moines gambler David Zelcer), Attell met with Burns and informed him that Rothstein had reconsidered the fix proposition and was now willing to finance it. The credulous Burns thereupon hastened to Cincinnati to rendezvous with the players on the eve of Game One.

In the meantime, the campaign to fix the Series had opened a second front. Shortly before the White Sox were scheduled to leave for Cincinnati, Gandil, Cicotte, Weaver, and other fix enlistees met privately at the Warner Hotel in Chicago. A mistrustful Cicotte demanded that his $10,000 fix share be paid in full before the team departed for Cincinnati. He then left the gathering to socialize elsewhere. The others remained to hear two men identified as "Sullivan" and "Brown" from New York. A confused Lefty Williams later testified that he was unsure if these men were the gamblers financing the fix or their representatives.

The first Warner Hotel fixer has always been identified as Gandil's Boston pal, Sport Sullivan, but the true identity of "Brown" would remain a mystery to fix investigators. Decades later, first Rothstein biographer Leo Katcher and thereafter Abe Attell asserted that "Brown" was actually Nat Evans, a capable Rothstein subordinate and Rothstein's junior partner in several gambling casino ventures. Whoever "Brown" was, $10,000 in cash had been placed under the bed pillow in Cicotte's hotel room before the evening was over. The Series fix was now on, in earnest.

The Warner Hotel conclave was unknown to Burns, then trying to finalize his own fix arrangement with the players. He, Attell, and Bennett/Zelcer met with all the corrupted players, save Joe Jackson, at the Sinton Hotel in Cincinnati sometime prior to the Series opener. After considerable wrangling, it was agreed that the players would be paid off in $20,000 installments following each White Sox loss in the best-five-of-nine Series.

Later that evening, Burns encountered an old acquaintance, Chicago sportswriter Hugh Fullerton. Like most experts, Fullerton had confidently predicted a White Sox triumph. But something in the tone of Burns's assurance that the Reds were a "sure thing" unsettled Fullerton. Burns made it sound as though the Series had already been decided. Almost simultaneously, betting odds on the Series shifted dramatically, with a last-minute surge of money transforming the once-underdog Reds into a slight Series favorite. To Fullerton and other baseball insiders, something ominous seemed to be afoot.

To those unaware of these developments, the Game One matchup typified the inequity between the two sides. On the mound for the White Sox was 29-game-winner Eddie Cicotte, a veteran member of Chicago's 1917 World Series champions and one of the game's finest pitchers. Starting for Cincinnati was left-hander Dutch Ruether, who, prior to his 1919 season's 19-win breakout, had won exactly three major-league games.

Aside from control master Cicotte plunking Reds leadoff batter Morrie Rath with his second pitch, the match proceeded unremarkably in the early going. Then Cicotte suddenly fell apart in the fourth. By the time stunned Chicago manager Kid Gleason had taken him out, the White Sox were behind 6–1. The final score was a lopsided Cincinnati 9, Chicago 1. Following their delivery of the promised loss, the players were stiffed, fix paymaster Attell reneging on the $20,000 payment due.

The White Sox fulfilled their side of the fix agreement in Game Two, in which Lefty Williams's sudden bout of wildness in the fourth inning spelled the difference in a 4–2 Cincinnati victory. With the corrupted players now owed $40,000, Burns was hard-pressed to get even a fraction of that from Attell. Accusations of a double-cross greeted Burns's delivery of only $10,000 to the players after the Game Two defeat. Still, he and Maharg accepted Gandil's assurance that the Sox would lose Game Three. The two fix middlemen were then wiped out, losing their entire wagering stake when the White Sox posted a 3–0 victory behind the pitching of Dickey Kerr.

Whether the Series fix continued after Game Two is a matter of dispute. Joe Jackson would later inform the press that the Black Sox had tried to throw Game Three, only to be thwarted by Kerr's superb pitching performance. Those maintaining that the White Sox were now playing to win often cite the decisive two-RBI single of erstwhile fix ringleader Chick Gandil.

With the Series now standing two games to one in Cincinnati's favor, Cicotte retook the mound for Game Four, the most controversial of the Series. Locked in a pitching duel with Reds fireballer Jimmy Ring, Cicotte exhibited the pitching artistry that had been expected from him at the outset. His fielding, however, was another matter, with the game turning on two egregious defensive misplays by Cicotte in the Cincinnati fifth. Those miscues provided the margin in a 2–0 Cincinnati victory.

Cicotte later maintained that he had tried his utmost to win Game Four, but whether true or not, Eddie had received little offensive help from his teammates. The White Sox, both Clean and Black variety, were mired in a horrendous batting slump that would see the American League's most potent lineup go an astonishing 26 consecutive innings without scoring. Chicago bats were silent again in Game Five, managing but three hits in a 5–0 setback that pushed the Sox to the brink of Series elimination.

Meanwhile, uncertainty reigned in gambling quarters. After the unscripted White Sox victory in Game Three, Burns, reportedly acting at the behest of Abe Attell, approached Gandil about resuming the fix. Gandil spurned him. But whether that brought the curtain down on the debasement of the 1919 World Series is far from clear. The Burns/Attell/Zelcer combine was not the only gambler group that the White Sox had taken money from. Admissions later made by the corrupted players make it clear that far more than the $10,000 post–Game Two payoff was disbursed during the Series. But who made these payoffs; when/where/how they were made; how much fix money in total was paid out by gambler interests, and how much of that money Gandil kept for himself, remain matters of conjecture.

More well-settled is the fact that awareness of the corruption of the World Series was fairly widespread in professional gambling circles. After the post–Game Two player/gambler falling-out, a group of Midwestern gamblers convened in a Chicago hotel to discuss a fix revival. Spearheading this effort were St. Louis clothing manufacturer/gambler Carl Zork and an Omaha bookmaker improbably named Benjamin Franklin, both of whom were heavily invested in a Reds Series triumph. The action, if any, taken by these Midwesterners is another uncertain element in the fix saga.

Back on the diamond, the White Sox teetered on the brink of elimination, having won only one of the first five World Series games. Their outlook turned bleaker in Game Six when the Reds rushed to an early 4–0 lead behind Dutch Ruether. At that late moment, slumbering White Sox bats finally awoke. Capitalizing on timely base hits from the previously dormant middle of the batting order (Buck Weaver, Joe Jackson, and Happy Felsch), the White Sox rallied for a 5–4 triumph in 10 innings. The ensuing Game Seven was the type of affair that sporting pundits had anticipated at the Series outset: a comfortable 4–1 Chicago victory behind masterly pitching by Eddie Cicotte and RBI-base hits by Jackson and Felsch.

Now only one win away from evening up the Series, the hopes of the White Sox faithful were pinned on regular-season stalwart Lefty Williams. Williams had pitched decently in his two previous Series outings, only to see his starts come undone by a lone big inning in each game. In Game Eight, disaster struck early. Lefty did not make it out of the first inning, leaving the White Sox an insurmountable 4–0 deficit. The Reds continued to pour it on against second-line Chicago relievers. Only a forlorn White Sox rally late in the contest made the final score somewhat respectable: Cincinnati 10, Chicago 5.

The next morning, the sporting world's approbation of the Reds' World Series triumph was widespread, tempered only by a discordant note sounded by Hugh Fullerton. In a widely circulated column, Fullerton questioned the integrity of the White Sox's Series performance. He also made the startling assertion that at least seven White Sox players would not be wearing a Chicago uniform the next season. More explicit but little-noticed charges of player corruption quickly followed in *Collyer's Eye*, a horse-racing trade paper.

Although a few other intrepid baseball writers would later voice their own reservations about the Series bona fides, Fullerton's commentary was not well-received by most in the profession. A number of fellow sportswriters characterized the Fullerton assertions as no more than the sour grapes of an "expert" embarrassed by the misfire of his World Series prediction. In a prominent *New York Times* article, special World Series correspondent Christy Mathewson also dismissed the Fullerton suspicions, informing readers that a fix of the Series was virtually impossible.

For its part, Organized Baseball mostly ignored Fullerton's charges, leaving denigration of Fullerton and his allies to friendly organs like *Baseball Magazine* and *The Sporting News*. In the short run, the strategy worked. Despite reiteration in follow-up columns, Fullerton's concerns gained little traction with baseball fans. By the start of the new season, the notion that the 1919 World Series had not been on the level was mostly forgotten—except at White Sox headquarters.

Unbeknownst to the sporting press or public, White Sox owner Charles Comiskey had not dismissed the allegations made against his team. While the 1919 Series was in progress, Comiskey had been disturbed by privately received reports that his team was going to throw the championship series. Shortly after the Series was over, club officials were dispatched to St. Louis to make discreet inquiry into fix rumors. Much to Comiskey's chagrin, disgruntled local gambling informants endorsed the charge that members of his team had thrown the Series in exchange for a promised $100,000 payoff.

Lingering doubt on that score was subsequently erased when in-the-know gamblers Harry Redmon and Joe Pesch repeated the fix details to Comiskey and other club brass during a late December meeting in Chicago.

Of the courses available to him, Comiskey opted to pursue the one of self-interest. Rather than expose the perfidy of his players and precipitate the breakup of a championship team, Comiskey kept his fix information quiet. Early in the new year, the corrupted players were re-signed for the 1920 season, with Joe Jackson, Happy Felsch, Swede Risberg, and Lefty Williams receiving substantial pay raises, to boot. Only fix ringleader Chick Gandil experienced any degree of Comiskey wrath; Gandil was tendered a contract for no more than his previous season's salary. When, as expected, Gandil rejected the pact, Comiskey took pleasure in placing him on the club's ineligible list. That suspension continued in force all season and effectively ended Chick Gandil's playing career. He never appeared in a major-league game after the 1919 World Series.

From a financial standpoint, Comiskey's silence paid off. Fueled by a return to pre-World War I "normalcy" and the unprecedented slugging exploits of a pitcher-turned-outfielder named Babe Ruth, major-league baseball underwent an explosion in popularity. With its defending AL champion team intact except for Gandil, the White Sox spent the 1920 season in the midst of an exciting three-way pennant battle with New York and Cleveland. With attendance at Comiskey Park soaring to new heights, club coffers overflowed with revenue. Then late in the 1920 season, it all began to unravel. The immediate cause was an unlikely one: the suspected fix of a meaningless late August game between the Chicago Cubs and Philadelphia Phillies.

At first the matter seemed no more than a distraction, the latest of the minor annoyances that bedeviled the game that season. That spring, baseball had been mildly discomforted by exposure of the game-fixing proclivities of Hal Chase, revealed during the trial of a breach-of-contract lawsuit instituted by black-sheep teammate Lee Magee. Then in early August, West Coast baseball followers were shaken by allegations that cast serious doubt upon the legitimacy of the 1919 Pacific Coast League crown won by the Vernon Tigers. In time, the PCL scandal would have momentous consequences, providing Commissioner Landis with instructive precedent for dealing with courtroom-acquitted Black Sox defendants. In the near term, however, the significance of these matters resided mainly in their effect upon Cubs president William L. Veeck Sr. Unhappy connection to both the Magee affair and the PCL scandal—Veeck's boss, Cubs owner William Wrigley, was livid over the prospect that his Los Angeles Angels might have been cheated out of the PCL pennant—prompted Veeck to make public disclosure of the Cubs-Phillies fix reports and to pledge club cooperation with any investigative body wishing to delve into the matter.

Revelation that the outcome of the Cubs-Phillies game might have been rigged engaged the attention of two of the Black Sox Scandal's most formidable actors: Cook County Judge Charles A. McDonald and American League President Ban Johnson. Only recently installed as chief justice of Chicago's criminal courts and an avid baseball fan, McDonald promptly empaneled a grand jury to investigate the game fix reports.

But within days, influential sportswriter Joe Vila of the *New York Sun*, prominent Chicago businessman-baseball fan Fred Loomis, and others were pressing a more substantial target upon the grand jury: the 1919 World Series. Privately, Johnson, a longtime acquaintance of Judge McDonald, urged a similar course upon the jurist. Like Comiskey, Johnson had conducted his own confidential investigation into the outcome of the 1919 Series. And he too had uncovered evidence that the Series had been corrupted. McDonald was amenable to expansion of the grand jury's probe, and by the time the grand jury conducted its first substantive session on September 22, 1920, inquiry into the Cubs-Phillies game had been relegated to secondary status. The panel's attention would be focused on the 1919 World Series.

The ensuing proceedings were remarkable for many reasons, not the least of which was the wholesale disregard of the mandate of grand jury secrecy. Violation of this black-letter precept of law was justified on the dubious premise that baseball would benefit from the airing of its dirty laundry, and soon newspapers nationwide were reporting the details, often verbatim, of grand jury testimony.

This breach of law was accompanied by another extra-legal phenomenon: almost daily public commentary on the proceedings by the grand jury foreman, the prosecuting attorney, and, on occasion, Judge McDonald himself. In a matter of days, the transparency of the proceedings permitted the *Chicago Tribune* to announce the impending indictment of eight White Sox players: Eddie Cicotte, Chick Gandil, Joe Jackson, Buck Weaver, Lefty Williams, Happy Felsch, Swede Risberg, and Fred McMullin—the men soon branded the Black Sox. For the time being, the charge against them was the generic conspiracy to commit an illegal act. The scandal spotlight then shifted briefly to Philadelphia, where a fix insider was giving the interview that would blow the scandal wide open.

In the September 27, 1920, edition of the *Philadelphia North American*, Billy Maharg declared that Games One, Two, and Eight of the 1919 World Series had been rigged. According to Maharg, the outcome of the first two games had been procured by the bribery of the White Sox players by the Burns/Attell/Bennett combine. The abysmal pitching performance that cost Chicago any chance of winning Game Eight was the product of intimidation of Lefty Williams by the Zork-Franklin forces, Maharg implied.

Wire service republication of the Maharg expose produced swift and stunning reaction. A day later, first Eddie Cicotte and then Joe Jackson admitted agreeing to accept a payoff to lose the Series when interviewed in the office of White Sox legal counsel Alfred Austrian. The two then repeated this admission under oath before the grand jury. Interestingly, neither Cicotte nor Jackson confessed to making a deliberate misplay during the Series. Press accounts that had Cicotte describing how he lobbed hittable pitches to the plate and/or had Jackson admitting to deliberate failure in the field or at bat were entirely bogus. According to the transcriptions of their testimony, the two had told the grand jury no such thing. While each had taken the gamblers' money, Cicotte and Jackson both insisted that they had played to win at all times against the Reds. The other player participants in the Series fix were identified by Cicotte and Jackson, but apart from laying blame on Gandil, neither man disclosed much knowledge of how the fix had been instigated or who had financed it.

This exercise repeated itself when Lefty Williams spoke the following day. Like Cicotte and Jackson, Lefty admitted joining the fix conspiracy and accepting gamblers' money, first confessing in the Austrian law office, and thereafter in testimony before the grand jury. But Williams also denied that he had done anything corrupt on the field to earn his payment. He said he had tried his best at all times, even during his dismal Game Eight start. For the grand jury record, Lefty officially identified the fix participants as "Cicotte, Gandil, Weaver, Felsch, Risberg, McMullin, Jackson, and myself." Williams also put names on some of the gambler co-conspirators. At the Warner Hotel in Chicago, they had been named "Sullivan" and "Brown." At the Sinton Hotel in Cincinnati, the fix proponents had been Bill Burns, Abe Attell, and a third man named "Bennett."

A similar tack was taken by Happy Felsch when interviewed by a reporter for the *Chicago Evening American*. Like the others, Felsch admitted his complicity in the fix plot and his acceptance of gamblers' money. But his subpar Series performance, particularly in center field, had not been deliberate, he said. Lest the underworld get the wrong idea, Felsch hastened to add that he had been prepared to make a game-decisive misplay, but the opportunity to do so had not presented itself during the Series. Unlike the others, Happy confined admission of wrongdoing to himself, although he had come to admire the way that Cicotte had demanded his payoff money up front. Felsch did not know who had financed the fix, but he was willing to subscribe to press reports that it had been Abe Attell.

A far different public stance was adopted by the other Black Sox. Chick Gandil, Swede Risberg, Fred McMullin, and Buck Weaver all protested their innocence, with Weaver in particular adamant about his intention to obtain legal counsel and fight any charges preferred against him in court. Those charges would not be long in coming. On October 29, 1920, five counts of conspiracy to obtain money by false pretenses and/or via a confidence game were returned against the Black Sox by the grand jury. Gamblers Bill Burns, Hal Chase, Abe Attell, Sport Sullivan, and Rachael Brown were also charged in the indictments.

The stage thereupon shifted to the criminal courts for a whirl of legal events, few of which are accurately described or well understood in latter-day Black Sox literature.

The return of criminal charges in the Black Sox case coincided with the Republican Party's political landslide in the November 1920 elections. An entirely different administration soon took charge of the Cook County State's Attorney's Office, the prosecuting agency in the baseball scandal. When the regime of new State's Attorney Robert E. Crowe assumed office, it found the high-profile Black Sox case in disarray. The investigation underlying the indictments was incomplete. Evidence was missing from the prosecutors' vault, including transcriptions of the Cicotte, Jackson, and Williams grand jury testimony.

Worse yet, it appeared that their predecessors in office had premised prosecution of the Black Sox case on cooperation anticipated from Cicotte, Jackson, and/or Williams, each of whom had admitted fix complicity before the grand jury. But now, the trio was standing firm with the other accused players, and seeking to have their grand jury confessions suppressed by the court on legal grounds. This placed the new prosecuting attorneys in desperate need of time to rethink and then rebuild their case.

In March 1921, prosecutors' hopes for an adjournment were dashed by Judge William E. Dever, who set a quick peremptory trial date. This prompted a drastic response from prosecutor Crowe. Rather than try to pull the Black Sox case together on short notice, he administratively dismissed the charges. Crowe coupled public announcement of this stunning development with the promise that the Black Sox case would be presented to the grand jury again for new indictments.

Before the month was out, that promise was fulfilled. Expedited grand jury proceedings yielded new indictments that essentially replicated the dismissed ones. All those previously charged were re-indicted, while the roster of gambler defendants was enlarged to include Carl Zork, Benjamin Franklin, David (Bennett) Zelcer, and brothers Ben and Lou Levi, reputedly related to Zelcer by marriage and long targeted for prosecution by AL President Ban Johnson.

With the legal proceedings now reverting to courtroom stage one, prosecutors had acquired the time necessary to get their case in better shape. That extra time was needed, as the prosecution remained besieged on many fronts. The State was deluged by defense motions to dismiss the charges, suppress evidence, limit testimony, and the like. Prosecutors were also having trouble getting the gambler defendants into court. Sport Sullivan and Rachael Brown remained somewhere at large. Hal Chase and Abe Attell successfully resisted extradition to Chicago, and Ben Franklin was excused from the proceedings on grounds of illness.

In the run-up to trial, however, prosecution prospects received one major boost. Retrieved from the Mexican border by his pal Billy Maharg (via a trip financed by Ban Johnson), Bill Burns had agreed to turn State's evidence in return for immunity. Now, prosecutors had the crucial fix insider that their case had been lacking.

Jury selection began on June 16, 1921, and dragged on for several weeks. Appearing as counsel on behalf of the accused were some of the Midwest's finest criminal defense lawyers: Thomas Nash and Michael Ahern (representing Weaver, Felsch, Risberg, and McMullin; McMullin did not arrive in Chicago until after jury selection had begun, and for this reason, the trial went on without him and the charges against him were later dismissed); Benedict Short and George Guenther (Jackson and Williams); James O'Brien and

John Prystalski (Gandil); A. Morgan Frumberg and Henry Berger (Zork), and Max Luster and J. J. Cooke (Zelcer and the Levi brothers). Cicotte, meanwhile, was represented by his friend and personal attorney Daniel Cassidy, a civil lawyer from Detroit.

Although outnumbered, the prosecution was hardly outgunned, with its chairs filled by experienced trial lawyers: Assistant State's Attorneys George Gorman and John Tyrrell, and Special Prosecutor Edward Prindiville, with assistance from former Judge George Barrett representing the interests of the American League in court, and a cadre of attorneys in the employ of AL President Johnson working behind the scenes.

About the only unproven commodity in the courtroom was the newly assigned trial judge, Hugo Friend. Judge Friend would later go on to a distinguished 46-year career on Illinois trial and appellate benches. But at the time of the Black Sox trial, he was a judicial novice, presiding over his first significant case. Although his mettle would often be tested by a battalion of fractious barristers, Friend's intelligence and sense of fairness would stand him in good stead. The Black Sox case would be generally well tried, if not error-free.

In a sweltering midsummer courtroom, the prosecution commenced its case with the witnesses needed to establish factual minutiae—the scores of 1919 World Series games, the employment of the accused players by the Chicago White Sox, the winning and losing Series shares, etc.—that the defense, for tactical reasons, declined to stipulate. Then, chief prosecution witness Bill Burns assumed the stand. For the better part of three days, Burns recounted the events that had precipitated the corruption of the 1919 World Series. Those who had equated Burns with his "Sleepy Bill" nickname were in for a shock. Quick-witted and unflappable, Burns was more than a match for sneering defense lawyers, much to the astonishment, then delight, of the jaded Black Sox trial press corps. Newspaper reviews of Burns's testimony glowed and, by the time their star witness stepped down, prosecutors were near-jubilant. Thereafter, prosecution focus temporarily shifted to incriminating Zork and the other Midwestern gambler defendants.

Halfway through the State's case, the jury was excused while the court conducted an evidentiary hearing into the admissibility of the Cicotte, Jackson, and Williams grand jury testimony. Modern accounts of the Black Sox saga often relate that the prosecution was grievously injured by the loss of grand jury documents. That was hardly the case. When prosecutors discovered that the original grand jury transcripts were missing, they merely had the grand jury stenographers create new ones from their shorthand notes. These second-generation transcripts were available throughout the proceedings, and Black Sox defense lawyers did not contest their accuracy.

What was contested was whether, and to what extent, the trial jury should be made privy to what Cicotte, Jackson, and Williams had told the grand jurors. According to the defense, the Cicotte, Jackson, and Williams grand jury testimony had been induced by broken off-the-record promises of immunity from prosecution. If this were true, the testimony would be deemed involuntary in the legal sense and inadmissible against the accused.

With testimony restricted exclusively to what had happened in and around the grand jury room, the proceedings devolved into a swearing contest. Cicotte, Jackson, and Williams testified that they had been promised immunity. Lead grand jury prosecutor Hartley Replogle and Judge McDonald denied it. During the hearing, grand jury excerpts were read into the record at length. After hearing both sides, Judge Friend determined that the defendants had confessed freely, without any promise of leniency. Their grand jury testimony would be admissible in evidence—but not before each grand jury transcript had been edited to delete all reference to Chick Gandil, Buck Weaver, or anyone else mentioned in it, other than the speaker himself. Once this tedious task was accomplished, the redacted grand jury testimony of Eddie Cicotte, Joe Jackson, and Lefty Williams was read to the jury, a prolonged and dry exercise that seemed to anesthetize most panel members.

The numbing effect that the transcript readings had on the jury was not lost on prosecutors. Wishing to close their case while it still enjoyed the momentum of the Burns testimony, prosecutors made a fateful strategic decision. They jettisoned the remainder of their scheduled witnesses (Ban Johnson, Joe Pesch, St. Louis Browns second baseman Joe Gedeon, et al.) and wrapped up the State's case with another fix insider: unindicted co-conspirator Billy Maharg. The affable Maharg provided an account of the fix developments that he was witness to, providing firm and consistent corroboration of many fix details supplied by Bill Burns earlier.

Pleased with Maharg's performance, prosecutors rested their case. Now they would be obliged to accept the cost of short-circuiting their proofs. In response to defense motions, Judge Friend dismissed the charges against the Levi brothers for lack of evidence. He also signaled that he would be disposed to overturn any guilty verdict returned by the jury against Carl

Zork, Buck Weaver, or Happy Felsch, given the thinness of the incriminating evidence presented against them. These rulings, however, did not visibly trouble the prosecutors, for they had plainly decided to concentrate their efforts on convicting defendants Gandil, Cicotte, Jackson, Williams, and the gambler David Zelcer.

The defense had long advertised that the Black Sox would be testifying in their own defense. But that would have to wait, as the gambler defendants would be going first. Once the Zelcer and Zork defenses had presented their cases, the Gandil defense took the floor, calling a series of witnesses mainly intended to make a liar out of Bill Burns.

Also presented was White Sox club secretary Harry Grabiner, whose testimony about soaring 1920 club revenues undermined the contention that team owner Comiskey or the White Sox corporation had been injured by the fix of the 1919 World Series. (Years later, jury foreman William Barry would tell Judge Friend that the Grabiner testimony had had more influence on the jury than that of any other witness.)

Then, with the stage finally set for Chick to take the stand, the Gandil defense abruptly rested. So did the other Black Sox. Little explanation for this change in defense plan was offered, apart from the comment that there was no need for the accused players to testify because the State had made no case against them. Caught off-guard by defense maneuvers, the prosecution scrambled to present rebuttal witnesses, most of whom were excluded from the testifying by Judge Friend. As little in the way of a defense had been mounted by the player defendants, there was no legal justification for admitting rebuttal.

The remainder of the trial was devoted to closing stemwinders by opposing counsel and the court's instructions on the law. Then the jury retired to deliberate. Less than three hours later, it reached a verdict. With the parties reassembled in a courtroom packed with defense partisans, the court clerk announced the outcome: Not Guilty, as to all defendants on all charges. A smiling Judge Friend concurred, pronouncing the jury's verdict a fair one.

With that, pandemonium erupted. Jurors shook hands and congratulated the men whom they had just acquitted. Some in the crowd even hoisted defendants onto their shoulders and paraded them around. Thereafter, defendants, defense lawyers, jurors, and defense followers gathered on the courthouse steps, where their mutual joy was captured in a photo published by the *Chicago Tribune*. Later, a post-verdict celebration brought the defendants and the jurors together once again at a nearby Italian restaurant. There, the revelry continued into the wee hours of the morning, closing with jurors and Black Sox singing "Hail, Hail, The Gang's All Here."

This extraordinary exhibition of camaraderie suggests that the verdict may have been a product of that courthouse phenomenon that all prosecutors dread: jury nullification. In a criminal case, jurors are carefully instructed to abjure passion, prejudice, sympathy, and other emotion in rendering judgment. They are to base their verdict entirely on the evidence presented and the law. But during deliberations in highly charged cases, this instruction is susceptible to being overridden by the jury's identification with the accused. Or by dislike of the victim. Or by the urge to send some sort of message to the community at large.

In the Black Sox case, defense counsel, notably Benedict Short and Henry Berger, worked assiduously to cultivate a bond between the working-class men on the jury and the blue-collar defendants. The defense's closing arguments to the jury, particularly those of Short, Thomas Nash, A. Morgan Frumberg, and James O'Brien, stridently denounced the wealthy victim Comiskey and his corporation. The defense lawyers also raised the specter of another menace: AL President Ban Johnson, portrayed as a malevolent force working outside of jury view to ensure the unfair condemnation of the accused.

In the end, of course, the underlying basis for the jury's acquittal of the Black Sox is unknowable all these years later. Significantly, the fair-minded Judge Friend concurred in the outcome. Still, jury nullification remains a plausible explanation for the verdict, particularly when it came to jurors' resolution of the charges against defendants Cicotte, Jackson, and Williams, against whom the State had presented a facially strong case.

Few others shared the jurors' satisfaction in their verdict, with many baseball officials vowing never to grant employment to the acquitted players. That sentiment was quickly rendered academic. Commissioner Kenesaw Mountain Landis had taken note of the minor leagues' prompt expulsion of the Pacific Coast League players who had had their indictments dismissed by the judge in that game-fixing case. Landis now utilized that action as precedent.

With a famous edict that began "Regardless of the verdict of juries," Landis permanently barred the eight Black Sox players from participation in Organized Baseball. And with that, Joe Jackson, Eddie Cicotte, Buck Weaver, and the rest were consigned to the sporting wilderness. None would ever appear in another major-league game. The Black Sox saga, however, was not quite over.

In the aftermath of their official banishment from the game, Buck Weaver, Happy Felsch, Swede Risberg, and Joe Jackson instituted civil litigation against the White Sox, pursuing grievances grounded in breach of contract, defamation, and restraint on their professional livelihoods.

Outside of Milwaukee, where the Felsch/Risberg/Jackson suits were filed, little attention was paid to their complaints. Jackson's breach-of-contract suit was the only one that ever went to trial. It was founded on the three-year contract that Jackson had signed with the White Sox in late February 1920, months after the World Series. The club had unilaterally voided the pact when it released Jackson in March 1921, and he had gone unpaid for the 1921 and 1922 baseball seasons.

In a pretrial deposition, plaintiff Jackson disputed that his termination by the White Sox had been justified by his involvement in the Series fix. On that point, Jackson swore to a set of fix-related events dramatically at odds with his earlier grand jury testimony. Jackson now maintained that he had had no connection to the conspiracy to rig the 1919 Series. He had not even known about it until after the Series was over, when a drunken Lefty Williams foisted a $5,000 fix share on Jackson, telling him that the Black Sox had used Jackson's name while trying to persuade gamblers to finance the fix scheme.

When the suit was tried in early 1924, its highlight was Jackson's cross-examination by White Sox attorney George Hudnall. Confronted with his grand jury testimony of September 28, 1920, Jackson did not attempt to explain away the contradiction between his civil deposition assertions and his grand jury testimony. Nor did he attempt to harmonize the two. Rather, Jackson maintained—more than 100 times—that he had never made the statements contained in the transcript of his grand jury testimony.

An outraged Judge John J. Gregory subsequently cited Jackson for perjury and had him jailed overnight. The court vacated the jury's $16,711.04 award in Jackson favor, ruling that it was grounded in false testimony and jury nonfeasance. After the proceedings were over, civil jury foreman John E. Sanderson shed light on the jury's thinking. Sanderson informed the press that the jury had entirely disregarded Jackson's testimony about disputed events. The foreman also rejected the notion that the panel had exonerated Jackson of participation in the 1919 World Series fix.

Rather, the jury had premised its judgment for Jackson on the legal principle of condonation. As far as the jury was concerned, White Sox team brass had known of Jackson's World Series fix involvement well before the new three-year contract was tendered to him in February 1920. Having thus effectively condoned (or forgiven) Jackson's Series misconduct by re-signing him, the club was in no position to void that contract once the public found out what club management had known about Jackson all along. Jackson was, according to the Milwaukee jury, therefore entitled to his 1921 and 1922 pay.

In time, the four civil lawsuits, including that of Jackson, were settled out of court for modest sums. Little notice was taken, as the baseball press and public had long since moved on. In the ensuing years, the Black Sox Scandal receded in memory, recalled only in the random sports column, magazine article, or, starting with the death of Joe Jackson in December 1951, the obituary of a Black Sox player.

Revival of interest in the scandal commenced in the late 1950s, but did not attract widespread attention until the publication of Eliot Asinof's classic *Eight Men Out* in 1963. Regrettably, this spellbinding account of the scandal was marred by historically inaccurate detail, attributable presumably to the fact that much of the criminal case record had been unavailable to Asinof, having disappeared from court archives over the years. This had compelled Asinof to rely upon scandal survivors, particularly Abe Attell, an engaging but unreliable informant.

Asinof also exercised artistic license in his work, creating, apparently for copyright protection purposes, a fictitious villain named "Harry F." to intimidate Lefty Williams into his dreadful Game Eight pitching performance. Asinof likewise embellished his tale of the Jackson civil case, inserting melodramatic events, such as White Sox lawyer Hudnall pulling a supposedly lost Jackson grand jury transcript out of his briefcase in midtrial, into *Eight Men Out* that are nowhere memorialized in the fully extant record of the civil proceedings.

Over the years, the embrace of such Asinof inventions, as well as the repetition of more ancient canards—the miserly wage that Comiskey supposedly paid the corrupted players, the notion that disappearing grand jury testimony hamstrung the prosecution, and other fictions—has become a recurring feature of much Black Sox literature.

In 2002 scandal enthusiast Gene Carney commenced a near-obsessive re-examination of the Black Sox affair. First in weekly blog posts and later in his important book *Burying the Black Sox: How Baseball's Cover-Up of the 1919 World Series Fix Almost Succeeded* (Potomac Books, 2006), Carney circulated his findings, which were often at variance with long-accepted scandal wisdom. Sadly, this work was cut short by Carney's untimely passing in July 2009. But the mission endures, carried on by others, including the membership of the SABR committee inspired by Carney's zeal.

That scandal revelations are still to be made is clear, manifested by events like the surfacing of a treasure trove of lost Black Sox documents acquired by the Chicago History Museum several years ago. As the playing of the 1919 World Series approaches its 100th anniversary, the investigation continues. And the final word on the Black Sox Scandal remains to be written.

SOURCES

This essay is drawn from a more comprehensive account of the Black Sox legal proceedings provided in the writer's *Black Sox in the Courtroom: The Grand Jury, Criminal Trial, and Civil Litigation* (Jefferson NC: McFarland & Co., 2013). Underlying sources include surviving fragments of the judicial record; the Black Sox Scandal collections maintained at the Chicago History Museum and the National Baseball Hall of Fame and Museum's Giamatti Research Center; the transcript of Joe Jackson's 1924 lawsuit against the Chicago White Sox held by the Chicago Baseball Museum; newspaper archives in Chicago and elsewhere; and contemporary Black Sox scholarship, particularly the work of Gene Carney, Bob Hoie, and Bruce Allardice.

46

Bill McKechnie

WARREN CORBETT

SABR's Biography Project was formed in 2002, and its website is home to more than five thousand biographies of baseball players and personnel. SABR could produce a book to honor this project alone. For now, the project's chairmen were asked to select a single biography to represent the five thousand articles, and they selected this one. Among his many contributions, its author Warren Corbett has written more than a hundred articles for the BioProject, always respecting the subject while bringing his story to life.

Twelve managers have won more games than Bill McKechnie. None has won more respect.

Deacon Bill McKechnie was the first to lead three different teams to the World Series and the first to win championships with two different teams. In 25 seasons as a manager, between 1915 and 1946, he earned respect as a baseball strategist and even more respect as a human being. "He is the sort of man that other decent men would want their sons to play for," baseball historian and Cincinnati Reds fan Lee Allen wrote.[1]

McKechnie achieved the stature of a baseball saint only late in his career. His bosses didn't always treat him with respect. His first two National League managing jobs ended in humiliation.

McKechnie was a gifted team builder. Even when he took over sorry clubs, he never had more than two losing seasons in a row. He built teams that were more than the sum of their parts by getting the most out of each individual. "McKechnie was a master handler of men," Allen wrote. "Some managers will never learn to handle personalities as long as they live. McKechnie in that department was without a peer."[2]

His secret was no secret, McKechnie said: "Just treat them the way you'd like to be treated."[3] He thought managers who delivered rah-rah speeches or clubhouse rants were showboats or fools. "A manager tries to pick his men carefully, keeping out the bad actors. But the average ballplayer plays [for] himself. He isn't hustling for the manager or the club owner. He's hustling for his own contract—his family and his future."[4]

Sounds simple. But in a time when most managers were tyrants like John McGraw or ironfisted disciplinarians like Joe McCarthy, McKechnie's fatherly approach was rare. In many ways he anticipated today's manager, who must persuade young multimillionaires to be team players.

McKechnie was also a throwback, a relic of the deadball game in the long-ball era. He emphasized defense and pitching above all else. Most managers give lip-service to the virtues of stingy defense. To McKechnie, that was not just a cliché but a religion. He played the percentages faithfully because he believed the percentages would always win in the long run. He pleaded guilty to managing by the book: "Show me a manager who isn't and I'll show you a manager who loses a lot of games he ought to win."[5]

William Boyd McKechnie was born in Wilkinsburg, Pennsylvania, near Pittsburgh, on August 7, 1886, one of 10 children of Scottish immigrants Archibald McKechnie and the former Mary Murray.[6] The household also included three adopted children. Bill remembered marching to church with his brothers, all wearing kilts. His parents were Presbyterian, but Bill became a pillar of the Mifflin Avenue Methodist Church. Although he was never a deacon, he sang baritone in the choir for much of his adult life. He married his high school girlfriend, Beryl Bien, who said, "He told me the first time he saw me, he got so excited, he swallowed his chewing tobacco."[7]

McKechnie's playing career was forgettable, but his eagerness and intelligence impressed some of the game's biggest names. A switch-hitting and seldom-hitting infielder, he dropped out of high school to play semipro ball, then graduated to the low minors. The Pittsburgh Pirates acquired his contract in 1907. When he made the big-league club three years later, the Pirates' superstar, Honus Wagner, took a liking to the hometown boy. McKechnie said Wagner taught him more about baseball than anyone else.

Landing with the New York Yankees in 1913, he became a favorite of the crusty manager, Frank Chance. Asked why he spent so much time with a benchwarmer, Chance replied, "Because he's the only man on this club who knows what baseball is all about."[8]

McKechnie's career was going nowhere, so he jumped to the outlaw Federal League in 1914. He batted .304 as the regular third baseman for the pennant-winning Indianapolis Hoosiers. After the franchise moved to Newark the next year, the 28-year-old McKechnie took over as manager in June and led the club to a 54-45 record and a fifth-place finish.

When the Federal League folded after the 1915 season, John McGraw of the New York Giants picked up McKechnie's contract along with that of his Newark teammate and friend, outfielder Edd Roush. In August 1916 McGraw traded his washed-up pitching ace, Christy Mathewson, to Cincinnati so Matty could become the Reds' manager. McGraw told Matty he could take two players with him; Matty picked Roush and McKechnie.

Roush became the Reds' star center fielder. McKechnie took up residence on the bench. He was sold back to Pittsburgh and finished his playing career in the minors in 1921.

The next year the Pirates hired him as a coach for manager George Gibson. Pittsburgh owner Barney Dreyfuss had already identified McKechnie as a future manager. The club was one game under .500 on June 30, 1922, when Gibson resigned and the 35-year-old McKechnie replaced him.

Despite their problems, the Pirates were a team on the rise. The lineup featured three future Hall of Famers: shortstop Rabbit Maranville, third baseman Pie Traynor, and center fielder Max Carey, the league's perennial stolen base leader. Lefty Wilbur Cooper and curveball specialist Johnny Morrison anchored the pitching staff. McKechnie brought the club home in third place with an 85-69 record.

Over the next two years, McKechnie and Dreyfuss methodically improved the team. Outfielder Kiki Cuyler cracked the lineup in 1924 and batted .354/.402/.539. McKechnie picked up a 31-year-old rookie pitcher, Remy Kremer, from the Pacific Coast League, and he won 18 games. Dreyfuss bought minor-league shortstop Glenn Wright. McKechnie took one look at Wright's powerful arm and moved Maranville to second base.

The tiny Maranville was one of the game's most popular players and one of its premier hell-raisers. In an effort to curb his night prowling, McKechnie roomed with him and his running mate, pitcher Moses Yellow Horse. One night the pair lured a flock of pigeons into the manager's hotel room and locked them in the closet for him to find. For some reason, the soused Rabbit became a favorite of the teetotaler McKechnie.

The Pirates won 90 games in 1924, but finished third for the third straight year. After the season Dreyfuss and McKechnie traded three players reported to be discipline problems—Maranville, Cooper, and first baseman Charlie Grimm—to the Chicago Cubs for second baseman George Grantham, pitcher Vic Aldridge, and a rookie first baseman.

Some writers thought the Cubs had locked up the pennant, but McKechnie had a plan. He shifted Grantham to first base and installed young Eddie Moore at second. With Wright and Traynor, all four Pirates infielders had started out as shortstops. An infield full of shortstops would become a McKechnie trademark as he sought to construct the strongest possible defense.

The refurbished 1925 team stood barely above .500 in June when Barney Dreyfuss, one of baseball's smartest and most successful owners, made a move so stupid it defies explanation. Fred Clarke, the Pirates' player-manager in the glory days of Honus Wagner, had bought stock in the team and was appointed vice president, chief scout, and assistant manager. Dreyfuss sent him to sit on the bench with McKechnie. Although Clarke had been out of the game for a decade, Dreyfuss evidently thought he would bring old-school fire to an underachieving club. It was an insulting vote of no-confidence in the young manager, but Clarke was a local hero and Dreyfuss was the boss. McKechnie had to take it or quit.

Clarke, who had struck oil on his Kansas ranch, didn't need the job and didn't covet McKechnie's; he hoped to buy the team from the aging Dreyfuss. The sportswriters dutifully reported that Clarke and McKechnie worked together in blissful harmony, but Clarke's hard-driving personality could not have been more different from the manager's, and he was never shy about voicing his opinion, whether the players wanted to hear it or not.

The Pirates charged into a tight pennant race with the Giants until Pittsburgh took command with a 16-3 run in August and September. The Pirates bludgeoned the rest of the league. They were the first National League club in the 20th century to score more than 900 runs, almost six per game, and led in batting average, on-base percentage, and slugging percentage. Pittsburgh's 95-58 record was 8½ games better than the Giants'.

The Pirates faced the defending champion Washington Senators in the World Series. The Senators took three of the first four games, with their saint, Walter Johnson, claiming two of the victories. Pittsburgh fought back to win the next two, forcing a Game Seven.

The deciding game played out in an unrelenting downpour. McKechnie's starter, Vic Aldridge, lasted only one-third of an inning as the Senators scored four times in the first. The Pirates hit Johnson hard and trailed by just 7–6 when they came to bat in the bottom of the eighth. Forbes Field was a swamp of mud sprinkled with sawdust, but Commissioner Kenesaw Mountain Landis was determined to complete nine innings.

With two out, Earl Smith and Carson Bigbee hit back-to-back doubles to tie the score. After a walk, Max Carey's grounder should have ended the inning, but Senators shortstop Roger Peckinpaugh threw the ball away—his record-setting eighth error of the Series. Bases loaded.

Washington manager Bucky Harris stuck with his weary ace. As the rain streamed down Johnson's face, writer Dan Daniel said, "He looked like he was crying his head off."[9] Kiki Cuyler sliced a line drive that bounded into the temporary bleachers in right field, bringing home the two winning runs.

It was Pittsburgh's first championship since 1909, when guess-who was the manager. Some sportswriters gave Clarke as much credit as McKechnie. Critics in the press believed McKechnie was too soft to be a leader. "Players behind his back laughed at him, kidded about his judgment," Regis M. Welsh of the *Pittsburgh Post* wrote later. "The general consensus was that the club won in spite of him."[10]

Dreyfuss added to the Pirates' powerful lineup for 1926 when he bought Paul Waner, a little left-handed batter who had hit .401 in the Pacific Coast League. Slashing line drives all over the field, Waner batted .336/.413/.528 in his rookie year. Pittsburgh had climbed into first place in August when it all fell apart.

Team captain Carey, slumping and sick of Clarke's carping, wanted the shadow manager removed from the dugout. Two other elders, pitcher Babe Adams and outfielder Carson Bigbee, agreed, but their teammates voted down the motion by a reported 18–6 landslide. Carey thought Clarke had intimidated the other players.

News of the vote inevitably leaked to the press. One headline screeched, "Mutiny."[11] The rebellious players were likened to anarchists and communists. At this critical moment, Barney Dreyfuss was on vacation in Europe, leaving his son, Sam, and Clarke in charge. Clarke decreed that the mutineers had to go, and Sam Dreyfuss swung the axe. Adams and Bigbee were released. Carey was suspended, then sold to the Brooklyn Dodgers.

The newspapermen agreed that the popular Clarke was an innocent victim of a sinister plot, but they couldn't agree on who was the greater villain, the mutinous players or the manager who had failed to quash the rebellion. The Pirates fell under .500 for the rest of the season and wound up in third place.

When Barney Dreyfuss returned home, he had little choice but to back his son's decision. And he claimed he had no choice but to fire the manager because the fans demanded it. One year after winning the World Series, McKechnie was unemployed.

Reflecting on the upheaval, the *Post*'s Regis Welsh gave the departing manager a kick on his way out of town: "McKechnie showed, more than ever, the weakness that had been typical of him."[12] The Pittsburgh mutiny could have ended McKechnie's career. He had been found guilty of a manager's unforgivable sin: He had lost control of the clubhouse. His failure was underscored the following year, when new manager Donie Bush, without Clarke's advice, led the Pirates to another pennant.

McKechnie found work as a coach for the St. Louis Cardinals under first-year manager Bob O'Farrell. The Cardinals had won their first pennant and World Series in 1926, but player-manager Rogers Hornsby was traded after the season because he couldn't get along with the owner, Sam Breadon (or practically anybody else). O'Farrell, a 30-year-old catcher who had been named NL Most Valuable Player in 1926, didn't want the job. He leaned heavily on McKechnie, occasionally calling time in mid-inning to go to the bench and consult his assistant.

The 1927 Cardinals won 92 games, three more than in their pennant year, and stayed in the race until the final weekend before finishing second. That wasn't good enough for Breadon, who panicked easily and often. He made McKechnie the Cardinals' fourth manager in four years.

As in Pittsburgh, McKechnie took over a strong team. Second baseman Frankie Frisch, acquired in a trade with the Giants for Hornsby, was the sparkplug. First baseman Jim Bottomley had his career year in 1928, and left fielder Chick Hafey wasn't far behind. McKechnie brought back Rabbit Maranville, who had dropped to the minors and quit drinking, to put a fourth future Hall of Famer in the lineup. A veteran trio—Bill Sherdel, Jesse Haines, and 41-year-old Grover Cleveland Alexander—led the pitching staff. The Cardinals moved into first place in June and won 11 of their last 15 games to outrun the Giants.

That set up a World Series rematch with the Yankees, the team St. Louis had defeated in seven games in 1926. The 1928 Series lasted only four. The Cardinals lost the first three, then took a 2–1 lead in Game Four. Babe Ruth and Lou Gehrig hit back-to-back home runs to finish them off. McKechnie's club was not only beaten, but swept; not only beaten and swept, but stomped. The Yankees outscored the Cardinals 27–10 and never even needed a relief pitcher.

Sam Breadon was not happy with the outcome, and when the owner was not happy the manager took the fall. Breadon had dumped Hornsby after he won a World Series. McKechnie could expect no better after losing one. The *New York Times*'s John Kieran wrote, "The charge against McKechnie is that 'he is one of the finest fellows in the world, but—.'"[13]

Breadon didn't just fire the manager; he demoted him to the minors. McKechnie swapped jobs with Billy Southworth, who had led the Cards' top farm club at Rochester to the International League pennant. Again, McKechnie had to swallow the humiliation to keep his paycheck.

Southworth had managed only one year in the minors. At 36, he was now managing major leaguers who had been his teammates two seasons before. Southworth decided he had to get tough to show the players who was in charge. He only succeeded in alienating most of the team.

The Cardinals lost a doubleheader on July 21 to fall 13½ games behind the first-place Pirates. Breadon, back in panic mode, spun his revolving door: Southworth and McKechnie swapped jobs again. Breadon admitted he had made a mistake when he sent McKechnie down.

The Cardinals played better under their new-old manager, but not particularly well. They went 34-29 and stayed in fourth place, finishing 20 games back. Even before the season ended, McKechnie signaled that he had had enough of Sam Breadon. He announced his candidacy for tax collector in his hometown, Wilkinsburg. "If elected, I'm through with baseball," he said. "If not, well, I guess I'll have to return to the old game."[14] Beryl McKechnie campaigned hard for her absent husband, and Cardinals vice-president Branch Rickey came to town to endorse him, but the voters rejected him in the September Republican primary.

McKechnie returned to the old game in a new spot. Breadon offered him a one-year contract to stay in St. Louis. Instead, he accepted a four-year deal to manage the Boston Braves in 1930. Security was all the new job had going for it. The Braves were a last-place team and had had one winning season in the past 13. The principal owner, Judge Emil Fuchs, managed the club in 1929 to save a salary. The Braves were usually near the bottom in attendance as well as in the standings.

The team's best players were on the downside of the hill. First baseman

George Sisler was a husk of the .400 hitter he had been. Shortstop Rabbit Maranville (him again) was 38. The rest of the roster was what you'd expect from a team that lost 98 games.

For the first time, McKechnie had full authority over player personnel. What he didn't have was money. Fuchs and McKechnie employed creative financing to acquire a new foundation player. They sold third baseman Les Bell to the Chicago Cubs and used the cash, reported to be at least $35,000, to buy center fielder Wally Berger from the Cubs' Los Angeles farm club. Berger had hit 40 home runs in the Pacific Coast League. In 1930 his 38 homers for Boston set a major-league rookie record that stood for more than half a century.

In three years McKechnie turned over the roster almost completely. The Braves reached .500 in 1932. The next year they made an unlikely run at the pennant.

On August 20 the Braves won a doubleheader from Pittsburgh and climbed into a virtual tie for second place, 7½ games behind the New York Giants. They went on to win eight in a row. McKechnie said his men thought they couldn't lose: "They're singing that song about being in the money and they mean every word of it."[15]

The season reached its high tide on August 31, when a victory over the Giants boosted the club within five games of first place. The next day a crowd estimated at 50,000 overflowed Braves Field for a Friday doubleheader, said to be the largest weekday turnout in Boston history. The Giants swept both games, then won the next two to pop McKechnie's pennant bubble.

In the season finale, Wally Berger, benched by the flu, came on as a pinch-hitter and powered a grand slam into the left-field stands to beat Philadelphia. The blow clinched fourth place with an 83-71 record, the Braves' first finish in the first division in a dozen years. The players were "in the money"; each man collected about $400 as a World Series share.

McKechnie had built a tight defense—second in the league in defensive efficiency—that transformed a staff of no-name pitchers into winners.[16] Left-hander Ed Brandt, who had developed under McKechnie, was fourth in the NL in ERA. Two others, Ben Cantwell and Huck Betts, were in the top 10. With just about the same team in 1934, the Braves finished fourth again, winning 78 games.

The club had been on shaky financial ground for years. Now the ground collapsed under Judge Fuchs. When he fell behind on the rent, his Braves

Field landlord threatened to void the lease and turn the ballpark into a dog-racing track. The National League assumed the lease, permitting Fuchs to remain in charge, and Boston civic leaders launched a campaign to sell tickets so the Braves could afford to go to spring training.

Fuchs took a desperate step to save the franchise. He signed the game's biggest drawing card and embarrassed his manager in the process.

Babe Ruth wanted to manage the Yankees. The Yankees wanted to be rid of him, but they needed to ease him out the door without alienating his fans. Fuchs offered Ruth a contract to join the Braves as a player, vice president, and assistant manager, with a wink that the Babe could become manager in a year. Yankees owner Jacob Ruppert agreed to release Ruth so he could take advantage of this wonderful opportunity in the city where his major-league career began.

When Fuchs put the offer in writing, he composed a masterpiece of law-yerly evasion, filled with half-promises, or maybe quarter-promises, that Ruth might manage the team if this and if that and if the other. The Bambino was being bamboozled.[17]

McKechnie was not consulted. In Florida preparing for spring training, he read in the papers that he might be kicked upstairs to the front office. He asked a reporter, "What would I do in an office?"[18]

Ruth was fat and 40, but Fuchs didn't care whether he could play as long as he sold tickets. On Opening Day 1935 everybody's dreams came true. Ruth slammed a homer off the league's best pitcher, Carl Hubbell, and accounted for all of Boston's scoring in a 4–2 victory over the Giants.

It went downhill from there. Opening Day was the only day the team was above .500. Ruth struck out 15 times in his first 15 games and was a statue in left field. He was ready to quit, but Fuchs persuaded him to make a road trip to the western cities, where his appearance had already been advertised. He summoned memories of his former self in Pittsburgh when he hit three home runs in one game, the last one clearing Forbes Field's roof and bouncing off a house an estimated 600 feet from the plate.

The sad end came on June 2. Ruth, batting .181, told the writers he was going on the voluntarily retired list, but Fuchs said he couldn't quit because the club had already released him.

The Braves' record stood at 9-24 when Ruth played for the last time. Their season was ruined, but not by him; they got worse after he left. McKechnie had no decent players to trade and no cash to buy new ones. The Braves' 115 losses were the most by a National League team in the 20th century until the expansion Mets were born.

Judge Fuchs had run out of money, credit, and hope. Before the 1936 season the National League took over the franchise and engineered a recapitalization with the longtime baseball executive Bob Quinn as principal owner. The 65-year-old Quinn had a knack for picking lost causes. He had owned the Red Sox after Harry Frazee plundered the team and then served as president of the debt-ridden Brooklyn Dodgers.

Quinn changed the team nickname to Bees but kept the manager. McKechnie started rebuilding again. He acquired a few useful players, including Al Lopez and Tony Cuccinello, possibly as an act of charity by the rest of the league, and improved the club's record by 33 wins in 1936, good enough for sixth place.

McKechnie overhauled his pitching staff for 1937. Still short of money, he tried out several veteran minor leaguers who came cheap because they were too old to be prospects. He molded two of them into the biggest surprises of the year. Jim Turner, an offseason milkman in Nashville, Tennessee, was 33 and had rattled around the minors for 14 seasons. Lou Fette turned 30 during spring training. Both were breaking-ball pitchers who induced ground balls, and McKechnie put the league's best defense behind them.

The 1937 Braves allowed the fewest runs and the fewest walks while leading the league with 16 shutouts. But they also scored the fewest runs. In the season's next-to-last game, the aged rookie Turner beat Philadelphia for his 20th victory and lowered his ERA to a league-best 2.38. The next day Fette won his 20th, a seven-hit shutout.

Boston closed with a rush, winning eight of the last 10 to finish fifth with a 79-73 record. *The Sporting News* named McKechnie Manager of the Year because "he has been able to make much out of little."[19] Gray-haired, wearing rimless bifocals on his sun-creased face, he was the National League's senior manager at age 51.

McKechnie had endured eight years of turmoil and poverty in Boston. Now he found himself in demand; four teams reportedly wanted him. The Cincinnati Reds bid highest. Their wealthy owner, Powel Crosley Jr., gave him a two-year contract at a reported $25,000, plus an attendance bonus. The salary was said to be third highest for any manager, behind Bill Terry and Joe McCarthy of the pennant-winning New York clubs.

The Reds were a last-place team, but for McKechnie they had an additional attraction beyond money. The general manager, Warren Giles, was a friend and admirer. He had been business manager at Rochester when McKechnie was in exile there. New to his job, Giles followed the manager's lead in decisions on playing personnel.

McKechnie's first three years in Cincinnati secured his place in baseball history. Taking on a habitual loser once more, he retooled the club to win two consecutive pennants and iced the cake with a World Series championship. That success earned him national recognition as the game's finest Christian gentleman since Christy Mathewson. And four decades later, when oral histories became popular, many of his Reds players were still alive to pump up his legacy.

Giles and McKechnie embarked on an extreme makeover. They kept Ernie Lombardi, the NL's best-hitting catcher, but dumped two faded stars, Kiki Cuyler and Chick Hafey, and handed center field to rookie Harry Craft, a light-hitting glove man. First base was awarded to Frank McCormick, who was big and slow but hit smoking line drives. McKechnie turned Lonnie Frey, a poor shortstop, into an excellent second baseman.

Midway through the 1938 season the Reds traded for Wally Berger, another power bat to go with Lombardi and right fielder Ival Goodman, and acquired Bucky Walters, a converted third baseman who had had little success on the mound. He perked up when he got away from the weak Philadelphia Phillies.

Johnny Vander Meer's back-to-back no-hitters were the highlight of the season. Lombardi won the batting title and the MVP award, McCormick led the league in hits, and Goodman belted a team-record 30 home runs (Giles had shortened Crosley Field's fences). Cincinnati scored the most runs per game in the league. In late June the Reds surged to within 1½ games of first place. They slipped back to finish fourth with an 82-68 record, only six games behind the pennant-winning Cubs.

The Reds completed their lineup makeover when they acquired third baseman Bill Werber from the Philadelphia Athletics during spring training in 1939. A three-time American League stolen base leader, he gave the team a speedy leadoff man, though he didn't steal many in McKechnie's conservative offense.

Werber, a confident and intense Duke University graduate, became the leader of the infield. He nicknamed the quartet "the Jungle Cats," calling himself "Tiger," shortstop Billy Myers "Jaguar," and second baseman Frey "Leopard." First baseman McCormick objected to Werber's teasing choice,

"Hippopotamus," so he became "Wildcat." Bucky Walters and the veteran workhorse Paul Derringer, both sinkerballers, turned into aces with the Jungle Cats pouncing on ground balls behind them. McKechnie made sure the infield grass at Crosley Field stayed high and damp to slow down those grounders.

McKechnie liked durable pitchers who threw strikes and finished what they started. Walters and Derringer filled the bill. They topped 300 innings apiece in 1939 and were first and second in the league in complete games. They started nearly half the Reds' games and recorded more than half of the club's 97 wins. Walters won the pitcher's triple crown, leading the league in victories (27, against 11 losses), ERA (2.29), and strikeouts (137, tied with Claude Passeau), and was named NL Most Valuable Player. Derringer was 25-7, 2.93, with five shutouts and barely more than one base on balls per nine innings. Derringer, who was prone to drinking and fighting, often in that order, said, "If a pitcher can't win for Bill McKechnie, he can't win for anybody."[20]

The Reds won 12 straight in May and climbed to the top of the standings, holding off the Cardinals to fly Cincinnati's first pennant in 20 years. Their home attendance of almost one million led both leagues, even though Cincinnati was the smallest market in the majors.

The World Series matched the Reds against the Yankees, winners of their fourth consecutive American League pennant. It was no contest. New York won in four straight. The memorable moment was "Lombardi's snooze," when two Yankees crossed the plate in the 10th inning of Game Four while the Cincinnati catcher lay helpless on the ground after baserunner Charlie Keller kicked him in the testicles. (Those were not the winning runs; the tie-breaker scored before Keller ran over Lombardi.)

In the offseason McKechnie acquired his antiquated Boston ace, Jim Turner, to add a third reliable starter. Second-year right-hander Junior Thompson made four. The Reds started strong in 1940 and gathered steam as the season wore on. In July they won 18 of 20 to open a comfortable lead.

But getting there wasn't easy. Injuries and batting slumps created holes in the outfield. Shortstop Myers left the Willard Hershberger club for several days in September, enraging his teammates. Worst of all, backup catcher Willard Hershberger killed himself on August 3.

Hershberger, filling in for the injured Lombardi, blamed himself for some lost games and became despondent. He was found dead in his hotel room with his throat slashed. "He told me what his problems were," McKechnie said. "It has nothing to do with anybody on the team. It was something personal. He told it to me in confidence, and I will not utter it to anyone. I will take it with me to my grave." He did.[21]

McKechnie's club weathered the shock. Beginning August 31 the Reds went on a 19-2 run to finish with 100 victories, 12 games ahead of second-place Brooklyn. At least they wouldn't have to face the Yankees in the World Series. The Detroit Tigers ended New York's string of four straight pennants.

This time the Series went the distance before Cincinnati won behind the pitching of Walters and Derringer, and contributions from a pair of unexpected heroes. Jimmy Ripple, a waiver pickup who plugged the hole in left field, slammed a homer and drove in six runs. Forty-year-old coach Jimmie Wilson went on the active list after Hershberger's suicide to replace Lombardi. Wilson caught six of the seven games and batted .353 while hobbling with charley horses in both legs.

The 1939 and 1940 Reds gave McKechnie his greatest triumphs. The teams not only won, they won his way: with pitching and defense. In both years Cincinnati allowed the fewest runs in the majors while recording the best defensive efficiency and the lowest opponents' batting average on balls in play. The 1940 club's 117 errors were the fewest in history to that point. The defensive efficiency rate—73 percent of batters retired on balls in play—tied for the all-time best. Sportswriter Edwin Pope commented that Cincinnati "guarded home plate like it was the last penny in Fort Knox."[22]

McKechnie won with a collection of mostly forgotten players. The Reds were the only team to win two straight pennants without a single Hall of Famer on the roster, until Lombardi was inducted nearly 50 years later. No other player came close to election.

When the club dropped to third place in 1941 and fourth in 1942, some of the players thought McKechnie showed too much loyalty to his slumping former stars. During the war years, as the military draft gutted the roster, McKechnie filled in with more over-the-hill veterans. In 1945 the depleted Reds fell to seventh place with their first losing record on McKechnie's watch.

The return of real major leaguers in 1946 brought little improvement. McKechnie's defense-first dogma produced a lineup that finished last in runs scored and sixth in the standings. While other teams basked in a postwar attendance bonanza, the Reds drew the smallest crowds in the league. Before the season was over, McKechnie resigned under pressure. "Those fans don't know what's good for them," general manager Giles lamented. "They've just forced me to fire the best manager in baseball."[23]

The 60-year-old McKechnie's unemployment may have been the shortest in history. Even before he got out of town, Cleveland owner Bill Veeck tracked him down to hire him as a coach. Veeck didn't think much of his manager, Lou Boudreau, who was also his star shortstop, but McKechnie insisted he would not manage again. Veeck made him the highest-paid coach in the game; his $25,000 salary was three or four times that of most coaches. The contract included a bonus based on attendance. When the Indians drew a record 2.6 million in 1948, McKechnie made around $47,000, more than any Cleveland player except Bob Feller.[24]

The arrangement was uncomfortable at first, bringing back echoes of Fred Clarke in Pittsburgh's dugout, but Boudreau came to rely on the man he called "Pops." McKechnie took primary responsibility for the pitching staff, which was the American League's best when Cleveland won the '48 pennant and World Series.

After Veeck sold the Indians in 1949, the new owners got rid of the high-priced coaches. McKechnie retired to his farm in Bradenton, Florida, where he grew tomatoes and citrus fruit. He had bought the land in partnership with his former catcher Jimmie Wilson and also owned a produce-shipping business. An investment in Texas oil wells with another of his former players, Randy Moore, paid off with comfortable incomes for McKechnie and several other baseball men, including Casey Stengel and Al Lopez. Edd and Essie Roush also retired to Bradenton; they lived just two blocks from the McKechnies, and the two wives were close friends.

When Boudreau became manager of the Red Sox in 1952, he wanted McKechnie as his pitching coach. At first McKechnie said he would only work with the team in spring training, but he agreed to a full-time job with his wife's encouragement. "I know he misses his friends in baseball," Beryl said. "I can tell every spring."[25]

The same week that McKechnie joined the Red Sox, his son Bill Jr. was named Cincinnati's farm director. Bill Jr. later served as president of the Triple-A Pacific Coast League. A grandson, also named Bill, was a minor league executive.

The Boston job lasted two years, until the team decided to go with younger and cheaper coaches. McKechnie retired for good. Beryl died in 1957. They had been married for 46 years and had two daughters and two sons.

In 1962 the Hall of Fame's Veterans Committee voted McKechnie into Cooperstown. He was the fifth man to be elected as a manager, following Connie Mack, John McGraw, Wilbert Robinson, and Joe McCarthy. McKechnie was inducted with Jackie Robinson, Bob Feller, and his friend Edd Roush. At the ceremony he said, "Anything I've contributed to baseball I've been repaid seven times seven."[26] That's how the newspapers reported it. McKechnie's daughter Carol heard him say "seventy times seven," a quotation from the Biblical book of Matthew.[27]

That summer two men barged into McKechnie's home wearing bags over their heads. One waved a gun, the other an iron pipe. They demanded cash. The 75-year-old tried to talk them out of it, but when that didn't work he grabbed a floor lamp and began swinging it like a Louisville Slugger. The thugs retreated as McKechnie hustled into his bedroom to get his shotgun. The frustrated pair got away without injury and without money.

In a fitting tribute, the city of Bradenton renamed its ballpark McKechnie Field. It is the spring home of the Pittsburgh Pirates and the home of their Class-A affiliate in the Gulf Coast League.

McKechnie contracted leukemia, which weakened his immune system, and died of pneumonia on October 29, 1965. His record shows 1,896 games won, 1,723 lost, with four pennants and two World Series championships, but his former players remembered his patience and decency. Pitcher Junior Thompson, who joined the Reds as a 22-year-old, said, "He and his wife were like parents to me."[28] Paul Waner recalled, "He could be a father to you when he felt he had to be and a taskmaster when that was needed."[29] Paul Derringer said, "In a sentence I'd say he was the greatest manager I ever played for, the greatest manager I ever played against, and the greatest man I ever knew."[30]

NOTES

1. Lee Allen, *The Cincinnati Reds* (New York: G. P. Putnam's Sons, 1948), 255.

2. Allen, *Cincinnati Reds*, 271.

3. Frank Graham, "Another Pennant for McKechnie?," *Look*, April 4, 1944, 42.

4. Ed Rumill, "An Interview with Bill McKechnie," *Baseball Magazine*, June 1950, 247.

5. Joe Williams, "Deacon Bill McKechnie," *Saturday Evening Post*, September 14, 1940, 89.

6. During his baseball career, McKechnie gave his birth year as 1887. He said he learned he was a year older when one of his sisters found the correct date in an old family Bible. In such a large family, it would be possible to confuse one child's birth date, but it seems equally probable that McKechnie, like many other players, had subtracted a

year for his "baseball age" and didn't want to admit it. *The Sporting News*, November 13, 1965, 25.

7. Graham, "Another Pennant," 44.

8. Frederick G. Lieb, "McKechnie, Flag-Winner in 3 Cities, Dead," *The Sporting News*, November 13, 1965, 25. Lieb is the source of several versions of the Chance quote, some more colorful than others.

9. Jerome Holtzman, *No Cheering in the Press Box* (New York: Holt, Rinehart, and Winston, 1974), 13.

10. Regis M. Welsh, "M'Kechnie Suffers Penalty of Indecision," *Pittsburgh Post*, October 19, 1926, 14.

11. "Two Veterans Walk Plank in Pirate Mutiny," *Chicago Tribune*, August 14, 1926, 13.

12. Welsh, "M'Kechnie Suffers Penalty."

13. John Kieran, "Sports of the Times," *New York Times*, October 23, 1928, 37.

14. 14 Al Abrams, "McKechnie's Plans Depend Upon Tax Collector Fight," *Pittsburgh Post-Gazette*, August 8, 1929, 17.

15. Burt Whitman, "'Let the Other Fellows Worry' Is McKechnie's Philosophy as Braves Resume War Dance," *Boston Herald*, August 26, 1933, 7. "We're in the Money" was a hit song from the Busby Berkeley movie musical "Gold Diggers of 1933."

16. Defensive efficiency rate measures a team's ability to convert batted balls into outs. The 1933 Braves' rate was 71.6 percent.

17. Fuchs's letter to Ruth is reprinted in Robert W. Creamer, *Babe: The Legend Comes to Life* (rpt.: New York: Penguin, 1983), 386–88.

18. "Bill McKechnie Goes About Business Despite Report Ruth Will Succeed Him," *Boston Herald*, February 27, 1935, 16.

19. Edgar G. Brands, "Barrow, McKechnie, Allen, LaMotte, Flowers and Keller Win '37 Accolades," *The Sporting News*, December 30, 1937, 2.

20. Bill McKechnie page at the National Baseball Hall of Fame website, http://baseballhall.org/hof/mckechnie-bill, accessed August 19, 2015.

21. William Nack, "The Razor's Edge," *Sports Illustrated*, May 6, 1991, http://www.si.com/vault/1991/05/06/124126/the-razors-edge-as-the-cincinnati-reds-chased-a-pennant-in-1940-a-dark-family-legacy-tortured-the-mind-of-catcher-willard-hershberger, accessed September 9, 2015.

22. McKechnie page at the HOF website.

23. Arthur Daley, "Sports of the Times," *New York Times*, February 8, 1962, 49.

24. Bill Veeck with Ed Linn, *Veeck as in Wreck* (rpt.: Chicago: University of Chicago Press, 2001), 155.

25. Bill Grimes, "Mrs. Bill McKechnie Hopes Hubby Stays with Red Sox," *Boston American*, February 29, 1952, 8.

26. "Feller, Robby, Two Veterans Join Famers," United Press International-*Boston Record-American*, July 24, 1962.

27. Mitchell Conrad Stinson, *Deacon Bill McKechnie* (Jefferson NC: McFarland, 2012), 214.

28. Talmage Boston, *1939: Baseball's Pivotal Year* (Fort Worth TX: Summit, 1990), 78.

29. Ed Rumill, "McKechnie Knew Plays, When to Use Them," *Christian Science Monitor*, November 4, 1972, 11.

30. *Bradenton Herald*, November 2, 1965, quoted in Stinson, *Deacon Bill McKechnie*, 212.

SOURCES

In addition to the sources cited in the notes, the author also consulted:

"Guillotine Quickly Puts Down Anti-Clarke Rebellion." *The Sporting News*, August 19, 1926.

Honig, Donald. *The Man in the Dugout*. Chicago: Follett, 1977.

Jackson, Frank, "Indian Summer at Braves Field." *Hardball Times*, March 27, 2015. http://www.hardballtimes.com/indian-summer-at-braves-field/.

Jaffe, Chris. *Evaluating Baseball's Managers*. Jefferson NC: McFarland, 2010.

James, Bill. *The Bill James Guide to Baseball Managers*. New York: Scribner, 1997.

Lowenfish, Lee. *Branch Rickey, Baseball's Ferocious Gentleman*. Lincoln: University of Nebraska Press, 2007.

Koppett, Leonard. *The Man in the Dugout*. New York: Crown, 1993.

Louisa, Angelo. "Fred Clarke." SABR BioProject.

Ritter, Lawrence. *The Glory of their Times*. New York: Macmillan, 1966.

Ruane, Tom. "A Retro-Review of the 1920s." Retrosheet.org, http://www.retrosheet.org/Research/RuaneT/rev1920_art.htm. Accessed August 19, 2015.

———. "A Retro-Review of the 1930s." Retrosheet.org. http://www.retrosheet.org/Research/RuaneT/rev1930_art.htm.

———. "A Retro-Review of the 1940s." Retrosheet.org. http://www.retrosheet.org/Research/RuaneT/rev1940_art.htm.

Swope, Tom. "On the Pennant Path," *Cincinnati Post*, August 16, 1939.

47

The Roster Depreciation Allowance

How Major League Baseball Teams
Turn Profits into Losses

STEPHEN R. KEENEY

Understanding the economics of owning a baseball team, particularly how a team can claim to be losing money every year while franchise sale prices keep escalating, has baffled fans and analysts for many decades. In this article, Stephen Keeney explores one piece of the puzzle—an accounting trick that big-league teams have long used to turn actual profits into paper losses. Keeney is a lawyer who works as a union staff representative in Dayton.

> "Under current generally accepted accounting principles, I can turn a $4 million profit into a $2 million loss, and I can get every national accounting firm to agree with me."
>
> —PAUL BEESTON, president of the Toronto Blue Jays

Major professional sports are big businesses. And owners of sports teams generally run them accordingly, seeking to strike a balance between costs—including taxes—and revenues which maximizes profits. As Paul Beeston's words show, sports franchises are even more profitable than leagues and owners like to admit. MLB Commissioner Bud Selig testified before Congress in 2001 that baseball teams were losing hundreds of millions of dollars per year.[1] The Congressional committee was skeptical, as was Forbes.com, which concluded that MLB teams likely had an operating profit of around $75 million.[2]

But if Paul Beeston can turn profits into losses under basic accounting principles, then perhaps Selig and Forbes were both technically "right." How can this be? One way is tax breaks. Taxing sports franchises is a challenge because the business model and profitability depend heavily upon intangible assets: things that create value but cannot be physically touched, such as television and trademark rights.[3] The issues and regulations regarding valuation of franchises are so complex that sports analysts often fail to fully understand them.[4]

This article discusses one such tax issue: the Roster Depreciation Allowance. The topic has been discussed in simple terms in the popular press, as in this quotation from *Time*: "Owners get to deduct player salaries twice over, as an actual expense (since they're actually paying them) and as a depreciating asset (like GM would for a factory or FedEx a jet)."[5] It has also been discussed in the academic field with in-depth mathematical and economic language and analysis.[6] This article presents a middle ground, delving into the history of the Roster Depreciation Allowance and presenting an understanding of the application and consequences of the Roster Depreciation Allowance that is more nuanced than the popular press but accessible to those without a strong background in mathematics or economics.

The Roster Depreciation Allowance (RDA) is a tax law that allows a purchaser to depreciate (or, more accurately, to *amortize*) almost the entire purchase price of a sports franchise. Depreciation is when a company takes the decrease in value of a tangible asset over a certain period of time as an economic loss in its accounting. If a landscaping company buys a riding mower, the company will take a certain percentage of that mower's cost each year for a certain number of years as a loss, which counts against the company's profits. The loss is economic because the company isn't actually losing any money on the mower, but because the mower is worth less than it was when the company bought it, companies are allowed to count that loss against their revenues for accounting purposes. By lowering the revenues and subsequently the profits of the company, depreciation lowers the company's taxable income.

The accounting principles behind depreciation are fairly simple. For every transaction, one account must increase, and one must decrease, both by the same dollar amount. When a company spends $1,500 on a riding lawn mower, assuming they pay in cash or an equivalent rather than with a loan, the company's bank account decreases by $1,500. But now the company owns a mower worth $1,500, so its asset account—the value of the stuff and money it owns—must go up by the same $1,500. That part is simple enough. But after the company uses the mower for several years the mower's value will be reduced to zero.[7] When the mower's value hits zero, the company's asset account would have essentially been reduced by $1,500 because they have $1,500 less stuff. But to keep their books balanced, there must be an equal increase somewhere else. That increase comes in the "depreciation expenses" category, which increases a company's expenses (the money a business spends conducting its business) just as if the company had paid money to an employee. The concept of depreciation simply allows the company to make those adjustments in smaller increments, say 10% per year for 10 years, instead of all at once.

The IRS puts out several rules and regulations which determine the percentage of the purchase price of any given item that is depreciable, over how many years the depreciation is spread, and what methods of depreciation are allowed. Amortization, as used here, is simply depreciation for intangible assets.[8] If a company buys an intangible asset, like a patent, it is amortized rather than depreciated, but the same basic process applies. To avoid confusion the rest of this paper will refer to the amortization that takes place under the RDA as depreciation.

The RDA is one of several "gymnastic bookkeeping techniques" businesses and sports franchises use to minimize tax liabilities.[9] The RDA is a depreciation of almost the entire purchase price of a sports franchise over 15 years. This means that each year for 15 years, the purchaser (or purchasers) of a professional sports franchise can take a tax deduction based on the purchase price of the franchise. The current RDA allows sports franchise purchasers to depreciate almost 100 percent of the purchase price over the first 15 years after the purchase; a tax deduction of about 6.67 percent of the purchase price per year.[10]

The RDA is not exactly unique because many businesses depreciate the costs of both tangible (physical, like lawn mowers) and intangible (not physical but still profitable, like patents) assets. But it is unique in that it deals with sports franchises. Unlike riding lawn mowers or patents, which are essentially worthless at some point in time, the value of sports franchises continues to increase. While depreciation generally allows companies to count the loss of value of their assets as costs of operation, the RDA allows companies to count losses on an asset whose value continues to rise.

The current RDA is fairly straightforward, but has not always been that way. Before the first RDA became law in 1976, nobody—not owners, lawyers, accountants, courts, or the IRS—could accurately depreciate the sports franchise as an asset with any consistency.[11] Because high barriers to entry meant that buying a sports franchise was and still is a relatively uncommon event, it took lawmakers a while to figure out what to do.

Before moving into the history of the RDA, it is important to understand a few key concepts. The first is the concept of franchise rights. Franchise rights refer to the full panoply of rights associated with being a franchise in a major sports league, such as rights to revenue sharing, rights to trademarks, trade names, licenses, and other intellectual property, rights to regional exclusivity, and all the other rights that come from being a member of the league.

The second concept is the distinction between player *contracts* and player *contract rights*. *Player contracts* state how much a player will make over how many years, and will set out what the player has to do to earn that money. In short, player contracts are about a player's salary. *Player contract rights* refers to the ownership of the right to enforce the contract and the duty to abide by it. So even though a player may have a $3 million per year salary, if he brings in $4 million in revenue, a person may only pay $500,000 for the contract rights, because he will pay the salary and the price of the contract rights for a total of $3.5 million in exchange for $4 million in revenue. But if the same $3 million player brings in $10 million in revenue a year, then someone may pay $5 million for his contract rights, for a total salary plus purchase price of $8 million in order to gain that $10 million in revenue. In an example that will be examined later, when Bud Selig bought the Seattle Pilots in 1970, he said that he paid $10.2 million to buy the *player contract rights* of the entire roster, even though the roster's total *salaries* were only $607,400.[12]

Two key court cases came about in the late 1920s which dealt with how baseball teams treat the costs of player contracts. The case of *Chicago Nat'l League Ball Club v. Commissioner*[13] dealt with the Chicago Cubs' 1927 and 1928 corporate tax returns and the case of *Commissioner v. Pittsburgh Athletic Co.*[14] dealt with the Pittsburgh Pirates' 1928–1930 corporate tax returns. Until 1928, the Pirates had been taking a tax deduction for the difference between all the player contracts they bought and all the player contracts they sold in a given year. But now both teams, the Cubs starting in 1927 and the Pirates starting in 1928, had begun taking the entire amount played for player contracts[15] in a given year as tax deductions in a that same year.

The reserve clause played a key role in these decisions because it essentially created a perpetual team option contract. Both teams argued that since all player contracts were technically only one-year contracts, they had useful lives of one year and thus the full amount was depreciable in the year in which they were purchased. The IRS argued that the amounts paid for player contracts should be deducted over a period of at least three years because the reserve clause essentially gave the contracts a useful life equal to a player's entire career. In both cases, the court relied on non-baseball precedent to say that even though a contract has an option to extend its duration, the life of the contract itself was not necessarily changed by the option. So in both cases, the team won.

An early version of the RDA was enacted just over a decade later. When sports entrepreneur Bill Veeck bought the Cleveland Indians in 1946, he persuaded Congress and the IRS to act. Veeck argued that the amount of the purchase price that went towards buying the rights to the player contracts should be treated as a depreciable asset.[16] Sports teams could then "double dip" by taking the RDA depreciation for the purchase price of the contracts, how much the new owners paid to old owners for the ability to enforce the contracts, and then deducting the salaries actually paid each year to players as labor costs. Moreover, unlike most assets which can only be depreciated once, the RDA applies anew each time a franchise is purchased.[17] This new, clear version of the rules increased the value of franchises, and Veeck quickly capitalized by selling the Indians in 1949.[18]

With the purchase price of player contracts now a depreciable asset, team buyers began doing what the *Chicago* court could not: determining how much of the purchase price was for the franchise rights (league membership, regional exclusivity, revenue sharing and licensing rights, etc.) and how much was for the player contracts. The IRS's stated position was that the price of the franchise rights was not depreciable because it did not have a determinable life (the NFL, NBA, or MLB and their franchises could potentially live on and be profitable forever), but the price of the player contracts was depreciable because they had a determinable life (the contract was only valuable for however many years the player was bound to the club).[19] While the franchise rights are the more valuable part of team ownership, buyers wanted to make as much of the purchase price depreciable as possible.[20] So buyers began allocating huge percentages of the purchase price to the player contracts and away from the franchise rights.

The NFL granted an expansion franchise in 1965 which became the Atlanta Falcons.[21] The new owners tried to depreciate both the cost of the contracts of the 42 players acquired via the expansion draft and the cost of the Falcons' franchise right to a share of the NFL television revenues.[22] The IRS asserted deficiencies, arguing that the owners allocated too much of the purchase price to the player contracts and not enough to the franchise rights.[23] The

IRS also argued that the "mass asset rule" should apply to prevent the Falcons from dividing the purchase price between the franchise rights and the player contracts. The "mass asset rule" prevents depreciation of intangible assets of indeterminate life (such as rights to television revenue) if they are inseparable from intangible assets of determinable life (such as player contracts). The IRS argued that it was impossible to separate the costs of becoming an NFL franchise and the costs expended to acquire the players on its roster, and that therefore the "mass asset rule" should apply.

The court disagreed. It held that the "mass asset rule" did not apply because the player contracts 1) had their own value separate from the franchise rights, and 2) had a limited useful life which could be ascertained with reasonable accuracy.[24] So the court allowed the Falcons to separate and depreciate the cost of player contracts from the rest of the intangibles.[25] The court also held that the television rights bundle could not be depreciated because it was of indeterminable length, running as long as the franchise is part of the NFL.[26] Thus, franchise owners benefitted the most when they attributed more of the purchase price to player contracts instead of to the franchise rights, so that's exactly what they started doing.

Former MLB commissioner Bud Selig took the practice of allocating costs towards player contracts in order to maximize depreciation deductions to new heights when he bought the Seattle Pilots in 1970. Selig bought the Pilots for $10.8 million.[27] He allocated 94 percent of the purchase price (or about $10.2 million) to the purchase of player contracts, even though the contracts themselves were only for $607,400 worth of salaries, according to Baseball-Almanac.com.[28] The remaining purchase price was allocated to the equipment and supplies ($100,000) and the value of the franchise ($500,000).[29] The court upheld this allocation.[30]

In response to Selig's allocation (but before the decision upholding it came down) the IRS and Congress acted to prevent such allocations in the future. Congress enacted Section 1056, which regulated the tax treatment of player contracts. Subsections (a)-(c) dealt with the "basis" of player contracts.[31] "Basis" is a tax term describing the amount of money "put into" an asset—minus any depreciation deductions taken—by the owner. This determines the amount of taxable profit/loss the owner will realize on a subsequent sale of the asset.[32] Subsection (d) creates a presumption that no more than 50 percent of the purchase price of a sports franchise could be allocated to player contracts, unless the purchaser establishes to the IRS that a higher percentage is proper. This amount could then be depreciated over a five-year period (rather than over the lives of the individual contracts). This law created the 50/5 rule: 50 percent of the total purchase price of the franchise could be depreciated over five years.

The 50/5 rule streamlined sports franchise bookkeeping by making all the purchased contract rights one large, depreciable asset. This may have been an attempt to get courts to stop evaluating the reasonableness of the contract rights purchase price first and allocating the remainder to franchise rights second.[33] However, since it created only a presumption and not a rule, the IRS continued to struggle against franchise buyers who argued that more than 50% of the purchase price was for the player contracts.[34]

Around the turn of the century, Congress drastically changed the RDA. In 1993, Congress had passed a tax law called Section 197, which gave all businesses the ability to depreciate the purchase price of intangible assets, but specifically excluded sports franchises.[35] So the 50/5 rule in Section 1056 continued to apply to professional sports franchises. Then Congress passed the American Jobs Creation Act of 2004. As part of this Act, Section 1056 was repealed, and the purchase price of sports franchises became subject to the 15-year depreciation rules applicable to other intangible assets under Section 197.[36] "Section 197 allows an amortized deduction for the capitalized costs of [things listed in Section 197]."[37] These intangibles include "workforce in place" (player contract rights), as well as "any franchise, trademark, or trade name."[38] Thus, the specific exclusion of sports franchises from intangible assets was ended.[39] Under this new 100/15 rule, almost the full purchase price of a franchise is depreciable over 15 years.[40]

The RDA is perhaps best understood through hypotheticals. An analysis of the 2004 rule gives the following example:

Buyer (B) pays Seller (S) $350 million for an MLB franchise. $40 million represents the costs of all tangible assets (uniforms, bats, balls, mascot costumes, etc.) and the intangible assets which are not the franchise itself or the player contracts (such as a stadium lease). The remaining $310 million is a depreciable asset, just as if B had bought a factory or patent.[41]

As this example illustrates, not all intangible assets are depreciable under the RDA, such as the stadium lease[42] mentioned above. This leaves room for the old-fashioned disputes about allocation, but the amount of money in contention is much smaller.

For an example of the difference between the old and new incarnations of the RDA, consider the following: Assume that an investor, or a group of investors, purchased a sports franchise for $150 million *total*. Under the old 50/5 rule, the franchise would be able to depreciate $75 million (50 percent) over five years, or $15 million dollars per year. That means that $15 million worth of revenues are not taxed. Assuming a tax rate of 35 percent, that $15 million in revenue would have generated income tax of $5.25 million.[43] Multiplied by five years means $26.25 million in tax savings for the franchise.

Now, let's use the same hypothetical for the current RDA. A purchaser or group of purchasers buys a sports franchise for $150 million, with $100 million of that being for the *franchise and player contract rights*.[44] Under the 100/15 rule, the franchise can depreciate $100 million over fifteen years, or about $6.67 million per year. That means that $6.67 million of revenues per year are not taxed. Assuming a tax rate of 35 percent, the franchise owners gain approximately $2.33 million in taxes, which they would have had to pay the IRS without the RDA. Multiplied by fifteen years, that equals about $35 million in tax savings.

These examples have two caveats. One is that, in the examples above, if an owner buys a team for $150 million he will almost certainly allocate far more than $100 million to the franchise and player rights ($100 million is only 67 percent of $150 million, but remember Bud Selig allocated 94 percent to player rights alone). Thus, the tax advantages to the owners under the current rules would be even greater than the example illustrates. The last 10 times a major sports franchise (NHL, NFL, NBA, or MLB) was sold, the prices ranged from $170 million to $2.15 billion, with five of those 10 between $200 and $600 million.[45] So, if a team were purchased for $400 million and the owners allocated $376 million to player rights and other depreciable intangibles ($376 million is 94% of the purchase price, which Bud Selig got away with), they could depreciate just under $25.1 million per year, which at a 35 percent tax rate would be savings of $8.77 million per year to the owners.

The second caveat is that nothing in this paper discusses changes to the depreciable amount. Theoretically, a franchise would acquire and sell the rights of individual players and would thus have to realize gains or losses on each sale, and likely apply the RDA to each new player contract it acquires, depending on how it does its accounting. Since these examples are illustrative only, we are only dealing with the initial purchase of all player contracts the franchise owns at the time of the sale.

This is a good point to provide greater context for the numbers we've been discussing to see the real impact of the RDA and the 2004 changes. As discussed earlier, the RDA creates tax savings for owners. But these breaks are only temporary. We have to remember the concepts of depreciation and basis discussed above. When you depreciate an asset, your basis in that asset decreases. If you sell that asset, you are taxed on the portion of that income which exceeds your basis. Remember that lawn mower from our landscaping company from before? Let's say the company buys a lawn mower for $1,500. Its basis in the lawn mower is $1,500. The company then depreciates $150 (10%) per year for six years, for a total depreciation of $900. The company's basis in the lawn mower is decreased by that $900 of depreciation, so that the company's basis is now $600. So after owning the lawn mower for six years, the company now sells it to someone else for $750. The company will have to pay tax on the difference between the $750 it received for the lawn mower and its $600 basis in the lawn mower, which is $150 of taxable income.

The same is true of sports franchises under the RDA. For every dollar a *franchise* takes as depreciation, the owners will have to pay taxes on another dollar of profit from the sale of the *franchise*. So the RDA itself does not really affect the dollar amount of taxes paid by a franchise. But it does do two other things. First, because the amount of the depreciation allowed was increased from 50% of the purchase price to almost 100% of the purchase price, it allows more revenue to go untaxed (see table 47.1). Second, by using the RDA and other accounting methods, franchises make revenue disappear from the profit line.

Table 47.1. Pre-2004 vs. post-2004 RDA taxable amounts

Pre-2004 RDA			
Purchase Price: $150m			
Year	Deduction ($)	Basis ($)	Revenue ($)	Rev. Taxed ($)
---	---	---	---	---
1	7.50	142.50	5.00	(2.50)
2	7.50	135.00	5.08	(2.43)
3	7.50	127.50	5.15	(2.35)
4	7.50	120.00	5.23	(2.27)
5	7.50	112.50	5.31	(2.19)
6	0.00	105.00	5.39	5.39
7	0.00	105.00	5.47	5.47

8	0.00	105.00	5.55	5.55
9	0.00	105.00	5.63	5.63
10	0.00	105.00	5.72	5.72
11	0.00	105.00	5.80	5.80
12	0.00	105.00	5.89	5.89
13	0.00	105.00	5.98	5.98
14	0.00	105.00	6.07	6.07
15	0.00	105.00	6.16	6.16
Total			83.41	45.91

Sale Price ($)	Basis ($)	Taxable ($)
200.00	105.00	95.00

Total Taxable Income Pre-2004 ($)

Sale	95.00
Revenue	45.91
Total	140.91

Post-2004 RDA

Purchase Price: $150m

Year	Deduction ($)	Basis ($)	Revenue ($)	Rev. Taxed ($)
1	10.00	140.00	5.00	(5.00)
2	10.00	130.00	5.08	(4.93)
3	10.00	120.00	5.05	(4.85)
4	10.00	110.00	5.23	(4.77)
5	10.00	100.00	5.31	(4.69)
6	10.00	90.00	5.39	(4.61)
7	10.00	80.00	5.47	(4.53)
8	10.00	70.00	5.55	(4.45)
9	10.00	60.00	5.63	(4.37)
10	10.00	50.00	5.72	(4.28)
11	10.00	40.00	5.80	(4.20)
12	10.00	30.00	5.89	(4.11)
13	10.00	20.00	5.98	(4.02)
14	10.00	10.00	6.07	(3.93)
15	10.00	0.00	6.16	(3.84)
Total			83.41	(66.59)

	Sale Price ($)	Basis ($)	Taxable ($)
	200.00	0.00	200.00
	Total Taxable Income Post-2004 ($)		
Sale	200.00		
Revenue	(66.59)		
Total	133.41		

These tax breaks create a type of deferred-tax situation—a situation where companies can use accounting to delay paying current taxes due until a later date—because they allow the franchise owners to keep more money now and make up for taxes due later. Because every $1 of depreciation decreases basis by $1, at a 35% tax rate the owners are saving $.35 now, but will have to pay that $.35 back later if they sell the franchise. Of course, these savings the owners get are going to be generating more income for them while the total they owe the IRS will stay the same, effectively acting as an interest-free loan from the government to the owners.[46] This article is not trying to decry some perceived injustice in the existence of the RDA—but it is something sports fans should be aware of when they are considering financial numbers put out by both the media and the teams themselves.

Congress placed sports franchises under the general law for intangible asset depreciation in 2004 for several reasons. First, it made the rules more uniform across industries. Second, the clearer rules were meant to minimize disputes regarding proper allocation, and in turn to reduce the IRS's administrative and enforcement costs.[47] Finally, supporters argued that it would increase tax payments by about $381 million over ten years.[48] While the deductible amount doubled, the amortization time period tripled, which would increase tax bills in the short term. As the above hypotheticals show, while the amortizable amount increased from 50 to almost 100 percent, the dollar amount amortized each year decreased; meaning that in the early years the teams would have more taxable income. While the 50/5 example above allowed an annual deduction of $5.25 million, the 100/15 example only allowed an annual deduction of $2.33 million, increasing the team's taxable income for the first five years. Of course, after those five years, as the depreciation continued to apply, the increased percentage meant that even more money was safe from taxation than before.

By doubling the amount of tax deductions a team could take the new

RDA increased franchise values. Higher depreciation totals meant more tax deductions and more untaxed profits for owners in the long run. Experts in the field theorized that the average values of sports franchises would increase by five percent.[49] One economic report argued that average value would in fact increase by 11.6 percent.[50]

Further, for many teams, even the lower depreciation amounts exceed taxable income for each of the 15 years, allowing the owners to pass the paper losses on to their personal income tax liability.[51] For example, a Los Angeles group of investors bought the Dodgers for $2.15 billion in 2012.[52] Thus, it can take over $143 million per year as a deduction, which is a tax savings of just over $50 million per year for the owners, again assuming a 35 percent tax rate.[53] The elongated time frame means that the Dodgers' new owners can extend the tax benefits to their private income taxes as business losses for ten years longer than under the old rules, but more importantly the extended coverage of the new RDA, from 50% to almost 100% of purchase price, allows them to almost double the total deductible about.[54] If Paul Beeston could turn a $4 million profit into a $2 million loss, just imagine how much profit the Dodgers' owners could turn into losses with $143 million in deductions.

There have been several examples in recent sports history that illustrate the effects of the RDA on the business of sports. In 1974, before the modern rules, only 5 of 27 professional basketball teams reported a profit.[55] This history of paper losses has continued under the new rules. In 2011, with the Collective Bargaining Agreement between the league and players expiring, the NBA stated that 22 of its 30 teams were losing money.[56] As a lockout loomed, NBA players argued that the "losses" suffered by teams were paper rather than real.[57] As a former director of the MLB Players Association once said, if "[y]ou go through *The Sporting News* of the last 100 years, and you will find two things are always true. You never have enough pitchers, and nobody ever made money."[58]

Forbes reported in August 2013 that the Houston Astros, who had finished with the worst record in Major League Baseball each year from 2011 through 2013, were on pace to make $99 million in profit in 2013—the most of any team in baseball history.[59] The Astros responded that their numbers were not near that amount. The difference is because the Astros, unlike *Forbes*, included non-cash losses, such as the RDA, in its calculation.[60] Current Astros owner Jim Crane bought the team in 2011. Between then and 2013, he cut player salaries from $77 million to $13 million.[61] According to the *Sports Business Journal*, Crane paid about $700 million for the team.[62] This means that the Astros would get about $46.7 million per year in paper losses associated with acquiring player contracts, despite paying actual salary amounts as low as $13 million. If you multiply the $46.7 million per year deduction by 35 percent, the RDA allows the team to keep about $16.3 million dollars per year which it would have had to pay in taxes. That's more than enough to double the salary of the entire 2013 roster. So, with the help of the RDA, the Astros are taking a large paper loss as well as decreasing labor expenses, greatly increasing their profit margin. If you subtract the $46.7 million in depreciation losses from the Forbes projection of $99 million in profits, it's easy to see why the Astros claimed the numbers were so far off. It's also easy to see how such vastly profitable businesses as sports franchises can say they are not making money with a straight face.

If you were to get on the public address system at any ballpark in America during a baseball game and ask for a show of hands on how many people are interested in how their teams account for depreciation of intangible assets, among the sea of boos you would probably find no hands up. But the people who run the teams are very interested in limiting their tax liability. It allows them to either pocket more money in profits or to pay better players to win more games. And as fans and society continue to take an increasingly academic look at professional sports, the Roster Depreciation Allowance is a crucial consideration to pay attention to in the economics of professional sports. The next time you see an article about the financial condition of your favorite team, you'll know that there is much more going on in the books than meets the eye.

NOTES

Epigraph: Dan Alexander, "Can Houston Astros Really Be Losing Money Despite Rock-Bottom Payroll?," Forbes.com, August 29, 2013, http://www.forbes.com/sites/danalexander/2013/08/29/can-houston-astros-really-be-losing-money-despite-rock-bottom-payroll/.

1. Richard Sandomir, "Selig Defends His Plan of Contraction to Congress," *New York Times*, December 7, 2001, http://www.nytimes.com/2001/12/07/sports/ baseball-selig-defends-his-plan-of-contraction-to-congress.html.

2. Michael Ozanian, "Is Baseball Really Broke?," *Forbes*, April 3, 2002, http://www.forbes.com/2002/04/01/0401baseball.html.

3. See Robert Holo and Jonathan Talansky, "Taxing the Business of Sports," 9 Fla. Tax Rev. 161 (2008): 184 (discussing current issues in taxing sports at the entity level).

4. *See* Tommy Craggs, "Exclusive: How an NBA Team Makes Money Disappear [Update With Correction]," Deadspin.com, June 30, 2011, http://deadspin.com/5816870 /exclusive-how-and-why-an-nba-team-makes-a-7-million-profit-look-like-a-28 -million-loss (misconstruing the nature of the allowance and implying that it is of unlimited duration rather than the current 15-year limit); and Larry Coon, "Is the NBA Really Losing Money?," espn.com, July 12, 2011, http://sports.espn.go.com/nba /columns/story?columnist=coon_larry&page=nbafinancials-110630 (asserting the pre-2004 law of the Roster Depreciation Allowance as current in 2011).

5. Gary Belsky, "Why $1.5 Billion for the Dodgers Might be a Bargain," Time.com, March 9, 2012, http://business.time.com/2012/03/09/why-1-5-billion-for-the-dodgers -might-turn-out-to-be-a-bargain/.

6. N. Edward Coulson and Rodney Fort, *Tax Revisions of 2004 and Pro Sports Team Ownership*, available at http://econ.la.psu.edu/~ecoulson/veeck.pdf.

7. The mower may have "scrap value" which a company may account for, but for practical and illustrative purposes we will assume the mower becomes worth $0 at the end of its useful life.

8. Amortization is a general name for the spreading out of payments over a long period of time into equal amounts. In terms of loans such as mortgages and car loan, amortization refers to spreading out the total debt into equal regular payments rather than paying it all at once at the end of the loan period. In terms of business assets, amortization refers to the process of spreading the cost of an intangible asset's depreciation into equal parts over a period of time, and taking the depreciation as a paper loss at regular intervals.

9. Ron Maierhofer, *No Money Down: How to Buy a Sports Franchise, A Journey Through an American Dream* (Indianapolis: Dog Ear Publishing, 2009), 27.

10. 26 U.S.C. § 197.

11. 26 U.S.C. § 1056, effective January 1, 1976 through 2004. See http://law.justia.com /codes/us/1996/title26/chap1/subchapo/partiv/sec1056 and http://uscode.house .gov/view.xhtml?req=granuleid:usc-prelim-title26-section1056&num=0&edition =prelim.

12. "1969 Seattle Pilots Roster," Baseball-Almanac.com, http://www.baseball-almanac.com /teamstats/roster.php?y=1969&t=sel. The $607,400 team total salary comes from adding together the salaries listed on the page cited.

13. *Chicago Nat'l League Ball Club v. Commissioner*, 1933 WL 4911 (B.T.A.) (1933), affirmed sub nom *Commissioner of Internal Revenue v. Chicago Nat'l League Ball Club*, 74 F.2d 1010 (1935).

14. *Commissioner of Internal Revenue v. Pittsburgh Athletic Co.*, 72 F.2d 883 (1934).

15. The distinction between player contract rights and player salaries is key here: the teams were deducting the costs of acquiring the rights of the player as business expenses, and also claiming the salaries paid to players as labor costs.

16. See Jason A. Winfree and Mark S. Rosentraub, *Sports Finance and Management* (Boca Raton FL: CRC Press, 2012), 428–29 (discussing the history of the RDA), and Coulson, *supra* note 7 (discussing Bill Veeck's role in creating the RDA and the economic consequences).

17. Winfree, *Sports Finance*, 429.

18. Winfree, *Sports Finance*, 429.

19. Winfree, *Sports Finance*, at 197. *See also*, Rev. Rul. 71–137, 1971–1 C.B. 104.

20. Talansky, "Taxing . . . Sports," 193.

21. "Atlanta Falcons Team Page," NFL.com, http://www.nfl.com/teams/atlantafalcons /profile?team=atl.

22. See *Laird v. U.S.*, 556 F. 2d. 1224, 1226–1230 (5th Cir. 1977) (upholding the Falcons' allocation of purchase price).

23. *Laird v. U.S.*

24. *Laird v. U.S.*, 1232–1233.

25. *Laird v. U.S.*, 1232–1233.

26. *Laird v. U.S.*, 1235–1237.

27. See *Selig v. U.S.*, 740 F. 2d. 572, 574 (7th Cir. 1984) (upholding the allocation made by Selig).

28. Winfree, *Sports Finance*, 429; "1969 Seattle Pilots Roster," Baseball-Almanac.com, http://www.baseball-almanac.com/teamstats/roster.php?y=1969&t=sel.

29. *Selig*, 740 F. 2d. at 575.

30. Talansky, "Taxing . . . Sports," 189 (one commentator referred to the opinion as one that "reads more like a Ken Burns paean to baseball than a legal opinion" because the court talked as much about the history of baseball in America as it did about the applicable law).

31. 26 U.S.C. § 1056.

32. For example, if you buy a house for $200,000 and make $50,000 in upgrades, your basis in the house is $250,000. If you are a landlord and you have depreciated $100,000 of the same house on your books, your basis is $150,000 ($250,000-$100,000). If you sell the house, your taxable income is the amount you got for the house minus your basis.

33. Talansky, "Taxing . . . Sports," 193.

34. Talansky, "Taxing . . . Sports," 197.

35. 26 U.S.C. § 197; "Notes," *26 U.S.C. § 197*, Cornell Law, https://www.law.cornell.edu /uscode/text/26/197.

36. Talansky, "Taxing . . . Sports," 200.

37. 26 C.F.R. § 1.197–2.

38. 26 U.S.C. § 197(d)(1)(C)(i); 26 U.S.C. § 197(d)(1)(F).

39. Talansky, "Taxing . . . Sports," 196. See also, *Complete Analysis of the American Jobs Creation Act of 2004, Chapter 300 Cost Recovery*, "315 Professional Sports Franchises are Made Subject to 15-Year Amortization; Special Basis Allocation and Depreciation Recapture Rules for Players Contracts are Repealed," 2004 CATA 315, 2004 WL 2318514 (briefly explaining the history of allocation debates between purchasers and the IRS).

40. The regular rules for depreciation of tangible assets continues to apply to all tangible things the new owners get, such as uniforms, bats, balls, equipment, etc.

41. See Complete Analysis, note 32 (paraphrased, not quoted).

42. Intangibles like the stadium lease, which are not related to franchise rights or player contracts, may be depreciable under other sections of the tax code, but they are not included in the RDA and their treatment is outside the scope of this paper.

43. I chose a 35% tax rate because it is the second-highest personal income tax rate and the highest corporate income tax rate. The *actual* tax rate—that rate the entity should pay under the tax code—will depend upon how the ownership entity is taxed (whether pass-through like a partnership or as an entity like a corporation), the net income of the individuals or entity, and whether the income is taxed at the much lower capital gains tax rate. The *effective* tax rate—the percent actually paid in taxes—will depend upon the expenses and deductions of the individual team or owners, and several other factors which may be too numerous to use in an illustrative example.

44. In both examples the team is purchased for $150 million, but in the post-2004 example the depreciation is based on $100 million rather than $150 million. This is because the pre-2004 50/5 rule applied to the *total* purchase price paid for the franchise, while the post-2004 100/15 rule applies *only* to the portion of the purchase price paid for *intangible assets* like franchise rights, player contract rights, and trademarks.

45. Dan Primack and Daniel Roberts, "American Sports Teams: All Worth More Than You Think," Fortune.com, http://fortune.com/2014/06/05/american-sports-teams -all-worth-more-than-you-think/.

46. This situation is very similar to a tax deferment. For more on tax deferments, see Stephen Foley, "The $62bn Secret of Warren Buffett's Success," *Financial Times*, FT.com, March 4, 2015, available at http://www.ft.com/cms/s/2/9c690e44-c1d2–11e4 -abb3–00144feab7de.html#slide0, and Joshua Kennon, "Using Deferred Taxes to Increase Your Investment Returns," available at http://beginnersinvest.about.com /od/capitalgainstax/a/Using-Deferred-Taxes-to-Increase-Your-Investment-Returns .htm.

47. Kennon, "Using Deferred Taxes."

48. Talansky, "Taxing . . . Sports," 202, and Coulson, "Tax Revisions of 2004," 1.

49. Talansky, "Taxing . . . Sports," 203, and Coulson, "Tax Revisions of 2004," abstract.

50. Coulson, "Tax Revisions of 2004," 18. Five or 11 percent might not sound like much, but when you consider that this is just one piece of the accounting puzzle and that we are talking about sums of hundreds of millions or billions of dollars, it adds up to a lot of money.

51. Depending on what type of business entity owned the team. Most teams are owned by partnerships, which generally allow the tax benefits to pass through to the owners' individual income tax liabilities.

52. Sean Leahy, "Bankrupt to Big Bucks: The New Economics of the Los Angeles Dodgers," San Diego State University Sports MBA '13, http://sandiegostatesmba13.blogspot.com/2012/09/bankrupt-to-big-bucks-new-economics-of.html.

53. Leahy, "Bankrupt to Big Bucks."

54. Alexander, "Can Houston Astros Really Be Losing Money." In fact, the last six World Series winners combined have made less than $99 million.

55. Talansky, "Taxing . . . Sports," 192–93.

56. Coon, "Is the NBA Really Losing Money?"

57. Coon, "Is the NBA Really Losing Money?"

58. Talansky, "Taxing . . . Sports," 184n71.

59. Dan Alexander, "2013 Houston Astros: Baseball's Worst Team is the Most Profitable in History," Forbes.com, August 26, 2013, http://www.forbes.com/sites/danalexander/2013/08/26/2013-houston-astros-baseballs-worst-team-is-most-profitable-in-history/.

60. Alexander, "Can Houston Astros Really Be Losing Money."

61. Alexander, "2013 Houston Astros."

62. Daniel Kaplan, "Crane's $220M Loan from BofA to Finance Purchase of Astros has 'Recession-Era Structure,'" SportsBusinessDaily.com, June 6, 2011, http://www.sportsbusinessdaily.com/Journal/Issues/2011/06/06/Finance/Astros.aspx.

48

Professional Woman Umpires

LESLIE HEAPHY

In 2017 SABR published *The SABR Book on Umpires and Umpiring*, a comprehensive look at the history and craft of the profession. This piece from that work examines the long but little-known history of women trying to make inroads into umpiring professional baseball, right up to the present day. Leslie Heaphy is a prolific researcher and writer in the areas of the Negro Leagues and women's baseball. She has been the chair of the Women in Baseball Committee since 1995, and in 2008 she became the founding editor of the journal *Black Ball*, published by McFarland. Leslie joined the SABR Board of Directors in 2010 and currently serves as its vice president.

"Are you blind?" is a familiar cry for fans sitting in the stands at any baseball diamond. Fans believe it is part of their job to harass the men in blue. But what happens when that man is a woman in blue? Do the insults change? Yes. Are fans so surprised some of them do not even know how to react? Yes. But baseball has been played professionally in the United States since the 1860s. Why are people still surprised by female umpires? Because they are absolutely still a novelty. Women have had limited success breaking in to the ranks of the arbiters of the game, though the few who have been allowed to participate have proved they know the rules and how to call a game. And why have both the NBA and professional football added female referees but not baseball?

Baseball made one concession to change in 2006 when the rules committee voted to acknowledge the presence of a female umpire. An amendment to Rule 2.00 in the Definition of Terms reads: "Any reference in these Official Baseball Rules to 'he,' 'him,' or 'his' shall be deemed to be a reference to 'she,' 'her,' or 'hers,' as the case may be, when the person is female."

Veteran big-league umpire Larry Young, a member of the Playing Rules Committee, voted in favor of the wording.[1] Those who voted believed it needed to be done.

Where does the story begin for the seven U.S. professional female umpires? One of the earliest women to be paid to umpire semipro games was Amanda Clement in the early 1900s. Her brother Hank helped get her started and people, while surprised, were impressed with her ability and knowledge. After Clement there was a long hiatus until Bernice Gera got her chance as the first professional. Gera was followed by Pam Postema and then there were Christine Wren and Theresa Cox. Ria Cortesio and Shanna Kook worked at the same time in 2003 and 2004. In addition to these ladies there is also Cuba's Yanet Moreno, who has been umpiring in the National Series since 2003. In 2015 Guam added a female umpire to its ranks with Jhen Senence Bennett. She umpired her first game with her father. And as recently as early 2016 Jen Pawol became the seventh after receiving a contract from the Gulf Coast League upon successful completion of umpire school.

Bernice Mary Shiner Gera was born on June 15, 1931, in Ernest, Pennsylvania but grew up in Erath, Louisiana. Gera graduated from high school in 1949, with a graduating class of three. She married Louis Thomas Jr. and after their divorce married freelance photographer Stephen Gera. She worked as a secretary before turning her hand to umpiring. A longtime baseball fan, Gera graduated in 1967 from the Jim Finley umpire school but no one came calling to give her a job professionally. Gera's experience came with local ballgames and semipro tournaments. Due to Organized Baseball's lack of acceptance Gera began a six-year battle to get a chance to umpire. She stated, "I was not out there fighting anybody's cause. I didn't do what I did because of women's liberation or anything like that. . . . I just wanted to be affiliated with baseball."[2] She received a contract in 1969 but it was invalidated by NAPBL President Philip Piton before she even got an opportunity. She finally won her lawsuit in 1972 when the New York Court of Appeals ruled in her favor. Gera signed her first and only contract on April 12, 1972. Her only officiated game took place on June 24, 1972, a Class-A game in Geneva, New York. She was supposed to ump a doubleheader between Auburn and the Geneva Senators but she left after the first game and never looked back. She retired after that one game. It was a tough game with at least three disputed calls, one of which led to her ejecting Auburn manager Nolan Campbell. Campbell said, "She should be in the kitchen, peeling potatoes."[3] After leaving the field Gera went to work for the New York Mets in community relations and promotions. When Gera died on September 23, 1992, from kidney cancer, her tombstone read, "Pro Baseball's First Lady Umpire."[4] A historical marker was also placed at Blue Spruce Park near the ball field close to her home in Pennsylvania.[5] Her uniform and equipment are on display at the Bridgeton Hall of Fame All Sports Museum.

After Gera left the game, Christine Wren had a short career in the 1970s. Wren played softball growing up in Spokane, Washington. She spent about 13 years playing fast-pitch softball, usually as the catcher. After being called out on a play at second that was clearly wrong, she decided she could be an umpire too. She attended umpire school in Mission Hills, California. When she finally got her chance to umpire, she commented, "I'm not a freak. I'm just somebody trying to do a job."[6] Wren umpired for two years in the Northwest League, in 1975 and 1976, and then in the Class-A Midwest League in 1977. In 1977 she made $250 a month plus $60 for travel expenses. Her most unusual experience came in an exhibition game when a Portland player came up to her and kissed her on the field. She gave him a warning and no one ever tried that again. Midwest League President Bill Walters was so impressed with Wren that he stated, "The girl is good and I want to convince Mr. (Bowie) Kuhn that she's good."[7] She managed the players on the field like any good umpire and ejected players only when needed. Her first ejection came in a Seattle Rainiers game against Boise. She ejected catcher Ron Gibson in the seventh inning over a pitch call.[8] Wren said she loved the work but hated the travel and the low pay. "The athlete in me, the ballplayer in me, always liked umpiring. It was something I always wanted to do."[9] After a few years Wren decided to call it quits and make her winter job a full-time one driving a delivery truck.[10]

After Gera and Wren left the game, Pam Postema was the next to try to break the barrier. Postema had the most success before Ria Cortesia made it to Triple A in the early 2000s.

Postema umpired for 13 years before filing a lawsuit against major-league baseball after her career stalled at the Triple-A level, following three years in the Pacific Coast League. Postema grew up in Willard, Ohio (born April 1954), playing softball and baseball with her brothers. She even played some football with her brothers growing up. Though she played the game she never thought about umpiring until she got older. She was waitressing at a Red Lobster when she read an ad about umpire school.

She started in the Gulf Coast League in 1977 after attending the Somers School in Daytona Beach, Florida, as one of 130 students. She wanted to be sure she made the cut because she was a good umpire and not because she was a woman. "And if I wasn't good enough I didn't want to make it then just because I was a woman."[11] Postema actually applied three times without ever getting even a reply. She decided to just show up and ask for a chance in person, which she got. After graduating 17th in her class, Postema got her first assignment in the Gulf Coast League. After her time in the Gulf Coast League Postema moved to the Class-A Florida State League and then the Double-A Texas League in 1991. By 1993 Postema found herself promoted to the Pacific Coast League, where she worked for four years before making her final move to the Triple-A American Association. Postema commented on her career saying, "I love every moment of my work."[12] No matter how much she loved her work, Postema still had to fight for everything she got. One of the more difficult things she had to deal with in many parks was the conditions in the locker rooms because they did not have accommodations for female umpires. At many parks the best that could be done was to hang a sheet to give her some privacy while she changed to go out onto the field.

Postema got the chance to umpire a spring-training game between the Cleveland Indians and San Francisco Giants in 1982. For her the game was like any other for an umpire trying to earn a chance to move up to the next level. Postema was assigned to "B"-level spring-training games to get more experience after umpiring the previous fall in the Arizona Fall League. She was working to earn her dues like any other umpire. She said she took no more abuse than any other umpire. She stated, "I get the same amount of harassment as any ump, I think, and there's been no favoritism, no prejudice. I've been really lucky and worked with super umps. It's no big deal being a woman ump."[13] Postema also commented that any umpire who was the least bit different would take flak, if they were fat, or black, or a woman. Her answer was the same as any other umpire: If you get too much flak you throw them out.[14]

As expected, reaction to Postema's work was mixed. Manager Jim Fregosi said, "I hardly noticed her so I guess she did okay." Pitcher Tim Burke commented on her calling balls and strikes, saying, "She's just another mask behind the plate." When she tossed batboy Sam Morris for not retrieving a chair thrown onto the field by his manager, the reaction was loud and wide. Postema believed she did the right thing and maintained that if she had been a man no one would have said anything at all.[15] Red Sox superstar Wade Boggs said, "I have no objection if she can do a good job. If she's there as a publicity stunt; I don't agree with that."[16] The real compliment for Postema's skills came from Louisville outfielder Jack Ayer who said, "Tell you the truth, I don't really recognize that she's a woman. I don't have time for that."[17] Randy Kutcher, a utility infielder for the Boston Red Sox, commented, "She does a good job. She's as good as anybody." Kutcher had a unique perspective, having had the chance to see Postema umpire for five years at Double A and Triple A.[18] Catcher Ozzie Virgil thought she did a good job. "I had no complaints. I was really impressed with the way she handled all the stuff people in the stands were yelling at her."[19]

In contrast, Bob Knepper asserted that God did not like what she was doing in a man's job.[20] Toby Harrah, manager of the Oklahoma City 89ers, got thrown out by Postema and was not complimentary in his reactions. Harrah stated, "She just doesn't grasp the game of baseball. If you haven't played the game—and I'm sure she hasn't—you miss the grasp."[21] Postema's reaction was simply that she was trying to make the major leagues like any other umpire. Dick Butler, who scouted umpires for the American League, said she was there and so why not give her a chance.[22] Postema's best chance at making the majors was lost when Commissioner Bart Giamatti died. He had seemed receptive to the idea of a woman moving up to the highest level of baseball.

Postema also had to deal with those who only saw her as a woman and never as someone who could control a game. A reporter in Cuba simply referred to her as "un mujer muy bonita, por cierto (a very pretty woman, by the way)."[23]

Postema's real trouble developed because she never got a chance to move beyond Triple A. By Organized Baseball rules there was a limit to the years one could spend in the minors without being called up to the majors. If one did not get the call then they were let go, as Postema was. She believed that she was let go because of her gender and not because she was unqualified. The interesting issue for Postema was that previously she had been ranked at the top of the list for umpires moving up and then without any indications or written concerns she dropped from the top to out of contention for an opening,

Postema filed suit in Manhattan District Court in 1991 because the league did not promote her to the majors even though she had excellent performance reviews. She sued for damages, money, and a job. U.S. District Judge Robert Patterson ruled that her case could go forward to trial.[24] Postema was able to bring suit against the National League but not the American because of the number of job openings each had and potential candidates for those jobs. After leaving baseball she went to work for Federal Express in San Clemente, California.[25]

After her career ended, Postema received a number of honors. In 2000 she was inducted into the Shrine of the Eternals. She also published a book about her experiences in 1992 entitled *You've Got to Have Balls to Make It in This League*. In the book she describes her view of why women have such a difficult time even getting a chance to umpire. "Almost all of the people in the baseball community don't want anyone interrupting their little male-dominated way of life. They want big, fat male umpires. They want those macho, tobacco-chewing, sleazy sort of borderline alcoholics."[26]

After attending the Wendelstedt umpire school in 1982, Perry Lee Barber began her still continuing (as of 2015) career; for her long and varied career, which included being assignor of umpires for the independent Atlantic League from 1998 to 2001, see her essay "The Stained Grass Window" in the SABR *Book of Umpires and Umpiring*.

Theresa Cox of Ohio (later Cox-Fairlady) had a short career after Postema and together they paved the way for Ria Cortesio and Shanna Kook. Cox went to the Harry Wendelstedt School for umpires and graduated fifth out of a class of 180. Cox never really got a fair chance as she was told her voice was too high and she could not really wear the uniform. When she tried to change the tone she was told her voice now sounded fake. Since Cox umpired college and high-school games, her voice was simply an excuse for not wanting her on the diamond. Wendelstedt challenged that view when he claimed Cox was "the best female candidate I've ever had."[27] He trained 28 women and 5,000 men so his view was certainly one to be taken seriously. In 1989 Cox worked two Double-A Southern League games before umpiring for two years, 1989–1990, in the Arizona Rookie League. She said that in her Arizona League season she walked 22 batters in her first game before the pitchers discovered her strike zone. Cox acknowledged that Postema's work helped her in trying to break into the game. "What she went through has made it easier for me, and if it's not me who is the first woman ump, then maybe I'll make it easier for somebody who follows after me. But we have to keep trying. It's like life, either you evolve or you die out."[28] In 2008 Cox-Fairlady had a chance to umpire a Mets spring-training exhibition game against the University of Michigan. The game was not that unusual but the umpiring crew was, since it included four women, one of whom was Cox-Fairlady. She was joined by Perry Barber, Ila Valcarcel, and Mona Osborne. When she was not umpiring Cox drove for UPS in Birmingham, Alabama, to supplement the money she made umpiring.[29]

Next in line was Ria Cortesio (real name Maria Papageorgiou), from Rock Island, Illinois, who got her start as a professional umpire in 1999. She decided to become an umpire when she was about 16, after talking with umpire Scott Higgins, who sat down with her and explained how the whole process worked.[30] Growing up she never got the chance to play since girls were expected to play softball and baseball was a boy's game. She played in her front yard with her cousins but never in organized ball. She graduated from the Jim Evans Umpire Academy in Kissimmee, Florida, after attending the five-week program in 1998 as her second try, having also attended in 1996. Cortesio was one of only two women each time she attended the school. In addition to umpire school, Cortesio was also a graduate of Rice University, graduating summa cum laude. Evans commented after her graduation from umpire school, "I don't think sex should be a criterion for umpiring in the big leagues."[31] Her goal was to work her way up through the ranks and win one of the 68 major-league umpiring jobs. She even cut her ponytail and lowered her voice so she would not stand out as much. But Cortesio was up against a large group of men working for the same goal. By 2006 she was umpiring the Futures game and home-run derby in Pittsburgh. In 2007 she got the opportunity to umpire a spring-training game between the Cubs and the Diamondbacks. Derek Lee, first baseman for the Cubs, stated, "It's awesome. I think it's about time. Female eyes are as good as male eyes. Why can't they be umpires?"[32]

During a 2007 Double-A game Cortesio received the ultimate compliment from a fan who said, "He might be young, but he looks like he's consistent. So far, he's called a good game."[33] The fan had no idea the umpire was female and therefore he judged the performance solely on the quality and not the gender. One of her fellow umpires, Jason Stein, got a chance to work with her in the Futures game and continued to be impressed. "She's good enough to be here," said Stein, who worked in the Double-A Texas League. "She's just as good as we are. If she gets the opportunity to advance to the big leagues and be successful, it would be a great thing. I'm pulling hard for her."[34] "She has inconsistencies but she's just as good as any other umpire," said Suns pitcher Joel Hanrahan, who also saw Cortesio in the Pioneer League in 2000 and in the Florida State League in 2002.[35]

Not all reactions were positive to Cortesio's work. While she seemed to get less criticism than Postema and the other early pioneers, there were still critics of her as a female umpire. One of those was George Steinbrenner who expressed displeasure over her strike zone when she called a rehab game for Roger Clemens. Told that Cortesio had once umpired Clemens's boys in Little League in Texas, the New York Yankees owner huffed: "Is that right? Well, that's good; I guess she'll go back there."[36]

Cortesio never really saw herself as a pioneer, just someone who wanted to umpire in the major leagues. "Until I work a regular-season major-league baseball game, I haven't done anything," Cortesio said. "I don't want to be a pioneer. I just want to do my job."[37] Another time, she said, "It never crossed my mind that because I was a female, I couldn't do this job. I was lucky to be raised by parents without barriers; that there is no difference between a male and female doing the same job. The guidelines should be equal for both as long as you can do the job."[38] At the same time Cortesio realized she could do a lot to get other women involved.

Cortesio got the call from Mike Fitzpatrick (executive director of the Professional Baseball Umpires Corporation, the umbrella organization for minor-league umpiring) telling her they were letting her go after the 2007 season. There were no openings at the Triple-A level and her ranking had fallen, making her ineligible for a promotion after nine years. Because there are few openings, senior umpires can be let go if they do not move up, to make room for new hires.[39]

Other major-league players and managers agreed with Derek Lee and thought Cortesio had earned her chance. Willie Randolph commented, "I hope she gets her shot, that's important." Felipe Alou believed a female umpire like Cortesio would be good for the game, claiming, "I believe a woman umpire would bring some good ingredients to the game and added interest."[40]

When asked in 2007 why baseball and not softball, Cortesio had the following to say,

> I bet you if you go to any high school or college softball team and ask any of the girls, probably most of them when they're growing up dreamed of playing major league baseball. You know, baseball is our national pastime, but for some reason half of the nation is shut out of it. There's this pretty ridiculous stereotype, I think, in this country that baseball is just for boys, and girls, go play with dolls or play softball or something.[41]

Cortesio, the last woman to rise through the minor-league ranks to the present day in 2016, helped mentor Canadian Shanna Kook; they were the only two ladies whose career overlapped.

In 2003 Torontoan Kook umpired in the Pioneer League (she spent two years there) after graduating from the Harry Wendelstedt Umpire School. Her first game she umpired was behind home plate in a game between Provo and Casper. Provo manager Tom Kotchman said, "I'll give her credit. She was not tentative. It's tough to tell from the side but our catcher said she called a very good game."[42] Before taking up her place on the diamond, Kook attended Clinton Street Public School, where she excelled in the classroom and on the diamond. Kook joined the school baseball team and helped lead it to a championship during her senior year. Kook then enrolled at McGill University, where she majored in music and played the viola. She missed baseball and wanted to return to the game as an umpire.[43]

Kook's view on umpiring was best stated when she said, "I really don't care if people notice me. Really the more I'm anonymous, the better. If people don't know who I am, that's fine, because then I am doing my job."[44] She learned her craft on the diamonds in Canada starting at the age of 16 and by 2002 she was the crew chief for the Women's World Series. She attended a clinic to get started at the community center level. After starting college and realizing she needed more money, she returned to umpiring and eventually rose to umpiring higher-level games. From there she was invited to attend a women's umpire clinic in Canada and then she went for one week to the Jim Evans Academy of Professional Umpiring. Kook was hooked on umpiring and left school to pursue her chance. She joined the small rank of professional female umpires.[45]

After Cortesio was let go, Kate Sargeant tried to earn a spot, attending the Wendelstedt School in Florida in 2007 after umpiring with her dad in the Peninsula Umpires Association. She made it to the final selection process but was not picked for a position. She was the last umpire on the eligible list and she did not get a call. She also had previously attended the Jim Evans School twice. Her only shot came in the independent New York State League, where she spent two years umpiring (2007–2008).[46] Those who worked with her had no qualms about being on the field with Sargeant, saying she knew all the rules. After her failed attempt, league officials were asked when they thought a woman might get an opportunity. When MLB Vice President Mike Teevan was asked if it might be at least another six years before a woman could break into the majors, he said, "Basing on the roads that most [umpires] traveled, that's fair to say." He added, however, that the league "would love to see" a woman officiate one day.[47] Sargeant continued to umpire high-school games for a bit longer but finally gave up her dream and became a forest ranger with Canada's National Forest Service.[48]

One of the most successful female umpires in recent years has been working under the radar in Cuba, Yanet Moreno. Moreno loved baseball as a child but just like other women had trouble playing because others, like her father, thought baseball was for boys and not girls.[49]

In 2016 one more female umpire was added to the ranks of professional baseball. Jen Pawol graduated from Minor League Baseball's umpire camp along with Annie Monochello. While both graduated, only Pawol got an official assignment with the Gulf Coast League, making her the first female umpire at the professional level since 2007. Pawol brought a lot of umpiring experience from both baseball and softball. She played soccer and softball at West Milford High School (New Jersey) before getting a scholarship to play at Hofstra from 1995–1998. Pawol earned All-American honors as a catcher, hitting .332 with 102 RBIs. She umpired for fast-pitch softball as well as being an NCAA Division I postseason umpire. She also umpired in the Big Ten Conference from 2013 to 2015. In her first Gulf Coast League game Pawol umpired behind home plate. She worked a flawless game with the Blue Jays manager Cesar Martin saying, "She did a great job. Controlling the game, all these things. It was a nice game."[50]

Pawol is also an artist. She earned her BFA from the Pratt Institute and then an MFA from Hunter College. When she was not umpiring in previous years she also worked part-time as an eighth grade art teacher. Pawol sees a lot of correlations between painting and baseball, the sounds, the rhythm of the game, the artistry of the players, etc. . . . Pawol stated, "I don't really view umpiring as a gender job, I just view it as, if you're good at it, and you like it, you should do it."[51]

The path to becoming an umpire is a long and arduous journey for anyone but especially for a woman. After the establishment of an umpire school for the minor leagues in 2011, only one woman attended and graduated, Sarah Allerding, who then decided to become a deaconess in the Lutheran Church. She said she always felt welcome and simply made the choice to join the church. If she had made the cut and decided to pursue umpiring, it still would have been a minimum of six years before there could have been a female umpire, based on how promotions work. So there have been only six women in the professional ranks and we are still years away from possibly seeing that glass ceiling broken in the United States, even though the NBA and NFL have both employed female referees. Some make the claim that because women do not play baseball as much that is why there are fewer female umpires, but you do not have to play to know the rules.[52]

Writer Derek Crawford ended his article on the trials of female umpires saying, "Baseball truly is a fraternity and a brotherhood, but we live in a society in which a woman can run for President, sit on the Supreme Court, fight on the front lines in combat, but can't put on a chest protector and call balls and strikes in a Major League ballpark for a living."[53]

NOTES

1. Ben Walker, "Just One of the Umpires," *Seattle Times*, July 9, 2006.

2. Craig Davis, "She Never Wanted to Be a Pioneer," *Chicago Tribune*, October 8, 1989.

3. Lisa Winston, milb.com, June 22, 2007.

4. vrml.k12.la.us/ehs/history/berniceshiner.htm.

5. Edward J. Shiner obituary, *New York Times*, August 14, 2014.

6. "Woman Umpire Has a Single Goal," *Oregonian* (Portland), July 1, 1976, C8.

7. "Woman Umpire Has a Single Goal," *Oregonian* (Portland), July 1, 1976, C8.

8. "Christine Wren Uses Her Thumb," *Seattle Times*, June 27, 1975, C3.

9. Howie Stalwick, "Spokane Native Paved the Way for Postema," *Spokesman Review* (Spokane WA), March 8, 1988.

10. "Kill the Ump. If It's Christine Wren, Kiss Her," *People Magazine*, July 14, 1975.

11. Linda Lehrer, "Sporting Chance," *Chicago Tribune*, June 21, 1992.

12. Mal Bernstein, "Who Is That Woman Behind the Mask," *Christian Science Monitor*, July 29, 1985.

13. AP, "Female Umpire Inches Toward Major Leagues," *Dallas Morning News*, March 14, 1982, 47.

14. Robin Finn, "Female Umpire Aims for Majors," *Lakeland* (FL) *Ledger*, July 28, 1987, 16.

15. "Batboy Ejected for Disobedience," *Mobile Register*, May 27, 1984.

16. Stephen Harris, "Woman Behind the Plate No Threat," *Boston Herald*, March 15, 1988, 97.

17. "Umpire Pam Postema Is Fighting Tradition," *Mobile Register*, July 6, 1987, 4D.

18. Stephen Harris.

19. Jayson Stark, "She Awaits a Call From the Majors," philly.com, March 13, 1988.

20. Bernie Lincicome, "Woman Umpire Balks at Spotlight," *Chicago Tribune*, March 20, 1988.

21. *Mobile Register*, July 6, 1987: 4D.

22. Jerome Holtzman, "Lady Ump Could Find Home in Majors," *Chicago Tribune*, April 6, 1986.

23. Luis Perez Lopez, "No Maten al Umpire. Que es Una Mujer!" *El Miami Herald*, June 2, 1980, 9.

24. *Mobile Press Register*, July 14, 1992, 3C.

25. "Former Major League Umpire Pam Postema Sues Baseball," *Orlando Sentinel*, December 20, 1991.

26. Pam Postema, *You've Got to Have Balls to Make It in This League* (New York: Simon and Schuster, 1992).

27. Anna Quindlen, "I Don't Know Why a Young Lady Would Want this Job," *Chicago Tribune*, September 3, 1991.

28. Robin Finn, "Ohioan on Deck," *New York Times*, December 25, 1989.

29. Perry Barber and Jean Ardell, "Women in Black," *Cooperstown Symposium*, 2011–2012, State University of New York, College of Oneonta, 2013, 55; "Cox Hopes Her Fate as Umpire Turns Out Better than Postema," *Spokesman Review*, December 25, 1989.

30. Michel Martin, "Baseball's Leading Lady," NPR, April 30, 1977.

31. Josh Robbins, "Female Umpire Hopes for Shot at Major Leagues," *Lawrence* (KS) *Journal-World*, May 12, 2007, 16.

32. Lisa Winston.

33. Josh Robbins.

34. Lyle Spencer, "Female Ump Gets Futures Game Nod," mlb.com, July 9, 2006.

35. Jeff Elliott, "Female Umpire Plays Out Dream," *Florida Times-Union* (Jacksonville), June 25, 2003.

36. Ben Walker, "Just One of the Umpires," *Seattle Times*, July 9, 2006.

37. Lyle Spencer.

38. Jeff Elliott.

39. Associated Press, "Baseball's Only Female Umpire Fired," *Houston Chronicle*, November 1, 2007.

40. AP story, "Ria Cortesio Is Hoping Not to Get Rung Up," *Quad-City Times*, September 8, 2005.

41. Michel Martin.

42. Jason Franchuk, "Umpire Story," *Daily Herald* (Provo UT), July 10, 2003.

43. Justin Skinner, "Clinton Street PS Looks for Past Grads to Celebrate 125 Years," InsideToronto.com, October 26, 2012.

44. Fran Chuck, "Umpire Story," *Toronto Daily Herald*, July 10, 2003.

45. Leslie Heaphy, ed. *Women in Baseball Encyclopedia* (Jefferson NC: McFarland, 2006), 57–58.

46. Pat Borzi, "Woman Umpires Are Striking Out in MLB," ESPNW, August 9, 2011.

47. Lucy McCalmont, "MLB Probably Won't Have a Female Umpire for at Least Six Years," *Huffington Post*, April 16, 2015.

48. Terry Mosher, "Female NK Grad Sargeant Made Run at Umpiring in Pros," *Kitsap Sun* (Bremerton WA), April 12, 2014.

49. Shasta Darlington, "In Cuba's Male Baseball League, Female Umpire Calls 'Em Like She Sees 'Em," cnn.com, January 6, 2010.

50. Paul Hagan, "Female Umpire Calls Game in Rookie Ball," mlb.com, June 24, 2016.

51. David Dorsey, "Jen Pawol Travels Rare Baseball Path as an Umpire," News-Press .com, July 10, 2016; David Wilson, "Jen Pawol Ends Female Umpire Drought on Opening Day of GCL," *Bradenton-Herald*, June 24, 2016.

52. Lucy McCalmont. Of course, even fewer women play football.

53. Derek Crawford, "Behind the Mask: Where Are the Women?," baseballessential .com, April 4, 2015.

49

The Struggle to Define "Valuable"

Tradition vs. Sabermetrics in the 2012 AL MVP Race

PETER B. GREGG

The onset of modern sabermetrics has led to increasing conflict in our formerly friendly debates over who should win awards or be considered for the Hall of Fame. Should the new measures replace the old in determining value, or can the old measures stick around? Peter Gregg, the author of this work, uses the 2012 AL MVP vote to examine the struggle among fans and writers between the old and new ways we evaluate players. Gregg is an assistant professor of emerging media at the University of St. Thomas, and his research interests include media history, production, and audiences. He is also a lifelong Detroit Tigers fan.

> "When you cannot express it in numbers, your knowledge is of a meager and unsatisfactory kind."
>
> —LORD KELVIN

> "One absolutely cannot tell, by watching, the difference between a .300 hitter and a .275 hitter. The difference is one hit every two weeks. It might be that a reporter, seeing every game that the team plays, could sense that difference over the course of the year if no records were kept, but I doubt it."
>
> —BILL JAMES (as quoted in *Moneyball*)

Today, statistics have become a fundamental component of the fabric of baseball analysis and have gained appreciation at the major-league level.[1] As Ron Von Burg and Paul E. Johnson note, "For many, statistics are the main way of understanding and relating to the game of baseball."[2] Broadcasters employ color commentators whose job entails unpacking the nuances of the game, including explicating various statistics and in-game strategies. Fans and media can go to websites like Baseball-Reference.com to see era-by-era comparisons of teams or players and new statistics like WAR ("wins above replacement") and WRC+ ("weighted runs created plus").

These newer statistics and data analyses fall under the label "sabermetrics," defined by Bill James as "the mathematical and statistical study of baseball records" and later broadened to "search for objective knowledge about baseball."[3] Fundamentally, sabermetrics is a search for new ideas in an old game. Nathaniel Stoltz points out, "As time has progressed and media have diversified, the sabermetric movement has made an increasingly sizeable impact on baseball discourse."[4] Being relatively new, sabermetrics is not steeped in baseball tradition, and this makes it a potential threat to more traditional ways of thinking about the game. Although Michael Lewis's *Moneyball* put these advanced analytics into the public's mind and teams have come to depend on these advanced analytics, sports journalists have been slower to appreciate or incorporate them, generally favoring traditional evaluation methods with which they are comfortable.[5] Detractors see sabermetrics as a threat to baseball's past because traditional statistics supposedly embody "intangibles" like heart, grit, and character in celebrating player achievement.[6] With the growth of sabermetrics, the traditional terminology employed when using those statistics is undergoing some transformation and causing a bit of upheaval in the process. One of these terms under scrutiny is "valuable" as used in the award for the "most valuable" player.

In Major League Baseball, the "Kenesaw Mountain Landis Memorial Baseball Award" is given by the Baseball Writers' Association of America (BBWAA) to the "most valuable" player (or "MVP") in each league, as voted by two organization members from each city. The vote follows consideration by and discourse among member and non-member journalists, bloggers, and fans in and outside the press. In their memo to voters, the BBWAA notes that there is no formal definition of "most valuable" and the meaning is left to the discretion of the voter.[7] Because the definition of "value" is the result of discourse and a majority consensus, it is fundamentally determined rhetorically, and as such it is not without debate or controversy.

Statistics are among the key criteria the writers use to determine for whom they should vote and around which the debate revolves in defining the value of the "most valuable" player; consequently, discourse around MVP races tends to focus on performance seen through a statistical lens. For example, in 1941, Joe DiMaggio beat out Ted Williams for MVP largely because of his notable 56-game hit streak despite Williams having a solidly better season.[8] In 1999, catcher Pudge Rodriguez beat out pitcher Pedro Martinez in part because some writers felt that a pitcher does not contribute enough to their team to merit "most valuable" because they are not everyday players.[9] In 2001, Ichiro Suzuki won the MVP award over Jason Giambi, whose supporters pointed out he led the league in on-base percentage and slugging and beat Ichiro in walks, home runs, and RBIs with 170 fewer at-bats.[10]

One of the more significantly controversial MVP debates in recent years occurred during the summer and autumn of 2012 on the merits of Miguel Cabrera of the Detroit Tigers and Mike Trout of the Los Angeles Angels of Anaheim, both of whom were having notable seasons (see table 49.1). Cabrera's supporters pointed out that he was on pace to win the Triple Crown, leading the league in batting average, home runs, and runs batted in, a historic feat that had not happened since 1967. Mike Trout was a rookie sensation; his supporters argued that not only was he running neck-and-neck with Cabrera for batting average and hitting for power, sabermetric analysis showed he was scoring runs and stealing bases at a historic pace, as well as being an exemplary defender.

Table 49.1. Traditional and sabermetric statistics for
Trout and Cabrera, 2012 season

	R	H	HR	RBI	AVG	OBP	SLG	OPS+	SB	Off	Def	WAR
Trout	129	182	30	83	.326	.399	.564	168	49	64.2	13.0	10.3
Cabrera	109	205	44	139	.330	.393	.606	164	4	46.4	-8.2	6.4

League leader is underlined. 2012 MLB Leaderboard, Fangraphs.com. "2012 Major League Leaderboards." Fangraphs.com. Accessed August 28, 2017. http://www.fangraphs.com/leaders .aspx?pos=all&stats=bat&lg=all&qual=y&type=1&season=2012&month=0&season1=2012& ind=0&team=0&rost=0&age=0&filter=&players=0.

This noteworthy public crisis between "traditional" and "sabermetric" player evaluation methods formed an important transition point in baseball discourse by the press regarding the use of sabermetrics to evaluate players. "Claims to know are claims of power,"[11] and in the case of the 2012 American League Most Valuable Player award, the debate hinged on what knowledge claims constituted the definition of "valuable." For Joe Posnanski, "The argument seemed to split baseball fans between those who embrace the new baseball metrics and those who do not."[12] This race served as an important representative anecdote in the ways that sports journalists talked about sabermetrics.[13]

In this paper, to examine the rhetorical strategies used by reporters to define "valuable," I apply Edward Schiappa's methodology for exploring "definitional ruptures."[14] I unpack the factions' stated purpose or intent of defining, the interests advanced by the definitions, and the consequences of the definition. This three-layer approach reveals that the heart of this tension revolves around the power to define "valuable" as an institutional norm among baseball journalists, with mainstream journalists relying on older statistics and baseball history and newer journalists using sabermetric measures to define "valuable." I then discuss the consequences of that tension in 2012 and beyond.

I examined published articles and analysis by sports journalists and bloggers starting from late July 2012 and continued through early November after the award was announced. I emphasized writing by BBWAA members and the responses to their articles. The articles constituted the primary discourse since they came from the BBWAA voters or in response to their analysis and argumentation.

Methods of Analyzing Definitional Ruptures

Schiappa notes that the "rhetorical analysis of definition . . . investigates how people persuade other people to adopt and use certain definitions to the exclusion of others."[15] He argues that definitions are strategies to respond to situations or questions, and they "posit attitudes about situations."[16] Definitions are constituted by "rhetorically induced social knowledge."[17] This social knowledge often comes in the form of authority-based "articulation of what particular words mean and how they should be used to refer to reality."[18] While most definitions are not contested, at times the meaning of a particular word or how it ought to be used is a site of dispute or controversy. The various sides involved in the dispute take on the "natural attitude" that their usage in that specific context is correct.[19] For example, a baseball fan who disagrees with an official scorer's definition of an error has in a small way participated in a definitional dispute; when a team petitions the league for a ruling change on the play, they are arguing over a definition.

These definitional controversies "can be understood, in part, as definitional ruptures."[20] This necessitates not treating definitions as factual claims based on observations about the world and instead treating them as attempts to establish social or institutional norms based on theories of how the world ought to be. Seen in this way, a struggle among journalists to define a term like "valuable" is a struggle for "denotative conformity," or intersubjective agreement about the meaning of a word.[21] Words with high denotative conformity are usually seen as factual observation statements, resulting from their agreed-upon usage and the context of the use. Words with low denotative conformity are usually seen as theory statements about the world. For example, the strike zone has a clear definition in the MLB rulebook, but the strike zone as defined in practice by umpires varies on many different constraints, including the catcher behind the plate.[22] Seen in this light, the sides in a definitional rupture in baseball journalism over the meaning of the word "value" use the same word with a different definition and thereby construct or endorse different institutional norms for how it should be used.

Definitions entitle something, giving both a label and a status to that which is defined.[23] This entitling places the phenomenon in a set of beliefs or frames about the world that includes what is real and what qualities constitute the phenomenon.[24] When a new definition arises in discourse, the interrelated attitudes and beliefs are brought into the debate, and they too must be negotiated. "Whole sets of normative and factual beliefs must be changed before someone may be convinced to accept a new institutional fact."[25] When advocates push for a new definition, they must persuade others to change their linguistic behavior.

Schiappa outlines three major areas for the critic to identify and analyze within a definitional rupture: purpose or intent, use of power, and definitional practice. In exploring purpose or intent, the critic should examine the shared purposes in defining the word, the interests and values advanced by the competing definitions, and the practical consequences of the definition as it affects "the needs and interests of a particular community of language users involved in a dispute."[26] In examining questions of power, the rhetorical critic should identify who has the power to define or speak as an authority and how that power is used within the social institution. "A proposed definition is a request for institutional norms: When should X count as Y in context C?"[27] and "[t]he acts of framing and naming always serve preferred interests, even if those interests are not noticed or are uncontroversial."[28] As it pertains to definitional practice, the critic should identify or discover questions within the rupture involving how members do (or do not) achieve denotative conformity with a definition or whether denotative conformity is a reasonable goal.[29]

Seeing "Valuable" as Definitional Rupture

The 2012 American League MVP race constituted a crisis among baseball journalists in defining "valuable" as an observation statement (with high denotative conformity) or a theory statement (with low denotative conformity) about the world. Because the BBWAA does not provide a definition for "valuable," the onus is on the voters themselves to create theory statements to determine it. For traditionalists, value is best defined by an already-recognized significant historical achievement and the success of the team; for sabermetricians, value is defined by stats like WAR, a complex statistical aggregate accounting for the entirety of play. Both factions' definitions of value included a sensitivity to fairness and egalitarianism. Traditional journalists' goal was to fairly and equally treat this season's achievements with the ways past seasons' achievements had been treated for other players. Sabermetrically-oriented journalists' goal was to fairly and equally represent all the achievements of players in a season and reward the player who contributed the most. Sean Hartnett contended, "You couldn't conceive two MVP candidates that provide such conflicting cases for their candidacy ... You'll have old guard writers who will cling to the importance of the Triple Crown and new-age writers who will favor sabermetric measures such as WAR and range factor (RF)—and you'll never get either side to agree with one another."[30] Ultimately Cabrera won the American League MVP vote, earning twenty-two first place votes over Trout's six. "After all the debate, all the rhetoric, all the statistical and historical analysis, it wasn't close."[31]

Purpose and Intent of Defining "Valuable"

The debate over the definition of "valuable" was an attempt to alter or maintain linguistic behavior. Supporters of both players had the shared purpose of wanting the award to go to the "most valuable" player. In their discourse, they frequently used "valuable" as the key term in determining their vote, and so it was "the term 'valuable' that appears to foster differing viewpoints."[32] Numerous other writers noted that the argument was less about statistics versus intangible qualities and more about which statistics should be counted.[33] For David Roth, "This vote ... was more than just the usual MVP vote. It was also a fairly impassioned contest between two different philosophies and between old-fashioned counting stats and new-fangled metrics."[34]

Schiappa notes that a definitional rupture "should be addressed in part by re-asking such questions as 'How should we use the word X?'"[35] For Trout supporters, the definition of valuable was driven by the need for statistical accuracy and precision and a search for fairness to other players that year. They generally attempted to quantify his contributions statistically and held a belief in statistical proof as more valid than unmeasurable contributions players might make to a team. Tim Britton suggested, "This is about recognizing Trout's uniquely comprehensive skill set and the myriad ways he contributed to his team winning baseball games. It's about appreciating the athletic versatility that baseball, let's face it, isn't always known for."[36]

For the supporters of Cabrera, the definition of valuable consisted of the player making significant contributions to a team that made the playoffs and one that included historically important statistical achievements as meriting the award, regardless of other measures of value. Bill Madden summarized the position:

> Here's a guy having one of the greatest offensive seasons in history, on the cusp of being the first Triple Crown winner since Carl Yastrzemski in 1967, and yet there is this clamor from the sabermetrics gallery that Cabrera must be penalized for his slowness afoot and supposed defensive shortcomings. To hear them tell it, if Cabrera winds up leading the league in batting, homers, RBI, slugging and total bases, and being second in hits and runs, it will still pale in comparison to L.A. Angels super rookie Mike Trout leading the league in runs, stolen bases and . . . WAR.[37]

Traditional sports journalists tended to emphasize baseball history and significant achievement in their definition of "value." Cabrera's Triple Crown played a decisive role in their votes for him. "The MVP is the Big Dog of individual awards in sports. It often serves as a Hall of Fame deal-breaker. Yet the word 'valuable' restricts it to those whose brilliance made a difference, even though the electors are specifically told that it really isn't tied to team performance. They decide their own criteria."[38] The fact that Cabrera played better in the last months of the season and the Tigers made the playoffs also contributed to his case for most valuable player. "We more 'traditional' baseball journalists do tend to weigh postseason appearances highly when it comes to the MVP because, really, what else is value for? Cabrera got his team to the playoffs. Trout did not."[39] Other Cabrera voters felt this was an opportunity to support Cabrera as the exemplar of valuable production. "If Cabrera wins the MVP it will repudiate nothing Trout did. It will simply be a . . . reaffirmation of value."[40] For Mark Feinsand, there was a distinction between best player and most valuable player. "I think Trout was the best overall player in the game this season, especially when you factor in his defense and baserunning. But that doesn't mean I thought he was the most valuable."[41]

The idea of fairness and equal treatment in a single season is partially what drove the Trout supporters to WAR as a key statistic in measuring value. "Baseball experts have spent decades trying to find a way to quantify all of a player's contributions and boil it down into one number. The best measurement we have right now is what's known as Wins Above Replacement (WAR)."[42] Traditional baseball statistics tend to be "counting" statistics, where an event is tallied: a batted ball leaves the field of play in fair territory without hitting the ground and is counted as a home run, the batter hits the ball in fair territory and reaches base safely without a fielding error and it is counted as a hit, and so forth. More complex statistics are derived from averages: average hits per at bat yields a "batting average," average of earned runs per nine innings equals "earned run average." Almost all are easily seen, tallied, and understood.

Advanced baseball statistics tend to be derived from more complex formulae. In the case of WAR for position players, the final number is the product of various measures including hitting, baserunning, and defense, some of which rely on other advanced statistics, and then that statistical value is normalized against the standard performance in that season. This formula allows the player to be compared against his peers and in a manner that includes the complex ways the player contributes that may not be easily tallied and seen. For Carl Bialik, "Wins above replacement [is] an imperfect stat that still does a better job than any other of encapsulating a player's overall on-field value,"[43] and for Neil Paine WAR is "the single-number metric of choice for most sabermetricians when it comes to measuring a player's all-around value."[44]

For sabermetricians in 2012, Trout clearly created the most value as a player. "Basically WAR—and some other advanced metrics—showed that whatever advantages Cabrera had in terms of power and batting average and timely hitting were swamped by Trout's advantages as a fielder, base runner and player who gets on base. The argument made sense to many of us who champion the advanced statistics and their power to get closer to a player's true value."[45] Journalists supporting Trout's case noted that not only did he lead the league in WAR, but he did so in a historically significant way. "Trout's is the clearest case in 99 years as the majors' MVP . . . That's just how much better he's been than his peers."[46] Writers also addressed some "intangible" or non-quantifiable factors often used by Cabrera supporters, as Mark Reynolds wrote at Bleacher Report:

> As long as you think the MVP award should go the player who produced the most value, then Trout should have been the winner because Cabrera's offense was not superior enough to make up for the difference in the other categories. Cabrera might have been great in the locker room, but there's no evidence that Trout wasn't a great teammate, too. Cabrera's team made the postseason, but Trout's team won more games.[47]

Many writers argued that the Triple Crown is overvalued. Zachary D. Rhymer notes that "the Triple Crown indeed *is* a relic. It's a novel accomplishment, but things have changed too much over the last half century for both writers and baseball fans to still believe that the Triple Crown is the ultimate measure of value."[48] For sabermetricians each leg of the Triple Crown represents older, less helpful statistics for evaluating player performance. The RBI (or "runs batted in") depends considerably on the quality of a hitter's teammates, because they need to be on base for the batter to drive them in for runs. The home run shows power potential but is also dependent on factors like the depth of the outfields where the batter hits; since a team plays half its games at home, some batters are fortunate to play half their games on a field that is favorable to hitting home runs. Batting average is a fine descriptor of how often the batter reaches base safely on a hit, but does not capture the ability of the batter to reach base without getting out or to reach base with a double or triple. For many sabermetricians, the preferred statistic is either on-base percentage (OBP) or on-base plus slugging average (or "OPS").

Use of Power

Craig Calcaterra thought that the "MVP award voting, at least in the American League, has taken on political and philosophical overtones."[49] Supporters of both players claimed to know what "valuable" meant within their individual set of criteria. Because the result comes via vote of two members from each American League city, the power to define ultimately resided in those (then) 28 members. Non-voting members and non-members could rally for particular perspectives on what they would or what members should do, but they did not actually vote. The debate over value continued the tension between traditional sports journalists and an emerging group interested in newer ways of evaluating players and making strategic choices. An overwhelming majority of established writers voted for Cabrera. "The Triple Crown winner's main constituency was old people in old media. Twenty-four of the MVP voters work for newspapers or newspaper groups; 21 of them (88 percent) voted for Cabrera . . . every voter 51 and above . . . sided with Cabrera, the old-guard candidate."[50]

Because the BBWAA nominates each season's voters, it is feasible that the balance of power in the organization will shift as one faction or the other jostles for power over the seasons, and so the stakes for a given debate should be seen as a part of a longer-term power struggle. The tension over Trout and Cabrera for Most Valuable Player was a struggle for authority in the press. It was a question over the type of knowledge needed to be regarded as a baseball expert. "The false Trout/Cabrera debate, stripped of Tigers and Angels fans, is just the latest in the ongoing battle between two camps in the baseball media, one of which has seen its longtime primacy usurped by new writers, mostly younger, who look at the game in different ways and have more in common with successful front offices."[51] Established writers saw sabermetricians as using advanced statistics to usurp their power and prestige. Sabermetricians saw established writers using traditional tools to support Cabrera and undermine the utility of sabermetric evaluation.

One technique used by traditionally-oriented journalists to subordinate the sabermetrically-oriented writers was to resort to name-calling. "The old-school columnists often trafficked in ignorance and name-calling—relying on the cliché that the statistical community consisted entirely of geeks still living in their mothers' basements."[52] This cliché is epitomized by Mitch Albom's claim:

> [Baseball] is simply being saturated with situational statistics. What other sport keeps coming up with new categories to watch the same game? A box score now reads like an annual report. And this WAR

statistic—which measures the number of wins a player gives his team versus a replacement player of minor league/bench talent (honestly, who comes up with this stuff?)—is another way of declaring, "Nerds win!"[53]

Commonly the tone was aggressive and characterized sabermetricians as effete and weak, a position in alignment with Michael L. Butterworth's findings regarding the treatment of statistical political and sports discourse.[54] In addition to calling sabermetricans "geeks," Madden worried advanced analytics is "turning baseball into an inhuman board game."[55]

The pro-Cabrera writers used their definition to defer to historical tradition and significance. For them, the power to decide the meaning of "value" should rest in the hands of the people who have always decided it, not up-and-coming sabermetrician journalists. For the traditionalists, WAR is seen as a statistic "for geeks who don't know baseball . . . the real argument that non-Tigers fans are making about Trout."[56] For sabermetricians, the 2012 MVP race was a way to add clarity to the ways people think about player value. In his discussion of the race, Jonah Keri argued that Cabrera won because a player's value is perceived by its cultural and financial incentives.[57] Players who hit home runs and drive in RBIs get emphasized more in the press, get more praise by their teammates, and get larger contracts, and as a result they are more likely to win the Most Valuable Player award, although Nate Silver noted that "the real progress in the statistical analysis of baseball is in the ability to evaluate the contributions that a player makes on the field in a more reliable and comprehensive way."[58]

Definitional Practice

The MVP debate arose from a lack of denotative conformity and was an attempt to attain intersubjective agreement. Unlike many definitional disputes, the MVP award is the product of a vote in which scoring reflects a majority preference. The Trout-Cabrera debate represented the changes in the makeup of the BBWAA. "There is most definitely a growing divide among the BBWAA and the plethora of talented writers online who either are not members of the BBWAA or members that get drowned out by their older cohorts in the association."[59] Ultimately, the definition used is the one that serves the preferred or powerful interests, since those members have the power to entitle the word with specific meaning and weight. The preferred interests establish the social or institutional norms. The Trout-Cabrera MVP vote re-entitled "value" with the traditional definition: the player with the most value is the one who makes historically significant contributions on a playoff team.

While the vote did not necessarily stop the discourse or guarantee denotative conformity, it offers a resolution to that specific definitional rupture. Josh Levin suggested, "The BBWAA's voting system empowers baseball's most-conservative voices and disenfranchises those with non-prehistoric views."[60] John Shipley was more optimistic, noting "Maybe someday WAR, BABIP (Batting Average on Balls in Play) and RC27 (Runs Created per 27 outs) will replace the old stats as the new standards. But for those who came up memorizing batting averages and RBI totals from the backs of baseball cards, they're still relegated to the fringes of the national pastime."[61]

Entitling "value" as sabermetrically-defined would give power to the individuals with the expertise, knowledge, and background to understand, analyze, and discuss it. This community is largely a newer, younger generation of writers struggling for power within sports journalism. Matthew Trueblood suggested that the 2012 MVP race was one of the last gasps of power by the old guard of baseball writers, noting that "Soon, the electorate for these awards will be overwhelmingly new-school."[62] Calcaterra argued that this struggle to determine which measures should be used to gauge the value of a player exemplify a struggle over the political economy of baseball discourse.[63] The established writers defended their power to determine who should win based on the criteria they chose, and they entitled and endorsed their particular definition as best they could because their jobs were disappearing and they were losing their place as authorities in the game. The new guard of sports writers were "defensive and insecure about being taken seriously as baseball authorities"[64] and treated as "second-class citizens"[65] among baseball journalists, an ironic position since baseball front offices have recognized the value of advanced analytics and have their own proprietary set of sabermetric statistics, putting team management on a more similar ground with newer writers than the established sports journalists.

Baseball front offices believe in statistics as the key way to evaluate players. Team officials know the value of defense and base-running and have proprietary ways of evaluating players statistically. Traditional writers and players consequently do not have the best tools to gauge the quality of a player, and Trout would almost certainly have the support of front offices but not many writers and players.[66] In recognizing the change of power in the BBWAA, Levin noted that "Eventually, reason will win out over superstition, the conventional wisdom will change, and the nerds will become the establishment. The voters of 2012 will not decide who wins the MVP in 2032, and for that we can all be thankful."[67] Two seasons later when Trout finally beat Cabrera for MVP after losing to him two seasons in a row, Paine noted, "In what's quickly becoming an annual rite of summer, Mike Trout of the Los Angeles Angels once again led the American League in wins above replacement (WAR), the single-number metric of choice for most sabermetricians when it comes to measuring a player's all-around value."[68] Perhaps the tide finally turned for sabermetrician journalists.

Aftermath of the Definitional Rupture

The Trout-Cabrera debate of 2012 was an attempt to reinforce or change institutional norms within baseball journalism, addressing the question of how player value should be defined in practice: How should we use "valuable" in determining the most valuable player? However, baseball is slow to change, and "The statistical revolution that's permeating the baseball world hasn't won widespread acceptance just yet."[69] Looking back at the race, Carrie Kreiswirth interviewed ESPN editor Scott Burton, who noted, "In following the MVP debate between Mike Trout and Miguel Cabrera, it was shocking to me to witness the backlash to the analytics argument in favor of Trout. It was like we were stuck in 1998. And the fact that Trout lost handily, despite being superior in almost every meaningful way to Cabrera—as encapsulated by WAR—represented a failure for the analytics community. We lost the fight, badly."[70]

As sabermetric discourse grows in media and front offices, it will change how writers and fans talk about and understand baseball. Any substantial shift in baseball discourse is important for the sport, a game grounded in history and tradition. In the time since Trout-Cabrera, the use of sabermetric analysis by commentators, analysts, managers, and players has increased considerably. Today, we find discussions of WAR happening during broadcasts, fans are more comfortable with advanced analytics, and sabermetricians are gaining even more control in baseball front offices.[71]

The rise in the use of the defensive shift, more attention to things like pitch framing by catchers and batting average on balls in play, and other new approaches to player evaluation and scouting all show greater sensitivity to sabermetric reasoning and optimizing choices, and show its increased persuasiveness on people who think about and play baseball.[72] Sabermetrics has a louder voice in baseball discourse, but there is also a risk in seeing statistics as the only way to "truth" in valuing (and evaluating) players. There is the possibility that a faith in traditional value is being replaced with a faith in statistical value, a shift from more qualitative and visual evaluation to more quantitative and abstract reasoning. Seeing baseball as a series of statistical events and choices that can and should be statistically optimized runs the risk of making baseball even more neo-liberal and governed by economic metaphors.

There also remains the possibility that with specialized discourse "that the manner in which we draw distinctions among the different spheres may, itself, contribute to the decline of public discourse."[73] As baseball becomes more advanced statistically, we may be seeing the shifting of the permitted "speakers" moving from practitioners and lay observers to experts in elevated theory or statistics. With that shift may come alienation between traditional fans and sabermetrically-oriented ones. For example, acronyms can function in the bureaucratization of a field, alienating the laity from the bureaucratic experts and thereby entrenching the experts' power in the field. We see this concern expressed in Albom's infamous tirade against sabermetricians' support of Trout: "There is no end to the appetite for categories—from OBP to OPS to WAR. I mean, OMG! The number of triples hit while wearing a certain-colored underwear is probably being measured as we speak."[74] While it is easy to write off Albom's ridicule as satire or sarcasm, his article also expresses a concern at the overvaluation of complex statistics and obfuscation by new acronyms over the practical or observational qualities of player evaluation and the potential alienation that results.

Baseball as an institution continues to be somewhat slower than individual teams and writers to accept the statistical revolution played out on the fields. For example, in 2015 after the heavy use of unconventional, sabermetrically-inspired defensive shifts depressed offensive statistics, MLB Commissioner Rob Manfred said he was open to banning particular types of those shifts because of their negative effect and their deviation from traditional defensive arrangement.[75] This move received considerable pushback from the press, something that pre-2012 seemed rather unlikely in two ways: these kinds of defensive shifts were significantly less common, and the press likely would treat this as a negative instance of sabermetrics intruding on baseball in a clear, practical way that should not be permitted.

Conclusion

This project explores a representative anecdote of where and how definitions matter, and it shows the flexibility of Schiappa's method in exploring definitional practice.[76] It does not claim to be the last word on the matter. Since this is a single example based on a brief snapshot of time, future research in tension between sabermetrics and "traditional" baseball could look at changing definitional practice longer term, gravitating toward different crises or debates: Felix Hernandez and pitcher wins used in determining the Cy Young Award, how the RBI has been valued over time, the case for Jack Morris and the Hall of Fame. This project could also be seen as a first step in the larger fusing of rhetorical criticism and sports statistics, a move toward exploring the rhetoric of sabermetrics: the ways that baseball statisticians use words to define reality.

NOTES

1. Alan Schwarz, *The Numbers Game: Baseball's Lifelong Fascination with Statistics* (New York: Thomas Dunne, 2004).
2. Ron Von Burg and Paul E. Johnson, "Yearning for a Past That Never Was: Baseball, Steroids, and the Anxiety of the American Dream," *Critical Studies in Media Communication* 26(4): 356.
3. Bill James, *1980 Baseball Abstract* (Lawrence KS: Self-published, 1980).
4. Nathaniel H. Stoltz, "Sabermetrics over time: Persuasion and symbolic convergence across a diffusion of innovations," (master's thesis, Wake Forest University, 2014), 5, https://wakespace.lib.wfu.edu/bitstream/handle/10339/39317/Stoltz_wfu_0248m _10600.pdf.
5. Michael Lewis, *Moneyball: The Art of Winning an Unfair Game* (New York: W. W. Norton, 2003); Travis Sawchik, *Big Data Baseball: Math, Miracles, and the End of a 20-Year Losing Streak* (New York: Flatiron Books, 2015); Ben Lindbergh and Sam Miller, *The Only Rule Is It Has to Work: Our Wild Experiment Building a New Kind of Baseball Team* (New York: Henry Holt, 2016); Brian Kenny, *Ahead of the Curve: Inside the Baseball Revolution* (New York: Simon & Schuster, 2016).
6. Lonnie Wheeler, *Intangiball: The Subtle Things That Win Baseball Games* (New York: Simon & Schuster, 2015).
7. "Voting FAQ," Baseball Writers' Association of America, accessed November 2, 2016, http://bbwaa.com/voting-faq.
8. "Baseball's Most Controversial MVP Winners," *Real Clear Sports*, May 17, 2013, accessed November 2, 2016, http://www.realclearsports.com/lists/top_10 _controversial_mvp_winners/.

9. Associated Press, "Rodriguez Wins AL MVP Award," *Los Angeles Times*, November 19, 1999, http://articles.latimes.com/1999/nov/19/sports/sp-35454.

10. Arad Markowitz, "MLB: Top 10 Most Undeserving MVPs of All Time," *Bleacher Report*, May 26, 2011, http://bleacherreport.com/articles/713962-mlb-top-10-most-undeserving-mvps-of-all-time/page/8.

11. Edward Schiappa, "'Spheres of Argument' as *Topoi* for the Critical Study of Power/Knowledge," in *Spheres of Argument*, Bruce E. Gronbeck ed. (Annandale VA: Speech Communication Association, 1989), 48.

12. Joe Posnanski, "Revisiting Trout vs. Cabrera MVP Debate—With a Twist," nbcsports.com, March 4, 2013, http://mlb.nbcsports.com/2013/03/04/revisiting-trout-vs-cabrera-mvp-debate-with-a-twist/.

13. Kenneth Burke, *A Grammar of Motives* (Berkeley: University of California Press, 1969).

14. Edward Schiappa, *Defining Reality: Definitions and the Politics of Meaning* (Carbondale: Southern Illinois University Press, 2003), 7.

15. Schiappa, *Defining Reality*, 4.

16. James W. Chesebro, "Definition as Rhetorical Strategy," *Pennsylvania Speech Communication Annual* 41 (1985): 10.

17. Schiappa, *Defining Reality*, 3.

18. Schiappa, *Defining Reality*, 3.

19. Schiappa, *Defining Reality*, 7.

20. Schiappa, *Defining Reality*, 10.

21. Schiappa, *Defining Reality*, 46.

22. Mike Fast, "Spinning Yarn: Removing the Mask Encore Presentation," *Baseball Prospectus*, September 24, 2011, http://www.baseballprospectus.com/article.php?articleid=15093. Scott Lindholm, "How Well Do Umpires Call Balls and Strikes?," *Beyond the Box Score*, January 27, 2014, http://www.beyondtheboxscore.com/2014/1/27/5341676/how-well-do-umpires-call-balls-and-strikes.

23. Burke, *Grammar of Motives*, 359–79.

24. Schiappa, *Defining Reality*, 116.

25. Schiappa, *Defining Reality*, 66.

26. Schiappa, *Defining Reality*, 178.

27. Schiappa, *Defining Reality*, 178.

28. Schiappa, *Defining Reality*, 154.

29. Schiappa, *Defining Reality*, 179.

30. Sean Hartnett, "Cabrera vs. Trout—Sorting Through the Great 2012 AL MVP Debate," *CBS New York*, October 4, 2012, http://newyork.cbslocal.com/2012/10/04/hartnett-cabrera-vs-trout-sorting-through-the-great-2012-al-mvp-debate/.

31. Jason Beck, "Miggy Beats Trout to Add AL MVP to Collection," mlb.com, November 15, 2012, http://m.mlb.com/news/article/40301568/.

32. Alden Gonzalez, "Definition of Most Valuable? MVP Voters Explain," Angels.com, November 15, 2013, http://wap.mlb.com/laa/news/article/2013111563941740/?locale =es_CO.

33. John Shipley, "MVP Numbers: Old School (Miguel Cabrera) vs. New Age (Mike Trout)," *St. Paul Pioneer Press*, September 20, 2012, http://www.twincities.com/ci _21603755/mvp-numbers-old-school-miguel-cabrera-vs-new; Nate Silver, "The Statistical Case Against Cabrera for MVP," *New York Times*, November 14, 2012, https:// fivethirtyeight.blogs.nytimes.com/2012/11/14/the-statistical-case-against-cabrera-for -m-v-p/?mcubz=1&_r=0; Jonah Keri, "Mike Trout is the Real MVP, Miguel Cabrera is the Players' MVP," *Grantland*, November 16, 2012, http://grantland.com/the-triangle /mike-trout-is-the-mvp-cabrera-is-the-players-mvp/?print=1.

34. David Roth, "Revenge Against Baseball's Nerds," *Wall Street Journal*, November 16, 2012, http://blogs.wsj.com/dailyfix/2012/11/16/revenge-against-baseballs-nerds.

35. Schiappa, *Defining Reality*, 89.

36. Tim Britton, "Why I Voted for Mike Trout," *Providence Journal*, November 15, 2012, http://www.providencejournal.com/article/20121115/sports/311159990.

37. Bill Madden, "SABR Geeks Sabotaging Cy and MVP Races," *New York Daily News*, September 29, 2012, http://www.nydailynews.com/sports/baseball/nowlin-geeks-stiff -dickey-miguel-cabrera-nl-cy-young-al-mvp-voting-means-war-article-1.1171008 (ellipsis in original).

38. Mark Whicker, "Cabrera Over Trout for MVP is the Right Call," *Orange County Register*, November 13, 2012, http://www.ocregister.com/2012/11/13/whicker-cabrera -over-trout-for-mvp-is-the-right-call/.

49. Susan Slusser, "Why I Voted for Miguel Cabrera," *San Francisco Chronicle*, November 15, 2012, http://blog.sfgate.com/athletics/2012/11/15/why-i-voted-for-miguel-cabrera/.

40. Whicker, "Right Call," 34 (ellipsis added).

41. Mark Feinsand, "Miguel, Not Trout, Hooks My MVP Vote," *New York Daily News*, November 16, 2012, http://www.nydailynews.com/sports/baseball/feinsand-miguel -not-trout-hooks-mvp-vote-article-1.1202954.

42. Steve Gardner, "Trout Deserved Better in MVP Voting," *USA Today*, November 16, 2012, https://www.usatoday.com/story/sports/mlb/2012/11/15/mike-trout-mvp-case /1707791/.

43. Carl Bialik, "The MVP Case for Mike Trout," *Wall Street Journal*, September 24, 2012, http://blogs.wsj.com/dailyfix/2012/09/24/the-mvp-case-for-mike-trout-vs-miguel -cabrera/tab/print.

44. Neil Paine, "Finally, Mike Trout is the MVP," *FiveThirtyEight*, November 14, 2014, https://fivethirtyeight.com/datalab/finally-mike-trout-is-the-mvp/.

45. Posnanski, "Revisiting Trout."

46. Bialik, "MVP Case."

47. Mark Reynolds, "Mike Trout vs. Miguel Cabrera: Revisiting the 2012 American League MVP Race," *Bleacher Report*, March 17, 2013, http://bleacherreport.com

/articles/1570961-mike-trout-vs-miguel-cabrera-revisiting-the-2012-american-league
-mvp-race.

48. Zachary D. Rhymer, "AL MVP Award 2012 Voting Results: Why Mike Trout Got Totally Screwed," *Bleacher Report*, November 15, 2012, http://bleacherreport.com /articles/1410684-al-mvp-award-2012-voting-results-why-mike-trout-got-totally -screwed.

49. Craig Calcaterra, "Mike Trout vs. Miguel Cabrera a Proxy Battle in a Larger Cold War," nbcsports.com, November 15, 2013, http://mlb.nbcsports.com/2013/11/15 /miketrout-vs-miguel-cabrera-a-proxy-battle-in-alarger-cold-war.

50. Josh Levin, "Miguel Cabrera is Mitt Romney," *Slate*, November 16, 2012, http://www .slate.com/articles/sports/sports_nut/2012/11/miguel_cabrera_is_mitt_romney_this _time_the_candidate_of_old_white_men_won.html.

51. Keith Law, "Trout the Rational Choice for AL MVP," espn.com, September 25, 2012, http://www.espn.com/blog/keith-law/insider/post?id=155.

52. Reynolds, "Revisiting."

53. Mitch Albom, "Miguel Cabrera's Award a Win for Fans, Defeat for Stats Geeks," *Detroit Free Press*, November 16, 2012, http://www.freep.com/article/20121116/col01 /311160108.

54. Michael L. Butterworth, "Nate Silver and Campaign 2012: Sport, the Statistical Frame, and the Rhetoric of Electoral Forecasting," *Journal of Communication 64* (2012): 895–914.

55. Madden, "SABR Geeks."

56. Law, "Rational Choice."

57. Keri, "Trout Real MVP."

58. Silver, "Statistical Case Against Cabrera."

59. Joe Lucia, "AL MVP Voting Causes Baseball Writers to Go Nuclear," *Awful Announc-ing*, November 16, 2012, http://awfulannouncing.com/2012-articles/al-mvp-voting -causes-baseball-writers-to-go-nuclear.html.

60. Levin, "Cabrera is Romney."

61. Shipley, "MVP Numbers."

62. Matthew Trueblood, "Good for Baseball: Miguel Cabrera Won the 2012 AL MVP over Mike Trout," *Banished to the Pen*, November 16, 2012, http://www.banishedtothepen .com/good-for-baseball-miguel-cabrera-won-the-2012-al-mvp-over-mike-trout.

63. Calcaterra, "Proxy Battle."

64. Calcaterra, "Proxy Battle."

65. Calcaterra, "Proxy Battle."

66. Buster Olney, "Framing the American League MVP debate," espn.com, September 19, 2012, http://www.espn.com/blog/buster-olney/insider/post?id=58.

67. Levin, "Cabrera is Romney."

68. Paine, "Finally Mike Trout."

69. Gardner, "Trout Deserved Better."

70. Carrie Kreiswirth, "*ESPN The Mag*'s 'The Analytics Issue' dissects debate," espnfrontrow.com, February 2013, http://www.espnfrontrow.com/2013/02/espn -the-mags-the-analytics-issue-dissects-the-miguel-cabrera-vs-mike-trout-al-mvp -debate.

71. Stoltz, "Sabermetrics Over Time."

72. Sawchik, *Big Data Baseball*.

73. Schiappa, "Spheres of Argument," 48.

74. Albom, "Stat Geeks."

75. Cliff Corcoran, "New Commissioner Rob Manfred's Talk of Banning Shifts Makes No Sense," *Sports Illustrated*, January 26, 2015, http://www.si.com/mlb/2015/01/26 /rob-manfred-defensive-shifts-mlb-commissioner.

76. Schiappa, *Defining Reality*.

50

From Usenet Joke to Baseball Flashpoint

The Growth of "Three True Outcomes"

D. B. FIRSTMAN

It has been more than twenty years since the term Three True Outcomes first became part of our language, and in the intervening years the term has become a stand-in for how the game of baseball has evolved or, if you prefer, for what is wrong with modern baseball. D. B. Firstman, perhaps best known for their humorous takes on the game at their blog, *ValueOverReplacementGrit.com*, ably tackles the subject in this article that first appeared in the *Baseball Research Journal* in 2018. Firstman's work has also appeared at ESPN, *Bronx Banter*, *Baseball Prospectus*, *The Hardball Times*, and in *The Village Voice*.

It all started as a lark. Back in the mid-1990s, during the Internet's infancy, Usenet bulletin boards were the virtual water coolers we all gathered around to discuss our favorite topics. Over on the *rec.sport.baseball* board, Christina Kahrl and a bunch of like-minded individuals were marveling over the statistical quirks of Rob Deer. Deer had the unusual ability to *not* put the ball in play. At a time when about a quarter of all plate appearances ended in a walk, home run, or strikeout, Deer managed that outcome nearly half the time.[1]

The members of the Usenet board organized a "Rob Deer Fan Club" and, as Kahrl says:

> We basically trolled people over how this was a guy playing the game the right way, because he was generating runs and avoiding double plays. I wrote a silly Conan/Robert E. Howard sort of backstory about how "The Deer" was inspired by the "ur-Deer" (Gorman Thomas, of course), and since we were already steeping it in our semi-ridiculous absolute faith in our hero, I referred to his delivering "the Three True Outcomes."[2]

Baseball Prospectus (BP) was the first major website to note the Three True Outcomes (TTO). In August 2000 on that site, Rany Jazayerli whimsically proclaimed:

> The Revolution that will spread the Gospel of the Three True Outcomes to every man, woman and child on Earth.
>
> What are the Three True Outcomes, you ask? They are:
>
> The Home Run, the weapon with which we fight the evil legions of Little Ball.
>
> The Strikeout, a symbol of our refusal to compromise.
>
> The Base on Balls, which brings balance to our cause.
>
> Together, the Three True Outcomes distill the game to its essence, the battle of pitcher against hitter, free from the distractions of the defense, the distortion of foot speed or the corruption of managerial tactics like the bunt and his wicked brother, the hit-and-run.[3]

The next year, TTO got a further boost in prominence and an actual air of legitimacy when BP's Voros McCracken wrote about seeking to determine what impact fielding had on pitching. His work referenced aspects of TTO, as components that the fielders had no control over:

> The first thing I did was create something called "Defense Independent Pitching Stats." DIPS are the representation of a pitcher's stat line without any possible influence from the defense behind the pitcher. I calculated the various rates for walks, strikeouts, home runs, hit batsmen, etc. as a function of batters faced, and inserted them into the pitcher's line.[4]

In the following years, BP's Keith Woolner reported on the annual leaders in TTO percentage and noted when a player broke the record for highest percentage in a season. In 2004, Woolner introduced an update to those calculations, normalizing individual player rates based on major-league averages.[5]

With each passing year, additional baseball websites dipped their toes into the TTO waters, reporting on the yearly leaders and/or trailers (most times without normalization to major-league average for that season). This author applied TTO analysis on the team level in a post to their own baseball blog in 2012, providing a look at the teams from 1973 through 2011 with the highest and lowest TTO percentages relative to major-league average. In so doing, it was discovered that a team's TTO rate had very little impact on its overall record. There had been winning and losing teams on both sides of the TTO spectrum.[6]

In August 2017, during a season in which the TTO rate in the majors would ultimately hit a record 33.5 percent, Michael Baumann of the Ringer offered up an immersive run-through of TTO's ever-increasing footprint on the game. The article was ominously titled "The End of Baseball As We Know It" and it proclaimed: "With the march of three true outcomes—walks, strikeouts, and home runs—the sport has been pushed to its efficient extreme. MLB has undergone a quiet revolution without anyone stopping to ask the question: Is this what we really want?" Baumann placed the TTO explosion within the context of the steroid era, the increasing height and weight of players, and the increasing velocity of pitchers.[7]

In this paper TTO growth will be examined and possible explanations for the upward trend will be presented.

Historical Growth in TTO Categories

Babe Ruth set an incredible standard as a TTO leader during his career, compiling the 10 highest all-time TTO rates relative to major-league average, as shown in table 50.1. For example, in 1920 the big-league TTO rate was 15.5 percent. Ruth's 46.1 figure nearly tripled that, and the nine other marks were also at least double the standard for the corresponding season.

Table 50.1. Top ten TTO percentage differences (all by Babe Ruth), by season

Season	Ruth TTO%	MLB TTO%	Pct. Diff.
1920	46.1%	15.5%	+197.1%
1923	43.5%	16.2%	+169.0%
1921	41.1%	15.4%	+166.8%
1927	41.4%	16.0%	+159.3%
1926	41.0%	16.1%	+154.0%
1922	40.1%	15.9%	+152.0%
1924	39.5%	15.6%	+153.0%
1933	41.3%	16.8%	+146.6%
1928	40.6%	16.6%	+145.1%
1932	39.6%	17.4%	+127.7%

Table 50.2 shows the highest single-season TTO percentage difference for each decade. Ruth of course dominates the list, and we see the aforementioned Deer and Thomas. Dave Nicholson set a then-major-league record with 175 strikeouts in 1963 as a part of his TTO stats.

Table 50.2. Highest single-season TTO percentage differences for batting title qualifiers, by decade

Decade	Season	Name	HR%	BB%	SO%	TTO%	MLB TTO%	Pct. Diff.
1910s	1919	Babe Ruth	5.4%	18.6%	10.7%	34.7%	15.8%	+119%
1920s	1920	Babe Ruth	8.8%	24.4%	13.0%	46.1%	15.5%	+197%
1930s	1933	Babe Ruth	5.9%	19.8%	15.7%	41.3%	16.8%	+147%
1940s	1941	Dolph Camilli	5.3%	16.2%	17.9%	39.5%	19.7%	+100%
1950s	1958	Mickey Mantle	6.4%	19.7%	18.3%	44.5%	24.0%	+85%
1960s	1963	Dave Nicholson	4.2%	12.1%	33.7%	50.0%	25.4%	+97%
1970s	1979	Gorman Thomas	6.7%	14.7%	26.2%	47.6%	23.1%	+106%
1980s	1987	Jack Clark	6.3%	24.3%	24.9%	55.5%	27.1%	+104%
1990s	1991	Rob Deer	4.6%	16.5%	32.5%	53.6%	26.0%	+106%
2000s	2007	Jack Cust	5.1%	20.7%	32.3%	58.2%	28.2%	+106%
2010s	2012	Adam Dunn	6.3%	16.2%	34.2%	56.7%	30.4%	+86%

As shown in figure 50.1, Three True Outcomes made up no more than 20 percent of all plate appearances from 1913 through 1945. The one-quarter threshold was broken in 1961, and the 30 percent mark was eclipsed for the first time in 2012. The rate jumped considerably in each of the last three seasons, from 30.3 percent to 30.7 percent in 2015, 32.3 percent in 2016, and finally the record of 33.5 percent this past year.

Walk rates have remained relatively static over time, and while home run rates did hit a record 3.3 percent of plate appearances in 2017,[8] they remain the smallest component of TTO. Figure 50.2 shows the rapid increase in strikeout rate across the majors, especially since the early 1990s. It is the increase in strikeouts that is driving the TTO explosion.

Major-league baseball set a record with 21.6 percent of all plate appearances ending in a strikeout in 2017, and as table 50.3 shows, the last ten years have seen a nearly 25 percent increase in the overall strikeout rate.

MLB Three True Outcome Percentage - 1913 to 2017

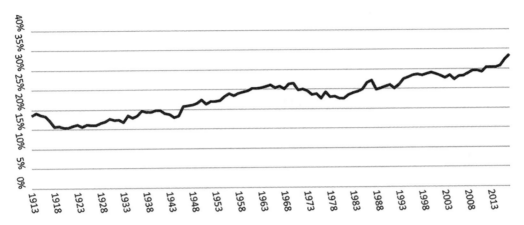

Fig. 50.1. Three True Outcome rates have been rising steadily, especially in the last 25 years.

MLB Homer, Walk and Strikeout Rates - 1913 to 2017

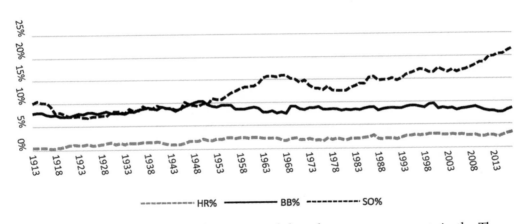

Fig. 50.2. Strikeout-rate growth has outpaced the other two components in the Three True Outcomes.

Table 50.3. Strikeout percentage in MLB, 2008–2017

Year	K%
2008	17.5%
2009	18.0%
2010	18.5%
2011	18.6%
2012	19.8%
2013	19.9%
2014	20.4%
2015	20.4%
2016	21.1%
2017	21.6%

Reasons for TTO Growth

With strikeouts being the largest component of TTO, it would make sense to examine the reasons for the increasing strikeout (and therefore TTO) rate. There are five main reasons:

Reason 1: March of the Relievers

The frequency of managers employing the strategy of "shortening" games—using seventh-inning relievers, setup men, lefty and righty specialists and the like to get the game to the closer—has risen sharply in the past decade. As shown in table 50.4, relievers took part in 38 percent of all plate appearances (PA%) in 2017, compared to only 33 percent back in 2005.[9]

This is important to the TTO discussion because relievers have higher strikeout rates than starters, going as far back as 1969.

Reason 2: Infusion of Youth in Game
Brought With It a Free-Swinging Attitude

Table 50.5 shows the percentage of plate appearances given to each of four distinct age groups in the major leagues. The year 2004 was chosen as that was the most recent nadir in terms of the youngest group's percentage of all plate appearances. "K Pct. Diff." is the difference between each group's strikeout rate and the majors as a whole that season. For example, in 2004 the "Ages <= 25" group had a strikeout rate of 19.4 percent against a major-league average of 16.9, for a "K Pct. Diff" of 15 percent above average. Similarly,

Table 50.4. Starter and reliever percentage of plate appearances, with strikeout and TTO rates, 2005–2017

	Starters			Relievers		
Year	PA%	K%	TTO%	PA%	K%	TTO%
2005	67%	16%	26%	33%	18%	30%
2006	65%	16%	27%	35%	19%	31%
2007	65%	16%	27%	35%	19%	31%
2008	65%	17%	27%	35%	19%	32%
2009	65%	17%	28%	35%	19%	32%
2010	67%	18%	28%	33%	20%	32%
2011	67%	18%	28%	33%	21%	32%
2012	66%	19%	29%	34%	22%	33%
2013	66%	19%	29%	34%	22%	33%
2014	66%	19%	29%	34%	22%	33%
2015	65%	19%	29%	35%	22%	33%
2016	63%	20%	31%	37%	23%	34%
2017	62%	21%	32%	38%	23%	36%

"TTO Pct. Diff" is the difference between the group's TTO percentage and the majors as a whole that season. In 2004 the "Ages <= 25" group had a 29.9 TTO percentage against a major-league average of 28.4, and was therefore 5 percent higher (29.9/28.4 = 105 percent).

Since 2004, the percentage of plate appearances given to "youngsters" has risen by 10 full points, offsetting a drop in that group's strikeout-percentage difference from 15 percent above average to 8 above average. Notice that in 2017, the younger the group was, the higher the strikeout rate and TTO percentage. The prospects and/or youngest players coming into the big leagues are driving the rising strikeout rate, which in turn raises the current TTO rate.[10]

Reason 3: "Small Ball" Is Waning

In 2011, there were 1,667 sacrifice bunts. In 2017, that number was down 45 percent to 925. There were 4,540 stolen base attempts and 1,274 sacrifice flies in 2011. Six years later, those numbers were 3,461 and 1,168 respectively.[11] It appears teams no longer play for one run unless absolutely necessary. The "Earl Weaver special" of a three-run homer is the weapon of choice nowadays, and TTO is taking over.[12]

Table 50.5. Comparison of strikeout and TTO rates with percentage differences, by age group in 2004 and 2017

| | 2004 (MLB 16.9 K%; 28.4 TTO%) | | | | | 2017 (MLB 21.6 K%; 33.5 TTO%) | | | | |
Split	PA%	K%	K pct. diff.	TTO%	TTO pct. diff.	PA%	K%	K pct. diff.	TTO%	TTO pct. diff.
Ages <= 25	16.9%	19.4%	+15%	29.9%	+5%	26.9%	23.4%	+8%	35.1%	+5%
Ages 26–30	49.0%	16.3%	-4%	27.4%	-3%	44.6%	21.6%	+/-0%	33.2%	-1%
Ages 31–35	24.7%	16.9%	+/-0%	29.1%	+2%	24.6%	20.1%	-7%	32.5%	-3%
Ages 36+	9.3%	15.3%	-9%	28.8%	+2%	4.0%	19.6%	-9%	31.6%	-6%

One look at an "expected runs matrix" should show why. Table 50.6 shows the 24 base-out states possible in an inning, along with the expected runs scored in each circumstance during 2017.[13]

Table 50.6. Expected runs matrix for MLB, 2017

Runners	0 outs	1 out	2 out
---	0.52	0.29	0.11
1--	0.89	0.54	0.23
-2-	1.11	0.69	0.33
--3	1.36	0.93	0.38
12-	1.48	0.94	0.46
-23	1.95	1.34	0.60
1-3	1.73	1.19	0.51
123	2.32	1.59	0.73

For example, with no outs and a runner on first, one should expect to score 0.89 runs. That expectancy actually drops to 0.69 runs if you sacrifice bunt or otherwise "productively" move the runner to second while making an out.

More and more, teams are forsaking small ball and relying upon the long ball. Table 50.7 shows the percentage of runs scored via the home run since 2007. The 42.3 percent figure in 2017 is an all-time record.[14]

This homer-happy thinking has been fueled by a dramatic increase in the percentage of fly balls that resulted in homers over the past few seasons. Table 50.8 shows that nearly 14 percent of all fly balls left the yard in 2017, a record since these data became available.[15]

Fly balls traveled an average of 316 feet in 2015. For whatever reason (batters changing their launch angle, which will be discussed shortly, or baseballs

Table 50.7. Percentage of runs scored in MLB via home run, 2007–2017	
Year	HR as % of Runs
2007	34.2%
2008	34.5%
2009	35.5%
2010	34.4%
2011	34.4%
2012	37.0%
2013	35.4%
2014	33.4%
2015	37.3%
2016	40.2%
2017	42.3%

Table 50.8. Homers as a percentage of fly balls, 2011–2017	
Year	HR/FB
2011	9.7%
2012	11.3%
2013	10.5%
2014	9.5%
2015	11.4%
2016	12.8%
2017	13.7%

being livelier, are two possibilities), that average jumped to 319 feet in 2016 and 321 feet in 2017.[16] Those five additional feet turn some routine outs into hits or even homers. Even if the fly ball doesn't go out, it has become less of a pox on batters. In 2014 batters hit .212 on fly balls. That average grew to .251 in 2017.[17] This leads into our next reason.

Reason 4: Advanced Analytics Have Made Launch Angle the "In" Thing
The 2015 introduction and growing use by teams of Statcast data, which tracks the movement of every ball and fielder in each park/game, has changed the way some players have approached hitting.[18] Where once hitters were limited to video review and advanced scouting of pitcher tendencies, now they have almost instantaneous access to the exit velocity and launch angle of their batted balls.[19]

A June 2017 article in the *Washington Post* went into great detail on this: "More batters are focusing not only on hitting the ball hard, but hitting the ball high into the air. The average launch angle—the angle at which the ball flies after being hit—rose from 10.5 degrees in 2015 to 11.5 degrees in 2016." By May 21, 2017, the average launch angle was up to 12.8. Those two degrees may not sound like much, but they can make the difference between a ground ball and a line drive. "Balls hit with a high launch angle are more likely to result in a hit. Hit fast enough and at the right angle [generally over 95 miles per hour at an angle between 25 and 35 degrees], they become home runs."[20]

The *Post* made Washington hometown hitter Daniel Murphy their example of a batter who adjusted his swing to hit the ball higher, noting that his "launch angle rose from 11.1 degrees in 2015 to 16.6 degrees in 2016" and "his batting average rose from .281 in 2015 to .347 in 2016. He also hit eleven more home runs."[21]

But when one swings hard and tries to hit the bottom half of the ball to generate loft, there will be an increased tendency to swing and miss, which leads brings us to the last reason.

Reason 5: The Strikeout Has Been Destigmatized

I've quit trying to hit home runs every time I go to bat. . . . From now on I'm just trying to keep from striking out. All I want to do is meet the ball. If I do that I'll have a good year.

—MICKEY MANTLE in April of 1956[22]

Ralph Houk . . . . has advised me to try choking up the bat when I'm up there left-handed and the pitcher has two strikes against me. I'm going to try it.

—MANTLE in January of 1961[23]

Back in the 1950s and '60s, Mickey Mantle was frequently criticized for his high strikeout totals, despite a high batting average, immense power, and, as it turned out, all his best intentions. Table 50.9 shows how in nearly every season of his career, including his MVP seasons of 1956, 1957, and 1962, Mantle far exceeded the major-league strikeout rate (and consequently one-upped the league TTO rate also).[24]

Table 50.9. MLB and Mickey Mantle's strikeout and TTO rates with percentage differences, 1951–1968

Year	MLB SO%	MLB TTO%	Mantle SO%	Mantle TTO%	SO Pct. Diff	TTO Pct. Diff
1951	9.7%	21.3%	19.2%	33.7%	+97%	+58%
1952	10.9%	22.0%	17.7%	33.4%	+62%	+52%
1953	10.7%	22.0%	16.7%	35.2%	+56%	+60%
1954	10.7%	22.2%	16.4%	36.3%	+54%	+63%

1955	11.4%	23.2%	15.2%	38.7%	+34%	+67%
1956	12.1%	23.9%	15.2%	40.3%	+26%	+69%
1957	12.5%	23.4%	12.0%	40.9%	-4%	+75%
1958	13.0%	24.0%	18.3%	44.5%	+41%	+85%
1959	13.3%	24.3%	19.7%	39.1%	+48%	+61%
1960	13.5%	24.6%	19.4%	42.9%	+44%	+74%
1961	13.6%	25.2%	17.3%	45.2%	+27%	+80%
1962	14.1%	25.3%	15.5%	45.8%	+10%	+81%
1963	15.3%	25.4%	15.0%	40.8%	-2%	+61%
1964	15.6%	25.7%	18.0%	41.6%	+15%	+62%
1965	15.7%	26.1%	17.5%	38.6%	+11%	+48%
1966	15.5%	25.4%	19.3%	39.7%	+25%	+56%
1967	15.9%	25.8%	20.4%	43.8%	+28%	+70%
1968	15.8%	25.1%	17.7%	40.4%	+12%	+61%

Contrast that with today's players and environment:

> There's no doubt the pitchers throw harder now than when I first
> got to the league, but there is also a different mentality from players
> these days. . . . They feel like if they strike out, it's not a big deal.
> I personally hate strikeouts . . . but that's my mentality. Yes, I see
> more homers and more strikeouts, but I guess that's, like, the new
> baseball.
> —CARLOS BELTRAN[25]

Beltran made the majors in 1998. During that season, 23 batting title
qualifiers ended the season with more walks than strikeouts.[26] Since 2012,
there have been no more than five qualifying players in any season.[27]

One need look no further than arguably the two best and most popular
players in the game, Bryce Harper and Mike Trout, to witness the new world
order of Strikeouts Are Okay. During his career, Harper has struck out 20.4
percent of the time, which coincidentally matches Mantle's worst season,
but is just a hair below the major league average of 20.5 percent.[28] No one
has suggested the five-time All-Star try cutting down his swing. Meanwhile,
Trout struck out an American League-leading 184 times in 2014, and still
led the league in offensive WAR and won the MVP that year.[29] He also strikes
out just above the major league average over his career (21.5 percent to 20.3

percent). There have been no reports of Mike Scioscia suggesting Trout choke up with two strikes against a tough righty.

Most recently, this past season, Aaron Judge became only the fifth rookie to qualify for the batting title while striking out in more than 30 percent of his plate appearances (table 50.10).[30] Note that four of these have occurred since 1995, and three of them have taken place in the last three seasons.

Table 50.10. Batting title qualifying rookies with 30 percent strikeout rate in season

Year	Player	K	PA	K%
2017	Aaron Judge	208	678	30.7%
2015	Kris Bryant	199	650	30.6%
1986	Pete Incaviglia	185	606	30.5%
2015	Michael Taylor	158	511	30.9%
1995	Benji Gil	147	454	32.4%

Judge also set a TTO rookie record in 2017 with an amazing 57.1 percent of his plate appearances ending in a walk, strikeout, or homer. According to Nate Silver, Judge became only the eighth player to lead his league in all three TTO categories in the same year.[31] Regardless of how voters felt about his TTO prowess, Judge earned the 2017 American League Rookie of the Year, and was a second-place finisher in AL Most Valuable Player balloting. Fans seemed more enamored with his rookie record 52 homers than concerned about his (also) rookie record 208 strikeouts, as he had the most popular jersey at MLBshop.com.[32]

Judge's assault on the TTO record this past season was actually upstaged by Joey Gallo, who broke Jack Cust's 2007 record of 58.2 percent TTO. Gallo's 58.6 TTO percentage means that three of the top 10 highest TTO rates occurred in 2017 (table 50.11).

Table 50.11. Top ten individual season TTO rates of batting title qualifiers, 1913 to 2017

Name	Season	TTO%
Joey Gallo	2017	58.6%
Jack Cust	2007	58.2%
Aaron Judge	2017	57.1%
Jack Cust	2008	57.0%

Mark McGwire	1998	56.8%
Adam Dunn	2012	56.7%
Jack Clark	1987	55.5%
Mark Reynolds	2010	54.7%
Ryan Howard	2007	54.5%
Chris Davis	2017	53.8%

Impact of TTO on Today's Game

Tickets sold to major-league games have declined relatively steadily from a 2007 peak of 79.5 million to 2017's 72.7 million.[33] Reasons for this decline have included the hot-button phrase "pace of play," as some believe that the increasing length of games (an average two hours and 49 minutes in 2005, which grew to three hours and eight minutes in 2017) has bored and/ or deterred fans.[34]

Some of this increase in game length can be attributed to the previously mentioned glut of relief appearances in today's game. Teams are using half a pitching appearance more on average per game in 2017 compared to 2005 (4.22 vs. 3.71). Additionally, pitches per plate appearance have increased from 3.74 in 2005 to 3.89 in 2017.[35] The longer plate appearances extend into time between pitches also. As of mid-June 2017, players were taking 1.1 seconds more between pitches in 2017 than 2016, an unprecedented one-year jump in the 11 seasons such records have been available.[36] As for game length being driven upward by increased offense, you can't blame it on more batters coming to the plate, as the average plate appearances per game has decreased slightly between from 2005 to 2017.[37]

A natural question to ask is whether TTO outcomes are to blame for longer plate appearances. To answer that, one would need to figure out how many pitches on average it took to achieve each of the TTO events, versus all other plate-appearance outcomes. Table 50.12 shows the results of taking Baseball Reference Play Index data for 2005 and 2017 and splitting out the pitch counts for strikeouts, walks, homers, and all other events.[38] The table reveals that the TTO outcomes—especially walks and strikeouts (both above the overall average in pitches)—lead to longer at-bats. In fact, it took more pitches in 2017 to finish *any* kind of plate appearance. Those longer at-bats are part of the reason for longer games.

Even though the average number of pitches to achieve a strikeout has increased only slightly between 2005 and 2017, there were nearly 10,000 more such events in 2017. An additional 46,473 pitches were thrown during strikeouts in 2017 compared to 2005. That works out to an average of 19 additional pitches per game, roughly one-half inning's worth.

Table 50.12. Pitches per plate appearance for various events in 2005 and 2017 (excluding zero-pitch intentional walks)

Outcome	2005			2017		
	Events	Tot. Pit.	Avg.	Events	Tot. Pit.	Avg.
SO	30,644	147,440	4.81	40,104	193,913	4.84
BB	15,207	83,723	5.51	15,083	86,224	5.72
HR	5,017	16,697	3.33	6,105	20,731	3.40
All other	135,424	448,306	3.31	124,003	423,776	3.42
Total	186,292	696,166	3.74	185,295	724,644	3.91

The Future of TTO

Still we've only had one run scored that was manufactured. It's millennial. This is millennial baseball right now. You get up, you take a big swing, you strike out. You don't try to get the runners over very often. Nobody bunts. Nobody hit-and-runs. We're a team that has to get guys on and we got five hits. I mean, six runs and five hits is what you call efficiency, except if you lose.

—STEVE GARVEY on Game Two of the 2017 World Series[39]

Game Two of the 2017 World Series featured 19 strikeouts, eight homers, and eight walks amid 90 plate appearances.[40] The Astros 7–6 win over the Dodgers had 35 three-true-outcome events, which was apparently too much for former major leaguer Garvey.

Regardless of whether you call it "millennial baseball" or TTO, there doesn't appear to be enough of a groundswell within Major League Baseball or the Players Association themselves to change the direction toward more TTO. Pace of play initiatives have focused on intentional walks, mound visit durations, and time between pitches and pitching changes.

From the player's perspective, why shouldn't they adopt a TTO approach, given the increasing use of defensive shifts on the infield? You can see the impact of infield shifts on batting average on balls in play (BABIP) in table 50.13. The normal BABIP in a season is right around .300. With shifts, balls on the ground resulted in a measly .237 BABIP in 2017—and that was the second highest figure in the last seven years.[41] So why put the ball in play on the ground?

Table 50.13. BABIP on groundballs hit into shifts, 2011–2017

Season	PA	H	BABIP
2011	1,602	342	.213
2012	2,827	649	.230
2013	3,742	803	.215
2014	6,639	1,474	.222
2015	10,723	2,430	.227
2016	15,071	3,594	.238
2017	14,193	3,362	.237

When you do put the ball in play, fielders are now as good as they've ever been, shifted or not. The .984 fielding average in the majors in 2017 was just below the all-time high of .985 in 2013.[42] There has been no tangible increase in batting average on balls in play in the past 25 years.[43] There is little in the way of new incentives to put the ball in play on the ground, and with whispers of a livelier ball being used since the middle of 2015, homers and other extra-base hits are easier to come by if you adjust your launch angle.[44]

With the rare exceptions of lowering the mound and reducing the strike zone in 1969, and the introduction of the designated hitter in 1973, baseball has not tinkered with the fundamental workings of the game in the past 50 years. Those changes were for the purposes of boosting offense and hopefully attendance along with them. If attendance continues to drop, baseball might be inclined to implement similar radical changes. Would MLB consider, for example, something as drastic as deadening the ball to reduce home runs? It's not that there is "too much offense" in the game right now; it's that the offensive strategies, on a "molecular" level, have dynamically changed the game flow. However, the TTO revolution, which started as an Internet goof and has become a reality due to the reasons addressed herein, is apparently here to stay.

NOTES

1. "Rob Deer Stats," Baseball-Reference.com, accessed October 29, 2017, https://www .baseball-reference.com/play-index/share.fcgi?id=jb3cC.

2. "Appreciating Tootblan and Other New Baseball Lingo," FOX Sports, June 29, 2015, http://www.foxsports.com/mlb/just-a-bit-outside/story/appreciating-new-baseball -lingo-tootblan-maddux-three-true-outcomes-062915.

3. Rany Jazayerli, "Doctoring the Numbers: The Doctor Is . . . Gone," *Baseball Prospectus*, August 15, 2000, https://www.baseballprospectus.com/news/article/724 /doctoring-the-numbers-the-doctor-is-gone/.

4. Voros McCracken, "Pitching and Defense: How Much Control Do Hurlers Have?," *Baseball Prospectus*, January 23, 2001, https://www.baseballprospectus.com/news /article/878/pitching-and-defense-how-much-control-do-hurlers-have/.

5. Keith Woolner, "Aim for the Head: Three True Outcomes, 2003," *Baseball Prospectus*, January 21, 2004, https://www.baseballprospectus.com/news/article/2518/aim-for -the-head-three-true-outcomes-2003/.

6. Diane Firstman, "Applying 'Three True Outcomes' to a Team," *Value Over Replacement Grit*, February 19, 2013, http://valueoverreplacementgrit.com/2012/02/06 /applying-three-true-outcomes-to-a-team/.

7. Michael Baumann, "The End of Baseball as We Know It," *The Ringer*, August 3, 2017, https://www.theringer.com/2017/8/7/16108098/the-end-of-baseball-as-we-know-it.

8. "2017 Major League Baseball Batting Ratios," Baseball-Reference.com, accessed October 29, 2017, https://www.baseball-reference.com/leagues/mlb/2017-ratio-batting .shtml.

9. "Team Pitching Split Finder," Baseball-Reference.com, accessed October 29, 2017, https://www.baseball-reference.com/tiny/qex8n.

10. "Team Pitching Split Finder."

11. "Major League Baseball Batting Year-by-Year Averages," Baseball-Reference.com, accessed October 29, 2017, https://www.baseball-reference.com/leagues/mlb/bat .shtml.

12. Diane Firstman, "Earl Weaver's Love Affair with the Three-Run Homer," *Value Over Replacement Grit*, January 22, 2013, http://valueoverreplacementgrit.com/2013/01 /20/earl-weavers-love-affair-with-the-three-run-homer/.

13. "Custom Statistics Report: Run Expectations," *Baseball Prospectus*, accessed October 29, 2017, http://legacy.baseballprospectus.com/sortable/index.php?cid=1918829.

14. "Statistics: Custom Statistic Reports: Team Batting," *Baseball Prospectus*, accessed October 29, 2017, http://legacy.baseballprospectus.com/sortable/index.php?cid= 2474935.

15. "Leaderboard, League Stats, Batting, Batted Ball," FanGraphs, accessed October 26, 2017, https://tinyurl.com/y7oztkcy.

16. "Statcast Search," BaseballSavant, accessed October 31, 2017, https://tinyurl.com /yaeakoxy.

17. "Major League Total Stats," 2017, Batters: Standard Statistics, FanGraphs Baseball, accessed November 1, 2017, https://tinyurl.com/ybpkgbyj.

18. "Glossary: Statcast," mlb.com, accessed December 27, 2017, http://m.mlb.com /glossary/statcast.

19. "Glossary: What Is a Exit Velocity (EV)? | Glossary," mlb.com, accessed December 27, 2017, http://m.mlb.com/glossary/statcast/exit-velocity; "Glossary: What Is a Launch Angle (LA)? | Glossary," mlb.com, accessed December 27, 2017, http://m.mlb.com /glossary/statcast/launch-angle.

20. Dave Sheinin, "Why mlb Hitters Are Suddenly Obsessed with Launch Angles," *Washington Post*, June 1, 2017, https://www.washingtonpost.com/graphics/sports /mlb-launch-angles-story/?utm_term=.5afef4d70b4b.

21. Shenin, "Why mlb Hitters Are Suddenly Obsessed."

22. Arthur Daley, "A Reformed Man," *New York Times*, April 22, 1956, http://www .nytimes.com/1956/04/22/archives/article-7-no-title-a-reformed-man.html.

23. Louis Effrat, "Mantle Accepts $75,000 Yankee Pact and Will Curtail Outside Interests," *New York Times*, January 17, 1961, https://timesmachine.nytimes.com /timesmachine/1961/01/17/118013388.html?pageNumber=43.

24. "Mickey Mantle Batting Stats: Ratio Batting," Baseball-Reference.com, accessed October 29, 2017, https://www.baseball-reference.com/players/m/mantlmi01-bat .shtml#batting_ratio::none.

25. Baumann, "The End of Baseball as We Know It."

26. "Batting Season Finder," Baseball-Reference.com, accessed October 31, 2017, https:// www.baseball-reference.com/tiny/Eaim7.

27. "Batting Season Finder," Baseball-Reference.com, accessed October 31, 2017, https:// www.baseball-reference.com/tiny/r8arr.

28. "Bryce Harper Batting Stats: Ratio Batting," Baseball-Reference.com, accessed October 29, 2017, https://www.baseball-reference.com/players/h/harpebr03-bat.shtml #batting_ratio::none.

29. "Mike Trout Stats," Baseball-Reference.com, accessed October 29, 2017, https://www .baseball-reference.com/players/t/troutmi01.shtml.

30. "Batting Season Finder," Baseball-Reference.com, accessed October 29, 2017, https:// www.baseball-reference.com/tiny/tjcSk.

31. Nate Silver, tweet, Twitter.com, September 30, 2017, https://twitter.com/natesilver538 /status/914230214955282432?lang=en.

32. "Aaron Judge's No. 99 is the best-selling jersey of 2017," si.com, accessed February 20, 2018, https://www.si.com/mlb/2017/10/03/aaron-judge-best-selling-jersey-2017 -mlb-season.

33. "Major League Baseball Miscellaneous Year-by-Year Averages and Totals," Baseball -Reference.com, accessed October 29, 2017, https://www.baseball-reference.com /leagues/mlb/misc.shtml.

34. "Misc. Year by Year," Baseball-Reference.com.

35. "Misc. Year by Year," Baseball-Reference.com.

36. Tom Verducci, "Baseball's Pressing Question: What Happens to a Sport When Nothing Happens?," si.com, June 20, 2017, https://www.si.com/mlb/2017/06/20/standstill-pace-play-cody-bellinger-clayton-kershaw.

37. "Misc. Year by Year," Baseball-Reference.com.

38. "Misc. Year by Year," Baseball-Reference.com.

39. Bill Baer, "Steve Garvey blames 'millennial baseball' for Game 2 of World Series," HardballTalk, October 26, 2017, http://mlb.nbcsports.com/2017/10/26/steve-garvey-blames-millennial-baseball-for-game-2-of-world-series/.

40. "2017 World Series Game 2, Astros at Dodgers, October 25," Baseball-Reference.com, accessed October 29, 2017, https://www.baseball-reference.com/boxes/lan/lan201710250.shtml.

41. "Splits Leaderboard," FanGraphs, accessed November 1, 2017, https://tinyurl.com/ybrf2ya5.

42. "Major League Baseball Fielding Year-by-Year Averages," Baseball-Reference.com, accessed October 29, 2017, https://www.baseball-reference.com/leagues/mlb/field.shtml.

43. "Major League Baseball Pitching Year-by-Year Averages," Baseball-Reference.com, accessed October 29, 2017, https://www.baseball-reference.com/play-index/share.fcgi?id=p3yyZ.

44. Baumann, "The End of Baseball as We Know It."